The Growth and Role of UK Financial Institutions 1880-1962

The Growth and Role of UK Financial Institutions 1880-1962

DAVID K. SHEPPARD

METHUEN & CO LTD
11 New Fetter Lane London EC4

First published in 1971
by Methuen & Co Ltd
11 New Fetter Lane, London EC4

Printed in Great Britain by
William Clowes & Sons, Limited
London, Beccles and Colchester

416 17680 1

Distributed in the USA
by Barnes & Noble Inc

Contents

List of tables vii

List of graphs x

Preface xi

Acknowledgements xiii

1 **The Growth of UK Financial Institutions and Changes in the Financial Environment 1880–1962** 1
Introduction 1
Changes in the Financial Environment 5
Conclusion 15

2 **The Growth of the UK Money Stock, Household Encashable Assets and Financial-Sector Credits by End Use 1880–1962** 17
Introduction 17
The Money Stock and other Encashable Assets 17
The UK National Savings Movement 22
Total Assets and Public and Private Credits of the Banking and Non-Banking Financial Institutions 25
UK Financial Sector's Savings and Investments 29
Conclusion 33

3 **Asset Preferences and the Money Supply in the United Kingdom 1880–1962** 35

4 **Estimation of Income Velocity, Asset Preferences and the Supply of Selected Institutional Liabilities in the UK 1880–1962** 52
Introduction 52
Income Velocity Estimates 52
Estimates of Households' Financial Asset Preferences 56
Estimates of Financial Institutions' Asset Preferences 60
Estimates of the Money Supply, the Size of Financial Intermediaries' Assets and of Credit Availability 64
Conclusion 67

5 **Money, Encashable Assets, Private Institutional Credits and Private Expenditure in the UK 1880–1962** 68
Introduction 68
Background 68
The Empirical Results 73
Conclusion 99

6 Conclusion: Some Historical Findings and Some Theoretical and Practical Implications 102

Appendix 109
Section 1 UK Banks 1880–1966 113
Tables (A)1.1–(A)1.14 116
Section 2 UK Non-Bank Financial Intermediaries 1880–1966 141
Tables (A)2.1–(A)2.12 142
Section 3 UK Money, Liquid Assets, National Savings and Institutional Private Credit Series 1880–1966 173
Tables (A)3.1–(A)3.8 176

Bibliography 193

Index 201

List of Tables

1.1 United Kingdom: Total Assets of Financial Institutions and Percentage Share Attributable to Each Component 1920–1962 3

2.1 United Kingdom: Household Encashable Assets and Percentage Share Attributable to Each Component 1880–1962 18

2.2 Total Assets and Government and Government-Guaranteed Security Holdings of Various UK Financial Institutions 1891–1962 30

3.1 Commercial Banks', Non-Bank Financial Institutions' and Private Sector's Average Asset Preferences in the UK 1892–1962 36

3.2 Some Determinants of the Money and Credit Supply in the UK 1892–1962 – Average and Coefficient of Variation 40

3.3 United Kingdom: Determinants of Money Stock 1881–1962 42

3.4 Contribution of Selected Determinants of the Money Stock UK and USA 1881–1962 and 1881–1960 48

3.5 Income Velocities – Average and Coefficient of Variation UK 1880–1962 49

4.1 Estimates of Income Velocity in the UK 1880–1962 54

4.2 Estimates of Selected Household Asset Preferences in the UK 1946–1962 58

4.3 Estimates of Commercial Banks' Asset Preferences in the UK 1921–1939 and 1947–1962 62

4.4 Estimates of Gross Non-Bank Financial Institutions' Liabilities and Gross Private Credit 1921–1939, 1947–1962 65

5.1 Pearson Correlation Coefficients between Financial Stocks and Private Expenditure in the UK 1881–1962 74

5.2 Expenditure Estimates – Consumption, Autonomous Expenditure and the Money Stock in Current Prices 1881–1962 76

5.3 Expenditure Estimates – Consumption, Autonomous Expenditure, Money Stock, Encashable Assets in Constant Prices 1881–1962 78

5.4 Expenditure Estimates – Gross Domestic Private Expenditure, Interest Rates and Stocks of Liquid Assets 1881–1914, 1921–1939 and 1947–1962 82

5.5 Expenditure Estimates in Constant Prices – Gross Domestic Private Expenditure, Interest Rates and the Money Stock 1881–1962, 1949–1967 84

5.6 Expenditure Estimates in Current Prices – Gross Domestic Private Expenditure, Gross Institutional Private Credit, Bank Private Credit, Autonomous Expenditure and the Money Stock 1881–1962 90

5.7 Expenditure Estimates in Constant Prices – Credit Availability Models 1881–1962 96

APPENDIX

Section 1

(A)1.1 United Kingdom Banks Combined Balance Sheets 1880–1966 116

(A)1.2 Joint-Stock Banks of England and Wales 1880–1966 118

(A)1.3 Joint-Stock Banks of Ireland 1880–1920 and Northern Ireland 1920–1966 120

(A)1.4 Joint-Stock Banks of Scotland 1880–1966 122

(A)1.5 Consolidated Balance Sheets of *The Economist*'s Private Bank Series, the Co-operative Wholesale Society Banks, and the Yorkshire Penny Bank 1891–1966 124

(A)1.6 United Kingdom Banks Combined Balance Sheet 1880–1966 126

(A)1.7 Co-operative Wholesale Society Limited Bank 1895–1966 128

(A)1.8 London Clearing Banks, End-of-year Consolidated Balance Sheet 1919–1966 130

(A)1.9 London Clearing Banks, Annual Average of Monthly Statements 1919–1966 132

(A)1.10 Bank Advances in Great Britain, Annual Averages 1936–8, 1946–66 134

(A)1.11 Bank Clearings, Great Britain 1880–1966 135

(A)1.12 Bank of England, Annual Average Wednesday Balance Sheet 1880–1966 136

(A)1.13 Combined Balance Sheets of Alexanders, National and the Union of London Discount Houses 1890–1966 138

(A)1.14 Compound Rates of Growth of Commercial Banks' Assets, Advances and Debit Clearings 140

Section 2

(A)2.1 Birmingham Municipal Bank Balance Sheets 1920–1967 142

(A)2.2 Post Office Savings Bank Balance Sheets 1862–1967 144

(A)2.3 Trustee Savings Banks of the United Kingdom 1880–1967 146

(A)2.4 Building Societies in Great Britain 1880–1967 150

(A)2.5 Insurance Companies Established in the United Kingdom 1880–1966 154

(A)2.6 Life and Other Type Insurance Funds, Great-Britain-Based Companies and Societies only 1880–1966 158

(A)2.7 Life and Other Types of Insurance Premiums Paid Yearly to UK-Based Companies and Societies on Business both Inside and Outside the UK 1880–1966 160

(A)2.8 Funds and Assets of the Various Societies Registered with the Registrar of Friendly Societies, which are Financial Institutions in Great Britain 1920–1966 162

(A)2.9 The Funds and the Number of Societies Registered Under the Friendly Societies and Provident and Industrial Assurance Societies Acts (Great Britain only) 1900–1966 166

(A)2.10 Balance Sheets of Hire-Purchase Finance Houses – Sample of Eight Companies 1920–1966 168

(A)2.11A Government-Sponsored Financial Institutions: The Finance Corporation for Industry Balance Sheet 1946–1966 170

(A)2.11B Government-Sponsored Financial Institutions: Industrial and Commercial Finance Corporation 1946–1966 171

(A)2.12 The Compound Rates of Growth of the Total Assets of Various UK Non-Bank Financial Intermediaries 172

Section 3

(A)3.1 United Kingdom National Savings 1860–1967 176

(A)3.2 Coin and Currency in Circulation in the United Kingdom 1880–1966 180

(A)3.3 United Kingdom Money Supply and Households' Liquid Assets 1880–1966 182

(A)3.4 UK Financial Institutions – Credit Series 1880–1966 184

(A)3.5 New Capital Issues in the United Kingdom 1920–1966 187

(A)3.6 Stocks Quoted on London Stock Exchange 1930–1966 188

(A)3.7 United Kingdom Rates of Interest 1860–1966 190

(A)3.8 The Compound Rates of Growth of National Savings, Money and Near-Money Stocks, and the Assets of the Financial Institutions 192

List of Graphs

(1)A	UK Financial Institutions: Credit Series 1892–1962	2
(2)A	UK Money Stock and Household Encashable Assets 1880–1962	20
(2)B	UK National Savings 1860–1962	24
(2)C	UK Financial Institutions: Bank and Other Financial Institutions' Assets 1880–1962	26
(2)D	UK Financial Institutions: Credit Allocation 1880–1962	28
(3)A	Money and High-Powered Money Stocks Outstanding in the UK 1881–1962	45
(3)B	Ratio of Commercial Banks' Deposits to Non-Bank Currency Outstanding and to Bank Reserves in the UK 1881–1962	46
(3)C	Ratio of Commercial Banks' Deposits to Non-Bank Currency Holdings and Bank Reserves in the USA 1881–1960	47
(3)D	Income Velocities in the UK 1880–1962	50

Preface

Monetary economics has recaptured some of its prominence of the pre-Keynesian era. As far as expenditure control is concerned, few economists question the hypothesis that changes in some 'monetary' variables may have a significant impact; more importantly, given the large financial demands of modern industry and the tendency, relative to these demands, towards a more equal distribution of *per capita* income, most economists probably agree that

> '... the existence of such financial arrangements (debt, financial assets, and financial institutions) is a necessary condition for the transfer of funds from savers to investors. Thus the ability of an economy to draw resources to their most efficient uses depends in a crucial way on the efficiency of its financial system.'[1]

Savers and spenders, whether Government, private or foreign, depend on the financial sector to accommodate a large portion of their marginal demands for assets or funds. As a consequence, monetary theory, or, more broadly, the theory of the financial sector, is once again receiving detailed consideration in its own right; a marked contrast to the peripheral position it occupied from the end of the 1930s to the mid-1950s. The amount and the composition of the assets and the liabilities of all and of particular groups of financial institutions are being reported and examined in various countries: '... financial statistics have stretched their tentacles upwards, sideways and intertwined them ...'[2] The record they reflect, as represented in the International Monetary Fund's *International Financial Statistics*, or in the sundry monthly or quarterly publications of various Government agencies, is striking: so much so that today monetary economics seems to be attracting more attention than any other area within the general field of macro-economics.

Unfortunately, before the mid-1950s, the coverage of the UK's financial statistics as published by the Bank of England or by Government agencies was far from comprehensive. Indeed, when reviewing the situation in 1959, H. Johnson observed '... it is remarkable (to say the least) how incomplete and inadequate monetary statistics available in this country are ...'[3] His remark echoed an earlier observation made by Mason and Sachs about the inadequacies of UK financial statistics in general; they held that the '... absence of regular comprehensive data regarding the general nature and movement of personal savings ...'[4] was probably one of the most serious practical constraints to an understanding of the saving–investment process. As a consequence, until quite recently, empirical studies even of aspects of the growth or of the role of the UK financial system have been impracticable – especially in the pre-1945 period. The deficiencies in the published record have made it impossible for econometricians to examine the various theories economists have put forward to explain either the growth or the role of this sector.

While certain economists such as Cairncross and Sayers successfully chastened the authorities into rectifying this deficiency in the post-1950 period, others have sought to fill in the gaps in the pre-1960 record. Johnson, Higonnet, Mitchell and Deane, Revell, Horne, Coppietiers, Barrett, Kavanagh, Walters and more recently Goodhart have made important contributions. Nevertheless, though considerably improved as a result of their efforts, the published series of UK financial statistics for the pre-1954 years are not comprehensive enough for study of the UK financial system to be nearly as detailed as analysis of the US financial system has been.

This book has been compiled with the intent of making this task more feasible. The annual data in the Appendix provide a considerable amount of the raw material required for such an assessment over a long time-period –

[1] D. Patinkin, 'Financial intermediaries and monetary theory', *American Economic Review* (March 1961), p. 95.

[2] J. J. Polak, 'Financial statistics and financial policy', *I.M.F. Staff Papers*, Vol. VII, No. 1 (1959), p. 1.

[3] H. G. Johnson, 'British monetary statistics', *Economica*, Vol. XXIV (February 1959), p. 1.

[4] J. J. Mason and D. Sachs, 'Statistics bearing on financial investment', *Journal of the Royal Statistical Society*, Vol. CXVIII (1955), Part 1, p. 96.

1880–1966. In conjunction, the first three chapters of the book have been designed both to set out the environmental framework in which the UK financial sector evolved, and to portray this evolution in a fashion which tends to identify some of the more important financial developments such as the growing importance of non-bank financial institutions, the revealed instability of certain important asset preferences, and the close correspondence between the growth of certain financial claims and the growth of economic activity. In the next two chapters, some of the theories which have been put forward to explain the changes in these asset preferences or the connection between certain financial claims and expenditure flows are tested against the data through the use of an ordinary least squares estimating procedure as applied to a single equation.

While the data in the Appendix should help to fill in the financial record, and while the descriptive account and the empirical examination of certain selected models of economic behaviour should be of assistance in appraising the growth and the role of the UK financial sector, it must be recognized that more should be done. This work is far from being definitive. The data represented in the Appendix provide only a portion of the required information; more importantly, the information they do provide is far from perfect, particularly in the pre-1920 period. The errors in the data undoubtedly introduce certain distortions in the descriptive account; more pertinently, by causing errors in variables, these imperfections make the results of the single equation estimators in the fourth and fifth chapters less accurate than they otherwise would be. In effect, the contents of this book are meant to provide a basis for a much more thorough examination of an important but complex topic: the role which the UK financial system played during the designated time interval – 1880–1962.

Acknowledgements

I thank A. A. Walters, C. A. E. Goodhart, R. Rhomburg, W. White, D. Williams, I. Palmer, G. Fisher and G. Dorrance for their comments and criticisms of earlier drafts of the text. I thank A. Smithies for his advice on the organization of the material, and I am very much in debt to R. S. Sayers whose lectures and publications gave me what I consider essential mental constructs with which to appraise the role of the selected financial institutions. I also appreciate the support the University of Birmingham, the Graduate Management Centre of the University of Aston and the International Monetary Fund gave to this project. The technical assistance of L. Harris at the latter institution was most helpful in obtaining the computed results. The research assistants in the economics department of the University of Birmingham, C. R. Barrett, C. Ash, D. Mussendon and F. Rakhshani also performed an important role: they helped to collect and check a considerable amount of the data represented in the Appendix. I thank the typists who coped competently with numerous drafts of the text. Finally, I thank Miss M. Ricketts, Miss L. V. Altman, Mrs A. Thomas and Mrs S. Lawrence for checking and editing the chapters, the footnotes, and the sources and notes of the tables in the Appendix.

1 The Growth of UK Financial Institutions and Changes in the Financial Environment 1880–1962

Introduction

Graph (1)A and Table 1.1 introduce an empirical account of the development of the UK financial structure since 1880. Together, they trace out the growth paths of the assets of many leading groups of financial institutions; and they show both the absolute share and the relative proportion of all of these assets that each of the selected groups had on an end-of-year basis from 1920 to 1962.

The record is not complete. Deficiencies in the published statistics made it impractical to incorporate the UK business of the overseas banks, the assets of the investment trusts, unit trusts, private trust and superannuation funds, and of the accepting houses and most of the merchant banks. Nevertheless, it seems unlikely that the UK business of the omitted institutions would exceed, say, £16,000 million – e.g. 50 per cent of the recorded evaluation of the included institutions' assets.[1] Moreover, in some respects, the omissions are salutary inasmuch as their inclusion would accentuate the tendency to incorporate inter-institutional claims and make it more difficult to standardize the method of asset evaluation.[2] As a consequence, the recorded data seem to be comprehensive enough to provide an indicative account of the main trends in the growth and the distribution of UK financial savings as well as outlining the development of the main UK-based financial institutions.

Graph (1)A and Table 1.1 indicate that there was a marked change in the consolidated total and in the assets of each of the selected groups of financial institutions over the period.

Between 1920 and 1962, for example, the table shows that the total financial assets of these institutions rose from £4·6 milliard to £32·6 milliard. Over the same period, the graph depicts that by group institutional assets rose as follows: the bank and discount companies' assets increased from £2·7 milliard to £10·8 milliard. Those of the insurance companies rose even more rapidly from £0·7 milliard to £8·5 milliard, and so did the assets of the building societies and the consolidated assets of the sample of eight leading hire-purchase companies. The building society assets increased from £90 million to £3,800 million, while those of the hire-purchase companies rose from £1 million to £440 million. Though their growth was less spectacular, the assets of both the Post Office Savings Bank and the trustee savings banks burgeoned over the years. The former's assets increased from £267 million to £1,760 million and the latter's rose from £94 million to £1,555 million. The overall increase in the consolidated assets of these institutions reflects a sizeable rise in the pace of financial activity; particularly when this increase is compared with the growth of GNP over the same period – £6 milliard to £25 milliard.

The graph illustrates that relative to each other the growth rates of the constituent groups of institutions changed considerably, and that there was also considerable variability in the growth rates of each group of institutions – except for the insurance companies, whose rate of asset accumulation barely deviated between 1892 and 1962.

For instance, while the graph shows that there were certain similarities between the rates of growth enjoyed by the trustee savings banks and the building societies throughout most of the period, it illustrates that the

[1] Some indication of the importance of the omitted institutions in the UK financial markets may be derived from the following statistics. In 1962, the combined assets of the investment and unit trusts amounted to over £2,200 million sterling on a market valuation. In the same year, the liabilities of the overseas banks operating in the UK were around £2,400 million; although it should be noted that a significant part of their funds was derived from depositors not resident in the UK. Similarly, the assets of UK-based pension funds reached quite a substantial level in 1962, £3,000 million, and undoubtedly the combined market valuation of the various trust funds administered by the clearing banks, the insurance companies and the office of the Public Trustee could not have been much below this level. On 31 December 1948, eight clearing banks administered trusts to the value of £800 million, and on 31 March of that year, the Public Trustee administered accounts which were valued at approximately £300 million.

[2] The assets of the unit trusts and investment trusts are usually valued at current market prices; whereas those of the banks and other deposit-receiving institutions are normally valued on the basis of an amortized historical cost or current market value – whichever is lower.

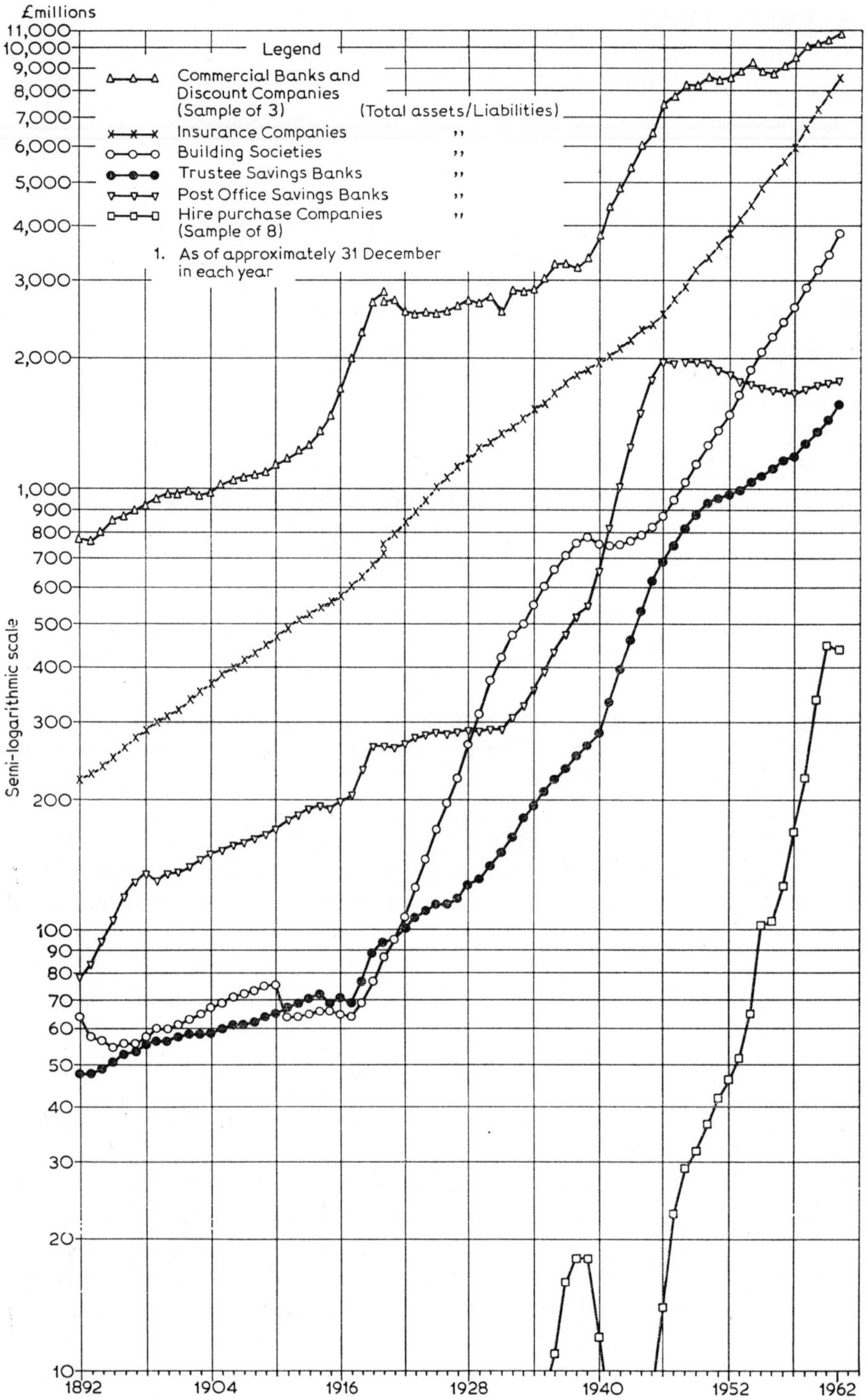

(1)A UK Financial Institutions: Credit Series 1892–1962

Source: See Appendix, Table (A)3.4

TABLE 1.1 **United Kingdom: Total Assets of Financial Institutions and Percentage Share Attributable to Each Component 1920–1962**

Year	*Total Financial Assets*[2]	*Percentage Contribution to Total Financial Institutions' Assets of Particular Intermediaries*							
		Banks and Discount Companies[1]	*Life Insurance Companies*	*Post Office Savings Bank*	*Building Societies*	*Trustee Savings Banks*	*National Savings Bonds*[2]	*Friendly Societies*	*Hire-Purchase Societies*
	£ millions								
1920	4,552	59·5	16·4	5·9	1·9	2·1	11·6	2·6	—
1921	4,695	58·2	16·9	5·6	2·0	2·0	12·6	2·5	—
1922	4,636	55·4	18·1	5·8	2·3	2·2	13·4	2·8	—
1923	4,707	53·6	19·0	5·8	2·7	2·3	13·7	3·0	—
1924	4,806	52·6	19·5	5·8	3·0	2·3	13·4	3·2	—
1925	4,929	51·1	20·4	5·8	3·4	2·3	13·4	3·3	—
1926	5,096	50·5	20·9	5·6	3·8	2·3	13·4	3·4	0·1
1927	5,257	50·0	21·4	5·4	4·2	2·3	12·8	3·5	0·1
1928	5,472	49·6	21·7	5·3	4·9	2·3	12·3	3·7	0·1
1929	5,553	48·2	22·5	5·1	5·6	2·3	12·0	3·8	0·1
1930	5,799	47·8	22·3	5·0	6·4	2·4	11·9	3·9	0·1
1931	5,704	45·0	23·5	5·1	7·3	2·6	11·8	4·3	0·1
1932	6,138	46·7	22·6	5·0	7·6	2·6	10·8	4·3	0·1
1933	6,270	45·3	23·1	5·2	8·0	2·9	10·6	4·5	0·1
1934	6,496	44·3	23·3	5·5	8·6	2·9	10·3	4·7	0·1
1935	6,852	44·4	23·1	5·7	8·8	3·0	9·8	4·7	0·1
1936	7,264	44·5	22·9	5·9	9·0	3·1	9·4	4·7	0·2
1937	7,558	43·3	23·1	6·2	9·4	3·1	9·5	4·8	0·2
1938	7,687	41·5	23·7	6·6	9·9	3·3	9·4	5·2	0·2
1939	8,126	41·3	23·2	6·8	9·5	3·2	10·3	5·0	0·2
1940	9,072	41·5	21·3	7·2	8·3	3·1	13·2	4·7	0·1
1941	10,458	42·2	19·2	7·9	7·2	3·2	15·6	4·4	0·1
1942	11,616	41·7	18·1	8·7	6·5	3·3	17·0	4·2	0·1
1943	13,020	41·3	16·9	9·5	5·9	3·5	18·3	4·0	0·1
1944	14,562	41·4	15·9	10·3	5·5	3·7	18·9	3·8	0·1
1945	15,779	40·7	15·0	11·3	5·2	3·9	19·5	3·7	0·1
1946	17,615	42·7	14·3	11·3	5·0	3·9	18·8	3·5	0·1
1947	18,303	42·8	14·8	10·6	5·2	4·1	18·3	3·6	0·1
1948	19,041	43·2	15·3	10·2	5·5	4·3	17·3	3·6	0·2
1949	19,525	42·4	16·1	10·0	5·8	4·5	16·8	3·7	0·2
1950	20,197	42·3	16·7	9·6	6·2	4·7	16·3	3·7	0·2
1951	20,395	41·3	17·6	9·2	6·7	4·7	16·1	3·9	0·2
1952	20,844	41·0	18·3	8·7	7·1	4·7	15·7	4·0	0·2
1953	21,543	40·8	19·0	8·1	7·6	4·6	15·2	4·1	0·2
1954	22,710	40·6	19·5	7·6	8·2	4·6	14·7	4·1	0·3
1955	22,955	38·2	21·0	7·4	9·0	4·7	14·6	4·2	0·4
1956	23,617	37·0	22·0	7·1	9·4	4·7	14·5	4·3	0·4
1957	24,627	36·9	22·7	6·8	9·8	4·7	13·9	4·3	0·5
1958	25,971	36·3	23·1	6·3	10·1	4·6	14·3	4·3	0·6
1959	27,956	36·0	23·4	6·0	10·4	4·5	14·2	4·2	0·9
1960	29,503	34·8	24·3	5·8	10·7	4·6	14·2	4·2	1·1
1961	30,982	33·6	25·4	5·6	11·1	4·6	13·7	4·2	1·4
1962	32,643	33·1	25·9	5·4	11·7	4·8	13·4	4·1	1·3

Source

D. K. Sheppard, 'UK Financial Statistics 1880–1962', *Birmingham University Discussion Papers*, Series A, Nos. 63–65 (August 1965).

[1] 'Bills discounted' and 'rebate' were added to the total assets of the sample of three discount houses from 1943 onwards, as these were included in the pre-1943 total assets in the published balance sheets.

[2] Excludes accrued interest earned on National Savings Certificates.

movements of both the commercial banks' and the Post Office Savings Bank's assets were quite dissimilar. In 1916, 1921–4 and 1954–6 the two sets of rates were negatively related. Moreover, the graph shows that in the post-1920 peacetime periods the building societies and the trustee savings banks did well; while the assets of the banks and of the Post Office Savings Bank either expanded slowly or declined. In contrast, from 1892 to 1914, from 1914 to 1920, and from 1939 to 1946 both the banks and the Post Office Savings Bank enjoyed periods of relatively high rates of growth, particularly during the periods of national emergency; whereas the assets of the building societies and to a lesser extent the trustee savings banks either declined or grew much more slowly. Finally, the graph highlights the extraordinarily rapid expansion of the sample of hire-purchase companies in the post-1919 period. From 1920 to 1939 their assets grew at a compound annual rate of 16 per cent and from 1946 to 1962 the rate was 24 per cent; it was 27 per cent from 1954 on to 1962.

Naturally, the sustained discrepancies between the growth rates of groups of institutions meant that over time each group's share of the market for loans and institutional claims changed significantly. Table 1.1 shows that in 1920 the banks accounted for 60 per cent of all institutional assets; by 1962, their share had fallen to 33 per cent; whereas the shares of the insurance companies and the building societies had risen from 17 per cent to 26 per cent and from 2 per cent to 12 per cent respectively. Moreover, it shows marked oscillations in the shares of these and the other groups. In effect, the graph and the table indicate that the UK financial structure changed considerably over the period, and that much of this change must be explained by sudden as well as slow changes in the financial environment. This is to say that qualitative factors, often exogenously determined, played an important role in the development of the financial sector.

The wars and the subsequent pressures which were exerted in the post-war reconstruction had a pronounced impact; so much so that in much of the post-1914 period the financial sector perhaps evolved as it did in response to particular needs: the needs of the Government to harness savings to finance the war effort; the needs of the household sector to satisfy its wartime deferred demand for houses and consumer durables. The radical changes in the sources of exercisable demand pressures for institutional loan accommodation were such that for purposes of analysis it seems that the statistical record should be examined in five sub-periods rather than in one.

While the wartime emergencies and the adjustments which followed them account for the major discontinuities in the series, shares and growth rates, other developments of a qualitative nature played a role in the evolution of the financial sector.

The pre-1880 changes in the institutional environment had a considerable influence at least up to 1914, in the sense that by 1880 nearly all the recorded institutions were operating financial intermediaries within a chosen or legislated area of specialization in the financial market.

From 1880 onwards, the Government became increasingly important as a decision-maker. It adjusted the established regulating legislative framework with greater ease to meet its needs; it stepped up the development of its own schemes for attracting savings, and by incentives and eventually directives it exerted increasing pressure on the portfolio choices of the privately controlled institutions to finance its needs or other desired social objectives, e.g. housing. As a side effect, its actions had considerable influence on the growth or retardation of the banks, the trustee savings banks, the Post Office Savings Bank and the building societies by altering the relative attractiveness of their obligations.

Less dramatically but significantly inasmuch as it affected the nature of the Government's directives and intervention, the long-run change in the UK's international economic position was influential. The decline in the British Empire and the accompanying erosion of sterling's role as an international currency affected the sources and placements of savings received and made by the institutions. The UK financial system slowly switched from being a net supplier to a net absorber of external short-term funds. The switch resulted in considerable changes in the operating practices of the established institutions, and it created opportunities for expansion which were readily seized by some of the more independently operated intermediaries – the merchant banks.

After 1880 the financial institutions also took steps which influenced the environment and therefore played a part in shaping the development of the financial sector. Each group established trade associations which it then proceeded to strengthen in order to regulate within-group competitive behaviour as well as to represent the group's interests to the Government. Through the expansion of the inter-group loan accommodation and/or equity ownership, the liaison between the separate groups improved. Within- and between-group conjectural variation became well recognized. Within-group borrowing and lending rates became standardized and knowingly geared to the rates of other groups to avoid undue competition. Equally important was the tendency, which often resulted from Government legislation, for each group to select a particular type of financial savings as well as a particular range of outlets in which to place its funds. The institutional lending and borrowing practices became segmented. The emerging gaps in the intermediating process, such as the excess demands for export finance, for consumer finance, for medium-term industrial loans, for loans to local authorities, only tended to be filled on Government sponsorship or, rather later, through the activities of intermediaries which were not absorbed by the close-knit institutional arrangements.

Naturally the external shocks, long-run influences and institutional generated market imperfections noted above were not the only factors which influenced the overall pattern of financial activity. The growth in tangible wealth, the growth and change in composition of expenditure, the growth and more equitable distribution of disposable income, the degree of unemployment, the level of prices, of interest rates, of tax rates, and expectations about these undoubtedly played a part in dictating the nature and composition of period changes in assets and liabilities of the institutions. After all, these institutions' liabilities and therefore assets would not have grown at all if the non-financial private sector had been unwilling to take up the readily realizable secure wealth claims they issued in exchange for this sector's savings. Nevertheless, I consider that the non-quantifiable factors were important too, and would urge that their influence should be borne in mind in designing and interpreting econometric relationships which are structured to explain the growth or the role of the financial sector.

The most important of these qualitative factors are set out below with an assessment of what seems to have been their likely effect in terms of their particular influence on the financial sector. The broad environmental background is outlined, and then the effects of the Government's intervention, of the institutions' own activities, and of the change in the international environment are traced and examined successively in the post-1880 period. Naturally this record is not complete and the interpretations of the intent as well as the effects of some of these developments are certainly contentious. Neither the authorities nor the institutional trade associations have been particularly eager to argue that they intended to channel the flow of private financial savings or that they had come to certain market-sharing arrangements.

Changes in the Financial Environment

The UK financial system was quite well developed by 1880. Most of the currently operating institutional groups were established, and the Government had already passed most of the statutes which now form their legislative environment. Moreover, the authorities had already become directly involved in the market through the creation of their own savings-collecting agencies, and they had developed the two rationales on which the future State's influence was based: stimulating and safeguarding low-income groups' savings and manipulating the portfolio preferences of the financial institutions so that the State's financial requirements might be more easily met.

The background

By 1880, the bulk of the statutory framework in which the UK banking system was to operate over the next eighty-two years had been formed. The Acts of 1826, 1833 and 1844 provided a large part of the framework for the subsequent rapid growth of deposit banking. In 1826 and 1833 stamp duties were imposed on bills of exchange written in amounts of less than £20 and £50 respectively. In addition, by the 1833 Act, joint-stock banks were permitted to operate in the London area providing that they refrained from issuing notes. These Acts, in conjunction with the Bank Act of 1844, which placed a rigid ceiling on all bank fiduciary note issues for the next seventy years, help to explain the subsequent expansion of the deposit-based joint-stock company banking system. Acceptable substitutes for deposits, small denomination bills of exchange or currency notes, were either heavily taxed or prevented from increasing by statute; whereas deposit-creating institutions received legislative stimulus.

Legislation in the 1850s and the 1860s further enhanced the growth of deposit banking. The usury laws were repealed; the stamp duty on bank cheques was reduced to 1*d*; the duty on internal bills of exchange was changed from a specific to an *ad valorem* tariff; severe penalties (transportation for life) were imposed for fraudulent cheque alterations, and, under the Companies Act of 1862, banks were accorded the privilege of limited liability. These developments coupled with the Bank of England's entry into the London Clearing House in 1864 and its acceptance of its position as a lender of last resort after the Overend and Gurney crisis in 1866 bolstered the expansion of joint-stock bank deposit liabilities. The legal impediment to a rise in their earnings through interest-rate regulation had been removed. The tax on the utilization of their liabilities had been reduced. Both the State and the Central Bank had passed legislation or adopted procedures to foster public confidence in their liabilities. In the meanwhile the expansion of other competing media of exchange was constrained by the authorities. The banks had been given a near monopoly over the creation of the new additions to the money stock. They used it. Their combined deposits tripled between 1880 and 1913.

By 1880 much of the important capital market and institutional savings' legislative framework had been set up too. The Company Acts of 1837, 1862 and 1867 broke the Crown's monopoly over the control of the formation of joint-stock companies with limited liability; this form of business organization, as it became more extensively utilized, both increased the demand for and the ease of issuance of institutional loan accommodation.

The various Friendly Society Acts of 1793, 1829, 1836, 1842, 1846, 1850 and 1855, and the Trustee Savings Bank Acts of 1817, 1820, 1824, 1828, 1833, 1835, 1844, 1860, 1863, 1877 and 1880 established much of the legislative environment in which these charitable or non-profit organizations were to operate in subsequent years.

The Friendly Society Acts were designed to promote and protect the growth of small savings by providing both incentives and safeguards to such asset accumulations. The benefits paid by the Friendly Societies were exempted from taxation and their transactions were exempted from stamp duties. To acquire such benefits Friendly Societies were required to register with the newly established office of the Registrar of Friendly Societies and to file annual reports with that office.

The trustee savings banks received similar treatment. All the proceeds of their ordinary deposits were required to be lodged in the account of the National Debt Commissioners at the Bank of England. They were paid a subsidized rate of interest on these funds, which in turn they were required to pass on to their depositors after allowing for expenses. The subsidization of small savings was assured by limiting the per annum deposit in 1828 to £30 and the maximum deposit to £150 per depositor; these limits remained unchanged until 1893.

The legislative ground rules which the Government set up to govern the operation of its own savings bank in 1861 were similar. A maximum rate of interest on Post Office Savings Bank deposits of 2½ per cent was prescribed – it remained unchanged over the next hundred years. The maximum total and per annum placements of deposits per depositor were controlled (£150 total and £30 per annum). In the same way, the funds received on deposit were handed over to the National Debt Commissioners for investment, and, in turn, the Government guaranteed both the principal and interest earnings of such savings placements.

By 1880 then the State had passed the basic legislative statutes and established the administrative machinery to regulate the activities of most of the institutional participants in the small-savings movement; in addition, it had powers to direct the composition of some of these savings institutions' investment placements and to regulate the means by which they competed for household savings. Only the statutory ground rules as they affected the building societies and the insurance companies had to be firmly framed.

The building societies were initially included under the Friendly Society legislation by the 1836 Act; however, the nature of their activities was such that they became subject to special legislation. By the Building Societies Act of 1874, they were allowed to incorporate; they were awarded limited borrowing powers of up to two-thirds of their outstanding mortgages, and they were prohibited from making property investments. Around the same time, the Treasury authorities began to reject the building societies' claim for a tax exempt status under the 1829 Friendly Societies Act as many of them straddled the boundary between the charitable and private financial institutions due to their close connection with property companies. In 1894, however, the building societies' position in the institutional savings structure was clearly delineated.

In the Building Societies Act of that year, the borrowing and investment powers incorporated in the 1874 Act were reiterated. In addition, the societies were prohibited from holding ballots for advances; they were required to furnish the Registrar of the Friendly Societies with an annual report which depicted all their property holdings, their past due mortgages, and all mortgage loans in excess of £5,000, and they were exempted from paying stamp duties. In the same year, the societies reached an agreement with the Inland Revenue authorities to the effect that their interest payments to their depositors should be taxed at approximately half the standard income-tax rate. The Act had the effect of firmly channelling the building society business towards the promotion of low-income group home ownership and away from the larger and more speculative real-estate ventures. They were incorporated within the charitable institutional framework.

The legislative framework as it directly affected the insurance companies was also not complete by 1880. Certainly, with respect to their life assurance business, much had been done. The concept of what was an assurable interest had been set out; and the Life Assurance Acts of 1867, 1870 and 1872 had set up the regulatory framework for this part of the insurance companies' business. Like the joint-stock banks under the 1844 Act, to engage in life assurance the respective companies had to have a minimum capital stock outstanding. In addition, they were required to make a sizeable deposit, some £20,000, with the Paymaster General, to separate their life assurance and accident insurance business records, and to file annual accounts with the Board of Trade. Moreover, they had obtained significant income-tax concessions for their policy holders.

The legislative framework which was to govern the full range of the insurance companies' activities was not, however, set out until later under the Assurance Companies Act of 1909. Then, in addition to the incorporation of the provisions of the earlier Acts, the companies were required to adhere to the deposit provision for each type of insurance business they engaged in as well as to maintain separate accounts for these. In addition, the form of their balance sheet was prescribed in considerable detail. In effect, they too were drawn into the State's supervisory network. In return, their life-policy holders continued to receive favourable income-tax treatment on their premium payments.

The pattern of the Government's direct involvement in the financial market was also well established by 1880. With the Montague Loan Bill of 1692, the legislative authority for issues of national debt was set forth; in the future, negotiable instruments bearing the State's guarantee were to become more plentiful on the market-place – particularly in the post-1914 era. Moreover, the Government had established the practice of making a market for its own obligations. Indeed the original Bank Charter Act of 1694 was primarily designed for this purpose, and, as Coppietiers notes: 'Every increase in privilege (to the Bank of England) coincided with increased advances to a Government in need to finance its wars.'[1] Furthermore, as the Post Office Savings Bank Act of 1861 showed, the State could and would create its own savings-collecting agency if the need arose. As P. Woodruff observed, this need extended beyond meeting the requirements of the security-conscious small savers to assisting the Government's demand for finance: 'Gladstone . . . was at that time in disagreement with the Bank of England regarding certain matters of finance, and doubtless contemplated that the establishment of such a bank would assure HM Treasury at least a measure of independence from City funds.'[2] The setting-up of the Military Savings Bank in 1842, of the Naval Savings Bank in 1866, the introduction of several Government annuity schemes between 1829 and 1880, and the direct sale of Government stock to individuals through the medium of the Post Office Register from 1880 indicate the pattern of the State's direct involvement in the savings and investment process. All funds collected by these agencies were either invested directly in Government obligations or lodged with the National Debt Commissioners.

As a consequence, by 1880 the Government had set up much of the framework within which both the collection and placement of savings were to be conducted. More importantly, it had set up its own yardstick competitors within the savings movement, and it had devised measures to assist such agencies to make their obligations attractive in the market-place. This pattern of State involvement in the financial markets was continued in the post-1880 period.

The development – the Government's post-1880 activities

The Government's direct involvement in the long-term capital market was particularly marked in the post-1880 period. The State did not neglect the precedents it had established for making a market for its own obligations. For instance, both the pre- and post-1880 legislation to regulate the management of charitable and private trusts, the Acts of 1853, 1855, 1860, 1862, 1869, 1888, 1893, 1900, 1906, 1925 and 1928, had a matching orientation: 'Namely to make borrowing for certain borrowers cheaper than it would be without the cachet of trustee status.'[3] Naturally, the State's own obligations were at all times incorporated in the permitted list.

Similarly, the State sought to make its obligations more attractive to the financial institutions. In the Savings Bank

[1] E. Coppietiers, *English Bank Note Circulation 1694–1954* (The Hague: Louvain Institute of Economic and Social Research, 1955), p. 18.

[2] P. Woodruff, 'British savings banks', *Banker's Magazine*, Vol. CXXXII (1931), p. 40.

[3] 'A plea for trustees', *The Economist* (19 January 1946), p. 102.

Act of 1891, it restricted their special investment departments' investments to the prescribed list of trustee securities and banned the establishment of any further special investment departments. These provisions were repealed in the Savings Bank Act of 1904, when the establishment of new special investment departments was re-authorized and the list of permitted investments for such departments was again extended to include loans to local authorities as well.[1] The Building Societies Act of 1894 had a similar provision to the Savings Bank Act of 1891 with respect to the societies' investments in securities.

Furthermore, the Government sought to speed up the process it had already engaged in of directly collecting financial savings. The opening-up of Government stock accounts in the Savings Bank in 1880 was one such measure; others followed. In 1882, it raised the maximum limit on the individual acquisition of Government annuities from £50 to £100; in 1893 it raised the savings-bank deposit limit from £150 to £200 and at the same time raised the limit on individual acquisition of Government stock through the Post Office Register from £300 to £500. These ceilings were raised in the succeeding years and removed altogether during periods of national emergency on deposit placements in the Post Office Savings Bank or in the ordinary department of the trustee savings bank. Indeed, as the period progressed, the Government's interest in the operations of the longer-term segment of the capital market became more extensive. For example, other measures were periodically introduced to stimulate the State's collection of longer-term household savings.

As far as the Post Office Savings Bank was concerned, sundry steps were taken. The State soon overlooked its intent, as expressed in the original Act, to set up branches only in areas which did not have any other form of savings bank. It engaged actively in the process of branch competition for the public's savings. By 1907, for instance, it had over 15,000 branches; whereas the joint-stock banks had just a little over 6,600 and the trustee savings banks, its main competitor, had about 400. In addition, it adopted new techniques to increase the relative attractiveness of the Post Office Savings Bank's deposits. By 1888, the authorized rate paid on ordinary deposits in the trustee savings banks had been reduced to that paid by the Post Office, and there it remained with minor oscillations until 1962. Moreover, by 1905 the State had passed legislation which required the building societies and trustee savings banks to issue only term liabilities; at the same time it allowed depositors at its own bank to withdraw small sums on demand. Finally, it stimulated the growth of this bank by such measures as requiring that all workmen's compensation money should be distributed through the Post Office, and by channelling service-separation allowances and post-war credits through this intermediary as well.

More significantly, and in response to the financial pressures of war emergencies, it supplemented its 1880-initiated direct collection of household savings through bond sales. In 1916, it launched a National Savings Scheme in which high-interest-yielding savings certificates were issued on a tax-free basis. The movement was an outstanding success, and, though its growth flagged as the incentives were reduced during the inter-war years, it was revived again with great success in the Second World War. It received further stimulus in the post-war period by the introduction of premium bonds in 1957.

As has been noted, the financial demands of the State induced by the First World War accentuated the speed of its involvement in the financial markets, and the atmosphere of a national emergency provided a suitable testing ground for further State financial intervention. The declaration of a prolonged bank holiday, the closure of the London Stock Exchange, the establishment of minimum prices on stock-exchange dealings, the unilateral extension of the maturity of all commercial bills for one month, the control of new issues, and the ban on investment abroad provided the State with a taste of its market power. A taste which in turn it exercised to meet the emergencies in the post-war period.

The means by which the Government chose to implement its post-war financial policies, as well as the rationales on which they were based, emerged as products of the various State-appointed advisory committees and commissions. Indeed, an examination of their reports traces out the chronological development of the Government's post-war financial policy quite accurately.

The report of the Farrington Committee of 1916, for instance, underlined the desirability of stimulating export finance to correct the balance-of-payments position. It resulted in the establishment of the British Trade Corporation in 1917, and the spelt-out rationales provided some of the stimulus to the proliferation of the State's schemes to stimulate export finance: the Overseas

[1] The post-1891 practice of Scottish trustee savings banks of establishing investment trusts to handle the business of their special investment departments seems to have been influential in removing the ban on the establishment of special investment departments.

Trade Act of 1920, the First Export Credit Guarantee Scheme of 1921, the Second Export Credit Guarantee Scheme of 1926 and the Export Credit Guarantee Act of 1937.

The Report of the Cunliffe Committee in 1917 set out the general prescripts for money-market intervention to eliminate the inflationary effects of war finance. An automatic deflationary policy was set aiming at a 3 per cent per annum reduction in the money supply until prices had fallen enough for the Gold Standard to be readopted at the pre-war exchange rate. A plan was prescribed for the absorption of all wartime issues of Treasury currency notes by the Bank of England, and this plan was designed to lead to the reintroduction of tight control over note issues as set out by the 1844 Bank Act. These ends were achieved in 1925 and 1928 respectively after a severe period of domestic deflation.

Following its committee's recommendations, the Government sought to channel a certain amount of credit to other sectors as well as to the export trade, and also to curtail the banks' market power and limit their advances.

By the issuance of a Government directive, Cmnd. 9052, in 1918, the banks agreed to desist from further amalgamations without Treasury approval; in 1920 they agreed to co-operate with the Government's deflationary programme by restricting advances.

On the credit-channelling front, the Government's intervention became more extensive. By the Housing and Town Planning Act of 1919 the State began its housing-subsidy programme.[1] By the passage of the Agricultural Credit Acts in 1923 and 1928 the Government sought to channel funds to the agricultural sector. Similarly, by persuasion through the offices of the Bank of England or by direct subsidy or both, the Government arranged for the organization of new financial institutions to channel funds to selected areas. By these means, in 1920 the Bank of England assisted in the formation of the United Dominion Trust to bolster hire-purchase finance; in 1928, the Agricultural Mortgage Corporation was established to provide long-term capital to the agricultural sector, and in 1929 and 1930 respectively, two new institutions were formed (the Securities Management Trust and the Bankers' Industrial Development Company) to channel funds to credit-needy sectors.

This committee–policy–committee cycle continued throughout the 1920 period. One Government committee after another was appointed to examine the condition of the UK financial markets – the Balfour, the Enfield and finally the Macmillan Committee. Their findings and their recommendations played an important role in shaping the State's overall financial policy in the 1930s.

The recommendations of the Macmillan Committee (the Committee on Finance and Industry) which spanned the early stages of the Great Depression (1929–31) were particularly persuasive, and they were to exert a decisive influence on future Government financial policy. Macmillan's own statement in the opening paragraphs of the final report was a portent for the future: '. . . in the case of our financial . . . institutions we may well have reached the stage when an era of conscious and deliberate management must succeed an era of undirected evolution'.[2]

The depression-induced exchange crises were soon to bring this era more openly into being. With the abandonment of the Gold Standard in September 1931, the establishment of the exchange equalization account and the concept of the sterling area, and the closing of the UK capital market to non-sterling-area issues in 1932, the stage was set for direct State financial management. By 1936, the utterances of Montague Norman, chairman of the Bank of England, suggest that this process was well under way: '. . . I assure the Ministers that if they will make known through the appropriate channels what they wish us to do in the furtherance of their policies, they will at all times find us willing with good will and loyalty to do what they direct as though we were under legal compulsion . . .'[3] The Government had established its control over the hub of the money market; a position which was formalized by the nationalization of the Bank of England in 1946.

As the Government's interest in the financial system developed, and as the pace of its intervention was stepped up in the money, the capital and the foreign exchange markets, it acquired and exercised additional powers to regulate the development and investment practices of the domestic financial institutions. To be sure, some of its post-1920 legislation was mainly orientated to make saving through these institutions more secure by eliminating undesirable business practices. The Building Societies Act of 1960, for instance, in which societies' loans to

[1] Substantial grants or low-interest loans were provided to stimulate the construction of low-cost housing in both the post-war intervals; though these forms of State housing subsidies became more restricted after the initial phase of the post-war periods.

[2] Committee on Finance and Industry, *Report*, Cmnd. 389, London: HMSO, 1931, p. 5.

[3] W. F. Crick, 'British monetary policy', *Banker's Magazine*, Vol. CXLV (1938), p. 238.

builders and property companies were curtailed, clearly had this intent. Nevertheless, the nature of many of the controls the Government subsequently placed on the private financial institutions clearly changed. Their freedom to place their assets as they wished became more constrained so that such asset placements meshed more closely with the State's plans. These constraints were particularly severe in the Second World War and in the early part of the post-war period.

By 1920, the 'directive' impact of the Government's powers was already noticeable. Parliamentary approval for the permanent establishment of the Birmingham Municipal Savings Bank in 1919 was only obtained on the understanding that a large proportion of its deposits would be invested in public funds. Later, the Treasury's conditions for authorizing the establishment of additional municipal savings banks in the post-1928 period had a similar orientation – 45 per cent of their funds were to be invested in Government securities. By the 1930s, a finding published by the Board of Trade Inquiry into the operations of unit trusts in 1936 is revealing: '. . . experience does not suggest that the movement is likely to have any serious repercussions on the rate of Government borrowing'.[1] Finally, with the implementation of the Defence Regulations in 1937 and the establishment of the Capital Issues Committee in 1939 the Government made sure that no privately controlled savings movement could have any serious repercussions on the rate of Government borrowing without the Government's prior permission.

The authorization for these credit-directing powers in the post-war period was set out in the Borrowing Act of 1946: Treasury permission had to be obtained on all company and local authority borrowings in excess of £50,000 and for all bank loans in excess of £10,000. In conjunction with its control of the Central Bank, with its powers to direct the lending practices of commercial banks under Section 4 of the Bank Act of 1946, and with its own large saving organization – the Post Office Savings Bank – and the National Savings Schemes, these powers gave the State a great deal of control over the savings and investment decisions of the UK financial sector during the post-war reconstruction period.

It should be clear that both indirectly through regulatory legislation and persuasive directives, and directly through the establishment of State-owned yardstick competitors, the Government played an increasingly significant role in shaping the development of the UK financial system. It should be noted too that changes in Government policy in the social and fiscal field also affected the way the financial sector developed. The rapid rise in the income-tax rate, the growing incidence of special legislation, the accompanying growth of the Government sector, the imposition and then the removal of building, rent, investment and consumption controls during the war and the post-war periods were obviously influential. Finally, of course, the State's extensive nationalization programme in the 1946–52 period had some important financial repercussions.

The income-tax rate, 2 per cent in 1880, rose to 6 per cent by 1914 and even more rapidly thereafter. From 1920 to 1939, it did not fall below 4*s* in the pound (20 per cent); indeed it was raised to 5*s* in the pound during the Depression (1929–32). Between 1946 and 1962 the rate was as high as 48 per cent and never fell below 39 per cent. Obviously, with rates at these levels, the yield and therefore the demand for partially tax-exempt institutional obligations – building-society shares and deposits and life insurance policies – was enhanced.

The State's aid to the housing industry in the post-war periods undoubtedly stimulated the growth of the building societies; moreover, its social legislation affected the development of the insurance companies. The Workmen's Compensation Acts of 1897, 1906 and 1932 undoubtedly stimulated industrial insurance business. Conversely, the Old Age Pension Acts of 1908, 1911, 1919 and 1925, the National Health Insurance Act and the Unemployment Income Act of 1911, the Blind Act of 1920, the War Pension Schemes Acts of 1915, the Widows, Orphans and Old Age Contributing Pensions Acts of 1925, and the further evolution of schemes up to the passage of the National Insurance Act of 1946, had a retarding influence inasmuch as they removed some of the demand for insurance companies' services.

Moreover, the nationalization of the Bank of England, of the coal mines, of the transportation system, of the gas and electrical systems and of the iron and steel industry between 1946 and 1951 had an effect on the investment policies of many of the major institutions. In five years, over £2,000 million of Government securities were issued in exchange for the retirement of a like amount of private obligations and equity issues. Given that the State obligations issued in the form of compensation bore lower yields than the private-debt obligations they replaced, and that the nationalized industries had been among the institution's largest private domestic borrowers, these

[1] 'Fixed or unit trusts' (Board of Trade Committee Report), *Banker's Magazine*, Vol. CXLII (1936), p. 342.

Acts had an impact on various financial institutions' portfolio policies – particularly on those of the insurance companies. The default risk on a large segment of their existing investments was eliminated; but the earnings on these were reduced and major avenues for investment in senior private-sector interest obligations had been drastically curtailed. Naturally, this consequence of nationalization worked as a catalyst in causing the institutions '... to reappraise the value of other types of securities, especially equities, in their anxious search for a higher rate of return on their funds'.[1] This search was progressively more easily satisfied as the Government gradually relaxed its controls over private-sector and local-authority borrowings after the Second World War.

Indeed, the selective reduction in the Government's comprehensive financial and expenditure controls in the post-1951 period, with the accompanying substitution of a more traditional form of money and credit control, also had a marked effect on the subsequent development of the British financial system.

The partial reduction, and then the complete elimination of capital issues control on the domestic market borrowings of the investment trusts, the unit trusts, and the hire-purchase companies from 1953 on had a stimulating effect on these institutions; particularly when coupled with other liberalizing legislation (the 1954 Hire Purchase Act) and the abolition of credit directives (the 1952 removal of the 1947 directive which pegged the level of bank advances to hire-purchase companies). From 1949 to 1962, the assets of UK investment trusts increased from £619 million to over £2,000 million; over the same period the assets of our sample of hire-purchase companies boomed – from £32 to £436 million, and between 1954 and 1962, as noted previously, they grew at a compound rate of more than 26 per cent per annum.

As in the 1920 to 1938 period the relaxation of building controls in 1952, coupled with the various State incentives to home ownership (the 1954 and 1955 Guarantee Schemes, the first steps towards abolishing rent control under the Rent Act of 1957, and the House Purchase Scheme of 1958) stimulated the demand for housing and thus for building-society loan accommodation, a demand which the favourable tax treatment of building-society interest earnings helped to fulfil. From 1946 to 1962 building-society assets increased from nearly £900 to over £3,800 million.

Conversely, the maintenance of the selective directives and the occasional imposition of ceilings on bank advances and loans (such as those imposed in the 1955–8 period), coupled with the traditional incidence of the post-1951 conventional application of monetary policy, stunted the growth of the banking system and stimulated the growth of its competitors.[2] The assets of UK commercial banks grew relatively slowly between 1946 and 1962 – at 2·3 per cent compound per annum. Indeed, by 1958 the authorities had apparently become aware of some of the implications of their policy approach. Heathcoat Amory, the Chancellor of the Exchequer at that time, observed '... [Quantitative bank credit] control is vexatious and frustrating and makes for inefficient banking, notably because it obliges the banks to restrict competition among themselves and yet exposes them to additional competition from outside institutions.'[3]

The subsequent post-1957 elimination of the maintenance of select directive and quantitative controls on bank credits seems to have had a quite pronounced effect. Late in 1958 the banks bought a controlling interest in nine of the twelve leading hire-purchase finance houses and began to compete directly for a more proportionate share of the personal loan market. Between the end of 1957 and the end of 1962 the increase in the banks' assets, some £1,600 million, was more than that of the previous eleven years.

The development – the influence of changes in international conditions

Naturally, the Government's interest in the domestic financial structure was partly a product of the change which occurred in the UK's economic position in the world community. Indeed, the consequent changes in the 'City's' and in sterling's position in the international environment must be sketched out in order to understand the significance of the decline of the British Empire on the business practices of the British-based financial institutions.

Before 1900, Britain's international position was preeminent. The 'City' was the hub of the world's financial market, and sterling, as a reserve currency, was as good as, or better than gold. However, the introduction of impediments to trade, tariffs, the rapid growth in the economic power of its trading rivals, and the two major wars which followed radically changed the situation.

[1] G. Clayton and W. T. Osborne, *Insurance Company Investment* (London: Allen & Unwin, 1965), p. 107.

[2] In December 1957, the London Clearing Banks' advances were slightly less than in December 1951. *Bank of England Quarterly Bulletin* (June 1969), p. 184.

[3] 'The new mandatory weapon – full description and appraisal', *The Banker* (August 1958), p. 493.

By 1960, instead of being a major international creditor, the country was a major international short-term debtor, and during the transition the activities of its financial institutions adjusted to the changing environment.

Beginning with the turn of the century, with Government pressure (Colonial Stock Act of 1900), the placements of UK financial savings abroad were first skewed so that the savings flowed towards the Empire; then they were constrained in their entirety as the Empire fragmented following the Second World War. The abandonment of the Gold Standard and the establishment of the Sterling Area in 1931 accentuated the first process, which in turn was practically completed with the establishment of the Government's Foreign Transactions Advisory Committee in 1936.

The implementation of the Defence regulations in the following year, which prohibited all capital issues without Treasury assent, effectively severed the erstwhile close connection between the UK's domestic and non-sterling areas' capital and money markets and set the stage for the severance of the old imperial connections as well. By the end of the Second World War and its aftermath – devaluation, the independence of India and the subsequent movement towards independence of other dependent territories – the imperial orientation of such overseas investment placements waned rapidly; particularly as the demands for domestic reconstruction expenditure and the burgeoning governmental social and economic programmes provided alternative outlets for investment placements.

In effect, over the period 1880–1962, the geographic confines of the UK financial mechanism changed considerably. From being in many ways the core of the international savings and investment scheme, a role which made the domestic financial system extremely sensitive to external financial pressure, the boundaries of its operations first shrank so that it just had an Empire orientation. Then, in the post-1946 periods a further contraction took place. New savings and investment commitments became progressively slanted to the domestic economy; while the financial ties with the newly independent ex-colonies tended to stagnate and decline. The results of this geographic contraction in the markets' lending practices were substantial.

The marked reduction in the relative share of sterling-denominated commercial bills in the banks' holdings of bills discounted between 1914 and 1920 from 95 per cent to 59 per cent and the parallel relative reduction from 41 per cent to 15 per cent between 1938 and 1946, for instance, indicates how wartime demands, as expressed through the issuance of Treasury Bills, pre-empted the UK money market's potential contribution to the supply of short-term international loans. Similarly the absolute reduction of some £130 million in the banks' holding of commercial bills in the inter-war period may be taken as a reflection of a withdrawal of the market from international lendings; whereas the rapid growth of the merchant banks and of local-authority temporary loans in the post-convertibility era (1958 on) may be partly taken as an indication of the growth in the market's net borrowings of international funds (from the Euro-dollar market) as well as the Bank of England's encouragement of city factoring in the international investment and savings process.

The change in the UK's international position had the effect of arresting and then reversing the London money market's role in the international money market with respect to its sterling position. Previously it had contributed, through its acquisitions of sterling and commercial bills, to the supply of international funds; more recently, though, reviving its position as a financial entrepôt, it had through the conversion of Euro-dollar deposits into sterling actually drawn on these funds to accommodate the loan demands of domestic borrowers.

The change in the UK's international position over the period 1920–62 had other effects too. The reduction in the bank holdings of commercial bills in the 1920s and 1930s, coupled with the long-sustained Government policy of domestic deflation throughout most of the period, reduced the banks' second line of liquid reserves (their money at call and at short notice and their bills discounted) by approximately £120 million between 1920 and 1938. It is reasonable to suppose that this development both acted as an impediment to the overall expansion of the joint-stock banks' business and tended to make them more cautious in their lending business; these banks were relatively unresponsive to the domestic demands for medium-term loans and consumer finance in the inter-war era.

From 1946 to 1958, the banks experienced a similar situation. Their holdings of bills discounted (including TDRs) fell from £2,269 million to £1,368 million, mainly in response to the Government's successful efforts to reduce the market's holdings of Treasury bills as part of its programme to restrain the growth of domestic demand. Similarly, the growth of the other components of their liquid reserves (money at call and at short notice) was far from sufficient to make up the deficiency (+£182 million).

As a consequence, it was not surprising for one observer to note in 1956 that '... the British banks have settled into a comfortable middle age, content to carry on in traditional grooves'.[1] The liquidity considerations coupled with the various quantitative and selective credit directives eliminated their ability to do much else. Nor, given the Government-underwritten full employment policy, was it surprising in the absence of much joint-stock bank competition that the growth of the hire-purchase companies and of various merchant banks was so rapid in the post-war era. The change in the UK's international position coupled with lethargic bank competition undoubtedly had an effect on both the growth rates and on the relative market shares of various UK financial institutions.

The development – the institutions' actions

Naturally, the response of the financial institutions to the changing legislative and general economic environment was not necessarily passive. Indeed, with respect to the statutory controls which either regulated their own activities or those of other financial institutions, their actions frequently both led to and at times actually dictated the nature of the Government intervention: they soon set up pressure groups in the form of trade associations to represent their interests. These responses are part of the record of important considerations to be taken into account in analysing the empirical account of the development of the financial institutions.

To be sure, during the early part of the period the influence of these associations was relatively weak, as the members of each group of institutions competed aggressively with each other for a growing share of the community's financial savings. However, when the net benefits of intra-group competition became more marginal as the numbers in the group were reduced (the number of joint-stock banks declined from 168 to 45 between 1891 and 1920, and the number of trustee savings banks and building societies shrank from 303 to 163 and from 4,320 to 1,271 respectively over the same period) the trade associations (the Committee of the London Clearing Banks, the Trustee Savings Bank Association, the Building Societies Association, etc.) were used to set out the norms of within-group behaviour as well as to represent the groups' collective interests with other members of the financial community and with the Government.

[1] R. F. Henderson, 'The economic effects of hire purchase', *Spring Lectures* (The Institute of Bankers, 1956), p. 110.

With time, then, the within-group behaviour of the various financial institutions tended to become cartelized. Norms with respect to interest paid or received tended to be established for those institutions not legally subject to State interest-rate regulation – the banks and the building societies. Similarly, the institutions' trade associations prepared within-group guidelines with respect to various types of non-price competition as well as to the character of the business which the institutions within the group should engage in.

As the relevant trade associations became more powerful and a more tightly knit oligopolistic market structure emerged, the financial activities of the various cartelized groups of institutions became, in turn, more clearly demarcated. In 1931, for instance, a member of the Macmillan Committee observed that the banks' balance sheets

> '... show a remarkable adherence to the conventional distribution of assets over a period of years, and this feature has to be kept in mind in considering the position of the commercial banks as the distributive agents for credit throughout the commercial, industrial and financial world'.[2]

This comment on the long-run adherence to a statutory or a convention-dictated asset distribution would have been even more relevant with respect to certain other large financial institutions – the building societies, the trustee savings banks, the Post Office Savings Bank and the insurance companies and with similar implications. The growing cartelization of the predominant parts of the financial system tended to lead to an inflexibility in loan placements which left gaps in the process of financial intermediation. The Macmillan Committee's observation that in 1930 there was a deficiency in the conversion process of financial savings into medium-term loans serves as an example of the results of the development of such market imperfections.

Indeed, the process of cartelization made it almost inevitable that the gaps should both emerge and grow without outside intervention. As the various groups of institutions grew, their representative trade associations made it more difficult for both within-group members and outside organizations to meet the new emerging demands for financial accommodation. Bank opposition

[2] Committee on Finance and Industry, *Report*, p. 38. This observation was not completely accurate in the sense that the percentage of bank asset holdings of Government securities and of loans and advances certainly changed. It is accurate, however, with respect to the nature and terms of their loans to the private sector.

led to the withdrawal of the first Bill to establish the Birmingham Municipal Bank on a permanent basis in 1916 and to the failure on the First and Second Export Credit Guarantee Schemes in 1926 and 1930. It formed the main barrier to the trustee savings banks' attempts to secure permission to introduce cheque-drawing facilities. 'The initial reaction of the commercial banks to this request was anything but favourable . . .'[1] In addition, the banks were far from amenable to suggestions that they or anyone else should provide clearing services which might tend to benefit their financial competitors. They introduced their credit-transfer clearing scheme in 1960 only on becoming aware that the Post Office had plans to implement a competing national giro system.[2]

The banks objected to the establishment of new entrants to deposit banking. They thought that all other savings organizations should be restricted to the term-deposit business. They were not inclined to assist their competitors, such as the finance houses, to capture an increasing share of the loan market by providing specialized clearing facilities. Other trade associations, such as the Trustee Savings Bank Association, the Building Societies Association, and the Council for the London Stock Exchange, also exerted dampening or restraining pressures on new entrants.[3] As a consequence, as the gaps emerged within the financial framework, attempts to fill them were usually initiated by some independent agency, such as the Bank of England, the Government, or, more recently, by certain merchant banks with their new-found source of independent finance – the Euro-dollar.

In the 1920s and 1930s, as noted, the Bank of England initiated the creation of the United Dominion Trust, the Security Management Trust, the Agricultural Mortgage Corporation, the Bankers' Industrial Development Corporation and, less directly, the first unit trust – Municipal and General Securities in 1931. Similarly the Government, with its direct subsidies to local-authority and privately sponsored low-cost housing projects, helped to eliminate the municipal and private unsatisfied demands for housing finance.

In the 1940s and 1950s, the Government and the Bank of England continued their financial innovating efforts. In 1945, the Bankers' Industrial Development Corporation was reorganized into two new agencies – the Finance Corporation for Industry and the Industrial and Commercial Finance Corporation, and, as in the 1930s, the established financial institutions, the banks and the insurance companies, were encouraged to provide overdraft facilities or else to take up the capital issues of the new organizations. Such State- or Bank-of-England-initiated innovations continued into the 1950s with the creation of the Ship Mortgage Finance Company, the Air Finance Company Ltd, and the Commonwealth Development Finance Company.

This Bank-of-England- or State-sponsored intervention had an important side effect. It tended to bolster private confidence in the institutions they chose to aid with the result that these institutions tended to grow rapidly. The hire-purchase companies, for instance, expanded rapidly following the establishment of the Bank-of-England-supported Dominion Trust in 1920. Similarly, the indirect assistance the Bank of England gave to the establishment of the first unit trust in 1931 seemed to have similar results. In 1931 there was one unit trust; in 1933 there were three; in 1936 there were 67 holding assets of over £50 million.[4]

While the Bank-of-England- or direct State-sponsored innovations noted above served to fill in some of the gaps created by the process of institutional cartelization, the effect of Government statutory regulations tended to ensure that the tendency towards market segmentation was sustained. The impact of the statutory framework, of the Government's general financial policy and of its selective quantitative controls and directives tended to cement the existing institutions even more firmly into their traditional grooves and to discourage any adventurous financial innovations. The institutions reinforced the tendency. They developed special relationships among themselves within and across the group boundaries in the form of loan accommodation, special financial arrangements, or direct ownership.

Special relationships, for instance, had existed between the banks and the building societies, and the insurance companies and the building societies for years. In the early 1900s building societies arranged financial stand-by agreements with insurance companies: for instance, in 1910 the Woolwich Equitable Building Society arranged a £100,000 stand-by tranche with a life insurance company at a cost of 10*s* 6*d* per £100 per annum.[5] In turn, no

[1] Lombard, 'Crux of the savings bank argument with Lombard Street', *Financial Times* (20 February 1964), p. 11.

[2] 'British banking', *The Economist* (30 June 1962), p. 1340. The introduction of this giro system was delayed until October 1968.

[3] Stockjobbers and stockbrokers regarded the unit-trust movement with disfavour until such savings instruments were traded in the stock exchange.

[4] 'Fixed or unit trusts', op. cit., p. 339.

[5] E. J. Cleary, *The Building Society Movement* (London: Elek Books, 1965), p. 158.

doubt, such insurance companies benefited by having fire and property insurance business directed their way. Similarly, as the building societies grew, they played an increasingly important role in funding the banks' construction loans; in turn, the banks provided them with short-term financial accommodation – in 1957 all the building societies had bank overdraft facilities.[1] Moreover, the banks' financial involvement with the sample of hire-purchase companies from 1924 on was extensive. They then provided slightly under 10 per cent of these institutions' financial requirements (£150,000); by 1930 bank financial accommodation had risen to nearly 40 per cent (£2,507,000), and in 1955 it reached 59 per cent (£60,174,000). Finally, in 1958 the banks bought a controlling interest in nine of the twelve members of the Finance Houses Association which in turn accounted for over 80 per cent of the finance-company HP debt outstanding.

Naturally, as these financial inter-group relationships were established, each group's interest was more readily recognized. The tendency towards market segmentation by the type and term of borrowings and by the type and term of savings was accentuated as interest rate competition was minimized both within and between groups. Moreover, within this framework, it seems probable that aspects of certain market-sharing arrangements to the mutual benefit of the close-knit groups of institutions were well recognized. For instance, as the hire-purchase companies grew in market stature they became an increasingly important source of second-line bank reserve – bills discounted, which the banks could with a modicum of ingenuity transpose into fully fledged banking deposit reserves.[2] Likewise, given that the banks' own lending business often encountered official restraints, it would hardly be surprising if the banks actually directed a fair number of their potential borrowers to such institutions for loan accommodation – particularly after the banks had acquired a controlling interest in them. The assets of the sample of hire-purchase companies, six of which were bank-owned in the post-1958 period, increased by over 260 per cent from the close of 1958 to 31 December 1962 (£166 million to £436 million).

As a consequence, the market-liberalizing tendencies of domestically sponsored innovations were muted. The overall growth and business practices of the newly emerging intermediaries were constrained to fit in with the needs of the dominant domestic financial groups of institutions. In contrast, the impact of the market innovations which stemmed from borrowings in the Euro-dollar market in the post-1957 convertibility period was, with respect to the amount of intervention and its effect on the market structure, much more extensive.

The subsequent growth of externally controlled money-market institutions' liabilities and the increase in their direct ownership in UK-issued liabilities were substantial. Between 1951 and 1957, the deposits of overseas banks with UK offices remained almost constant at around £700 million; similarly, changes in their overall investments in UK obligations were minimal. During the period 1957–62 a marked change took place. The total deposits of these banks grew from £700 million to over £2,300 million; more significantly their acquisitions of certain UK obligations increased more rapidly – their holdings of local-authority paper increased from £6 million to £168 million. Similarly, the growth of certain domestically controlled financial institutions – the accepting house-merchant banks – was staggering; the presence of the Euro-dollar market provided part of the necessary finance. From 1957 to 1962 their deposit liabilities increased from £151 million to £658 million and their holdings of local-authority paper rose from £8 million to £290 million.[3]

In effect, convertibility and rapid subsequent growth in the international capital market provided a sharp stimulus to institutions existing on or beyond the fringe of the control of the domestic financial oligopolies to step up their financial activities in the UK market. They responded, and the magnitude of their response tended to break down the existing market arrangements. Financial intermediation became more sensitive to interest differentials than to market-sharing arrangements. So much so, in fact, that by the mid-1960s the monetary authorities were forced to extend their credit-curbing requests to all types of financial institutions, including the overseas banks, in their efforts to contain the growth of domestic credit expansion.

Conclusion

The national, the international and the inter-institutional historical developments discussed above played an important part in shaping the growth of the UK financial

[1] Committee on the Working of the Monetary System, *Principal Memoranda of Evidence*, Vol. 2, p. 20.

[2] In 1965, the authorities imposed an upper limit on the banks' ability to create commercial bills and hence liquid assets. Commercial bills were incorporated in the loan ceilings imposed in that year.

[3] *Bank of England Quarterly Bulletin* (December 1960) and Central Statistical Office, *Financial Statistics* (April 1963).

system. Moreover, many of these developments help to explain the trends of relative market shares of the various competing institutions which are set out in Table 1.1.

In the early part of the period, Government intervention obviously enabled the joint-stock banks to acquire a virtual monopoly of the money market; it led to the banks' monopolistic position as suppliers of monetary assets – bank deposits. Similarly, Government intervention played a key role in channelling the growing amounts of low-income saving into a particular set of institutions – the Friendly Societies, the Post Office Savings Bank, the trustee savings banks, the building societies and the insurance companies. Its directives also largely determined how these institutions invested these funds. In addition the expansion of the State's legislative influence, its growing demands for financial accommodation, and the concomitant expansion of its decision-making powers over the amount and composition of domestic expenditure played an even more important role after 1914 in determining the nature of the evolution of the UK financial system.

The institutions' response to the State's intervention and to intra- and inter-institutional group competition also had an increasingly powerful impact as the period progressed. Their representative trade associations became increasingly influential as widespread amalgamation movements increased the incidence of intra-group institutional concentration. Intra-group institutional competition was modulated, and the boundaries of each group of institutions' operations as borrowers and lenders in the financial markets tended to become more sharply delineated. In all, the process of institutional cartelization tended to reinforce the impact of the State's intervention on the main market structure. The financial market tended to become more segmented and the type of competition within each segment became more oligopolistic. The institutional accommodation of the financial demands of borrowers became less sensitive to the return the borrower was willing to make and more sensitive to the conventional or Government-dictated guideline regarding the type of business the lenders should engage in.

Efforts were made to fill the resultant gaps by the process of financial intermediation. In particular, the Government and the Bank of England sponsored the development of several new innovations to channel finance to credit-needy sectors in the 1920s and in the decade following the Second World War. In a limited sense, some of their efforts were highly successful – the authorities' stimulus to the hire-purchase companies and the unit-trust movement was particularly effective. Nevertheless, as the State-sponsored intermediaries grew, they in turn formed close-knit relationships with the existing cartel-dominated institutions. The latter in turn tended to regulate the competitive practices of new entrants.

In effect, by the late 1950s, the UK financial institutional system had evolved into a carefully segmented type of market system in which each set of institutions had acquired a tacitly agreed monopoly over a certain section of the loan market, and in which each institution in turn endeavoured to avoid direct interest-rate competition with its competitors for its share of household savings.

From the late 1950s, however, the interlocking market-sharing cartel arrangements tended to break down as foreign banks and domestic merchant banks, drawing on the growing pool of Euro-dollars, stepped up their intervention in the domestic market-place. Interest incentives became increasingly important in both allocating credit and in attracting domestic savings. The dominant domestic institutions, the banks, the insurance companies, the building societies and savings banks, were forced to compete more aggressively to retain their market shares.

2 The Growth of the UK Money Stock, Household Encashable Assets and Financial-Sector Credits by End Use 1880–1962

Introduction

An empirical base is presented in this chapter to illustrate the changes in the UK financial system over the 1880–1962 period. It is a counterpart of the previous chapter describing the qualitative environmental developments which influenced the financial structure over these years. The graphs and tables record the absolute amounts and the rates of growth of the consolidated assets and liabilities of the main UK financial institutions. In turn, these assets and liabilities are disaggregated in order to show the levels and the growth rates of certain important financial variables: bank and non-bank financial institutions' assets, the money stock broadly and narrowly defined, the financial institutions' public- and private-sector credits, and the liabilities of the State-run savings schemes. Indicatively, on some of the graphs, gross domestic private expenditure has been plotted so as both to show the graphical association between it and some of the financial stocks which are held to affect it, and to illustrate the relative size and rates of growth of some of these financial stocks. At a glance it seems that the existence of these stocks warrants consideration.[1]

The empirical evidence is presented so that it fits into four broad categories: the money supply and other institutionally generated liquid claims – encashable assets, National Savings, the growth and composition of the financial institutions' assets and public and private financial-sector credits. The discussion of each category highlights the significant overall changes as well as those which occurred in each of the three peacetime periods and the two wars.

[1] In this respect the following matrix of the simple Pearson correlation coefficients between certain financial stocks and gross domestic private expenditure is suggestive.

Pearson correlation coefficient: GDPE and certain financial stocks

Period	*Money Stock*	*Money Stock lagged by Six Months*	*All Encashable Assets*	*Gross Private Credit*
1882–1914	0·96	0·96	0·98	0·98
1922–1939	0·68	0·71	0·61	0·63
1948–1962	0·98	0·97	0·98	0·98

The Money Stock and other Encashable Assets

This statistical account of the UK financial sector traces out the growth of household encashable assets – M_3 and its components: those institutional and State-issued obligations which may be regarded as the non-corporate private sector's 'liquid' stock of financial assets.

Table 2.1 records the yearly consolidated total of the stock of household encashable assets and it delineates the percentage shares attributable to its component parts. Encashable assets are composed of 'quasi-money' – M_2 plus all National Savings Certificates and savings bonds, and life assurance funds. The latter stock is taken as a proxy of the cash value of issued policies. Quasi-money in turn consists of net money – M_1 plus all savings bank deposits and all building societies' deposits and shares. Net money consists of currency outstanding and net bank deposits; both the components of M_1 have been compiled so as to exclude estimates of commercial banks' currency holdings and inter-bank deposits.

Graph (2)A supplements Table 2.1 by illustrating the growth trends and the yearly levels of encashable assets and its key components – quasi-money, net money and currency (H). In addition, by representing the annual levels of gross domestic private expenditure, Graph (2)A provides a yardstick with which to measure the size of these stocks; a comparison which has some significance in monetary theory.

As Graph (2)A depicts, all four of the represented financial stocks (H, M_1, M_2, M_3) grew quite rapidly over the entire period except during the 1920s and early 1930s. The overall per annum compound rates of growth of these stocks (currency, money, quasi-money and encashable assets) were 3·4, 3·9, 4·3 and 4·6 per cent respectively from 1891 to 1962. The graph also shows that over the whole period there was a fairly close association between the level of private expenditure and

TABLE 2.1 **United Kingdom: Household Encashable[1] Assets and Percentage Share Attributable to Each Component 1880–1962**

Year (approx. (31 Dec.)	*Total Encashable Assets £ mil.* I	*Currency* % II	*Net Bank Deposits* % III	M_1 % IV	*Savings Bank Deposits* % V	M_2 % VI	*Life and Annuity Funds* % VII	*National Savings Bonds, etc.* % VIII
1880	802	19·1	49·1	68·2	10·0	84·4	15·5	0·1
1881	835	18·7	49·6	68·3	9·9	84·6	15·3	0·1
1882	872	18·4	49·5	67·9	9·9	84·8	15·1	0·1
1883	897	17·6	50·0	67·6	10·0	84·6	15·2	0·2
1884	916	16·5	50·7	67·2	10·3	84·4	15·3	0·3
1885	926	15·8	50·9	66·7	10·5	84·2	15·4	0·3
1886	922	14·9	50·8	65·7	11·0	83·8	15·8	0·3
1887	940	14·0	51·2	65·2	11·2	83·5	16·0	0·5
1888	969	12·7	52·7	65·4	11·2	83·5	16·0	0·5
1889	1006	12·4	53·5	65·8	11·1	83·4	16·0	0·6
1890	1043	12·5	53·7	66·2	11·1	83·5	15·9	0·6
1891[2]	1086	12·7	54·3	67·0	11·0	83·7	15·6	0·6
1892	1102	12·2	54·7	66·9	11·1	83·4	16·0	0·6
1893	1101	12·2	54·1	66·4	11·5	82·8	16·6	0·6
1894	1147	11·9	54·4	66·3	11·9	82·8	16·6	0·6
1895	1215	11·4	55·3	66·7	12·2	83·1	16·4	0·6
1896	1276	11·6	54·9	66·5	12·5	83·0	16·4	0·6
1897	1307	10·9	54·8	65·7	12·9	82·6	16·8	0·6
1898	1350	10·4	55·0	65·4	13·2	82·4	17·0	0·6
1899	1398	10·1	54·9	65·0	13·3	82·2	17·0	0·8
1900	1445	10·2	54·7	64·9	13·3	82·1	17·0	0·9
1901	1453	9·8	54·2	64·0	13·6	81·5	17·6	1·0
1902	1478	9·3	54·1	63·4	13·7	81·0	17·9	1·1
1903	1479	9·7	52·9	62·6	13·7	80·3	18·5	1·2
1904	1502	9·3	52·8	62·1	13·7	79·8	18·9	1·3
1905	1534	8·9	53·3	62·2	13·7	79·5	19·3	1·2
1906	1581	8·2	53·3	61·5	13·6	79·3	19·4	1·3
1907	1604	8·3	53·1	61·4	13·5	79·1	19·6	1·3
1908	1636	7·9	53·2	61·1	13·5	78·7	20·0	1·3
1909	1672	7·8	53·0	60·8	13·6	78·5	20·1	1·4
1910	1734	7·7	53·3	61·0	13·4	78·4	20·1	1·4
1911	1783	7·6	54·0	61·5	13·6	78·4	20·2	1·5
1912	1841	7·7	54·1	61·7	13·5	78·4	20·1	1·5
1913	1908	7·5	54·5	62·0	13·4	78·6	20·0	1·4
1914	2081	8·4	54·8	63·2	12·5	78·6	18·7	2·6
1920	4224	10·9	55·8	66·7	8·5	77·1	10·4	12·5
1921	4275	9·5	55·5	65·0	8·4	75·4	10·7	13·9
1922	4167	9·0	53·3	62·3	8·9	73·6	11·5	14·9
1923	4181	8·8	51·9	60·7	9·1	72·5	12·1	15·4
1924	4215	8·8	50·8	59·6	9·3	72·1	12·6	15·3
1925	4283	8·4	49·8	58·3	9·4	71·3	13·3	15·4
1926	4395	8·1	49·4	57·5	9·2	70·7	13·8	15·5
1927	4500	7·8	49·3	57·2	9·0	70·8	14·2	15·0
1928	4655	7·4	49·2	56·7	9·0	71·0	14·5	14·4
1929	4686	7·3	48·1	55·4	9·0	70·6	15·2	14·3
1930	4885	6·9	47·9	54·8	8·9	70·9	15·0	14·1
1931	4783	7·1	45·6	52·7	9·3	70·2	15·8	14·0
1932	5180	6·5	47·7	54·2	9·2	71·9	15·3	12·8
1933	5275	6·5	46·4	52·9	9·8	71·6	15·8	12·6
1934	5449	6·4	45·5	52·0	10·2	71·8	15·9	12·3
1935	5733	6·3	45·8	52·1	10·6	72·5	15·8	11·7

1880–1962

Year (approx. 31 Dec.)	*Total Encashable Assets £ mil.* I	*Currency* % II	*Net Bank Deposits* % III	M_1 % IV	*Savings Bank Deposits* % V	M_2 % VI	*Life and Annuity Funds* % VII	*National Savings Bonds, etc.* % VIII
1936	6092	6·5	45·9	52·4	11·0	73·4	15·5	11·2
1937	6345	6·9	44·4	51·4	11·4	73·2	15·5	11·3
1938	6419	7·0	42·7	49·7	12·1	72·8	15·9	11·3
1939	6777	6·8	42·6	49·4	12·3	72·2	15·4	12·4
1946	16050	8·3	40·7	49·0	17·1	71·2	8·2	20·6
1947	16551	8·1	41·4	49·5	16·6	71·4	8·4	20·2
1948	16865	7·3	41·9	49·2	16·8	71·6	8·8	19·6
1949	17108	7·2	41·2	48·4	16·9	71·6	9·2	19·2
1950	17531	7·1	41·2	48·3	16·7	71·7	9·6	18·8
1951	17676	7·3	40·5	47·8	16·4	71·3	10·1	18·6
1952	18070	7·6	40·3	47·9	15·8	71·3	10·6	18·1
1953	18664	7·8	40·3	48·1	15·0	71·4	11·1	17·5
1954	19565	7·9	39·9	47·8	14·5	71·3	11·6	17·1
1955	19680	8·4	37·6	46·0	14·4	70·3	12·6	17·1
1956	20271	8·7	36·6	45·3	14·2	69·8	13·2	16·9
1957	21039	8·8	36·5	45·2	13·8	69·9	13·8	16·3
1958	22120	8·6	35·9	44·5	13·1	68·7	14·5	16·8
1959	23647	8·3	35·6	43·9	12·7	68·2	15·0	16·8
1960	24770	8·3	34·4	42·7	12·6	67·1	16·0	16·9
1961	25892	8·3	33·3	41·6	12·8	66·6	16·9	16·4
1962	27182	7·9	32·9	40·8	12·4	66·1	17·8	16·1

Sources

Same as those of Graph (2)A.
Col. I = Col. VI + Col. VII + Col. VIII.
Col. VI = Col. IV + Col. V + Building Societies' Deposits and Shares.
Col. IV = Col. II + Col. III.

Notes

[1] Encashable Assets: Currency + Bank Deposits + Savings Bank Deposits + Building Societies' Deposits and Shares + Life and Annuity Funds + National Savings Certificates, Defence Bonds, Premium Bonds and other bonds recorded on the Post Office Register.

[2] Cols. I and III have been adjusted in the 1880–90 period so as to preserve the continuity of the series. In 1891 various banks' balance sheets were published for the first time in *The Economist*'s 'Banking Number'. The adjustment took the form of inflating the net deposit figures in the pre-1891 period by multiplying them by a splicing factor.

the various categories of encashable assets. Finally, it indicates that though the growth rates of these stocks were quite similar, the discrepancies between them were substantial enough to bring about major changes in their market shares of total encashable assets over the period.

An examination of the record for the whole period shown in Table 2.1 underlines this point. The currency-outstanding share of encashable assets fell from 19 to 8 per cent. The money stock's contribution was reduced from 68 to 41 per cent, whereas the residual components of encashable assets increased their share from 32 to 59 per cent. Moreover, the table demonstrates that a large portion of this increase is directly attributable to the growth of the State's direct-placement savings schemes. The share of such State-issued obligations rose from 0 to 16 per cent from 1880 to 1962. The record for the whole period shows that household encashable assets increased from £800 million in 1880 to £27,000 million in 1962; and it illustrates that as this growth took place there was a marked shift in householders' preferences away from zero- or low-interest-yielding encashable assets (currency and bank deposits) to those wealth claims which provided a greater post-tax interest yield to their holders.[1]

On a sub-period basis, the graph and table illustrate

[1] Deposit accounts as opposed to current accounts earned interest which was generally set at about 2 per cent below 'bank rate'.

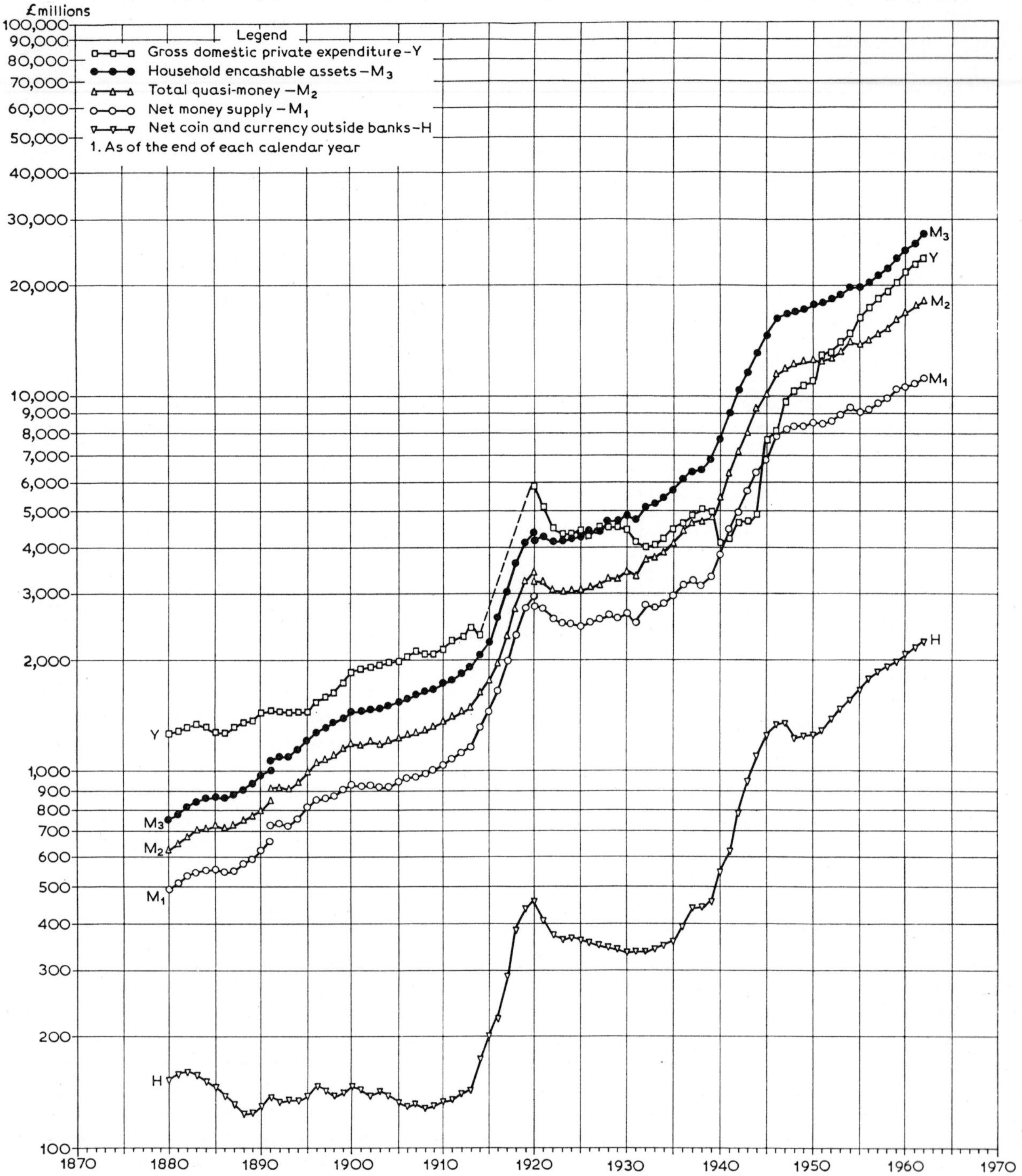

(2)A UK Money Stock and Household Encashable Assets 1880–1962

Source: See Appendix, Table (A)3.3

that very pronounced divergences in the rates of growth and changes in the distribution of these household liquid assets took place over relatively short periods, particularly during the war years. The magnitude and the variation in these sub-period changes should be regarded as indicative in the sense that they reflect the responsiveness of the financial sector to external stimuli. This variable record warrants examination.

The table and the graph show there was an absolute decline in the currency stock and in its relative share before 1914; a trend which no doubt reflects the continued influence of the 1844 Bank Act. Conversely, bank deposits increased substantially. Their growth more than offset the influence that the declining currency stock had on the money supply; it increased, though there was some reduction in its share of total encashable assets. Apart from the currency-to-deposit switch, the expressed relative asset preferences remained fairly stable over these years, probably reflecting the sustained environmental stability. The rates of growth of the net money supply, of total quasi-money and of total potential encashable assets were nearly identical: 2·6, 2·6 and 2·9 per cent per annum from 1891 to 1914.

The 1914–20 period produced some sharp discontinuities. The stock of currency outstanding and of bank deposits more than doubled; consequently the money stock rose sharply over the six-year period, increasing from £1·2 milliard at the close of 1913 to about £3 milliard by the end of 1920. During the war years the compound growth rates of currency, deposits and of the money stock were approximately 18, 14 and 16 per cent respectively; the money stock's share of encashable assets rose from 63 to 67 per cent from 1914 to 1920. There were even more marked changes in the growth and in the shares of other encashable assets too. The share of life assurance funds fell by nearly 50 per cent – 18·7 to 10·4 per cent. The share of National Savings Bonds, etc., quintupled – 2·6 to 12·5 per cent. Parallel types of movement occurred elsewhere. Deposits with Post Office Savings grew rapidly, while the obligations of the privately sponsored trustee savings banks and building societies declined. Over all, in the First World War period there was a marked expansion in bank deposits, and, consequently, the money supply. Other less liquid forms of encashable assets grew rapidly also; but nearly all the growth in these financial savings was in the form of either institutionally placed or directly issued Government obligations. The pressures stemming from the national emergency were obviously potent.

From 1920 to 1939, owing at least in part to the post-war reconstruction demands, nearly all the trends of the 1914–20 interval were completely reversed. The stock of currency outstanding increased by only three million pounds – less than 0·7 per cent over the entire twenty-year period. Indeed from 1920 to 1930 it decreased steadily, year in year out (excluding 1924), from £429 to £337 million, i.e. by over 25 per cent. Similarly, and in contrast with the 1914–20 period, currency's share of total encashable assets decreased from nearly 11 per cent in 1920 to just under 7 per cent in 1930. It remained around this level up to 1939. The changes in the other component of the money supply, bank deposits, did not offset these movements. The market share of bank deposits rose in only three of the twenty years, falling from 56 per cent in 1920 to just under 43 per cent in 1939. Bank deposits actually declined between 1920 and 1930. As a consequence the market share of the money supply fell from 67 to 49 per cent over the period; the size of the outstanding stock oscillated downwards between 1920 and 1931 and then rose slowly. Over this period, its compound rate of growth per annum was under 1 per cent; this was 2 per cent less than in the 1891–1914 period, and 21 per cent lower than in the 1914–18 interval. These developments were partly a product of deliberate Government policies.[1]

For the other components of encashable assets the wartime trends were also reversed. The compound rate of growth and the market share rose more slowly for the least liquid portion, National Savings issues and life assurance funds, than for savings bank and building society shares and deposits – $(M_2 - M_1)$. The former's share increased from 23 to 28 per cent – about £900 million; the latter's share rose from 10 to 23 per cent – about £1,100 million. In addition, in both these categories of encashable assets, the division of new savings placements was heavily skewed in favour of the privately run institutions. In the savings bank sector, the growth of building society shares and deposits was phenomenal. They rose from £80 million to £700 million and accounted for over 50 per cent of the overall increase in this asset category. In the less liquid category, too, the growth of life assurance funds was substantial: they rose by over £600 million, as compared with the £300 million increase in National Savings Certificates and Bonds, accounting for over 65 per cent of the increase in the growth of the least liquid component of encashable assets.

During the inter-war period, then, both the distribution

[1] See previous chapter.

of encashable assets between the three classifications and the shares of the components within each classification changed considerably. The most liquid asset classification, money, declined in relative importance, and its most liquid component, currency, fell faster than did bank deposits. In the next category, M_2, savings bank and building society deposits and shares increased markedly, particularly the building society liabilities which had remained relatively stagnant since 1880. The increase in the share of the last and most illiquid component of encashable assets, life and annuity funds and National Savings certificates, etc., was much smaller – about 5 per cent; but here too there was a pronounced shift towards the accumulation of private as opposed to State-issued encashable obligations. In all, over the period there was a marked shift in household encashable asset preferences away from the most liquid component – money – and towards less liquid, higher yielding assets offered by private financial institutions.

In many ways the record reflected by Table 2.1 and Graph (2)A in the Second World War parallels that of the First, reflecting once more the pronounced impact of the 'emergency'. The stock of currency outstanding rose rapidly, growing at a compound rate of over 16 per cent per annum (22 per cent per annum in 1914–18). Bank deposits also increased sharply, growing at a compound rate of 12 per cent per annum (14 per cent per annum in 1914–18), and the overall stock of money increased by 13 per cent per annum rising from £3·3 milliard in 1939 to £7·9 milliard in 1946. As Table 2·1 illustrates, however, there was a divergence from the 1914–18 record. The relative shares of the three broad groups of liquid assets barely changed. The marked increase in the money stock was matched by increases in the less liquid components of encashable assets. Nevertheless, as in the First World War and unlike the record of the inter-war period, the expansion within each of the components was concentrated in the form of State-underwritten obligations. Moreover, the relative shares of both the building society liabilities and of life and annuity funds of total encashable assets declined sharply from 10 to 5 per cent and 15 to 8 per cent respectively. Over all, the impact of the war-induced demands on the financial sector was quite as powerful as in the First World War; this time, however, the organization of the Government's fund-raising programme was better managed so that its impact was more evenly spread over the financial system.

Again, the elimination of the wartime pressures and the emerging reconstruction demands influenced the post-war development. The record for the post-1946 period is quite similar to that for the inter-war era. The stock of currency outstanding declined initially and the period growth in bank deposits was so restrained – 2·3 per cent compound per annum – that the share of the money-stock component of encashable assets fell from 49 to 40 per cent. The shift from State- to privately issued obligations paralleled the inter-war experience. The market shares of both building society shares and deposits and life and annuity funds more than doubled – from 5 to 13 per cent and from 8 to 18 per cent respectively. The former grew at a compound rate of 9·6 per cent per annum and the latter at a rate of 5 per cent per annum. The outstanding obligations of their State competitors, the Post Office Savings Bank deposits and National Savings Bonds and Certificates, either declined or were just sustained.

In summary, the sub-period examination shows that the wartime emergencies produced quite substantial variations in the data. During these periods, for instance, much of the whole-period growth in the money supply took place; over half of the £10,500 million increase occurred in these twelve critical years. Over all, however, even the war-induced pressure did not mask the important long-run change in household asset preferences. In peace and war the expressed preference for a positive net tax return on encashable asset holdings steadily became more pronounced.

The UK National Savings Movement [1]

The growth of the State-sponsored small-savings schemes, and particularly the Government's successful efforts to directly place its own obligations, are reflected in the growth and the composition of the stock of household encashable assets. National Savings – all savings bank deposits, National Savings Certificates, Defence Bonds, and other securities listed on the Post Office Register – are included in encashable assets. The movement's share of these liquid assets rose considerably from 1880 to 1962: from 10 to 28 per cent. By 1962 these savings instruments were an important part of the private sector's holdings of liquid assets; their contribution to the outstanding stock of such claims was only 5 per cent less than that of the commercial banks.

The growth of the movement over the period mirrors three other important financial developments. It shows

[1] The official definition of National Savings has been extended to incorporate the Birmingham Municipal Savings Bank's deposits as well.

how successful the State-sponsored or -controlled savings schemes have been in competing with privately controlled institutions. It illustrates the extent to which this competition has been channelled through State-owned or -controlled institutions – the Post Office Savings Bank and the trustee savings banks – rather than by the direct issue of Government savings instruments to households. Finally, given that most of the collected National Savings are invested in Government debt instruments, it demonstrates how useful the movement has been in serving as a financial intermediary for the channelling of private savings to finance public expenditure.

Graph (2)B shows the development of the movement from 1860 to 1962. It depicts the total level of National Savings, of the deposits of the savings banks, of National Savings Certificates, and of Defence Bonds and other direct security issues, in each year. Here too it is clear that a sub-period examination of this record would be revealing, as marked changes in the trend both of National Savings and of its constituent components occurred either at the beginning or shortly after the end of the periods of national emergency – 1914–18 and 1939–45.

From 1880 until 1914, the State-controlled or -regulated savings banks dominated the movement; though, to be sure, the direct placement of Government stock with households, via the Post Office Register, had been growing quite rapidly since 1900. From 1914 to 1922, however, the situation changed. The growth of the old rnd the new direct savings schemes burgeoned, so that by 1922, their combined share of total National Savings had risen to 60 per cent after having been 9 per cent in 1914.[1] During this eight-year period, total National Savings rose from £290 million to £990 million, an increase which was more than two and a half times as large as the total additions to National Savings in the previous fifty-odd years.

With the re-establishment of peacetime conditions, the growth of the movement and of its components changed markedly. The compound rate of growth, which averaged 22 per cent per annum from 1914 to 1918, plummeted. It levelled out to a mean of 2·9 per cent in the inter-war era – a rate which was considerably below that of its growth in the pre-war era – 3·8 per cent. Within the movement, the State's direct-placement savings programme lost ground. Households ran down their holdings of such savings instruments at a compound rate of just over 0·8 per cent per annum. In the meanwhile, the combined deposits of the Post Office, the trustee and the Birmingham Municipal savings banks continued to grow slightly faster than they had done in either of the two previous sub-periods, averaging out at 4·7 per cent per annum. By 1939, these State-directed or State-owned financial intermediaries had recaptured some of the ground they had lost during the First World War – their market share of total National Savings had risen and that of the direct savings schemes had fallen by 20 per cent over the interval.

As the graph shows, however, during the Second World War the trends which had dominated the movement during the First World War were repeated. Again the annual compound rate of growth of National Savings soared from 2·9 to 21·3 per cent – just slightly below the First World War rate. Again the growth of the direct security sales programme accelerated dramatically; the total book value of the outstanding stock quadrupled from approximately £800 million to £3,100 million between the end of 1939 and the end of 1945. Moreover, (and reflecting better management by the National Savings Committee) this time the movement's financial intermediaries, the trustee savings banks, the Post Office Savings Bank and the Birmingham Municipal Bank, enjoyed a substantial rate of growth too. Their combined deposits rose at a rate of over 18 per cent compound per annum, moving from approximately £800 million to £2,400 million. Over the six years the movement's share of encashable assets rose from 25 to 38 per cent – an absolute increase of £3,500 million, which was just £500 million short of the increase of the money supply over the interval.

In the post-1946 period, the pattern of the inter-war era was not duplicated, although to be sure there were some similarities. Instead of continuing to grow, even if at a much reduced rate, National Savings actually declined in each year from 1948 to 1954. However, as in the inter-war years, the experiences of the different savings-collecting agencies varied markedly. From 1946 to 1962, for instance, the deposits held at the Post Office Savings Bank declined by over £200 million; whereas the special investment deposits at the trustee savings banks, which paid a higher rate of return, almost sextupled, rising from about £110 million to £600 million. A similar effect was seen with the movement's two major types of direct-savings instruments. The relatively high-paying National Savings Certificates continued to be accumulated throughout the period, rising by some £700 million;

[1] This was probably due to the fact that during this period the post-tax yield on such securities was substantially higher than on savings bank deposits.

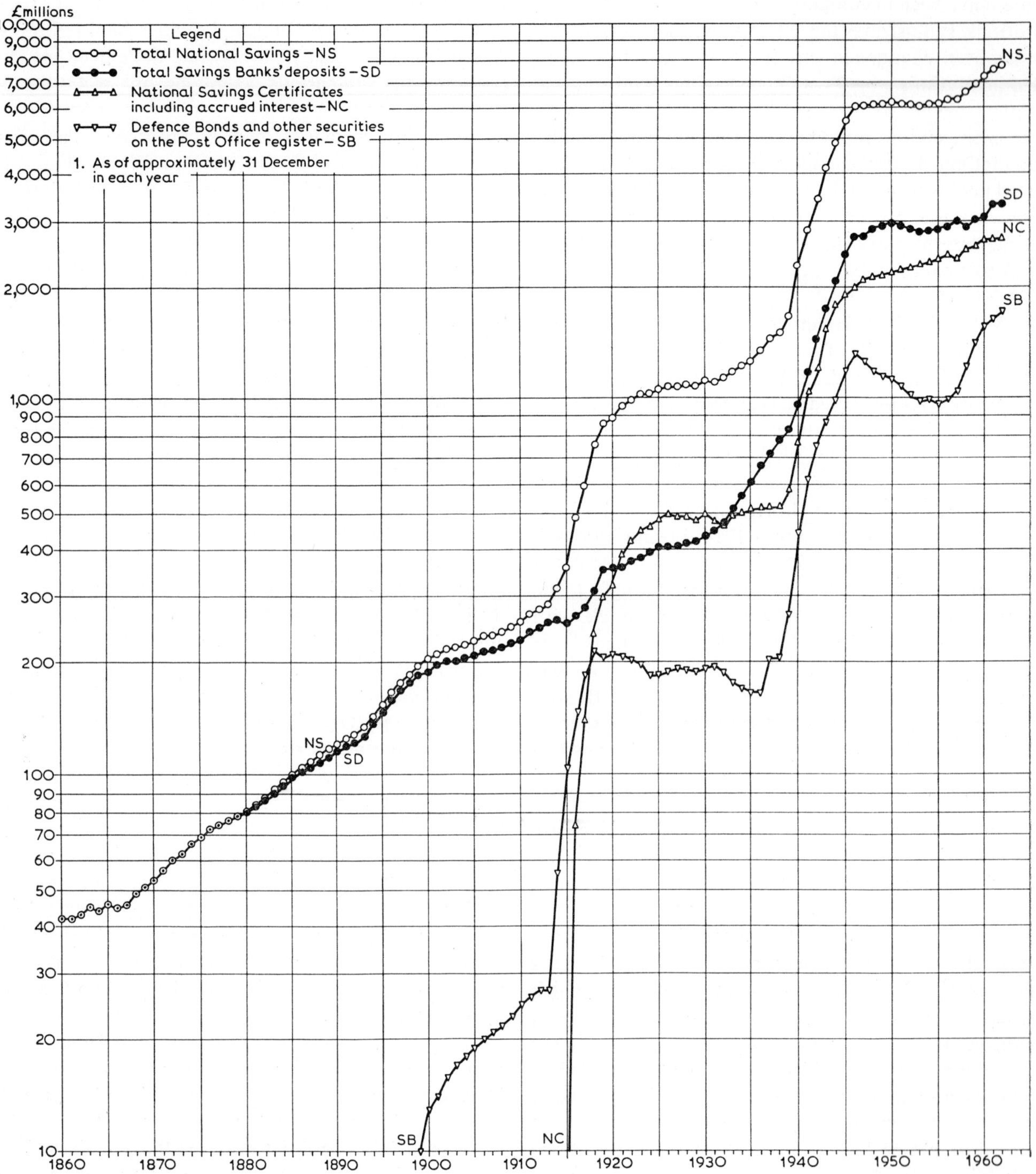

(2)B UK National Savings 1860–1962

Source: See Appendix, Table (A)3.1

while the lower-yielding direct-security issues holdings declined by about 30 per cent from 1947 to 1957, when their growth was revived with the introduction of 'premium' bonds. In all, over this period, the movement's progress was far from satisfactory. Its average compound growth rate of 1·6 per cent per annum was about half what it had achieved in the inter-war era, and it was substantially less than that of any of the other financial intermediaries it competed with for a share of household savings. Correspondingly, its share of household encashable assets sagged from 39 per cent in 1946 to just under 30 per cent in 1962 while between 1920 and 1939 its share had increased from 21 to 25 per cent.

Taken as a whole, this examination of the development of the National Savings movement is quite indicative. It reveals just how successful a movement like this may be, given the right conditions. It suggests that the National Savings instruments offered must bear a competitive rate of return if the movement's share of the market is to be sustained, and that they should bear a slightly higher rate of return if the authorities desire this share to be increased. Finally, as noted, the marked fluctuations in the rate of growth of the movement between peace and war periods illustrate to a large extent how large the changes in household savings placements were between such periods. The extent of these changes, particularly after the Second World War, could in theory at least account for some of the successes and for some of the failures the authorities have experienced in controlling the growth and the impact of the financial sector.

Total Assets and Public and Private Credits of the Banking and Non-Banking Financial Institutions

The long-run change in the composition of encashable assets and the marked variations in the growth of the National Savings movement indicate that there was a fairly large reduction in the banks' share of institutionally collected financial savings over the period; and that within this period there were also fairly pronounced fluctuations in the allocation of all institutionally collected savings. The recorded slow post-war growth of bank deposits and the rapid growth of building society shares and deposits and of life insurance funds, coupled with the relative stagnation of the National Savings movement, had a marked effect. An examination of the growth and composition of the sample of institutional assets substantiates both points, and sets them out in more detail.

Graph (2)C shows the total institutional assets, A; the assets of the banks and non-banking financial institutions, D' and Q; commercial bank loans and advances, L_B; and a measure of domestic expenditure, Y (Gross Domestic Private Expenditure). It shows that the period rate of growth of the consolidated institutional assets was substantial – a 4·6 per cent compound increase per annum between 1891 and 1962. Moreover, it indicates that the rate of growth was reasonably stable, and that what instability there was appeared to be mainly due to the checkered growth path of bank assets. Indeed, apart from a sharp rise in the rate of accumulation, the growth path for the assets of the non-banking financial intermediaries is quite remarkable for its stability. Before 1918, this increased steadily at a compound rate of approximately 3·5 per cent per annum; after 1917, it rose steadily at an annual rate of 6·4 per cent per annum. In all, the graph shows that between 1891 and 1962 total financial institutional assets increased from £1,200 million to £28,200 million, that bank assets rose from £800 million to £10,800 million; that the assets of the savings-orientated institutions grew from £400 million to £17,400 million; the corresponding levels of Y were £1,300 million and £24,000 million respectively.[1]

A more detailed examination of this graph shows that the change in the banks' share of total institutional assets varied markedly over the period, and the main changes occurred during the wars and in the inter-war and post-war periods. The previous discussion of the sub-period movements in encashable assets and of National Savings, and in particular the emphasis on the impact of the two national emergencies on these series is indicative.

During the war years, presumably due to the magnitude of the State's demand for finance, the banks grew rapidly in comparison with the other institutions – 14 per cent versus 3·6 per cent per annum in 1914–18 and 12·2 versus 8·1 per cent in 1939–46. During the inter-war and post-war eras the situation was completely reversed. Between 1918 and 1939 the banking sector's assets grew at a compound rate of 1·8 per cent per annum while those of the other institutions rose at 6·6 per cent per annum, and between 1946 and 1962 the respective rates were 2·3 and 6·1 per cent. In turn, the small comparative increase in banking assets in these peacetime periods could well reflect the known substantial change in the State's financial policy and perhaps the change in the composition and the amount of realizable private demand for

[1] Phyllis Deane and W. A. Cole, *British Economic Growth 1688–1959*, pp. 332–3. See also Central Statistical Office, *National Income and Expenditure* (London: H.M.S.O., 1965).

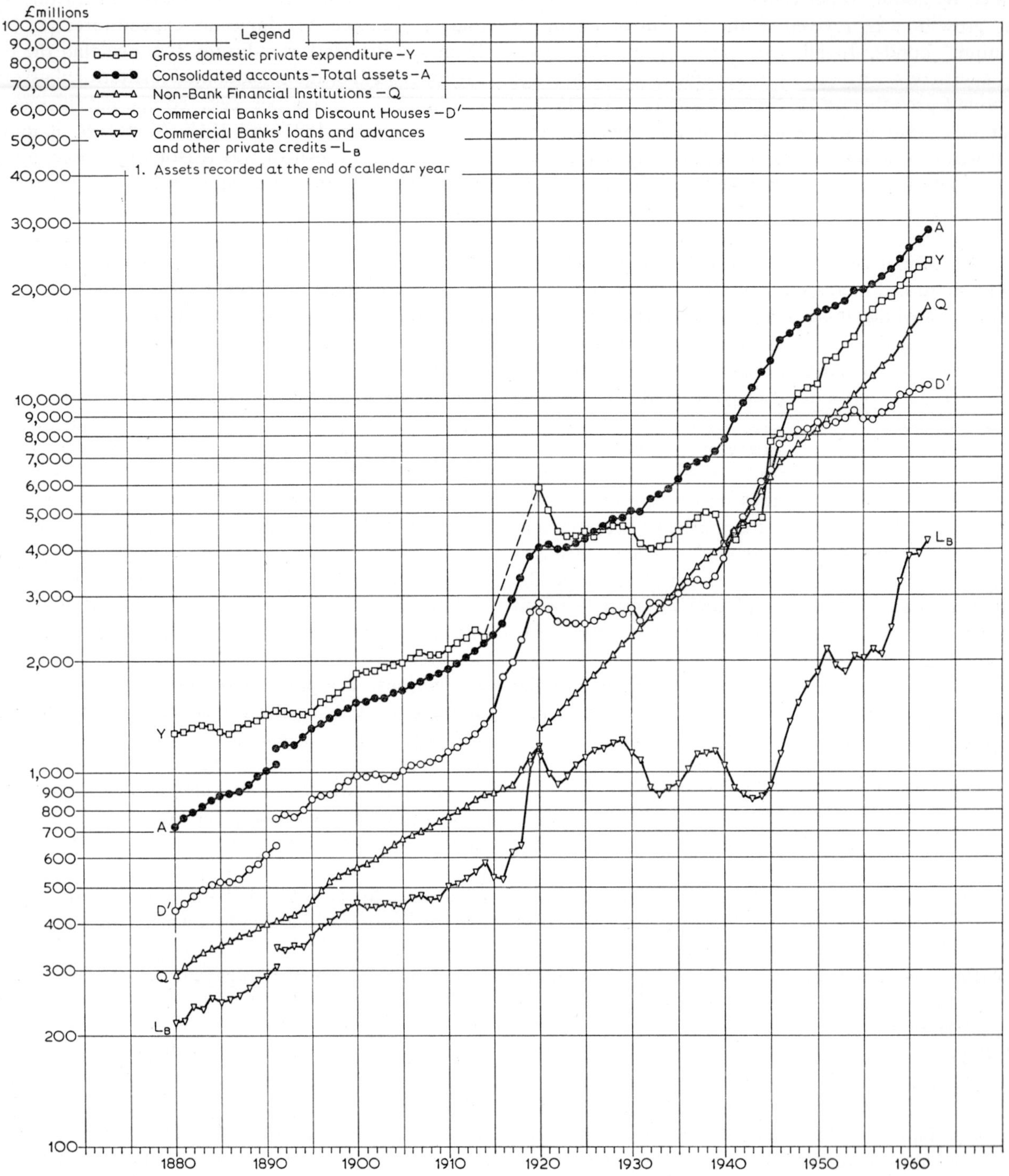

(2)C UK Financial Institutions: Bank and Other Financial Institutions' Assets 1880–1962

Source: See Appendix, Table (A)3.4

financial loan accommodation. In accord with the noted change in the rate of growth of bank as opposed to non-bank institutional assets, the banks' share of the consolidated financial assets fell from 63 per cent to 58 per cent between 1891 and 1914; it rose from 58 to 73 per cent between 1914 and 1920; it declined from 73 to 46 per cent between 1920 and 1939; it increased from 46 to 52 per cent from 1939 to 1946, and it fell again from 52 per cent to 38 per cent, between 1946 and 1962.

Graph (2)D sets out the growth paths of the selected financial institutions' loan placement. It shows that, in conjunction with the increase in the 'savings', there were also changes in the institutions' share of consolidated total assets and the allocation of institutional credits between the private and public sector. In the wars, as indicated, there was a pronounced switch in institutional credit placements in favour of the public sector; during the inter-war and post-war periods, the wartime movement was completely reversed. Over the whole period too, the non-bank financial institutions with their greater rate of growth eventually exceeded the bank share of the market for public and private credits. This can be seen by examining the movements of A (total institutional assets), of L (gross private institutional loans)[1] and of L'_B (the commercial bank and discount company private credits), and the movements between them.

In more detail, the graph shows that over the whole period the non-bank financial institutions' private credit extensions grew considerably more rapidly than those of the banks – 4·4 as opposed to 3·6 per cent compound rate per annum between 1891 and 1962. In nominal terms, the private credits of the 'savings type' of institutions rose from £260 million to £11,420 million; while the banking-sector private loans increased from £540 million to £5,550 million between these two dates. Concomitantly, the other assets of the non-bank financial institutions, mainly Government debt, rose from £150 million to £6,030 million; while the banks' residual assets (cash, premises and Government securities) increased from £220 million to £5,270 million. In conjunction with the overall growth of the total consolidated institutional assets noted above, these developments reflect the long-run growth in the importance of institutional financial intermediation both in the collection and investment of household savings; moreover, they underline the fact that in both processes the non-bank financial institutions played a role that became progressively more important.

On a sub-period basis, the graph illustrates the extent to which the trends in the recorded institutional private credit placements were disrupted by the two wars, and it shows how the subsequent peacetime growth in such institutional assets mirrored or differed from the pre-war pattern.

All forms of the financial intermediaries' private credits, total private credit, L, the banking sector's private credit, L'_B, and institutional mortgages, M, declined absolutely during the early phases of the national emergencies, and they did not regain their pre-war levels until after the cessation of hostilities. These facts, in conjunction with the noted extraordinarily rapid growth of total financial institutional assets, A, in these war years, of approximately 10·2 per cent compound rate per annum, indicates the extent to which these institutions' portfolio preferences were slanted to help meet the Government's demands for financial accommodation.

The graph shows that the trends in the post-war as opposed to the pre-war variations in the banking sector's private credit extensions were quite different. In the 1891 to 1914 interval, these credits grew relatively steadily; in the inter-war era in contrast they showed marked variations round a slowly falling trend; in the post-1945 period they grew in two discontinuous spurts from 1946 to 1951 and from 1957 to 1962. These changes perhaps suggest how sensitive such credits are to the volume of private expenditure and to the financial constraints imposed by the monetary authorities.

Finally, the graph illustrates the extraordinary growth in institutional mortgages in both the inter-war and post-war years. From 1890 to 1914, these credits rose slowly at a compound annual rate of 1·4 per cent per annum increasing from £140 million to £190 million. From 1918 to 1939, the rate of accumulation averaged 9·3 per cent per annum and between 1946 and 1962 it amounted to 10·9 per cent per annum. Correspondingly, institutional mortgages rose from £160 million to £1,050 million and from £910 million to £4,770 million over the same time periods. These inter-war and post-war rises in mortgage credits were presumably caused in part by the released war-deferred housing demand as abetted by the State's assistance to the housing industry. Over all, the sub-period trends in the growth of these mortgage credits, like the sub-period trends in bank advances, suggest that environmental developments had a pronounced impact

[1] Gross private credit was derived by adding together the total assets of the banks, the assurance companies, the savings banks, the building societies, the various Friendly and provident societies, and of the sample of eight hire-purchase companies *after* deducting these institutions' holding of cash, Government obligations and recorded foreign credits.

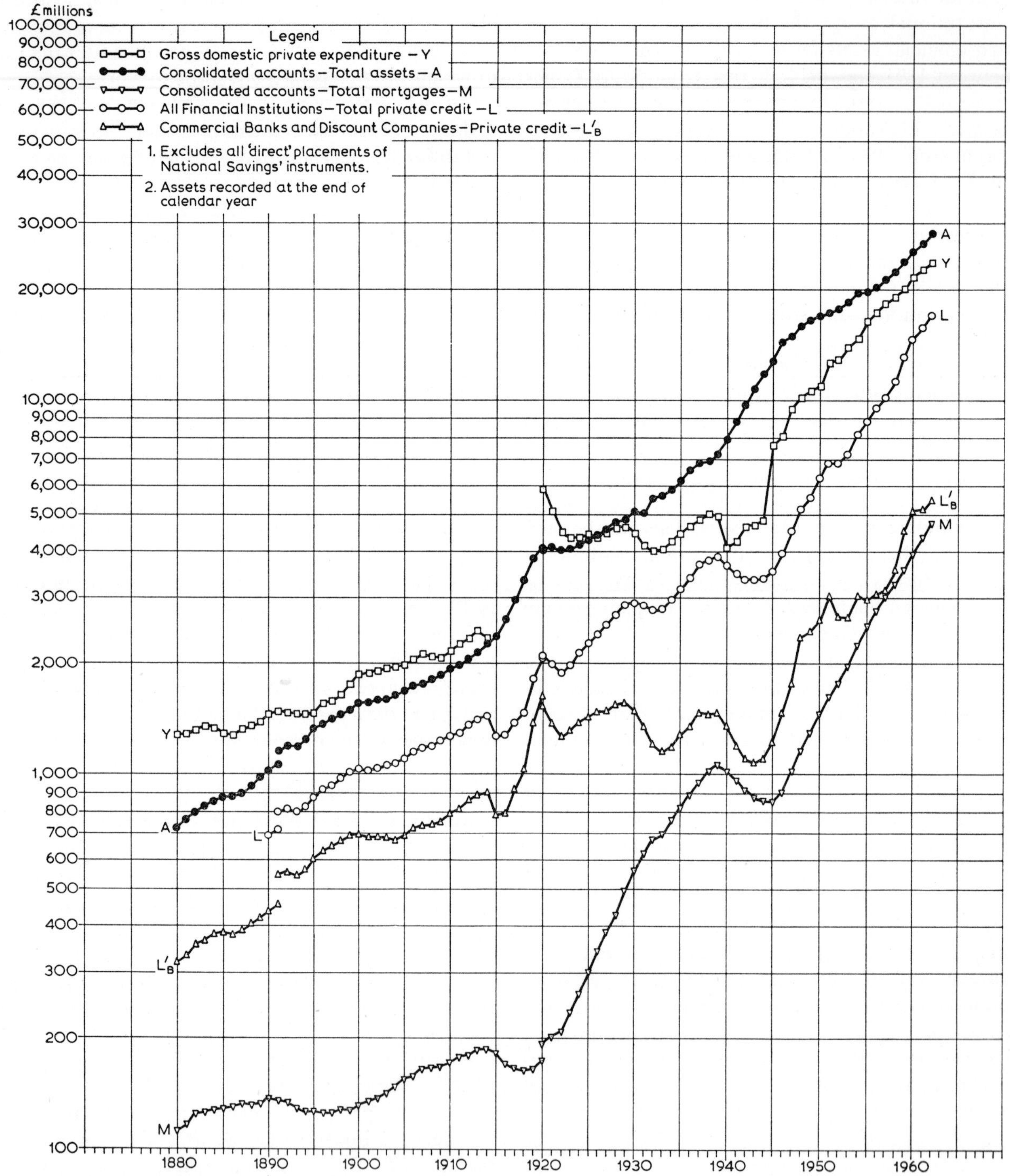

(2)D UK Financial Institutions: Credit Allocation 1880–1962

Source: See Appendix, Table (A)3.4

on the subsequent growth and pattern of the financial institutions' credit placements.

UK Financial Sector's Savings and Investments

While the graph depicts the growth of the operating financial institutions' assets and indicates in general the nature of their credit disbursements, it understates both the growth and allocation of financial savings in that the proceeds of the State's direct security sales under the National Savings programme have not been included. As noted, these State-managed savings schemes grew very rapidly over the period, particularly during the wars, so that their investments and their liabilities are quite significant.[1] This is shown in Table 2.2, which also analyses the composition of some of the financial institutions' asset holdings.

Table 2.2 shows how the financial sector's savings-collecting agencies' asset preference for Government or private paper changed between 1891 and 1962.[2] As noted above, the supporting data differ from those in Graphs (2)C and (2)D in that they incorporate the book value of the State's direct-security placements outstanding as sold through the National Savings programme. As a result, due to this inclusion, the table provides a more accurate picture of the growth of voluntary household savings – compulsory contributions to various State-run superannuation schemes are not included.

The table illustrates that from 1891 to 1962 there was a substantial increase in financial savings. As an indication of this, column 1 shows that the assets of the collecting institutions rose from £1,200 million to £32,000 million over the 73 years. It shows that, as these assets were accumulated, an increasing proportion of them were placed in Government debt instruments. In 1891, for instance, the banks held approximately 10 per cent of their assets, £80 million, in Government paper and the other institutions invested approximately 29 per cent of their funds in the State's obligations – £120 million. By 1962, the banks held 30 per cent of their assets in such instruments – £4,200 million, and the other institutions' holdings of Government debt had risen to 42 per cent – £8,950 million. These facts give an indication of the growth of the institutionalization of savings as well as suggesting how useful the movement was as a source of Government finance.

The inclusion of the State's direct-savings placements as part of the financial sector's assets has a considerable effect on the bank versus non-bank shares of the market assets. In particular, it makes the recorded divergence between the movement of bank and non-banking assets much more marked after 1914. As a consequence, the bank and discount company share of the adjusted total of financial assets are shown to fall below 50 per cent in 1930 rather than in 1934, and, except for a very modest recovery in the war years, this downward trend is sustained right up to 1962 when their share accounted for 34 per cent of the outstanding financial sector's assets.

The incorporation of these National Savings instruments, besides raising the level of the financial sector's assets and changing the banking sector's share, has had other effects on the records. It accounts for a large portion of the increase of the other financial agencies' assets in the war periods, and it partly explains the phenomenal increase in their revealed preference for Government securities during the emergencies. From 1914 to 1918, as shown by column 7, this relative preference nearly doubled – it rose from 31 to 60 per cent; from 1939 to 1946 it nearly doubled again – it increased from 39 to 71 per cent. Equally significant, as noted in the section on the history of the National Savings movement, was the impact that the abrupt curtailment in the expansion of such direct-security issues in the inter-war and the post-war years had on the peacetime movement of the 'preference' ratio. It fell from 60 to 39 per cent from 1920 to 1939 and from 71 to 42 per cent from 1946 to 1962.

The table also shows that the revealed preferences of the various privately controlled financial institutions for Government obligations varied widely between wartime and peacetime. These changes contributed to the impact that the variable growth of the National Savings Movement had on the allocation of total savings between Government and private obligations. Moreover, in line with explanations of how wartime-accrued liquid assets influenced subsequent peacetime spending, the peacetime changes in these revealed preferences suggest that these institutions treated their Government security holdings as a kind of potential credit inventory. One

[1] The inclusion of the business of the various governmental and privately managed pension schemes would have affected the record too. However, as the savings flowing into these schemes are often obligatory, the omission is perhaps fortunate.

[2] Before 1946, and in particular before 1920, the recorded percentage asset distributions are sometimes heavily dependent on estimates.

TABLE 2.2 **Total Assets and Government and Government-Guaranteed Security Holdings of Various UK Financial Institutions 1891–1962.[1,5] (In £ millions)**

Year[2]	*Total Assets All Institutions*[7]	*Total Assets Banks and Discount Cos.*[3,7]	*Banks+ Discount Cos. Total Assets / Total Assets All Institutions*	*Banks+ Discount Cos. Gov. and Gov. Gty. / Total Assets Banks and Discount Cos.*	*Banks+ Discount Cos. Treas. Bills +TDR's etc. / Total Assets Banks and Discount Cos.*	*Banks+ Discount Cos. Total Cash / Total Assets Banks and Discount Cos.*	*Share of Government and Gov. Gty. Holdings of Non-Bank Financial Institutions to their Total Assets*	*Share of Cash Holdings of Non-Bank Financial Institutions to their Total Assets*	*Selected Institutions' Holdings of Gov. and Gov. Gty. to their Total Assets: Building Socs.*	*Assurance Cos.*	*Trustee Savings Banks*
	1	2	3	4	5	6	7	8	9	10	11
			%	%	%	%	%	%	%	%	%
1891	1,172	760	65	10	—	9	29	3	0	3	91
1892	1,198	777	65	10	—	9	30	2	0	2	91
1893	1,195	767	64	11	—	9	30	2	0	2	98
1894	1,251	802	64	10	—	10	31	2	0	2	98
1895	1,323	853	64	9	—	10	34	2	1	2	98
1896	1,371	872	64	9	—	8	34	2	1	2	98
1897	1,417	893	63	8	—	10	35	2	1	2	99
1898	1,470	925	63	8	—	10	35	1	1	2	98
1899	1,508	950	63	8	—	10	34	1	1	2	98
1900	1,557	983	63	8	1	10	33	1	1	2	98
1901	1,569	980	62	8	1	11	33	1	1	3	98
1902	1,607	994	62	8	1	11	33	1	1	3	98
1903	1,612	972	60	8	1	10	33	1	1	3	98
1904	1,645	986	60	9	1	11	32	1	1	3	98
1905	1,703	1,018	60	10	1	11	31	1	1	2	91
1906	1,752	1,048	60	8	1	11	31	1	1	2	89
1907	1,783	1,058	59	8	1	11	30	1	1	2	89
1908	1,826	1,080	59	8	1	12	30	1	1	2	87
1909	1,873	1,098	59	8	1	12	29	1	1	2	85
1910	1,938	1,136	59	7	1	11	29	1	1	2	84
1911	1,999	1,175	59	7	1	12	29	1	0	1	83
1912	2,072	1,219	59	6	1	12	29	1	0	1	82
1913	2,153	1,272	59	6	1	12	29	1	0	1	81
1914	2,295	1,361	60	8	1	17	31	2	0	1	80
1915	2,471	1,480	61	20	4	16	37	2	1	9	79
1916	2,843	1,701	62	20	6	19	47	1	2	13	80
1917	3,252	1,991	63	19	8	16	53	1	4	19	80
1918	3,760	2,301	63	19	10	16	60	1	8	26	82
1919	4,289	2,704	64	19	8	16	63	1	10	30	84
1920[4]	4,529	2,874	64	16	7	14	62	2	9	32	83
1920	4,482	2,707	61	16	7	14	60	2	9	32	83
1921	4,613	2,731	60	17	13	15	60	2	9	32	81
1922	4,535	2,567	57	20	10	15	61	2	10	35	79
1923	4,582	2,521	55	20	8	15	59	2	9	34	78
1924	4,713	2,530	54	18	7	15	56	2	7	32	78
1925	4,826	2,520	52	16	6	15	54	2	5	30	76
1926	4,972	2,570	52	15	7	15	51	2	4	28	75
1927	5,135	2,630	51	14	7	14	48	2	4	25	72
1928	5,348	2,712	51	14	7	15	46	2	5	23	69
1929	5,426	2,676	51	14	7	14	44	2	4	20	65
1930	5,674	2,770	49	16	10	14	42	2	4	19	62
1931	5,605	2,569	46	17	11	13	44	2	4	21	59

1933	6,169	2,842	46	28	12	12	42	2	3	24	57
1934	6,387	2,877	45	29	9	13	41	2	2	24	56
1935	6,733	3,039	45	29	9	13	40	2	2	23	58
1936	7,137	3,231	45	29	8	13	39	2	2	22	60
1937	7,414	3,271	44	28	7	13	39	2	2	21	61
1938	7,547	3,187	42	28	7	13	38	2	2	21	62
1939	7,980	3,360	43	25	11	14	39	3	1	20	62
1940	8,915	3,767	44	28	16	14	48	3	3	26	65
1941	10,280	4,409	45	32	23	14	55	2	4	29	70
1942	11,414	4,837	44	32	27	14	60	2	6	33	75
1943	12,787	5,377	43	31	31	14	64	2	8	35	80
1944	14,394	6,033	43	29	34	14	68	1	10	39	83
1945	15,476	6,428	42	29	33	14	71	1	11	41	86
1946	17,284	7,517	44	28	33	12	71	1	10	40	87
1947	17,936	7,837	44	28	30	12	69	2	8	36	89
						—[6]					
1948	18,638	8,222	44	28	28	8	69	2	7	39	90
1949	19,090	8,277	43	27	26	8	66	2	6	37	90
1950	19,684	8,535	43	27	26	8	64	2	4	33	91
1951	19,936	8,415	42	32	15	9	62	2	5	32	91
1952	20,338	8,536	42	33	19	9	60	2	4	30	90
1953	21,019	8,796	42	35	19	9	58	2	4	30	88
1954	22,165	9,213	42	34	17	9	55	2	5	28	84
1955	22,359	8,772	39	31	19	9	52	2	5	26	82
1956	23,093	8,738	38	30	18	9	51	2	6	23	78
1957	24,124	9,081	38	29	20	9	49	2	6	21	76
1958	25,517	9,427	37	29	17	9	48	2	7	21	75
1959	27,463	10,075	37	22	16	9	46	2	7	19	74
1960	29,001	10,264	36	18	15	9	45	2	7	18	73
1961	30,523	10,426	34	16	16	9	43	2	7	17	72
1962	32,104	10,812	34	17	13	9	42	2	7	18	69

Sources

See Appendix tables. The primary sources of these papers were as follows: Banks: *The Economist*'s 'Banking Supplement', and the Bank of England, *Quarterly Bulletin*; insurance companies: *British Parliamentary Papers* and C.S.O. *Annual Abstract*; building societies: C.S.O. *Annual Abstract* and *Building Societies' Year Book*; Post Office Savings Bank: *Annual Report of the Postmaster General*; trustee savings banks: *Annual Report of the Trustee Savings Banks Inspection Committee*; Friendly Societies: *Annual Report of the Registrar of Friendly Societies*; Co-operative Wholesale Society Bank and the Birmingham Municipal Savings Bank: Annual Balance Sheets; hire-purchase companies: Company Records at Somerset House.

Notes

[1] Institutions: *Banks*: London clearing banks, excluding the National Bank (Ireland) from 1920 on; the Scottish and Irish, and from 1920 the Northern Irish banks, *The Economist* Private Bank Series, the Co-operative Wholesale Society Bank and the Yorkshire Penny Bank. *Discount Companies*: Alexanders, National and Union Discount Cos. In 1962 those three companies accounted for 61 per cent of the total assets of all discount companies. *Non-Bank Financial Institutions*: Birmingham Municipal Savings Bank, building societies of Great Britain, life insurance companies of the United Kingdom; various Friendly Societies: Reg. Friendly Societies, trade unions, Certified Loan Societies, Collecting Societies, Superannuation Societies, Railway Savings Bank, eight hire-purchase companies: Bowmaker, British Wagon, Forward Trust, Mercantile Credit, Midland Counties, Mutual Finance, United D.T., Unit-Motor Finance, Post Office Savings Bank, the trustee savings banks, and all outstanding National Savings financial instruments.

[2] Year-end varies between 31 March and 31 December; however, most of the institutions' balance sheets are struck on or about 31 December.

[3] The three discount companies: Alexanders, National and Union accounted for about 57 per cent of the total discount companies' assets between 1953 and 1962.

[4] Discontinuity due to exclusion of Southern Irish banks, and inclusion of the hire-purchase companies, the various Friendly Societies, and the Birmingham Municipal Bank.

[5] The recorded principal holdings of National Savings Certificates, Defence Bonds, and Premium Savings Bonds are published as of 31 March each year. As a consequence, in order to approximate a 31 December figure, the posted figures were held to represent the holdings as of 31 December in the preceding year – e.g., National Savings Certificates outstanding on 31 March 1963 are treated as those outstanding on 31 December 1962.

[6] Cash holdings of the banks have not been adjusted for window dressing which was particularly large in the pre-1948 period. In 1947, 8 banks were asked to stop this practice.

[7] From 1943 on, the rebates and rediscounts of the sample of discount houses have been added to their total assets as posted in the balance sheets before the same were incorporated in col. 2 in order to maintain the consistency of the series.

which, perhaps because of the Central Bank's concern to maintain an orderly market for Government obligations, seems to have given the institutions a substantial degree of freedom in adjusting the supply of private credits to the demand once the war-imposed quantitative credit controls were removed.

The suggestion that the changes in the privately controlled institutions' Government security/total asset ratios were particularly sensitive to demand conditions seems to be substantiated by an examination of columns 4 and 5, and columns 9, 10 and 11. The first two show the percentage of banking-sector assets held in long- and short-term Government securities, and the last three show the percentage of their assets the building societies, the insurance companies and the trustee savings banks respectively invested in Government paper.

This examination illustrates that, for all the recorded institutions, Government/total asset ratio certainly responded to the Government's wartime demands for financial accommodation. The banking sector's ratio rose from 7 to 29 per cent from 1913 to 1918; while the ratios of the building societies, the insurance companies and the trustee savings banks increased from 0 to 8 per cent, 1 to 26 per cent and 81 to 82 per cent respectively. During the Second World War this pattern was repeated. The percentage of the banking sector's assets invested in long- and short-term Government securities rose from 35 per cent in 1938 to 62 per cent in 1945; over the same interval the building societies increased their commitment from 2 to 11 per cent, the insurance companies from 21 to 41 per cent and the trustee savings banks from 62 to 86 per cent. An examination of the supporting balance-sheet data shows that in each period of national emergency the building societies, the insurance companies and the trustee savings banks invested more than 100 per cent of the total increase in their assets in Government debt. Their marginal propensity to invest in Government debt with respect to their savings receipts was greater than one. In aggregate, of the total increase in the assets of the banks and the other institutions of £1,150 million between 1913 and 1918, 65 per cent were placed in Government obligations. Between 1938 and 1945 the Government's share of the growth of these institutions' investment was even bigger – it accounted for 93 per cent of the £4,200 million rise in their assets.

In the inter-war and post-1945 periods, as noted, the war-stimulated increase in the relative share of Government securities in the portfolios of the non-bank financial institutions was almost eradicated. The non-bank financial institutions which experienced the most rapid peacetime growth were those that were orientated towards meeting the rising private demand for credit, particularly for mortgages. Between 1920 and 1938, the increase in the assets of the building societies, the insurance companies and the special investment departments of the trustee savings banks accounted for nearly 70 per cent of the increase in the non-banking financial agency assets – £2,800 million. Over this period, these institutions showed an average marginal propensity to invest in Government securities of approximately 0·08 as compared with over 1·0 in the war interval. Again in the 1946 to 1962 period, these institutions accounted for over 80 per cent of the £11,500 million increase in the non-banking financial sector's assets, and again their average marginal propensity to acquire Government securities fell from over 1·0 to approximately 0·08. Indeed, when one compares the growth record of the building societies and the insurance companies during the period between the two world wars with that of the banks or the National Savings movement, it seems that in peacetime too the term, the nature – public or private – and the growth of aggregate demand, coupled with the lending biases of the particular financial institutions, explain the discrepancy. Both the building societies and the insurance companies, benefiting from favourable tax treatment which made the terms offered on their liabilities very competitive, readily placed their rapidly expanding share of financial savings in meeting the post-war demand for reconstruction finance.

In contrast, the table indicates that the banking sector, precluded by custom from providing mortgage finance or other long-term credits, experienced difficulty in placing their funds in the inter-war period. The recurrent intervals of depressed business conditions obviously curtailed the private sector's demand for bank loans. Bank advances and loans outstanding fell by 10 per cent during the 1920–3 recession and by about 25 per cent from 1929 to 1933; correspondingly, and indicating the absence of credit-worthy borrowers, their holdings of government obligations rose from 23 to 33 per cent and from 21 to 40 per cent. Over all, columns 4 and 5 illustrate the unsatisfactory nature of their inter-war investment record. The share of their assets invested in Government securities rose from 23 per cent in 1920 to 35 per cent in 1938; this meant that over the period their average marginal propensity to invest in Government securities with respect to the increase in their assets was greater than one.

In the period after the Second World War as well, demand conditions seem to have had a pronounced impact on the investment strategy of the monetary institutions. Though hampered by quantitative controls and directives, the record suggests that the banks exerted considerable efforts to obtain a full share of the private demand for credit induced by full employment. While their assets increased by about £4,000 million from 1945 to 1962, their advances alone increased by £3,000 million. Moreover, both relatively and absolutely they reduced their holdings of Government obligations. For the banking sector as a whole, the share of their assets invested in Government securities and money-market instruments fell from 62 per cent in 1945 to 30 per cent in 1962; in absolute terms this amounted to a net liquidation of such assets of about £300 million. On average, then, and completely at variance with their revealed portfolio choices in the inter-war and the Second World War periods, the banking sectors showed a negative marginal propensity to invest in the State's market obligations in these post-war years.

This net liquidation of Government securities coupled with the monetary sector's marked preference for private obligations could well be taken as a partial explanation of the monetary institutions' post-war growth as compared with their stagnation in the inter-war years. The strong private demand for loans which faced the banks was largely met, despite the general incidence of a fairly tight monetary policy, by readjusting portfolios to obtain both the reserves and uncommitted funds to permit such credit extensions.

In summary, the data brought together in this section illustrate that over the 1880–1962 interval substantial changes took place in the financial sector. The extent of the financial institutions' intermediation in the saving-investment process grew considerably more rapidly than did national income. There were also marked changes in the way that the privately operated institutions' share of the growing pool of financial savings was divided up. The dominant proportion of the sector's business held by the commercial banks and discount companies was reduced; while the shares of the insurance companies and particularly those of the building societies increased considerably. In concert, mortgage loans, medium-to-long-term private credits, and, latterly, consumer credits extended by the rapidly growing hire-purchase companies accounted for an increasing proportion of the financial sector's private business. Finally, the Government's share of the assets of the selected financial institutions and savings agencies' increased substantially.

Over all, the record for the whole period reflects a marked growth in the institutionalization of the saving-investment process; which, in turn, by facilitating the process of capitalizing the income streams of certain borrowers, was accompanied by very considerable changes in the financial structure over the eighty-three years.

Conclusion

This chapter provides a quantitative record of the end-year assets and liabilities of a large sample of UK financial institutions from 1880 to 1962. It portrays the growth of the money stock, in other institutional liabilities which could be taken as potential money substitutes, and the growth in all of the selected institutions' assets by sector (Government or private) of allocation, and in one instance by end use – mortgages. Similarly, it depicts the variation in the market shares of total financial institutional assets for some of these intermediaries, and it provides a considerable amount of information on how these institutions' asset preferences changed over the period. While its purpose is primarily descriptive, the record was designed to present the data in a manner which should be useful in examining its causal significance.

As an historical narrative, the account underlines several interesting financial developments. It shows how rapidly the non-bank financial institutions grew from 1920 to 1962 and depicts the accompanying erosion of the market share of the commercial banks. It illustrates how quickly the State-sponsored savings agencies stepped up their activities during the periods of national emergency; as well as the promptness with which the privately controlled institutions reorientated their investment policies to meet the exponentially growing demands of the Government for financial accommodation. It gives an indication of how wartime developments disrupted the financial structure and how the development of this structure was influenced by the consequent economic and political pressures following the national emergencies.

More suggestively, the account seems to underline the growing importance of the financial institutions' intermediating function by demonstrating that, through what might well be called the process of creditization, they enabled selected borrowers to capitalize a fair portion of their income streams to finance certain approved forms of expenditure. In this respect they obviously facilitated the growth of Government expenditure in the UK and stimulated the realized demand for housing. By implication, this suggests that whatever may have been the effect on aggregate expenditure of the growth of the money stock, of all encashable assets, or of the available financial credits, the financial institutions' lending practices did influence the composition of that expenditure and therefore production and factor allocation.

3 Asset Preferences and the Money Supply in the United Kingdom 1880–1962

While the size and growth of the money stock, of other forms of household liquid assets, and of total financial institution assets are regarded as important by many economists, so also is the composition of these assets. Specifically, details of the composition of any of these three broad groups of assets by such categories as currency, demand deposits, time deposits, holdings of Government securities and of Treasury Bills depict the revealed preferences households or financial institutions have for various sub-sets of assets. These preferences provide data for models which are designed to predict the portfolio behaviour of both the household sector and the financial institutions. In turn, the predicted portfolio behaviour, expressed as a relative asset preference such as a deposit/currency ratio or income velocity, plays a critical role in models which are designed either to explain the growth of the money or credit stock or else to predict the impact which these financial stocks have on private expenditure.

In this chapter the value of many of the relative asset preferences which are regarded as important in such models are recorded annually; their average values and their variation round these averages in three sub-periods are reported, and finally, for illustrative purposes, the effect of changes in two of these relative asset preferences on the money stock is assessed.

The data which record the size, variations and effects of changes in these relative asset preferences are set out in the five tables (3.1–3.5) and four graphs ((3)A–(3)D). Table 3.1 and Table 3.2 have been arranged so that they delineate the yearly level as well as the period variability in certain financial ratios which represent relative asset preferences featuring in discussions of credit allocation and money-stock generation. Table 3.3 and Graphs (3)A, (3)B and 3(C) depict the value which a few of these ratios attained both in the United Kingdom and in the United States along with the size of the money stock and of high-powered money in each year. Table 3.4 shows the impact which changes in two of these relative asset preferences and the changes in the stock of high-powered money had on the money stock, within the framework of the Friedman and Schwartz format: '. . . the hypothetical changes in M that would have occurred if each of the determinants in turn changed as it did, while the others had remained at their initial values'.[1] Finally, Graph (3)D and Table 3.5 illustrate the annual values, the average values and the coefficients of variation of income velocity in the UK over the whole period, 1881–1962, and for three sub-periods; 1881–1914, 1920–39 and 1946–62.

Table 3.1 shows the liabilities of the bank and the non-bank financial institutions,[2] the sum of their joint liabilities, and the quotients of various financial ratios which represent aspects of their revealed portfolio preferences.[3] The notation in the table coincides with that used in the article 'Financial Credit Multipliers and the Availability of Funds' so that the reported statistics may be substituted for the literal numbers used in the models contained therein.[4] Table 3.2 provides a measure of central tendency and of the range of the values of some of the ratios round their average values over selected time intervals.

In Table 3.1, columns 4–15 represent certain financial asset preferences of the three main groups of decision-takers: the banking institutions, the financial intermediaries, and householders and non-financial business entities. They delineate the non-financial sector's preference for financial intermediaries' liabilities relative to its preference for those of the banks (column 4) and similarly this sector's preference for high-powered money with respect to its ownership of banking liabilities and those of all financial institutions (columns 11 and 13). Similarly, they show the revealed preferences of banking institutions for certain types of assets in relation to their total assets (columns 5, 6, 7 and 14), and the revealed selected asset

[1] M. Friedman and A. J. Schwartz, *A Monetary History of the United States 1867–1960* (Princeton University Press, 1963), p. 795.

[2] For the purposes of exposition, non-bank financial institutions will be called financial intermediaries from now on.

[3] The ratios were computed by taking the average of the year-end data.

[4] D. K. Sheppard and C. R. Barrett, 'Financial credit multipliers and the availability of funds', *Economica* (May 1965), pp. 198–214.

TABLE 3.1 **Commercial Banks', Non-Bank Financial Institutions' and Private Sector's Average Asset Preferences in the UK, 1892–1962[1] (£ millions)**

Period as of Approx. 30 June	Liabilities of Non-Bank Financial Institutions[2] Q 1	Total Bank and Discount Co.'s Liabilities[3] D 2	$D+Q$ 3	$h=\frac{Q}{D}$ 4	$k=\frac{S_B}{D}$ 5	$t=\frac{T_B}{D}$ 6	$d=\frac{H_B}{D}$[4] 7	$j=\frac{S_I}{Q}$ 8	$f=\frac{D_I+H_I}{Q}$ 9	$\frac{H_p+H_I}{D}$ 10	$e=\frac{H_p}{D}$[5] 11	$\frac{H_p+H_I}{D+Q}$ 12	$v=\frac{H_p}{D+Q}$[5] 13	$\frac{L_B}{D}$ 14	$\frac{L_I}{Q}$ 15
1892	417	768	1,185	0·543	0·103	—	0·052	0·293	0·026	0·188	0·173	0·122	0·112	0·845	0·681
1893	425	772	1,197	0·551	0·106	—	0·049	0·299	0·024	0·190	0·178	0·123	0·114	0·845	0·677
1894	438	785	1,223	0·558	0·104	—	0·057	0·306	0·021	0·189	0·177	0·121	0·113	0·839	0·673
1895	459	828	1,287	0·554	0·097	—	0·057	0·325	0·022	0·184	0·171	0·118	0·110	0·846	0·653
1896	485	863	1,348	0·562	0·092	—	0·052	0·338	0·019	0·191	0·181	0·122	0·116	0·856	0·643
1897	512	882	1,394	0·580	0·087	—	0·054	0·344	0·016	0·176	0·166	0·111	0·105	0·859	0·640
1898	535	909	1,444	0·589	0·082	—	0·057	0·350	0·015	0·169	0·161	0·107	0·101	0·861	0·635
1899	551	938	1,489	0·587	0·080	—	0·055	0·343	0·015	0·164	0·156	0·103	0·098	0·865	0·642
1900	566	967	1,533	0·585	0·081	—	0·057	0·334	0·014	0·168	0·159	0·106	0·100	0·862	0·652
1901	581	982	1,563	0·592	0·081	0·012	0·059	0·334	0·014	0·160	0·154	0·100	0·097	0·848	0·652
1902	601	987	1,588	0·609	0·083	0·013	0·062	0·333	0·013	0·154	0·146	0·096	0·091	0·842	0·654
1903	626	983	1,609	0·637	0·083	0·013	0·056	0·331	0·013	0·160	0·152	0·098	0·093	0·848	0·656
1904	650	979	1,629	0·664	0·087	0·013	0·061	0·328	0·012	0·156	0·148	0·094	0·089	0·839	0·660
1905	672	1,002	1,674	0·671	0·094	0·013	0·064	0·320	0·013	0·145	0·137	0·087	0·082	0·829	0·667
1906	695	1,017	1,712	0·683	0·090	0·013	0·063	0·312	0·013	0·141	0·133	0·084	0·079	0·834	0·675
1907	715	1,053	1,768	0·679	0·084	0·010	0·061	0·308	0·013	0·141	0·132	0·084	0·079	0·845	0·679
1908	736	1,069	1,805	0·688	0·082	0·007	0·065	0·302	0·012	0·134	0·125	0·079	0·074	0·846	0·686
1909	761	1,089	1,850	0·699	0·079	0·008	0·065	0·297	0·013	0·133	0·124	0·078	0·073	0·848	0·690
1910	789	1,118	1,907	0·706	0·073	0·009	0·064	0·293	0·013	0·131	0·122	0·077	0·072	0·859	0·694
1911	813	1,151	1,964	0·706	0·070	0·009	0·067	0·293	0·012	0·129	0·121	0·076	0·074	0·859	0·695
1912	839	1,197	2,036	0·701	0·065	0·007	0·065	0·293	0·012	0·129	0·121	0·076	0·071	0·863	0·695
1913	867	1,245	2,112	0·696	0·059	0·006	0·069	0·291	0·013	0·126	0·117	0·074	0·069	0·866	0·696
1914	908	1,317	2,225	0·689	0·068	0·006	0·096	0·297	0·014	0·153	0·143	0·090	0·084	0·830	0·689
1915	962	1,420	2,382	0·677	0·144	0·024	0·092	0·340	0·018	0·167	0·155	0·099	0·092	0·740	0·642
1916	1,066	1,591	2,657	0·670	0·202	0·056	0·113	0·421	0·015	0·161	0·151	0·097	0·091	0·629	0·564
1917	1,201	1,846	3,047	0·650	0·194	0·073	0·098	0·501	0·012	0·180	0·172	0·109	0·104	0·635	0·487
1918	1,360	2,146	3,506	0·634	0·186	0·090	0·098	0·570	0·012	0·198	0·190	0·121	0·116	0·626	0·418
1919	1,522	2,502	4,024	0·608	0·189	0·089	0·100	0·615	0·012	0·192	0·185	0·120	0·101	0·622	0·373
1920	1,620	2,789	4,409	0·581	0·177	0·075	0·080	0·625	0·018	0·182	0·171	0·115	0·108	0·668	0·357
1921[2]	1,829	2,719	4,548	0·673	0·161	0·099	0·088	0·602	0·018	0·164	0·152	0·098	0·091	0·65'	0·380
1922	1,925	2,649	4,574	0·727	0·184	0·114	0·086	0·605	0·016	0·156	0·141	0·091	0·082	0·616	0·379
1923	2,014	2,544	4,558	0·792	0·199	0·092	0·082	0·599	0·016	0·160	0·148	0·089	0·082	0·627	0·385
1924	2,122	2,526	4,648	0·840	0·186	0·074	0·082	0·578	0·016	0·160	0·146	0·087	0·079	0·658	0·406
1925	2,246	2,525	4,771	0·890	0·167	0·065	0·082	0·553	0·017	0·160	0·145	0·085	0·077	0·686	0·430
1926	2,355	2,545	4,900	0·925	0·153	0·068	0·079	0·527	0·017	0·155	0·140	0·081	0·073	0·700	0·456
1927	2,454	2,600	5,054	0·944	0·144	0·070	0·077	0·497	0·017	0·150	0·133	0·077	0·069	0·709	0·486
1928	2,571	2,671	5,242	0·962	0·141	0·069	0·075	0·473	0·018	0·148	0·131	0·075	0·067	0·715	0·509
1929	2,694	2,694	5,388	1·000	0·140	0·068	0·071	0·451	0·017	0·141	0·124	0·070	0·062	0·721	0·532
1930	2,828	2,733	5,561	1·035	0·147	0·084	0·071	0·431	0·018	0·136	0·118	0·067	0·058	0·698	0·551
1931	2,970	2,670	5,640	1·112	0·164	0·106	0·069	0·424	0·020	0·141	0·119	0·067	0·056	0·661	0·556
1932	3,108	2,717	5,825	1·144	0·204	0·134	0·072	0·422	0·023	0·137	0·111	0·064	0·052	0·590	0·555
1933	3,254	2,853	6,107	1·141	0·258	0·139	0·077	0·421	0·023	0·134	0·109	0·063	0·051	0·526	0·556
1934	3,418	2,860	6,278	1·195	0·287	0·106	0·078	0·417	0·021	0·136	0·110	0·062	0·050	0·529	0·562
1935	3,602	2,958	6,560	1·218	0·291	0·087	0·076	0·408	0·021	0·125	0·110	0·061	0·059	0·546	0·571

1936	3,800	3,135	6,935	1·212	0·290	0·085	0·073	0·397	0·019	0·138	0·115	0·062	0·052	0·552	0·584
1937	4,024	3,251	7,275	1·238	0·285	0·079	0·073	0·391	0·019	0·147	0·123	0·066	0·055	0·563	0·590
1938	4,252	3,229	7,481	1·317	0·280	0·080	0·077	0·387	0·020	0·149	0·125	0·064	0·053	0·563	0·593
1939	4,490	3,274	7,764	1·371	0·267	0·088	0·078	0·389	0·024	0·153	0·120	0·064	0·051	0·567	0·587
1940	4,884	3,564	8,448	1·370	0·270	0·134	0·074	0·439	0·027	0·166	0·129	0·070	0·054	0·522	0·534
1941	5,510	4,088	9,598	1·348	0·300	0·196	0·073	0·518	0·022	0·164	0·134	0·070	0·057	0·431	0·460
1942	6,218	4,623	10,841	1·345	0·319	0·247	0·071	0·577	0·018	0·179	0·155	0·076	0·066	0·363	0·405
1943	6,988	5,102	12,090	1·369	0·317	0·287	0·072	0·623	0·016	0·195	0·172	0·082	0·073	0·324	0·361
1944	7,836	5,696	13,532	1·375	0·300	0·327	0·071	0·663	0·015	0·187	0·167	0·079	0·070	0·302	0·322
1945	8,654	6,222	14,876	1·391	0·289	0·339	0·073	0·696	0·014	0·210	0·191	0·088	0·080	0·299	0·290
1946	9,407	6,958	16,365	1·352	0·286	0·331	0·071	0·710	0·014	0·199	0·180	0·085	0·077	0·312	0·273
1947	9,932	7,660	17,592	1·297	0·283	0·315	0·072	0·700	0·015	0·187	0·167	0·081	0·073	0·330	0·285
1948	10,258	8,003	18,261	1·282	0·280	0·291	0·069	0·688	0·016	0·165	0·144	0·072	0·063	0·360	0·296
1949	10,615	8,211	18,826	1·293	0·275	0·272	0·068	0·675	0·017	0·163	0·141	0·071	0·061	0·385	0·308
1950	11,008	8,361	19,369	1·317	0·270	0·260	0·068	0·651	0·017	0·160	0·138	0·069	0·060	0·402	0·332
1951	11,346	8,416	19,762	1·348	0·294	0·202	0·069	0·629	0·017	0·164	0·141	0·070	0·060	0·435	0·354
1952	11,645	8,426	20,071	1·382	0·326	0·167	0·069	0·609	0·018	0·172	0·146	0·072	0·061	0·438	0·373
1953	12,011	8,628	20,639	1·392	0·340	0·189	0·069	0·587	0·019	0·178	0·151	0·074	0·063	0·402	0·394
1954	12,588	8,954	21,542	1·406	0·345	0·180	0·069	0·564	0·018	0·181	0·155	0·075	0·065	0·406	0·418
1955	13,290	8,938	22,228	1·487	0·326	0·179	0·070	0·539	0·017	0·193	0·167	0·078	0·067	0·425	0·444
1956	13,991	8,714	22,705	1·606	0·304	0·185	0·071	0·516	0·017	0·211	0·184	0·081	0·071	0·440	0·467
1957	14,698	8,866	23,564	1·658	0·295	0·189	0·072	0·497	0·017	0·216	0·188	0·081	0·071	0·444	0·486
1958	15,565	9,196	24,761	1·693	0·288	0·182	0·071	0·482	0·017	0·215	0·187	0·080	0·069	0·459	0·501
1959	16,739	9,693	26,432	1·727	0·254	0·165	0·071	0·471	0·016	0·210	0·182	0·077	0·067	0·510	0·513
1960	18,062	10,115	28,177	1·786	0·199	0·157	0·071	0·458	0·016	0·210	0·181	0·075	0·065	0·573	0·526
1961	19,384	10,292	29,676	1·884	0·165	0·157	0·072	0·441	0·017	0·216	0·184	0·075	0·064	0·606	0·542
1962	20,658	10,566	31,224	1·955	0·161	0·146	0·071	0·425	0·017	0·211	0·178	0·071	0·060	0·622	0·558

Notation

Q = Total non-bank financial liabilities.
D = Total bank and discount houses liabilities.
S_B = The banks' and discount companies' holdings of British Government and Government-guaranteed securities.
T_B = The banks' and discount companies' holdings of Treasury bills, Treasury deposit-receipts and special deposits at the Bank of England.
S_I = The non-bank financial institutions' holdings of Government and Government-guaranteed securities.
D_I = The non-bank financial institutions' holdings of bank liabilities.
H_I = The non-bank financial institutions' holdings of high-powered money.
H_p = The non-financial private-sector holdings of high-powered money.
L_B = The gross private-sector loans made by the banks and discount companies.
L_I = The gross private-sector loans made by the non-bank financial institutions.
H = High-powered money outstanding = bank deposits at Bank of England + private deposits at Bank of England + currency outstanding.

Sources

All the data, 1892–1962, Appendix, Sections 1, 2 and 3.

Notes

[1] All the end-year balance sheet data were processed so as to reflect the mid-year average. In addition, where the year-end was recorded as of 31 March, the data were assumed to reflect the amounts outstanding as of 31 December in the previous year.

[2] Non-bank financial institutions' liabilities: National Savings Certificates, Defence and Premium Savings Bonds, life insurance, building societies, Post Office Savings Banks, trustee savings banks; and after 1920, hire-purchase co. – sample of 8; Friendly Societies, collecting societies, registered trade unions and superannuation funds, Birmingham Municipal and Railway Savings Banks.

[3] Includes most of the commercial banks whose business is primarily in the United Kingdom, and three discount houses: Alexanders, National and Union. The Banks of Eire and the National Bank were excluded from 1921 on. From 1943 onwards, 'rediscounts' and 'rebates' were added to total liabilities of the discount houses as they were included in this total in earlier years.

[4] The currency holdings of the commercial banks and discount houses: 1921–62 B.O.E. *Statistical Summary*, January 1939, and the C.S.O. *Annual Statistical Abstract*. Before 1921, the balance sheet bank cash was used after adjusting it for window dressing by multiplying such statistics by λ. $\lambda = \sum_{1921}^{1925}$ actual bank cash$/\sum_{1921}^{1925}$ balance sheet bank cash $= 0{\cdot}562$. Bankers' deposits at the Bank of England were extracted from its balance sheets.

[5] These ratios were computed on the assumption that $D_I = 0$; i.e. the non-bank financial institutions hold no bank liabilities.

preferences of the financial intermediaries with respect to their total asset placements (columns 8, 9 and 15). Moreover, they show the non-banking sector's combined preference for high-powered money in relation to the stock of bank deposits and of financial intermediary liabilities (columns 9, 10 and 12). In effect, the table provides a fairly detailed account of the revealed asset preferences of the three groups of private economic actors in the financial markets; in addition, it depicts the recorded amounts of bank deposits and financial intermediary liabilities outstanding annually over the period.

As noted, these liabilities and some of the relative asset preferences are often referred to in the literature. For example $d = H_b/D$ and $e = H_p/D$ are the two basic components in the denominator of the simple bank deposit multiplier as represented by A. Gambino.[1] Likewise, $t = T_B/D$, which, with d, accounts for the predominant portion of the denominator in Sayers's bank deposit multiplier model.[2] Moreover, $k = S_B/D$, $j = S_I/Q$, $f = (D_I + H_I)/D$, L_B/D and L_I/D have been considered to play an important role in both the determination of bank deposits and the allocation of financial institutions' assets.[3] Finally, $h = Q/D$, which shows the private sector's preference for the liabilities of financial intermediaries to those of the banks, has also attracted attention. This ratio reflects the degree of the banking sector's power in the financial market. Its growth over time indicates that this power has been steadily eroded away, and, in contrast, it shows the rising importance which these intermediaries' portfolio decisions have had in the process of credit allocation.

This table serves three other useful ends. Obviously it enables one to compare the UK record of portfolio selections with those of similar economic actors in other countries where similar statistics are available. Next, it provides a basis for evaluating the accuracy of published observations which purport to represent the asset preferences of certain members of the UK financial community. Finally, it is an empirical basis which one may use to assess the validity of certain assumptions of portfolio behaviour which have been used in financial theory and to modify them if necessary.

On the inter-country basis, the asset preferences of the UK's financial institutions may be readily compared with those of American institutions. In this respect, it is interesting to observe that the UK bank holdings of Government securities and of short-term Government obligations as a portion of their total assets ($S_B/D + T_B/D$) substantially exceeded the corresponding ratio for American banks. In 1900, 1912, 1929, 1933, 1939, 1945 and 1952 the percentages of UK and US bank assets invested in such debt instruments were as follows: 9 and 5 per cent, 7 and 3 per cent, 21 and 7 per cent, 39 and 18 per cent, 37 and 35 per cent, 61 and 56 per cent and 49 and 37 per cent respectively.[4] Moreover, in line with Goldsmith's observations of developments in the US financial structure, in both countries there was a reduction in the banking sector's share of the outstanding wealth claims of the financial sector and a considerable increase in the countries' financial institutions' holdings of Government obligations relative to their total assets over the period; a development which was unequivocally associated with the magnitude of these Governments' financial demands in two major wars.

When the table is used to test certain assertions about the portfolio selections of the financial institutions, there appears to be a tendency for the accuracy of the observations to be correlated with time. Undoubtedly, the more recent observations have benefited from the post-1950 growth in the collection and publication of financial statistics by various Government agencies.

Turning to some early observations on institutional asset preferences, the statistics in Table 3.1 challenge a few of the findings of the *Macmillan Report* with respect to bank portfolio behaviour. For example, the statistics in Table 3.1 do not fully support one of the important findings of this report that bank balance sheets '. . . show a remarkable adherence to the conventional distribution of assets over a period of years. . . .'[5] Admittedly, in the pre-1914 period and in the 1920 to 1930 interval an examination of these balance sheets suggests that the distribution of bank funds between types of assets, advances, discounts, investments, cash and money at call, was more stable than in succeeding years. Nevertheless, even these so-called stable periods showed some sizeable oscillations. In the 1920–9 interval, for instance, the percentage of their asset which banks placed in bills discounted ranged between 20 and 10 per cent, and the ranges in the percentages placed in advances and investments were 48 to 37 per cent and 25 to 17 per cent

[1] A. Gambino, 'Money supply and interest rate in recent macroeconomic conception', *Banca Nazionale del Lavoro Quarterly Review* (September 1954).

[2] R. Sayers, 'The determination of the volume of bank deposits', *Banca Nazionale del Lavoro Quarterly Review* (December 1955).

[3] D. K. Sheppard and C. R. Barrett, op. cit., pp. 203–12.

[4] R. W. Goldsmith, *Financial Intermediaries in the American Economy since 1900* (Princeton University Press, 1958), p. 195.

[5] Committee on Finance and Industry, *Report*, p. 8.

respectively. The table indicates that the impact of these variations was borne by the markets for both Government- and private-sector-issued debt obligations. The range in quotient of S_B/D, for instance, between 1892 and 1914 was 10 to 6 per cent and between 1920 and 1929, it was 20 to 14 per cent. These oscillations in bank asset placements must have exerted a considerable impact on financial market conditions given that up to 1930 total bank assets accounted for a full 50 per cent of the sample of total financial institutions' assets.

With respect to the general bias which underlies bank portfolio behaviour, however, the data indicate that statements on bank policy made by bankers at the Macmillan Committee hearings in 1930 were as accurate as those made in the 1950s. In 1930, for example, Mr F. Hyde, the managing director of the Midland Bank, stated '. . . we distribute our assets over a variety of different forms of employment so as to secure two objects, first of all, liquidity, and secondly, profits'.[1] In 1954 Mr J. Wadsworth, the Midland Bank's economist, reiterated Mr Hyde's representation of the bank's portfolio management targets with the provision that the revealed demands and directives of the Government exerted an important influence too. Wadsworth held that the banks' policy was to utilize '. . . their resources profitably, in so far as this is consistent with safeguarding liquidity, in providing short-term Government finances, avoiding undue capital losses, and complying with official guidance on bank lending'.[2] The table shows that their observations were accurate.

Comparing column 7, $d=H_B/D$, with column 9, $f=(D_I+H_I)/Q$, for instance, one quickly observes the importance the banks attach to primary liquidity. On balance, the bank primary reserve ratio was four times the size of that of the other institutions. Moreover, noting that the banks' holdings of Government securities relative to their total assets were generally less than half the size of the ratio for corresponding financial intermediaries (columns 5 and 8), the table demonstrates the short-term orientation of the banks' investment placements as compared with those of their institutional competitors for financial savings. The validity of this point is accentuated if one records the relatively high percentage of their assets that the banks and discount houses placed in short-term Government obligations (column 6), which ranged between 7 and 34 per cent in the 1920–62 period. In contrast, the other institutions had minimal holdings of these obligations. Finally, the oscillations in the bank L_B/D ratio (column 14) during the war years and in the period after the Second World War indicate the sensitivity of the banks to official guidance on bank lending. In both emergencies, there was a considerable reduction in the relative proportion of bank loans to the private sector in relation to their total assets – 83 to 63 per cent and 56 to 30 per cent. Moreover, during the 1950s, when the banking sector bore the main burden of official directives with respect to their loan placements, the percentage of the total credit they extended to the private sector (column $14=L_B/D$), fluctuated between 40 and 45 per cent; while those of the financial intermediaries rose from 35 to 50 per cent in the same period.

While the data contained in Table 3.1 seem to substantiate the point that the 1930 and the 1954 representations of bank portfolio strategy had substance, they also confirm the accuracy of recent observations on their actual asset distributions. Dacey, in *Money Under Review*,[3] for instance, and Brechling and Clayton in their article, 'Commercial Banks' Portfolio Behaviour',[4] represent that over time there is a kind of see-saw movement between bank advances and bank holdings of Government securities. Column 5, S_B/D, and column 14, L_B/D, when jointly considered, indicate that this finding is empirically verified. Similarly, Dacey's observation that the share of bank holdings of investments rarely falls below 15 per cent of their total assets and that the maximum amount banks placed in advances rarely exceeded 60 per cent appears to be correct; especially when it is noted that the numerator of column 5, S_B, only includes long-term Government obligations, and that in turn the numerator of column 14, L_B, contains several other forms of bank private credit extensions as well as advances. An examination of the underlying data confirmed these contentions. Throughout the whole period, 1880–1962, the quotient of the ratio of bank advances to total banking assets did not exceed 51 per cent; similarly the quotient of the ratio of their investments to their total assets did not fall below 15 per cent. The observed facts that the composition of the bank portfolio changes, and that the share of a particular group of assets oscillates within a relatively large range, have a distinct theoretical

[1] Ibid., p. 38.

[2] J. Wadsworth, 'United Kingdom of Great Britain and Northern Ireland', in *Banking Systems*, ed. B. H. Beckhart (New York: Columbia University Press, 1954), p. 790.

[3] W. Manning Dacey, *Money Under Review* (London: Hutchinson, 1960), p. 48.

[4] F. Brechling and G. Clayton, 'Commercial banks' portfolio behaviour', *National Economic Development Office Mimeograph* (1962), p. 4.

import; a consideration of Table 3.2 and the subsequent discussion is relevant.

The period averages and the coefficients of variation shown in Table 3.2 supplement the findings drawn from Table 3.1. If the reported period coefficient of variation is small, then the relative asset preference in question is reasonably stable. If the coefficient of variation is large, however, say around 20 per cent, and if in particular the average ratio is large too, then this indicates that both on a relative and on an absolute basis a considerable change in the placement of funds occurred during the selected time period.

TABLE 3.2 **Some Determinants of the Money and Credit Supply in the UK 1892–1962 – Average and Coefficient of Variation**

Variable	*1892–1914*		*1920–1939*		*1946–1962*	
	$\bar{x}$	*c.v.*(%)	$\bar{x}$	*c.v.*(%)	$\bar{x}$	*c.v.*(%)
$d = \frac{H_B}{D}$	0·06	14·7	0·08	6·3	0·07	2·1
$t = \frac{T_B}{D}$	—	—	0·09	23·5	0·21	27·5
$\frac{H_P+H_I}{D+Q}$	0·10	17·2	0·08	19·1	0·08	5·9
$e = \frac{H_P}{D}$	0·16	14·3	0·13	12·8	0·17	11·0
$h = \frac{Q}{D}$	0·63	9·3	1·02	21·1	1·52	14·2
$k = \frac{S_B}{D}$	0·08	14·2	0·21	27·6	0·26	32·2
$(1-t-d-k) = \frac{L_B}{D}$	0·85	1·3	0·63	10·5	0·44	19·3
$\frac{L_I}{Q}$	0·67	3·0	0·50	16·2	0·42	22·6
$j = \frac{S_I}{Q}$	0·32	6·1	0·48	15·3	0·57	16·6
S_A / Total assets of life assurance companies	0·02	30·4	0·25	20·1	0·28	27·6

Notes

(i) The subscripts, A, B, I, and P denote the asset holders – assurance companies, banking sector, non-bank financial institutional sector, and the non-financial institutional private sector.

(ii) The symbols D, H, Q, S, T, and L denote particular types of assets – bank deposits, high-powered money, non-bank financial institutions' liabilities, Government and Government-guaranteed securities, Treasury bills + Treasury deposit receipts + special deposits and total assets of financial institutions minus their holdings of Government obligations and foreign assets respectively (see Table 3.1).

It is interesting to observe the growing stability of the bank cash reserve ratio over the three periods.[1] The average quotient of the H_B/D ranged between 6 and 8 per cent over the three selected time intervals; while the coefficient of variation fell from 15 per cent in the 1892–1914 period, to 6 per cent in 1920–39, and then to 2 per cent in the 1946–62 period. In contrast, the table demonstrates the rising instability of the banks' L_B/D and their S_B/D ratios with the passage of time. Starting with the first period, the quotient of the average L_B/D ratio fell from 85 to 63 per cent and then to 44 per cent; while the corresponding coefficient of variation rose from 1 to 10 per cent and to 19 per cent so that at least on a relative basis this portion of banking assets was subject to increasing variations. The average value of the S_B/D ratio increased considerably, from 8 to 21 to 26 per cent; moreover, its coefficient of variation rose: from 14·2 to 27·6 to 32·2 per cent. Therefore, given that total banking assets increased over time, both proportionately and absolutely bank holdings of gilt-edged securities became increasing variable. These facts should be of considerable interest to architects of debt management and monetary policies.

It is interesting to note that the 1946–62 yearly variations in S_B/D correspond to the observations made by Shearer in the United States and those of Brechling and Clayton in the UK on the changes in the ratio of bank investment to total-liability ratio (I_B/D) as shown by quarterly data for 1954–61 and 1951–61 periods respectively. Shearer found that the US ratio had 'a significant cyclical pattern superimposed on a falling trend'.[2] Brechling and Clayton, when engaged in testing Dacey's see-saw thesis for the UK came to much the same conclusion. Moreover, the coefficients of variation reported by Brechling and Clayton for the average I_B/D and $L_B{}^*/D$ ratios for 1951–61, 20·8 per cent and 19·9 per cent, are fairly similar to those reported in the table for the whole post-war period, 32·2 and 19·3 per cent respectively.[3] In theory, the size of the variations in the I_B/D ratio in both the United States and the United Kingdom in the post-war era has some significance; particularly if one holds, like Shearer, that the value of the bank deposit

[1] In the last period, the Government's directive to the clearing banks to cease the practice of window-dressing obviously had a marked effect. They stopped.

[2] Ronald A. Shearer, 'The expansion of bank credit – an alternative approach', *Quarterly Journal of Economics* (August 1963), p. 496.

[3] Brechling and Clayton, op. cit., p. 3. Note $L_B{}^*/D$ = (Advances/Total liabilities) ratio.

multiplier 'is very sensitive to both the reserve ratio and the security asset ratio'.[1]

It should be noted too that over time, most of the other ratios shown in Tables 3.1 and 3.2 have been identified as reflecting a portfolio decision which has some impact on the amount of the money stock.

The ratio H_B/D, which may be taken as the bank reserve ratio, has been regarded as being the sole portfolio decision which influenced deposit creation. Here, a comment by Mr Hyde before the Macmillan Committee in 1930 is instructive: 'When we lend the surplus it does not destroy that surplus; it comes back to us, taking the banks as a whole, from some other quarter, so we have still got it to lend, but we have nine-tenths instead of ten-tenths . . .'[2] Obviously, if this traditional view is correct, then the value and observed stability of $d=H_B/D$ to which Mr Hyde refers is certainly important.

Again, in May 1939 an early echo of the Sayers's liquid asset ratio approach to the determination of the supply bank deposits was set out. In particular, it was held that for money-supply determination the size and stability of the T_B/D ratio and the H_B/D ratio should be considered together. The author of the article in the 'Banking Supplement' assumed that currency and Treasury Bills were perfect substitutes for each other, and that, therefore, the Exchange Equalization Account's trade in Treasury Bills did not insulate the economy from a surplus or deficit on the foreign account: 'So . . . each change in our gold stocks must bring a corresponding change in the total supply of credit.'[3]

Other ratios, besides $t=T_B/D$ and $d=H_B/D$, have been given a prominent place in more recent money and credit supply formulations. As noted, Clayton and Brechling and then Shearer have paid close attention to the inverse relationship between S_B/D and L_B/D. Using US data, Shearer shows quantitatively that changes in the bank holdings of Government securities may offset the direct effects of open-market operations.[4] Portfolio adjustments of the non-institutional private sector too, as represented by the movements in $e=H_P/D$ and $h=Q/D$, and by the financial intermediaries, as illustrated by changes in $j=S_I/Q$, $f=(D_I+H_I)/Q$, and L_I/Q, are held to play a role. In particular, for instance, in 1954, Gambino represented that bank liabilities $D=H/(d+e)$, and he stressed, as Meade and Goodwin had done in the 1930s, that the e term in the denominator was particularly important in view of its size and the range in its oscillations.[5] Table 3.1 shows the upper and lower limits of e to be 19 and 11 per cent after 1920, a large range when compared with the equivalent values of d of 9–7 per cent. This suggests that variations in the private sector's demand for currency relative to its demand for deposits has been important.

Finally, in a review article in *Economica* in 1965, C. R. Barrett and I developed a series of models which illustrate how most of these ratios, as reflections of financial institutions' and private individuals' portfolio decisions, *may* affect bank deposits, non-bank financial institutions' liabilities, and the amount of institutional credit which is extended to the private and public sector: L_B+L_I and $S_B+S_I+T_B+H_B+T_I$ respectively.[6] However, the effective utilization of the more complicated models by the monetary authorities to regulate the money supply presupposes that the authorities have accurate estimates of the expected values of such ratios as h, j, k, t, etc., in the planning period. Since the likelihood of this assumed knowledge of institutional and non-institutional private-sector portfolio decisions is low, the Gambino model and the Sayers's liquid-asset formula $[D=(H+T)/(d+t)]$ have received the most attention in practical banking literature.

Tables 3.3 and 3.4 and graphs (3)A, (3)B and (3)C show how such a simplified model may be applied to describe the determination of the money stock in the UK and the USA over the period. The model, identical to the one Friedman and Schwartz used in *A Monetary History of the United States 1867–1960*, is a simple transposition of the Gambino representation; namely:

$$M = \frac{H.b(1+p)}{b+p},$$

in which M, money, is defined as being equal to currency plus deposits; H is defined as being equal to currency plus the banks' deposits at the central bank; b is defined as being equal to $1/d=D/H_B$, and p is defined as being equal to $1/e=D/H_P$. By definition $H_B+H_P=H$ as they delineate the banks' and the non-banking private sector's holdings of high-powered money – those assets which banks are constrained to use to back their deposit liabilities.

[1] Shearer, op. cit., p. 495.

[2] Committee on Finance and Industry, *Minutes of Evidence*, Vol. I (London: H.M.S.O., 1931), p. 59.

[3] 'Monetary policy, 1844–1939', *The Economist*'s 'Banking Supplement' (20 May 1939), p. 6.

[4] Shearer, op. cit., p. 498.

[5] Gambino, op. cit.

[6] Sheppard and Barrett, op. cit., pp. 198–214.

TABLE 3.3 **United Kingdom. Determinants of Money Stock 1881–1962 (£ millions)**

Period	*Bank Deposits – I.B.D.*[1]	*Bank Reserves*	*Non-Bank Currency Holdings*	*High-powered Money*	*Deposit/Reserve Ratio* b	*Deposit/Currency Ratio* p	*Money* I+III
	I	II	III	IV	V	VI	VII
	(*mid-year average*)		(*annual average*)				
1881	389	27	164	191	14·41	2·37	553
1882	409	27	168	195	15·15	2·43	577
1883	425	27	167	194	15·74	2·54	592
1884	444	27	159	186	16·44	2·79	603
1885	455	29	155	184	15·69	2·94	610
1886	458	30	146	176	15·27	3·14	604
1887	464	30	140	170	15·47	3·31	604
1888	485	33	131	164	14·70	3·70	616
1889	515	35	133	168	14·71	3·87	648
1890	541	37	139	176	14·62	3·89	680
1891	566	39	148	187	14·51	3·82	714
1892	585	40	144	184	14·63	4·06	729
1893	589	38	146	184	15·50	4·03	735
1894	598	45	147	192	13·29	4·07	745
1895	636	47	152	199	13·53	4·18	788
1896	671	45	165	210	14·91	4·07	836
1897	692	48	155	203	14·42	4·46	847
1898	716	52	154	206	13·77	4·65	870
1899	741	52	154	206	14·25	4·81	895
1900	764	55	162	217	13·89	4·72	926
1901	775	58	157	215	13·36	4·94	932
1902	779	61	152	213	12·77	5·13	931
1903	778	55	157	212	14·14	4·96	935
1904	773	60	153	213	12·88	5·05	926
1905	790	64	146	210	12·34	5·41	936
1906	816	64	144	208	12·75	5·67	960
1907	833	64	148	212	13·02	5·63	981
1908	846	69	143	212	12·26	5·92	989
1909	864	71	145	216	12·17	5·96	1,009
1910	892	71	147	218	12·56	6·07	1,039
1911	928	77	149	226	12·05	6·23	1,077
1912	964	78	155	233	12·36	6·22	1,119
1913	1,003	86	157	243	11·66	6·39	1,160
1914	1,062	126	201	327	8·43	5·28	1,263
1915	1,167	130	237	367	8·98	4·92	1,404
1916	1,301	180	257	437	7·23	5·06	1,558
1917	1,534	180	333	513	8·52	4·61	1,867
1918	1,798	210	424	634	8·56	4·24	2,222
1919	2,118	250	481	731	8·47	4·40	2,599

Sources

Col. I Bank deposits, D. K. Sheppard, 'Financial statistics – UK banks 1880–1962', Birmingham University, *Discussion Papers*, Series A, No. 63, August 1965.

Col. II Bank reserves = bankers' deposits at Bank of England + estimates of banks' currency holdings 1880–1962, *Bankers' Deposits at Bank of England*, D. K. Sheppard, op. cit.. The pre-1920 bankers' deposits estimated as the recorded figures to 1919 only contain deposits of London bankers' head offices. Method:

Total private deposits at the Bank of England was multiplied by $\lambda = 0{\cdot}6707$, where $\hat{\lambda} = \sum_{t=1920}^{1924}$ bankers' deposits at Bank of England/ $\sum_{t=1920}^{1924}$ total private deposits at the Bank of England.

Banks' currency holdings: 1881–1920 estimated method: Banks balance sheet cash. $\hat{\theta}$, where $\hat{\theta} = 0{\cdot}562$ and $0{\cdot}562 = \sum_{1921}^{1925}$ actual bank cash/ $\sum_{1921}^{1925}$ balance sheet cash.

1921–38, Bank of England, *Statistical Summary*, January 1939, p. 4.

1939–62, Central Statistical Office, *Annual Statistical Abstract*, various issues.

Col. III equals col. IV minus col. II.

Col. IV High-powered money = currency outstanding plus bankers' and private deposits at the Bank of England.

1881–1962, *Private and Bankers' Deposits*, D. K. Sheppard, op. cit.

Period	Bank Deposits – I.B.D.[1] I	Bank Reserves II	Non-Bank Currency Holdings III	High-powered Money IV	Deposit/Reserve Ratio b V	Deposit/Currency Ratio p VI	Money I+III VII
	(mid-year average)		*(annual average)*				
1920[2]	2,380	222	507	729	10·72	4·69	2,887
1920	2,246	210	502	712	10·70	4·47	2,748
1921	2,323	239	445	684	9·72	5·22	2,768
1922	2,262	224	414	638	10·10	5·46	2,676
1923	2,156	208	406	614	10·37	5·31	2,562
1924	2,116	206	404	610	10·27	5·24	2,520
1925	2,097	207	403	610	10·13	5·20	2,500
1926	2,114	202	395	597	10·47	5·35	2,509
1927	2,157	200	389	589	10·78	5·54	2,546
1928	2,217	202	384	586	10·98	5·77	2,601
1929	2,237	192	380	572	11·65	5·89	2,617
1930	2,266	194	373	567	11·68	6·08	2,639
1931	2,229	184	377	561	12·11	5·91	2,606
1932	2,294	196	372	568	11·70	6·17	2,666
1933	2,421	221	384	605	10·95	6·30	2,805
1934	2,424	223	389	612	10·87	6·23	2,813
1935	2,514	225	399	624	11·17	6·30	2,913
1936	2,668	231	431	662	11·55	6·19	3,099
1937	2,767	238	477	715	11·63	5·80	3,244
1938	2,747	250	481	731	10·99	5·71	3,228
1939	2,772	257	500	757	10·79	5·54	3,272
1940	3,014	262	593	855	11·50	5·08	3,607
1941	3,484	299	671	970	11·65	5·19	4,155
1942	3,962	330	827	1,157	12·01	4·79	4,789
1943	4,382	369	993	1,362	11·88	4·41	5,375
1944	4,917	407	1,165	1,572	12·08	4·22	6,082
1945	5,390	454	1,307	1,761	11·87	4·12	6,697
1946	6,011	493	1,385	1,878	12·19	4·34	7,396
1947	6,603	550	1,432	1,982	12·00	4·61	8,035
1948	6,855	555	1,319	1,874	12·35	5·20	8,174
1949	6,966	562	1,335	1,897	12·40	5·22	8,301
1950	7,045	566	1,337	1,903	12·45	5·27	8,382
1951	7,076	582	1,380	1,962	12·16	5·13	8,456
1952	7,139	582	1,446	2,028	12·27	4·94	8,585
1953	7,317	599	1,532	2,131	12·22	4·78	8,849
1954	7,570	620	1,619	2,239	12·20	4·68	9,189
1955	7,520	627	1,727	2,354	11·99	4·35	9,247
1956	7,333	623	1,841	2,464	11·77	3·98	9,174
1957	7,457	641	1,916	2,557	11·63	3·89	9,373
1958	7,727	656	1,977	2,633	11·78	3·91	9,704
1959	8,090	684	2,033	2,717	11·83	3·98	10,123
1960	8,368	715	2,127	2,842	11·70	3·93	10,495
1961	8,500	740	2,218	2,958	11·49	3·83	10,718
1962	8,693	754	2,227	2,981	11·53	3·90	10,920

1881–1962, Currency outstanding: D. K. Sheppard, 'Financial statistics, a provisional money, liquid asset and credit series for the UK, 1880–1962', Birmingham University, *Discussion Papers*, Series A, No. 65.
Col. V equals col. I/col. II.
Col. VI equals col. I/col. III.
Col. VII equals col. I plus col. III.

Notes

[1] Prior to 1891, the deposits of some banks included in the post-1890 series were not recorded. As a consequence, the deposits in the pre-1891 period were inflated by a factor = 1·135 which represents the ratio of the two series in 1891. *I.B.D.* equals inter-bank deposits and items in transit.

[2] Two rows for 1920 are given to reflect the establishment of the Republic of Ireland in 1921.

Table 3.3 depicts net bank deposits, bank reserves, non-bank currency holdings and the money stock outstanding on a mid-year basis as well as the derived determinants *H*, *b* and *p* in the UK. In accord with Friedman and Schwartz's approach, bank deposits include both current and deposit accounts in the commercial banks. Bank reserves consist of bank currency holdings and bankers' deposits at the Bank of England. Non-bank currency holdings are adjusted to include private deposits at the Bank of England as well as notes and coin. Money is defined as being equal to column I, bank deposits, plus column III, non-bank currency holdings.

Graph (3)A and Graph (3)B isolate the movements of these two stocks and these two ratios for examination.

There seems to be a fairly close correlation between the movements in high-powered money and money; moreover, an examination of the underlying data also shows a close correspondence between the trends in high-powered money and bank deposits. The Pearson correlation coefficient between *H* and *M* was 0·81 for the 1921–39 interval and 0·95 for the period after the Second World War. These findings tally with those made by Friedman and Schwartz in the United States.

The movements of *b* and *p* in the UK, however, do not correspond as closely to the US experience – see Graph (3)C, *USA Ratio of Commercial Banks' Deposits to Non-Bank Currency Holdings and Bank Reserves*. Nevertheless, there are similarities, the *p* ratio in both countries declined during periods of national emergency and rose fairly steadily in the pre-1914 era; moreover the within-country movements in *b* and *p* were in the same general direction in the 1920s and in the 1950s. There, however, the similarity ends. In the post-1920 period the movements in the US ratios were much more substantial and their trends were often in the opposite direction to those of their UK counterparts.

From 1881 to 1913, for instance, the UK's D/H_P ratio rose from 2·4 to 6·4, while the matching US *p* ratio increased from 2·2 to 7·6; over the same period the UK's deposit/reserve ratio fell from 14·4 to 11·7; whereas the US *b* ratio rose from 5·3 to 8·6. After the First World War years the discrepancies between the slopes of the trends of these ratios on an inter-country basis were even more pronounced. From 1929 to 1933, the United States deposit/currency ratio and deposit/reserve ratio fell from 11·0 to 5·2 and from 13·0 to 8·4; during the corresponding period in comparison, the UK ratios hardly changed at all: *p* moved upwards from 5·9 to 6·3 and *b*, in comparison, fell slightly from 11·7 to 11·0. As a consequence, in so far as the movements in these ratios can be regarded as significant indicators of monetary developments during the period, they reflect a substantial difference between the monetary histories of the respective countries. In particular they suggest that the US unit banking system was much more subject to speculative excesses and crises of confidence than the branch banking system in the UK. This suggestion is supported by the historical record.

Turning to the two UK graphs (3)A and (3)B and examining them in conjunction with the upper section of Table 3.4 it is interesting to see how the movements in the various determinants may, in a Friedman and Schwartz fashion, be fitted into British monetary history.

Taking the relationship between high-powered money and the money stock first; as noted, Graph (3)A depicts a close correlation between these two magnitudes for the whole period. Moreover, Table 3.4 shows that for the whole period and for all but one of the selected sub-periods, that of 1881–1913, the change in high-powered money would have accounted for the main portion of the change in the money stock if the two key ratios *b* and *p* had remained constant. Of the whole period change in the money stock of some £10·4 milliard, the calculation shows that the change of high-powered money contributed 92 per cent. Similarly, in all periods the sign of the impact of the variations in high-powered money was positive, indicating that its movement was in the same direction as the change in the money stock. These observations support the claim made in *The Economist* in 1939 that the implementation of the Cunliffe Committee's recommendation in 1917 to reduce the currency stock was unnecessarily deflationary: 'This was tantamount to a progressive reduction, regardless of the nation's needs.'[1] As noted elsewhere, particularly in the *Macmillan Report*, sundry economists and industrialists held that the accompanying reduction of the money stock from 1920 to 1925 of some £237 million had a fateful impact on the pace of reconstruction and development just after the First World War.

Graph (3)B and Table 3.4 suggest that the movements in the other two determinants of the money supply, *b* and *p*, were also influential. The upward drift in *p* in the pre-1914 era (the deposit/currency ratio nearly tripled) exerted a sharp stimulus to the money stock.[2] Table 3.3 shows that this impact would have accounted for 77 per

[1] 'Monetary policy, 1844–1939', op. cit., p. 4.

[2] Some economists have argued that this movement really reflects the pace of the bank amalgamations movement. I doubt it.

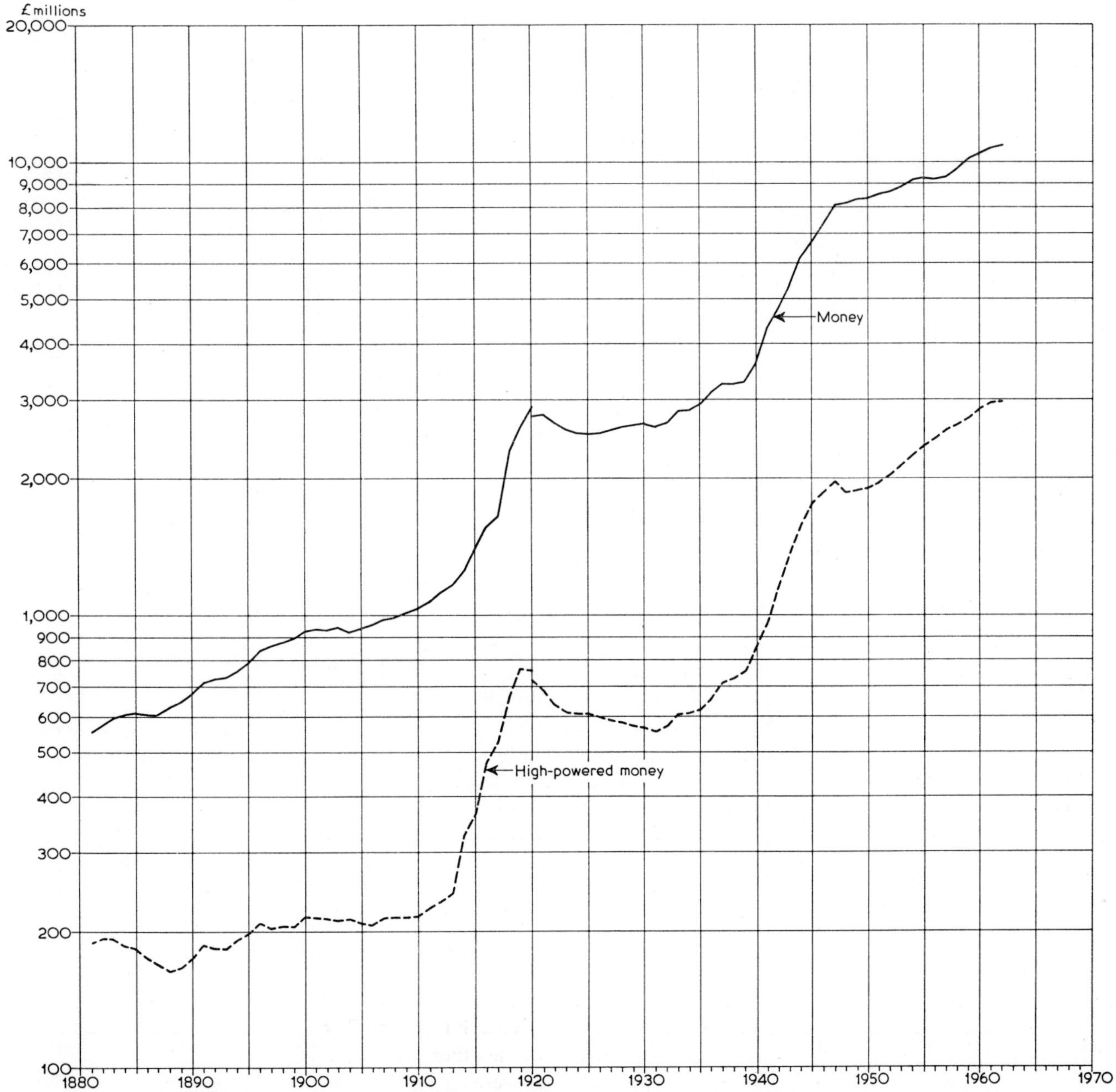

(3)A Money and High-Powered Money Stocks Outstanding in the UK 1881–1962[1]

[1] As of approximately 30 June in each year

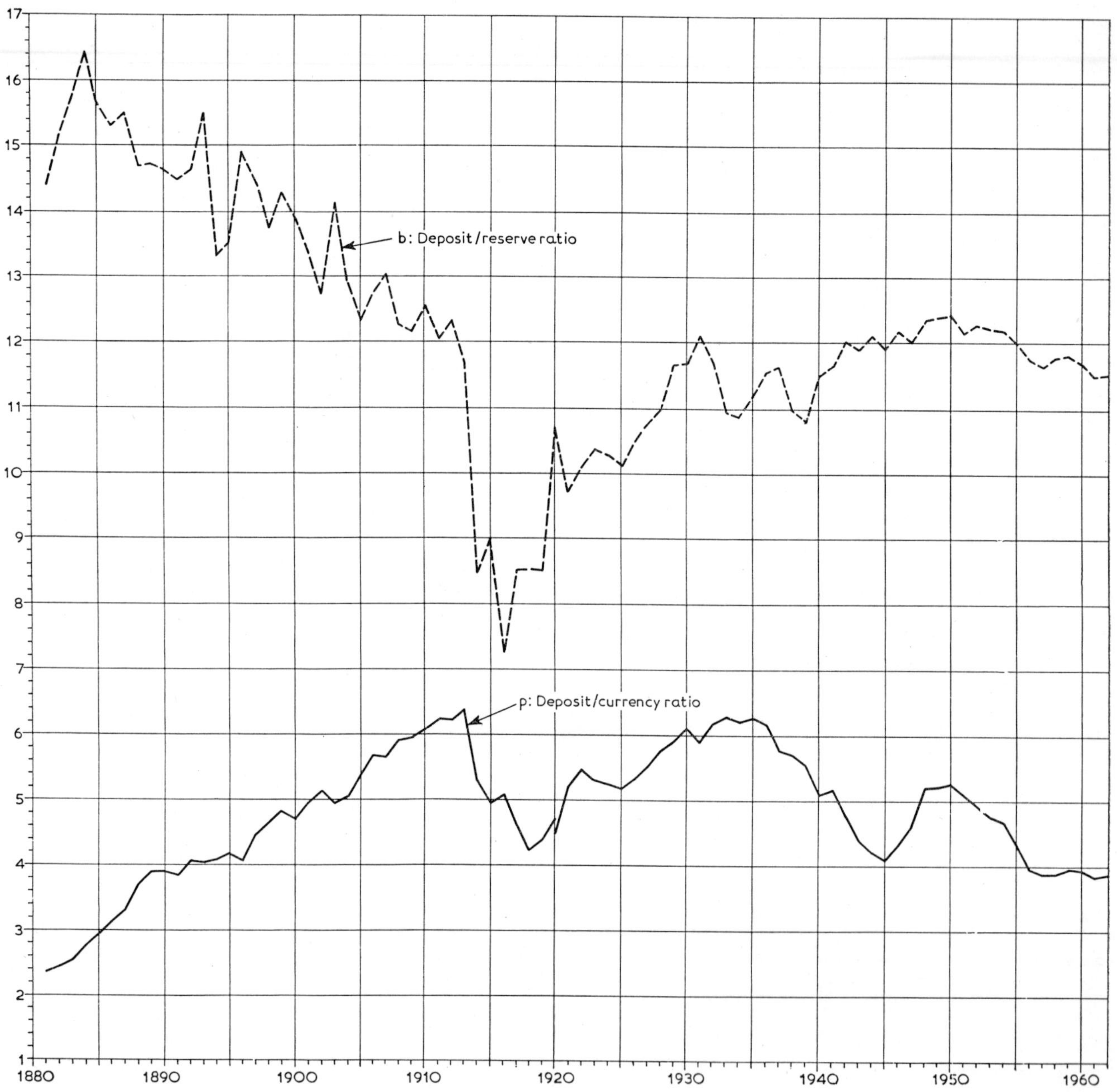

(3)B Ratio of Commercial Banks' Deposits to Non-Bank Currency Outstanding and to Bank Reserves in the UK 1881–1962[1]

[1] Computed as of approximately 30 June in each year

(3)C Ratio of Commercial Banks' Deposits to Non-Bank Currency Holdings and Bank Reserves in the USA 1881–1960[1]

Source: M. Friedman and A. J. Schwartz, *A Monetary History of the United States 1867–1960* (Princeton University Press, 1965), pp. 799–808

[1] Computed as of approximately 30 June in each year

cent of the change in the money supply if the other two determinants had remained constant. The upward tendency in both b and p in the 1921–9 period also may be seen as exerting a powerful influence; a combined effect which in turn offset the deflationary impact of official monetary policy by two-thirds. In contrast, in the First World War, the downward movements in b and p offset the inflationary influence of rapid increase in high-powered money by approximately a third. In the Second World War, the dampening influence of changes in these two ratios would have again been quite substantial if the war-issued Treasury Deposit Receipts had been included in bank reserves.

Finally, it is interesting to note how much more important the role of p, the deposit/currency ratio, has been than that of b, the deposit/reserve ratio, throughout most of the period – and particularly from 1948. From 1948, the decline in p would have induced a 55 per cent reduction in the money stock, *ceteris paribus*, as shown by the Friedman and Schwartz format; whereas the role of

TABLE 3.4 **Contribution of Selected Determinants of the Money Stock UK and USA 1881–1962 and 1881–1960**

Period	*Change in M*	*Impact of ΔH (%)*	*Impact of Δb (%)*	*Impact of Δp (%)*	*Interaction (%)*
	(£ millions)	*United Kingdom*			
1881–1962	+10,367	92·1	−1·2	+9·6	−0·6
1881–1960	+9,942	91·4	−1·1	+9·9	−0·6
1881–1913	+607	32·5	−4·4	+77·0	−5·0
1913–1920	+1,727	120·5	−3·4	−17·8	−0·6
1913–1918	+1,062	147·5	−18·6	−33·4	+4·4
1921–1929	−152	319·3	−105·5	−105·2	−8·8
1921–1939	+503	60·7	+20·2	+17·9	+0·8
1929–1933	+188	80·8	−30·6	+50·0	−1·4
1933–1939	+467	146·4	−4·6	−42·1	+0·4
1939–1946	+4,124	111·2	+5·1	−15·5	−0·8
1948–1962	+2,747	160·4	−7·2	−54·6	+1·4
1948–1960	+2,322	160·6	−6·3	−59·4	+1·2
	$ milliards	*United States*			
1881–1960	+206·0	+85·7	+2·8	+8·8	+2·7
1881–1913	+13·1	+62·4	+6·4	+23·8	+7·4
1913–1920	+19·0	+93·1	+11·9	−4·4	−0·6
1913–1918	+11·0	+107·8	+5·8	−12·3	−0·5
1921–1939	+16·2	+239·7	−144·9	+1·0	−0·6
1921–1929	+13·7	+24·1	+14·6	+57·0	−0·4
1929–1933	−16·0	−33·4	+58·0	+95·5	−20·5
1933–1939	+18·5	+163·0	−84·5	+31·0	−14·1
1939–1946	+90·0	+89·4	+31·4	−12·3	−6·8
1948–1960	+60·7	+18·5	+42·5	+31·2	+7·7

Notes

Given $M=H.b(1+p)/(b+p)$, where $b=D/H_b$ and $p=D/H_p$, the effect of the change in the value of the determinants on the change in the money stock between, say, two points in time, $t=0$ and $t=1$, is as follows:

effect of a change in H = $(\log H_1-\log H_0)/(\log M_1-\log M_0)$

effect of a change in b = $[\{\log b_1-\log b_0-\log (b_1+p_0)+\log (b_0+p_0)\}/(\log M_1-\log M_0)]$

effect of a change in p = $[\{\log (1+p_1)-\log (1+p_0)-\log (b_0+p_1)+\log (b_0+p_0)\}/(\log M_1-\log M_0)]$

Interaction = $[\{-\log (b_1+p_1)+\log (b_1+p_0)+\log (b_0+p_1)-\log (b_0+p_0)\}/(\log M_1-\log M_0)]$

Proof

See M. Friedman and A. Schwartz, *A Monetary History of the United States*, pp. 794–5.

changes in the deposit/reserve ratio is shown as minimal. The main reason why the changes in p were so much greater than those in b is that it was official policy to keep the banks' cash ratio at around 8 per cent.[1]

[1] R. S. Sayers, *Modern Banking*, 6th edn. (Oxford: Clarendon Press, 1964), p. 38.

When we look at the USA, however, and examine the impact of changes in b and p on the money supply we find that the order of magnitude of each ratio's contribution was the reverse of what it was in the UK – see the bottom section of Table 3.4. The changes in the deposit/reserve ratio, b, exerted a more powerful influence on the changes in the money stock than did the changes in the deposit/currency ratio – p – particularly since 1932. Taking the absolute sum of all the percentage contributions of the changes in these ratios over the same periods in each country the 'impact' of b in the United States amounted to 402·8 per cent; whereas the 'effect' of b in the United Kingdom was 211 per cent. Similarly, p contributed 277 per cent in the United States and 428 per cent in the United Kingdom. In the post-1932 period; the relative divergence was even more pronounced. The absolute sum of the contribution of the American b amounted to 158·4 per cent, whereas in the United Kingdom b accounted for just 16 per cent of the money supply change. The corresponding impact of deposit/currency ratio was 74·5 per cent in the United States and 117·1 per cent in the United Kingdom.

Over all, then, to the extent that the Friedman and Schwartz simple money-supply model has some practical validity, it is obvious that changes in both asset preferences must be accurately estimated if the model is to be of much use in policy formulation. Moreover, to the extent that Treasury Bills serve as high-powered money substitutes and that changes in the desired Government security/total asset ratios of the banks and the financial institutions are seen to have a sizeable impact on these institutions' private credit extensions, then other asset preferences warrant consideration.

Finally, and naturally with respect to the influence that the money stock is asserted to have in the economy, it is of interest to examine the data to see how stable the private sector's demand for money has been with respect to either total private expenditure or Gross National Product. The revealed stability of this ratio, income velocity, either as an historical constant or as a variable which slowly changes over time, would obviously do much to substantiate the early expressions of the quantity theory formulations of the role of money in the economy.[2]

[2] $M^dV_y=P_yO=V_yM^s$ – the superscripts d and s stand for demand and supply, P_y for the level of prices of final goods and O for the output of these final goods. The term V_yM^s has been added to the right-hand side (though it is generally omitted) as, usually, M^d is meant to be equal to M^s in equilibrium – the assumption on which the model is usually based.

Marked variations in this ratio, however, either as oscillations round a constant value or resulting from pronounced changes in trend, invalidate a mechanistic approach. Income velocity V_y, then, should have been regarded as an economic variable which varied; and these variations in turn should have been examined in the context of a more sophisticated money-demand relationship which acknowledged that there were other uses for money besides being a medium of exchange.[1]

Graph (3)D, and Table 3.5 illustrate that the changes in income velocity have been such as to make clear that the quantity theory approach to expenditure determination, like the simple bank deposit multiplier approach to credit allocation and deposit creation, needs modification; even if the underlying behavioural relationship is valid. Like the implicit assumptions about the stability of institutional portfolio preferences in the deposit generation approach, the constancy assumptions with respect to the value of velocity are not substantiated by the record. Similarly the evidence suggests that naive estimations, those based on its value in the last period or extrapolated from past trends are also likely to be too unreliable for policy purposes. The graph and chart indicate that more sophisticated stochastic techniques are needed to obtain a reliable estimate of the value of this variable.

The graph provides other interesting information. In agreement with US experience, as reported by Friedman and Schwartz, the secular trend in this variable was negative from 1880 until 1939 in the UK; similarly, since 1946 the trend has been positive. These findings hold if GNP is substituted for GDPE in the numerator and various other definitions of money are substituted in the denominator as well.

It is also apparent that if money, defined in the broadest sense as encashable assets, is used as the denominator, the range in the value of the variable is considerably reduced, and that this substitution produces results that show that

[1] Keynes's liquidity preference function was such a formulation.

TABLE 3.5 **Income Velocities – Average and Coefficient of Variation UK 1880–1962[1]**

Variable x	*1880–1962*[1]		*1880–1914*		*1920–1939*		*1946–1962*	
	$\bar{x}$	*c.v.* (%)	$\bar{x}$	*c.v.* (%)	$\bar{x}$	*c.v.* (%)	$\bar{x}$	*c.v.* (%)
GDPE / Currency	11·52	20·8	12·27	22·1	12·17	5·7	9·21	13·5
GDPE / Net bank deposits	2·24	19·6	2·55	11·8	1·92	10·7	1·99	22·8
GDPE / Money	1·85	16·0	2·06	7·0	1·66	9·6	1·64	21·0
GDPE / Quasi-money	1·41	20·2	1·64	6·3	1·30	16·1	1·08	18·1
GDPE / Encashable assets	1·09	28·5	1·34	7·9	0·94	17·7	0·75	16·3
GNP / Currency	11·82	20·6	12·52	23·4	12·26	5·7	9·84	13·5
GNP / Net bank deposits	2·30	18·9	2·59	10·3	1·94	11·0	2·13	23·1
GNP / Money	1·90	15·6	2·09	6·4	1·67	9·9	1·75	21·3
GNP / Quasi-money	1·45	19·1	1·67	5·4	1·31	16·1	1·15	18·4
GNP / Encashable assets	1·12	24·9	1·37	6·6	0·95	17·9	0·80	16·7

All assets computed on a mid-year basis.
GDPE = Gross Domestic Private Expenditure.
GNP = Gross National Product.
Currency = Currency outstanding.
Net bank deposits = Privately owned deposits.
Money = Currency + bank deposits = M_1.
Quasi-money = Money + savings bank deposits + building society deposits and shares = M_2.
Encashable assets = Quasi-money + all National Savings Bonds and Certificates + life assurance funds = M_3.

[1] The years 1915–19 and 1940–5 are omitted.

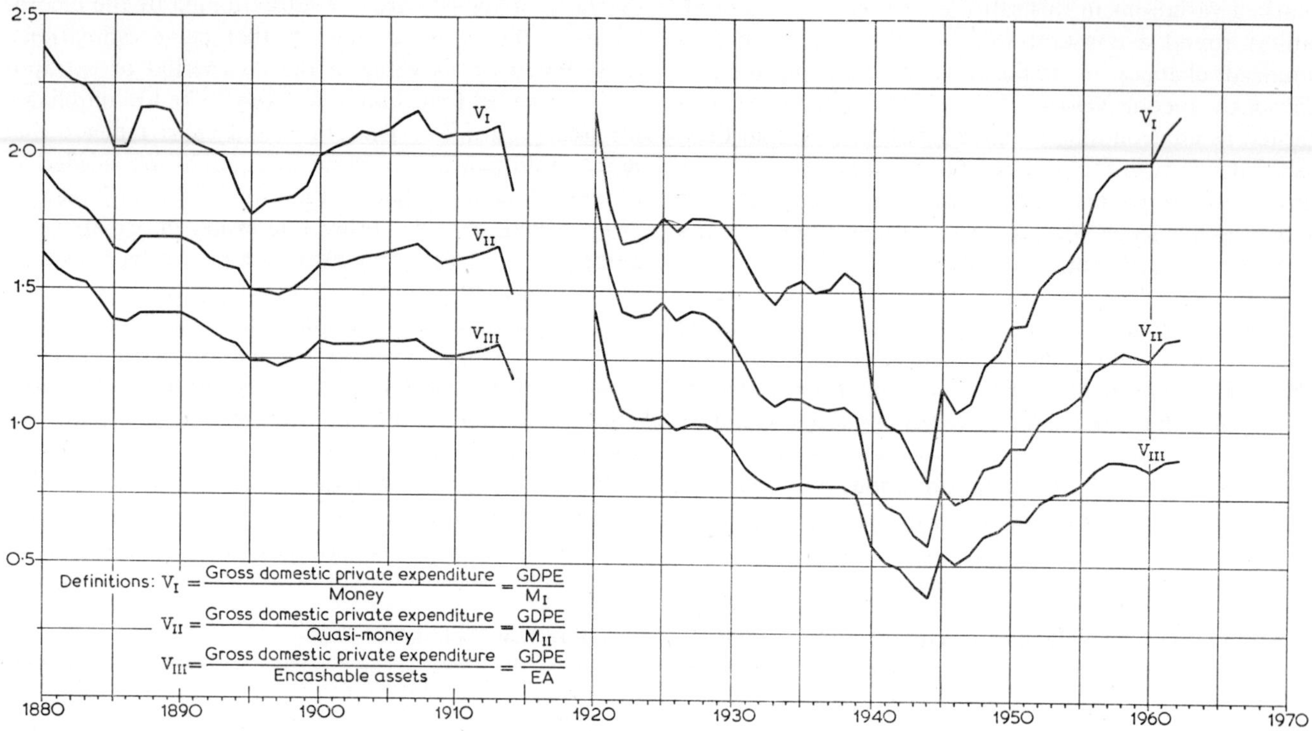

(3)D Income Velocities in the UK 1880–1962

Source: See Appendix, Table (A)3.3

the value of the variable has been relatively constant over fairly long periods: 1899–1913, 1923–9, 1932–9 and 1956–62. Perhaps this could be taken as an indication of stable wealth-holding practices during periods of economic stability.

Moreover, examining the movements of income velocity in the less stable periods, it is interesting to observe that the decline in its value seems to be associated with periods of recession, and, conversely, that upward oscillations in its value accompany periods of relatively rapid economic resurgence. Examinations of US data by C. Warburton support this finding. This is particularly true of the more conventional definition: (GDPE/M_I) – see the recessionary periods of 1882–6, 1892–5, 1908, 1920–3, 1926, 1930–2 and the upswings of 1887–91, 1896–1907, 1909–13, 1924, 1927–9, 1933–8 and the post-war period. These observed movements of income velocity fit in well with the proposition that its value is positively correlated with interest rates, with the level of prices and other rationales which would engender more or less economy in the utilization of money balances, as stores of value – as assets as well as being a means of making payments.

In conclusion, the data set out by the tables and graphs in this chapter indicate that considerable changes occurred in both the household asset preferences and in those of the financial institutions during the period. In particular, it is shown that there were fairly pronounced changes in certain ratios reflecting certain asset preferences which in turn are held to be important in determining both the amount of institutional finance allocated to the public and the private sector and also the sum of these institutions' liabilities; part of which, bank deposits, is a major component of the money stock. In turn, the role of the changes in certain of these asset preferences, *p* and *b*, are examined within a particular model of money-supply generation in which the independent effects of such changes on the money stock have been isolated – they appear to have been quite potent during certain periods. Finally, and with respect to a way in which the stock of money is purported to influence economic activity, the data have been processed to see how stable the revealed preference for money has been in relation to private expenditure or total national expenditure between 1880 and 1962. Again, as with most of the financial asset ratios, this expenditure/asset ratio, income velocity, with both the numerator and the denominator being redefined in various ways, has been shown to be a variable and not a constant, and, therefore, likely to change. In all, these annually averaged recorded asset preferences, their trends and their deviations from these trends through time, and the data on financial stocks provide another facet to the descriptive account of the growth and evolution of the UK financial sector.

4 Estimation of Income Velocity, Asset Preferences and the Supply of Selected Institutional Liabilities in the UK 1880–1962

Introduction

In the first three chapters, the annual growth of certain financial institutions' assets and liabilities is set out from 1880 through to 1962. In addition, the changes in some of the revealed asset preferences of these institutions and of the household sector for such institutions' liabilities are recorded. In this chapter, I examine the use of a simple bank deposit multiplier model to explain a facet of this growth, the growth of the money supply, and I test some of the rationales which have been used to explain the changes in such preferences. In the next chapter, I shall utilize sections of the reported data, money stock and financial institutions' private credits, to see if there is any direct relationship between the levels or changes in these stocks and those in certain forms of private expenditure. To be sure, the underlying models of explanatory behaviour and the statistical techniques which are used to evaluate them are relatively simple. As a consequence, the recorded results are only indicative. Nevertheless, they should help to indicate the variables that might be included in a more comprehensive investigation of the growth and the role of the financial sector. They, like the data, provide the essential foundation for such a study.

As noted in the previous chapter, certain asset preferences are regarded as important in monetary theory. Income velocity and certain financial ratios which reflect selected institutional and household asset preferences, for instance, are critical components of some of the basic models which have been used to explain the role and growth of an important financial variable – the money supply. In turn, many versions of these models have utilized an assumption which contrasts sharply with the facts. The models are presented with an assertion that the influential asset preferences are constant, so that, for example, only a change in the stock of high-powered money needs to be considered as the critical determining variable. In the UK many of these ratios have not been even approximately constant as the size of their coefficient of variation shows.[1] These constancy assumptions should be dropped if these models of economic behaviour are to be useful. In turn, the values of these ratios should be estimated, and the explanatory or predictive content of the adjusted models re-examined.

[1] See Chapter 3.

Income Velocity Estimates

The assumption that income velocity is constant has been dropped from most theoretical formulations. The barrage of empirical evidence to the contrary, such as that provided by Holmans in his study of velocity changes in twelve countries since the Second World War, seems to have eradicated the tendency to use this convenient rationale.[2] Nevertheless numerous suggestions have been made as to the way this behavioural norm may be validated. The denominator of the ratio should be redefined so as to incorporate good money substitutes or to exclude those money balances not held by the household sector. The numerator should be redefined so that it excludes all income receipts of the corporate and Government sectors. Alternatively, both numerator and denominator should be adjusted so that they reflect the permanent income and the money holdings in terms of permanent prices, and that the test of stability of the underlying behavioural relationship should be measured against the long-term trend of the adjusted ratio, not its average value. Despite these suggestions, however, the tendency to regard the observed unadjusted income velocity as the relevant variable and to estimate it through the use of econometric techniques now seems to be becoming established in line with the growing acknowledgement of the importance of money.

This movement towards the estimation of income velocity has been strengthened by the fact that some of the suggested adjustments to either the numerator or the denominator of the observed velocity ratio have not produced the desired results. For example, as shown in the previous chapter, no matter which definition of the money stock one uses, in the UK from 1880 to 1962 the coeffici-

[2] A. E. Holmans, 'The quantity of money, Gross National Product and the price level', *Scottish Journal of Political Economy* (February 1961), p. 30.

ents of variation of the various measures of velocity were large. They ranged from 16 per cent when the traditional definition of money was used in the denominator to 28 per cent when all encashable assets were substituted for it.[1] The sub-period record did not produce much improvement; despite the fact that when all encashable assets were included in the denominator, the actual value of the redefined income velocity remained stable over a number of years, 1900–13, 1933–9 and 1956–62. In effect, in the 1880–1914, the 1920–39 and the 1946–62 intervals, the ranges in the recorded coefficient of variations of the different definitions of velocity were 6 per cent to 22 per cent, 6 per cent to 18 per cent and 14 per cent to 21 per cent respectively. More significantly, the size of the coefficient of variation was not reduced with the passage of time by the inclusion of money substitutes in the denominator. Indeed, in the first period, the coefficient of variation of currency-based income velocity was the highest – 22 per cent; in the subsequent two periods it was the lowest – 6 per cent and 14 per cent. Moreover, on comparing the sub-period coefficient of variations of the different definitions of velocity during between-periods, it is interesting to observe that the minimum value of this measure of variability was more than twice as high in the period after the Second World War as in the pre-1914 or inter-war periods. Finally, these results hold with very minor discrepancies if Gross National Product is substituted for Gross Domestic Private Expenditure in the numerator.

The variations noted in velocity and the rising interest in money's direct impact on expenditure soon produced results in the form of statistical estimates of income velocity.

T. H. Lee, using annual US data over the 1934–64 period, found that he obtained satisfactory results using a logarithmic relationship. As regards the determinants of velocity, he reported a significant negative regression coefficient with respect to real income and a significant positive regression coefficient with respect to the log of the short-term interest rate as adjusted for bank charges.[2]

In the UK, conducting a similar study over a longer time period (1877–1961), N. J. Kavanagh and A. A. Walters came up with a matching set of results on examining the relationship between the percentage changes in the Cambridge k, $1/V_y$, and the percentage changes in real income and in the consol rate (long-term interest rate) in selected time periods; though the regression coefficient of the percentage change in the consol rate was not significant in the latter half of the period – 1920–61.[3] However, when they regressed the log of k on the log of the consol rate and the log of real income, for the 1923–61 period, the coefficient of the consol rate, in keeping with Lee's findings, was both large ($-0{\cdot}553$) and highly significant ($s_b=0{\cdot}063$). None the less, in the same regression they found that the coefficient of the log of real income for the UK was both significant and negative in contradiction to Lee's results and their own estimates of the regression coefficient of the log of real income for the whole period. Similarly, in terms of goodness of fit, they reported rather low $\bar{R}^2$'s for their logarithmic regression relationships of 0·40 for the 1877–1961 period and 0·70 for the 1923–61 period.[4] In effect, though indicative, Kavanagh and Walters's results suggest that their investigations might be complemented by further studies with respect to the estimation of income velocity in the UK.

Table 4.1 contains the results of such an exercise. Before examining the results, however, these points should be noted. First, a preliminary investigation of the relationship between velocity and the selected explanatory variables suggested that a linear rather than a logarithmic function gave the best fit. Next, unlike Lee, Kavanagh and Walters, I decided to omit real income as an explanatory variable, and substitute a retail price index and the standard rate of income tax, the latter expressed in decimals of a pound, in its place. Walters and Kavanagh, whose money series was drawn from the same basic source as mine, had obtained rather puzzling results with respect to the relationship between the log of real income and the log of the Cambridge k. As noted above, the sign of the regression coefficient changed over time. This suggested that in the latter half of the period, the expected positive wealth effect was undermined, perhaps by the improvement in payment practices and/or the growth of money substitutes which accompanied the rise in real income. Finally, as the underlying simple correlation matrices indicated the presence of multicollinearity between some of the explanatory variables, particularly the consol rate and the price index in the 1946–62 period, the results of the simple regressions between each of the selec-

[1] Chapter 3, Table 3.5.

[2] T. H. Lee, 'Substitutability of non-bank intermediary liabilities for money: the empirical evidence', *The Journal of Finance* (September 1966), p. 447.

[3] N. J. Kavanagh and A. A. Walters, 'Demand for money in the UK 1877–1961: some preliminary findings', *Bulletin Oxford University Institute of Economics and Statistics* (May 1966), p. 106.

[4] Ibid., p. 105.

TABLE 4.1 Estimates of Income Velocity in the UK 1880–1962

Period	*Dependent Variable*	*Constant*	*Independent Variables* r_c	r_t	P	t_y	$\overline{Rsq}$	*DW*	$\overline{See}$	$\overline{Sct}$ (%)
1880–1962[1]	V_y	0·918 / 13·4	−0·020 / 0·5	—	—	—	0·00	0·13	0·299	16·20
		1·505 / 24·2	—	0·125 / 6·2	—	—	0·34	0·21	0·241	13·10
		2·000 / 34·7	—	—	−0·004 / 3·2	—	0·12	0·15	0·280	15·12
		2·079 / 52·4	—	—	—	−1·226 / 7·7	0·45	0·27	0·022	11·92
		1·790 / 51·4	—	0·060 / 5·1	0·011 / 7·6	−2·799 / 12·0	0·85	0·80	0·114	6·14
1880–1914	V_y	0·997 / 3·5	0·367 / 3·8	—	—	—	0·28	0·27	0·125	6·05
		1·822 / 21·9	—	0·084 / 3·0	—	—	0·19	0·27	0·132	6·43
		0·918 / 3·4	—	—	0·061 / 4·2	—	0·33	0·27	0·120	5·82
		2·120 / 33·8	—	—	—	−1·561 / 1·0	0·00	0·22	0·147	7·11
		0·694 / 3·2	—	0·050 / 2·3	0·008 / 5·8	−5·436 / 5·4	0·65	0·62	0·086	4·20
1920–1939	V_y	0·873 / 7·4	0·193 / 6·8	—	—	—	0·70	1·18	0·089	5·36
		1·445 / 45·4	—	0·080 / 8·1	—	—	0·77	1·47	0·078	4·71
		0·567 / 4·0	—	—	0·028 / 7·8	—	0·76	0·82	0·081	4·83
		1·697 / 8·1	—	—	—	−0·151 / 0·2	0·00	0·44	0·168	10·14
		0·901 / 8·2	—	0·033 / 2·9	0·022 / 5·0	−0·659 / 2·0	0·91	1·86	0·050	1·66
1946–1962	V_y	0·252 / 2·5	0·324 / 14·2	—	—	—	0·93	0·85	0·096	5·88
		1·174 / 20·6	—	0·174 / 9·9	—	—	0·86	1·18	0·134	8·17
		−0·329 / 4·8	—	—	0·023 / 29·1	—	0·98	1·73	0·048	2·95
		5·723 / 7·7	—	—	—	−9·456 / 5·3	0·62	0·50	0·216	13·24
		0·480 / 1·7	—	0·017 / 1·2	0·019 / 12·3	−1·233 / 2·3	0·99	2·26	0·038	2·35

Notation

V_y = Gross Domestic Private Expenditure/money stock.
r_c = Consol rate of interest.
r_t = Treasury Bill rate of interest after 1920, and high-class bill rate up to 1920.
P = Retail price index – 1958=100.
t_y = Standard rate of income tax as a decimal fraction of a £.
$\overline{Rsq}$ = square of correlation coefficient corrected for number of degrees of freedom. *DW*=Durbin-Watson statistic. $\overline{See}$=Standard error of estimate corrected for degrees of freedom. $\overline{Sct}$=Corrected standard error of estimate as percentage of average of dependent variable.

Note

[1] The war years 1915–19 and 1940–5 have been omitted.

ted explanatory variables and income velocity in turn are reported as well, so that the reliability of the multiple regression estimates of the regression coefficients may be more easily assessed.

In terms of *a priori* expectations, income velocity is expected to increase as the long-term rate of interest increases; that is as fixed-interest-bearing obligations become more attractive media for storing value than money in view of the prospective potential capital gain. Similarly, income velocity is expected to rise as the short-term rate of interest rises and as the price level rises too. The short-term rate represents the opportunity cost of holding money balances as an alternative to running down one's utilization of bank credit or some other short-term loan. The price index may be regarded as an implicit cost of holding money as a long-term asset instead of holding other durable assets whose monetary values move with the price level. Alternatively, income velocity is expected to fall as the standard rate of income tax rises, as the net of tax return on income-earning assets will be less, and, perhaps more importantly, the demand for money as a means of tax payment and possibly as a means of tax evasion will be accentuated. With just one exception (see the sign of the regression coefficient of P in the whole period), all the significant regression coefficients of these variables in both the single and multiple regressions are shown to exert their effect on V_y in the expected direction. In this respect, the empirical results tend to validate the noted expectations.

However, over the whole period and in the first sub-period, the degree of validation except for the sign is not impressive. The coefficients of determination, the $\overline{Rsq}$'s, are fairly low, particularly in the simple regressions, and the degree of autocorrelation in the residuals, as shown by the Durbin-Watson statistic, is severe enough to invalidate the relevance of the significance tests of the regression coefficients. Nevertheless, in the last two periods, 1920–39 and 1946–62, the $\overline{Rsq}$'s and the Durbin-Watson statistics of both the simple and the multiple regression are much more acceptable; in the latter the $\overline{Rsq}$'s are shown to be 0·91 and 0·99 respectively and the DW statistics indicate an absence of autocorrelation at the 5 per cent level. These findings, coupled with the low standard error of the residuals and the almost immoderately large t-ratios of many of the chosen explanatory variables, suggest that these variables in turn were quite influential in determining the household sector's preference for money relative to income, or its reciprocal V_y, and, fittingly, that these explanatory variables became more influential as the period progressed; that is as other assets, particularly financial assets, were more readily available as a means of storing wealth in addition to money.

Examining the results in more detail, it is interesting to observe that the regression coefficient of the long-term rate of interest, r_c, is between two to four times the size of the short-term rate of interest, r_t, in each of the sub-periods, and also that in the first and the last of these three sub-periods, the use of the long-term rate of interest seems to explain more of the variations in V_y than the short-term rate of interest does.[1] The $\overline{Rsq}$'s of the respective simple regressions are 0·28 as opposed to 0·19 and 0·93 to 0·86 respectively. Given that the wealth effect of a 1 per cent move in the long-term rate is much greater than that of a 1 per cent move in the short-term rate, this finding is quite consistent with the treatment of money as an asset, as a store of value, particularly as a variable one.

In this respect, too, it is interesting to observe that when the long-term rate of interest was included in the multiple regression as an explanatory variable, its regression coefficient was not significant in either the whole period or any of the sub-periods.[2] Its effect seems to have been swamped by the effect of the price index, with which, as the underlying correlation matrices showed, it was well correlated.[3] Therefore, in the multiple regressions reported in Table 4.1: the long-term rate of interest was omitted as an explanatory variable since the simple regression results showed that the price index, P, as a proxy for price expectations, was a far more potent measure of the opportunity cost of holding money balances as a store of value than the long-term rate of interest was. Indeed, the presence of r_c in the relationship distorted the regression coefficient of the other explanatory variables slightly and did not contribute to the significance of the results.[4] The above points suggest that this particular

[1] In the 1920–39 interval, it seems reasonable to suppose that the Government's extremely restrictive monetary policy in the 1920s as coupled with the confidence crises of the recession years, make V_y more sensitive to the short-term rate – e.g. more sensitive to money market conditions.

[2] When r_c, the consol rate, was included in addition to the other explanatory variables in the regression relationships, the results were as tabulated at the top of p. 56.

[3] Over the whole period the Pearson correlation coefficient of r_c with P was 0·74; while the Pearson correlation coefficient of r_t, the short-term rate, with P was just 0·16.

[4] In the other regressions, the regression coefficient of r_c is not significant in either the whole or any of the sub-periods. Moreover, its inclusion made no noticeable difference to the size of either the coefficient of determination or the index of autocorrelation. Its main effect was simply to reduce the t-ratios of the other independent variables with which it was well correlated.

Period	*Dependent Variable*	*Constant*	r_c	r_t	P	t_y	$\overline{Rsq}$	DW	$\overline{See}$	$\overline{Sct}\%$
1880–1962	V_y	1·762 / 27·1	0·016 / 0·5	0·054 / 3·1	0·010 / 7·5	−2·848 / 11·2	0·85	0·78	0·114	6·17
1880–1914	V_y	0·586 / 2·6	0·158 / 1·4	0·048 / 2·2	0·058 / 3·2	−5·521 / 5·6	0·66	0·63	0·085	4·13
1920–1939	V_y	1·024 / 7·3	−0·065 / 1·3	0·054 / 2·8	0·023 / 5·3	−0·597 / 1·8	0·91	2·32	0·049	2·93
1946–1962	V_y	0·452 / 1·6	0·042 / 1·3	0·015 / 1·1	0·017 / 7·2	−1·102 / 2·1	0·99	2·28	0·037	2·28

relative household asset preference, income velocity, is strongly influenced by the movements in variables which affect householders' expectations of how the value-storing capacity of their holdings of money will compare with that of other stores, bonds and, more potently, tangible assets and perhaps claims on these – equities.

Estimates of Households' Financial Asset Preferences

Like the variations in income velocity, the changes in the composition of the financial assets held by the financial and the non-financial private sector have been quite substantial in the UK over the 1880–1962 period. Similarly, as more attention has been paid to the growth and role of the financial sector, the oscillations in household holdings of the liabilities of the constituent institutions and of these intermediaries' holdings of the liabilities of the non-financial private sector have attracted attention too – particularly after 1950. With reference to the financial sector's role in expenditure generation, for instance, in 1963 R. Shearer argued that '... the influence of commercial banks on aggregate demand is exerted more by changes in direct bank credit than by changes in total bank credit or bank-generated changes in the money supply'.[1] And, referring to the control of the growth of bank liabilities, in 1966 G. W. Mitchell clearly indicated that changes in household asset preferences could exert a significant effect.[2] In turn, as economists have endeavoured to explain the changes in these relative asset preferences, they often selected the same explanatory variables as are used in velocity studies – real income, prices and interest rates.

With respect to changes in household asset preferences, interest rates, that is long rates, short rates, or the size of the differentials between deposit rates, have long been regarded as important determinants by a substantial number of economists. In the UK, for instance, Kavanagh and Walters found in their study of demand for money, 1877–1961, that on an annual basis there was a significant '... negative relationship between money and the rate of interest'.[3] In the USA, using quarterly post-war data, Hamburger found '... a significant relationship between money balances and other asset yields for the household sector....'[4] In effect, he showed that the percentage change in the short-term rate and the percentage change in the yield on equities each contributed about the same amount to the percentage change in money balances, while the contribution of the percentage change of income had the wrong sign and was not statistically significant. The implications of these interest-rate findings for the demand for other financial assets had already been broached and disputed in the literature.

In the UK, for example, Radice had argued in 1939 that working-class savings were positively correlated with the rate of interest.[5] In 1947, Horne provided some interesting historical evidence to buttress this point and to demonstrate how sensitive trustee savings banks' depositors were to the presence of interest differentials on competitive savings instruments; though perhaps the degree of financial acumen of his sample of depositors was somewhat influenced by the fact that they were mid-nineteenth-century Scots.[6] In 1965, Cleary in his study of the building society movement stated that between 1951

[1] R. A. Shearer, 'The expansion of bank credit – an alternative approach', *Quarterly Journal of Economics* (August 1963), p. 489.

[2] G. W. Mitchell, 'Interest rates versus interest rate ceilings in the allocation of credit flows', *American Finance Association Papers and Proceedings* (28 December 1966), p. 17.

[3] Kavanagh and Walters, op. cit., p. 108.

[4] M. J. Hamburger, 'The demand for money by households, money substitutes and monetary policy', *Journal of Political Economy* (December 1966), p. 616.

[5] E. A. Radice, *Savings in Great Britain* (London: Oxford University Press, 1939), p. 8.

[6] H. O. Horne, *A History of Savings Banks* (London: Oxford University Press, 1947), p. 223.

and 1963 the fund placements of investors in these institutions were similarly influenced. In particular, he held that the movement's share of the public's total saving depends '... a good deal on whether the interest rate offered is favourable in relation to that offered by competing institutions'.[1] In the same year, Clayton and Osborn emphasized the importance of interest-rate differentials as the major determinant of the substantial changes in building society funds over the years. 'These fluctuations are a direct result of the notorious stickiness of the rates which building societies offer their shareholders and depositors.'[2] And in Canada and the United States, as noted in the Porter Commission's report and in Mitchell's address to the American Finance Association, monetary economists in other countries have held that interest-rate differentials play an important role in influencing the composition of the demand for financial assets.

While the interest-rate differences have been widely used as a rationale to explain changes in the composition of financial assets, its applicability has been questioned. Sayers, in the sixth edition of *Modern Banking*, observed that the Post Office Savings Bank depositors' asset preferences appear '... insensitive to the appeal of rates of interest offered elsewhere in excess of the unvarying 2½ per cent....'[3] Cleary, in his study of the building societies, also made it clear that considerations other than a positive interest differential, particularly the development of an encompassing institutional branch network, accounted for part of the rapid rate of growth of these institutions' liabilities. In the *Monetary History of the United States*, Friedman and Schwartz argued that income velocity and, indirectly, the demand for money balances were relatively insensitive to interest rates. On a similar tack, using Canadian data over the 1946–62 period, Salyzn found evidence which discredited the Porter Commission's findings that '... the rate paid on deposits is also a very important factor in attracting funds....'[4] He held the change in the share of each of the competing institutions' holdings of total savings was much more sensitive to the change in the ratio of the number of their branch outlets, and he endorsed the earlier observation of D. and C. Alhadeff in the February 1958 issue of the *Quarterly Journal of Economics* '... that interest-rate differences are discredited as the explanation for the relative decline of commercial bank savings....'[5] It seems worthwhile to see if interest differentials played a role in determining the composition of UK financial savings.

In Table 4.2, I have endeavoured to see if some of the recorded changes in asset preferences in the UK may be explained by interest differentials. Unfortunately it was possible to use only the data for the period after the Second World War to examine the postulated relationship since the rates of return paid on a number of the selected savings instruments, building societies' shares and deposits, and the special deposits in the trustee savings banks, are not available before 1914 or for most of the inter-war period. Moreover, the data on the number of branches each of the selected institutional groups had in operation are both incomplete and difficult to evaluate in assessing how many of these branches were effective savings outlets. As a result, Salyzn's alternative hypothesis, that the ratio of one institution's branches with respect to those of another explained the ratio of their liabilities outstanding, could not be examined.

The relationships, which underlie the regression results depicted in Table 4.2, are based on the premise that relative asset preferences, as expressed by the ratio or the log of the ratio of the holdings of one form of asset with respect to another, are influenced by the difference or the log of the difference between rates of return on the two types of assets considered. Implicitly, as well, inasmuch as this postulated relationship is valid, one would expect that the relative asset preferences, as expressed by the ratio of the holdings of one asset to those of another, would also be related to the ratio of their respective rates of return. Indeed, this proved to be the case. Where the differences in the rates of return were significant, so too were the ratios of the respective rates of return. The results of roles of the ratios of the rates of return, however, are not reported because they were inferior. For example, in the case of the second regression the $\bar{R}^2$ was reduced from 0·94 to 0·90 and the Durbin-Watson statistic fell from 0·86 to 0·65.

In the first two regressions in Table 4.2, the ratio and the log of the ratio of building society shares to Post Office Savings Bank deposits are regressed on the difference or the log of the difference between the rates paid

[1] E. J. Cleary, *The Building Society Movement* (London: Elek Books, 1965), p. 280.

[2] G. Clayton and W. T. Osborn, *Insurance Company Investment* (London: Allen & Unwin, 1965), p. 23.

[3] R. S. Sayers, *Modern Banking*, 6th edn. (Oxford: Clarendon Press, 1964), p. 154. As shown below, this particular insensitivity does not seem to be supported by the empirical record.

[4] V. Salyzn, 'The competition for personal savings deposits in Canada', *Canadian Journal of Economics* (August 1966), p. 327.

[5] Ibid., p. 333.

TABLE 4.2 **Estimates of Selected Household Asset Preferences in the UK 1946–1962**

Dependent Variables	Constant Term	Independent Variables			$\overline{Rsq}$	DW	$\overline{See}$	$\overline{Sct}$%
1. $\frac{S_{bs}}{D_{psb}}$	$\frac{0{\cdot}061}{0{\cdot}9}$	r'_{bpsb} $\frac{0{\cdot}620}{13{\cdot}5}$			0·92	0·89	0·143	14·79
2. $\log\left[\frac{S_{bs}}{D_{psb}}\right]$	$\frac{-0{\cdot}177}{29{\cdot}5}$	$\log r'_{bpsb}$ $\frac{0{\cdot}987}{15{\cdot}4}$			0·94	0·86	0·081	8·21
3. $\log\left[\frac{S_{bs}}{(D_{tsb}+S_{bs})}\right]$	$\frac{-0{\cdot}216}{61{\cdot}6}$	$\log r'_{btsb}$ $\frac{0{\cdot}252}{18{\cdot}5}$			0·96	1·08	0·014	n.a.
4. $\frac{S_{bs}}{S_{bs}+D_{bs}}$	$\frac{0{\cdot}587}{27{\cdot}4}$	r_{bsd} $\frac{0{\cdot}093}{2{\cdot}6}$		*Trend* $\frac{0{\cdot}011}{7{\cdot}2}$	0·98	0·97	0·007	0·82
5. $\log\left[\frac{D_{bda}}{D_{bca}}\right]$	$\frac{-6{\cdot}092}{3{\cdot}7}$	$\log r_t$ $\frac{-0{\cdot}485}{1{\cdot}6}$	$\log NNI$ $\frac{2{\cdot}165}{4{\cdot}0}$	*Trend* $\frac{-0{\cdot}070}{4{\cdot}9}$	0·92	1·90	0·019	8·68

Notation

S_{bs} = Shares in building societies.
D_{psb} = Deposits in Post Office Savings Bank.
r'_{bpsb} = Interest paid on building societies' shares adjusted for income tax exemption minus $2\frac{1}{2}$ per cent interest paid on Post Office Savings Bank's deposits.
D_{tsb} = Ordinary deposits in trustee savings banks.
r'_{btsb} = Interest paid on building societies shares adjusted for income tax exemption minus $2\frac{1}{2}$ per cent paid on ordinary deposits in the trustee savings banks.
D_{bda} = Deposit accounts in London clearing banks.
D_{bca} = Current accounts in London clearing banks.
D_{bs} = Deposits in building societies.
r_t = Interest rate paid on Treasury Bills.
NNI = Net National Income.
$\overline{Rsq}$ = Square of correlation coefficient corrected for number of degrees of freedom.
DW = Durbin-Watson statistic.
$\overline{See}$ = Standard error of estimate corrected for number of degrees of freedom.
$\overline{Sct}$ = $\overline{See}$ as a percentage of dependent variable.

on these two types of savings instruments net of tax. Throughout the period, that is from 1946 to 1962, the net of tax rate paid on such shares was greater than that paid on Post Office Savings Bank deposits and the spread widened rapidly as the period progressed; the ratio of such shares to such deposits increased too. It was 0·33 in 1946 and 1·83 in 1962. The results show that the ratio was well correlated with the difference in the rates paid on these types of savings instruments: in both regressions the coefficients of determination exceed 0·90. Moreover, the results suggest that even the presence of a relatively small differential, say 1 per cent, has quite a marked influence on savers' revealed preference between these two types of financial assets.

To be sure, the Durbin-Watson statistics in both regressions indicate that the coefficients of the independent variables are not necessarily efficient. More significantly, they point to the fact that the underwritten *t*-ratios, as tests of their significance, are unreliable. Nevertheless, the coefficients, though not efficient, are unbiased and consistent, and the recorded *t*-ratios are so high that it seems most unlikely that the elimination of the autocorrelation would result in the recomputed *t*-ratios falling below the acceptable level – 2·2. The findings support the hypothesis that savers' asset preferences are sensitive to the spread between the rates of return paid on fairly similar sorts of savings instruments.[1]

The third regression in the table was designed to examine the relationship between savers' preferences for building society shares, relative to their preference for such shares plus ordinary deposits at the trustee savings banks, and the spread between the post-tax yields of such household assets. In turn, the fourth regression was structured to see if the difference in the rate of return paid by the building societies on the two types of their issued liabilities, shares and deposits, seemed to influence savers' preferences and, therefore, the composition of these institutions' liabilities. In addition, given that building society shares increased rapidly over the period while their deposits remained relatively constant, a linear time trend was introduced into the fourth regression to counteract the influence on the dependent variable of the pull of the high-share interest rate from other forms of savings instruments. Again the results of the regressions suggest that the presence of interest-rate differentials is influential.

The results of the third regression suggest that the household sector's choice between building society shares and ordinary deposits in the trustee savings banks is influenced by the size of the spread between the interest rates paid on these two types of assets. The regression coefficient of the log of this spread is positive, large (0·252) and highly significant, having a t-ratio of 18·5; moreover the adjusted coefficient of determination of 0·96 is satisfactory as a measure of goodness of fit. To be sure the Durbin-Watson statistic, having a value of 1·08, suggests that there might be a certain amount of positive serial correlation existing in the residuals; its value falls within indeterminate range at the 5 per cent level. Nevertheless, it seems reasonable to suppose that the regression coefficient is reasonably efficient and that it is also quite significant.

In the fourth regression too, the results indicate that savers' relative preference for building societies' obligations is sensitive to the spread between the two types of liabilities. A 1 per cent spread in favour of shares over deposits is shown to account for a little over 9 per cent of the ratio. On average over the period the spread was approximately $\frac{1}{2}$ per cent. However, though the $\overline{Rsq}$ is again satisfactory and the Durbin-Watson statistic is in the inconclusive range, the time trend, representing external factors, obviously played a dominant role. Still, the rate differential is shown to have exerted an influence – its partial correlation coefficient was 0·195.

The fifth and last regression in this table was designed to see what variables appeared to influence savers' preference for deposit accounts at commercial banks with respect to their holdings of current accounts with such banks. Again it seemed relevant to see if this particular preference, as expressed by a ratio of deposit accounts to current accounts, was sensitive to some measure of the spread between the yields on these two types of deposits. As in the fourth regression, it appeared advisable to incorporate a time trend and some other variable, such as Net National Income, as additional explanatory variables in the relationship.

The rate paid on deposit accounts, 1 per cent to 2 per cent below bank rate, was not particularly competitive with the rates offered by other institutions net of tax. These interest-bearing deposits, unlike current deposits whose utility presumably resides in their transaction function, would tend to be more adversely affected by the presence of such differentials; paradoxically, though, the London Clearing Banks' figures show that they grew relatively much faster than current deposits: £1,700 million to £3,400 million as opposed to £3,400 million to £4,200 million between 1946 and 1962. In this regression then, the log of the Treasury Bill rate, r_t, was used as a proxy for the difference between the rates paid on deposit accounts and current accounts. Its expected effect on the dependent variable was positive. Net National Income was used as a proxy for deposit holders' wealth, and, as deposit accounts were interest-bearing, its expected effect was positive in that to this extent at least deposits would represent better claims on that store than current deposits. Finally, the time trend was interpreted as acting as a proxy for the external pull of the presence of better wealth claims – that is those yielding a higher implicit rate of return. Accordingly its expected effect was negative.

As shown by the results, however, the expected effects were not necessarily realized; though in terms of goodness of fit and the indicated absence of any serial correlation, the regression result is quite good.

Explicitly, either the Treasury Bill rate does not act as a good proxy for the spread between the rates paid on

[1] It is interesting to record that from 1946 to 1962, building societies' shares outstanding increased from £646 million to £3,265 million. In contrast, the deposits placed in the Post Office Savings Bank fell from £1,982 million to £1,780 million. During this period the difference between their respective rates of return, post tax, rose from 0·6 per cent to 2·6 per cent in favour of the building societies.

these two types of bank liabilities, or, if it is a good proxy, then the results suggest that deposit holders' relative preferences for the deposit accounts as compared with current accounts were insensitive to this spread. The t-ratio of 1·6 indicates that the regression coefficient of r_t is not significantly different from the null hypothesis that this variable has no impact. The bank rate was also tried and found wanting.

This finding with respect to the log r_t is perhaps fortuitous as the actual regression coefficient has the wrong sign – it is negative not positive. Though, as suggested later, this *bonne chance* is perhaps fortunate if the bill rate is regarded as a good proxy for the cost of bank credit. In these circumstances, to the extent that deposit accounts are more sensitive than current accounts to interest rates, it would be reasonable to assume that the ratio would be negatively affected by a rise in costs of bank credits in the sense that deposit accounts would be more likely to be run down so as to minimize the rising cost of bank borrowing. This rationale (coupled with the fact that the recorded regression coefficients of log r_t and log *NNI* were very sensitive to errors as these independent variables were well correlated with each other (0·90)) indicates that a negative and significant regression coefficient of log r_t might be expected, if the multicollinearity had been removed. Of course, this expectation would splice in with the hypothesis that asset choices are sensitive to the spread between their relative prices, that is the spread between their rates of return.

Turning away from the somewhat fast-footed rationalizations of the role of the log r_t, the results do show that the other two variables behaved in accord with *a priori* expectations; though the time trend term obviously has little significance as compared with the contribution the log of *NNI* makes to the reduction of the residual variance. Indeed, the size of the positive and fully significant regression coefficient of log *NNI* – 2·165/4·0 – is quite striking. It suggests, *ceteris paribus*, that there was a fairly pronounced switch in the demand for bank liabilities from a transaction-orientated to a savings type of asset as income rises; this suggestion, in turn, could well be taken as a poignant indicator as to how British banks could retain their market share of UK financial savings. They should introduce new types of savings instruments which are designed to benefit from the substitution effect too by offering a more competitive rate of return.[1]

[1] Such an innovation was introduced in 1968. The banks issued sterling certificates of deposits, which bear competitive rather than institutionally rigged low rates of return.

Estimates of Financial Institutions' Asset Preferences

As efforts were made to explain the observed changes in income velocity and the revealed variations in household asset preferences, several economists have endeavoured to explain the oscillations in the asset preferences of certain financial institutions – particularly the banks' broad preferences for the obligations of the private and the public sector. These attempts to specify the functional relationships which underlie such institutional asset preferences are important on two counts. First, the historical record shows that certain financial institutions' selected asset/total asset ratios have exhibited a marked degree of instability. Second, the expected values of some of these ratios play an important role in the design of monetary policy; the ratios act as key variables in the underlying theoretical formulations of money supply and credit availability determination. Moreover, as with income velocity and certain household asset preferences, the evidence shows that the constancy assumptions of these relative asset preferences have been invalid. Therefore, efforts to explain these ratios are useful, even if they just draw attention to the need for respecifying the traditional money and credit supply formulations.

In this respect, given the importance ascribed to banking within the financial sector, it is not surprising that estimation of the behavioural patterns of bank portfolio management has received most of the attention. Moreover, in the UK, in view of the authorities' supposed control over the total amount of banking liabilities, deposits, it is not surprising that this attention has been somewhat limited before 1960. Perhaps, too, the emergence of the new money supply orthodoxy and the knowledge of sustained official directives and guidelines on bank asset holdings dampened much of the academic interest; despite the fact that even between 1920 and 1939 the record shows that there were substantial oscillations in the percentage of their credits the banks advanced the private and the public sectors. The coefficient of variation of bank holdings of long-term Government securities to bank deposits, S_B/D, and of total bank private credits to deposits, L_B/D, were 27·6 per cent and 10·5 per cent respectively; a marked increase over the corresponding measurement of variation in the 1880–1914 period of 14·2 per cent and 1·3 per cent.[2] In any event, after 1960 there was increased interest in bank portfolio preferences in the UK following the abandonment of official credit directives in 1958, and it

[2] See Chapter 3, Table 3.2.

accompanied the rising interest in the credit availability interpretation of the financial sector's external influence.

Naturally, most of the recent efforts which have been made to explain the changes in the absolute or relative asset preferences of the banks highlight the recorded historical instability of these preferences. In his attempt to explain the change of bank loan accommodation of the private sector, L_B, Shearer drew attention to the fact that US banking data revealed that bank holdings of all long-term securities, I_B, had oscillated in a significant pro-cyclical fashion round a falling trend.[1] Similarly, in their 1962 National Economic Development Office monograph, Brechling and Clayton drew attention to the size of the coefficient of variation of various bank asset/bank liability ratios – I/D, L/D and A/D – as computed from quarterly data from 1951 until 1961. They found the coefficients of variation of the corresponding investment, the liquid asset and the bank advance ratio to be 20·8 per cent, 8·5 per cent and 19·9 per cent respectively.[2]

All three economists interpreted their findings as having a policy import. Shearer, Brechling and Clayton, on testing the responsiveness of such asset preferences against movements in interest rates and demand pressures, found that the results were significant and that they contradicted the established *a priori* expectation put forward by Roosa in the presentation of his well-known locking-in effect of interest-rate increases. Their results indicated that the assumed stability of bank holdings of securities during periods of monetary stringency – rising interest rates – was invalid.

In 1965, Brechling and Clayton published a version of their 1962 paper which incorporated quarterly observations for two additional years – 1962 and 1963. Their findings agreed with those of their earlier investigations and the results of their modified regression relationships explaining L/D, I/D and A/D improved considerably giving an $\overline{Rsq}^2$ of 0·91, 0·86 and 0·90 for the 1951–63 period.[3] Pertinently, referring to the changes in bank asset preferences they concluded that '. . . there seems to be one group of asset-holders who react 'perversely' to changes in the bond rate'.[4] In effect, both in the UK and the USA investigations suggest that not only are bank asset preferences variable, but that the recorded variability may be explained as being the product of rational bank asset management: that of rearranging their asset holdings so as to obtain resources to meet the burgeoning demands of their private borrowers in boom periods.

The behavioural models which underlie the estimates of commercial banks' asset preferences shown in Table 4.3 broadly parallel those used by Brechling and Clayton. It should be noted, however, that the dependent variables, S_B/D and L_B/D, differ. S_B, for instance, includes only bank holdings of long-term Government securities, and L_B incorporates bank holdings of commercial bills and money at call as well as the banks' other loans to the private sector. In effect S_B is slightly smaller than I – bank investments – though it is included in the latter and L_B is larger than A – non-negotiable bank loans to the private sector – though it incorporates the latter. However, D, bank liabilities, is the same.

In contrast, as well, the estimates contained in the table are based on annual year-end data as recorded in the banks' consolidated balance sheets and annual averages of the various rates of interest and the standard rate of taxation; whereas Clayton and Brechling used quarterly statistics. Moreover, as Brechling and Clayton were interested in explaining the size of each of the three main groups of bank asset/total liability ratios, I/D, A/D and L/D, they used three rates of interest, the short-term bond rate, the bank rate and the Treasury Bill rate as independent variables to approximate the rates of return on each type of asset – investments, advances and liquid assets. In Table 4.3, however, I am interested in estimating the sensitivity of two particular bank asset/bank liability ratios, S_B/D and L_B/D, with respect to the long-term rate of interest, r_c, and with respect to the degree of monetary ease or of fiscal restraint as indicated by the spread between the long- and short-term rates on Government paper and the standard rate of income tax.

On examining the four regression results in the table, it may be seen at a glance that the results are reasonably indicative. The $\overline{Rsq}$'s are large. The *t*-ratios of at least two of the three explanatory variables in each regression equation indicate that the regression coefficients above them are highly significant; moreover the reported Durbin-Watson statistics suggest that the values of these ratios are reasonably accurate inasmuch as there is little if any autocorrelation. In addition, the standard errors of the residuals as percentages of the means of the dependent variables, the $\overline{Sct}$, are reasonably small; they are all between 2·5 and 6·7 per cent. On considering the size of the

[1] Shearer, op. cit., p. 496.

[2] F. Brechling and G. Clayton, 'Commercial banks' portfolio behaviour', *National Economic Development Office* (University of Liverpool, 1962), p. 3. I=Investments, L=Liquid assets and A=Bank advances; D stands for Total bank liabilities.

[3] F. Brechling and G. Clayton, 'Commercial banks' portfolio behaviour', *Economic Journal* (June 1965), p. 303.

[4] Ibid., p. 314.

TABLE 4.3 **Estimates of Commercial Banks' Asset Preferences in the UK 1921–1939 and 1947–1962**

Period	*Dependent Variable*	*Constant Term*	*Independent Variables*				$\overline{Rsq}$	*DW*	$\overline{See}$	$\overline{Sct}$ (%)
			r_c	(r_c-r_t)	t_y	*Trend*				
1921–1939	S_B/D	0·538 9·7	−0·012 7·9	−0·002 0·4	0·485 4·7	−0·003 2·8	0·95	1·74	0·013	6·40
	L_B/D	0·284 4·3	0·112 7·2	−0·011 1·5	−0·655 5·3	0·007 4·7	0·95	1·72	0·016	2·50
					GNP	*Trend*				
	S_B/D	0·434 7·3	−0·101 9·0	—	0·00005 3·8	−0·003 2·0	0·92	1·23	0·017	8·00
				(r_c-r_t)	t_y	*Trend*				
1947–1962	S_B/D	−0·270 1·9	−0·091 4·9	−0·033 5·5	1·969 6·5	0·017 3·8	0·89	2·68	0·018	6·70
	L_B/D	0·275 1·9	0·070 3·8	0·030 5·0	−0·487 1·6	0·004 0·9	0·95	2·10	0·018	4·10
					GNP	*Trend*				
	S_B/D	1·107 5·1	−0·020 0·5	—	−0·00009 2·9	−0·093 3·1	0·61	0·85	0·035	12·70

Notation

S_B = Bank holdings of long-term Government securities – those listed under the heading 'Investments' in the banks' balance sheets.
L_B = All bank assets excluding S_B, bank holdings of Treasury Bills, Treasury deposit receipts, special deposits, currency and deposits at the Bank of England.
D = Total banking liabilities – this includes deposits, capital and reserves and other liabilities.
r_c = Current yield on consols – the long-term interest rate.
r_t = Yield to maturity on three-month Treasury Bills – the short-term rate.
GNP = Gross National Product.
t_y = Standard rate of income taxation expressed in decimals.
$\overline{Rsq}$ = Square of correlation coefficient corrected for number of degrees of freedom.
DW = Durbin-Watson statistic.
$\overline{See}$ = Standard error of estimate corrected for number of degrees of freedom.
$\overline{Sct}$ = $\overline{See}$ as a percentage of the average of the dependent variable.

Note

The *t* statistic is depicted beneath each of the regression coefficients; the latter are significant at the 95 per cent level if this statistic equals or exceeds 2·145 in the first period and 2·179 in the second period.

coefficients of variation of the two ratios in the two periods, the estimates seem quite satisfactory.[1]

Taking each regression equation in turn, these findings emerged from the investigation.

In the first period, a 1 per cent rise in the long-term rate of interest was associated with a 0·102 reduction in the S_B/D ratio; similarly, a 1 per cent rise in the standard rate of taxation was accompanied by a 0·005 increase in the S_B/D ratio given that the other explanatory variables remained unchanged. Conversely, over this period, a 1 per cent rise in the consol rate was matched by a 0·112 increase in the L_B/D ratio, and a 1 per cent rise in the standard rate of income tax corresponded to a 0·007 reduction in the L_B/D ratio, given the same constancy assumptions. The *t*-ratios of the second explanatory variable (r_c-r_t) are too low to ascribe much significance to the size or sign of the regression coefficient of this variable in the years before the Second World War. However, the time trend[2] was significant in both the S_B/D and L_B/D

[1] In 1920–9 the coefficients of variation of S_B/D and L_B/D were 27·6 per cent and 10·5 per cent. From 1946 to 1962 the size of this measure of their variability was even larger – 32·2 per cent and 19·3 per cent respectively.

[2] The time trend was inserted as an explanatory variable to take account of the fact that at the beginning of each period bank holdings of Government securities were disproportionately high.

formulations, and it indicates that each year the S_B/D ratio fell by 0·3 per cent and that the L_B/D ratio increased by 0·7 per cent, given the underlying *ceteris paribus* assumption that the other determining variables remained constant, a movement which seems a reasonably good adjustment of the composition of bank portfolios to peacetime conditions. In the second period, 1947–62, the findings are generally of a similar nature; though in this period the regression coefficients of the second explanatory variable $(r_c - r_t)$ are highly significant in both formulations; whereas the significance of t_y as a determinant of L_B/D is questionable since its t-ratio, 1·6, is below the usual acceptable level of 2·2.

The results of the regression show that given the underlying constancy assumptions with respect to the other explanatory variables, a 1 per cent rise in the long-term rate of interest, a 1 per cent increase in the spread between the long- and short-term interest rates, or a 1 per cent increase in the standard rate of income tax will be associated with a 0·091 reduction, a 0·033 decrease, and a 0·020 increase respectively in the S_B/D ratio. Similarly a 1 per cent rise in r_c, a 1 per cent increase in the spread between r_c and r_t, and, less certainly due to the low value of its t-ratio, a 1 per cent increase in t_y, will be associated with a 0·070 rise, a 0·030 increase and a 0·005 decrease in the L_B/D ratio. In the second period, the time trend term is significant only in the S_B/D regression. It indicates that with the passage of each year that the S_B/D ratio will rise by 0·017, a finding which is somewhat surprising in view of the fact that this ratio fell from 0·286 to 0·161 between 1947 and 1962.

Taking a positive view, and assuming that the direction of causation flows from right to left, it seems that the findings may be interpreted as follows: a rise in the long-term rate of interest induces the banks to reduce their holdings of Government securities and increase their advances to the private sector relative to the total funds they have at their disposal – D. This suggests that the banks treat their Government security holdings as secondary reserves for satisfying increased private demands for loan accommodation. In addition, and in accord with Brechling and Clayton's findings on quarterly data, the findings support the Treasury view that sales of Government securities during periods of rising interest rates are difficult to sustain. Conversely, however, the regression results suggest that during periods of monetary or fiscal stringency, that is when the gap between r_c and r_t is narrowed or reversed or when the standard rate of tax, t_y, is increased, the *banks' S_B/D ratio is increased* and *their L_B/D ratio is reduced.* In effect, and in partial contradiction to the interpretation that Shearer, Brechling and Clayton gave to their results, it seems *that banks do manage their portfolios in an anti-cyclical fashion in response to monetary and/or fiscal pressure*: though, to be sure, the offsetting coefficient of the long-term rate substantially exceeds that of the $(r_c - r_t)$ in both periods, which suggests that the narrowing or the elimination of the yield gap will be insufficient as long as the long-term rate continues to rise *pari passu*.

On assessing these findings, it should be recorded that the measure of monetary stringency, a narrowing in the $r_c - r_t$ gap indicated monetary tightness in 1920, 1923–6, 1929, 1931, 1934–5, 1939, 1952–3, 1955–6 and 1960. The value of the spread became negative in 1920, 1929, and 1956 indicating extremely tight monetary conditions. Similarly, the index of fiscal restraint, a rise in the standard rate of income tax, occurred in 1930, 1931, 1936, 1937, 1938, 1939 and 1951. In the other years, 1920–9, 1946–50, and 1952–62 it was either constant or it was reduced. Over all, the tax rate fell from 30 per cent to 20 per cent and then rose again to 30 per cent in the first period; it was gradually reduced, with one exception, from 45 per cent to 39 per cent in the period after the Second World War. Moreover, in terms of movements in the long-term rate of interest, r_c, and the retail price index, p, 1958 = 100, in the first period, 1920–39, the long-term rate of interest fell from 5·3 per cent in 1920 to 2·9 per cent in 1935 and rose to 3·8 per cent in 1939; this movement was practically paralleled by the fall in the retail price index from 54 in 1920 to 34 in 1933 and a slight rise to 38 in 1939. In the 1946–62 period, with a few deviations, the consol rate moved steadily upwards from 2·6 per cent in 1946 to 6·0 per cent in 1962 and the index of retail prices increased every year rising from 60 in 1946 to 108 in 1962. These observations provide additional material which should be helpful in interpreting the regression results.

The movements in the measures of monetary and fiscal tightness, for instance, suggest that in the first period between 1920 and 1931 the authorities relied primarily on monetary policy to restrain demand pressures; whereas after 1932, the burden was primarily placed on fiscal policy. The movements in prices and interest rates, moreover, suggest that during the first period, the tendency towards excess capacity and slack domestic demand became increasingly prevalent with the exception of a slight recovery towards the end of the period. In contrast, in the 1946–62 period, the measures of monetary and fiscal restraint suggest that, with one exception – 1951 – monetary measures played the major restraining role after the imposed quantitative controls of the war years were reduced and then removed. Similarly, the sustained upward movement in prices and the long-term rate of interest indicate that this was a period of rising domestic demand and full capacity utilization.

These observations, which generally conform with the historical record, in conjunction with the regression results, indicate that the period changes in S_B/D and L_B/D responded to the degree of capacity utilization.[1] In effect, if unchecked by fiscal or monetary measures, a buoyant private demand for bank loan accommodation tends to generate its own supply due to bank asset substitution – a finding to which Shearer and Brechling and Clayton allude in their analyses of quarterly data.

Estimates of the Money Supply, the Size of Financial Intermediaries' Assets and of Credit Availability

The variability in the asset preferences of banks, non-bank financial institutions, and the private sector casts some doubt on the reliability of the traditional money supply model – $M_s = H/(d+e) + H_p$. Here d and e represent the average propensities of the banks and the private sector to hold high-powered money, H, with respect to the deposit liabilities outstanding. As shown, the above model only acquires explanatory relevance in its reduced form if both H and d are set independently by some outside agency; and, even then, given that e is a variable, accurate estimates of e have to be obtained in order to forecast M_s. Indeed, it sometimes is questionable if changes in H and/or d may be regarded as being prescribed by the central authority. Moreover, when H or either of the two asset preferences changes, and these changes are induced by changes in final demand, one can use Sayers's argument, '. . . it is business that wags the money supply. . . .'[2] In short, in these circumstances the money supply is demand determined.

In much the same way, the variations in asset preferences noted above blur the validity of the assumption that the amount of non-bank financial institutions' liabilities outstanding is proportionately linked with the existing level of bank deposits. That is that Q, the non-banking institutions' liabilities, is equal to hD; where h may be taken as some constant reflecting the non-banking institutions' liabilities/bank deposit ratio that the private sector desires to hold.[3] The expression, $Q=hD$, explains nothing, even if the size of Q exerts no influence on D, unless h, being a variable, is accurately predicted. Similarly, the observed oscillations in the fraction of the total assets the banks and the non-banking financial institutions hold in Government obligations, S_B/D, T_B/D, H_B/D and S_I/Q, T_I/Q, H_I/Q respectively, where S, T and H stand for Government securities, Government Treasury Bills, and Government-issued currency or currency substitutes, create parallel difficulties. The success one achieves on extrapolating from the determination of D and Q to predict the total amount of institutional credit which will be extended to the private sector in a given time-period depends upon the reliability of the estimates of these fractions. In effect, the revealed changes in the UK's institutional and non-institutional private sectors' relative asset preferences, as shown in Tables 3.1 and 3.2 in Chapter 3, invalidate the frequently made assumption that the relevant ratios may be treated as constants in models of deposit creation or of institutional credit allocation. The financial coefficients change. And such changes must be accurately estimated if these models are to be useful in explaining the observed stock of deposits, of other institutional liabilities outstanding, and of institutional credit allocations.

The explicit incorporation of functional relationships to determine the value of the relevant financial coefficients within the traditional money supply model, however, creates problems. The simplicity of the single-equation approach has to be abandoned. The substitute, a simultaneous-equation system, is difficult to construct in the sense that the relevant system may well turn out to be a model of the national economy. Finally, the operational significance that the resulting model has for the formulation of monetary policy may be impeded by the presence of data time lags of activity in certain key sectors. The same set of problems applies with equal validity to the estimation of the amount of non-bank financial institutions' liabilities which will be outstanding, or as to how

[1] It may be of interest to record that on regressing S_B/D on the consol rate, r_c, the Gross National Product and a trend term in each period, I found a significant positive coefficient for GNP in the 1920–39 period and a significant negative coefficient for GNP in the last period. In effect, the regression coefficients indicated that an increase in GNP of £1,000 million would have increased the S_B/D ratio 0·05; whereas in the second period the same increase in GNP was associated with a decline in the S_B/D ratio of 0·09. Over the first period, GNP fell from the £5,100 million in 1920 to around £4,000 million in 1932, and then rose again to approximately the 1920 level by 1939. In the 1946–62 period GNP rose in each year from approximately £8,800 million in 1946 to £25,000 million in 1962.

[2] R. S. Sayers, 'Alternative views of central banking', *Economica* (May 1961), p. 320.

[3] D. K. Sheppard and C. R. Barrett, 'Financial credit multipliers and the availability of funds', *Economica* (May 1965), p. 202.

the financial institutions as a group will allocate their assets between the private and the public sector. As a consequence, though it is desirable to construct a model of the whole economy, it does seem worthwhile to see if the traditional single-equation estimators may be redesigned so that they predict with a reasonable degree of accuracy the phenomena they are designed to explain.

The task of redesigning the traditional formulations is facilitated by the fact that the underlying asset preferences which have to be estimated are average rather than marginal relationships, and that each pertains to the aggregate, rather than the individual, preferences of a select group of economic actors. As a consequence, even though the critical financial coefficients do change over time, it is reasonable to suppose that in many instances their values in one period serve as a good estimate of their values in the next. This supposition gains credibility if one examines the historical record and notes that the simple correlation coefficients between successive annual values of these ratios is usually 0·90 or higher. As a result, it seems reasonable to substitute the values of the determining asset preferences in one period for their recorded values in the subsequent year, and then to examine the adjusted model to see how well it performs.

Such substitutions were made in the traditional models used in Table 4.4. These when so adjusted, were applied to see how well they performed as determinants of the variables they were designed to explain: the change in bank deposits, the level of financial intermediaries

TABLE 4.4 **Estimates of Gross Non-Bank Financial Institutions' Liabilities and Gross Private Credit 1921–1939, 1947–1962**

Period	*Dependent Variable*	*Constant*	*Independent Variables*			$\overline{Rsq}$	*DW*	$\overline{See}$	$\overline{Sct}$%
1921–1939	ΔD_t		$\frac{\Delta H_t}{(d+e)_{t-1}}$						
		21·249 12·0	0·480 3·6			0·402	1·29	51·439	—
1947–1962	ΔD_t	181·265 3·3	−0·062 0·2			−0·060	1·01	183·403	—
			$\log h_{t-1}$	$\log D_t$	*Trend*				
1921–1939	$\log Q$	2·833 8·4	0·041 0·5	0·122 1·1	0·020 10·8	0·999	0·50	0·003	0·10
1947–1962	$\log Q$	0·683 1·1	0·655 6·8	0·830 5·3	0·007 4·2	0·996	1·30	0·006	0·16
			$D'_t(1-c_{npb})_{t-1}$	$Q_t(1-c_{np})_{t-1}$					
1921–1939	C_{pft}	100·658 0·4	0·726 5·4	0·932 3·7	−5·636 0·2	0·985	0·86	76·607	2·65
1947–1962	C_{pft}	−321·503 1·2	0·723 4·8	1·101 10·1	−7·697 0·2	0·997	1·36	188·988	2·11

Notation

D = Commercial bank deposits.
D' = Total bank liabilities.
d = Recorded reserve/deposit ratio – reserve = banks' holdings of currency and bankers' deposits at the Bank of England.
e = Recorded non-bank currency/deposit ratio – currency includes note and coin holdings plus non-bank private deposits at the Bank of England.
H = High-powered money – currency plus bankers' and private deposits at the Bank of England.
Q = Non-bank financial institutions' total liabilities.
h = Q/D'.
C_{pft} = Total private credit extended by all financial institutions.
c_{npb} = Ratio of non-private credit to total credit extended by the banks.
c_{np} = Ratio of non-private credit to total credit extended by the non-banking financial institutions.

outstanding, Q, and the amount of credit all the financial institutions in the chosen sample extended to the private sector during the two time periods, 1921–39 and 1947–62. The results are interesting.

The application of the traditional model which is used to explain changes in bank deposits was reasonably successful in the inter-war interval. The regression coefficient of 0·480, though considerably below its postulated value of 1, is highly significant given that its *t*-ratio is 3·6. Similarly, the coefficient of determination $\overline{Rsq}$ is reasonably high, 0·40, and the Durbin-Watson statistic is such that one may be reasonably confident of the measure of the regression coefficient's significance. Indeed, when the level of deposits and the level of high-powered money outstanding were substituted for their changes in the relationship, which in turn was then put in a logarithmic form in order to separate the effects of H_t and $(d+e)_{t-1}$, both the regression coefficients were large, significant, and with the expected sign (+0·866/15·0 and −0·764/10·9). Moreover the $\overline{Rsq}$ of 0·95 and the Durbin-Watson statistic of 1·00 were reasonably satisfactory; though the latter suggested that some autocorrelation might exist since it lay within the indeterminate range (0·86–1·85). In the 1947–62 period, however, in the sense that the $\overline{Rsq}$ is −0·06, the model in the first differences fails to give any insight into how the change in bank deposits is determined; though in the underlying stock model, the results were reasonably good. The regression coefficients of the log H_t and the log $(d+e)_{t-1}$ were quite large and fully significant 0·632/7·6 and −0·380/2·5) and the $\overline{Rsq}$ and the *DW* statistic were 0·90 and 1·1 respectively. In effect, while the model performed reasonably well in the inter-war period, it did not perform at all between 1947 and 1962 in the first differences, though the underlying stock models performed satisfactorily in both periods.

These two contrasting findings in the first differences might fit in with Sayers's new orthodoxy with respect to deposit creation which is so well represented in the literature: that is, that the traditional model does not coincide with the representative model of the 1950s; high-powered money should be extended to include Treasury Bills, commercial bills and money at call, and that similarly, the currency deposit ratio and the reserve deposit ratio should be adjusted accordingly. However, the contrast supports the new orthodoxy only in the sense that the traditional model does not seem to work in the first differences in the 1947–62 period and the validity of the new orthodoxy itself can be established only by a direct examination of its applicability. Unfortunately, this examination cannot be made owing to the unavailability of relevant statistics – totals of Treasury and commercial bills outstanding.[1]

While the deposit change supply model used in Table 4.4 did not have any predictive value in the post-war period, as with the deposit model the formulations which are used to account for the *level* of non-bank financial intermediary liabilities and the total stock of financial institutions' credits to the private sector produced more satisfactory results, though the results in the 1921–39 period were inferior.

In the model which was designed to estimate the financial intermediaries' liabilities, of the variables which are meant to determine the value of log Q, neither log h_{t-1}, nor log D_t had regression coefficients which were significant in the 1921–39 period. Only the trend term was significant. This disappointing result is probably partly due to the fact that there is a considerable amount of correlation between the two independent variables, 0·73, which might well have led to the poor *t*-ratios. The underlying simple correlation between log Q and log h_{t-1} and log Q_t and log D_t was 0·88 and 0·98 respectively. However, in the second period, 1947–62, the values of *t*-ratios of the two independent variables were satisfactory, 6·8 and 5·3 respectively, though in this period too, the problem of multicollinearity was certainly present.

The results of the regression model which was designed to predict the stock of institutional private credits were more satisfactory. As determinants of the value of C_{pfi}, apart from the suggestion of some positive serial correlation, the naive estimators provided good results in both periods. The *t*-ratios of the partial regression coefficients are satisfactory; moreover, the values of the individual regression coefficients are quite similar in both periods – a fact which suggests that the values of the respective coefficients would be approximately the same for the whole period, that is from 1921 to 1962 excluding the 1940–46 interval. This indeed proved to be the case; their values were 0·810 and 1·093 respectively, and their *t*-ratios were extremely large – 12·2 and 31·0. These results seem to confirm the expectation that if good estimates are available of both bank and non-bank financial institutions' lia-

[1] It is of more than passing interest to note that whereas the simple correlation coefficients between H and D in each period were 0·78 and 0·94 respectively, the correlation between the changes in these two stocks in the same two periods varied considerably. It was 0·64 in 1921–39 and −0·07 in 1947–62, a fact which suggests that in the latter period the high correlation between the stocks' high-powered money and bank deposits was due to a uniform trend factor and was not a response to any causal nexus between them.

bilities, D_t and Q_t, and the previous year's data reflecting the division of their assets between Government and private-sector obligations are known, it might be possible to obtain reasonable estimates of the financial institutions' credit extensions to the private or to the public sectors in the current period: a consideration which might prove useful in the design of a credit availability model.[1]

Conclusion

Over all, however, for predictive purposes, the degree of success of the estimators of the log Q_t and C_{pfi} is only partly indicative. Their dependence on the presence of good estimates of D_t and D_t', the values of which may well be considerably influenced in turn by the *ex ante* demands the non-institutional sector has for Q_t and particularly institutional credit – C_{pfi}, circumscribes their applicability. Moreover, given that the composition of both the institutional and non-institutional demands for assets changes, and that these changes may also exert an influence on D_t and D_t', the predictive powers of the chosen estimators may vaporize completely to the extent that interest differentials, prices, tax rates, and levels of expenditure exert an important influence. In effect, the weight of evidence presented in this chapter suggests that single-equation estimators of the money supply, of income velocity, of the stock of other money substitutes, or of the supply of institutional credit are mainly useful to the extent that they facilitate interpretation of the historical record. For predictive purposes, such as meeting the demand for good estimates of the final impact of the application of some monetary measure, a considerable part of the underlying *ex ante* flow of funds matrix will have to be accurately specified.

[1] This idea was used quite successfully in some 'credit' impact private expenditure models: see Chapter 5, pp. 87ff.

5 Money, Encashable Assets, Private Institutional Credits and Private Expenditure in the UK 1880–1962

Introduction

This chapter is designed to serve as a basis for an examination of what H. G. Johnson has called '. . . the fundamental issue . . . in the history of monetary theory'.[1] The issue is whether monetary economists should concentrate on endeavouring to obtain a correct specification of the demand for and the supply of money in order to get a good estimate of a variable, the rate of interest, whose changes in turn are asserted to have an influence on the change in activity in the product and factor markets; or, alternatively, whether they should concentrate on the equation-of-exchange approach which suggests that changes in the nominal (or by some the real) stock of money transmits a direct influence on the expressed demands in both markets. Below, the historical record is examined to see what empirical support may be found in the UK for the direct 'effect' hypothesis, and to appraise whether the support for the direct expenditure effect is improved by broadening the definition of the money stock or substituting in its place a measure of the private credits granted by the financial sector to private borrowers.

The findings have been mainly derived from a preliminary statistical investigation of the degree of association between the year-end balance sheet figures of the main UK financial institutions and various expenditure flows over the 1880–1962 period. They should be interpreted cautiously and should not be regarded as showing causation even if they seem predictive; especially as the estimating procedure, ordinary least squares applied to a single equation, though widely used, is subject to a serious limitation – the problem of identification as employed below. The assumed exogeneity of the explanatory variables is questionable as well. It is also important to note that the backing data on financial stocks, and on expenditure flows, are not exact, owing to the deficiencies in the published record in the pre-1946 period: so that in addition the results are distorted by errors in variables. The pre-1946 regression coefficients are unlikely to be consistent. Nevertheless, the products of the calculations should be useful. They, like the results of similar types of studies conducted in the United States, are designed to help to select the most fruitful avenues for further study of the financial sector's effect on the pace of economic activity.[2]

Background

Monetary economists have long claimed that money has a direct impact on the level of economic activity: changes in the stock of money will induce changes in aggregate expenditure.

Lavington, when outlining the 'Theory of Money', summarized the pre-1930s position with his representation of the underlying quantity theory of money: $P=(MV)/T$, where P stands for the average price per transaction, T represents the number of transactions and M and V are defined as equal to the money stock and the transaction velocity of that stock in the transaction period. Given that T and V were either constants or variables which were determined exogenously, an increase in the money stock would simply engender a proportional increase in the price level.[3]

The current quantity theory position, which is probably best represented in the writings of Milton Friedman, is broadly similar; though Q, real expenditure, replaces T and appears along with P in the left-hand side of the equation, and, more importantly, the V, now income velocity, is regarded as a behavioural variable which is a stable function of the level of permanent income and of permanent prices. Again, given that V changes slowly, if there is an excess supply of money and the money supply is exogenously determined, then equilibrium is only restored by an increase in the price level and/or an increase in real expenditure: an increase in private

[1] H. G. Johnson, 'Monetary theory and policy', in *Surveys of Economic Theory*, Vol. I (London: Macmillan, 1967), p. 20.

[2] M. Friedman and D. Meiselman, 'The relative stability of monetary velocity and the investment multiplier in the United States, 1897–1958', in *Stabilization Policies* (Englewood Cliffs: Prentice Hall, 1963), p. 174.

[3] F. Lavington, *The English Capital Market* (London: Methuen, 1929), p. 23.

expenditure in terms of current prices. Naturally a corollary to this theory for policy is that '... the effects of monetary policy may be expected to operate more than would otherwise be supposed through the direct effect of changes in the stock of money on spending, and rather less through indirect effects on rates of interest, thence on investment, and thence on income.'[1]

This theory and its corollary have been vigorously disputed; particularly after Keynes published his *General Theory* which laid the foundations for the development of a compelling rival hypothesis – the income-expenditure approach to demand determination. Advocates of Keynes's views held that exogenously determined changes in income and not exogenously determined changes in the money stock were mainly responsible for changes in expenditure in constant prices; changes in the money stock only exerted an influence indirectly inasmuch that they affected the rate of interest, which in turn might change the amount of the exogenously determined expenditure flow. In many instances such advocates suggest that the primacy of the income-expenditure approach holds in current prices too.

Monetary economists reacted. The attractiveness of their alternative propositions, however, has been somewhat diffused by their variety; that is whether money or credit or both have a direct influence on nominal expenditure, or whether (directly countering Keynes's argument) changes in real money balances exert a direct impact on real expenditure and therefore on income. This discord between monetary economists has been long-standing; it existed before Keynes's major contribution, and it is reflected in the difficulty these economists have had in defining exactly what the components of the crucial financial variable might be – that is the components of money or credit.

In the nineteenth century, for instance, as shown by the currency versus banking school controversy, economists disagreed as to whether or not commercial bank deposits should be added to bank notes and gold specie in determining the money stock. The argument was centred around two interlocking issues; that is whether bank deposits were perfect substitutes for notes and coin or not, or, if they were perfect substitutes, whether the authorities' control over the size of the note issue allowed them to prescribe the amount of bank deposits outstanding as well. Even today, elements of this old controversy still have to be settled, as there is still a substantial amount of disagreement as to which type of bank deposits, demand or time, should be included in the money magnitude.

In the 1920s, Lavington interjected another complexity. He suggested that credit, that is the power to borrow '... multiplies the stock of standard money into a much larger stock of general purchasing power in the form of promises to pay ...'[2] Moreover, he made it clear that the utilization of this credit also had a direct expenditure effect: '... in modern conditions ... production takes time and is based largely on contracts involving future payments'.[3] The availability of bank *and* non-bank credits, contracts involving future payments, could, if rationed, affect both the amount and the composition of output and thereby income. Credit was regarded as having an independent direct influence, as well as having an effect through its impact on standard money. The hypothesis that the availability of credit mattered had been unequivocally made.

In the 1930s, various aspects of Lavington's arguments were well established in the literature. They had the effect of making the rigid quantity theory approach to expenditure determination appear even more nebulous.

In 1933, Robertson, for instance, argued that in certain conditions the existence of other institutional savings instruments also had a direct expenditure effect. 'It is of the utmost importance that under certain conditions money which has been imprisoned in what Mr Keynes calls the "savings deposits" and "business deposits" may seep out, raise aggregate income and "income deposits" and drive up *P*.'[4] In 1935, Hicks amplified Robertson's position when he suggested that the presence of non-bank financial institutions' liabilities would '... act as a substitute for money in one of its uses, and thus diminish the demand for money....'[5] Given that these non-monetary financial assets had grown substantially, from about £300 million in 1880 to £2,700 million in 1935, Hicks's amplification of Robertson's point implied, in quantity theory terms, that the suggested seepage was both important and continual. By implication, it seemed that other assets, as well as bank deposits and currency, should be incorporated in the definition of the money stock.

[1] M. Friedman, 'The demand for money: some theoretical and empirical results', *Journal of Political Economy* (August 1959), p. 351.

[2] Lavington, op. cit., p. 52.

[3] Ibid., p. 52.

[4] D. H. Robertson, 'A note on the theory of money', in *Readings in Monetary Theory* (London: Allen & Unwin, 1962), p. 157.

[5] J. R. Hicks, 'A suggestion for simplifying the theory of money', *Economica* (February 1935), p. 10.

By the 1960s, this suggestion had been explicitly taken up by Sayers who in addition thought that Lavington's concept of 'credit' should also be added as a component of the critical financial factor. Money is composed of those assets '. . . which are used as media of exchange and stores of value'.[1] As such, '. . . money is the creation of the public that chooses to impute certain qualities to certain claims'.[2] These claims, Sayers argues, would include such non-bank institutional liabilities as savings deposits at the Post Office and trustee savings banks.

> It is this wide concept of liquid assets that we must put, in the place conventionally occupied by "the supply of money", as the monetary quantity influencing total effective demand for goods and services. And we must interpret it widely enough to include credit that can be brought into existence concurrently with a decision to exercise demand.[3]

This broadening of the definition of the money stock leads to problems of measurability and of independence of the determining financial variable. For these and associated reasons, a considerable number of economists have opposed the attempt to broaden the definition of money. Others, while acknowledging the Lavington type of credit effect, held that the supply of such credit is closely geared to the stock of money. M. J. Hamburger, for instance, tackling the broader definition, could '. . . find no compelling reason to extend the definition of money to include savings accounts at financial institutions'.[4] Friedman and Meiselman, looking at the credit effect, acknowledged that it could be important in setting the level of autonomous expenditure, but held, nevertheless, that such credit was itself dependent on the money stock.[5] It seems that in general there has been a marked reluctance on the part of many theorists to accept Sayers's definition of 'liquidity' or to subscribe to his view that the broadened definition of money should be substituted for the more traditional definition in the quantity theory approach to expenditure determination.

Naturally, the variations in definitions of the money stock have a functional base: that is whether money's main influence is on the rate of interest, on prices, or on the level of employment – the level of real expenditure, or as a mirror image of the above positions, whether equilibrium in the money market is achieved primarily through a change in interest rates, in prices or in real private expenditure.[6]

There are several main positions. Friedman and those economists who adhere to the view of the Chicago School hold that the prime effect of changes in the money supply is on prices – on expenditure in current prices. Patinkin represents the view that it is the change in the real as opposed to the nominal stock of money that matters, and its prime effect is to induce a change in the real level of domestic expenditure in the same direction. Other economists, particularly in the neo-Keynesians, assert, in contrast, that the direct effect of a change in the money supply is to induce the rate of interest to change in the opposite direction. Kaldor's statement before the Radcliffe Committee summarizes the most extreme form of this view: 'It cannot be emphasized too strongly that there is no direct relationship in a modern community between the amount of money in circulation . . . and the amount of money spent on goods and services per unit of time.'[7] Finally, Sayers gives money a rather more open-ended role inasmuch as he suggests that while money has an expenditure effect it is also partly demand-determined. As noted, the variety in these views over money's role has led to a considerable number of disputes in the literature.

While the controversy continues as to whether the money supply or expenditure in current prices is the senior partner in the quantity-theory formulation, with the alternative notion that changes in the real value of money balances directly induce some changes in real private expenditure, it is generally accepted that credit availability has a direct impact on expenditure.

This near unanimity seems to have been sustained over time too. In the nineteenth century, both Tooke and Mill held that the extension or contraction in trade credit exerted a similar effect on expenditure, and, as Haberler has recorded, changes in the supply of credit featured prominently in many of the 'deficiency of savings' types of business-cycle models in the pre-1930s. Keynes too, in his discussion with Sir R. M. Kindersley in the Macmillan Committee hearings, indicated that he thought that credit, or more accurately the lack of it, could stunt

[1] R. S. Sayers, 'Monetary thought and monetary theory in England', *Economic Journal* (December 1960), p. 711.

[2] Ibid., p. 722.

[3] Ibid., p. 729.

[4] M. J. Hamburger, 'The demand for money by households, money substitutes and monetary policy', *Journal of Political Economy* (December 1966), p. 613.

[5] Friedman and Meiselman, op. cit., p. 166.

[6] D. Patinkin, *Money, Interest and Prices*, 2nd edn. (New York: Harper & Row, 1965), p. xxiii.

[7] Committee on the Workings of the Monetary System, *Principal Memoranda of Evidence*, Vol. 3 (London: H.M.S.O., 1960), p. 146.

the demand for heavy capital goods.[1] Indeed, his pre-occupation with the potential amount of bank advances testified to his interest in the credit availability approach to expenditure determination in general. Again, noted adherents to the modern quantity theory approach, such as Friedman, also suggest that credit, paper claims, exert an influence on the realized demand for capital goods. More recently R. A. Shearer,[2] and R. Shapiro[3] have produced evidence or arguments which suggest that credit availability is important as a determinant of private expenditure. Finally, even the neo-Keynesian critics of Friedman and Meiselman's work seem to suggest that there is substance in the credit availability argument: 'There is urgent need for some way of assessing quantitatively the extent of non-price rationing of credit.'[4] The rationale behind the alleged credit effect seems to have been accepted: now the significance of this effect, its validity as a consideration in policy formation, must be derived from an empirical examination.

The request for quantitative assessment and its satisfaction is certainly topical. Today the general popularity of any of the particular explanations of expenditure determination seems to be rooted in the degree of support for it which may be marshalled by an examination of the empirical record. In this respect it has recently been shown by empirical studies that both the quantity theory and to a lesser extent, credit availability seem to influence private expenditure decisions in current prices. And, perhaps more pertinently, as a direct contrast to Keynes's approach, a few studies have shown a very high degree of statistical association between the levels and changes in the levels of real money balances and the levels and changes in the levels of real income. The positive results of quantitative examinations of the historical record have been responsible for the increased attention paid to the financial sector's role in the process of expenditure determination in recent years.

With respect to the relationship between the money stock and the level of nominal expenditure, in the United States Warburton and then Friedman produced a considerable amount of empirical support for the thesis that money does have such a direct effect on the level of economic activity. In particular, in the early 1960s, M. Friedman and D. Meiselman published a detailed statistical study which contrasted the direct monetary effect with the direct autonomous expenditure effect on aggregate income in current prices, on the basis of an examination of annual data over the 1897–1958 interval. They showed that both the simple and the partial correlation coefficients between money and consumption were substantially higher than the matching coefficients between the autonomous expenditure and consumption over the whole period, and for eleven of the twelve sub-periods they selected. Using quarterly data, they reached the same conclusion for the period since the Second World War, and, even more significantly, they found that the primacy of the monetary effect over the autonomous expenditure effect was accentuated when they examined the correlation coefficients between the money stock lagged by six months and the level of current consumption expenditure.

Some reviewers of Friedman and Meiselman's study found its results partially convincing.

> The correlation between consumption and the stock of money reported by Friedman and Meiselman is uniformly so high, that one cannot fail to be impressed, especially if one holds, as we do, that money is an important factor contributing to the determination of the level of income.[5]

Or again, two other reviewers, this time appraising the results of their own calculations, concluded that they were '... in general agreement with Friedman and Meiselman's positive conclusion that money is important'.[6] The support given to the quantity theory by these empirically based observations has had a marked effect on the way the money stock is regarded by economists in the United States: money *matters*.

In the UK too, examinations of the empirical evidence indicated that the money stock warrants consideration in models which are designed to explain the level of aggregate economic activity.

In 1957, Higonnet noted, as Warburton had in the United States, that there seemed to be a close association between the movements of the money stock and changes

[1] Committee on Finance and Industry, *Minutes of Evidence*, Vol. I, p. 97.

[2] R. A. Shearer, 'The expansion of bank credit – an alternative approach', *Quarterly Journal of Economics* (August 1963), p. 498.

[3] Robert Shapiro, 'Financial intermediaries, credit availability and aggregate demand', *Journal of Finance* (September 1966), p. 475.

[4] A. Ando, E. Brown, R. Solow and J. Kareken, 'Lags in fiscal and monetary policy', *Stabilization Policies* (Englewood Cliffs: Prentice Hall, 1963), p. 7.

[5] A. Ando and F. Modigliani, 'Velocity and the investment multiplier', *American Economic Review* (September 1965), p. 707.

[6] M. Deprano and T. Mayer, 'Tests of the relative importance of autonomous expenditure and money', *American Economic Review* (September 1965), p. 747.

in the level of income.[1] Much more affirmatively, and basing their findings on tests of the models of consumption determination that Friedman and Meiselman had used, A. A. Walters and C. R. Barrett concluded: 'Our results suggest that both money and autonomous expenditure have been important factors in the determination of aggregate expenditure.'[2] Later, Walters reviewed his empirical work on the role of the money stock in two articles. In one, he observed that his study showed that money had been an efficient '. . . predictor of the level of, or change in, income . . .' over much of the period.[3] In the other, he held, like Friedman, that one of the main implications of his empirical work '. . . is that the Government should stabilize the growth of the quantity of money'.[4]

In the UK too, the effect of these empirical studies seems to be producing a consensus that money matters as a determinant of national expenditure in current prices.

A limited amount of empirical work has also been done to see what credence may be placed in the hypothesis that oscillations in the real value of the money stock will engender a change in the real value of aggregate expenditure. At present this type of work has been restricted to an examination of US data.

The most affirmative findings were again produced by Friedman and Meiselman. They tested the relationship between consumption and autonomous expenditure and consumption and the money stock in all constant prices,

$$C_t = \alpha+\beta_1 A_t+\beta_2 P_t \quad \text{and} \quad C_t = \alpha+\beta_1 M_t+\beta_2 P_t,$$

over the 1897–1958 period. The Keynesian model performed dismally: '. . . the correlations between consumption and autonomous expenditure in real terms were either nearly zero or negative in all sub-periods except one'.[5] In contrast they found the correlations between real consumption and real money were remarkably high in '. . . every sub-period excluding World War I and World War II'.[6] The correlations were positive and the underlying regression coefficients were usually highly significant having t-ratios often exceeding 10.

This evidence of a remarkably high degree of correlation between real money balances and real consumption could well be interpreted as providing backing for Patinkin's hypothesis that oscillations in real balances have a direct and potent impact on real expenditure. Friedman and Meiselman, however, noting that there were good grounds to suppose that the level of real money balances as contrasted with nominal money balances was endogenously determined, argue that these highly favourable results should be interpreted differently; in effect, that real balances rather than real consumption should be looked at as the dependent variable.[7]

Finally, turning to the role that credit availability is asserted to play in the process of expenditure determination, there have been a few empirical studies which seem to substantiate the contention that the availability of credit does have an impact on subsequent expenditure decisions.

In the United States, Shearer's study stands out as an example, and it seems reasonable to suppose that the Federal Reserve Board has some evidence which supports this contention, given the weight the Board ascribes to this approach in its policy recommendations. In the UK, J. Ball and P. Drake marshalled additional empirical support for this theory, in their study of the determinants of demand for consumer durables.[8] They found that the size of the down payment and the term of loan variables, which they assert are good proxies for the availability of new consumption credits, exerted a significant influence on the realized expenditure on consumer durables in each quarter.

[1] R. P. Higonnet, 'Bank deposits in the United Kingdom, 1870–1914', *Quarterly Journal of Economics* (August 1957), p. 33.

[2] C. R. Barrett and A. A. Walters, 'The stability of Keynesian and monetary multipliers in the United Kingdom', *The Review of Economics and Statistics* (November 1966), p. 405.

[3] A. A. Walters, 'Monetary multipliers in the UK 1880–1962', *Oxford Economic Papers* (November 1966), p. 282.

[4] A. A. Walters, 'Money in boom and slump', *Hobart Papers*, No. 44 (January 1969), p. 52.

[5] Friedman and Meiselman, op. cit., p. 208. Actually their results show that the correlation between consumption and autonomous expenditure in constant prices was positive and significantly greater than zero in three of the chosen sub-periods, 1920–9, 1921–33 and 1929–39; though the value of the correlation coefficients in the first two periods is quite low – 0·611.

[6] Ibid., p. 208.

[7] This interpretation, rather than the results, seems to have biased the nature of the subsequent UK studies. In them, only the relationship between nominal expenditure and the nominal money stock and/or the nominal amount of autonomous expenditure have been examined in impact monetary multiplier formulations. This is unfortunate. The relationship which Friedman and Meiselman examined was pointedly directed towards settling an outstanding controversy. This focused on whether the aggregate real demand function for goods and services is homogeneous in the degree zero with respect to movements in real money balances through time or not; e.g. given that the nominal amount of money balances is fixed exogenously, do movements in the absolute price level matter? It should be noted that to a certain extent movements in the price level may be determined exogenously too; particularly those movements associated with a rise in import prices or Government intervention in the form of price or wage controls.

[8] R. J. Ball and Pamela S. Drake, 'Impact of credit controls on consumer durable goods spending in the United Kingdom 1957–1961', *The Review of Economic Studies* (October 1963).

Nevertheless the evidence which has been published is not particularly impressive when compared with the quantity theory results on the determination of nominal expenditure. There is still an urgent need for further empirical investigations of the asserted relationship, and perhaps an even more urgent need to see if there is some substance in a closely related hypothesis, i.e. that the change of the level of private credit in constant prices has a direct impact on the change of the level of real private expenditure.

The regression results presented below should help to meet this need for quantitative assessment of the role that real and nominal private credit play in the execution of aggregate private expenditure decisions. In addition, they should be useful in indicating how the money stock, broadly or narrowly defined and in nominal or constant prices, serves as a catalyst to the execution of such expenditure decisions. The results should compare usefully with the findings derived from the empirical studies mentioned above; moreover, they should provide some indication as to whether money or credit has had the greater direct impact on private expenditure in the UK.

The Empirical Results

The tables of regression results show the degree of association there was between certain financial stocks and certain expenditure flows in both nominal and real terms in the UK over the 1880–1962 period excluding the war years. In three ways the evidence may be regarded as indicative. First, more often than not, the explanatory variables have been lagged; in this sense the models are predictive. Next, as far as the data permit, the noted expenditure flows represent the realized spending decisions of the private sector; the money stock and encashable assets represent the holdings of certain liquid assets by this sector; similarly, the credit series used represents the institutional credits which were advanced to that sector. In this sense, the models may be taken as having been designed to explain realized private expenditure decisions.

The main results are reported in three sections:

A. Consumption and Money and Consumption and Autonomous Expenditure,
B. Private Expenditure and Money and Private Expenditure, Encashable Assets and Interest Rates and
C. Private Expenditure, Financial-Sector Private Loans and Interest Rates.

To the extent that the relationships in these sections may be interpreted causatively, they serve as rough tests of the validity of the underlying theories of private expenditure determination. Prior to their introduction, however, Table 5.1 is presented to illustrate the degree of correlation between these expenditure flows and these financial stocks and to delineate their components.

A glance at Table 5.1 shows that in the whole period, and in the first and last sub-periods, the correlation between total private expenditure and each of the financial stocks, lagged or otherwise, barely deviated from 1·00. Moreover, the correlation between consumption and each of these stocks and consumption and autonomous expenditure, lagged or otherwise, in these periods is similarly high. Nevertheless while all of the correlation coefficients have the right sign (they are all positive), these results are neutral with respect to any causal connotation, in the sense that both of the well-correlated time series may have similar trends each of which is determined independently. Despite this fact, the sizes and the signs of the correlations are such that they suggest further investigation is certainly warranted; though to be sure, in these periods the uniformity of their values gives no indication as to which approach to expenditure determination will be most fruitful.

The notes at the bottom of the table set out the definitions of the dependent and the main independent variables which were used in the regression analysis. It should be noted that most of the stock data were derived from the year-end balance sheets of the relevant financial institutions, and that the notation M_t', and EA_t' and L_t' are averages of these stocks as recorded at the end of the current and preceding year. They are designed to represent the money stock, the stock of encashable assets, and the gross private institutional credits outstanding as of approximately 30 June. In particular, attention should be paid to the definitions of encashable assets and of autonomous expenditure. The former variable includes the money stock and all those assets which householders may with little difficulty turn into a readily usable store of purchasing power: savings bank deposits, deposits and shares at building societies, National Savings Certificates, Defence and Premium Bonds, stocks held on the Post Office Register, and life assurance funds which are used as a proxy for the cash value of life assurance policies outstanding. The latter variable, autonomous expenditure, is composed of those expenditure components which seem to be least likely to be affected by householder expenditure decisions. Inventory investment, imports and

TABLE 5.1 **Pearson Correlation Coefficients between Financial Stocks and Private Expenditure in the UK 1881–1962[1]**

Period	*Expenditure Flow*	*Financial Stocks*						*Income Flows*	
		M'_t	M_{t-1}	EA'_t	EA_{t-1}	L'_t	L_{t-1}	A_t	A_{t-1}
1881–1962[1]	Y_t	0·98	0·97	0·99	0·99	0·99	0·99	—	—
1881–1914	Y_t	0·96	0·96	0·98	0·99	0·98	0·98		
	C_t	0·97	0·97	0·99	0·99	0·99	0·99	0·98	0·97
1921–1939	Y_t	0·68	0·71	0·61	0·62	0·63	0·58		
	C_t	0·76	0·77	0·64	0·65	0·62	0·62	0·78	0·58
1947–1962	Y_t	0·98	0·97	0·98	0·98	0·98	0·98		
	C_t	0·98	0·98	0·98	0·98	0·98	0·98	1·00	0·98

Notation

Y=Gross Domestic Private Expenditure=consumption+gross fixed capital formation+foreign investment.
C=Consumption expenditure.
A=Autonomous expenditure: Gross fixed capital formation+exports+Government expenditure.
M'=Mid-year money stock. The average of net bank deposits as recorded on 31 December of the current year and of the preceding year plus currency outstanding, e.g.

$$M'_t=\frac{D_t+D_{t-1}}{2}+\text{currency}.$$

M=End-year money stock. This is composed of the net bank deposits outstanding as of 31 December plus annual average currency outstanding.
EA=End-year encashable assets. This equals M_t plus all deposit and share liabilities of the building societies, of the trustee savings banks, and the deposits of the Post Office Savings Banks, plus life assurance funds, all National Savings Certificates and Premium Bonds, and all other holdings of Government securities as recorded on the Post Office Register of approximately 31 December.
EA'=Average of EA outstanding as of 31 December in the current and in the previous year.
L=Gross private credit extended by a sample of UK financial institutions as of 31 December.
L'=Average of gross private credit extended by these institutions as of the end of the current and of the preceding year.

Sources

Y=Deane and Cole, *British Economic Growth 1688 to 1959* (Cambridge, 1962). After 1950 the series was revised in accord with Jeffrey and Walters, 'National income and expenditure of the United Kingdom 1870 to 1952', *Income and Wealth Series*, 5 (London, 1955), and from 1953 on, in accord with the data given in 'Key statistics of the British economy', *London and Cambridge Economic Bulletin*.
C=Feinstein, 'National income and expenditure of the United Kingdom 1870 to 1963', *L.C.B.*, No. 50 (1964). Gross fixed capital formation; Feinstein, op. cit.
Exports: Mitchell and Deane, *Abstract of British Historical Statistics* (Cambridge, 1962), pp. 283–4. After 1948, these data were taken from the C.S.O. *Annual Abstract of Statistics*.
Government Expenditure: 1880–1939 – Mitchell and Deane, op. cit.; 1946–1962 – Pember and Boyle, *British Government Securities in the Twentieth Century* (August 1963).

Note

[1] The war years 1915–19 and 1940–5 were omitted.

tax receipts have not been allowed for as the inclusion of such endogenous increments or leakages might well reduce the significance of autonomous expenditure as a determinant of consumption.[1] Finally, before the regression results are presented, it must be noted that the pre-1914 financial stocks and expenditure flows are much more likely to be distorted from their true values than they are in the subsequent sub-periods. Consequently, due to the likelihood of these errors in measurement in the first period and due to the pronounced structural changes which the two wars induced, only the sub-period regression results have been generally recorded.

[1] Deprano and Mayer, op. cit., p. 734.

A. *Consumption, the Money Stock and Autonomous Expenditure*

As the theories which underlie the relationships examined in Table 5.2 have been discussed above and elsewhere, the models do not require much elaboration. The relationships represent simplified versions of the Keynesian and the quantity theory approach to income determination, or the mixed form, in which both the money stock and autonomous expenditure are used jointly to explain the same. To facilitate a comparison between these two approaches, consumption is substituted for total expenditure in accord with the findings of M. Friedman and G. Becker.[1] In line with most of the other exploratory work in this field the models are of the impact multiplier type – the impact that the explanatory variable or variables has in the relationship is worked out as it affects expenditure in just one income period.

It should be noted that the 'pure' Keynesian approach and the Chicago school quantity theorists' approach are not really competitive. Keynes's approach to expenditure determination was cast in constant prices; whereas Friedman and other quantity theorists postulate that their approach to expenditure determination holds only in current prices. Indeed, taking it that the level of real as opposed to nominal money balances is endogenously rather than exogenously determined, adherents to this branch of the quantity theory school are quite clearly Keynesian in their view that the level of real income determines the real stock of money rather than the other way round.[2] In nominal terms then, an evaluation of the two approaches requires that the Keynesian approach be recast in terms of current prices, and in this sense the issue as to their relevance might be regarded as an appraisal of two possible determinants of demand pull inflation: the money stock or autonomous expenditure. Alternatively, a comparison between the explanatory force of either the Keynesian or the real balance quantity theory approach is best measured when both are couched in constant prices and where the real balances are lagged to preserve a degree of exogeneity.

Taken together, the results of the first three and the last three regressions – 1, 2, 3, 5, 6 and 7 are quite interesting, particularly when they are compared with the findings of Friedman and Meiselman for the United States and Walters and Barrett for the UK.[3]

In the first three regressions, it appears that both money and autonomous expenditure were important determinants of consumption in each of the three periods. This finding corresponds with the results reported by Walters and Barrett; but it contrasts with those of Friedman and Meiselman, who reported that autonomous expenditure, though differently defined, played a very modest role in the relationship. In their multiple regression, the coefficient of A_t was often negative and rarely both positive and significant in most of the sub-periods they examined over much the same time interval – 1897 to 1958.[4] However, in all of these three similar studies of consumption determination the regression results indicate that the underlying functional relationship was somewhat unstable. In particular, the marginal income velocity varied substantially between the selected sub-periods. It fell from 1880 to 1939 and then rose substantially in the post-1946 interval in the UK. Moreover, in this study both the significance of the overall results and the identification of each of the explanatory variables' independent effects were distorted by the presence of serial correlation in the residuals, and in the third equation by multicollinearity.

In the last three regressions, 5, 6 and 7, Table 5.2 shows that the change in autonomous expenditure, as opposed to the change in the money stock, was by far the most potent determinant of the change in nominal consumption in the first and second periods. Indeed, the contribution of the change in the money stock is shown to be unimportant in all three sub-periods, as measured by the coefficient of determination; whereas the impact of the change of autonomous expenditure appears to be particularly potent in the second period – the $\overline{Rsq}$ is as high as 0·61 and the Durbin-Watson statistic is relatively satisfactory.

These results correspond roughly with those found by Walters and Barrett when they examined the relationship between the percentage changes of similar variables in the United Kingdom over roughly the same time periods. In their rendering of the seventh regression between 1921 and 1938, they found the $\overline{Rsq}$ was 0·81, the Durbin-Watson statistic was 2·61, and the t-ratios of the regression coefficients of the percentage change in M and A were 2·3 and 4·1 respectively. In Table 5.2 for the 1921–39 interval, the change in M and the change in A were nearly as successful in explaining the change in consumption; similarly, as their t-ratios show, autonomous expenditure played the more decisive role. In the period after the Second World War, the findings in the first differences were again broadly identical. Table 5.2 shows that neither the change in M nor the change in A had any obvious relationship with the change in C; Walters and Barrett recorded that they found hardly any correlation between the percentage changes in such variables and the percentage changes in consumption between 1948 and 1963.

In contrast, in the US, using quarterly data, Friedman

[1] M. Friedman and G. Becker, 'A statistical illusion in judging Keynesian models', *Journal of Political Economy* (February 1957).

[2] Friedman and Meiselman, op. cit., p. 179.

[3] Ibid., p. 179, and Barrett and Walters, op. cit.

[4] Friedman and Meiselman, op. cit., p. 224.

TABLE 5.2 **Expenditure Estimates – Consumption, Autonomous Expenditure and the Money Stock in Current Prices 1881–1962 (£ millions)**

Eq.	*Period*	*Dependent Variables*	*Constant*	*Independent Variables*			$\overline{Rsq}$	*DW*	$\overline{See}$	$\overline{Sct}$%
				A_t	M'_t	M_{t-1}				
1	1881–1914	C_t	383·566 / 9·0	2·062 / 27·3			0·96	0·78	66·058	4·38
2	1881–1914	C_t	170·979 / 2·8		1·600 / 22·8		0·94	0·24	78·310	5·19
3	1881–1914	C_t	240·211 / 8·4	1·188 / 11·1	0·742 / 8·8		0·99	0·78	36·193	2·40
4	1881–1914	A_t	−90·088 / 2·0			0·767 / 14·0	0·86	0·46	56·615	10·39
1	1921–1939	C_t	3116·226 / 17·6	0·603 / 5·3			0·60	0·83	150·844	3·72
2	1921–1939	C_t	2033·139 / 5·3		0·729 / 5·2		0·59	0·76	151·875	3·75
3	1921–1939	C_t	2124·642 / 7·9	0·413 / 4·4	0·465 / 4·2		0·80	1·39	107·339	2·65
4	1921–1939	A_t	1840·044 / 2·8			0·675 / 2·6	−0·24	0·52	271·865	17·55
1	1947–1962	C_t	−351·631 / 2·2	1·300 / 21·0			0·96	0·98	660·929	5·32
2	1947–1962	C_t	−19191·000 / 12·2		3·472 / 20·4		0·96	0·82	681·724	5·48
3	1947–1962	C_t	−10100·000 / 5·6	0·680 / 5·8	1·739 / 5·5		0·99	0·59	384·898	3·10
4	1947–1962	A_t	−16376·730 / 8·9			2·891 / 14·4	0·93	1·29	699·192	7·00
				ΔA_t	ΔM_t					
5	1882–1914	ΔC_t	21·842 / 16·7	0·559 / 3·3			0·40	1·63	23·831	—
6	1882–1914	ΔC_t	19·410 / 3·2		0·413 / 1·4		0·04	1·18	30·147	—
7	1882–1914	ΔC_t	11·911 / 2·6	0·571 / 5·2	0·467 / 2·3		0·47	1·78	22·404	—
5	1921–1939	ΔC_t	−27·380 / 0·9	0·653 / 5·4			0·61	0·94	138·198	—
6	1921–1939	ΔC_t	−63·999 / 3·7		1·235 / 2·0		0·13	0·69	206·397	—
7	1921–1939	ΔC_t	−45·791 / 3·9	0·603 / 5·0	0·671 / 1·6		0·64	1·14	132·340	—
5	1947–1962	ΔC_t	705·761 / 14·7	−0·004 / 0·0			−0·07	1·82	203·886	—
6	1947–1962	ΔC_t	637·056 / 10·3		0·301 / 1·1		0·01	1·91	195·907	—
7	1947–1962	ΔC_t	568·514 / 4·8	0·086 / 0·7	0·433 / 1·3		−0·03	2·21	199·782	—

Notation

C = Consumption.
A = Autonomous expenditure
M'_t = Mid-year money stock.
M_{t-1} = Money stock as of 31 December in the previous year.

and Meiselman found that the change in the money stock lagged by six months correlated very well with the change in current consumption over the 1948–57 period; and, moreover, that the change in autonomous expenditure, though differently defined, had either an insignificant or a perverse impact – the change in the lagged money stock dominated the relationship. However, their pro-quantity theory findings were somewhat modified by the work of Deprano and Mayer who found, using US data, that in the first differences both money and autonomous expenditure defined as in Table 5.2 played an important role in determining the change in consumption over the 1929–63 period excluding the war years, and that in the 1948–63 interval autonomous expenditure, as defined in Table 5.2, was the more influential variable though the change in the money stock still mattered.[1]

In both countries, then, the evidence suggests that both the change in autonomous expenditure and the change in the money stock are important as determinants of the change in consumption, but that in the UK the change in the money stock has not been as influential.

Switching away from the relationship between money balances or autonomous expenditure and consumption expenditure all in current prices, the hypotheses, Pigouvian and Keynesian, that the prime effect is to be found between the real balances or autonomous expenditure and consumption measured in constant prices, are examined in Table 5.3. In it the relationships have been transferred into logarithms to the base 10, which has the effect of tending to reduce the impact of recording errors and also the problem of heteroscedasticity.

As in Table 5.2, the results recorded in Table 5.3 are divided into two parts. In the first part, the log of real consumption expenditure $(C/P)_t$ was regressed on the log of the levels of the real money stock and on the stock of real encashable assets outstanding as of 31 December in the previous year, and on the log of the level of real autonomous expenditure in the same time period:

$$\left(\frac{M}{P}\right)_{t-1}, \quad \left(\frac{EA}{P}\right)_{t-1}, \quad \text{and} \quad \left(\frac{A}{P}\right)_t.$$

In the second part of the table, the first differences in the log of real private expenditure were regressed on the first differences of the real values of these stocks and flows. In effect, the first three regressions show the relationship between these stocks and the flows; the last four equations, 4 to 7, show the relationships between their percentage changes. The results of both parts contrast sharply in some ways with the reported findings in Table 5.2.

At a glance, the first three regressions show that in real terms both the lagged value of the money stock and that of encashable assets are well correlated with the real value of consumption expenditure in the subsequent period; whereas, and in contrast to the results recorded in Table 5.2, the level of autonomous expenditure for the same period, now measured in constant prices, does not seem to be particularly influential. It seems to play a relatively modest role in the 1881–1914 period, but in the others, 1921–39, and 1947–62 it plays no role at all as the underlying t-ratios show that its regression coefficients were not significant at the 95 per cent level. Moreover, it is interesting to observe how stable the relationship in real terms seems to have been, and for that matter, how the lagged value of the log of the real balances acts as the dominant explanatory variable in terms of its contributions to the coefficient of determination in the last two periods; whereas the time trend term, though generally significant, plays a relatively modest role in most of the regressions. Over all, the results are surprisingly good; all the coefficients of determination are large, the standard errors of the residuals are small and as the Durbin-Watson statistics show, the distortion due to autocorrelation is fairly minimal in sharp contrast with most of the stock flow results in Table 5.2.

The results of the first differences of the logs of real consumption expenditure, real autonomous expenditure, and the real value of encashable assets are represented by equations 4 to 7. Broadly, the results in the percentage changes of the real expenditure flow and of the real stocks of monetary and encashable assets are in accordance with the results of the first three equations in Table 5.3, and differ considerably from the results of the first difference regressions of these stocks and flows reported in Table 5.2.

The synchronous percentage change in the real level of autonomous expenditure is fairly well correlated with the percentage change in the real level of consumption expenditure in the first period, 1882–1914; thereafter, however, the contribution of the percentage change in autonomous expenditure measured in constant prices falls off sharply: in the 1948–62 interval, neither this variable nor its lagged value correlates significantly with the percentage change in real consumption expenditure. In contrast, the percentage change in the annual average stock of real money balances, in the annual average stock of real encashable assets, or in the values of these variables

[1] Deprano and Mayer, op. cit., p. 740.

TABLE 5.3 **Expenditure Estimates – Consumption, Autonomous Expenditure, Money Stock, Encashable Assets in Constant Prices 1881–1962 (£ millions)**

Eq.	*Period*	*Dependent Variable*	*Constant*	*Independent Variables*			*Trend*	$\overline{Rsq}$	*DW*	$\overline{See}$	$\overline{Sct}$%
				$\log\left(\frac{M}{P}\right)_{t-1}$	$\log\left(\frac{EA}{P}\right)_{t-1}$	$\log\left(\frac{A}{P}\right)_t$					
1	1881–1914	$\log\left(\frac{C}{P}\right)_t$	1·074 / 20·7	0·468 / 13·3			0·003 / 9·6	0·99	0·88	0·009	0·46
2	1881–1914	$\log\left(\frac{C}{P}\right)_t$	0·810 / 12·1		0·584 / 14·3		0·001 / 3·1	0·99	1·38	0·008	0·44
3	1881–1914	$\log\left(\frac{C}{P}\right)_t$	0·721 / 10·4		0·528 / 12·6	0·143 / 3·4	0·001 / 1·2	0·99	1·59	0·007	0·37
1	1921–1939	$\log\left(\frac{C}{P}\right)_t$	1·566 / 9·4	0·227 / 2·4			0·004 / 3·7	0·98	0·97	0·007	0·34
2	1921–1939	$\log\left(\frac{C}{P}\right)_t$	1·456 / 8·7		0·262 / 3·0		0·003 / 1·5	0·98	1·15	0·006	0·29
3	1921–1939	$\log\left(\frac{C}{P}\right)_t$	1·456 / 7·8		0·262 / 2·9	−0·000 / 0·0	0·003 / 1·5	0·98	1·15	0·006	0·29
1	1947–1962	$\log\left(\frac{C}{P}\right)_t$	1·235 / 5·7	0·393 / 3·9			0·012 / 13·4	0·96	1·88	0·009	0·44
2	1947–1962	$\log\left(\frac{C}{P}\right)_t$	1·301 / 6·4		0·318 / 3·8		0·010 / 18·0	0·96	1·78	0·009	0·44
3	1947–1962	$\log\left(\frac{C}{P}\right)_t$	0·706 / 1·4		0·250 / 2·4	0·396 / 1·5	0·006 / 2·0	0·95	1·08	0·010	0·46
				$\Delta\log\left(\frac{A}{P}\right)_t$	$\Delta\log\left(\frac{A}{P}\right)_{t-1}$	$\Delta\log\left(\frac{EA'}{P}\right)_t$	$\Delta\log\left(\frac{EA}{P}\right)_{t-1}$				
4	1882–1914	$\Delta\log\left(\frac{C}{P}\right)_t$	0·006 / 12·2	0·195 / 3·3				0·24	1·98	0·008	—
5	1882–1914	$\Delta\log\left(\frac{C}{P}\right)_t$	0·007 / 9·7		0·096 / 1·3			0·02	1·92	0·009	—
6	1882–1914	$\Delta\log\left(\frac{C}{P}\right)_t$	0·002 / 2·0			0·463 / 5·2		0·45	1·74	0·006	—
7	1882–1914	$\Delta\log\left(\frac{C}{P}\right)_t$	0·006 / 4·0				0·190 / 1·6	0·04	2·28	0·008	—
4	1922–1939	$\Delta\log\left(\frac{C}{P}\right)_t$	0·007 / 3·6	−0·003 / 0·0				−0·06	1·27	0·008	—
5	1922–1939	$\Delta\log\left(\frac{C}{P}\right)_t$	0·007 / 3·4		−0·025 / 0·6			−0·04	1·34	0·008	—
6	1922–1939	$\Delta\log\left(\frac{C}{P}\right)_t$	0·005 / 2·5			0·121 / 1·0		0·00	1·55	0·008	—
7	1922–1939	$\Delta\log\left(\frac{C}{P}\right)_t$	0·002 / 1·0				0·256 / 2·6	0·24	1·78	0·007	—
4	1948–1962	$\Delta\log\left(\frac{C}{P}\right)_t$	0·008 / 4·5	0·179 / 0·9				−0·01	2·25	0·011	—
5	1948–1962	$\Delta\log\left(\frac{C}{P}\right)_t$	0·009 / 33·0		−0·085 / 0·8			0·03	2·19	0·012	—
6	1948–1962	$\Delta\log\left(\frac{C}{P}\right)_t$	0·009 / 45·0			0·542 / 5·2		0·65	2·23	0·007	—
7	1948–1962	$\Delta\log\left(\frac{C}{P}\right)_t$	0·009 / 23·0				−0·039 / 0·2	−0·07	2·30	0·012	—

Notation

C = UK consumption expenditure.
A = UK autonomous expenditure = exports + Government expenditure + gross fixed capital formation.
M' = Average money stock – average of year-end money stocks.
M = End-year money stock.
P = Retail price index – 1958 = 100.
EA = End-year encashable assets – money stock + Post Office and other savings bank deposits + outstanding National Savings instruments + life assurance funds.
EA' = Average encashable assets – average of year-end stocks.
DW = Durbin-Watson statistic.
$\overline{Rsq}$ = Square of correlation coefficient corrected for number of degrees of freedom.
$\overline{See}$ = Standard error of estimate corrected for number of degrees of freedom.
$\overline{Sct}$ = Standard error of estimate corrected for degree of freedom as a percentage of the average of the dependent variable.

lagged by 6 months, are shown to make a surprisingly potent contribution in each period. Though not reported, the partial correlation coefficients of $\Delta \log (M'/P)_t$ and of $\Delta \log (M/P)_{t-1}$ were 0·25 and 0·18 over the 1882–1914 interval; they were −0·06 and 0·34 in the 1922–39 period, and they were 0·52 and −0·05 in the years 1948–62. The reported corresponding values for $\Delta \log (EA'/P)_t$ and $\Delta \log (EA/P)_{t-1}$ are shown to be 0·45 and 0·04, 0·00 and 0·24, and 0·65 and −0·00.[1]

These findings suggest that with respect to planning percentages in their real consumption expenditure, householders are directly more influenced by the concurrent or previous change in the percentage change in the real value of their spendable assets than they are by the concurrent or previous percentage changes in the real spending decisions of foreigners, their employers or their government. This observation is supported by the results of regressions of the log of real consumption on the log of the real value of householders' holdings of money and other encashable assets; and it is consistent with the *a priori* arguments of Patinkin over the direct role money plays; particularly in an industrial environment where individual householders tend to be price takers rather than price makers.

Over all, then, the results do suggest that both autonomous expenditure and the money stock influenced aggregate consumption expenditures over much of the period.

Explicitly, with reference to the first seven regression results in Table 5.2 it seems that an exogenously induced inflationary gap or deflationary gap, brought about by a change in the level of autonomous expenditure, did have an impact on consumption in current prices; similarly, it seems that the actual level of the money stock, and far less certainly the change in that level, had the expected impact on consumption in current prices too. However, in the first differences, neither the income expenditure approach nor the quantity theory approach seems to have worked in the UK in the period after the Second World War. These null results in the last period which conflict with the positive findings derived from similar models of economic behaviour in the United States, might be described as a product of the greater degree of Government management of aggregate demand in the UK in the post-war period than in the USA.

Turning to the real monetary effect, that is that real consumption expenditure is an increasing function of the level of real balances, the findings as shown by equations 1 to 7 in Table 5.3 suggest that there is substance in this proposition in all periods; especially when the definition of the monetary balances was extended to include other forms of liquid financial savings as well as bank deposits and the currency issue. Later, as shown below, these results also hold with respect to the real monetary effect on aggregate real domestic private expenditure.

B. *Private Expenditure, the Money Stock, Encashable Assets and Interest Rates*

The empirical studies, conducted by Friedman and Meiselman in the USA and Walters and Barrett in the UK which compared the efficiency of money and autonomous expenditure as predictors of consumption, were, as their authors recorded, a facet of a more general study of the role played by money in generating economic activity. Indeed, these and other monetary economists argue that consumption is a better proxy variable for permanent income than observed income measures – GNP, and therefore its use as the dependent variable is particularly meaningful in either the quantity theory or

[1] The Durbin-Watson statistics show that the reported regression coefficients are not biased by the presence of any significant degree of serial correlation in the residuals.

the income expenditure models of demand determination. Nevertheless, despite its relevance as the dependent variable, and it certainly seems more relevant as a measure of induced expenditure than national income or Gross National Product, many economists still continue the tradition of examining the money stock's impact on GNP or on disposable income in their empirical studies. The use of GNP or national income as the dependent variable in quantity theory formulations, being a better measure of aggregate economic activity than consumption expenditure, was presumably designed so as to capture the overall effect of money on aggregate expenditure, a utilization which would seem to extend the basic quantity theory model so that it purports to explain not only household expenditure, but corporate, Government and the foreign sector's expenditures too.

Not surprisingly, with this view of the work that the money stock was set to do, empirical investigations soon after the Second World War into the validity of the simple quantity theory model ($GNP=\alpha+\beta\,\text{money}+\varepsilon$) produced somewhat disheartening results with respect to the stability of the model's regression coefficients, despite the fact that the coefficients of determination, the $\bar{R}^2$'s, were relatively high.

A study by Jucker-Fleetwood for instance, using UK and USA quarterly data over the 1950–7 period, showed that the marginal income velocity was not equal to the average income velocity: the constant term was significant and different from zero; moreover marginal income velocity was variable and it tended to increase over time.[1]

Holman, in 1961, studied the movements in income velocity for twelve countries since the Second World War and came to much the same conclusion. Post-war income velocity was rising, whereas previously it had been falling. Such explanations of this phenomenon as war-incurred excess liquidity or the growth of quasi-money substitutes, failed the test of empirical verification.[2]

Again in 1962, Drakatos, investigating the movements of marginal and average income velocity in the UK and using quarterly data over the 1954–61 period, arrived at similar findings. He showed that average and marginal velocity were unequal and were not stable in the UK.[3]

Indeed, until the publication of the findings of Friedman and Meiselman in 1963, results, such as the above, had had the tendency to discredit the quantity theory approach to expenditure determination. The movements in the money impact multiplier, marginal income velocity, were both sizeable and seemingly unpredictable.

The Friedman and Meiselman study revived interest in the money stock as an important economic variable. Besides showing that both the money stock and lagged changes in the money stock were well correlated with the level and the change in the level of consumption expenditure in the USA over the 1897–1958 period, their findings indicated that money also seemed to have a considerable influence on the level and the change in the level of total *private* expenditure, which they simulated by using aggregate disposable income as a proxy. Moreover, they showed that the definition of the money stock mattered in predicting the dependent variable. M_2 (currency plus all forms of deposits at commercial banks) was a better explanatory variable than M_1 (currency plus demand deposits) or M_3 (M_2 plus time deposits placed with savings and loan associations). Moreover, their analysis of quarterly data for the 1948–57 interval suggested that most of the impact money had on nominal expenditure took place after a 6 months' lag. Finally, in many of the sub-periods they examined, their yearly data results showed that the average velocity was equal to the marginal income velocity – the regression coefficient of the intercept was either zero or not statistically significant, and equally important, they illustrated that the between-period variation in marginal income velocity was considerably less as derived from annual data than Jucker-Fleetwood had found using quarterly statistics.

In the USA, as a result, it seemed by 1963 that money had a direct impact on expenditure, and, though the variation in the impact multiplier (the marginal income velocity) was quite substantial (it ranged from 1·3 to 2·2 omitting the war periods), Friedman and Meiselman's application of relatively simple statistical estimating techniques to the quantity theory model of expenditure causation certainly suggested that money mattered.

Shortly after Friedman and Meiselman's findings were published, a group of economists led by A. A. Walters at the University of Birmingham began to publish studies

[1] Erin E. Jucker-Fleetwood, 'The key role of the velocity of circulation of money and credit', *Oxford Economic Papers* (October 1958), p. 307.

[2] A. E. Holman, 'The quantity of money, Gross National Product and the price level', *Scottish Journal of Political Economy* (February 1961), p. 39.

[3] C. Drakatos, 'Short-term fluctuations in the velocity of circulation of money in the UK 1954–1961', *The Banker*, Vol. CXLIV (1962), pp. 408–15.

which showed that in the UK too, over a broadly similar period, the degree of statistical association between the money stock and total aggregate expenditure (actually GNP), as well as consumption, was significant enough to warrant attention. To be sure, when dealing with stocks and expenditure flows, they found the presence of positive serial correlation in the residuals eliminated much of the significance of their regression results – Friedman and Meiselman seemed to be unconcerned over this issue – and as a consequence they attributed most of their pro-money findings to the first differences results they obtained in their log linear quantity theory formulations. They found on the basis of the adjusted coefficient of determination of such regressions, that the change in the money stock was associated with the subsequent change in GNP in both the 1880–1913 interval and from 1922 to 1938, but, unlike Friedman and Meiselman, they found that the relationship seemed to disappear in the interval after the Second World War. The '... most striking result of this study is the efficiency of the money stock as a predictor of the level of, or change in, income for the years before 1939 and especially before 1914, compared with the inefficiency of money after 1955'.[1]

The regression results recorded in Tables 5.4 and 5.5 are designed to complement the exploratory empirical studies, noted previously, of the direct expenditure effect of the growth or change in the money supply in the UK. Before examining these results, however, a few points should be considered.

The substitution of gross private expenditure for GNP, which was used as the dependent variable in Walters's studies of the determination of aggregate expenditure, seems to make the underlying models better suited to predict the impact of money stock on the private sector's behaviour. In any event, the substitution produced more statistically significant results than when GNP was used as the dependent variable, and it made the relationships derived from UK data more comparable with those Friedman and Meiselman found in the States. In addition, fitting in with one of the side products of Friedman and Meiselman's study, three different definitions of the money stock were used in the regressions, M, M_2 and EA and, in accord with a number of the issues that Walters has raised, adjustments were made to reduce the degree of autocorrelation and heteroscedasticity in the time series by inserting a time trend term, taking first differences, lagging the independent variables, and transforming the recorded values of the logarithms.[2] Moreover, in keeping with the results of the velocity estimates in the previous chapter the short-term rate of interest (the Treasury Bill rate $= r_s$) and the long-term rate of interest (the consol rate $= r_c$) were introduced as independent variables. Finally, as in the consumption section, the relationship between money and expenditure was examined in constant prices in order to see if the stock or the change in the stock of real balances played a role in predicting the level or the change in the level of real aggregate private expenditure.

In the first three regression equations in Table 5.4, private expenditure was regressed on the lagged values of the money stock (M_1), the equivalent of Friedman's M_2, on encashable assets, (EA), on the current short-term rate of interest (r_s), and on a time trend term. At a glance it is evident that the trend term plays a potent role in the relationships, particularly in the first and last periods. Nevertheless, in each period, the lagged stock of encashable assets plays a role in reducing the residual variance, and the money stock and the short-term rate of interest are shown to have had some impact as well. Over all, it seems that both regressions suggest that the financial variables, money, encashable assets, and the rate of interest, have been significant determinants of expenditure, but their separate or combined impacts are far from being either decisive, or easily interpreted.

A closer examination of these results supports this conclusion. The positive sign of the coefficient of the short-term rate of interest in equations 1 and 2 seems to *clash* with one's expectations. Moreover, comparing the results on a sub-period basis, it is obvious that the relationship between expenditure and the chosen explanatory variables is somewhat unstable. The constant terms are quite dissimilar, and there is quite considerable variation in the size of the regression coefficients of each explanatory variable over time. However, from a quantity theorist's view, the positive correlation between Y_t and r_s could be expected, in that the short-term rate of interest represents a cost of holding money balances. Income velocity increases as r rises. Moreover, the recorded instability of the relationships over the period does seem to fit in with the pronounced structural changes which the wars and the post-war reconstruction induced. More positively, the results recorded for the

[1] A. A. Walters, 'Money multipliers in the UK 1880–1962', *Oxford Economic Papers* (November 1966), p. 282.

[2] $M_2 = M_1$ + building societies' deposits and shares ± all savings banks' deposits. The results of its use as an explanatory variable are unrecorded as they were inferior to M_1 and EA.

1921–39 interval and the 1947–62 period are quite good statistically. There is little autocorrelation in any of the relationships, and the regression coefficients of EA_{t-1} and less certainly that of M_{t-1} are reasonably significant. Finally, the results suggest that though money may have mattered as a determinant of expenditure, other variables too, particularly autonomous expenditure, as indicated in the consumption section, should be included in the relationship.

In the next two regressions, equations 4 and 5, this suggestion is taken up directly. After the data have been transformed into logarithms, the mixed form model, in which money and autonomous expenditure are used as determinants of private expenditure, seems to produce useful results; especially in the second and third periods in the unlagged model, where, as the Durbin-Watson statistic shows, the significant regression coefficients are fairly efficient. To be sure, as shown in the previous section, and particularly during the 1947–62 period, the independent variables are serially correlated, and the use of $\log A_t$ as a determinant of $\log Y_t$ might be as questionable as correlating C on Y. Nevertheless, the size of the residual standard error, $\overline{See}$, and more particularly, the significance of the coefficients of the lagged values of the

TABLE 5.4 **Expenditure Estimates – Gross Domestic Private Expenditure, Interest Rates and Stocks of Liquid Assets 1881–1914, 1921–1939 and 1947–1962**

Eq.	*Period*	*Dependent Variable*	*Constant*	*Independent Variables*				*Trend*	$\overline{Rsq}$	*DW*	$\overline{See}$	$\overline{Sct}$%
				M_{t-1}	EA_{t-1}		r_s					
1	1881–1914	Y_t	−699·622 4·2	0·376 1·2			84·756 6·7	26·174 4·7	0·98	0·77	56·855	3·30
2	1881–1914	Y_t	175·556 1·2		1·085 4·8		60·203 5·5	−1·151 1·6	0·99	0·99	43·661	2·53
3	1881–1914	Y_t	−79·288 0·4		1·644 5·9			−17·981 2·0	0·97	0·72	60·936	3·54
1	1921–1939	Y_t	1305·864 1·3	1·079 3·0			112·809 2·0	−10·503 0·6	0·30	2·66	251·208	5·53
2	1921–1939	Y_t	1328·145 1·1		0·727 2·9		103·296 1·8	−71·566 2·2	0·28	2·49	254·919	5·61
3	1921–1939	Y_t	223·015 0·2		0·614 2·4			−80·340 2·3	0·17	2·10	273·323	6·12
1	1947–1962	Y_t	1041·067 0·2	0·862 1·7			67·487 0·5	774·827 6·3	0·99	1·51	393·301	2·51
2	1947–1962	Y_t	1951·666 3·5		0·388 2·4		13·033 1·2	67·198 7·4	0·99	2·02	303·256	1·93
3	1947–1962	Y_t	2755·390 1·9		0·330 3·5			753·171 12·1	0·99	1·73	308·781	1·97
				$\log M'_t$	$\log M_{t-1}$	$\log A_t$	$\log A_{t-1}$					
4	1881–1914	$\log Y_t$	0·895 1·5	0·320 7·0		0·514 1·3			0·99	0·64	0·011	0·34
5	1881–1914	$\log Y_t$	0·823 1·3		0·398 7·1		0·458 9·5		0·98	1·01	0·013	0·40
4	1921–1939	$\log Y_t$	2·006 7·1	0·218 2·4		0·263 6·0			0·77	1·26	0·014	0·39
5	1921–1939	$\log Y_t$	1·408 4·6		0·448 5·2		0·221 5·8		0·79	1·16	0·014	0·39
4	1947–1962	$\log Y_t$	−1·467 1·4	0·515 1·3		0·904 6·2			0·98	1·36	0·018	0·43
5	1947–1962	$\log Y_t$	−4·247 2·8		1·559 2·6		0·569 2·5		0·94	0·91	0·031	0·74

TABLE 5.4—*continued*

Eq.	*Period*	*Dependent Variable*	*Constant*	*Independent Variables*				*Trend*	$\overline{Rsq}$	*DW*	$\overline{See}$	$\overline{Sct\%}$
				$\Delta \log M'_t$	$\Delta \log r_s$	$\Delta \log A_t$	$\Delta \log Y_{t-1}$					
6	1882–1914	$\Delta \log Y_t$	0·006 / 3·0	0·152 / 0·8	0·056 / 4·0				0·31	2·00	0·010	—
7	1882–1914	$\Delta \log Y_t$	0·004 / 2·0	0·000 / 0·0		0·374 / 7·0	0·023 / 0·2		0·61	2·53*	0·007	—
6	1922–1939	$\Delta \log Y_t$	−0·007 / 3·5	1·102 / 2·5	0·044 / 1·6				0·23	1·27	0·022	—
7	1922–1939	$\Delta \log Y_t$	−0·002 / 0·6	0·370 / 1·1		0·167 / 2·0	0·305 / 1·8		0·60	1·64*	0·013	—
6	1948–1962	$\Delta \log Y_t$	0·023 / 0·5	0·535 / 1·2	0·027 / 1·3				0·03	2·13	0·014	—
7	1948–1962	$\Delta \log Y_t$	0·050 / 3·8	−0·679 / 1·0		−0·385 / 1·3	−0·231 / 1·0		0·09	2·72*	0·013	—
				$\Delta \log M'_t$	$\Delta \log r_c$							
8	1882–1914	$\Delta \log Y_t$	0·005 / 2·5	0·181 / 0·8	0·339 / 2·5				0·08	1·63	0·011	—
8	1922–1939	$\Delta \log Y_t$	−0·006 / 2·3	0·856 / 1·9	0·209 / 1·3				0·19	1·07	0·22	—
8	1948–1962	$\Delta \log Y_t$	0·017 / 3·4	0·631 / 1·7	0·250 / 2·5				0·23	2·12	0·012	—

Notation

M'_t, M_{t-1}, EA_{t-1}, A_t, A_{t-1}, Y_{t-1}. See Table 5.3.

r_s = Short-term interest rate.

r_c = Consol rate.

Note

* Due to the inclusion of the lagged value of the dependent variable as an independent variable, the Durbin-Watson statistic is biased – see *Biometrika*, 1951.

independent variables suggest that the relationships are meaningful in a predictive sense. Indeed, even taking into account the noted limitations and the elementary design of the regression relationship, it is interesting to note, in keeping with Friedman's and Walters's findings, that the coefficients of the lagged value of the money stock, lagged by 6 months, are consistently bigger than those of the unlagged values; whereas the coefficients of $\log A_{t-1}$ are consistently smaller than those of $\log A_t$. The lagged value of the log of the money stock seems to perform quite well as a predictor of the log of Y_t.

Following Walters's approach, as shown in the sixth, seventh and eighth regressions, the above models were examined in the first differences to see if the percentage changes in the money stock, in autonomous expenditure, in various rates of interest, and in the lagged value of private expenditure were statistically well correlated with the percentage change in private expenditure in the current period. The results, like those of Walters, suggest that the percentage change of the money stock has been of some significance, but the standard errors of its regression coefficients in all periods are too large to place much confidence in them, and in general the other selected independent variables account for most of the reduction in the residual variance.

Despite the defects, the results are interesting.

In all periods, the positive sign of the coefficient of the percentage change in the money stock agrees with the theoretical expectation. The positive signs of the coefficient of the percentage change in the short- and the long-term rates of interest might be expected too, since these variables are respectively interpreted as being either the annual percentage change in the implicit cost of holding money balances, or as a measure of the percentage change in the marginal efficiency of expenditure.[1] Moreover, it is not surprising that the percentage change in autonomous expenditure played such a potent role in the first two periods: the results are in accord with those of the consumption section. Similarly, and noting that this form of expenditure is defined as gross fixed capital formation, exports and Government expenditure, it may seem surprising that its contributions, in the first differences, disappeared in the last period. However, this last result could well be explained by the actions of the Government. Income taxes were much higher, and Government regulation of domestic private expenditure, particularly consumption, was much more severe in the 1948–62 period.

In real terms, however, as illustrated in Table 5.5, it seems that in both the logs and in the first differences of the logs the lagged real monetary effect on real private expenditure was more decisive.

As shown by equations 1 and 2, in each period real money balances and real encashable assets, lagged by 6

[1] This positive interest rate coefficient, in contrast with the Keynesian expectation, seems to fit the quantity theory formulation quite well. For example, taking r_s as the cost of money and r_c as a proxy for the marginal efficiency of investment, $(\partial V_Y)/\partial r_s)$ and $(\partial V_Y)/\partial r_c)$ should both be greater than zero. Such findings are often obtained in empirical studies of the determinants of income velocity.

TABLE 5.5 **Expenditure Estimates in Constant Prices – Gross Domestic Private Expenditure, Interest Rates and the Money Stock 1881–1962, [1]1949–1967**

Eq.	*Period*	*Dependent Variable*	*Constant*	*Independent Variables* $\left(\frac{M}{P}\right)_{t-1}$	$\left(\frac{EA}{P}\right)_{t-1}$	r_c	*Trend*	$\overline{Rsq}$	*DW*	$\overline{See}$	$\overline{Sct}$%
1	1882–1914	$\left(\frac{Y}{P}\right)_t$	48·240 3·4	0·628 3·4		−0·352 0·1	1·002 5·8	0·98	1·24	2·301	2·483
2			37·280 2·7		0·652 4·3	0·329 0·1	0·525 2·1	0·98	1·64	2·134	2·302
1	1921–1939	$\left(\frac{Y}{P}\right)_t$	45·701 1·4	0·810 2·0		3·010 1·0	0·412 0·6	0·89	1·20	3·571	2·938
2			50·882 1·5		0·474 1·8	2·963 0·9	−0·512 0·4	0·88	1·10	3·676	3·024
1	1947–1962	$\left(\frac{Y}{P}\right)_t$	56·900 4·6	0·653 2·7		0·540 0·1	6·004 4·6	0·95	2·26	5·276	2·98
2			74·770 3·2		0·284 2·9	−0·724 0·3	5·593 4·7	0·95	2·19	5·159	2·90
				$\Delta \log \left(\frac{M'}{P}\right)_t$	$\Delta \log \left(\frac{EA'}{P}\right)_t$		$\Delta \log r_c$				
3	1881–1962[1]	$\Delta \log \left(\frac{Y}{P}\right)_t$	0·005 2·7	0·440 3·8			0·182 2·6	0·17	2·29	0·013	—
4			0·003 1·3		0·486 3·8		0·188 2·6	0·16	2·20	0·013	—
3	1881–1914	$\Delta \log \left(\frac{Y}{P}\right)_t$	0·003 1·1	0·417 2·9			0·200 1·3	0·18	1·78	0·011	—
4			0·000 0·2		0·592 3·5		0·228 1·5	0·24	1·75	0·010	—

TABLE 5.5—*continued*

Eq.	*Period*	*Dependent Variable*	*Constant*	*Independent Variables* $\Delta \log \left(\frac{M'}{P}\right)_t$	$\Delta \log \left(\frac{EA'}{P}\right)_t$	$\Delta \log r_c$	$\overline{Rsq}$	*DW*	$\overline{See}$	$\overline{Sct}$%
3 4	1921–1939	$\Delta \log \left(\frac{Y}{P}\right)_t$	No significant results. None of the regression coefficients was statistically significant and the adjusted coefficients of determination, $\overline{Rsq}$, each had a zero or negative value.							
3	1947–1962	$\Delta \log \left(\frac{Y}{P}\right)_t$	$\frac{0{\cdot}013}{3{\cdot}0}$	$\frac{0{\cdot}953}{4{\cdot}1}$		$\frac{0{\cdot}282}{2{\cdot}5}$	0·54	1·85	0·013	—
4	1947–1962	$\Delta \log \left(\frac{Y}{P}\right)_t$	$\frac{0{\cdot}009}{1{\cdot}8}$		$\frac{0{\cdot}824}{3{\cdot}2}$	$\frac{0{\cdot}228}{1{\cdot}8}$	0·41	1·76	0·015	—
				$\%\Delta \left(\frac{M'}{P}\right)_t$		r_c				
5	1949–1967[2]	$\%\Delta \left(\frac{Y'}{P}\right)_t$	$\frac{2{\cdot}77}{4{\cdot}3}$	$\frac{0{\cdot}70}{3{\cdot}5}$			0·36	1·82	2·70	—
6	1949–1967[2]	$\%\Delta \left(\frac{Y'}{P}\right)_t$	$\frac{9{\cdot}45}{3{\cdot}2}$	$\frac{0{\cdot}89}{4{\cdot}7}$		$\frac{-1{\cdot}30}{2{\cdot}3}$	0·49	2·09	2·42	—

Notation

$\%\Delta \left(\frac{Y'}{P}\right)_t$ = Percentage change in real private expenditure = gross fixed domestic capital formation plus consumption expenditure plus value of volume of physical increase in stocks and works in progress all deflated through by P = price index.

$\%\Delta \left(\frac{M'}{P}\right)_t$ = Percentage change in the money stock in constant prices, where the money stock is set equal to the net deposits at the London clearing banks (average of monthly figures) and the average of the estimated currency in circulation during the year in question. Again, the stock so derived is deflated through by the price index.

r_c = Gross yield on consols – average of working days.

P = retail price index – 1958 = 100.

M and M' = Money stock end-year and money stock average of end-year respectively.

EA and EA' = Total encashable assets end-year and total encashable assets average of end-year respectively.

Y = Gross domestic private expenditure.

Stock data may be found in the Appendix, section 3.

Sources

Blue Book, *Annual Abstract of Statistics* (1949–67) and Appendix (1882–1962).

Note

[1] The war years, 1914–19 and 1940–5, are excluded.

[2] I thank Dr C. E. Goodhart for providing the above information. Dr Goodhart also examined the above model against quarterly data from 1956 to 1967 and found that the relationship was significant:

$$\% \text{ change in } \Delta \left(\frac{Y}{P}\right)_t = \frac{0{\cdot}45}{2{\cdot}1} + \frac{0{\cdot}64}{3{\cdot}2} \%\Delta \left(\frac{M'}{P}\right)_t . \ \overline{Rsq} = 0{\cdot}20 \ DW = 2{\cdot}29.$$

months, contributed considerably to the size of the coefficients of determination in each period. The signs of the regression coefficients are positive and their coefficients are fully significant especially in the first period. To be sure, the current long-term rate of interest, r_c, proved to be ineffective. There seems to be little evidence that the wealth effect of movements in the interest rate had the expected impact. Nevertheless, the results seem to be indicative. The lagged level of real balances does seem to have some impact on real expenditure, and these results were substantiated when the regressions were run in logarithmic form – see Table 5.3.

When the same relationships were run in the first differences in the logarithms, the results were quite positive too, except in the inter-war era. As shown by an examination of the third and fourth regressions, in the period 1947–62, the regression coefficients of the percentage change in the real value of the money stock and of the percentage change in the real value of encashable assets are highly significant. Note, also, that in the last period the underlying partial correlation coefficients of these variables in the third and fourth regressions were 0·518 and 0·370 respectively; this underlines their contribution to the coefficients of determination of 0·54 and 0·41. Moreover, the fifth and sixth regressions show that in real terms the percentage change in money balances was well correlated with the percentage change in real private expenditure over the 1949–67 period.[1] And, as indicated in the footnotes to the table, the relationship was also significant when the model was run using quarterly data over the 1956–67 time interval. The coefficient of the percentage change in the real money stock was quite similar to the annual model, 0·64 as opposed to 0·70; though as expected, the coefficient of determination was considerably smaller – 0·20 as to 0·36. In real terms then, it seems that the percentage change in the money supply was well correlated with the percentage change in expenditure over much of the period, and that this correlation seems to have become even stronger in the period after the Second World War.

If one glances back over the results in Table 5.5, several features stand out.

Looking at equations 1 and 2, it is interesting to observe that the regression coefficient of $(M/P)_{t-1}$ was similar in each of the three periods. A one million pound rise in the lagged value of real money balances predicts a rise in the real level of private expenditure six months hence of between £630,000 and £810,000. As an aside, a similar stability was observed when the data were transformed into logarithms and the regression was re-run – the resulting elasticity of real expenditure with respect to the real stock of money balances lagged by 6 months was 0·362, 0·372 and 0·308 in each of the three sub-periods. Then, passing over the impact of the consol rate, r_c, since its regression coefficient was not significant, the significance and the change in the size of the trend term attracts attention. It was highly significant from 1882 to 1914. It was not significant in the inter-war era. Again it was fully significant in the post-war era. Moreover, in the first period its coefficient was 1·0, in the second it was 0·4 and in the third it was 6·0. It would seem that the trend term could be taken as a proxy for spenders' expectations with respect to the permanence of their income and employment – the strength in demand for their services. This would explain the divergence between the size of its coefficient in the first and third periods, and it would account for the negative sign of this coefficient in the second regression in the second period.

Then, examining the next two regression results, equations 3 and 4, in line with the above argument about the interpretation of the economic significance of the trend term results, one notes that in the first differences in the logs neither real money balances nor the real value of encashable assets served to predict the percentage change in real expenditure in the inter-war period. In effect, the results suggest that in so far as the real balance effect is operative, its immediate effect is somewhat dampened during a period of price deflation, as opposed to a period of price inflation, due to the impact such price movements have on expectations.[2] The change in the size of the regression coefficients of the percentage change in the real money balances from 0·417 in the 1881–1914 interval, to 0·096 in the inter-war period, and to 0·953 from 1947 to 1962 supports this suggestion.[3]

Finally, it is interesting to observe that in equations 3 and 4 the sign of the percentage change in the long-term interest rate is positive in all periods where the coefficient is significant; whereas it was negative but not significant in the 1921–39 period. However, in equation 6, where the actual level of the long-term rate is regressed against the percentage change in real expenditure, the sign is negative (−1·30) and quite significant. This creates difficulties in interpretation. However, as noted above, it seems best to regard the percentage change in r_c as a proxy for the percentage change in the opportunity cost of holding money balances, so that as this cost rises, one might expect the percentage change in real expenditure to rise too. This would account for the positive coefficient. More adventurously, with respect to the percentage change in real expenditure, one may interpret the actual level of r_c as a rough proxy for the degree of credit tightness or of the degree of official restraints on the rate of growth of real private expenditure. One would then expect the coefficient of r_c to be negative if the policy worked.

[1] It is of interest to see that the level of the long-term rate of interest r_c, as opposed to its percentage change, did have a negative effect on the percentage change of real private expenditure.

[2] It is of interest to note that in Table 5.3 in the inter-war period, the lagged values of the percentage change of EA/P were shown to be significantly correlated with the percentage change in C/P in the current time periods; whereas in the pre-1915 and post-1946 periods their contribution to the reduction of the residual variance was either very marginal or non-existent.

[3] In line with the analysis of the income velocity estimates in the previous chapter, these movements in the percentage change impact multiplier could be interpreted as the effect which price changes have on the demand for real money balances; though this in turn is quite a similar argument since expectations of price movements affect expectations of the relative value of real money balances.

Over all, as in the consumption section, the above investigations agree with Walters's findings as to the influence nominal holdings of money balances had on nominal expenditure in the UK over the 1880–1962 period. The correlation between the stock of money and the level of private expenditure is both positive and quite high in all three periods; though, when the autocorrelation was removed from the residuals, as in the regressions in the first differences, the degree of association between the changes in nominal money balances and the changes in nominal private expenditure was much reduced. In fact it appears to be non-existent in the third period. This last finding, though consistent with Walters's results, clashes with the positive findings of Friedman and Meiselman in the United States.

However, the lack of significance of a change in the money stock, or for that matter a change in autonomous expenditure as a predictor of the change in private expenditure in the 1947–62 period, probably should not be taken as an indication of a marked divergence in the private sector's behaviour with respect to its expenditure decisions in these two developed countries.[1] Instead, it seems more reasonable to interpret the absence of any positive evidence of a relationship between the change in the money stock or the change in autonomous expenditure and the change in total private expenditure in the UK as simply reflecting the extent of official regulation of private-sector expenditure in this country during the post-war period, a suggestion which seems to be warranted on examination of the real relationship. Indeed, as in the consumption section, in both the stock-flow relationships and in the changes in these, when the financial stocks and expenditure flows were measured in constant prices, the money or encashable asset impact on expenditure was accentuated, with the exception of the first difference results for the inter-war period. In particular, the correlation between the percentage change in real money or real encashable assets and the percentage change in real private expenditure was higher in the period after the Second World War than in the two earlier periods 1882–1914 and 1921–39. These findings indicate that the degree of interaction between the product sector and the financial sector was more direct than the Keynesian model suggests.

C. *Gross Domestic Private Expenditure, Financial-Sector Private Loans and Interest Rates*

Like the quantity theory and the income expenditure approach, credit availability may be used as a rationale to explain both the generation of demand pull inflation and increases or decreases in real income. As with the quantity theory approach, its direct effect upon the amount of economic activity in current prices has been ascribed to the presence of market imperfections in the financial markets. Similarly, its indirect effects on the product market are seen to operate either by affecting the costs of loans or by influencing the returns paid on household savings and thereby affecting their placement.

Unlike both the quantity theory of money and the income expenditure approach, however, the direct effect that changes in credit availability had on expenditure was usually seen in the past to have its impact on the pace of activity in a particular sector (manufacturing, inventory investment, ship-building) rather than on economic activity in general. This micro-, as opposed to macro-, orientation to its influence on expenditure, in conjunction with the widespread expenditure effects attributed to changes in the money stock, seems to have shrouded the thesis that Lavington put forward that changes in credit, as well as changes in the money stock, influence the pace of general economic activity.[2] In any event, to date, with a few important exceptions – notably J. Duesenberry and R. Shearer – the attention paid to credit availability in theoretical models of aggregate expenditure determination has been modest; moreover, there are hardly any published empirical studies that are designed to measure its influence on such broad expenditure aggregates as total consumption, investment or domestic private expenditure.

To be sure, the influence of credit availability on activity in particular sectors during the inter-war era, and especially in the post-1950 period, has been acknowledged by representatives of industry, finance and

[1] M. Keran has recently published an article in the Federal Reserve Bank of Saint Louis's *Monthly Bulletin* which substantiates this point. Keran shows that there was a positive and statistically significant correlation between the change in GNP and the change in the lagged level of money stock in the UK and seven other developed countries over the 1953–63 period. According to P. Jay of *The Times*, specifically Keran found that 35 per cent of the quarterly change of GNP in the UK measured in current prices was explained by the quarterly change in the money stock eighteen months previously. Jay also reports that compared with Keran's results for other countries, the time taken for the change of the money stock to have its impact in the UK was abnormally long – it was six months in the United States. The length of this lag probably accounts for the 'null' results reported above – it was not expected, and therefore not allowed for in the regressions. P. Jay, 'The economic challenge from Saint Louis', *The Times* (26 February 1970), p. 25.

[2] Lavington, op. cit., p. 272.

Government as well as by certain academic economists. It is also clear that as these arguments about the particular effects of credit availability have been developed, they have proliferated, so that nowadays there are few if any expenditure decisions which monetary economists would regard as being uninfluenced by credit conditions. As a consequence, through the back door as it were, through argument and experience of the particular effects of credit market imperfections and of credit controls sanctioned by national emergencies, the credit availability approach now vies with the quantity theory of money as a mental construct which may be useful in explaining the financial sector's contribution to economic activity. In this respect, and from a monetary official's viewpoint, A. Hayes's reflection on '... the connection between monetary policy and our basic economic objectives ...'[1] is interesting.

> The linkage, of course, runs from specific monetary policy actions (open market operations, changes at the discount window and in reserve requirements) to the cost and availability of credit (and especially bank credit), thence to changes in real economic activity, use of resources, price relationships, and international payment flows.[2]

In this section of the chapter, again using the statistical techniques employed in the other two sections, I have endeavoured to see how well an aspect of the linkage to which Hayes alludes fits the UK experience over the 1880–1962 period.

Certainly, the results for or against the null hypothesis as recorded in the tables of regression relationships should only be regarded as indicative of whether or not credit availability influenced aggregate private expenditure in real or nominal terms. Errors in variables undoubtedly distort the results in the early years, and in all periods it seems unlikely that the main explanatory variable, credit, may be assumed to be exogenous – that is unaffected by the current or preceding level of private expenditure. More importantly, in general, I have used as a measure of credit availability, the recorded stock of various financial institutions' end-year total assets after netting out their cash holdings, and their holdings of Government and foreign securities as reported on their balance sheets – gross private domestic credit. This measure is theoretically defective in that it shows the amount of institutional credits which had been taken up and not the amount of private credit which the same sample of institutions might have made available on the same terms if the private loan demand had been greater than it actually was. Nevertheless, given that the included institutions (banks, insurance and assurance companies, building societies, trustee savings banks) generally offer their loans on more favourable terms than most other lending agencies, it seems reasonable to assume that throughout most of the period, the amount of credit that these institutions extended to the private sector was all they cared to provide, given their appraisal of market risks, the statutory controls on their portfolio selections, and, in the post-1946 period, the presence of Government guidelines or lending directives. In any event, whether this rationalization of the defect in the measure is accepted or not, the absence or presence of a high degree of association between private expenditure and these credits does provide some useful information which should help in appraising the need for, as well as the design of, empirical tests of the credit availability effect.

The empirical results are divided into two sub-sections which are designed to show the degree of statistical association there is between credit and expenditure in current prices and between credit and expenditure in constant prices. Each sub-section in turn is divided so as to show the strength in the relationship between the selected financial stocks and the selected expenditure flows, as well as changes or percentage changes in these stocks and flows. Moreover, in a number of the regressions the stock of institutional private credits has been lagged by six months: L_{t-1} stands for the stock of these credits outstanding as of approximately 31 December in the previous year; while Y_t stands for the average annual flow of private expenditure in the current year.

Table 5.6 records the results of five multiple regressions in three time periods: 1881–1914, 1921–39 and 1947–62. In the first three Y_t, private expenditure, is regressed respectively on L_{t-1}, the previous end-year stock of private credit, on L'_t, the average stock of private credit outstanding in the current year and on a time trend term. In the fourth regression, following Friedman's suggestion, A_t, autonomous expenditure, is regressed on L_{t-1} and on a time trend term. In the fifth regression Y_t is regressed on H_{t-1}, high-powered money outstanding in the previous time period, on $(L_B/D^*)_{t-1}$, the banks' lagged private asset credit/total asset ratio, on $(L_I/Q)_{t-1}$, the non-banking financial institutions' lagged private credit/total asset ratio, and on $(D/C)_{t-1}$, the lagged deposit/currency

[1] A. Hayes, 'Interest rates and monetary policy in perspective', *Federal Reserve Bank of New York Monthly Review* (February 1966), p. 22.

[2] Ibid., p. 22.

ratio the public chose to hold in the previous period. It should be noted that in theory there are good reasons to believe that the *ex ante* stock of credit available should be an increasing function of each of the four independent variables.[1]

In equations 1, 2 and 3, in each time interval, the regression coefficients of L_{t-1} and L'_t are fully significant at the 95 per cent level; whereas the significance of the coefficient of L'_{Bt}, total bank private credits, is not satisfactory in any of the periods: a result which seems a little surprising in view of the stress such credit extensions receive in the literature. Certainly, in the first period, the Durbin-Watson statistic indicates that a considerable amount of positive autocorrelation is present in each of the regressions, which distorts the relevance of these observations for the 1881–1914 interval; however, in the other two periods, the *DW* statistic is satisfactory for the first two regressions.

The change in the size of the regression coefficients of L_{t-1} and of L'_t between periods also attracts attention. In each case the reduction is quite substantial: 1·7 to 0·9 to 0·3 and 1·8 to 1·2 to 0·4 from 1881–1914 to 1921–39 to 1947–62. This change, as with the change in the regression coefficient of the money stock (see Table 5.4), could be interpreted as indicating a rising income elasticity of demand for institutional loan accommodation or, alternatively, as evidence of marked between-period leakages from the expenditure effect of credit extensions due to the increased weight of Government economic intervention. The standard rate of income tax did not rise above 8 per cent in the £ in the 1880–1914 period, nor fall below 20 per cent and 39 per cent in the £ in the 1920–39 and the 1946–62 periods respectively.

It also is interesting to observe the similarity in explanatory power of the first two credit availability models in this table and the third quantity theory model in Table 5.4, in which the lagged value of encashable assets and a time trend term are used as the variables in determining private expenditure. All three have approximately the same performance record: they yield seemingly significant but distorted results in the first period. They all have low coefficients of determination in the second period though each financial variable does play a role in reducing the residual variation. They all perform remarkably well in the last period.

In sum, the first two regressions in the table suggest that private expenditure was closely linked with private institutional credit over much of the time period, and that the lagged value of private credit should be useful in predicting the value of current private expenditure in near to full employment periods. Surprisingly, they indicate that total institutional private credit serves better than total bank private credit in the relationship. None the less, and noting that L_{t-1} and EA_{t-1} are well correlated in all three time periods, it could be argued that the stock of private credit is nothing more than a good proxy for the stock of household encashable assets, and that this test of the availability effect is really just a disguised quantity theory formulation. The lagged level of encashable assets performed well as an explanatory variable in the quantity theory type regressions.

The fifth regression result sheds some light on this issue. In addition, it illustrates that together the four independent variables which are held to determine 'credit availability' perform reasonably well; though again the results of the first period are distorted by the presence of autocorrelation in the residuals.

In this regression, as a means of delineating between the quantity theory and availability effect, the first and the last independent variables H_{t-1} and $(D/C)_{t-1}$ (high-powered money and the deposit/currency ratio) are regarded as the variables which have the most influence on the money stock;[2] whereas the second and third variables, $(L_B/D^*)_{t-1}$ and $(L_I/Q)_{t-1}$ (the banks' private credit/total asset ratio and the non-banking financial institutions' private credit/total asset ratio) serve as indicators as to how liberal or stringent the banks and the other institutions are likely to be in meeting the private credit demand in the forthcoming period. As a consequence, in so far as the underlying regression relationship has some explanatory power, it seems reasonable to argue that the liquidity or quantity theory effect is strongest if the first and/or the last independent variable dominate the relationship (as shown by their partial correlation coefficient); or alternatively, that the credit availability effect plays a dominant role if the second and/or the third variables are shown to have a similar potency.

In order to interpret the regression coefficient in this model, it should be noted that in the first period, a £1 million rise in H in the previous period, *ceteris paribus* is associated with a £6·6 million rise in private expenditure in the following period. Similarly, a 0·01 rise in $(L_B/D^*)_{t-1}$, or in $(L_I/Q)_{t-1}$, or in $(D/C)_{t-1}$ is associated

[1] D. K. Sheppard and C. R. Barrett, 'Financial credit multipliers and the availability of funds', *Economica* (May 1965), p. 210.

[2] The coefficient of variation of the banks' cash/deposit ratio was quite small over most of the period.

TABLE 5.6 Expenditure Estimates in Current Prices – Gross Domestic Private Expenditure, Gross Institutional Private Credit, Bank Private Credit, Autonomous Expenditure and the Money Stock 1881–1962

Eq.	*Period*	*Dependent Variable*	*Constant*	*Independent Variables*				$\overline{Rsq}$	*DW*	$\overline{See}$	$\overline{Sct\%}$
				L_{t-1}	L'_t	L'_{Bt}	*Trend*				
1	1881–1914	Y_t	202·568 / 1·0	1·722 / 4·4			−4·883 / 0·5	0·96	0·57	69·491	4·04
2	1881–1914	Y_t	144·133 / 0·7		1·807 / 4·7		−7·355 / 0·8	0·97	0·45	67·193	3·90
3	1881–1914	Y_t	669·887 / 2·8			1·849 / 1·8	18·629 / 2·5	0·94	0·30	84·373	4·90
4	1881–1914	A_t	−135·552 / 0·9	0·843 / 3·0			−5·742 / 0·9	0·89	0·59	49·846	9·06
1	1921–1939	Y_t	2945·888 / 4·1	0·899 / 2·1			−87·9 / 2·1	0·13	1·92	279·654	6·27
2	1921–1939	Y_t	2380·305 / 0·3		1·206 / 3·0		−122·5 / 2·9	0·28	2·09	254·252	5·70
3	1921–1939	Y_t	3515·276 / 4·5			0·912 / 1·2	−1·8 / 0·1	0·00	1·57	302·816	6·78
4	1921–1939	A_t	−679·683 / 1·0	1·245 / 3·3			−112·008 / 2·9	0·34	0·58	252·898	16·33
1	1947–1962	Y_t	6811·749 / 25·2	0·306 / 3·2			734·20 / 10·4	0·99	1·52	315·541	2·01
2	1947–1962	Y_t	6203·219 / 17·1		0·449 / 2·8		658·70 / 8·6	0·99	1·69	284·944	1·79
3	1947–1962	Y_t	7142·435 / 21·8			0·409 / 1·5	892·40 / 18·6	0·99	1·10	393·419	2·46
4	1947–1962	A_t	4673·831 / 19·1	0·229 / 2·7			393·50 / 6·1	0·99	1·41	285·803	2·86
				H_{t-1}	$\left(\frac{L_B}{D^*}\right)_{t-1}$	$\left(\frac{L_I}{Q}\right)_{t-1}$	$\left(\frac{D}{C}\right)_{t-1}$				
5	1882–1914	Y_t	−2031·172 / n.a.	6·595 / 5·6	428·307 / 0·4	1688·809 / 2·4	203·998 / 10·1	0·97	0·78	66·516	3·84
5	1921–1939	Y_t	684·946 / n.a.	5·127 / 3·2	1074·379 / 0·9	1890·860 / 1·5	−168·502 / 0·6	0·71	1·17	169·150	3·75
5	1948–1962	Y_t	14200·000 / n.a.	5·273 / 4·9	4685·118 / 2·02	28850·653 / 12·2	860·879 / 2·6	0·99	2·36	198·320	1·26
				$\log L_{It-1}$	$\log L_{Bt-1}$		$\log Y_{t-1}$				
6	1881–1914	$\log Y_t$	0·160 / 1·4	0·047 / 0·5	0·118 / 1·4		0·819 / 9·0	0·98	1·39*	0·012	0·36
6	1921–1939	$\log Y_t$	1·145 / 2·7	0·066 / 2·3	0·112 / 0·1		0·620 / 5·4	0·66	0·82*	0·017	0·48
6	1948–1962	$\log Y_t$	0·791 / 4·4	0·253 / 3·2	−0·006 / 0·1		0·597 / 5·3	0·99	2·96*	0·010	0·23

TABLE 5.6—*continued*

Eq.	*Period*	*Dependent Variable*	*Constant*	*Independent Variables*				$\overline{Rsq}$	*DW*	$\overline{See}$	$\overline{Sct}$%
				$\Delta \log L'_t$	$\Delta \log L_{t-1}$	$\Delta \log r_{s_t}$	$\Delta \log r_{c_{t-1}}$				
7	1882–1914	$\Delta \log Y_t$	0·003 1·4	0·401 1·4		0·048 3·4		0·34	1·86	0·009	—
8	1882–1914	$\Delta \log Y_t$	−0·001 0·2	0·780 2·2				0·11	1·33	0·010	—
9	1882–1914	$\Delta \log Y_t$	0·005 1·2		0·267 1·0		−0·038 0·2	0·00	1·36	0·021	—
7	1922–1939	$\Delta \log Y_t$	−0·022 3·1	0·980 2·8		−0·007 0·2		0·29	0·87	0·021	—
8	1922–1939	$\Delta \log Y_t$	−0·015 3·5	0·935 5·1				0·60	1·22	0·013	—
9	1922–1939	$\Delta \log Y_t$	−0·018 3·4		0·999 4·6		−0·342 2·5	0·53	1·73	0·140	—
7 8 9	1948–1962		No significant results – all adjusted $\overline{Rsq}$'s were either zero or negative, and none of the regression coefficients was significant.								

Notation

Y_t, A_t, M'_t, representing gross domestic private expenditure, autonomous expenditure and average of two end-year money stocks are defined at the bottom of previous tables.

L_{t-1} = gross amount of private credit extended to UK borrowers by the sample of UK financial institutions (banks, insurance companies building societies, trustee savings banks, hire-purchase companies) as of approximately 31 December of the previous year. The gross private credit extensions were derived by summing these institutions' total assets after extracting the amounts they held in cash, lent to the Government, or invested in foreign securities.

n.a. = Not computed.

* = The *DW* statistic is biased.

L'_t = Average of consecutive gross private credit extensions (L_t) as of 31 December in the current and in the preceding year.

L'_{Bt} = Average of gross private credit advanced by the banks as of 31 December in the current and in the preceding year.

H_{t-1} = Average amount of high-powered money outstanding in the previous year = private sector currency holdings plus bankers' and private deposits at the Bank of England.

$(L_B/D^*)_{t-1}$ = Ratio of banks' total gross private credit extensions to their total assets – D^*, as of approximately 31 December in the previous year.

$(L_I/Q)_{t-1}$ = Ratio of the other financial intermediaries' gross private credit extensions to their total assets – Q as of approximately 31 December in the previous year.

$(D/C)_{t-1}$ = Ratio of deposits to currency outstanding held by the non-banking private sector in the previous year.

r_s = Treasury Bill rate.

r_c = Consol rate.

L_{It} = Stock of gross private credit extended by the non-bank financial institutions as of 31 December in the previous year.

with rises of £4·3 million, of £16·9 million, or of £2·0 million respectively in private expenditure in the next time interval. The results of the fifth regression are now examined.

On the basis of the interpretation given above, it seems that the quantity theory effects were dominant in the first period. The regression coefficients of H_{t-1} and $(D/C)_{t-1}$ are very significant; moreover, these two variables changed quite considerably over the period – from £191 million to £243 million and from a ratio of 2·43 to one of 6·6 – whereas each of the other two ratios changed very little: only by 0·01. Private expenditure increased by £1,000 million over the interval and the two monetary variables dominate in the regression.

In the next period, 1921–39, in which private expenditure increased by £500 million, only high-powered money seems to have played much of a role: it increased by just £47 million. The regression coefficients of

$(L_B/D^*)_{t-1}$, of $(D/C)_{t-1}$, and $(L_I/Q)_{t-1}$ are not significant enough to justify much confidence in their computed values. The monetary variable (H_{t-1}) was most influential.

In the third period, it seems that all four variables had some influence on private expenditure: all the regression coefficients are fully significant within the 95 per cent confidence interval, and all the variables changed substantially over the period. High-powered money increased by £976 million, the bank private loan/total asset ratio and the non-bank private loan/total asset ratio rose from 0·33 to 0·60 and from 0·28 to 0·54 respectively; whereas the deposit/currency ratio fell from 4·80 to 4·11. Again high-powered money played a sizeable role in reducing the residual variance; nevertheless, in this last period $(L_I/Q)_{t-1}$ exerted an even more potent influence – its partial $\bar{R}^2$ was 0·906. In contrast with the 1882–1914 or the 1922–39 periods, in the 1948–62 period credit, and particularly the way non-banking financial institutions chose to allocate it between the private and the public sectors, seems to have played a dominant role in the relationship.

To some extent, the suggestion that the results of the fifth regression indicate that financial factors were important in the determination of domestic private expenditure might seem to be marred by a marked between-period change in some of the regression coefficients. The regression coefficients in the second and third variables show a marked between-period variation – 428 to 1074 to 4685 and 1689 to 1891 to 28851; only the regression coefficient of H_{t-1} seems to be reasonably stable. However, these results are consistent with the thesis that credit, particularly institutional credit, played an increasing role in the process of expenditure generation, as they are consistent with the fact that the denominators of the two ratios, D^* and Q, increased substantially over the war periods. Each 0·01 increase or decrease in either ratio in the inter-war and the post-war period represents a substantial increase or decrease in credit extended, as compared with a 0·01 change in the respective ratios in the previous time interval. The banking sector's assets, D^*, increased at a 14 per cent and a 12 per cent compound rate per annum in the war intervals; moreover, in the inter-war and post-war periods the per annum rates of growth of D^* and particularly of Q were quite marked – Q grew at a compound rate of approximately 6 per cent per annum in the peacetime periods. In effect, to the extent that private expenditure is an increasing function of available credit tranches, the between-period upward trend in the regression coefficients of the ratios is expected as long as D^* and Q have increased too. The between-period change in size in the regression coefficients seems to contribute to the argument that institutional credit is becoming increasingly important in the process of private expenditure determination.

The period results of the fourth regression, in which autonomous expenditure is regressed on L_{t-1} and on a time trend term, also suggest that credit availability played a role in the formulation of the private sector's investment decisions in accord with Friedman's suggestion. To be sure, the significance of the role of L_{t-1} in the relationship is undermined by the presence of a considerable degree of autocorrelation in the first and second periods; though the $\overline{Rsq}$'s of 0·89 and 0·34 imply that there is some substance in the relationship. This suggestion seems to be strengthened by the results in the third period. The autocorrelation is hardly significant, whereas the t-ratio of the regression coefficient of L_{t-1} is again very large. Moreover, it is interesting to observe that on comparing the results of the regression of A_t on L_{t-1} in this table and A_t on M_{t-1} in Table 5.2, the residual standard error adjusted for degrees of freedom, $\overline{See}$, is considerably smaller when L_{t-1} rather than M_{t-1} is used as the explanatory variable: an observation which seems to indicate that inasmuch as some financial stock has an effect on the realization of autonomous expenditure decisions, the availability of private credit, as measured by L_{t-1}, rather than the availability of money, as measured by M_{t-1}, has the most effect.[1]

The suggestion that L_{t-1} seems to have become somewhat more important than M_{t-1} as the financial stock which serves as a predictor or, more adventurously, a determinant of autonomous expenditure, seems also to hold for total private expenditure, inasmuch as L'_{B_t}, bank advances, might be taken as a proxy variable for the money supply. This may be seen by an examination of the regression coefficients and t-ratios of L'_t and L'_{B_t} in equations 2 and 3 of this table. In any event, as indicated in equation 5 and as shown in the log linear autoregressive model in equation 6, it certainly appears that non-bank institutional private credits, as opposed to the banking system's private credits, played a more important role in the post-war peacetime periods. Indeed, in the

[1] The superiority of L_{t-1} over M_{t-1} as a determinant of the amount of autonomous expenditure did not hold when the amount of gross fixed capital expenditure was substituted for A_t as the dependent variable. In effect, regressing K_t on a constant and on M_{t-1} or L_{t-1} respectively in each period, 1881–1914, 1921–39, 1947–62, the partial correlation coefficients of the explanatory variables were 0·51 and 0·41, 0·69 and 0·62, and 0·96 and 0·97.

inter-war and post-war periods equation 6 shows that $L_{B_{t-1}}$ played no readily observable role in the regression other than to reduce the degrees of freedom; whereas the coefficient of $L_{I_{t-1}}$, non-bank institutional private credits, was fully significant in both periods. Moreover, when the recorded expenditure elasticities of 0·066 and 0·253 in each period aıe adjusted to reflect the lag structure, the rise in the size of the elasticities over the two periods is quite substantial: 0·174 and 0·628. The results of the first, second, third, fifth and sixth regressions all indicate that total private credit, L, and particularly non-bank institutional private credit, L_I, have become an increasingly important financial determinant of the level of nominal private expenditure; similarly, they suggest that bank credits, L_B, have not been directly influential in the post 1914–18 peacetime intervals.[1]

The suggested primacy of the direct credit effect over the direct monetary effect with respect to nominal domestic private expenditure also seems to hold in the first differences as may be seen on examining equation 6 in Table 5·4 and equations 7, 8 and 9 in Table 5·6.

The seventh, eighth and ninth regressions in this table show that there was a fairly strong positive correlation between private expenditure and the stock of private credit (lagged and unlagged) in the first differences in the logs over the 1882–1939 peacetime periods. Glancing at the eighth regression, for instance, in which the percentage change in Y is regressed on the percentage change in L'_t, the regression coefficients of $\Delta \log L'_t$ are fully significant in the 1882–1914 and the 1921–39 intervals, and pertinently, fitting in with the suggested increase in the importance of private institutional credit extensions over time, the explanatory power of the percentage change in private credit increased substantially between the periods – the $\overline{Rsq}$ rose from 0·11 to 0·60. It seems significant, too, on examining the ninth regression, that the percentage change in private credit over the previous calendar year played a significant role in the 1921–39 period whereas its impact in the 1882–1914 interval was sub-marginal. Together these findings suggest that over the time period in which the financial sector was not subject to extensive Government regulation – quantitative credit restrictions and the like – the changes in credit availability had an increasing impact on the change in private expenditure and that its impact extended into at least one subsequent income period.

As with the regression of the percentage change of private expenditure on the percentage change in the money stock, on the percentage change in autonomous expenditure, on the percentage change of the short-term rate of interest or on $\Delta \log Y_{t-1}$, in Table 5.6 all three regressions indicate that in the 1947–62 period the degree of statistical association between the $\Delta \log Y_t$ and either the $\Delta \log L'_t$ or the $\Delta \log L_{t-1}$ was minimal. The coefficients of determination adjusted for degrees of freedom were not significantly different from zero in each of these regressions; the t-ratios were so low that no significance could be ascribed to the size of the regression coefficients, and these coefficients either had a zero value or a negative value. These results are also markedly different from the positive correlations found in the expenditure flow credit stock findings for the 1947–62 period. In effect, taking both sets of seemingly contradictory findings together, the evidence suggests that while the stock of available institutional credit seems to be exerting a greater impact on aggregate private expenditure, the influence of a change in this stock on the present or immediately subsequent change in expenditure has waned considerably. These peculiar results might again be explained by the effect of the post-war increased incidence of Government financial regulations and budgetary measures which were levied to control private expenditure, coupled with the full employment policy that was officially imposed after 1946. Together these Government actions would tend to extend and smooth out the private sector's plans to discount its future income stream through the use of financial credits. In this context, the conflict between the levels and the first difference results seems resolvable.

Over all then, with respect to the hypothesis that private credit availability has a direct impact on private nominal expenditure, the above results show that the degree of statistical association between the level of expenditure and private credit, lagged and unlagged, was substantial in the post-1945 period; it was modest in the inter-war years, and it was sizeable but perhaps spuriously

[1] It is of interest to note that L_I increased from approximately £570 million in 1920 to £2,400 million in 1939, whereas bank advances, L_B, hardly changed at all – they just ranged between £880 million to £1,140 million and they were only £25 million higher in 1939 than they were in 1920. In the 1946–62 period L_I increased from £2,470 million to £11,420 million while L_B rose from £1,120 million to £4,198 million, with most of the increase (over £2,000 million) taking place in the post-1958 period. In effect, a rough perusal of the statistical record shows and a reading of the institutional history confirms that relative to their institutional competitors, the banking sector as a whole performed dismally in their attempt to retain their market share of the private loan market in the 1920–39 and 1946–62 periods.

so in the pre-1914 period as the residuals of the regressions in the earlier years were well correlated. Moreover, in the models which were designed to see whether this purported credit effect became in reality a disguised monetary effect (regressions two, three, five and six), the results suggested that the credit effect was more important, particularly in the post-1946 period, though the monetary effect was still present. This finding seems to be consistent with those obtained in Table 5.2 which shows that total encashable assets rather than the money stock seem to exert the most influence in the simple quantity theory relationship. The examination suggests that the nominal amount of private credit outstanding does have a direct influence on the level of nominal expenditure in the same and in the subsequent year.

With respect to the impact that the percentage change in nominal private credit has, lagged or unlagged, on the percentage change in private expenditure, the seventh, eighth and ninth regressions suggest that the impact was certainly positive over the 1882–1939 peacetime periods, and was very potent between the wars. Between 1921 and 1939 the results indicate that during that time a 1 per cent change in the credit stock was matched by or followed by an approximately 1 per cent change in nominal expenditure. Moreover, and significantly – in terms of *a priori* expectations – the sign of the $\%\Delta r_{c_{t-1}}$, the lagged consol rate, was negative: a 1 per cent increase in the consol rate being associated with a 0·34 per cent decline in private expenditure in the next period *ceteris paribus*. Both the percentage change in the quantity and in the cost of credit seem to have influenced the percentage change in private expenditure in the expected direction. However, in the post-1946 period, as noted above, the results show no association between the $\Delta \log L'_t$ or $\Delta \log L_{t-1}$ and $\Delta \log Y_t$. This finding does seem to coincide with the greater attention the state paid to 'fine tuning', or, perhaps more appropriately, frequent tuning of the financial sector's portfolio decisions and the private sector's expenditure plans in the 1947–62 interval.

In constant prices, that is when private expenditure flow and the private credit stock variables have been deflated by the 1958-based retail price index, it seems from Table 5.7 that the degree of statistical association between private expenditure and credit was sustained in each of the time periods – 1881–1914, 1921–39 and 1947–62. The results suggest that the real stock of private credit has a direct impact upon the real stock of private expenditure in the subsequent income period; a finding which is wholly consistent with the direct real monetary effect recorded in Table 5.5, and which provides further corroboration that the influence of financial factors, and particularly the presence of certain financial stocks, may have had quite a substantial effect on both the real and the nominal levels of economic activity in the United Kingdom.

In the first two regressions reported in Table 5.7, real private expenditure $(Y/P)_t$ is regressed respectively on the lagged value of the stock of real private credit $(L/P)_{t-1}$, on the Treasury Bill rate (r_{s_t}), on a time trend term, and then $(L/P)_{t-1}$ and the spread between the consol rate and the Treasury Bill rate $(r_c - r_s)$. In these regressions $(L/P)_{t-1}$ is used as a proxy for the available stock of institutional real private credit in the current time period and its expected impact is positive. In turn, r_s serves as an index of the cost of short-term credit, and its expected impact on private expenditure is negative. The time trend acts as an index of any slowly changing factors influencing real expenditure, including the lagged effect of $(L/P)_{t-2}$, and the expected value of its impact is positive. Finally $(r_c - r_s)$ represents the degree of financial 'ease' as opposed to tightness in the capital markets (the extent to which credit granting facilities are under-utilized), and the expected sign of its impact is negative.

The first regression indicates that the interest rate, r_s, had relatively little influence on real private expenditure. None of the regression coefficients of r_s was significant at the 95 per cent level; in two periods, the first and last, this coefficient was positive, not negative as expected, and in all periods its partial correlation coefficients adjusted for degrees of freedom were zero. Such results coincide with the findings reported in equations 1 and 2 in Table 5.5, in which the contribution of the long-term interest rate r_c, as a determinant of real private expenditure, was also negligible. In contrast, the direct effect of $(L/P)_{t-1}$ seems to have been quite substantial and in the expected direction in both the first and the last periods, and its impact in the inter-war period would perhaps have been substantial, as suggested by the second regression, if the degree of its serial correlation with r_s had been somewhat lower.[1] Finally, and in contrast to the results in current prices as shown in equation 1 of Table 5.6, it is interesting to observe that while the time trend played a significant role in reducing the residual variance in the early period, its effect was minimal in the inter-war and the post-1946

[1] The Pearson correlation coefficient between $(Y/P)_t$ and $(L/P)_{t-1}$ was 0·98, 0·95 and 0·95 in each period. The Pearson correlation coefficient between $(L/P)_{t-1}$ and r_{s_t} in the 1921–39 interval was $-0{\cdot}70$.

periods: a fact which suggests that institutional credit or its availability played a progressively important role in influencing the real amount of private expenditure throughout the period.

The results of the second regression seem to support this supposition. The coefficient of $(L/P)_{t-1}$ is positive, large and very significant in all periods. Moreover, the degree of autocorrelation in the first and the last intervals was non-existent; so its regression coefficients were not distorted by this bias, and the high recorded *t*-ratios indicate that these coefficients are very significant. Similarly, it is interesting to note the role that the index of financial ease played in the relationship. In the first period, a 1 per cent spread between the long- and short-term interest rates, would *ceteris paribus* account for a reduction of £211 million in private expenditure as measured in 1958 prices; whereas in the last period, 1947–62, a similar spread would account for a reduction of £461 million in the same prices. This finding could almost be taken as showing that private expenditure had a perverse sensitivity to the costs of credit, as well as indicating how difficult it has been to curb private real expenditure through the imposition of traditional market tightening techniques – that is, those techniques which do not directly link or reduce the amount of institutional credit made available. In turn, this perverse reaction fits in well with the changes observed in bank portfolio behaviour during periods of rising interest rates as observed by Clayton and Brechling in the UK and by Shearer in the USA in the post-1946 period.

The third regression in the table is directly comparable to equation 5 in Table 5.6, except that this time expenditure in constant prices is regressed on high-powered money, lagged in constant prices, in addition to the other three ratios: $(L_B/D^*)_{t-1}$, $(L_I/Q)_{t-1}$ and $(D/C)_{t-1}$. As before, the first variable $(H/P)_{t-1}$ and the last $(D/C)_{t-1}$ are intended to be interpreted as proxies for the *ex ante* stock of total real financial credit outstanding in the subsequent period, particularly the money stock, while the other two variables $(L_B/D^*)_{t-1}$ and $(L_I/Q)_{t-1}$ are meant as proxies as to how the financial institutions, the banks and then the non-banking financial intermediaries, will allocate their assets in the form of loans to the private sector with respect to their total assets in the forthcoming income period. The model is designed to contrast the real monetary effect with the real credit effect as two alternative rationales of real private expenditure determination.

On balance, as in the first and second regressions, the results in constant prices seem to be somewhat better than those in nominal prices, particularly in the 1881–1914 interval. Moreover, with respect to the difference between the significant regression coefficients of the same independent variables for the different periods, it appears that the relationship, as measured in constant prices, is more stable over the long run. Like the regression in current prices, however, in each period the dominant explanatory variable in this regression is identical – $(D/C)_{t-1}$ accounts for most of the reduction in the residual variance in the first period: $(H/P)_{t-1}$ dominates the relationship in the second interval, and $(L_I/Q)_{t-1}$ exerts the most potent influence in the 1948–62 era. These findings fit neatly into the historical record.[1]

In two respects, however, the comparison of the results in nominal and in constant prices is puzzling. First, there seems to be a considerable divergence between the significant coefficients of the same variable in like periods, excluding the ones posted for H_{t-1} and $(H/P)_{t-1}$. Second, the sign of the coefficient of $(L_I/Q)_{t-1}$ is negative in the first period, which is contrary to expectations, whereas it is positive in both the other periods and in all periods when the relationship was cast in current as opposed to constant prices.

The first difficulty, however, is mainly illusory due to the fact that the flow variable was deflated by the 1958 price index – 1958 = 100, rather than 1958 = 1 – so that in 1958 prices, the coefficients of the variables which are ratios should be raised by 10^2, e.g. the decimal place should be shifted two places to the right. In effect, a 0·01 rise in $(L_I/Q)_{t-1}$ in the 1948–62 period should be associated with a subsequent increase of approximately £293 of expenditure in 1958 prices as compared with a rise of £289 in current prices.

The second problem is more difficult to rationalize as there seems to be no obvious statistical explanation for the negative sign. There is, however, an intuitive argument to explain it. Assurance companies' debenture holdings accounted for an important component of L_I in the 1880–1914 period. As such, it certainly seems possible that an increase in this ratio $(L_I/Q)_{t-1}$ could well be reflected in the form of a purchase of non-UK-based railroad obligations, etc. – long-term capital exports, the proceeds of which were used to finance UK capital

[1] There was a rapid growth of deposits relative to currency in the pre-1914 time period. Official restrictions almost eliminated the growth of the high-powered money stock in the inter-war era. In the post-1947 period, non-bank institutional private credits rose extremely rapidly after the quantitative restrictions on such credits had been lifted.

TABLE 5.7 **Expenditure Estimates in Constant Prices – Credit Availability Models 1881–1962**

Eq.	*Period*	*Dependent Variable*	*Constant*[1]	*Independent Variables*				*Trend*	$\overline{Rsq}$	*DW*	$\overline{See}$	$\overline{Sct}$%
				$\left(\frac{L}{P}\right)_{t-1}$	$(r_c - r_s)_t$		r_{s_t}					
1	1881–1914	$\left(\frac{Y}{P}\right)_t$	35·500 / n.a.	0·921 / 2·4			0·733 / 1·2	0·503 / 2·4	0·97	1·23	2·154	2·32
2	1881–1914	$\left(\frac{Y}{P}\right)_t$	23·033 / n.a.	1·462 / 35·4	−2·112 / 3·8				0·98	2·02	2·210	2·38
1	1921–1939	$\left(\frac{Y}{P}\right)_t$	82·310 / n.a.	0·725 / 1·3			−1·049 / 1·1	−1·102 / 0·5	0·89	0·98	3·741	3·10
2	1921–1939	$\left(\frac{Y}{P}\right)_t$	84·123 / n.a.	0·565 / 6·0	0·497 / 0·3				0·82	0·88	4·575	3·94
1	1947–1962	$\left(\frac{Y}{P}\right)_t$	110·814 / n.a.	0·436 / 2·8			3·217 / 1·7	1·613 / 1·3	0·96	2·45	5·111	2·92
2	1947–1962	$\left(\frac{Y}{P}\right)_t$	97·402 / n.a.	1·085 / 9·5	−4·609 / 2·0				0·91	1·94	7·155	4·08
				$\left(\frac{H}{P}\right)_{t-1}$	$\left(\frac{L_B}{D^*}\right)_{t-1}$	$\left(\frac{L_I}{Q}\right)_{t-1}$	$\left(\frac{D}{C}\right)_{t-1}$					
3	1882–1914	$\left(\frac{Y}{P}\right)_t$	117·604 / n.a.	0·847 / 0·9	16·025 / 0·5	−148·473 / 3·5	11·363 / 20·3		0·98	1·82	2·154	2·32
3	1921–1939	$\left(\frac{Y}{P}\right)_t$	9·834 / n.a.	3·990 / 3·3	19·906 / 0·8	36·117 / 1·1	2·498 / 0·6		0·90	1·10	3·551	2·94
3	1947–1962	$\left(\frac{Y}{P}\right)_t$	−78·077 / n.a.	3·093 / 2·3	25·860 / 0·5	292·746 / 3·7	8·292 / 1·0		0·96	2·70	5·175	2·95
				$\log\left(\frac{L_I}{P}\right)_{t-1}$	$\log\left(\frac{L_B}{P}\right)_{t-1}$		$\log\left(\frac{Y}{P}\right)_{t-1}$					
4	1881–1914	$\log\left(\frac{Y}{P}\right)_t$	0·311 / 2·7	0·077 / 0·9	0·099 / 1·2		0·722 / 5·8		0·98	2·29[2]	0·011	0·56
4	1921–1939	$\log\left(\frac{Y}{P}\right)_t$	1·007 / 2·8	0·107 / 2·7	−0·025 / 0·3		0·454 / 2·3		0·90	1·31[2]	0·012	0·61
4	1947–1962	$\log\left(\frac{Y}{P}\right)_t$	1·042 / 3·1	0·364 / 2·9	−0·021 / 0·3		0·266 / 1·1		0·93	2·84[2]	0·016	0·71
				$\Delta\log\left(\frac{L'}{P}\right)_t$	$\Delta\log r_s$		$\Delta\log\left(\frac{Y}{P}\right)_{t-1}$					
5	1882–1962[3]	$\Delta\log\left(\frac{Y}{P}\right)_t$	0·000 / 0·1	0·569 / 5·6	0·010 / 1·1		−0·001 / 2·2		0·32	1·84[2]	0·012	—
5	1882–1914	$\Delta\log\left(\frac{Y}{P}\right)_t$	0·002 / 0·1	0·626 / 4·5	0·024 / 2·6		−0·001 / 1·6		0·43	1·82[2]	0·009	—
5	1922–1939	$\Delta\log\left(\frac{Y}{P}\right)_t$	0·007 / 0·1	0·500 / 2·2	−0·025 / 1·6		−0·001 / 0·9		0·21	2·00	0·011	—
5	1948–1962	$\Delta\log\left(\frac{Y}{P}\right)_t$	0·005 / 0·1	0·664 / 2·9	−0·004 / 0·2		−0·001 / 2·0		0·43	1·4	0·012	—

Notation

Y/P, L_I/P, L_B/P, L'/P, L/P, H/P are respectively, gross domestic private expenditure, non-bank institutional credits to the private sector, bank institutional credits to the private sector, total financial institutional credits to the private sector and the stock of high-powered money all in constant prices.

r_s = Short-term rate of interest – Treasury Bill rate.

r_c = Long-term rate of interest – consol rate.

$(L_B/D^*)_{t-1}$ and $(L_I/Q)_{t-1}$ and $(D/C)_{t-1}$ stand for the ratios of gross private-sector loans made by the banks to their total assets, of gross private-sector loans made by other financial institutions to their total assets, and of the non-banking private sector's holdings of deposits to their holdings of high-powered money respectively in the previous year.

Notes

[1] Where n.a. is reported, the standard error of the constant term was not computed.

[2] The DW statistic is biased due to the inclusion of the lagged endogenous variable.

[3] Excludes the years 1915–21 and 1940–7 – i.e. sixty-six observations in all.

equipment exports. This type of loan placement practice, as coupled with the use to which these funds were put, might have had a greater inflationary effect than the allocation/use practices had in the subsequent periods when L_I was more closely geared to financing domestic investment and housing. In this sense, the expected value of the correlation between $(Y/P)_t$ and $(L_I/Q)_{t-1}$ could well be negative in the first period, whereas the sign of the correlation between $(Y/P)_t$ and $(L_I/Q)_{t-1}$ in the last two periods, as well as Y_t and $(L_I/Q)_{t-1}$ in all periods could well be positive – coinciding with the results obtained in Tables 5.6 and 5.7. In effect, it is argued that the pre-1914 selected financial intermediaries' portfolio preferences for foreign debt issues tended to stimulate the rise of domestic prices but to dampen the growth in real output by diverting savings from domestic to foreign capital formation.

In the fourth regression of Table 5.7, the log of real private expenditure is regressed on the log of real non-bank private institutional loans, $(L_I/P)_{t-1}$, on the log of real bank private loans, $(L_B/P)_{t-1}$, and on the log of the lagged value of real private expenditure $(Y/P)_{t-1}$. The results compare favourably with those of the fifth regression in Table 5.6 in which the same 'explanatory model' was used in nominal terms – current prices. In this regression over time, that is comparing period with period, the elasticity of real realized private demand with respect to the lagged value of real institutional private loans becomes larger and more significant, and thereby plays an increasingly important role in reducing the residual variance. Significantly, log $(L_B/P)_{t-1}$ played no role of note; moreover, the decline in the importance of the lagged endogenous variable is marked – its partial correlation coefficient adjusted for degrees of freedom fell from 0·49 to 0·11 and then to 0·00. To the extent that this variable, log $(Y/P)_{t-1}$, stands as a proxy for the echo effect on log $(Y/P)_t$ of the lagged values of log (L_I/P) and log (L_B/P) in previous periods, the decline in its impact suggests that in real terms the expenditure effect of the other two independent variables was more quickly worked out with the passage of time. Over all, the regressions in current and constant prices indicate that the lagged value of non-bank private sector loans as opposed to the lagged value of bank private sector loans has become a better predictor of the value of subsequent private expenditure.[1] This finding tends to support the contention that the direct credit effects have become an increasingly important determinant of the level of economic activity.

The positive correlation observed between the level of real private institutional credit and the subsequent amount of private expenditure holds in the first differences, as an examination of the fifth regression results in Table 5.7 indicates. In this regression, the percentage

[1] These rather positive credit availability as opposed to quantity theory impact multiplier results, however, should at best be regarded only as a rough empirical validation of either approach. For besides the noted inadequacies of the estimating techniques, the partial regression coefficients obtained in this last regression are evidently distorted by the presence of a considerable degree of multicollinearity, as an examination of the underlying correlation matrix shows. This problem was particularly acute in the first period, in which all the independent variables were very well correlated with each other – the simple Pearson correlation coefficient ranged between 0·96 and 0·99 – which might well account for the poor t-ratios, high standard errors, of the coefficient of log $(L_I/P)_{t-1}$ and log $(L_B/P)_{t-1}$ in the 1882–1914 period. In the subsequent periods, the correlation between the independent variables reached more tolerable levels with the exception of the relationship between log $(L_I/P)_{t-1}$ and log $(Y/P)_{t-1}$ which remained in the 0·90+ region throughout. This high correlation would tend to distort the partial regression coefficients of both variables in all periods, and it perhaps accounts for the lack of statistical significance of log $(Y/P)_{t-1}$ in the last period.

change of real private expenditure, $\Delta \log (Y/P)_t$, was regressed on the percentage change of the mid-year level of private institutional credit in constant prices, $\Delta \log (L'/P)_t$, on the percentage change of the short-term interest rate, $\Delta \log r_{s_t}$, and on the percentage change of the lagged dependent variable, $\Delta \log (Y/P)_{t-1}$. The first two 'independent' variables were included to measure the rationing and the 'cost' effect of credit on expenditure. The expected sign of the rationing effect is positive; the expected sign of the cost effect is negative. The last variable $\Delta \log (Y/P)_{t-1}$, is included in order to measure the lagged impact of previous values of the explanatory variables on $\Delta \log (Y/P)_t$; if there is no lagged impact, the coefficient of this term should not be significantly different from zero.

The results tend to support the rationing effect of the percentage change of real credit availability and to contradict the indirect effect of the percentage change of the cost of such credits. The coefficient of $\Delta \log (L'/P)_t$ is positive and fully significant in the whole period regression and for each of the three sub-periods. Moreover, there is not much between-period variation in this coefficient; it ranges between 0·500 and 0·664. The coefficient of $\Delta \log r_{s_t}$, however, is sometimes positive and sometimes negative; it is significant only in the first period, 1882–1914, and then it has the 'wrong' sign. The coefficient of $\Delta \log (Y/P)_{t-1}$ is significant only over the whole period and in the last period, and the size of its coefficient then suggests that the lagged impact is sub-minimal with respect to the current impact of the other independent variables.[1] In percentage change terms, the results suggest that the relationship between a percentage change in private credit and private expenditure in constant prices is prompt; that the effect is a rationing rather than a cost of credit effect, and that this relationship has been persistently stable over a long period of time and has been quite strong too. The $\overline{Rsq}$'s for the whole period, and for each of the consecutive sub-periods are shown to be 0·32, 0·43, 0·21 and 0·43. Fittingly, the rationing effect is shown to be weakest in the 1922–39 interval when there was presumably least demand for such credit. It is only in this period that the coefficient of the percentage change of interest has the expected sign and is almost significant – 0·025/1·6.[2]

Finally, the results of the fifth regression, as coupled with the results of the other regressions of the first differences in the logarithms in Tables 5.3, 5.4, 5.5 and 5.6 suggest that in the first differences also the chosen financial stocks can be ranked with respect to their association with the change in total private expenditure in either current or constant prices.

A comparison of the findings in Tables 5.4 and 5.6 indicates that the percentage change in private credit was much more closely associated with the percentage change in private expenditure in both the 1882–1914 and the 1922–39 intervals than the percentage change in the money stock was. Neither of these two financial variables, however, seems to have had much 'effect' in the post-war period. Moreover, even in the earlier periods, Tables 5.4 and 5.2 suggest that, with respect to first differences, the change in autonomous expenditure was a considerably more potent explanatory variable of the change in private expenditure than was the change in either of the financial stocks; nevertheless it too was completely ineffective in the 1947–62 interval.

With respect to the change or the percentage change in the dependent and independent variables in constant prices, much the same conclusions may be drawn from Tables 5.3, 5.5 and 5.7 with one major and two minor exceptions. In general, in real terms, the percentage change in credit was much more effective than the percentage change in the money stock or of encashable assets as a determinant of the percentage change in private expenditure. In the whole period and in each of the sub-periods the regression coefficient of this variable was remarkably stable and fully significant; whereas Tables 5.3 and 5.5 show that there was a considerable variation between the effect of the percentage changes in real money balances, in real autonomous expenditure and in encashable assets in constant prices respectively on the percentage change in real private expenditure.

[1] Regressions were run in which the lagged value of the percentage change in real private credit and the percentage change in the lagged consol rate were used as explanatory variables. The lags were approximately 6 months and one year respectively. In all periods the impact of the percentage change in $(L/P)_{t-1}$ was not significantly different from zero; while the percentage change in $r_{c_{t-1}}$ did have a significant negative impact in the first and second periods; but it was very small.

[2] It should be noted though, that in each of the periods, regressions were run to see what the correlation was between the percentage changes in real private expenditure and the percentage change in real private credit lagged by 6 months. In all such regressions, none of the coefficients of determination was significantly different from zero. In each of the periods, too, regressions were run in which the lag structure was reversed – the change in the real stock of private credit was computed by taking the difference between the end-year rather than the annual average levels. In each period, the coefficients of determination were quite large – 0·52 and 0·27 and 0·41. These results suggest that the change in the stock of private credit in constant prices is influenced by the preceding change in real private expenditure.

In Table 5.3, for instance, the percentage change in real autonomous expenditure is actually shown to have played a contributing role in the first period, *and no role at all* in the other periods in relation to the percentage change in real consumption. In contrast, the percentage change in encashable assets in the same table is shown to have played a greater role in the first period and an even more potent role in the third ($\overline{Rsq}=0{\cdot}65$) but it had no influence between the wars; unless the lagged value of this variable's effect is considered. Table 5.5 shows that though both the percentage change in the money stock and in encashable assets in constant prices were reasonably well correlated with the percentage change in real private expenditure (including consumption) in the first and the last periods too, there was a marked variation in the size of the significant coefficients of the independent variables between each time interval. Moreover, neither the percentage change in real balances nor the percentage change in real encashable assets had any impact on the synchronous percentage change in real private expenditure in the inter-war period, and only the percentage change in the real money stock outperformed the percentage change in real credit and then only in the last period.

Again then, credit outperformed any of the other selected financial variables (money, encashable assets and interest rates) as a determinant of private expenditure in every period but the last. Moreover, and in contrast to the results in nominal prices, its impact as a determinant of the percentage change in real expenditure was much greater than that of the change in real autonomous expenditure in all three periods. In accord with the financial stock expenditure flow relationships then, in real terms the change in money, encashable assets or credit certainly seemed to have had a direct impact throughout the period on the change or percentage change in real private expenditure; whereas their indirect effects, as in the current price relationships, as expressed through changes in the interest rates, generally contradicted theoretical expectations or were completely insignificant.

Conclusion

The empirical investigation of the relationships between various financial stocks or changes in these stocks and the level or the change in the level of certain forms of private expenditure conducted in the second section of this chapter has produced some interesting results. The results splice in well with those of similar studies carried out in the USA and the UK of the financial sector's 'effect' on economic activity. In particular, inasmuch as an 'effect' may be read into the sign, the significance of regression coefficients, and the variables' contribution to the reduction of the residual variance, it appears that the financial sector's effect stems directly from its provision of liquid assets or credit. In contrast, its indirect effect on such expenditures, as expressed by the regression relationships between the long- or the short-term interest rates and the level of expenditure, was either hardly recordable or perverse. In some of the regressions the rate of interest or the change in the log of this rate was positively correlated with the level or the change in the log of the level of private expenditure. Moreover, the results seem to add a complement to the published studies. Surprisingly, they suggest that this financial sector's direct effect is considerably more potent in influencing the level or the change in the level of private expenditure in *constant* prices than it is in current prices. In effect, the investigation implies that the process of monetization or alternatively creditization, that is the expansion of the process of financial intermediation, has played an important role in the growth of real economic activity in the UK during peacetime over the 1880–1962 period.

The investigation is set out on a step-by-step basis. In Table 5.1 the simple Pearson correlation coefficients between the level of private expenditure or consumption, and the level of the money stock, the level of encashable assets, the level of private credit and the level of autonomous expenditure, lagged or unlagged, in current prices are set out for examination. In Tables 5.2, 5.3, 5.4, 5.5, 5.6 and 5.7 the regression results of various single equation models in current and constant prices are reported, and these in turn were designed to indicate the direct impact of the money stock, of encashable assets, of autonomous expenditure and of institutional credits on consumption or on total private expenditure in the same or in the succeeding income period.

Over all, as Table 5.1 illustrates, the degree of correlation between private expenditure and the synchronous or lagged values of the various financial stocks was quite high enough to justify further investigation into the nature of the relationship. The findings also indicated that autonomous expenditure should be considered as an equally and perhaps even a more dominant variable in models of expenditure determination.

Tables 5.2 and 5.3 give the results of some regressions which were designed to test further the degree of association of consumption expenditure with the money stock, with encashable assets, and with autonomous expenditure in current prices and in constant prices. In current prices, autonomous expenditure seemed to act as the dominant explanatory variable over much of the period (particularly in the first differences) though the contribution of the synchronous and lagged (six months) levels of the money stock seemed to be significant enough to make it unwise to disregard its influence in the design of more sophisticated models of consumption determination. In constant prices, however, in both the levels and in the first differences, real money balances and real encashable asset balances were shown to be more potent determinants of consumption expenditure than autonomous expenditure. Indeed, in the first differences, the role of real autonomous expenditure seemed to wane over the period whereas the role of the real value of encashable assets seemed to become increasingly potent. In the 1948–62 interval, for instance, the percentage change of encashable assets in constant prices had a partial correlation coefficient adjusted for degrees of freedom of 0·65; whereas the partial correlation of the percentage change of autonomous expenditure in constant prices was 0·01.

In Tables 5.4 and 5.5, the results of broadly similar regressions are reported; though total private expenditure was substituted for consumption expenditure as the dependent variable. Basically, much the same findings were obtained. In current prices, the lagged value of the money stock and of encashable assets seemed to have played a role; but one which tended to be relatively marginal when compared with the impact of autonomous expenditure – especially in the first differences of the logs in the 1882–1914 and the 1922–39 periods. In real terms, however, the lagged values of the money stock and of encashable assets were shown to be good 'predictors' of the subsequent level of real private expenditure in each of the intervals. And in the regressions in the first differences in the logs of the dependent flow and the independent stock variables in constant prices the results are also reasonably satisfactory except in the inter-war interval. Again, in the last period it is interesting to record that, as shown by the third and sixth regressions in Table 5.5 (i.e. from 1947–62 and from 1949–67), the correlation between the percentage change in real money balances and the percentage change in real private expenditure was quite high and that the respective regression coefficients of the explanatory variables were both highly significant and quite similar. The coefficients of determination were 0·54 and 0·49 and the regression coefficients and *t*-ratios were 0·953/4·1 and 0·89/4·7 respectively in these two overlapping post-1946 time intervals.

Tables 5.6 and 5.7 record the results of other single equation regressions models in which the stock of institutional private credits, or proxies for the availability of these credits, are substituted for the money stock or encashable assets as the explanatory variables. As in the other tables, the models were run in current and constant prices to separate the real effect from that of the effect in current prices. In addition, some of the underlying relationships were designed to reveal what degree of association there was between the lagged credit stock and autonomous expenditure, and to show whether it was possible to compare the force of 'liquidity' with that of credit availability as determinants of private expenditure in the subsequent income period.

Table 5.6 shows that credit effect was quite influential in the expenditure flow/financial stock relationships in current prices. Significantly, too, it shows that the lagged stock of financial credit seemed to be well correlated with the current amount of autonomous expenditure – particularly in the post-1946 years. In particular, the fifth regression (the rudimentary model which was designed to separate out the credit and the monetary effects) indicates that over time the credit effect became dominant, though of course the monetary effect had an influence in each of the three time periods. In the first differences, however, though the percentage change in credit was well correlated with the percentage change in current private expenditure before the First World War and particularly in the inter-war era, in the post-1946 period there was no discernible relationship. This finding was repeated when the percentage change in autonomous expenditure in current prices was used to predict the percentage change in consumption expenditure as noted in Table 5.2. It seems that these null post-1946 results are explained by the increased weight of Government regulation of the change in pace of economic activity.

In constant prices the results in Table 5.7 show that the lagged stock of institutional credits served well as a predictor of the real level of private expenditure in each period; whereas as in the current price relationship, the effect of the explicit price of credit, as represented by the interest rates, was unimportant. Again, too, as in the current price relationships, the credit effect, as opposed to the monetary effect, became dominant in constant prices as the period progressed (see equation 3 in Table 5.7), and as a supporting aside, as in current prices, non-bank financial institutions' private credits as opposed to bank private credits played an increasingly important role in the regressions – see equation 4 in Table 5.7, and equations 2 and 3 in Table 5.6. Finally, the fifth regression in Table 5.7 illustrates that in constant prices, the percentage change in credit was reasonably well correlated with the percentage change in private expenditure in all three periods. In particular this regression indicates that the impact of the percentage change in the real stock of private credit was both significant and quite stable in each of the sub-periods, which contrasts with the null results found in the percentage changes of the impact of real balances in the inter-war interval.

Over all then, the results suggest that money, encashable assets and the stock of institutional private credits are directly associated with the level of economic activity as represented by private expenditure in current prices. Moreover, they indicate that the indirect effects of these stocks, as represented by the level or the percentage change in the level of interest rates, are very weak or perverse. However, they also suggest, especially in the first differences, that autonomous expenditure had a more potent direct association with total private expenditure in current prices throughout most of the period; though to be sure the actual amount of autonomous expenditure was fairly well correlated with the lagged financial stocks and particularly the lagged stock of private credit. In current prices then, the income-expenditure approach to the determination of aggregate private sector demand seems to warrant particular consideration on the basis of this examination. Nevertheless, in constant prices, each one of the financial stocks seems to outperform autonomous expenditure as a predictor of the real level of economic activity; moreover, in the first differences of the stocks and the expenditure flows or in the percentage changes, this real financial effect seems to be even more dominant, particularly the real credit effect, if only for the reason that after the first period the real autonomous expenditure effect seems to fade away completely. The empirical evidence suggests that the income expenditure effect seems to work best in current prices whereas the real balance quantity theory or credit availability effect seems to work best in constant prices.[1]

[1] This result might be partly explained by the argument that the process of financialization fosters a gradual lengthening of the realizable discountable time horizons of purchasers and producers. This facilitates the process of capital deepening and the application of more sophisticated cost-saving productive techniques, thereby tending to stimulate the growth of real output in the Böhm Bawerk tradition. Whereas, in contrast, though the growth of autonomous expenditure stimulates aggregate demand considerably, its immediate effect on the real supply schedule is much less so that it induces a price rise rather than a real increase in output. It should be noted that from 1920 on, Government expenditure was by far the largest component of autonomous expenditure; as a consequence it might be expected that the 'pay off' in terms of growth of real productivity would be somewhat protracted. This argument might be couched in traditional demand-supply relationships in which the interaction of the two schedules determined the price level measured on the ordinate and the real amount demanded and supplied on the abscissa. 'Financialization' tends to push both schedules out to the right and to make them more elastic by lengthening the feasible planning time horizons of buyers and sellers. Autonomous expenditure has the effect of mainly pushing the demand schedule to the right and leaving the supply relatively unaffected; therefore, it is a more potent determinant of demand pull inflation than a catalyst which induces a fairly prompt increase in real output.

6 Conclusion: Some Historical Findings and Some Theoretical and Practical Implications

The end-year balance sheet data of leading UK financial institutions which are set out in the Appendix, the empirically couched description of their development which is represented in the first three chapters of this book, and the results of quantitative tests of various models of financial portfolio preferences and of private expenditure decisions should complement the reviving interest in the growth and role of the financial sector in the UK. The data provide a considerable amount of the necessary statistical material to make assessments. An inspection of the descriptive section suggests that there is a need to make such assessments; the revealed record is at times considerably different from that which one would expect either from reading the literature or from appraisal of the theoretical structures which have underwritten various Government policies. Moreover, the results of the quantitative tests of certain models of financial behaviour and of private expenditure decisions indicate that this need may be quite pressing. In particular, the degree of association between the levels of certain financial stocks and certain expenditure flows, or the change in these levels and the change in these flows, is sizeable enough to warrant a thorough investigation simply on the pragmatic basis of national macro-economic management. This study indicates that account should be taken of the role the financial sector plays in influencing activity in the product markets.

While this study, like other recent empirical studies of the role of the financial sector conducted in both the US and the UK, indicates a need for a reappraisal as well as an explicit incorporation of financial factors in models of aggregate demand management, it, like them, contains information which might make this reappraisal and this incorporation easier to achieve. Such considerations and approaches are set out below in more detail.

The data in the Appendix, the text, and the various tables and graphs in the first three chapters provide a fairly comprehensive descriptive account of the growth of several leading UK financial institutions' assets and liabilities, an account which reflects to a large extent the evolution of the UK financial sector over the 1880–1962 period. In the next two chapters, the data are used to examine various theories which purport to explain certain bank and non-bank asset preferences, the growth of the money supply, and the effect which certain financial variables (money, credit or the rate of interest) have on the level or the change in the level of economic activity. Neither the empirical record nor the results which have been derived from it, however, should be regarded as definitive. Nevertheless, the data should provide a basis, and the results should indicate the avenues of an approach which should serve to make a more accurate assessment of the growth and role of the UK financial sector during the chosen time interval.

Chapter 1 provides a qualitative account of certain environmental developments which undoubtedly influenced the chosen financial institutions and the financial markets between 1880 and 1962. The World Wars, Government stimulus to building and to the National Savings movement, and the official changes in the various incentives and controls relating to the placement and disposition of household financial savings obviously had a significant impact on the overall growth and on the composition of these savings and of institutional investments. So, for that matter, did the establishment of certain trade associations, and the special inter-institutional group relationships which tended to establish market-sharing arrangements – arrangements which, when reinforced by Government directives and increasing concentration within each of the sub-groups of institutions, tended to make the financial markets somewhat uncompetitive and to blunt movements towards financial innovation. In turn, the emerging gaps in the savings-lendings process, such as shortfalls in mortgage credits, medium-term credits, consumer credits, ship-building and agricultural credits, usually were only partly filled, and then only as a result of direct or indirect state sponsorship. This was the case until the influx of foreign money and foreign institutions in the post-1958 period broke the power of the domestically based financial cartels and made their participants compete more actively. Over all, the account in this chapter suggests that as the period progressed mutual interdependence between the Government and the institutions, and between the various groups of the financial institutions, became well recognized, and that, moreover, the two World Wars and the subsequent reconstruction legislation tended to make the State's influence on this recognition and on the financial structure generally dominant. From 1914 on, the qualitative record indicates that the Government's decisions had an increasing impact on the UK financial system – the era of conscious state management of the financial sector's operations had begun.

The descriptive empirical records provided in the next two chapters tend to support this suggestion. They show, for example, what a profound impact the two World Wars had on the financial structure. Well over 50 per cent of the whole period increase in the currency stock, in bank deposits, and in the money supply occurred during the eleven years of hostilities. Nearly £3,000 million of the period's £5,000 million increase in the State's direct security sales to households were made during the wars. Just as significantly, the asset side of the balance sheets of the sample of financial institutions shows that they radically readjusted their portfolio strategy in order to accommodate the State's demands for finance during the emergencies.

In the following reconstruction periods, the empirical record again tends to substantiate the growing impact of the State's objectives. In the first period, the impact of the Cunliffe Committee's recommendations in 1917 – a rigid deflationary programme – is reflected by a sizeable reduction in the stock of currency, in the stock of bank deposits outstanding and in the size of the money supply over the next ten years. The annual average of the stock of coin and notes outstanding increased by less than 1 per cent between 1920 and 1939. Alternatively, the State's stimulus to the building industry and the accompanying encouragement it gave to the building societies, to the insurance companies and to the hire-purchase companies, which had hardly grown at all in the pre-1914 period, burgeoned. The shares and deposits of the first increased from £80 million to £711 million; the liabilities of the last increased from £1 million to £17 million; whereas life assurance company funds more than doubled over the same period. In the second reconstruction period much the same patterns were repeated. In the war, currency, bank deposits the money supply and National Savings instruments had grown rapidly. After the hostilities, the currency stock was again reduced; bank deposits grew much more slowly; the National Savings movement's growth was retarded; whereas the building societies, the insurance companies and the hire-purchase companies soon reattained their rapid peacetime levels of asset accumulation.

Besides buttressing the assessments made in Chapter 1 with an empirical foundation, the two descriptive chapters also yield some interesting information. They delineate the annual growth in the money stock, in savings deposits, in other near-money substitutes and in total encashable assets over the entire period, and they show also the changes in the market shares of each component of total encashable assets. Similarly, they trace out the amounts and market shares of each of the constituent institution's assets, and they show the amounts and the percentage shares of their total assets which these institutions invested in certain types of obligations – mortgages, bank advances, cash, Government securities, Treasury Bills and private credits. At a glance, these chapters demonstrate that the portfolio preferences of both the households and the institutions have not been constant over the years. Householders' preferences for near-money substitutes rather than deposits or currency obviously became more accentuated. The householders' preference for deposits with respect to their currency holdings have been quite variable. Similarly, the institutions' preferences for Government-issued as opposed to privately issued obligations changed markedly. In all, the chapters illustrate that over the period there was both a marked growth in the UK financial system and that the composition of this system changed. Total financial savings grew considerably faster than national income; an increasing proportion of these savings tended to be placed with the non-banking institutions; concurrently, relative to the banks, these other institutions became increasingly important both as sources of credit and as providers of relatively liquid savings instruments.

Besides its descriptive content, the material in these two chapters has theoretical implications. In theory, the presence of these changes indicates that the financial sector never achieved what has been represented as a stationary state, and, inasmuch as financial equilibrium was achieved, it was achieved in a dynamic and not in a static context. In this sense, aspects of the standard representations of the Keynesian model of the financial sector's effect are only of practical relevance if one takes account of yearly shifts as well as changes in slope of the *LM* curve – a consideration which is of some interest in view of the strong positive correlation between real private expenditure and the real value of the money stock as recorded in Chapter 5. It is in this dynamic context that the portrayal of gross domestic expenditure along with the money stock, the stock of total encashable assets and the stock of private credit outstanding on the various graphs in Chapter 2 was not accidental. It was done quite deliberately in order to represent the graphical association between this flow and these stocks in accord with the quantity theory or credit availability theory of expenditure determination. After all, it is in this context that financial factors are asserted to generate expenditure effects such as in the deficiency of savings models of the business cycle.

Given the nature of the financial environment as represented in the descriptive section, that is that the financial market was far from perfect and, as often as not, the condition of the market could be described as being in dynamic disequilibrium (there seems to be little evidence of any steady-state growth path), it seems that models which are designed to explain the nature of the revealed financial evolution (such as the change in various asset preferences or the growing dominance of non-banking financial institutions) or to represent the financial sector's effect on the spending decisions of the private sector should be cast in a dynamic context and structured to take account of the noted market imperfections. This type of assessment was attempted in the next two chapters.

In these two chapters, 4 and 5, the models which were designed to explain the represented asset preferences, the change of the money supply, the change in the amount of financial institutions' private credits, and the impact which certain financial variables (money, credit, interest rates) have on aggregate private expenditure in current and in constant prices are tested using an ordinary least squares estimating procedure as applied to a single equation. Within the limitations of the estimating procedure, the results are quite interesting; pertinently they are directly comparable with the results of similar tests conducted by Friedman, Meiselman and Shearer in the United States, and by Walters, Kavanagh, Barrett, Clayton and Brechling in the UK.

Chapter 4 represents the results of single equation models which were designed to estimate income velocity, various household and financial institutions' relative asset preferences, the change in the money supply, and the levels of non-bank financial institutions' private credits outstanding in selected time periods – 1880–1962, 1880–1914, 1920–39 and 1946–62. The findings are interesting, though the single equation estimating approach should be replaced by a simultaneous equation estimating procedure in order to obtain a more reliable assessment.

The estimates of income velocity produces a very good fit in the last two sub-periods, and it is interesting to note that the retail price index was the most potent explanatory variable. Apparently, money holders are sensitive to loss engendered in the real purchasing power of these balances as the price level increases.

The estimates of household asset preferences, as expressed by the ratio of the holdings of one type of interest-earning asset with respect to their holdings of some other interest-earning financial asset, indicate that these relative preferences are quite sensitive to the difference in the net of tax returns paid on such assets. This finding indicates that the presence of such yield differentials has a considerable impact on the composition of financial savings; though, as an exception, the composition of bank deposits between time and current accounts seemed insensitive to this spread.

Institutional asset preferences were similarly sensitive. Both the long-term rate and the spread between the long-term and the short-term rates worked well as determinants of the banks' S_B/D and L_B/D ratios, and the standard rate of taxation was also effective. The sensitivity of the S_B/D and the L_B/D ratio to the level of the consol rate is in accord with Brechling and Clayton's findings that banks manage their portfolios in a pro-cyclical fashion. However, the impact of the two other explanatory variables, the spread between the long and the short interest rates and of the income tax rate, suggests that this pro-cyclical behaviour pattern is modulated as the authorities ease or tighten monetary or fiscal policy.

Finally, in the last section of the chapter, the application of the estimating procedure to the Gambino model of the determination of bank deposits which would have been induced by a change in high-powered money *ceteris paribus* produced rather paradoxical results. In the 1921–39 period, the model worked quite well – the coefficient of determination was 0·40; in the 1947–62 period, however, it did not work at all – the coefficient of determination was zero and even the regression coefficient of the explanatory variable, $\Delta H_t/(d+e)_{t-1}$, though not statistically significant, was negative instead of positive. This result, though only indicative, does suggest that economists have cause to be somewhat suspicious of the traditional model of the money supply in the UK after the Second World War. Perhaps Sayers's liquid asset multiplier approach would give better results (unfortunately the data to test this model are still unavailable) or perhaps, given the degree of support the authorities have given to the gilt-edged market, in the UK during these post-war years changes in the money supply were determined by demand rather than by supply conditions.

This view that the money supply is demand-determined rather than being exogenously proscribed by the central authorities is not so heretical either with respect to the history of economic thought or practice. As Friedman notes, in the United States the dependence of the domestic money stock on balance of payment conditions was quite possible in the pre-1914 conditions.[1] After all, that is how the gold-specific flow mechanism was meant to work through the money stock and therefore to domestic prices in order to re-create external equilibrium. Again in the UK the experience of the First and Second World Wars causes sundry observers to note that the war-induced financial demands were responsible for the marked increase in currency and deposits. In 1952, H. G. Johnson observed: '... it may be safely concluded that much the larger part of banking operations over the past decade consisted in the creation of deposits against government debt'.[2] Indeed, certain demand considerations, such as the assumption that demand conditions are such that the money stock will be taken up (e.g. there will be no excess reserves), are present in every known model of the money supply. In this sense, the positive and then the null results of the application of the modified traditional model of bank deposit determination are not surprising for these two periods – 1921–39 and 1947–62. Demand conditions varied markedly between them, with the result that one might expect supply considerations to be more important in the former period – particularly given the Government's deflationary policy – and to be less important in the latter. As an aside, the noted contrasting findings, of course, underline one of the main weaknesses of the estimating procedure – that is, the strong *ceteris paribus* assumption of the single equation approach that the demand or supply conditions, depending on what one is estimating, adjust as necessary.

In much the same vein, the answer to the question whether the explanatory variables in Chapter 5, the money stock, encashable assets, private credits, interest rates and autonomous expenditure, may really be regarded as independent variables, independent of the dependent expenditure flow they are held to determine, is generally negative. As Friedman and Schwartz point out when they appraise the role the money stock played in the US economy: 'Changes in the money stock are therefore a consequence as well as an independent source of change in money income and prices ...'[3] As a consequence, unless for instance the quantity of money '... can be shown to be a stable function of a few key variables, [it] ... must be a subordinate and not a strategic element in both the explanation and the control of economic activity'.[4] The same considerations hold for the other independent variables – they should either be regarded as being predetermined or accurately estimated along with the variable they are designed to explain or predict if accurate estimates of their actual roles are to be obtained.

Notwithstanding these considerations the results contained in Chapter 5 are of interest. As in Friedman and Meiselman's work and in Walters and Barrett's in the UK, they suggest the money stock has a direct impact on future income and prices. 'Changes in the money stock ... once they occur ... produce in their turn still further effects on income and prices.'[5] Similarly they suggest that the stock of encashable assets and slightly more certainly that the stock of private credit advanced by the financial institutions have a similar lagged impact on future private expenditure. In other words, no matter how these 'independent' variables were determined, to the extent that the regressions show that they have a lagged direct impact on the next period's private expenditure in current prices, they, along with product market variables, such as autonomous expenditure, should be included in models which are designed to predict the aggregate level of economic activity.

In constant prices, the results of the regressions in Chapter 5 are perhaps even more indicative, as no matter which part of the whole period is examined, the findings consistently suggest that the lagged value of the money stock, of encashable assets, or of private credit have a potent influence on the subsequent level of real economic activity. Certainly these results are open to statistical and behavioural criticisms. The fact that both the dependent and most of the independent variables were deflated

[1] M. Friedman and A. J. Schwartz, *A Monetary History of the United States 1867–1960* (Princeton University Press, 1963), p. 695.

[2] H. G. Johnson, 'Clearing bank holdings of public debt, 1930–50', *Reprint Series*, No. 54 (Cambridge University Press, 1952), p. 6.

[3] M. Friedman and A. J. Schwartz, op. cit., p. 695.

[4] H. G. Johnson, 'Monetary theory and policy', *Surveys of Economic Theory*, I (London: Macmillan, 1967), p. 15.

[5] M. Friedman and A. J. Schwartz, op. cit., p. 695.

through by the same price index may be shown to introduce spurious correlation, though the theoretical significance of this bias is not of much note unless the price index used contains large errors which by the deflating process are then inserted in both sides of the equation.[1]

On a more fundamental level, one may argue like Friedman, who, incidentally, along with Meiselman obtained similar results with respect to the relationship between real money balances and real consumption expenditure, that there is much more reason to believe that in constant prices, it is the level of real expenditure which determines the size of the real balances held rather than the other way round. In other words, the real financial stock rather than the real expenditure flow should be looked on as the dependent variable. Nevertheless, and though this criticism of these real balance or real credit effect findings is certainly as valid as Friedman's own criticism of his quantity theory findings – that the money stock in current prices is partly demand-determined, again, and using his own argument in which he justifies his approach, it is interesting to see that the actual level of the money stock, of encashable assets, or of credit, all measured in constant prices, is well associated with the level of consumption expenditure or of total private expenditure in the subsequent period also measured in constant prices. In turn, this interest is accentuated, when one examines the role that autonomous expenditure played in the constant price regression models. Except in the first period, 1881–1914, the results show that it played no significant role in determining the level of real consumption in either the same or the subsequent period. In effect, these findings in constant prices suggest that financial factors are now more closely associated with real levels of economic activity than they are with the level of this activity measured in current prices – an observation which has interesting theoretical implications.

In substance, the empirical findings in this chapter indicate that it is probably unwise to disregard the possible disequilibrium expenditure effects which may be engendered by a change in liquid asset holdings or of credit availability. They suggest that even simple equation models of aggregate private expenditure are reasonably predictive when financial stocks are included as explanatory variables. Period by period over a long time interval the expenditure effects of the lagged level of some financial stock are consistently shown to have the *a priori* expected positive impact on private expenditure. Moreover, though there is some variability in the size of the regression coefficients of the explanatory variables, this variability is often quite small in the constant price relationships. Finally, in keeping with the last observation, the results imply that the postulated relationship between the levels of such financial stocks and the concurrent or subsequent flow of private expenditure is much more direct than is often imagined. The impact of certain financial variables is only partially siphoned off through price level variations. The real amount of private expenditure undertaken in any period is shown to be strongly enough correlated with the level of the real values of these stocks to warrant detailed consideration.

The consideration which the results seem to warrant should not necessarily be constrained to a theoretical reappraisal of the role the financial sector plays in a dynamic adjustment process as coupled with a more sophisticated quantitative assessment of their effects. To a modest extent, it seems that the findings, and particularly those which are supported by other similar types of empirical studies, could well be used as a guide for practical policy formation in the UK now, given that some policies seem to have been applied without much preliminary empirical investigation – for instance the selective employment tax or even the common application of the traditional tools of monetary regulation. The type of information which may be derived from these explanatory estimations has some immediate practical application in the sense that it gives an quantitative prediction of what the effect of the measure will be.

For example, the historical record suggests and the subsequent single equation least squares tests of household and institutional portfolio preferences confirm that these preferences are sensitive to the existence of interest rate differentials. In effect, to the extent that the State is interested in such asset management considerations, and,

[1] As an exercise designed to test the extent of the spurious correlation induced by the deflation of the independent and dependent variables by the same price index, I selected two series of random numbers, deflated them through by the price index used, and regressed one upon another. In addition, I regressed one of the random number series on the other, and I transformed both sets of series into first differences, into logs and into first differences in the logs, and regressed the deflated and undeflated series on each other, both for the whole period, 1880–1962, and for each of the sub-periods. In the whole period, no significant correlation was found between the two sets of undeflated random numbers however transformed. In contrast, for the whole period, the correlation between the deflated series was 0·54 when untransformed; it was 0·16 in the first differences; it was 0·37 in the logs and 0·01 in the first differences in the logs. In the sub-periods, however, the induced correlation dropped markedly, and it rarely exceeded the correlation recorded between the transformed or untransformed undeflated series of random numbers for the same time period.

in particular, to the extent that the State is interested in assuring a firm market for its own obligations, it should take account of the impact of these differentials in framing its policies. In particular, to the extent that the Government is interested in stimulating its National Savings programme, the record suggests that the programme will be very effective so long as the State ensures that the rewards offered for such savings are fully competitive. In this sense, there would seem to be a good case for making such a favourable rate of return very explicit and for regulating the National Savings premium, say yearly, along with the budget, in accord with the State's needs to attract more or hold on to existing funds.

In much the same way in the task of monetary regulation, that is to the extent the central bank is interested in regulating the stock of money, of total encashable assets, or of the total stock of credit that the banks and the non-bank financial institutions are likely to make available to the private sector, the Bank of England should accept the fact that relative asset preferences must be looked at as being economic variables unless they may be constrained through decree (quantitative credit ceilings). As pertinently, in designing its monetary policies, it should take account of the above results, and perhaps those of Brechling and Clayton or Shearer which show that such preferences may be in part explained by movements in interest rates, the level of income taxation, by the pressure of private demand for financial accommodation or the degree of tightness in the financial markets. To be sure, the effectiveness of such policies which bear these considerations in mind might be somewhat erratic. There may well be a tendency to undershoot or overshoot the official target; nevertheless, the chances of hitting this target in any planning period would seem to be considerably improved as compared with neglecting to give such factors any stochastic consideration.

In the area of expenditure regulation the findings seem indicative enough to warrant incorporation within the official strategy of regulating the pace of economic activity. The evidence suggests that in an empirical setting, that is out of the stationary state conjectures of armchair musing, financial factors play a role in the determination of consumption and private expenditure plans as measured in current or constant prices. As such, and given that the State believes that it is its duty to regulate private expenditure, there seems to be no good reason why the State should neglect the role of such variables which preliminary surveys show may account for 30 or 40 per cent (and in some cases more) of the reduction in the residual variance of expenditure forecasts. This argument for a more positive consideration of financial factors in national economic planning is strengthened by the ease with which the State may exercise its control over certain financial variables in the UK.

Certainly, the case for much fine tuning on the basis of the results of the private expenditure and financial stock relationships in current prices might be called questionable on the basis of the findings in this study in the 1947–62 period. The regressions of the change or the percentage change of consumption or of total private expenditure on the change or the percentage change of various financial stocks (money, encashable assets, private credits) were decidedly unsatisfactory. Nevertheless, though such changes in financial factors were shown to be ineffective determinants of the change in current expenditure, so too was the change in autonomous expenditure. Moreover some of the changes in the financial variables, particularly private credit, and the change in autonomous expenditure were shown to have had an impact in early periods. In effect, given that the regression relationships between the levels of these financial stocks and the level of the flow of the subsequent year's private expenditure are fully significant in the period after the Second World War, it would seem that the null results obtained in the differences are most likely to be a product of the impact of official intervention (rationing, wage and price controls) and other exogenous developments (devaluation, changes in the terms of trade, the growth of administrative pricing) than to any major defect in the basic behavioural relationship.

This finding seems to be substantiated by the recorded results of the regressions between the changes or the percentage changes in the various financial stocks and the changes or percentage changes in the two measures of private expenditure in constant prices. In all periods, one or other of the financial stocks worked well as a determinant of private expenditure. In particular, the percentage change in the stock of private credit was shown to be consistently quite influential. Moreover, and fitting in with the results obtained by Keran of the Federal Reserve Bank of St Louis, some recent tests I have done of the relationship between the change in consumption expenditure and the change in the money stock in current prices in the post-1947 period have produced significant results too. In the 1948–66 period, for instance, regressing the annual change of consumption on the annual change in the money stock, the regression coefficient of $\Delta M'_t$ was 1·057; its t-ratio was 4·4 and the $\overline{Rsq}$ and DW statistics were 0·55 and 1·2 respectively. In the 1948–68 period, and this time using money stock and expenditure flow statistics as recorded in International Financial Statistics, again I obtained similar and significant results. The regression coefficients of the $\Delta M'_t$ was 1·070; its *t*-ratio was 6·1 and the $\overline{Rsq}$ and *DW* statistics were 0·672 and 1·37 respectively.[1]

Finally, with respect to the real amount of resources which the private sector uses per income period, as noted the regression results suggest that these amounts are closely correlated with the amounts of various financial stocks outstanding as measured in constant prices in the preceding year. These findings held in the first differences as well. These degrees of association seem to be substantial enough to warrant attention in national economic programmes which are designed to regulate the share and perhaps the composition of real resources this sector uses in any time period. Certainly, though the regression coefficients are quite stable, say for lagged values of private credit in constant prices or for the changes in its value, the results should only be regarded as indicative. Indicative of a reasonably based presumption that if the Government is able to find the means of regulating the real value of the credit made available to the private sector, it should be able to develop an additional policy tool which the record suggests would have a fairly prompt impact on the level of real private expenditure.

Over all, the data, the descriptive section and the inferences which may be drawn from the regression results in Chapters 4 and 5 indicate that the UK financial structure grew, changed and had a varying impact over the eighty-three years. Part of the growth and the subsequent changes were undoubtedly due to the long-run change in the UK's economic position, to the sudden shock of wars and to the corresponding growth in the influence of the Government sector. Part of the growth and subsequent changes were undoubtedly endogenously induced, however. Along with the standardization of working hours, with the acceptance of the principle of unemployment, industrial accident and health insurance, as well as the broadening demand for home ownership, a varied and complex set of demands for financial services was set up, services which could be readily provided once the ground rules, and hence the investors' confidence, in the financial institutions had been established.

As noted, most of the necessary legislative framework had been laid by 1880. From then on, the record suggests that in peace and war the financial sector played a progressively more important role in helping to reallocate both private and public savings to their preferred uses, and, as these uses changed, given that the borrowing and lending activities of the leading institutions had become compartmentalized, the influence of any particular set of institutions in this process changed also. In the early part of the period, the descriptive section of the text shows that the banking sector exerted a dominant influence in the financial market-place. Fittingly the statistical results show that their liabilities, mainly bank deposits, were well correlated with the different forms of private expenditure in both current and constant prices up to 1914. In the inter-war period and in the post-1945 period, however, the descriptive section of the text shows that the banks' dominance of the financial markets waned. Fittingly, again, the statistical results show that as the banks' influence waned, other forms of assets, such as total encashable assets or total private institutional credits tended to outperform the money stock as a determinant of the two chosen forms of private expenditure.

In all, the record suggests that in seeking to explain the growth, or to assess the role of the UK financial system, it may be very misleading to be dogmatic. The financial system, that is the institutions, the markets and the borrowers and lenders, is continually making and being influenced by innovations. As new primary or secondary securities gain acceptance, new lines of credit are being laid. As a consequence, it is perhaps dangerous to set up a functional definition for some particular finance stock, say money or certain institutional private credits, just because over a certain period of time this easily identifiable stock works well in a financial stock-expenditure-flow relationship. When it is functionally defined, for instance, as Sayers notes over time, 'there is no hard and fast line between what is and what is not money'.[2] There are no immutable rules to follow, other than to note that the financial sector matters and to make assessments of its impact which take account of important recent developments as well as of past market conditions.

[1] I obtained similar significant results in processing my own updated data – see Appendix – and correlating these with expenditure flows extracted from I.F.S. Regressing the ΔC_t on the $\Delta M'_t$ for the 1948–66 period the regression coefficient of $\Delta M'_t$ was 1·106, its *t*-ratio was 4·4, and the $\overline{Rsq}$ and *DW* statistics were 0·52 and 1·49 respectively. Moreover, I obtained even more significant results when I regressed the change in private expenditure (ΔY_t) on the change in gross private credit ($\Delta L'_t$) over the 1950–66 period. The regression coefficient of the one explanatory variable $\Delta L'_t$ was 0·557; its *t*-ratio was 6·8, and the $\overline{Rsq}$ and *DW* statistics were 0·72 and 1·87 respectively.

[2] R. S. Sayers, *Central Banking after Bagehot* (Oxford: Clarendon Press, 1958), p. 5.

Appendix

SECTION 1 UK Banks 1880–1966
Tables (A)1.1–(A)1.14

SECTION 2 UK Non-Bank Financial Intermediaries 1880–1966
Tables (A)2.1–(A)2.12

SECTION 3 UK Money, Liquid Assets, National Savings and Institutional Private Credit Series 1880–1966
Tables (A)3.1–(A)3.8

Appendix

A preliminary edition of the attached tables was issued in mimeograph form in August 1965.[1] Since then, the material has been updated to include the four years from 1963 to 1966, and has undergone revision in accord with advice from the Bank of England and the suggestions of a number of my colleagues. The coverage of the UK financial system is still not complete, and the data, drawn from institutional balance sheets, not yet free of errors. The familiar problems of time and funds imposed limitations of scope; as importantly, inadequacies in the early accounting practices reflected in many of the recorded institutions' end-year balance sheets created difficulties in splicing these early accounts with those presented in later years. Nevertheless, the coverage is sufficiently comprehensive, and the recorded statistics sufficiently accurate, for the revised series to constitute a guide to both the evolution of the UK financial system and the growth of several important groups of financial institutions over the period 1880–1966. These revised series should, in fact, supply a good deal of the raw material necessary for empirical studies related to either the growth and role of the system itself or to the function and development of particular sets of institutions within it.

Though the statistics should be useful as a basis for further investigation (and they have been compiled with this aim in mind), before they are used the sources and notes accompanying each of the relevant tables should be examined, and the introductory text at the beginning of each section should be carefully read. This introductory text outlines the contents in each section; it depicts the more general difficulties encountered in their collection, and it illustrates the degree of comparability between some of the data in these tables and similar data which may be derived from other published sources. The sources are of obvious importance in giving the precise derivation of the data in the tables, and in supplying, where published material is absent, the methods of deriving the estimates. The notes explain the reasons for any discontinuities and provide additional information to assist interpretation.

When using these tables, one should realize that the reported statistics provide only a rough guide to the actual values of the time series one is interested in, and that the accuracy of this guide deteriorates as it goes back through time and as one turns one's attention away from the recorded institutional liabilities and begins to inspect the asset side of the balance sheets. This partly reflects the lack of official interest in quantifying the operations of the financial system in the pre-Radcliffe Committee period, and it is partly also a product of the vagaries of financial accounting practices for balance sheet purposes both within and among the various groups of institutions. As a consequence, the reader may with justification feel that some of the data, particularly those based on rough estimators, are not sufficiently accurate for his purposes. Nevertheless, and noting that such estimates are clearly distinguished from the data which have been obtained from published sources, he should find the residual data useful if only to provide a basis for his own estimating procedures: e.g. building societies' holdings of Government securities will not exceed their total holdings of investments.

As noted above, financial accounting varied considerably both within and among the various groups of institutions. Before 1920, for instance, several banks included acceptances with bills discounted; others merged discounts with investments, and some incorporated their discounts under the caption 'Cash, Money at Call and at Short Notice'. The combined building societies' balance sheet was compiled from end-year balance sheets which were struck up at widely different dates over the whole period; moreover, it was not until 1958 that such balance sheets were obtainable in a form in which their holdings of Government securities were separated from their total holdings of investments. Again, the balance sheets of the assurance companies are far from satisfactory. No aggregate accounts were published by the Board of Trade between 1915 and 1921 or from 1938 to 1944; these figures had to be estimated. Moreover, owing to Board of Trade regulations, the actual data reported in these accounts are probably based on a different system of valuation from that chosen by most of the other institutions. The word 'probably' is important, as there are no clear-cut rules to guide the other institutions on how to value their assets. Finally, until the early 1950s none of the available consolidated balance sheet statements for any of the groups of institutions contained information on their holdings of Treasury Bills; as a

[1] D. K. Sheppard, 'Financial statistics – UK banks 1880–1962'; 'Financial statistics – UK financial intermediaries 1880–1962'; and 'A provisional money, liquid asset and credit series for the UK 1880–1962', *Birmingham University Discussion Papers*, Series A, Nos. 63, 64 and 65 (August 1965).

consequence, the recorded institutional holdings of such bills in the pre-1950 years are based on estimates.

There were further difficulties in compilation. Frequently, different issues of the same basic source for much of the data – *The Economist*'s 'Banking Supplement' or 'Banking Number', and the Board of Trade or Central Statistical Office's *Annual Abstract of Statistics* – gave different totals for the same item in identical years. On such occasions it was assumed that the more recent statistics were more accurate, and the older series was discarded.

Again, certain developments during the period induced distortions that could not be isolated and identified. Other developments and their effects were clearly located and in these cases the resulting discontinuity could be shown in the tables. For example, after the establishment of the Irish Republic in 1922 the branches of the Post Office Savings Bank and the trustee savings banks in Ireland fell outside the UK; years passed before the assets and liabilities of these institutions were excluded from the UK totals. This difficulty did not arise in assembling the banking data as the separate balance sheets of all Irish banks were available over the whole period. As a result, the effect of the separation is shown as of one date – actually 1920 rather than 1922, as this fits in with the division made in the collection of national income statistics. The same type of adjustment for a discontinuity in the series was made in 1891 in order to reflect the fact that *The Economist*'s 'Banking Number' did not publish the consolidated balance sheet figures of the private banks until that year.

Passing over the problems in the compilation of the tables, it should be noted that much of the formative work which made this collection possible had already been done. The special sections in *The Economist* provided the main source of the banking data up to the early 1950s; though the Radcliffe and the Macmillan Committee Reports, along with a very useful study by H. G. Johnson were valuable supplementary sources. Published official documents provided most of the source material for the non-banking financial institutions, and these in turn were well complemented by such useful books as Mitchell and Deane's *Abstract of British Historical Statistics* and Horne's *A History of Savings Banks*. In addition, a considerable amount of unpublished information was provided by various public agencies, private corporations and individuals. These contributions particularly those of the Bank of England, the Royal Mint, the Registrar of Friendly Societies, the London Stock Exchange, the Secretary of the Inspection Committee of Trustee Savings Banks, and the General Manager of the Co-operative Wholesale Society Bank, filled in a large number of the gaps in the published record.

As noted, the data are presented in three sections:

(1) UK Banks 1880–1966.
(2) UK Non-Bank Financial Intermediaries 1880–1966.
(3) UK Money, Liquid Assets, National Savings and Institutional Private Credit Series 1880–1966.

Each section is introduced by a short note setting out some of the more general facts which should be considered when examining it. Moreover, the tables in each section have adequate footnotes, so that inasmuch as the raw data were adjusted to take account of the deficiencies noted above, the corrections, the estimates, the splicing factors and the estimators are delineated.

Section 1. UK Banks 1880–1966

Table (A)1.1 is a consolidation of Tables (A)1.2–(A)1.5, which in turn represent the end-year balance sheet figures of the joint-stock banks of England and Wales, the joint-stock banks of Ireland and (from 1920) of Northern Ireland, the joint-stock banks of Scotland, and then a consolidation of the balance sheet figures of some private banks along with the balance sheet figures of both the Yorkshire Penny Bank and the Co-operative Wholesale Society Bank. The definitions of the various column headings are relatively straightforward with one exception; the heading of column 11, Treasury deposit receipts, which took the form of a special deposit levy between 1940 and 1951. These deposits, renamed special deposits, were called again in the 1960s as shown in Tables (A)1.1, (A)1.2 and (A)1.4. In addition, it should also be noted that column 3 in the first four tables and column 2 in the fifth table do not include column 8 (column 7 in Table (A)1.5), 'Acceptances and Endorsements or Customer Liability for the same', as this inclusion would lead to some double counting and therefore exaggeration of the banks' liabilities. In essence, the banks as a group undoubtedly discounted a large portion of the bills they collectively accepted, and the bills they accepted are already incorporated in their balance sheets along with their other holdings of discounted bills.

The banks which have been incorporated in these five tables were all UK-based banks engaged primarily in banking business in the UK. No colonial or foreign-owned joint-stock banks which had London offices were included; in fact a few domestically based banking institutions were excluded. Hambros, for instance, formerly the British Bank of Northern Commerce, was omitted as it was carried in *The Economist*'s 'Banking Supplement' and in *The Bankers' Almanac and Year Book* as a 'British Bank Trading Abroad' over much of the period. The Birmingham Municipal Bank was also excluded; this bank is much more akin to a savings bank, or a savings and loan association, in that its depositors could not draw cheques against their accounts; the amount they could withdraw on demand was limited by statute; and the bank's investment of these deposits was placed either with the National Debt Commissioners or in certain prescribed forms – such as loans to the City of Birmingham Corporation. On rather similar grounds – in that its operations became increasingly dominated by the public sector, and nationalization ensued in 1946 – the Bank of England was omitted too; its balance sheet appears separately as Table (A)1.12. Finally, of course, a few small banks such as the Scottish Co-operative Wholesale Society Bank had to be left out on the grounds of consistency. This bank, founded in 1948, took over the banking business of several small co-operative banks and lending societies, such as the People's Bank. Unfortunately, the balance sheet data of its predecessors for the 1891–1914 and 1937–50 periods seem to be well intertwined with the accounts of the Co-operative Retail and Wholesale Trading Societies. However, as the Scottish Co-operative Society Bank's total assets did not exceed £20 million in the post-1950 period, this omission is not particularly serious. In sum, it seems unlikely that the consolidated accounts of the other omitted banks would alter the series in any substantial way, given the concentration in the British banking system – the eleven London Clearing Banks' total assets alone accounted for over 80 per cent of total banking assets from 1920 onwards.

Table (A)1.6 represents the *Percentage Distribution of the Combined UK Banks' Balance Sheets*; Tables (A)1.8 and (A)1.9 detail respectively, the *End-year* and *Annual Average Balance Sheets of the London Clearing Banks*.

The first column of Table (A)1.6 duplicates the third column of Table (A)1.1; it depicts the gross liabilities, excluding acceptances and endorsements of the sample of UK banks from 1880 to 1966. The next three columns indicate the percentage market shares of this total which the banks of England and Wales, the banks of Scotland and the banks of Ireland respectively held over the period – the residual of these three columns when subtracted from 100 per cent gives the share of the private banks, of the Co-operative Wholesale Society Bank and of the Yorkshire Penny Bank in the post-1890 period. The other columns indicate the percentage share of column 1, the total liabilities or assets of the consolidated banking system, the banks as a group owed in certain forms of liabilities, deposits, notes in circulation, etc., or, alternatively, invested in certain forms of assets – investments and loans and advances. The table illustrates in considerable detail the distribution in percentage terms of the banking system's asset preferences.

Tables (A)1.8 and (A)1.9, presenting respectively the end-year and the annual average balance sheet position of the London Clearing Banks, indicate when taken together, the degree of comparability between annual average and end-year UK banking statistics over the years. For example, the end-year deposit figures are invariably larger than the annual average deposit figures, and the margin is such (£300 million in 1950 and £600 million in 1962) that quite obviously the use of these end-year data to compute the money stock makes the year-end money estimates in this appendix considerably larger than the annual average money stock figures which have been published elsewhere.

Tables (A)1.7, (A)1.10–(A)1.13 and (A)1.14, complete this section. Table (A)1.7, the balance sheet data of the Co-operative Wholesale Society Bank (kindly provided by the Bank's head office) has been included as these statistics have not been published in this form elsewhere. Table (A)1.10, *Bank Advances in Great Britain*, indicates how banks have allocated their loans by end use in the last twenty-odd years of the period. Table (A)1.11 gives details on the volume in millions of pounds of certain forms of cheque clearings. Table (A)1.12 represents the Bank of England balance sheet figures. Table (A)1.13 presents the combined balance sheet figures of three leading discount houses, and Table (A)1.14 presents the compound rates of growth of all bank assets, of the various groups of bank assets and of debit clearings and bank advances over selected time periods.

While the tables provide a considerable amount of information which should be useful for an analysis of the operations of the UK banking sector over a long time period, the reader should take prior note of two additional points. The first is certainly the more important: in the post-1962 period, the tables contained in the Central Statistical Office's *Financial Statistics* provide a more comprehensive and accurate coverage of banking sector statistics. Its publication depicts the balance sheet positions of *all* banks which operate in the UK, not just the British-based banks, as well as presenting the full balance sheet positions of the discount houses and the accepting houses. Moreover, it provides these data for various dates during the year, as well as at the end of the year or near to it. It is partly for this reason that the analysis in the previous sections of the text was terminated in 1962.

The second point is less important though in some ways more interesting as it implies that certain sections of the data in this table are less reliable than series published elsewhere. It would seem that the gross deposit figures in column 4 of Table (A)1.1 should be quite similar to those derived by Higonnet from apparently the same basic source from 1891 onwards; moreover, presumably the deposit figures in this column should bear a close resemblance to the Bank of England's deposit figures which were published for the 1905–31 period.

Higonnet's series, however, were derived from estimates made by the compilers of *The Economist*'s 'Banking Number' and not directly from the consolidated balance sheet statistics *The Economist* published in the 'Banking Number' during the 1880–1947 period. No doubt, if one could actually identify what these compilers incorporated (Higonnet indicates that they incorporated the note issue of all banks prior to some date in the 1890s), their series, when adjusted, would provide a more accurate deposit series than the one in Table (A)1.1. But in any case, after 1891 the discrepancy between the two series is quite small. For example, Table (A)1.1 shows total deposits to be £595 million in 1891, whereas Higonnet's series show them to be between £670 and £690 – a difference of between £75 million and £95 million; however this discrepancy is reduced by at least £38 million and possibly by an additional £14 million as Higonnet's series include all deposits at the Bank of England (shown as £38·2 million in 1891 in Table (A)1.12) and possibly the banks' note issue as well (shown as £14·4 million in column 6 of Table (A)1.1). In other words, the discrepancy between the deposits given in Table (A)1.1 and those extracted by Higonnet from *The Economist*'s estimates is between £23 million and £43 million – i.e. my figures are perhaps between 4 per cent and 8 per cent too low. In 1900 the deposit figures in Table (A)1.1, when adjusted for total Bank of England deposits, correspond closely to Higonnet's series giving a total of £799 million plus £50 million, or £849 million in total, as compared with Higonnet's estimate of total deposits of between £840 million and £850 million. In 1910, again the deposit figures given in Table (A)1.1 of £939 million when adjusted for the deposits at the Bank of England of £30·0 million agree with the estimates Higonnet gives: £970 million to £980 million.[1] In effect, the discrepancy between the two series is not large in the 1890s and it is barely recordable after 1900.

In much the same way, that is after making allowances for their composition, a detailed comparison of the gross deposit figures given in Table (A)1.1 and those given by the Bank of England in its *Statistical Summary* of November 1932 for the 1905–31 period shows that there is a close correspondence between these series as well. From 1905 to 1931, after adjusting the deposits given in Table (A)1.1 to include deposits at the Bank of England (other than 'Bankers' Deposits'), and from 1921 on adding in the deposits of the banks of Eire, the two series are very similar. They deviate from each other between ½ and 2 per cent over the entire period. In all but two years, 1905 and 1914, when the adjusted deposit figures in Table (A)1.1 were £3 million and £11 million less than those given in the *Statistical Summary*, the deposit figures in the table slightly exceeded those in the *Summary*. The amount of this excess suggests that the Bank of England figures did not include the deposits of the Co-operative Wholesale Society Bank over these years.

[1] B. R. Mitchell and Phyllis Deane, *Abstract of British Historical Statistics* (Cambridge University Press, 1962), p. 447.

TABLE (A)1.1 **United Kingdom Banks Combined Balance Sheets 1880–1966[1,6,7] (Figures for Bank of England excluded. Assets and liabilities £ millions[5])**

Year-End Approx. 31 Dec.[2]	*Banks*	*No. of Branches*[3]	*Total Assets and Total Liabilities*[4]	*Deposits and Other Accounts*	*Misc. Liabilities*	*Notes in Circulation*	*Paid-up Capital and Reserves*	*Acceptances and Endorsements*	*Premises and Other Assets*	*Cash, Money at Call and at Short Notice*		*Treasury Deposit Receipts or Special Deposits*	*Discounts*		*Investments*		*Loans and Advances and Other Accounts*
										Total	*Cash*		*Total*	*Treasury Bills*[9]	*Total*	*British Government and Government-Guaranteed*	
	1	2	3	4	5	6	7	8	9	10 A	10 B	11	12	13	14	15	16
1880	108	2712	432·3	342·4	4·7	12·7	72·5	21·5	7·5	74·1	**38·5**[10]	—	55·5	—	73·3	40·0	218·9
1881	112	2752	452·6	360·1	3·5	14·0	75·0	22·2	9·6	81·8	**42·5**	—	62·5	—	76·5	41·1	222·3
1882	119	2869	474·9	376·6	3·4	15·5	79·4	22·4	8·9	82·6	**42·8**	—	64·7	—	79·1	38·8	242·3
1883	123	2937	492·5	391·8	3·8	14·0	82·9	22·0	12·4	84·5	**43·6**	—	69·9	—	85·4	43·0	239·4
1884	126	2910	509·3	406·6	1·9	13·4	85·4	18·5	10·6	83·6	**43·1**	—	63·6	—	100·0	45·5	255·1
1885	129	2807	517·1	414·2	0·0	13·1	85·8	16·9	11·5	89·6	**45·9**	—	62·6	—	103·4	45·9	248·3
1886	128	2918	517·1	414·3	3·7	13·0	86·1	16·0	10·9	92·4	**47·6**	—	62·2	—	99·6	47·3	251·9
1887	128	3032	527·0	424·9	3·6	12·6	85·9	16·6	11·2	94·8	**48·5**	—	60·3	—	102·6	45·7	258·9
1888	130	3105	559·2	454·1	3·8	13·4	87·9	18·3	11·7	104·2	**53·4**	—	62·7	—	112·4	48·8	268·5
1889	122	3319	585·5	478·7	4·1	14·2	88·5	22·2	8·4	110·9	**56·8**	—	64·7	—	118·9	54·3	282·1
1890	123	3634	611·4	498·8	5·3	14·3	93·0	26·7	12·9	114·5	**58·6**	—	65·3	—	129·2	60·3	289·5
1891[8]	125	3685	641·4	523·8	11·2	13·9	92·5	19·5	12·7	121·2	**62·4**	—	62·8	—	137·1	64·7	307·4
1891	168	3685	725·2	594·8	11·2	14·4	104·8	22·1	12·7	139·2	**69·2**	—	64·2	—	164·5	74·8	342·2
1892	168	3776	739·6	608·1	11·1	14·0	106·4	26·4	15·2	144·5	**71·0**	—	66·8	—	172·1	79·4	339·3
1893	166	4003	732·1	600·5	10·9	14·0	106·7	24·9	14·8	138·9	**67·9**	—	60·1	—	169·9	81·1	347·3
1894	164	4120	763·3	632·2	10·4	14·2	106·5	25·9	14·8	161·8	**80·0**	—	65·2	—	175·4	77·7	345·1
1895	162	4204	810·8	677·1	12·1	14·8	106·8	30·2	16·0	167·7	**82·5**	—	69·7	—	187·3	78·1	368·3
1896	146	4576	834·6	700·7	12·7	14·6	106·6	28·1	17·0	163·4	**81·3**	—	69·7	—	192·6	77·2	392·4
1897	137	5180	856·4	721·7	13·2	14·8	106·7	28·2	17·0	170·8	**85·7**	—	67·3	—	195·2	74·2	405·8
1898	135	5335	885·6	749·4	11·6	15·1	109·5	25·3	17·4	183·2	**91·8**	—	66·6	—	195·9	74·2	420·7
1899	130	5486	913·7	774·3	13·1	15·5	110·8	27·9	17·8	183·9	**92·2**	—	68·6	—	197·9	75·0	442·4
1900	119	5375	941·7	798·9	14·2	15·8	112·8	26·6	20·6	196·1	**98·5**	—	68·9	**7·3**[10]	200·9	77·5	456·1
1901	115	5679	938·9	796·9	12·8	15·0	114·2	29·0	20·1	204·3	**102·6**	—	66·1	**9·0**	203·1	79·2	442·9
1902	108	5946	954·1	808·8	14·5	15·5	115·3	29·8	21·4	214·9	**108·3**	—	71·7	**9·1**	201·5	81·3	442·4
1903	102	6059	934·0	790·2	13·2	15·2	115·4	32·2	18·6	195·4	**98·3**	—	69·1	**9·1**	193·8	78·9	454·6
1904	98	6164	944·4	802·0	12·6	14·6	115·2	33·9	16·8	211·5	**106·7**	—	71·3	**9·1**	196·7	87·8	450·0
1905	95	6344	971·6	828·0	14·0	14·0	115·6	44·0	20·8	226·2	**114·1**	—	77·5	**9·1**	200·6	85·4	447·4
1906	90	6529	998·1	853·8	14·0	14·5	115·8	47·6	19·6	227·2	**114·6**	—	81·7	**8·4**	199·1	86·3	470·1
1907	86	6616	1003·6	861·8	12·5	14·5	114·9	50·2	19·9	225·9	**113·3**	—	82·5	**5·1**	194·9	85·8	478·8
1908	83	6754	1023·9	883·8	11·1	14·0	115·1	47·7	19·5	243·5	**123·3**	—	86·7	**5·5**	207·9	86·1	464·3
1909	77	6862	1039·8	899·6	11·8	14·0	114·4	47·6	19·3	251·3	**127·0**	—	86·2	**6·5**	212·5	80·7	469·2
1910	76	7086	1081·1	939·4	12·9	14·5	114·3	57·1	20·1	250·7	**127·2**	—	87·1	**6·4**	212·2	78·9	507·8
1911	75	7314	1118·0	977·6	11·3	14·6	114·5	55·1	24·6	269·0	**136·0**	—	100·1	**6·5**	212·7	78·2	510·9
1912	75	7485	1156·1	1012·3	13·5	15·1	115·2	68·9	25·6	277·3	139·6	—	109·1	**4·1**	208·0	74·2	531·5
1913	71	7747	1205·0	1059·4	13·8	16·0	115·8	69·1	26·7	299·4	151·9	—	119·3	**4·7**	205·4	70·3	552·3
1914	66	7815	1312·6	1163·2	14·0	20·6	114·8	55·0	28·2	346·3	224·4	—	115·3	**6·0**	241·0	100·4	581·3
1915	64	7981	1428·0	1272·4	14·0	27·9	113·7	67·7	31·4	338·9	230·5	—	85·7	**38·9**	437·2	298·9	534·8
1916	61	7944	1636·3	1473·4	15·7	34·9	112·3	76·0	28·7	461·4	320·5	—	166·7	**81·2**	452·2	340·4	526·5
1917	61	8019	1913·3	1736·6	18·0	41·6	117·1	71·9	24·7	536·4	320·8	—	248·6	**125·7**	474·7	371·6	628·3
1918	53	8598	2221·9	2024·5	14·1	56·3	127·0	64·3	34·5	623·9	373·5	—	389·8	**196·8**	531·9	421·9	640·8
1919	47	9328	2611·8	2398·2	14·6	57·5	141·5	159·6	23·9	594·3	423·7	—	320·7	**172·1**	617·0	513·6	1055·4
1920	44	9807	2771·2	2537·7	15·1	54·3	163·6	110·9	26·8	584·8	402·3	—	400·2	**164·4**	571·0	469·8	1177·4
1920	38	9156	2604·1	2397·6	15·1	37·3	154·1	110·3	26·2	551·5	379·9	—	392·9	**159·5**	508·2	417·5	1115·3
1921	38	9535	2620·1	2420·0	13·7	30·6	155·8	79·4	30·6	546·6	416·2	—	520·7	**290·7**	530·1	451·9	991·4
1922	41	9854	2461·2	2261·2	13·6	28·5	157·7	91·9	31·5	523·4	372·7	—	353·4	**207·3**	610·4	516·1	939·7
1923	37	10156	2408·0	2210·1	12·8	27·3	157·8	118·6	34·5	506·2	370·4	—	315·3	**158·8**	573·7	489·6	978·0
1924	35	10393	2397·9	2194·2	13·3	27·2	163·2	142·5	35·9	525·7	380·9	—	269·2	**115·9**	526·9	441·6	1039·1
1925	35	10661	2390·6	2184·3	12·8	26·2	167·3	136·3	37·1	528·5	377·0	—	256·0	**110·2**	469·0	390·4	1099·1
1926	34	10924	2432·6	2222·9	12·7	24·9	172·1	118·6	39·5	528·3	378·3	—	265·1	**123·4**	453·5	374·9	1145·8
1927	34	11225	2487·9	2274·7	14·0	25·3	173·9	150·7	41·0	584·3	367·1	—	263·8	**127·6**	436·3	353·8	1162·3
1928	34	11464	2570·9	2351·7	15·8	25·1	178·3	255·4	49·4	591·3	392·1	—	287·6	**128·3**	441·8	373·1	1199·1
1929	34	11704	2535·8	2314·5	15·8	25·2	180·3	197·1	48·3	571·6	384·4	—	253·1	**117·9**	439·8	357·7	1222·7
1930	34	11997	2622·9	2396·0	14·2	25·1	187·6	142·9	50·9	570·7	373·5	—	371·0	**190·5**	507·5	420·6	1125·1
1931	34	12154	2440·2	2225·5	13·0	24·7	177·0	121·4	58·0	501·6	335·0	—	290·5	**207·7**	516·8	427·8	1071·7
1932	34	11988	2722·2	2509·6	10·2	24·3	178·1	107·7	56·2	546·9	347·8	—	450·0	**349·6**	754·7	654·3	924·4
1933	34	12146	2697·8	2484·9	12·5	22·5	177·9	133·9	57·4	542·9	348·3	—	341·7	**265·7**	881·1	774·2	881·3

1935	33	12245	2891·3	2672·8	11·2	25·4	181·9	129·0	56·3	609·0	398·6	—	317·6	**198·8**	967·9	847·8	939·3
1936	33	12213	3072·2	2855·8	6·0	26·9	183·5	107·9	83·4	677·0	419·7	—	300·4	**196·9**	1026·5	904·7	1016·4
1937	32	12245	3113·2	2887·7	10·4	27·5	187·6	141·3	53·2	635·9	420·5	—	294·3	**175·5**	1005·1	885·3	1124·0
1938	31	12310	3034·3	2810·4	7·5	27·8	188·6	158·7	53·3	613·9	412·5	—	244·3	**143·9**	996·0	875·8	1121·9
1939	30	11857	3190·0	2961·5	11·1	30·9	186·5	137·9	53·9	672·9	452·5	—	347·8	**251·7**	974·6	840·6	1140·1
1940	30	11753	3595·4	3359·7	12·5	36·4	186·8	126·9	54·0	743·4	530·1	336·0	278·2	**187·9**	1154·0	1020·3	1033·6
1941	30	10574	4220·1	3973·8	9·8	47·3	189·2	132·0	50·9	812·8	616·0	797·5	183·8	**120·6**	1444·2	1338·5	920·5
1942	30	10197	4604·9	4345·3	10·3	60·3	189·0	107·7	50·4	882·7	675·1	943·0	212·5	**188·7**	1627·0	1514·5	885·1
1943	30	10122	5113·8	4840·4	11·6	69·0	192·5	120·1	49·5	968·3	747·6	1356·5	157·0	**133·9**	1729·6	1613·5	853·4
1944	30	10139	5726·2	5440·5	16·3	75·0	194·4	123·3	49·1	1100·5	820·5	1734·5	177·2	**151·8**	1795·3	1677·6	869·6
1945	30	10195	6107·6	5822·2	11·7	76·7	197·0	138·1	49·0	1199·8	872·3	1596·5	397·1	**338·1**	1934·2	1793·6	929·6
1946	30	10927	7058·2	6763·7	13·2	80·8	200·5	219·8	48·9	1428·4	911·5	1626·5	641·6	**547·6**	2193·7	2042·1	1118·2
1947	30	11192	7363·8	7073·9	8·4	78·7	202·8	280·1	113·5	1486·3	910·6	1342·0	825·4	**721·5**	2271·2	2108·9	1371·9
1948	30	11332	7663·5	7313·1	63·5	74·9	212·0	305·6	51·3	1252·6	652·5	1449·0	770·7	**598·6**	2226·6	2088·8	1542·2
1949	30	11423	7656·6	7306·3	62·0	75·7	212·6	313·3	48·2	1372·1	688·7	820·0	1138·1	**997·3**	2226·7	2082·7	1732·3
1950	28	11742	7831·5	7475·8	64·3	77·0	214·4	443·0	51·8	1408·6	703·0	476·5	1438·5	**1301·9**	2222·4	2079·2	1881·9
1951	28	—	7782·9	7464·8	21·9	82·8	213·4	536·8	52·3	1420·7	721·4	109·0	999·3	803·5	2598·8	2471·1	2161·3
1952	28	—	7907·1	7590·0	5·8	91·1	220·2	417·3	53·9	1402·0	751·3	—	1285·4	1211·9	2772·4	2648·3	1939·6
1953	27	—	8161·5	7848·3	3·2	96·6	213·4	363·6	57·6	1361·4	749·6	—	1450·3	1364·9	2946·4	2805·9	1877·1
1954	27	—	8503·1	8174·9	3·7	102·1	222·4	384·2	58·3	1417·8	799·8	—	1346·7	1221·3	3047·2	2887·6	2079·7
1955	26	—	8130·0	7782·8	3·3	109·1	234·8	515·4	60·4	1418·9	803·6	—	1446·4	1305·6	2648·8	2491·7	2033·7
1956	26	—	8168·2	7806·0	5·6	118·9	237·7	509·0	70·1	1422·1	818·8	—	1465·0	1309·5	2585·1	2428·6	2138·7
1957	26	—	8472·1	8102·0	4·1	124·5	241·5	568·1	79·0	1500·8	861·5	—	1598·8	1452·0	2630·5	2475·7	2091·8
1958	26	—	8749·0	8366·7	5·3	125·2	251·8	547·0	77·1	1539·5	842·2	—	1368·0	1218·3	2670·1	2496·2	2471·7
1959	25	—	9333·2	8888·0	2·8	127·7	314·7	624·3	85·3	1627·8	890·0	—	1432·0	1243·4	2232·2	2036·9	3253·5
1960	25	—	9534·8	9043·4	4·2	130·3	356·9	750·5	97·2	1754·4	925·6	151·3	1231·3	1042·7	1746·8	1551·3	3803·5
1961	25	—	9691·2	9172·2	5·3	132·9	380·8	606·3	106·1	1901·4	949·5	232·5	1423·7	1154·5	1556·3	1373·1	3854·6
1962	25	—	10083·8	9507·2	4·1	127·8	444·7	504·5	121·5	2018·2	962·9	—	1387·3	1098·0	1741·1	1551·8	4197·9
1963	25	—	10844·3	10188·8	8·4	130·6	517·5	522·1	142·4	2050·6	995·8	—	1367·8	1032·8	1704·3	1513·6	4891·6
1964	25	—	11294·5	10608·3	14·7	134·0	537·5	565·3	168·2	2097·4	1050·1	—	1240·0	795·7	1534·7	1347·4	5499·7
1965	25	—	12081·3	11325·3	11·6	137·2	607·2	660·8	215·8	2404·0	1127·7	95·8	1305·6	828·9	1562·4	1354·4	5667·3
1966	25	—	12194·8	11401·7	12·1	137·0	644·0	663·9	246·7	2713·9	1203·1	198·1	1165·3	698·0	1626·7	1382·9	5654·0

Sources

Cols. 1–4, 6–10B, 12, 14, 15, 16 (1880–1946), composed by extracting the consolidated balance sheets of the joint-stock banks of England and Wales net of the Bank of England, of the Irish banks, of the Scottish banks, of *The Economist*'s 'Private Banks Series', and post-1914, of the balance sheet figures of the Yorkshire Penny Bank (now Yorkshire Bank), of Erlangers, of the British International, and of Farrows Bank from *The Economist*'s 'Banking Supplement', or 'Banking Number', published in May of the relevant years. These were summed and added to the balance sheet figures of the Co-operative Wholesale Society Bank. It should be noted that col. 10B (Cash), was largely estimated up to the year 1912, as will be seen in the accompanying tables.

Col. 11 (1880–1946), extracted from the *Bankers' Almanac*; it should be noted that the reported figures in *The Economist* for Total Discounts for the three main groups of banks were reduced by a like amount as the Total Discount figures reported included Treasury Deposit Receipts in the years 1940–50.

(1880–1962) col. 5 = col. 3 – [col. 4 + col. 6 + col. 7].

Cols. 1–4, 7–10B, 12, 14, 16 (1947–50), compiled as above from figures reported in the 'Banking Supplement', of *The Economist*'s *Records and Statistics*, vols. 1–12, and the *Bankers' Almanac*.

Cols. 6, 11, 15 (1947–50), composed as above and extracted from 'British Banks', found in the annual issue of the *Bankers' Almanac*.

Cols. 1, 3, 4, 9–16 (1951–62), composed as above and extracted both from the Bank of England's *Quarterly Bulletin* I, No. I, III No. 3, Dec. 1960, and Sept. 1963, and from the *Bankers' Almanac*.

Cols. 5–8 (1951–62) composed as above and extracted from the annual issues of the *Bankers' Almanac*. It should be noted that these aggregated end-of-year figures may only be found by aggregating the separate balance sheet figures of the 26-odd banks. The clearing bank element of these columns is as of 30 June.

Col. 13 (1900–50), Treasury Bills, is primarily estimated on the basis of the Macmillan Report and the H. Johnson series for the relevant London Clearing Banks, and on the Government + Government-guaranteed/total investment holdings of the Irish and Scottish banks over the relevant years.

(1963–6), all columns derived by summing the balance sheets of joint-stock banks of England and Wales, joint-stock banks of Ireland, joint-stock banks of Scotland, private banks, Yorkshire and Co-operative Bank.

Notes

[1] As for 1962, these banks consisted of the ten London Clearing Banks (excluding the National Bank of Ireland), the five Scottish banks, the three banks of Northern Ireland, Barings Bank, the Isle of Man Bank, the Co-operative Wholesale Society Bank, Blydenstein, C. Hoare, S. Japhet and the Yorkshire Bank.

[2] In the earlier years in particular, the year-ends of some of the banks' individual balance sheets varied somewhat from 31 December.

[3] The branch figures only refer to the branches of the joint-stock banks of England, the Irish and then Northern Irish banks, and the Scottish banks. The branches of the CWS Bank and the Yorkshire (Penny) Bank, and *The Economist*'s private banks are omitted throughout.

[4] Total liabilities/total assets excludes the banks' liabilities for acceptances and endorsements as far as possible. It should be noted that in the pre-1930 period some banks – Barings in particular – included customer's liability for endorsements and acceptances in their loans and advances; where possible, such items were netted out of the reported figures.

[5] The Bank of England figures for the London Clearing Banks in the 1951–62 period were reported to the nearest million with the result that the decimal place in the 1951–62 period is statistically not too relevant.

[6] Banks' accounting practices were far from consistent, particularly in the earlier, pre-1920 years. Where possible, as will be seen on the accompanying balance sheets, the various anomalies and observed accounting practices and changes in these are pointed out. Nevertheless, there is no doubt that the division between discounts and advances and the separation between money at call and Treasury Bills, and Treasury Bills and British Government-guaranteed is fairly rough.

[7] As far as possible, the balance sheet figures obtained have been selected so as to reflect the banking business or banks whose main area of operations is in the UK. As a consequence all British banks operating primarily abroad, such as Hambros, have been omitted. Several other small banks such as Harrods Bank and the People's Bank – now the Scottish Co-operative Wholesale Society Bank – have been omitted, as have several of the merchant banks – S. Montague, N. Rothchilds, etc. Unfortunately, data on such banks are not readily available on a consistent basis over the period concerned.

[8] In 1891, *The Economist* commenced publishing its 'Private Banks Series'. This accounts for the indicated discontinuity.

[9] Series estimated 1900–50.

[10] All estimates set in bold type.

TABLE (A) 1.2 **Joint-Stock Banks of England and Wales 1880–1966 (Figures for Bank of England excluded (Assets and liabilities £ millions))**[1,2]

Year-End Approx. 31 Dec.[3]	Banks	No. of Branches	Total Assets and Liabilities[4]	Deposits and Other Accounts	Misc. Liabilities: Total	Misc. Liabilities: Credit Rebates	Notes in Circulation	Paid-Up Capital and Reserves	Acceptances, Endorsements and Customer Liability for same[4]	Premises and Other Assets	Cash, Money at Call and at Short Notice: Total	Cash, Money at Call and at Short Notice: Cash	Treasury Deposit Receipts or Special Deposits	Investments: Total	Investments: British Government & Government-Guaranteed	Discounts: Total	Discounts: Treasury Bills	Loans and Other Accounts
	1	2	3	4	A 5	B	6	7	8	9	A 10	B	11	12	13	14	15	16
1880	89	1335	278·2	226·6	1·9	1·8	1·1	48·6	17·8	3·8	53·4	28·3	—	38·4	21·3	31·9	—	147·8
1881	93	1369	296·0	241·7	2·3	2·3	1·2	50·8	17·1	5·9	58·1	30·8	—	40·6	22·5	39·6	—	151·9
1882	100	1487	315·7	257·3	2·1	2·1	1·4	54·9	18·4	5·2	59·1	31·3	—	43·0	23·5	41·6	—	170·0
1883	104	1553	331·0	269·3	2·3	2·3	1·4	58·0	18·7	8·8	60·8	32·2	—	46·9	25·1	46·2	—	167·2
1884	107	1542	348·9[i]	283·9	3·0	3·0	1·4	60·6	15·1	7·1	61·0	32·3	—	56·7	28·4	42·1	—	182·0
1885	110	1498	359·8	294·2	2·7	2·4	1·4	61·3	14·0	7·6	66·1	35·0	—	62·8	30·3	42·0	—	181·2
1886	109	1546	364·1	299·2	2·0	2·0	1·4	61·5	12·7	7·2	67·6	35·8	—	63·9	31·5	42·1	—	183·1
1887	109	1655	373·0	308·2	2·1	2·1	1·3	61·4	13·8	7·3	68·1	36·1	—	66·7	30·4	40·8	—	190·8
1888	111	1710	400·5	333·5	2·4	2·4	1·3	63·3	15·4	7·7	75·9	40·2	—	71·3	32·1	42·7	—	203·0
1889	103	1918	420·2	352·6	2·6	2·6	1·3	63·7	19·0	4·2	79·6	42·2	—	75·1	35·4	44·6	—	216·6
1890	104	2203	441·4	368·7	3·7	3·5	1·2	67·8	22·7	8·8	84·0	44·5	—	82·8	41·5	44·4	—	221·5
1891	106	2244	470·0	391·9	9·5	6·2	1·1	67·5	15·6	8·4	91·0	48·2	—	90·2	45·9	38·5	—	241·8
1892	102	2326	475·1	396·6	9·3	5·4	1·1	68·1	20·4	10·7	93·4	49·5	—	94·8	49·0	43·2	—	233·0
1893	99	2515	471·4	393·6	7·8	4·4	1·0	69·0	19·0	10·6	87·9	46·6	—	94·5	49·8	36·0	—	242·4
1894	99	2624	496·8	419·0	7·9	4·8	1·0	68·9	20·1	10·5	106·4	56·4	—	98·1	51·0	41·3	—	240·5
1895	99	2695	535·0	455·6	9·2	6·2	1·0	69·2	23·7	11·6	111·2	58·9	—	107·5	52·3	45·6	—	259·2
1896	94	3051	577·7	495·3	9·5	6·4	1·0	71·9	21·8	12·6	115·8	61·4	—	117·4	50·6	46·6	—	285·2
1897	90	3454	609·8	527·3	8·2	5·0	1·0	73·3	22·0	12·6	125·9	66·7	—	124·2	51·9	43·5	—	303·6
1898	87	3577	633·4	548·6	8·3	4·8	0·9	75·6	21·0	12·9	136·8	72·5	—	124·8	51·6	42·3	—	316·6
1899	83	3826	652·1	566·1	8·5	4·8	0·9	76·6	22·0	13·5	135·5	71·8	—	127·1	52·7	43·9	—	332·0
1900	77	3757	677·3	586·7	11·0	7·0	0·8	78·8	21·5	16·0	144·4	76·5	—	127·7	53·7	45·0	**6·3**[d]	344·1
1901	74	3935	674·2	584·9	8·7	4·8	0·6	80·0	23·9	15·0	153·9	81·5	—	130·0	56·4	45·3	**8·2**[d]	330·0
1902	68	4146	692·7	600·3	10·2	6·1	0·6	81·6	25·0	16·3	164·4	87·1	—	130·8	59·0	47·5	**8·2**[d]	333·6
1903	65	4334	680·5	588·5	9·6	6·0	0·5	81·9	27·4	13·5	149·1	79·0	—	125·8	57·5	46·3	**8·2**[d]	345·1
1904	61	4415	693·7	602·5	9·0	5·4	0·5	81·7	29·2	11·6	165·8	87·8	—	128·5	63·0	49·4	**8·2**[d]	341·8
1905	59	4558	719·5	627·5	9·6	3·1	0·4	82·0	39·2	15·5	179·5	95·1	—	131·7	63·1	54·5	**8·2**[d]	338·2
1906	55	4722	740·7	648·0	10·1	4·4	0·4	82·2	41·7	14·2	178·7	94·7	—	131·0	63·7	58·8	**7·5**[d]	358·0
1907	52	4822	738·8	648·6	8·2	3·9	0·4	81·6	44·4	14·5	174·5	92·4	—	125·8	63·5	58·6	**4·2**[d]	365·3
1908	50	4963	764·5	674·7	7·3	3·3	0·3	82·2	42·2	14·0	194·1	102·9	—	136·8	63·4	64·5	**4·7**[d]	354·3
1909	46	5022	774·5	685·0	8·1	4·1	0·1	81·3	41·3	13·8	199·7	105·8	—	137·3	56·7	65·3	**5·7**[d]	358·4
1910	45	5202	809·8	720·7	8·0	4·2	0·1	81·0	52·3	14·4	199·7	105·8	—	137·7	54·2	66·9	**5·7**[d]	391·1
1911	44	5410	836·3	748·6	7·6	3·7	0·1	80·0	48·8	19·1	211·7	112·2	—	133·8	54·1	78·5	**5·7**[d]	393·8
1912	44	5577	864·6	774·0	9·3	1·7	0·1	81·2	61·3	20·0	216·0	114·5	—	127·2	50·8	85·9	**3·2**[d]	413·2
1913	43	5797	901·4	809·4	9·8	1·3	0·1	82·1	61·7	21·1	235·6	124·9	—	121·2	47·8	92·4	**3·7**[d]	430·7
1914	38	5869	987·1	895·6	9·5	1·4	0·1	81·9	47·8	22·0	276·0	187·7	—	146·5	71·4	88·4	**5·1**[d]	454·1
1915	37	6027	1084·3	992·6	9·6	1·4	0·2	81·7	62·5	23·9	262·5	189·0	—	310·8	236·8	62·8	**30·0**[b]	424·4
1916	35	5993	1247·5	1154·9	11·3	1·9	0·2	81·1	68·7	22·2	369·5	266·0	—	323·0	258·5	119·4	**60·9**[b]	413·4
1917	34	6004	1462·8	1365·3	12·8	6·7	0·2	84·5	65·8	17·7	427·8	252·4	—	339·6	279·5[a]	183·1	**96·2**[b]	494·6
1918	26	6501	1683·8	1583·4	7·3	1·4	0·2	92·9	58·9	28·1	481·2	288·7	—	347·2	282·8[a]	307·3	**159·8**[b]	520·0
1919	21	7195	1986·8	1874·2	6·1	0·6	0·2	106·3	151·1	17·3	452·8	339·6	—	398·6	345·4[a]	263·0	**144·7**[c]	855·3
1920	20	7612	2097·4	1961·5	7·5	0·7	0·2	128·2	102·9	20·1	449·2	318·9	—	368·7	309·6[a]	328·9	**131·6**[c]	930·4
1921	20	7963	2111·2	1974·9	7·0	0·7	0·2	129·1	74·2	25·1	438·5	350·8[e]	—	375·6	311·9	445·5	**249·5**[c]	826·5
1922	20	8235	1970·5	1834·0	7·1	0·7	0·2	129·2	85·7	25·9	423·1	321·6[e]	—	424·4	361·0	301·3	**177·8**[c]	794·7
1923	19	8491	1958·3	1822·1	7·0	0·4	0·2	129·0	111·5	28·9	413·5	322·5[e]	—	404·4	340·0	281·5	**140·8**[c]	830·0
1924	18	8676	1952·7	1813·5	7·0	0·2	0·1	132·1	132·3	30·2	437·9	332·8[e]	—	361·4	298·6	238·3	**100·1**[c]	884·7
1925	18	8873	1948·8	1806·8	7·1	0·2	0·1	134·8	125·0	31·5	441·8	331·4[e]	—	317·6	258·9	227·1	**95·4**[c]	930·8
1926	18	9105	1994·0	1848·2	7·0	0·2	0·1	138·7	108·7	33·4	444·0	333·0[e]	—	307·7	250·0	237·0	**109·0**[c]	972·2
1927	17	9381	2039·2	1892·9	6·8	0·2	0·1	139·4	140·2	35·0	492·7	321·0[e]	—	290·5	231·1	237·4	**114·0**[c]	983·6
1928	16	9595	2100·1	1951·5	7·0	0·2	0·1	141·5	237·1	44·3	493·8	341·7[e]	—	293·2	251·2	259·3	**114·1**[c]	1009·6
1929	16	9815	2059·6	1911·0	6·9	0·2	0·1	141·6	179·3	42·3	481·3	335·4[e]	—	285·2	232·5	224·3	**103·2**[c]	1026·5
1930	16	10082	2127·7	1976·8	6·5	0·2	0·1	144·3	128·0	45·0	472·4	325·6[e]	—	329·3	275·6	316·4	**158·2**[c]	964·6
1931	16	10178	1961·8	1821·0	6·2	0·2	0·1	134·5	109·7	52·0	414·5	288·8[e]	—	329·5	275·6	234·1	**173·2**[c]	931·7
1932	16	10066	2205·6	2064·3	6·0	—	0·1	135·2	96·7	50·2	446·2	296·9[e]	—	520·9	458·9	389·2	**311·3**[c]	799·1
1933	16	10060	2166·8	2025·2	6·1	—	0·1	135·4	122·1	51·4	446·1	300·8	—	612·3	544·1	292·8	**234·2**[c]	764·2
1934	16	10086	2206·0	2061·9	6·3	—	0·1	137·7	131·2	50·9	477·4	311·9	—	638·8	566·3	255·2	**181·1**[c]	785·7
1935	15	10118	2316·7	2172·7	6·2	—	0·1	137·7	109·1	50·2	498·9	340·5	—	653·7	570·2	304·2	**191·6**[c]	809·7
1936	15	10074	2473·8[i]	2329·1	6·1	—	0·1	138·5	85·8	77·3	566·7	361·8	—	691·6	604·5	289·5	**191·0**[c]	884·4
1937	15	10097	2496·4	2348·2	6·0	—	0·1	142·1	117·9	47·3	522·1	361·9	—	663·9	583·0	282·4	**169·4**[c]	980·6

1940	13	9702	2924·4	2777·6	5·2	—	0·2	141·3	108·9	46·0	601·2	445·3	313·5	793·9	712·1	266·5	**181·2**[c]	903·3
1941	13	8626	3453·0	3306·6	4·8	—	0·2	141·4	111·6	44·9	653·9	516·3	757·5	1020·0	948·6	174·1	**114·9**[c]	802·7
1942	13	8326	3748·6	3601·4	5·0	—	0·2	142·0	93·5	44·3	695·5	559·8	895·0	1141·1	1071·8	198·8	**178·9**[c]	773·0
1943	13	8279	4159·5	4010·5	5·2	—	0·2	143·6	100·9	43·3	760·2	617·6	1306·0	1172·9	1101·4	135·3	**117·7**[c]	741·7
1944	13	8295	4662·6	4512·2	5·2	—	0·2	145·0	105·4	43·0	865·7	677·7	1665·0	1183·6	1110·6	149·7	**128·7**[c]	755·6
1945	13	8326	4964·0	4811·9	5·1	—	0·2	146·8	118·5	42·9	965·4	727·8	1522·0	1253·0	1162·0	371·4	**319·4**[c]	809·2
1946	13	9003	5799·8	5645·4	5·3	—	0·2	148·9	194·7	42·7	1163·9	748·9	1558·5	1445·6	1347·5	613·1	**527·3**[c]	976·0
1947	13	9244	6054·7	5898·2	6·1	—	0·2	150·2	252·5	107·1	1221·4	756·5	1287·0	1502·8	1396·2	799·6	**703·6**[c]	1196·9
1948	13	9374	6316·0	6104·4	53·6	—	0·1	157·9	273·3	44·2	974·1	496·5	1396·0	1458·2	1385·2	744·6	**580·8**[c]	1338·5
1949	13	9377	6321·3	6109·5	52·7	—	0·1	159·0	278·2	40·8	1091·7	527·0	792·5	1486·9	1397·7	1115·2	**981·4**[c]	1484·7
1950	12	9533	6484·1	6269·3	53·9	—	0·1	160·8	399·0	43·9	1123·4	536·0	455·5	1504·2	1413·9	1411·7	**1284·6**[c]	1605·1
1951	12	9690	6464·0	6288·4	14·2	—	0·1	161·3	481·5	44·1	1117·9	524·0	101·5	1953·3	1871·2	975·8	791·0	1834·3
1952	12	8641	6577·8	6410·7	2·2	—	0·1	164·8	372·2	45·2	1065·2	543·9	—	2137·2	2060·4	1251·2	1182·0	1638·8
1953	12	—	6803·1[f]	6640·6	1·1	—	0·1	161·3	323·7	46·2	1025·7	533·6	—	2263·2	2178·2	1419·5	1338·0	1584·2
1954	12	—	7054·3	6884·8	1·5	—	0·1	167·9	338·3	47·3	1048·9	561·0	—	2341·7	2245·5	1316·4	1199·0	1754·7
1955	12	—	6738·0	6558·1	0·6	—	0·1	179·2	462·5	49·2	1051·1	554·7	—	2007·8	1915·8	1403·9	1271·0	1716·3
1956	12	—	6783·4	6600·6	0·7	—	0·1	182·0	451·5	53·0	1052·4	559·4	—	1973·6	1882·0	1420·5	1275·0	1802·2
1957	12	—	7064·4	6867·7	2·2	—	0·1	184·4	504·1	57·7	1101·7	589·0	—	2039·6	1948·4	1541·8	1403·0	1745·0
1958	12	—	7331·4	7135·5	2·3	—	0·1	193·5	491·8	63·4	1149·4	574·2	—	2093·1	1981·5	1322·8	1185·0	2092·5
1959	12	—	7847·4	7597·4	0·0	—	0·1	249·9	581·0	69·5	1221·3	621·4	—	1700·2	1576·1	1382·3	1215·0	2778·1
1960	12	—	8041·9	7761·7	0·2	—	0·1	279·9	690·6	79·6	1345·4	644·9	143·4	1266·9	1142·4	1185·7	1017·0	3280·0
1961	12	—	8167·2	7865·6	1·1	—	0·1	300·4	544·0	87·2	1483·7	648·6	220·1	1115·7	999·6	1358·6	1106·0	3291·6
1962	12	—	8527·4	8166·6	1·1	—	—	359·7	440·2	101·5	1598·3	684·5	—	1314·0	1190·3	1338·2	1067·0	3579·7
1963	12	—	9221·1	8793·7	0·6	—	—	426·8	457·4	120·2	1620·8	713·8	—	1279·3	1158·1	1309·3	996·0	4226·7
1964	12	—	9605·9	9160·7	0·6	—	—	444·6	490·9	144·0	1657·5	752·5	—	1150·8	1027·4	1186·9	764·0	4754·5
1965	12	—	10315·7	9808·4	0·6	—	—	506·7	556·3	189·4	1914·5	806·5	91·0	1179·7	1033·5	1236·9	784·0	4904·3
1966[5]	13	—	10548·4	9999·7	3·8	—	—	544·9	573·6	217·2	2255·6	917·9	188·0	1222·1	1070·4	1108·0	651·0	4930·1
1966*	12	—	10385·0	9842·7	3·7	—	—	538·6	571·6	215·2	2199·1	917·0	188·0	1196·8	1045·6	1106·0	651·0	4851·9

Sources

Cols. 1–4, 5B–10B, 12–14, and 16 (1880–1946) were extracted from 'The Banking Number' or 'The Banking Supplement', carried annually in *The Economist*, usually in the May issue. Col. 11 (1940–50) and cols. 13 and 15 (1948–50) found in the annual issues of the *Bankers' Almanac*.

It should be noted that col. 14 for 1940–7 reported by *The Economist* has been adjusted downwards to account for the reported Treasury Deposit Receipts.

Cols. 1–4, 6–10B, 12, 14, 16 (1947–50) extracted from the 'Banking Supplement' in *The Economist*'s issues of *Records and Statistics*, Vols. 1–13, over these years.

Cols. 1–4, 6–16 (1951–2) extracted jointly from the Bank of England's *Quarterly Bulletin*, Vol. 1 (Dec. 1960), and *The Economist*'s *Records and Statistics*. The Bank of England's London Clearing Banks figures were adjusted downwards so as to exclude the figures in *Records and Statistics* for the National Bank of Ireland and upwards for the relevant balance sheet data of Barings and the Isle of Man.

Cols. 1–4, 6–16 (1953–62) extracted jointly from the Bank of England's *Quarterly Bulletin*, Vol. 1 (1963) and from the annual issues of the *Bankers' Almanac*, Vols. 110–19. The data were processed as for the 1951–2 period so as to maintain the consistency of coverage of the series.

Col. 5A (1880–1962) computed on a residual basis, e.g. col. 5A = col. 3 – (4 + 6 + 7) in any year.

Col. 15 (1900–14), see note (*d*) below.

Col. 15 (1915–50), see notes (*b*) and (*c*) below.

Cols. 4, 10A–16 (1963–6) from the Intelligence Department at the Bank of England. Cols. 5–9, together with National Bank of Ireland, Barings and Isle of Man Bank data, for adjustment from *Bankers' Almanac and Year Book*. Col. 3 = col. 4 + 5 + 6 + 7 (1963–6).

Notes

[1] An inspection of the main sources for the pre-1947 part of the table – *The Economist* 'Banking Number' and 'Banking Supplement' – will at times be somewhat perplexing inasmuch as different issues give slightly different figures for the same item. As a consequence, the actual annual balance sheet data were used rather than the time series accounts.

[2] The banks in this series contain all those joint-stock banks of England and Wales whose main business is primarily concentrated in the UK. In 1936 they were as follows: Barclays, Barings, British Mutual, Coutts, District, Glyn Mills, Isle of Man, Lloyds, London Merchant, Martins, Midland, National Provincial, Union of Manchester, Westminster and W. Deacons. In 1962 it consisted of Barclays, Barings, Coutts, District, Glyn Mills, Isle of Man, Lloyds, Martins, Midland, National Provincial, Westminster and W. Deacons. The reader will note that a slightly more comprehensive, though less processable series exists in the annual issues of the *Bankers' Almanac and Year Book* for the period 1920–52. While the coverage of this series is slightly more comprehensive with respect to banks covered, it does not have such a good asset breakdown – it omits holdings of Government and Government-guaranteed stock for instance – and also does not extend well back into the pre-1920 period.

[3] In the pre-1951 period, some banks' balance sheets were not drawn up on 31 Dec. After 1951, the bulk of the figures reported in cols. 6, 7, 8, were from 30 June rather than 31 Dec. of the relevant year. It should be noted that cols. 6 and 7 are relatively constant.

[4] Liability for acceptance has not been included in the bank's total asset liabilities figure.

[5] The National Bank of Ireland sold the Irish part of the business in 1966. Consequently the clearing bank figures do not have to be adjusted after 1965 for this bank. The second row for 1966 shows figures that are consistent with the rest of the series by interpolation (starred line*).

[a] Includes some Treasury Bills.

[b] Treasury Bills (1915–18). Estimated on basis of

$$\frac{\text{Government} + \text{Government-guaranteed Stock}}{\text{Total Investment}}$$

ratio of the banks for the relevant year multiplied by the Total Discounts in that year and by a splicing factor ϵ, where

$$\epsilon = \left(\frac{\text{Actual Treasury Bills}}{\text{Estimated Treasury Bills}}\right)_{1919} = 0{\cdot}64,$$

where the numerator was found as indicated in (*c*) below.

[c] Treasury Bills (1919–50) from Treasury Bills figures given for London Clearing Banks by Committee of Finance and Industry, *Report*, Cmd. 389, London: H.M.S.O. 1931, pp. 284–9, for the 1919–30 period and H. G. Johnson, 'Clearing bank holdings of public debt, 1930–50', *Reprint Series*, No. 54 (University of Cambridge, 1952), pp. 1–8. Note: prior to 1915, outstanding market Treasury Bills were relatively insignificant in sum. For instance, Pember and Boyle estimate this sum to be £13·0 million in 1914, and £16·1 million in 1900.

[d] Treasury Bills (1900–14) estimated on basis of

$$\frac{\text{Banks' total Treasury Bills Holdings in 1915}}{\text{Total Treasury Bills outstanding in 1915}}$$

= 0·39 times the total outstanding Treasury Bills in that year.

Figures for total market Treasury Bills 1900–44 may be found in Pember and Boyle, *British Government Securities in the 20th Century*, 2nd Edn. (London, 1961), p. 277.

[e] Cash figures adjusted to include certain amounts reported in *The Economist* not separated from money at call.

[f] From 1953 on, total asset and liability figures estimated on the basis of sums of the banks' reported liabilities, which the reader will note excluded undivided profit.

[i] Total liability figure reported in *The Economist* adjusted upwards as it is obviously wrong.

TABLE (A) 1.3 **Joint-Stock Banks of Ireland[1] 1880–1920 and Northern Ireland 1920–1966 (Assets and liabilities £ millions)**

Year	Banks	No. of Bran-ches	Total Assets and Liabili-ties[3]	Deposits and Other Accounts	Misc. Liabilities, Credits, Rebates, etc.		Notes in Circu-lation	Paid-up Capital and Reserves	Acceptances, Endorse-ments and Customer Liability for same[3]	Pre-mises and Other Assets	Cash, Money at Call and at Short Notice		Treasury Deposit Receipts or Special Deposits	Investments		Discounts		Loans, Ad-vances, Other Ac-counts, Total
					Total	Credit and Rebate					Total	Cash		Total	British Government and Government-Guaranteed	Total	Treasury Bills	
	1	2	3	4	5 A	5 B	6	7	8	9	10 A	10 B	11	12	13	14	15	16
1880[c]	9	500	55·4	38·1	1·4	0·2	6·0	9·9	0·0	0·5	8·4	5·4	—	13·6	5·0	6·6	—	26·3
1881[c]	9	500	56·8	39·1	0·6	0·2	7·2	9·9	0·0	0·6	9·8	6·3	—	15·0	6·1	6·2	—	25·2
1882[c]	9	498	57·2	39·1	0·0	0·0	8·3	9·8	0·0	1·0	9·0	5·8	—	14·7	4·9	5·8	—	26·1
1883[c]	9	491	56·3	39·3	0·0	0·2	6·7	10·1	0·0	0·9	8·6	5·5	—	15·2	7·3	6·0	—	25·6
1884[c]	9	437	55·0	39·3	0·0	0·0	6·1	10·0	0·0	0·8	8·0	5·1	—	15·2	5·1	5·9	—	25·1
1885	9	374	53·8	38·2	0·0	0·0	5·9	9·7	0·0	0·8	6·7	4·3	—	13·1	7·7	5·9	—	18·9
1886	9	423	51·2	34·5	0·9	0·8	5·9	9·9	0·0	0·9	8·5	5·4	—	14·3	7·9	5·9	—	21·6
1887	9	427	50·0	34·3	0·3	0·3	5·5	9·9	0·0	0·9	7·8	5·0	—	14·4	7·2	5·8	—	21·2
1888	9	432	52·6	36·1	0·2	0·2	6·3	10·0	0·1	0·9	8·7	5·6	—	16·0	7·7	5·8	—	21·3
1889	9	437	54·7	37·8	0·1	0·1	6·7	10·1	0·1	0·9	9·9	6·3	—	16·3	7·7	5·8	—	21·8
1890	9	456	55·8	38·5	0·3	0·3	6·6	10·4	0·3	0·8	9·1	5·8	—	17·1	7·4	5·8	—	23·0
1891	9	455	56·3	39·5	0·5	0·3	6·2	10·1	0·2	0·8	9·5	6·1	—	17·0	7·3	5·7	—	23·2
1892	9	455	57·4	40·6	0·5	0·3	5·9	10·4	0·1	0·9	9·0	5·8	—	17·2	7·5	5·6	—	24·7
1893	9	486	57·4	40·5	0·6	0·2	6·1	10·2	0·1	0·9	9·0	5·8	—	16·1	7·9	5·7	—	25·7
1894	9	489	59·5	42·7	0·4	0·2	6·2	10·2	0·2	0·9	11·7	7·5	—	16·6	6·9	5·8	—	24·5
1895	9	496	61·4	44·4	0·7	0·2	6·1	10·2	0·3	1·0	10·2	6·5	—	17·9	7·3	5·9	—	25·3
1896	9	509	62·6	45·6	0·6	0·2	6·1	10·3	0·3	0·9	9·4	6·0	—	18·2	7·0	6·3	—	27·8
1897	9	579	62·6	43·7	2·4	2·0	6·1	10·4	0·2	0·9	9·3	6·0	—	17·8	6·8	6·1	—	28·5
1898	9	580	63·1	45·9	0·8	0·3	5·9	10·5	0·2	1·0	9·5	6·1	—	17·6	7·4	6·0	—	28·9
1899	9	589	66·0	48·2	0·7	0·4	6·5	10·6	0·2	0·7	10·2	6·5	—	18·0	6·9	6·4	—	30·7
1900	9	543	67·8	49·4	0·8	0·2	6·7	10·9	0·2	0·9	11·7	7·5	—	17·7	7·7	6·1	**0·2**	31·3
1901	9	664	67·2	49·1	0·8	0·3	6·3	11·0	0·2	1·0	10·8	6·9	—	18·3	6·9	5·8	**0·2**	31·3
1902	9	685	69·0	50·2	0·9	0·2	6·8	11·1	0·4	0·9	11·8	7·6	—	18·9	7·5	5·9	**0·2**	31·5
1903	9	593	70·4	51·5	0·8	0·3	6·8	11·3	0·2	0·9	10·8	6·9	—	19·4	7·7	5·8	**0·2**	33·4
1904	9	604	71·6	53·0	1·0	0·6	6·3	11·3	0·1	0·9	10·3	6·6	—	19·5	8·9	5·9	**0·2**	34·9
1905	9	627	71·8	53·6	0·9	0·7	6·0	11·3	0·2	0·9	10·4	6·7	—	19·1	8·3	6·1	**0·2**	36·6
1906	9	631	73·4	54·7	0·9	0·7	6·4	11·4	0·3	0·9	11·0	7·0	—	19·3	8·4	5·8	**0·2**	37·5
1907	9	639	76·3	57·5	0·9	0·5	6·6	11·3	0·2	0·9	11·5	7·4	—	19·7	8·5	6·2	**0·2**	38·0
1908	9	613	77·8	59·3	0·7	0·3	6·4	11·4	0·2	0·9	12·2	7·8	—	21·0	9·0	5·7	**0·2**	38·0
1909	9	655	79·3	60·5	0·8	0·3	6·6	11·4	0·2	0·9	13·1	8·4	—	23·1	9·7	5·4	**0·2**	36·8
1910	9	663	82·1	62·5	0·9	0·3	7·2	11·5	0·1	1·0	13·8	8·8	—	23·2	11·0	5·2	**0·2**	38·9
1911	9	679	84·8	65·5	0·8	0·3	7·1	11·4	0·2	0·9	14·5	9·3	—	24·4	10·2	5·1	**0·2**	39·9
1912	9	683	86·0	66·9	0·7	0·2	7·2	11·2	0·4	1·0	14·0	8·9	—	24·0	9·1	5·2	**0·2**	41·7
1913	9	710	90·5	70·7	0·6	0·2	8·1	11·1	0·4	1·1	17·2	10·5	—	23·9	8·6	5·1	**0·2**	43·2
1914	9	693	97·3	74·5	0·7	0·2	10·9	11·2	0·5	1·2	22·4	15·8	—	26·0	10·2	5·3	**0·2**	42·4
1915	9	703	104·4	77·7	0·7	0·2	15·0	11·0	0·4	1·4	23·3	17·3	—	35·3	20·1	5·1	**2·4**	39·2
1916	9	708	114·4	83·7	0·8	0·2	19·1	10·8	0·8	1·4	32·6	24·2	—	38·1	26·4	4·1	**2·3**	38·1
1917	9	773	133·6	99·3	0·7	0·2	22·3	11·3	0·9	1·2	40·1	28·9	—	42·1	30·9[b]	4·4	**2·7**	45·8
1918	9	848	175·2	131·6	0·9	0·2	30·9	11·8	0·5	1·3	56·8[a]	39·9	—	65·3	54·2[b]	4·8	**3·3**	47·0
1919	9	869	209·1	166·2	1·0	0·2	29·1	12·8	0·5	1·5	55·1[a]	33·5	—	77·2	62·0	6·1	**4·0**	69·2
1920	9	912	239·0	200·4	1·0	0·1	24·7	12·9	1·4	1·7	46·7	31·5	—	81·0	67·9	8·9	**6·1**	100·7
1920[2]	3	261	71·9	60·3	0·5	0·1	7·7	3·4	0·8	0·4	13·2	9·1[e]	—	18·2	15·6	1·6	**1·2**	38·6
1921	3	264	68·9	59·9	0·4	0·1	5·2	3·4	0·3	0·5	12·3	8·1[e]	—	17·2	14·7	3·5	**2·1**	35·5
1922	3	267	65·6	56·7	0·5	0·1	5·0	3·4	0·1	0·6	8·2	6·7[e]	—	23·2	21·8	1·5	**1·2**	32·1
1923	3	248	61·3	52·0	0·5	0·1	5·0	3·8	0·2	0·6	6·9	6·1[e]	—	21·3	19·7	1·2	**0·9**	31·3
1924	3	249	60·7	51·1	0·6	0·2	4·9	4·1	0·2	0·6	6·7	5·9[e]	—	21·5	18·9	0·7	**0·5**	30·9
1925	3	252	59·2	50·1	0·5	0·1	4·4	4·2	0·2	0·5	6·0	5·2[e]	—	18·9	16·8	0·5	**0·4**	33·0

1927	3	255	59·9	49·3	2·2	1·9	4·0	4·4	[illegible]	[illegible]	[illegible]	[illegible]	[illegible]	[illegible]	[illegible]	[illegible]	[illegible]	32·3
1928	3	255	60·3	49·6	2·3	1·9	3·9	4·5	0·1	0·6	7·3	7·3	—	19·6	17·3	0·3	**0·3**	32·3
1929	3	256	59·9	49·5	2·1	1·9	3·7	4·6	0·0	0·6	6·2	6·2	—	20·5	18·1	0·3	**0·3**	32·3
1930	3	256	59·6	49·1	2·1	1·9	3·6	4·8	0·0	0·6	5·8	5·8	—	21·6	18·5	21·7	**15·4**	9·8
1931	3	258	59·1	49·1	2·2	2·1	3·2	4·6	0·0	0·6	5·8	5·8	—	21·5	18·7	20·8	**14·8**	10·1
1932	3	259	62·1	53·9	0·4	0·1	3·2	4·6	0·1	0·9	8·0	8·0	—	21·5	18·7	24·1	**17·4**	7·7
1933	3	260	59·5	51·2	0·4	—	3·2	4·7	0·1	0·6	5·7	5·7	—	25·6	22·4	18·8	**14·5**	7·4
1934	3	259	59·1	50·5	0·4	—	3·4	4·8	0·1	0·7	7·2	7·2	—	25·8	22·4	0·2	**0·2**	25·0
1935	3	259	59·7	50·9	0·4	—	3·6	4·8	0·1	0·7	7·2	7·2	—	27·1	23·6	0·2	**0·2**	24·4
1936	3	259	58·9	49·9	0·5	—	3·7	4·8	0·1	0·6	7·0	7·0	—	27·3	23·7	0·2	**0·2**	23·6
1937	3	259	58·3	49·1	0·4	—	3·9	4·9	0·1	0·6	5·8	5·8	—	26·7	23·2	0·2	**0·2**	24·9
1938	3	259	57·3	47·8	0·7	—	3·9	4·9	0·3	0·7	6·0	5·9	—	25·9	22·4	0·2	**0·2**	24·1
1939	3	252	59·9	49·8	0·5	—	4·6	5·0	0·2	0·6	9·9	9·8	—	25·3	21·8	0·3	**0·3**	23·5
1940	3	252	64·5	52·9	0·6	—	6·0	5·0	0·2	0·6	12·9	12·8	—	28·3	19·2	0·2	**0·2**	22·1
1941	3	251	79·1	65·1	0·4	—	8·6	5·0	0·2	0·6	19·7	19·7	—	38·3	35·4	0·1	**0·1**	20·3
1942	3	251	87·4	71·2	0·3	—	10·8	5·1	0·1	0·6	23·6	23·6	—	43·0	40·1	0·1	**0·1**	19·8
1943	3	250	94·9	77·5	0·6	—	11·7	5·1	0·1	0·6	26·5	26·5	—	47·6	44·6	0·1	**0·1**	20·0
1944	3	250	100·7	83·7	0·3	—	11·5	5·2	0·1	0·6	27·7	27·7	—	51·0	48·1	0·1	**0·1**	21·2
1945	3	250	106·4	89·0	1·4	—	10·7	5·3	0·5	0·6	26·0	26·0	—	56·7	53·8	0·3	**0·3**	22·3
1946	3	250	117·2	100·4	0·8	—	10·2	5·8	0·6	0·6	30·2	30·2	—	59·9	56·9	0·2	**0·2**	25·7
1947	3	250	124·3	109·0	0·3	—	8·9	6·1	0·3	0·8	20·5	20·5	—	62·0	59·0	0·3	**0·3**	32·5
1948	3	250	130·5	116·2	0·4	—	7·8	6·1	0·6	0·6	21·9	21·9	—	61·3	58·3	0·8	**0·8**	37·0
1949	3	284[d]	132·9	119·2	1·0	—	6·6	6·1	1·0	0·6	27·1	27·1	—	61·9	58·2	0·3	**0·3**	39·3
1950	3	448[d]	137·1	123·1	2·0	—	5·8	6·2	1·9	0·8	25·2	25·2	—	61·9	56·9	0·3	**0·3**	45·9
1951	3	441	133·9	120·4	2·0	—	5·4	6·1	1·7	0·8	21·5	21·5	—	55·3	51·4	0·3	**0·3**	52·7
1952	3	436	136·9	125·0	0·4	—	5·4	6·1	1·0	0·8	27·7	27·7	—	54·9	52·7	0·3	**0·3**	47·6
1953	3	—	140·4	129·8	0·1	—	4·2	6·3	1·1	0·9	26·4	26·4	—	65·2	63·9	0·2	**0·2**	47·5
1954	3	—	146·9	136·4	0·0	—	4·3	6·3	1·8	1·0	26·7	26·7	—	67·0	65·0	0·2	**0·2**	52·1
1955	3	—	141·7	131·3	0·0	—	4·2	6·3	1·9	1·1	22·6	22·6	—	62·7	60·8	0·2	**0·2**	55·1
1956	3	—	144·1	129·7	2·3	—	6·0	6·3	1·4	1·1	23·7	23·7	—	60·9	59·0	0·2	0·2	58·3
1957	3	—	151·9	139·6	0·0	—	5·9	6·4	1·4	1·3	28·8	28·8	—	58·9	57·0	0·2	**0·2**	62·7
1958	3	—	155·3	142·7	0·7	—	5·4	6·5	0·8	2·1	25·8	25·8	—	58·4	56·7	0·1	**0·1**	68·9
1959	3	—	160·7	148·3	0·4	—	5·2	6·8	1·1	2·3	24·0	24·0	—	54·6	52·5	0·5	**0·4**	78·9
1960	3	—	163·3	150·5	1·1	—	4·9	6·8	1·8	3·4	26·6	26·6	—	47·5	46·6	0·2	0·0	85·6
1961	3	—	176·7	161·2	1·2	—	5·0	9·3	1·7	3·9	30·2	30·2	—	47·9	46·6	1·8	1·6	91·3
1962	3	—	188·7	172·8	0·1	—	4·7	9·1	3·2	3·2	29·9	29·9	—	55·7	54·5	1·1	0·7	97·1
1963	3	—	200·7	182·1	4·8	—	4·7	9·1	4·6	4·3	30·2	30·2	—	55·8	46·4	2·5	1·5	105·2
1964	3	—	209·2	184·3	11·0	—	4·6	9·3	6·5	5·1	31·0	31·0	—	53·0	44·0	2·3	1·0	113·1
1965	3	—	227·8	206·0	7·4	—	5·0	9·4	6·9	5·5	39·1	39·1	—	57·0	47·5	4·3	1·0	117·8
1966	3	—	243·0	222·1	4·5	—	6·1	10·3	8·6	5·8	46·0	46·0	—	59·5	50·6	3·6	0·0	122·8

Sources

Cols. 1–4, 5B–10B, 12–14, 16 (1880–1946), were extracted from 'The Banking Number' or 'The Banking Supplement', carried annually in *The Economist*, usually in the May issue.

Cols. 1–4, 7–10, 12, 14, 16 (1947–52), extracted from 'The Banking Supplement', in *The Economist*'s issues of *Records and Statistics*, Vols. 1–13, over these years.

Cols. 6 and 13 (1947–52), extracted from the annual issues of the *Bankers' Almanac* over these years, Vols. 103–109.

Cols. 1–4, 5B, 6–10B, 12–14, 16 (1953–62). Ibid., Vols. 110–119

Col. 15 (1959–62). Ibid., Vols. 116–119.

Col. 5A=col. 3−(4+6+7) (1880–1966); col. 11, Treasury deposit receipts or special deposits were zero throughout. Col. 15 (1915–58) figures are all estimates. Method, estimated on basis of

$$\left(\frac{\text{Holdings of Government Stock}}{\text{Total Investment}}\right)_t \times \text{Total Discount}_t \times \hat{\lambda}$$

where $\hat{\lambda}$, the adjustment/splicing factor, was assumed to be equal to its value in 1959 – 0·83; e.g.

$$\left(\frac{\text{Treasury Bills/Total Discounts}}{\text{Government Stock/Total Investment}}\right)_{1959} = 0{\cdot}83 = \hat{\lambda}$$

Col. 15 (1900–15), figures are estimated on basis of joint-stock banks of England and Wales holdings of same, which are in turn also estimates.

Cols. 1–4, 6–12, 16 (1963–6), from *Bankers' Almanac and Year Book*.

Cols. 13–15 (1963–6), from the Bank of England's *Quarterly Bulletin*.

Notes

[1] Banks of Ireland, 1880–1920: Bank of Ireland, Northern Bank, Provincial Bank of Ireland, Belfast Banking Company, National Bank, Ulster Bank, Hibernian, Royal Bank of Ireland, Munster and Leinster Bank; 1920–62: Belfast Banking Company, Northern and Ulster Banks.

[2] The Irish Free State Agreement Act was passed into law on 31 March 1922. However, it was decided to break the series in 1920 rather than 1922 so as to make the series comparable with the UK Incomes series which also uses 1920 as the terminal date.

[3] It will be noted that acceptances have not been included in Total Assets/Liabilities as the series has been compiled in order to depict the actual credit the banks have extended.

[a] Includes some Treasury Bills not exceeding £12·4 millions in 1918 and £13·0 millions in 1919.

[b] Includes some Treasury Bills.

[c] For 1880–1 only figures for four banks recorded, and for 1882–4 figures for eight banks recorded. As a consequence the reported figures have been adjusted upwards on the basis of the nine banks' figures in 1885.

[d] Includes sub-agencies after 1949.

[e] Cash 1920–7 contained varying amounts of money at call at one bank. As a result the figures for those years have been adjusted downwards to account for same. There is reason to suppose that the post-1927 figures may also contain some money at call, but unfortunately figures indicating the amount are not given.

TABLE (A) 1.4 **Joint-Stock Banks of Scotland 1880–1966[2] (Assets and liabilities £ millions)**

Year-End, Varying Dates for Each Bank[1]	*Banks*	*No. of Branches*[c]	*Total Assets or Liabilities*	*Deposits and Other Accounts*[d]	*Misc. Liabilities, Credits, Rebates, etc.*		*Notes in Circulation*	*Paid-up Capital and Reserves*	*Acceptances, Endorsements and Customer Liability for same*	*Premises and Other Assets*	*Cash, Money at Call and at Short Notice*[e]		*Treasury Deposit Receipts or Special Deposits*	*Investments*[a]		*Discounts*		*Loans, Other Accounts, Total*[b]
					Total	*Credits and Rebates*					*Total*	*Cash*[e]		*Total*	*British Government and Government-Guaranteed*	*Total*	*Treasury Bills*	
	1	2	3	4	5 A	5 B	6	7	8	9	10 A	10 B	11	12	13	14	15	16
1880	10	877	98·7	77·7	1·4	1·3	5·6	14·0	3·7	3·2	12·3	**4·8**	—	21·3	13·7	17·0	—	44·8
1881	10	883	99·8	79·3	0·6	0·6	5·6	14·3	5·1	3·1	13·9	**5·4**	—	20·9	12·5	16·7	—	45·2
1882	10	884	102·0	80·2	1·3	1·3	5·8	14·7	4·0	2·7	14·5	**5·7**	—	21·4	10·4	17·3	—	46·2
1883	10	893	105·2	83·2	1·3	1·3	5·9	14·8	3·3	2·7	15·1	**5·9**	—	23·3	10·6	17·7	—	46·6
1884	10	931	105·4	83·4	1·3	1·2	5·9	14·8	3·4	2·7	14·6	5·7	—	28·1	12·0	15·6	—	48·0
1885	10	935	103·5	81·8	1·1	1·1	5·8	14·8	2·9	3·1	16·8	**6·6**	—	27·5	7·9	14·7	—	48·2
1886	10	949	101·8	80·6	0·8	0·8	5·7	14·7	3·3	2·8	16·3	**6·4**	—	21·4	7·9	14·2	—	47·2
1887	10	950	104·0	82·4	1·2	1·2	5·8	14·6	2·8	3·0	18·9	**7·4**	—	21·5	8·1	13·7	—	46·9
1888	10	963	106·1	84·5	1·2	1·2	5·8	14·6	2·8	3·1	19·6	**7·6**	—	25·1	9·0	14·2	—	44·2
1889	10	964	110·6	88·3	1·4	1·2	6·2	14·7	3·1	3·3	21·4	**8·3**	—	27·5	11·2	14·3	—	43·7
1890	10	975	114·2	91·6	1·3	1·3	6·5	14·8	3·7	3·3	21·4	**8·3**	—	29·3	11·4	15·1	—	45·0
1891	10	986	115·1	92·4	1·2	1·2	6·6	14·9	3·7	3·5	20·7	**8·1**	—	29·9	11·5	18·6	—	42·4
1892	10	995	115·3	92·6	1·2	1·1	6·5	15·0	3·5	3·6	19·6	**7·6**	—	30·2	11·2	17·0	—	44·8
1893	10	1002	115·9	91·9	2·3	1·5	6·5	15·2	3·5	3·3	21·4	**8·3**	—	30·7	13·5	16·9	—	43·7
1894	10	1007	117·0	93·3	2·1	1·1	6·6	15·0	3·0	3·4	21·8	**8·5**	—	30·5	10·5	16·4	—	44·9
1895	10	1013	119·2	94·6	2·2	1·3	7·3	15·1	3·3	3·4	22·8	**8·9**	—	30·8	9·5	15·8	—	46·4
1896	10	1016	120·7	95·7	2·4	1·4	7·3	15·3	3·6	3·5	22·0	**8·6**	—	30·5	12·5	15·2	—	49·5
1897	10	1147	122·4	96·9	2·5	1·6	7·5	15·5	3·5	3·5	22·7	**8·9**	—	31·1	10·1	16·2	—	48·9
1898	11	1178	124·5	98·6	2·4	1·3	7·8	15·7	3·1	3·5	23·0	**9·0**	—	31·3	9·7	16·6	—	50·1
1899	11	1071	129·3	102·8	2·6	1·6	7·9	16·0	4·1	3·6	24·8	**9·7**	—	30·5	9·8	16·4	—	54·1
1900	10	1075	133·9	107·2	2·4	1·4	8·1	16·2	3·6	3·7	26·4	**10·3**	—	33·4	10·6	16·9	**0·8**	53·5
1901	10	1080	134·4	107·3	2·7	1·5	8·0	16·4	4·0	4·1	26·9	**10·5**	—	33·2	10·5	13·0	**0·6**	57·2
1902	11	1115	134·8	106·9	3·2	2·0	8·0	16·7	3·4	4·2	26·0	**10·1**	—	33·0	10·1	15·5	**0·7**	56·0
1903	11	1132	131·6	104·3	2·7	1·5	7·8	16·8	3·6	4·2	24·8	**9·7**	—	31·2	9·6	14·8	**0·7**	56·6
1904	11	1145	129·1	101·9	2·5	1·5	7·7	17·0	3·7	4·3	23·9	**9·3**	—	31·5	11·6	14·7	**0·7**	54·7
1905	11	1159	128·7	100·6	3·4	1·8	7·5	17·2	3·6	4·4	24·1	**9·4**	—	31·4	9·5	15·3	**0·7**	54·3
1906	11	1176	133·0	105·2	2·9	1·7	7·6	17·3	4·6	4·5	26·1	**10·2**	—	31·2	10·1	14·9	**0·7**	56·3
1907	10	1155	136·5	108·7	3·3	2·1	7·4	17·1	4·6	4·5	27·0	**10·5**	—	32·0	9·7	16·0	**0·7**	57·0
1908	10	1178	133·3	105·8	3·0	1·9	7·2	17·3	4·3	4·6	25·7	**10·0**	—	33·5	10·3	14·3	**0·6**	55·2
1909	9	1185	134·3	106·7	2·9	1·6	7·2	17·5	5·0	4·6	25·7	**10·0**	—	34·5	11·0	13·3	**0·6**	56·1
1910	9	1221	134·3	106·7	2·9	1·7	7·1	17·6	3·6	4·7	25·6	**10·0**	—	33·3	10·2	12·1	**0·5**	58·6
1911	9	1225	140·2	112·2	3·0	1·8	7·3	17·7	4·8	4·6	30·1	**11·7**	—	33·9	10·2	13·3	**0·6**	58·2
1912	9	1225	147·5	118·8	3·6	0·2	7·7	17·4	5·7	4·6	33·9	13·2	—	36·6	10·5[a]	14·5	**0·7**	57·9
1913	9	1240	154·3	125·9	3·4	0·1	7·7	17·3	5·5	4·5	34·0	13·9	—	38·0	10·1[a]	18·0	**0·8**	59·7
1914	9	1253	162·3	132·7	3·4	0·1	9·5	16·7	5·7	4·6	34·6	18·3	—	44·8	14·1[a]	15·3	**0·7**	63·0
1915	9	1251	173·0	140·6	3·6	n.a.	12·6	16·2	4·0	5·6	36·7	20·1	—	67·0	35·8[a]	11·8	**3·5**	51·9
1916	8	1243	201·5	166·6	3·8	n.a.	15·5	15·6	5·9	4·6	42·0	24·8	—	69·7	47·0[a]	29·6	**11·2**	55·5
1917	8	1242	236·1	196·5	4·5	n.a.	19·0	16·1	4·5	5·2	47·8	33·0	—	71·6	52·0[a]	47·3	**19·9**	64·2[b]
1918	8	1249	269·6	222·1	5·8	n.a.	25·1	16·6	4·1	4·5	57·3	37·8	—	93·9	69·5[a]	63·6	**26·7**	50·3[b]
1919	8	1264	312·0	259·6	7·4	0·1	28·0	17·0	6·8	4·5	65·6	44·6	—	112·0	86·9	35·4	**15·6**	94·5[b]
1920	8	1283	333·6	279·2	7·1	n.a.	29·4	17·9	5·6	4·5	73·0	45·3	—	103·0	79·3	42·7	**18·8**	110·4[b]
1921	8	1308	341·1	291·1	6·3	—	25·2	18·5	3·9	4·5	71·2	52·7	—	114·5	108·6	49·9	**26·9**	101·0
1922	8	1352	316·8	267·8	6·0	—	23·3	19·7	5·0	4·5	63·8	39·2	—	126·0	119·6	32·0	**17·3**	90·4
1923	8	1417	295·1	247·2	5·3	—	22·1	20·5	4·3	4·5	64·0	39·9	—	112·1	104·2	25·2	**13·4**	89·1
1924	8	1468	293·1	242·6	5·7	—	22·2	22·6	5·6	4·6	61·3	40·7	—	103·9	97·6	22·1	**11·9**	100·9
1925	8	1536	291·7	240·9	5·2	—	21·7	23·9	6·1	4·6	60·3	38·8	—	95·2	89·6	21·0	**11·3**	110·3
1926	8	1565	288·9	238·8	4·8	—	20·7	24·6	4·8	4·9	59·6	37·8	—	91·2	85·2	18·8	**10·0**	114·3
1927	8	1589	293·4	242·0	5·0	—	21·2	25·2	5·0	4·9	61·2	38·4	—	88·6	81·9	18·5	**9·6**	120·3
1928	8	1614	301·0	248·8	5·2	—	21·1	25·9	7·0	4·0	63·3	41·3	—	83·4	76·7	19·8	**10·3**	129·8
1929	8	1633	304·9	250·9	4·8	—	21·4	27·8	6·5	4·9	62·3	40·3	—	83·7	76·6	21·7	**11·3**	132·5
1930	8	1659	312·7	256·1	5·1	—	21·4	30·1	4·8	4·8	63·8	40·2	—	98·1	88·9	24·6	**12·8**	124·5
1931	8	1718	299·6	243·6	3·9	—	21·4	30·7	4·8	4·8	60·4	39·4	—	101·4	91·5	28·7	**14·6**	104·3
1932	8	1663	332·5	276·5	4·2	—	21·0	30·8	5·1	4·7	68·1	42·0	—	136·7	125·0	30·3	**15·8**	102·7

1933	8	1826	337·3	281·7	3·3	—	19·2	30·9	6·3	4·8	66·0	40·9	—	157·7	145·6	22·0	**11·4**	[illegible]
1934	8	1852	342·6	286·7	3·5	—	21·4	31·0	10·0	4·8	70·5	43·2	—	161·1	146·5	11·6	**6·0**	94·8
1935	8	1868	385·4	308·5	3·8	—	21·7	31·4	13·6	4·8	75·9	46·4	—	177·7	163·1	12·5	**6·5**	94·6
1936	8	1880	377·5	317·3	5·5	—	23·1	31·6	14·8	4·7	76·0	47·5	—	186·3	171·7	9·9	**5·1**	95·4
1937	8	1889	390·3	330·5	3·5	—	23·5	32·8	16·6	4·7	83·3	51·6	—	187·5	170·2	9·5	**4·9**	105·3
1938	8	1900	385·9	328·6	0·0	—	23·8	33·5	19·0	4·7	80·0	52·8	—	184·3	168·1	8·4	**4·4**	105·3
1939	8	1854	394·5	331·1	3·1	—	26·2	34·1	16·9	4·7	88·8	57·4	—	181·4	159·1	10·0	**5·0**	109·4
1940	8	1799	433·1	364·4	4·2	—	30·2	34·3	15·3	6·8	104·2	71·0	22·5	196·9	177·8	7·7	**3·9**	98·4
1941	8	1697	494·6	417·3	4·4	—	38·5	34·4	17·3	4·8	113·5	78·5	40·0	241·7	223·1	5·7	**3·0**	88·8
1942	8	1620	541·4	453·1	4·5	—	49·3	34·5	14·1	4·9	130·4	90·0	48·0	264·3	246·8	7·1	**3·8**	86·8
1943	8	1593	591·3	493·8	5·5	—	57·1	34·9	16·2	5·0	146·5	101·7	50·5	296·6	279·0	8·1	**4·4**	84·6
1944	8	1594	651·3	542·5	10·3	—	63·3	35·2	14·5	4·9	165·8	111·2	69·5	316·2	299·6	9·5	**5·1**	85·4
1945	8	1619	696·5	590·4	4·6	—	65·8	35·7	15·3	4·9	170·5	114·3	74·5	347·0	330·2	10·8	**5·8**	88·7
1946	8	1674	771·6	657·8	7·0	—	70·4	36·4	20·1	5·0	196·7	129·7	68·0	383·8	366·1	13·2	**7·1**	104·8
1947	8	1698	812·0	703·6	1·8	—	69·6	37·0	21·8	5·0	203·3	131·5	55·0	407·9	388·5	12·5	**6·8**	123·0
1948	8	1708	856·5	743·3	8·4	—	67·0	37·8	25·2	5·9	216·3	132·7[f]	53·5	419·6	389·4	12·8	**6·9**	146·4
1949	8	1762	851·0	736·0	8·1	—	69·0	37·9	28·3	6·2	215·1	132·8[f]	27·5	413·4	395·0	12·6	**6·8**	170·6
1950	7	1761	871·3	754·8	7·3	—	71·1	38·1	38·2	6·5	222·0	140·1[f]	21·0	410·0	394·0	18·2	**9·8**	187·0
1951	7	—	874·4	754·4	4·4	—	77·3	38·3	45·5	6·8	237·3	174·0	7·5	384·2	373·5[f]	14·0	7·5	221·7
1952	7	—	884·0	756·0	2·0	—	85·6	40·4	40·7	7·3	259·0	177·7	—	382·2	369·7	27·1	24·3	200·7
1953	7	—	908·3	775·7	1·7	—	92·3	38·6	37·9	8·5	263·3	187·6	—	416·6	403·7	23·3	21·4	191·8
1954	7	—	977·0	837·0	1·5	—	97·7	40·8	42·7	8·0	291·7	209·5	—	430·5	419·0	21·4	15·9	217·8
1955	6	—	925·0	776·4	2·1	—	104·8	41·7	49·4	8·1	297·7	223·4	—	378·1	364·9	28·9	22·3	200·4
1956	6	—	918·7	762·3	2·0	—	112·8	41·6	53·7	14·0	302·5	232·8	—	359·4	345·2	32·3	24·8	204·8
1957	6	—	944·8	782·6	1·1	—	118·5	42·6	59·2	17·9	320·7	240·5	—	361·7	339·3	44·5	37·6	206·9
1958	6	—	955·1	791·3	1·3	—	119·7	42·8	51·1	9·7	317·2	239·1	—	349·1	335·6	31·4	25·7	235·6
1959	5	—	1003·8	831·2	2·5	—	122·4	47·7	36·5	11·5	331·0	241·1	—	313·5	289·0	29·5	23·2	311·6
1960	5	—	996·3	809·0	2·9	—	125·3	59·1	52·7	12·0	332·0	250·4	7·9	265·8	240·1	26·2	20·1	342·7
1961	5	—	1008·2	817·9	2·8	—	127·8	59·7	55·8	12·8	333·6[g]	267·2[g]	12·4	235·3[f]	209·1	49·9[h]	40·5	360·4[h]
1962	5	—	1032·4	842·5	2·8	—	123·1	64·0	55·2	14·1	335·4	244·5	1·9	224·2	198·5	32·9	23·8	402·6
1963	5	—	1076·0	878·7	2·7	—	125·9	68·7	54·8	15·4	346·5	251·8	—	232·7	203·8	40·3	30·0	422·5
1964	5	—	1127·0	924·9	3·1	—	129·4	69·6	61·3	16·5	344·7	266·6	—	200·8	169·9	33·9	21·4	497·4
1965	5	—	1171·9	961·5	3·6	—	132·2	74·6	89·3	18·2	385·8	282·1	4·8	191·1	159·2	46·4	33·6	502·9
1966	5	—	1193·7	981·7	3·9	—	130·9	77·2	75·0	19·9	402·4	290·9	10·1	208·9	174·1	37·2	22·8	493·8

Sources

Col. 15 (1900–49), holdings of Treasury Bills are estimates. Method (1900–14):

$$(\text{Total Discounts})_t . \left(\frac{\text{Estimated Holdings of Treasury Bills in 1915}}{\text{Total Treasury Bills outstanding in 1915}} \right) = \text{T.B.}_t ,$$

where market T.B. outstanding in the pre-1915 period are given in Pember and Boyle's *Government Securities in the Twentieth Century*.

Method, 1915–50:

$$\text{T.B.}_t = \frac{(\text{Government} + \text{Government Guaranteed})_t}{(\text{Investment})_t} \times (\text{Total Discounts})_t . \lambda . \quad \text{Where}$$

$$\lambda = \frac{\dfrac{\text{Actual Treasury Bill Holdings in 1951}}{\text{Total Discounts 1951}}}{\dfrac{\text{Government} + \text{Government Guaranteed 1951}}{\text{Investments 1951}}} = 0{\cdot}56$$

Cols. 1–4, 5B–10A, 12–14, 16 (1880–1946), were extracted from 'The Banking Number', or 'The Banking Supplement', carried annually in *The Economist*, usually in the May issue.

Cols. 1–4, 6–10B, 12, 14, 16 (1947–50), were abstracted from 'The Banking Supplement', in *The Economist*'s issues of *Records and Statistics*, Vols. 1–13 over these years.

1880–1950, col. 5A = col. 3 − (4 + 6 + 7).

Col. 11 (1940–50), col. 13 (1947–50), were obtained from the annual issues of the *Bankers' Almanac*.

Cols. 1, 4, 9–16 (1951–62), were derived from the Bank of England's *Quarterly Bulletin*, Vol. 1, Dec. 1960, and Vol. 3, March 1963.

Cols. 5A, 6–9 (1951–62), were extracted from the annual issues of the *Bankers' Almanac*, Vols. 110–119.

1951–62, col. 3 = cols. 5A + 6 + 7 + 4.

Col. 10B (1880–1911), estimated:

$$\frac{\text{Cash in 1912}}{\text{Total Cash} + \text{Money at Call and at Short Notice in 1912}}$$

= 0·39 times Column 10A over the relevant years.

Col. 10B (1912–46), see *The Economist*'s 'Banking Number', or 'Supplement'.

Cols. 5A–9 (1963–6), *Bankers' Almanac and Year Book*.

Cols. 4, 11–16 (1963–6), Bank of England *Quarterly Bulletin*.

1963–6, col. 3 = cols. 4 + 5A + 6 + 7.

Col. 10B (1963–6), 'Balances with other banks, items in transit', C.S.O. *Annual Abstract of Statistics* + 'Coins, notes, etc.', Bank of England *Quarterly Bulletin*.

1963–6, col. 10A = col. 10B + 'Money at call and short notice', Bank of England *Quarterly Bulletin*, various issues.

Notes

[1] Prior to 1951, the end-of-year dates for the various banks' balance sheets varied from February to September of the previous year; after 1951, all data excluding cols. 5A, 6–9 are 31 Dec. figures.

[2] In 1954, the Scottish banks were as follows; the Bank of Scotland, British Linen Bank, Clydesdale Bank, Commercial Bank of Scotland, National Bank of Scotland, Royal Bank of Scotland, and the Union Bank of Scotland. In 1962 they were: The Bank of Scotland, British Linen Bank, Clydesdale Bank, National Bank of Scotland and the Royal Bank of Scotland.

[a] 1912–18, British Government and Government-guaranteed figures include some money at call and at short notice.

[b] 1917–20, total loans and advances include some Treasury Bills.

[c] The accuracy of the number of branches figure is questionable as different issues of *The Economist* give varying figures for the same year.

[d] As with c, deposit figures for respective years vary slightly according to the particular *Economist* chosen.

[e] Includes deposits at other banks, plus items in transit, 'float'.

[f] Figures reported by *The Economist* and later by the Bank of England adjusted downwards as inspection of figures indicates Treasury deposit receipts added to cash in 1948, 1949, 1950 and to investments in 1961.

[g] Cols. 10A and 10B for 1961 and 1962 reported in Bank of England *Quarterly Bulletin* adjusted upwards to include items in transit so as to maintain the consistency of the series.

- - - - - Indicates a slight discontinuity.

[h] From 1961 onwards, col. 16 excludes refinanciable export credits which in turn are included in col. 14 in the same year.

TABLE (A) 1.5 **Consolidated Balance Sheets of *The Economist*'s Private Bank Series, The Co-operative Wholesale Society Banks and The Yorkshire Penny Bank 1891–1966[1] (Assets and liabilities £ millions)**

Year-End, Approx. 31 Dec.	*No. of Banks*	*Total[2] Assets or Liabilities*	*Deposits and Other Accounts*	*Misc. Liabilities*	*Notes in Circulation*	*Paid-up Capital and Reserves*	*Acceptances and Endorsements*	*Premises and Other Assets*	*Cash, Money at Call and at Short Notice*		*Investments*		*Discounts*		*Loans and Advances*
									Total	*Cash*	*Total*	*British Government and Government-Guaranteed*	*Total*	*Treasury Bills*	
	1	2	3	4	5	6	7	8	9	10	11	12	13	14	15
1891	43	83·8	71·0	—	0·5	12·3	2·6	n.a.	18·0	**6·8**	27·4	**10·1**	1·4	—	34·8
1892	47	91·8	78·3	—	0·5	12·9	2·4	n.a.	22·5	**8·1**	29·9	**11·7**	1·0	—	36·8
1893	48	87·4	74·5	—	0·4	12·3	2·3	n.a.	20·6	**7·2**	28·6	**9·9**	1·5	—	35·5
1894	46	90·0	77·2	—	0·4	12·4	2·6	n.a.	21·9	**7·6**	30·2	**9·0**	1·7	—	35·2
1895	44	95·3	82·5	—	0·4	12·3	2·9	n.a.	23·5	**8·2**	31·1	**9·8**	2·4	—	37·4
1896	33	73·6	64·1	—	0·2	9·1	2·4	n.a.	16·2	**5·3**	26·5	**7·1**	1·6	—	29·9
1897	28	61·6	53·8	—	0·2	7·5	2·5	n.a.	12·9	**4·1**	22·1	**5·4**	1·5	—	24·8
1898	28	64·6	56·3	—	0·5	7·7	1·0	n.a.	13·9	**4·3**	22·2	**5·5**	1·7	—	25·1
1899	27	66·3	57·2	—	0·2	7·6	1·6	n.a.	13·4	**4·2**	22·3	**5·6**	1·9	—	25·6
1900	23	62·7	55·6	—	0·2	6·9	1·3	n.a.	13·6	**4·2**	22·1	**5·5**	0·9	—	27·2
1901	22	63·1	55·6	—	0·1	6·8	0·9	n.a.	12·7	**3·7**	21·6	**5·4**	2·0	—	24·4
1902	20	57·6	51·4	—	0·1	5·9	1·0	n.a.	12·7	**3·5**	18·8	**4·7**	2·8	—	21·3
1903	17	51·5	45·9	—	0·1	5·4	1·0	n.a.	10·7	**2·7**	17·4	**4·1**	2·2	—	19·5
1904	17	50·0	44·6	—	0·1	5·2	0·9	n.a.	11·5	**3·0**	17·2	**4·3**	1·3	—	18·6
1905	16	51·6	46·3	—	0·1	5·1	1·0	n.a.	12·2	**2·9**	18·4	**4·5**	1·6	—	18·3
1906	15	51·0	45·9	—	0·1	4·9	1·1	n.a.	11·4	**2·7**	17·6	**4·1**	2·2	—	18·3
1907	15	52·0	47·0	—	0·1	4·9	1·0	n.a.	12·9	**3·0**	17·4	**4·1**	1·7	—	18·5
1908	14	48·8	44·0	—	0·1	4·2	1·0	n.a.	11·5	**2·6**	16·6	**3·4**	2·2	—	16·8
1909	13	51·7	47·4	—	0·1	4·2	1·1	n.a.	12·8	**2·8**	17·6	**3·3**	2·2	—	17·9
1910	13	54·9	49·5	—	0·1	4·2	1·1	n.a.	11·6	**2·6**	18·0	**3·5**	2·9	—	19·2
1911	13	56·7	51·3	—	0·1	5·4	1·3	n.a.	12·7	**2·8**	20·6	**3·7**	3·2	—	19·0
1912	13	58·0	52·6	—	0·1	5·4	1·5	n.a.	13·4	**3·0**	20·2	**3·8**	3·5	—	18·7
1913	10	58·8	53·4	—	0·1	5·3	1·5	n.a.	12·6	**2·6**	22·3	**3·8**	3·8	—	18·7
1914	10	65·9	60·4	—	0·1	5·0	1·0	0·4	13·3	**2·6**	23·7	**4·7**	6·3	—	21·8
1915	9	66·3	61·5	—	0·1	4·8	0·8	0·5	16·4	**4·1**	24·1	**6·2**	6·0	**3·0**	19·3
1916	9	72·9	68·2	—	0·1	4·8	0·6	0·5	17·3	**5·5**	21·4	**8·5**	13·6	**6·8**	19·5
1917	10	80·8	75·5	—	0·1	5·2	0·7	0·6	20·7	**6·5**	21·4	**9·2**	13·8	**6·9**	23·7
1918	10	93·3	87·4	—	0·1	5·7	0·8	0·6	28·6	**7·1**	25·5	**15·4**	14·1	**7·0**	23·5
1919	9	103·9	98·2	—	0·2	5·4	1·2	0·6	20·8	**6·0**	29·2	**19·3**	16·2	**7·8**	36·4
1920	7	101·2	96·6	—	—	4·6	1·0	0·5	15·9	**6·6**	18·3	**13·0**	19·7	**7·9**	35·9
1921	7	98·9	94·1	—	—	4·8	1·0	0·5	24·6	**4·6**	22·8	**16·7**	21·8	**12·2**	28·4
1922	10	108·1	102·7	—	—	5·4	1·1	0·5	28·3	**5·2**	36·8	**13·7**	18·6	**11·0**	22·5
1923	7	93·3	88·8	—	—	4·5	2·6	0·5	21·8	**1·9**	35·9	**25·7**	7·4	**3·7**	27·6
1924	6	91·4	87·0	—	—	4·4	4·4	0·5	19·8	**1·5**	40·1	**26·5**	8·1	**3·4**	22·6
1925	6	90·9	86·5	—	—	4·4	5·0	0·5	20·4	**1·6**	37·3	**25·1**	7·4	**3·1**	25·0
1926	5	89·9	85·3	—	—	4·6	4·6	0·6	18·3	**2·1**	35·7	**23·4**	8·8	**4·0**	26·4
1927	6	95·4	90·5	—	—	4·9	5·5	0·5	22·7	**1·6**	38·4	**24·3**	7·4	**3·6**	26·1
1928	7	109·5	101·8	—	—	6·4	11·2	0·5	26·9	**1·8**	45·6	**27·9**	8·2	**3·6**	27·4
1929	7	111·4	103·1	—	—	6·3	11·3	0·5	21·8	**2·5**	50·4	**30·5**	6·8	**3·1**	31·4
1930	7	122·9	114·0	—	—	8·4	10·1	0·5	28·7	**1·9**	58·5	**37·6**	8·3	**4·1**	26·2
1931	7	119·7	111·8	—	—	7·2	6·9	0·6	20·9	**1·0**	64·4	**42·0**	6·9	**5·1**	25·6
1932	7	122·0	114·9	—	—	7·5	5·8	0·4	24·6	**0·9**	75·6	**51·7**	6·4	**5·1**	14·9
1933	7	134·2	126·8	—	—	6·9	5·4	0·6	24·5	**0·9**	85·5	**64·1**	7·0	**5·6**	14·5
1934	7	137·2	126·8	—	—	7·8	6·1	0·6	28·2	**2·5**	95·3	**76·2**	0·6	**0·4**	11·3
1935	7	149·5	140·7	—	—	8·0	6·2	0·6	27·0	**4·5**	109·4	**90·9**	0·7	**0·5**	10·6
1936	7	162·0	159·5	—	—	8·6	7·4	0·6	27·3	**3·4**	121·3	**104·8**	0·8	**0·6**	13·0
1937	6	168·2	159·9	—	—	7·8	6·7	0·6	24·7	**1·2**	127·0	**108·9**	2·2	**1·0**	13·2
1938	5	174·2	165·2	—	—	8·0	6·7	0·6	23·3	**1·2**	132·9	**113·6**	1·3	**1·0**	14·8
1939	6	170·4	161·3	—	—	7·1	3·5	0·6	18·0	**1·1**	135·3	**111·9**	3·1	**2·3**	13·2

1941	6	193·4	184·8	—	—	8·4	2·9	0·6	25·7	**1·5**	144·2	**131·4**	3·9	**2·6**	8·7
1942	6	227·5	219·6	—	—	7·4	0·0	0·6	33·2	**1·7**	178·6	**155·8**	6·5	**5·9**	5·5
1943	6	268·1	258·9	—	—	8·9	2·9	0·6	35·1	**1·8**	212·5	**188·5**	13·5	**11·7**	7·1
1944	6	311·6	302·1	—	—	9·0	3·3	0·6	41·3	**3·9**	244·5	**219·3**	17·9	**17·9**	7·4
1945	6	340·7	330·9	—	—	9·2	3·8	0·6	37·9	**4·2**	277·5	**247·6**	14·6	**12·6**	9·4
1946	6	369·6	360·1	—	—	9·4	4·4	0·6	37·6	**2·7**	304·4	**271·6**	15·1	**13·0**	11·7
1947	6	372·8	363·1	—	—	9·5	5·5	0·6	41·1	**2·1**	298·5	265·2	13·0	10·8	19·5
1948	6	360·5	349·2	—	—	10·2	6·5	0·6	40·3	**1·4**	287·5	255·9	12·5	10·1	20·3
1949	6	351·4	341·6	—	—	9·6	5·8	0·6	37·2	**1·8**	264·5	231·8	10·0	8·8	37·7
1950	6	339·0	328·6	—	—	9·3	3·9	0·6	38·0	**1·7**	246·3	214·4	8·3	7·2	43·9
1951	6	310·6	301·6	—	—	7·7	8·1	0·6	44·0	**1·9**	206·0	175·0	9·2	4·7	52·6
1952	6	308·4	298·3	—	—	8·9	3·4	0·6	50·1	**2·0**	198·1	165·5	6·8	5·3	52·5
1953	5	309·7	302·1	—	—	7·2	0·9	2·0	45·0	**2·0**	201·4	160·1	7·3	5·3	53·6
1954	5	324·9	316·7	—	—	7·4	1·4	2·0	50·5	**2·7**	208·0	158·1	8·7	6·2	55·1
1955	5	325·3	317·0	—	—	7·6	1·6	2·0	47·5	**2·9**	200·2	150·2	13·7	12·1	61·9
1956	5	322·0	313·4	—	—	7·8	2·4	2·0	43·5	**2·9**	191·2	142·4	12·0	9·5	73·4
1957	5	321·1	312·1	—	—	8·1	3·7	2·1	49·6	**3·2**	180·3	131·0	12·3	11·2	77·2
1958	5	307·2	297·2	—	—	9·0	3·3	1·9	47·1	**3·1**	169·5	122·4	13·7	7·5	74·7
1959	5	321·3	311·1	—	—	10·3	5·7	2·0	51·5	**3·5**	163·9	119·3	19·7	4·8	84·9
1960	5	333·3	322·2	—	—	11·1	5·4	2·2	50·4	**3·7**	166·6	122·2	19·2	5·6	95·5
1961	5	339·1	327·5	—	—	11·4	5·3	2·2	53·9	**3·5**	157·7	117·8	13·4	6·4	111·3
1962	5	337·3	325·3	—	—	11·9	5·9	2·7	54·6	**4·0**	147·2	108·5	15·1	6·5	118·5
1963	5	347·2	334·3	—	—	12·9	5·3	3·0	53·1	**3·9**	136·6	105·3	15·7	5·3	137·2
1964	5	352·4	338·4	—	—	14·0	6·6	3·1	64·2	**4·7**	130·1	103·7	16·9	9·3	134·7
1965	5	365·9	349·4	—	—	16·5	8·3	3·3	64·6	**4·8**	134·6	100·0	18·0	10·3	142·3
1966	5	373·1	355·2	—	—	17·9	8·7	3·5	66·4	**4·8**	161·5	106·2	18·5	12·4	152·7

Sources

Cols. 1–3, 5–8, 9, 11. All banks, with the exception of the Co-operative Wholesale Society Bank and the Yorkshire Penny Bank (1891–1946) (1891–1914), *The Economist*'s 'Banking Number', or 'Banking Supplement', May issue over relevant years.

Cols. 1–3, 5–8, 9, 11–15 (1947–52), *The Economist*'s *Record and Statistics*, Vols. 1–13, 1947–53, and *Bankers' Almanac and Year Book*, Vols. 103–108.

(1895–1962), data on the Co-operative Wholesale Society Bank were kindly provided by the General Manager of the Banking Department. Prior to 1895 the Co-operative Society did not separate its bank balance sheets from the societies' collective accounts and as a consequence it was assumed for the purpose of continuity that the balance sheet data reported in 1895 were substantially similar to those in the immediately preceding four years, and entries were made accordingly. Cols. 1–3, 5–7, 8, 11 (1891–1913), representing the assets and liabilities of the Yorkshire Penny Bank. In August 1911 the Yorkshire Penny Bank became a limited company with its share capital wholly owned by eleven other banks. Prior to this date, no published data on its balance sheets appear to be available. The Secretary of the bank, however, kindly provided the total assets and total deposits figures for the 1891–1913 period from the bank's own records. The other items on the balance sheets were estimated on the basis of the asset distributions of *The Economist*'s 'Private Banks' in the relevant years adjusted by a splicing factor so as to tie in such estimates with the actual balance sheet figures reported in *The Economist* for 1914.

Col. 13 (1891–1947), Discounts of 'Private Banks Series' were estimated by subtracting col. 15 for such banks from the given total advances and discount figures for such banks.

Col. 15 (1891–1947), loans and advances of the 'Private Banks Series' were estimated on the basis of the holdings of the same by the joint-stock banks of England and Wales in relation to the total assets of such banks over the relevant years.

Cols. 12 and 14 (1896–1947), the 'Private Bank' holdings of Government securities and Treasury Bills were estimated on the basis of the joint-stock banks of England and Wales' holdings of the same in relation to such banks' holdings of total investments and total discounts over the relevant years.

Col. 10 (1891–1966), cash holdings of the private banks were partly estimated on the basis of S. Japhet's holdings of the same (1933–9), and for the rest of the period on the joint-stock banks of England and Wales' holdings of cash relative to total cash, money at call and short notice in the relevant years.

All cols. (1953–62), excluding the contribution of the Co-operative Wholesale Society Bank, were extracted from the *Bankers' Almanac and Year Book*, Vols. 110–119, by summing up the balance sheets of the banks concerned.

All cols. (1963–6), *Bankers' Almanac and Year Book*, and from the General Manager of the Co-operative Wholesale Society Bank by summing the balance sheets.

Notes

[1] Composition of series (1891–6), Channel Island Bank, Dumbell's Banking Company, Isle of Man Banking Company, Manx Bank, Yorkshire Penny Bank, Co-operative Wholesale Society Bank and those banks reported in *The Economist*'s 'Private Bank Series'.

(1897–8), as above, excluding the Channel Island Bank, which was absorbed by the Midland Bank.

(1899), as above, excluding Dumbell's Banking Company, which was liquidated; the Guernsey Bank is now included.

(1900–12), as above, excluding the Manx Bank which was absorbed.

(1913), as above, excluding the Isle of Man and Guernsey Bank which are reported in *The Economist*'s 'Joint-Stock Banks of England and Wales'.

(1914–15), as above, with the addition of British International.

(1916–17), as above, excluding the British International.

(1917–19), as above, with the addition of Farrows Bank.

(1920–8), the same, excluding Farrows. From 1924, *The Economist*'s 'Private Bank Series', incorporated here consists of C. Baker, B. W. Blydenstein, C. Hoare, and S. Japhet.

(1929–52), the same, with the addition of Erlanger. C. Baker excluded from *The Economist*'s, 'Private Bank Series', from 1937.

(1953), as above excluding Erlangers.

[2] Omissions: Various small banks, such as Harrods, which are not contained in the above series, Grindlays, except for the 1922–3 period, and Hambros (prior to 1920 The British Bank of Northern Commerce) have been excluded. While the omission, fund-wise, is fairly significant (Grindlay's had deposits of £25·7 millions and Hambros had deposits of £53·8 millions in 1956), there are grounds to suppose that Hambros in particular and Grindlays less positively should be excluded from a British-based bank series. Grindlay's assets figures were very small in the pre-war era, particularly in the 1920 period; as a consequence, their inclusion in 1922 and 1923 does not produce much of a discontinuity. Hambros, for instance, has such extensive foreign affiliations that it was reported as a British Bank Trading Abroad in the pre-1947 period. Grindlay's capital was taken over from National Provincial in November 1948 by the National Bank of India, and was amalgamated with that bank in 1958. The Scottish Co-operative Wholesale Society Bank founded in 1948 with assets of £16·0 millions in 1952 has been omitted on grounds of consistency as the figures for this and other co-operative banks (The Peoples' Bank) are not available from published series from 1937–51, and prior to 1915.

TABLE (A) 1.6 **United Kingdom Banks Combined Balance Sheet 1880–1966**

Year	Liabilities Total £ millions	Total Assets % of Total of all UK Banks' Assets			Deposits %	Misc. Liabilities %	Notes in Circulation %	Paid-up Capital %	Acceptances[c] %	Premises %	Cash, Money at Call and Short Notice		Treasury Deposit Receipts %	Bills Discounted		Investments		Loans, Advances %
		Eng.	Scot.	Ire.							% Total	% Cash		% Total	% Treasury Bills	% Total	% British Government Securities	
	A	B	C	D							A	B						
1	2		3		4	5	6	7	8	9	10		11	12	13	14	15	16
1880	432·3	64·4	22·8	12·8	79·2	1·1	2·9	16·8	5·0	1·7	17·1	8·9	—	12·8	—	17·0	9·3	50·6
1881	452·6	65·4	22·1	12·5	79·6	0·8	3·1	16·6	4·9	2·1	18·1	9·4	—	13·8	—	16·9	9·1	49·1
1882	474·9	66·4	21·5	12·1	79·3	0·7	3·3	16·7	4·7	1·9	17·4	9·0	—	13·6	—	16·6	8·2	51·0
1883	492·5	67·2	21·4	11·4	79·6	0·8	2·8	16·8	4·5	2·5	17·2	8·9	—	14·2	—	17·3	8·7	48·6
1884	509·3	68·5	20·7	10·8	79·8	0·4	2·6	16·8	3·6	2·1	16·4	8·5	—	12·5	—	19·6	8·9	50·1
1885	517·1	69·5	20·1	10·4	80.1	—	2·5	16·6	3·3	2·2	17·3	8·9	—	12·1	—	20·0	8·9	48·0
1886	513·1	70·4	19·7	9·9	80·1	0·7	2·5	16·7	3·1	2·1	17·9	9·2	—	12·0	—	19·3	9·1	48·7
1887	527·0	70·7	19·7	9·6	80·6	0·7	2·4	16·3	3·1	2·1	18·0	9·2	—	11·4	—	19·5	8·7	49·1
1888	559·2	71·6	19·0	9·4	81·2	0·7	2·4	15·7	3·3	2·1	18·6	9·5	—	11·2	—	20·1	8·7	48·0
1889	585·5	71·7	18·9	9·4	81·8	0·7	2·4	15·1	3·8	1·4	18·9	9·7	—	11·1	—	20·3	9·3	48·2
1890	611·4	72·2	18·7	9·1	81·6	0·8	2·3	15·2	4·4	2·1	18·7	9·6	—	10·7	—	21·1	9·9	47·4
1891[a]	641·4	73·3	17·9	9·0	81·7	1·7	2·1	14·4	3·0	2·0	18·9	9·7	—	9·8	—	21·4	10·1	47·9
1891	725·2	64·8	15·8	7·7	82·0	1·5	2·0	14·5	3·0	1·8	19·2	9·5	—	8·9	—	22·7	10·3	47·2
1892	739·6	64·2	15·5	7·8	82·2	1·5	1·9	14·4	3·6	2·1	19·5	9·6	—	9·0	—	23·3	10·7	45·9
1893	732·1	64·4	15·8	7·8	82·0	1·5	1·9	14·6	3·4	2·0	19·0	9·3	—	8·2	—	23·2	11·1	47·4
1894	763·3	65·1	15·3	7·3	82·8	1·4	1·8	14·0	3·4	1·9	21·2	10·5	—	8·5	—	23·0	10·2	45·2
1895	810·8	65·9	14·7	7·6	83·5	1·5	1·9	13·2	3·7	2·0	20·7	10·2	—	8·6	—	23·1	9·6	45·4
1896	834·6	69·2	14·5	7·5	84·0	1·5	1·7	12·8	3·4	2·0	19·6	9·7	—	8·4	—	23·1	9·2	47·0
1897	856·4	71·2	14·3	7·3	84·3	1·5	1·7	12·5	3·3	1·9	19·9	10·0	—	7·9	—	22·8	8·7	47·4
1898	885·6	71·5	14·1	7·1	84·6	1·3	1·7	12·4	2·9	2·0	20·7	10·4	—	7·5	—	22·1	8·4	47·5
1899	913·7	71·4	14·1	7·2	84·7	1·4	1·7	12·1	3·1	2·0	20·1	10·1	—	7·5	—	21·7	8·2	48·4
1900	941·7	71·9	14·2	7·2	84·8	1·5	1·7	12·0	2·8	2·2	20·8	10·5	—	7·3	0·8	21·3	8·2	48·4
1901	938·9	71·8	14·3	7·2	84·9	1·4	1·7	12·2	3·1	2·1	21·8	10·9	—	7·0	1·0	21·6	8·4	47·2
1902	954·1	72·6	14·1	7·2	84·8	1·5	1·6	12·1	3·1	2·2	22·5	11·3	—	7·5	1·0	21·1	8·5	46·4
1903	934·0	72·8	14·1	7·5	84·6	1·4	1·6	12·4	3·4	2·0	20·9	10·5	—	7·4	1·0	20·7	8·4	48·7
1904	944·4	73·4	13·6	7·6	84·9	1·3	1·5	12·2	3·6	1·8	22·4	11·3	—	7·5	1·0	20·8	9·3	47·6
1905	971·6	74·0	13·2	7·4	85·2	1·4	1·4	11·9	4·5	2·1	23·3	11·8	—	8·0	0·9	20·6	8·8	46·0
1906	998·1	74·2	13·3	7·3	85·5	1·4	1·4	11·6	4·8	2·0	22·8	11·5	—	8·2	0·8	19·9	8·6	47·1
1907	1003·6	73·6	13·6	7·6	85·9	1·2	1·4	11·4	5·0	2·0	22·5	11·3	—	8·2	0·5	19·4	8·5	47·7
1908	1023·9	74·6	13·0	7·6	86·3	1·1	1·4	11·2	4·7	1·9	23·8	12·0	—	8·5	0·5	20·3	8·4	45·3
1909	1039·8	74·4	12·9	7·6	86·5	1·1	1·3	11·0	4·6	1·9	24·2	12·2	—	8·3	0·6	20·4	7·8	45·1
1910	1081·1	74·9	12·4	7·6	86·9	1·2	1·3	10·6	5·3	1·9	23·2	11·8	—	8·1	0·6	19·6	7·3	47·0
1911	1118·0	74·8	12·5	7·6	87·4	1·0	1·3	10·2	4·9	2·2	24·1	12·2	—	9·0	0·6	19·0	7·0	45·7
1912	1156·1	74·7	12·7	7·4	87·6	1·2	1·3	10·0	6·0	2·2	24·0	12·1	—	10·3	0·4	18·0	6·4	46·0
1913	1205·0	74·8	12·8	7·5	87·9	1·1	1·3	9·6	5·7	2·2	24·8	12·6	—	9·1	0·4	17·0	5·8	45·8
1914	1312·6	75·2	12·4	7·4	88·6	1·1	1·6	8·7	4·2	2·1	26·4	17·1	—	8·8	0·5	18·4	7·6	44·3
1915	1428·0	75·9	12·1	7·3	89·1	1·0	2·0	8·0	4·7	2·2	23·7	16·1	—	6·0	2·7	30·6	20·9	37·5
1916	1636·3	76·2	12·3	6·9	90·0	1·0	2·1	6·8	4·6	1·8	28·2	19·6	—	10·2	5·0	27·6	20·8	32·2
1917	1913·3	76·4	12·3	6·9	90·7	0·9	2·2	6·1	3·8	1·3	28·0	16·8	—	13·0	6·6	24·8	19·4	32·8
1918	2221·9	75·7	12·1	7·8	91·1	0·6	2·5	5·7	2·9	1·6	28·1	16·8	—	17·5	8·9	23·9	19·0	28·8
1919	2611·8	76·0	11·9	8·0	91·8	0·6	2·2	5·4	6·1	0·9	22·8	16·2	—	12·3	6·6	23·6	19·7	40·4
1920	2771·2	75·7	12·0	8·6	91·6	0·5	1·9	5·9	4·0	1·0	21·1	14·5	—	14·4	5·9	20·6	17·0	42·5
1920[b]	2604·1	80·5	12·8	2·7	92·1	0·6	1·4	5·9	4·2	1·0	21·2	14·6	—	15·1	6·1	19·5	16·0	42·8

1923	2408·0	81·3	12·2	2·5	91·8	0·5	1·1	6·6	4·9	1·4	21·0	15·4	—	13·1	6·6	23·8	20·3	40·6
1924	2397·9	81·4	12·2	2·5	91·5	0·6	1·1	6·8	5·9	1·6	21·9	15·9	—	11·2	4·8	22·0	18·4	43·3
1925	2390·8	81·5	12·2	2·5	91·4	0·5	1·1	7·0	5·7	1·5	22·1	15·8	—	10·7	4·6	19·6	16·3	46·0
1926	2432·6	81·9	11·8	2·4	91·4	0·5	1·0	7·1	4·9	1·6	21·7	15·6	—	10·9	5·1	18·6	15·4	47·1
1927	2487·9	81·9	11·9	2·4	91·4	0·6	1·0	7·0	6·1	1·6	23·5	14·8	—	10·6	5·1	17·5	14·2	46·7
1928	2570·9	81·6	11·7	2·3	91·5	0·6	1·0	6·9	9·9	1·9	23·0	15·3	—	11·2	5·0	17·2	14·5	46·6
1929	2535·8	82·6	12·0	2·3	91·3	0·6	1·0	7·1	7·8	1·9	22·5	15·2	—	10·0	4·6	17·3	14·1	48·2
1930	2622·9	81·1	11·9	2·3	91·3	0·5	1·0	7·2	5·4	1·9	21·8	14·2	—	14·1	7·8	19·3	16·0	42·9
1931	2440·2	80·4	12·2	2·4	91·2	0·5	1·0	7·3	5·0	2·4	20·6	13·7	—	11·9	8·5	21·2	17·5	43·9
1932	2722·2	81·0	12·2	2·3	92·2	0·4	0·9	6·5	4·0	2·1	20·1	12·8	—	16·5	12·8	27·7	24·0	34·0
1933	2697·8	80·3	12·5	2·2	92·1	0·5	0·8	6·6	5·0	2·1	20·1	12·9	—	12·7	9·8	32·7	28·7	32·7
1934	2744·9	80·3	12·5	2·1	92·0	0·5	0·9	6·6	5·4	2·1	21·8	13·3	—	9·7	6·8	33·5	29·6	33·4
1935	2891·3	80·1	12·6	2·0	92·4	0·4	0·9	6·3	4·5	1·9	21·1	13·8	—	11·0	6·9	33·4	29·3	32·5
1936	3072·2	80·6	12·3	1·9	93·0	0·2	0·9	6·0	3·5	2·7	22·0	13·7	—	9·8	6·4	33·4	29·4	33·1
1937	3113·2	80·2	12·5	1·9	92·8	0·3	0·9	6·0	4·5	1·7	20·4	13·5	—	9·5	5·6	32·3	28·4	36·1
1938	3034·3	79·6	12·7	1·9	92·6	0·3	0·9	6·2	5·2	1·8	20·2	13·6	—	8·1	4·7	32·8	28·9	37·0
1939	3190·0	80·4	12·3	1·9	92·8	0·3	1·0	5·8	4·3	1·7	21·1	14·2	—	10·9	7·9	30·6	26·4	35·7
1940	3595·4	81·3	12·0	1·8	93·4	0·4	1·0	5·2	3·5	1·5	20·7	14·7	9·3	7·7	5·2	32·1	28·4	28·7
1941	4220·1	81·8	11·7	1·8	94·1	0·2	1·1	4·5	3·1	1·2	19·3	14·6	18·9	4·4	2·9	34·2	31·7	21·8
1942	4604·9	81·4	11·7	1·9	94·3	0·2	1·3	4·1	2·3	1·1	19·2	14·7	20·5	4·6	4·1	35·3	32·9	19·2
1943	5113·8	81·3	11·6	1·8	94·6	0·2	1·3	3·8	2·3	1·0	18·9	14·6	26·5	3·1	2·6	33·8	31·5	16·7
1944	5726·2	81·4	11·4	1·7	95·0	0·3	1·3	3·4	2·2	0·9	19·2	14·3	30·3	3·1	2·7	31·3	29·3	15·2
1945	6107·6	81·2	11·4	1·7	95·3	0·2	1·2	3·2	2·3	0·9	19·6	14·3	26·1	6·5	5·5	31·7	29·4	15·2
1946	7058·2	82·1	10·9	1·7	95·8	0·2	1·1	2·8	3·1	0·7	20·2	12·9	23·0	9·1	7·8	31·1	28·9	15·8
1947	7363·8	82·2	11·0	1·7	95·9	0·1	1·1	2·8	3·8	1·5	20·1	12·4	18·2	11·2	9·8	30·8	28·6	18·6
1948	7663·5	82·4	11·2	1·7	95·4	0·8	1·0	2·8	4·0	0·7	16·3	8·5	18·9	10·0	7·8	29·0	27·2	20·1
1949	7656·6	82·6	11·8	1·8	95·4	0·8	1·0	2·8	4·1	0·6	17·9	9·0	10·7	14·9	13·0	29·1	27·2	22·6
1950	7831·5	82·8	11·1	1·7	95·4	0·8	0·9	2·7	5·7	0·8	18·0	9·0	6·1	18·4	16·6	28·4	26·5	24·0
1951	7782·9	82·3	11·2	1·7	95·8	0·3	1·1	2·7	6·9	0·7	18·2	9·3	1·4	12·8	10·3	33·4	31·7	27·8
1952	7907·1	83·2	11·2	1·7	96·0	0·1	1·1	2·8	5·3	0·7	17·7	9·5	—	16·3	15·3	35·0	33·5	24·5
1953	8161·5	83·4	11·1	1·7	96·2	0·0	1·2	2·6	4·5	0·7	16·7	9·2	—	17·8	16·7	36·1	34·4	23·0
1954	8503·1	83·0	11·5	1·7	96·1	0·0	1·2	2·6	4·5	0·7	16·7	9·4	—	15·8	14·4	35·8	34·0	24·5
1955	8130·0	82·9	11·4	1·7	95·7	0·0	1·3	2·9	6·3	0·7	17·4	9·9	—	17·8	16·1	32·6	30·6	25·0
1956	8168·2	83·0	11·2	1·7	95·5	0·1	1·5	2·9	6·2	0·9	17·4	10·0	—	17·9	16·0	31·6	29·7	26·2
1957	8472·1	83·3	11·1	1·7	95·6	0·0	1·5	2·8	6·9	0·9	17·7	10·2	—	18·9	17·1	31·0	29·2	24·7
1958	8749·0	83·8	10·9	1·8	95·5	0·1	1·4	2·9	6·2	0·9	17·6	9·6	—	15·6	13·9	30·5	28·5	28·2
1959	9333·2	84·1	10·7	1·7	95·2	0·0	1·4	3·4	6·7	0·9	17·4	9·5	—	15·3	13·3	23·9	21·8	34·8
1960	9534·8	84·3	10·4	1·7	94·8	0·0	1·4	3·7	7·9	1·1	18·4	9·7	1·6	12·9	10·9	18·3	16·3	39·9
1961	9691·2	84·3	10·4	1·8	94·6	0·0	1·4	3·9	6·3	1·1	19·6	9·8	2·4	14·6	11·9	16·0	14·2	39·7
1962	10083·8	84·6	10·2	1·8	94·2	0·0	1·3	4·4	5·0	1·2	20·0	9·5	—	13·8	10·9	17·3	15·4	41·6
1963	10844·3	85·0	10·0	1·7	94·0	0·1	1·2	4·8	4·8	1·3	18·9	9·2	—	12·6	9·5	15·7	14·0	45·1
1964	11294·5	85·0	10·0	1·9	93·9	0·1	1·2	4·8	5·0	1·5	18·6	9·3	—	11·0	7·0	13·6	11·9	48·7
1965	12081·3	85·3	9·7	1·9	93·8	0·1	1·1	5·0	5·5	1·8	19·9	9·3	0·8	10·8	6·9	12·9	11·2	46·9
1966	12194·8	85·3	9·6	2·0	93·5	0·1	1·1	5·3	5·4	2·0	22·3	9·9	1·6	9·6	5·7	13·3	11·3	46·4

Sources

Same as Table (A)1.1.

Notes

[a] Discontinuity due to the addition of *The Economist*'s 'Private Banks', the Yorkshire Penny Bank, and the Co-operative Wholesale Society Bank.

[b] Discontinuity due to the exclusion of the banks of Eire which were previously included in the Irish Bank series.

[c] Acceptances are not included in Col. 2, therefore cols 4+5+6+7=100% of col. 2.

TABLE (A) 1.7 **Co-operative Wholesale Society Limited Bank 1895–1966[1] (Assets and liabilities £ millions)**

Year	No. of Branches	Total Assets and Liabilities[2]	Deposits and Other Accounts	Misc. Liabilities (Credit Rebates)	Paid-up Capital and Reserves	Accept-ances	Cash, Money at Call and at Short Notice		Investments		Discounts		Loans, Advances and Other Accounts
							Total	Cash	Total	British Government and Govern-ment-Guaranteed	Total	Treasury Bills	
							A	B	A	B	A	B	
	1	2	3	4	5	6	7		8		9		10
1895	1	1·1	1·1	—	0·0	—	0·5	0·0	0·5	0·2	—	—	0·1
1896	1	1·2	1·2	—	0·0	—	0·5	0·0	0·6	0·1	—	—	0·1
1897	1	1·0	1·0	—	0·0	—	0·1	0·0	0·7	0·1	—	—	0·2
1898	1	1·3	1·3	—	0·1	—	0·4	0·0	0·6	0·0	—	—	0·3
1899	1	1·3	1·3	—	0·1	—	0·1	0·0	0·6	0·0	—	—	0·6
1900	1	1·4	1·4	—	0·1	—	0·1	0·0	0·5	0·0	—	—	0·8
1901	1	1·6	1·5	—	0·1	—	0·5	0·0	0·3	0·0	—	—	0·8
1902	1	1·6	1·5	—	0·1	—	0·7	0·0	0·2	0·0	—	—	0·7
1903	1	1·5	1·4	—	0·1	—	0·6	0·0	0·2	0·0	—	—	0·7
1904	1	1·5	1·4	—	0·1	—	0·4	0·0	0·2	0·0	—	—	0·9
1905	1	2·0	1·9	—	0·1	—	1·0	0·0	0·2	0·0	—	—	0·8
1906	1	2·1	2·0	—	0·1	—	0·9	0·0	0·4	0·0	—	—	0·8
1907	1	2·5	2·4	—	0·1	—	1·1	0·0	0·6	0·0	—	—	0·8
1908	1	2·5	2·4	—	0·1	—	0·5	0·0	0·9	0·0	—	—	1·1
1909	1	3·0	2·9	—	0·1	—	1·1	0·0	0·9	0·0	—	—	1·0
1910	1	3·2	3·1	—	0·1	—	0·9	0·0	1·2	0·2	—	—	1·1
1911	1	4·3	4·2	—	0·1	—	0·9	0·0	2·3	0·2	—	—	1·1
1912	1	5·3	5·2	—	0·1	—	1·3	0·0	2·9	0·3	—	—	1·1
1913	1	6·3	6·1	—	0·2	—	1·5	0·0	3·6	0·4	—	—	1·2
1914	1	7·0	6·8	—	0·2	—	1·7	0·0	4·0	0·7	—	—	1·3
1915	1	7·9	7·8	—	0·1	—	2·0	0·0	4·5	0·9	—	—	1·4
1916	1	9·2	9·1	—	0·1	—	3·7	0·0	4·5	1·5	—	—	1·0
1917	1	9·7	9·6	—	0·1	—	4·6	0·0	4·0	1·8	—	—	1·1
1918	1	10·6	10·6	—	0·0	—	5·0	0·0	4·0	2·4	—	—	1·6
1919	1	10·8	10·8	—	0·0	—	0·5	0·0	4·2	2·7	—	—	6·1
1920	2	16·0	16·0	—	0·0	—	4·9	0·0	3·9	2·7	—	—	7·2
1921	3	16·4	16·3	—	0·1	—	7·7	0·0	5·7	2·7	—	—	3·0
1922	4	22·3	22·2	—	0·1	—	11·3	0·0	8·2	3·9	—	—	2·8
1923	4	26·0	25·8	—	0·2	—	10·2	0·0	12·2	4·9	—	—	3·6
1924	4	29·2	28·9	—	0·3	—	10·0	0·0	15·5	4·9	—	—	3·7
1925	4	30·7	30·4	—	0·3	—	9·7	0·0	14·6	3·7	—	—	6·4
1926	4	28·5	28·1	—	0·4	—	7·4	0·0	13·4	5·2	—	—	7·7
1927	4	32·9	32·3	—	0·6	—	12·2	0·0	14·5	3·6	—	—	6·2
1928	4	40·5	39·7	—	0·8	—	14·2	0·0	20·9	7·4	—	—	5·4

10

1930	4	55·5	54·5	—	1·0	—	14·5	0·0	34·6	16·6	—	—	6·6
1931	4	60·4	60·1	—	0·3	—	10·0	0·0	42·4	24·4	—	—	8·0
1932	4	68·3	67·9	—	0·4	—	12·6	0·0	50·0	31·6	—	—	5·7
1933	4	77·1	76·5	—	0·6	—	12·6	0·0	58·7	41·1	—	—	5.8
1934	4	86·0	83·3	—	0·7	—	14·0	0·0	67·9	52·2	—	—	4·1
1935	4	95·0	94·1	—	0·9	—	11·7	0·0	80·7	65·3	—	—	2·6
1936	4	105·1	104·0	—	1·1	—	10·9	0·1	91·3	76·7	—	—	2·9
1937	4	109·3	108·1	—	1·2	—	10·2	0·1	96·3	79·3	—	—	2·8
1938	4	113·6	112·1	—	1·5	—	10·7	0·1	99·4	81·3	—	—	3·5
1939	4	113·9	112·2	—	1·7	—	7·3	0·1	102·3	81·4	—	—	4·3
1940	4	116·9	115·0	—	1·9	—	14·9	0·1	100·1	80·0	—	—	1·9
1941	4	129·7	127·6	—	2·1	—	12·1	0·1	115·9	96·2	—	—	1·7
1942	4	155·4	153·1	—	2·3	—	16·4	0·1	138·0	118·2	—	—	1·0
1943	4	186·0	183·4	—	2·6	—	16·3	0·1	168·8	148·8	—	—	0·9
1944	4	217·9	215·2	—	2·7	—	19·3	0·1	197·2	176·7	—	—	1·4
1945	4	236·4	233·5	—	2·9	—	18·1	0·2	215·3	191·0	—	—	3·0
1946	5	259·6	256·5	—	3·1	—	17·6	0·4	237·5	210·4	—	—	4·5
1947	12	258·9	255·7	—	3·2	—	19·2	0·5	228·4	197·9	—	—	11·3
1948	13	247·1	242·7	—	3·4	1·0	22·2	0·6	212·3	182·7	1·0	—	11·6
1949	13	235·2	232·4	—	2·7	0·1	19·5	0·7	197·0	166·2	0·1	—	18·6
1950	14	221·5	218·6	—	2·8	0·1	20·8	0·7	179·5	149·4	0·1	—	21·1
1951	14	197·9	193·4	—	1·3	3·2	24·8	0·9	142·5	113·4	3·2	—	27·4
1952	15	191·7	190·1	—	1·4	0·2	27·6	0·8	137·1	105·9	0·2	—	26·8
1953	15	196·5	194·8	—	1·6	0·1	25·6	0·9	140·7	100·2	0·1	—	30·1
1954	15	205·9	204·0	—	1·8	0·1	28·3	1·1	147·5	98·5	0·1	—	30·0
1955	16	203·3	201·2	—	2·0	0·1	24·3	1·1	144·1	92·3	2·5	2·4	35·4
1956	16	198·8	196·0	—	2·2	0·6	21·6	1·1	132·5	84·9	0·6	—	44·1
1957	16	195·2	192·0	—	2·5	0·7	26·8	1·2	121·0	73·7	0·7	—	46·7
1958	16	176·1	173·1	—	2·7	0·3	23·8	1·2	109·7	64·3	0·3	—	42·3
1959	16	177·8	172·8	—	3·0	2·0	26·1	1·2	104·9	63·6	2·0	—	44·8
1960	16	182·6	178·1	—	3·3	1·2	24·2	1·1	105·9	65·8	1·7	0·5	50·8
1961	16	184·1	180·2	—	3·6	0·3	27·4	1·3	97·0	61·3	0·3	—	59·4
1962	16	176·6	171·6	—	3·9	1·1	24·5	1·2	85·0	52·5	1·1	—	66·0
1963	—	178·3	173·4	—	4·2	0·7	26·2	1·2	74·0	48·6	—	—	77·4
1964	—	171·9	167·1	—	4·5	0·2	33·3	1·3	67·7	44·7	—	—	70·5
1965	—	179·2	174·0	—	4·9	0·3	34·4	1·6	73·1	50·6	—	—	71·3
1966	—	177·0	171·6	—	5·3	0·2	34·6	1·5	96·5	45·4	—	—	80·3
1967	—	201·5	195·4	—	5·5	0·6	37·9	1·6	106·8	53·0	—	—	94·1

Sources

The above data were kindly provided by the General Manager of the CWS Bank. Comparable data may be found for the period 1915–36 and 1951–62 in the annual reports of the Registrar of Friendly Societies and the odd *Bankers' Almanac.*

Notes

[1] Since the balance sheet is drawn up in January the data for the year t are from the accounts of the year $t+1$.

Data not available prior to 1895.

[2] Total assets and liabilities includes acceptances when recorded – 1948 onwards.

TABLE (A) 1.8 **London Clearing Banks, End-of-year Consolidated Balance Sheet 1919–1966[1] (Assets and liabilities £ millions)**

Year-End 31 Dec.[3]	*No. of Banks*	*Total Assets or Liabilities*[4]	*Deposits and Other Accounts*	*Misc. Liabilities Credits, Rebates, etc.*	*Notes in Circulation*	*Paid-up Capital and Reserves*	*Acceptances, Endorsements and Customer's Liability for same*[4]	*Premises and Other Assets*	*Cash, Money at Call and at Short Notice*		*Treasury Deposit Receipts or Special Deposits*	*Discounts*		*Investments*		*Loans, Advances Other Accounts*
									Total	*Cash*		*Total*	*Treasury Bills*[5]	*Total*	*British Government and Government-Guaranteed*	
	1	3	4	5	6	7	8	9	A 10	B	11	12	13	14	15	16
1919	10	1841·5	1736·6	4·6	4·5	95·8	123·2	15·4	428·9	335·2	—	224·7	**144·7**	371·7	331·7	710·0
1920	10	1965·9	1838·3	6·0	4·1	117·5	88·6	18·8	429·6	316·5	—	292·2	**131·6**	356·9	306·7	798·9
1921	10	1978·5	1850·7	6·3	3·1	118·4	59·5	23·9	413·4	346·7	—	412·7	**249·5**	358·8	305·9	693·8
1922	10	1851·0	1724·0	5·6	2·8	118·6	73·1	27·0	396·3	316·8	—	282·2	**177·8**	402·1	352·3	675·2
1923	10	1846·1	1718·5	5·7	2·6	119·3	99·3	27·0	393·0	318·6	—	267·4	**140·8**	380·2	329·6	717·8
1924	10	1840·0	1707·5	7·1	3·2	122·2	115·6	27·8	412·7	327·5	—	219·2	**100·1**	343·5	291·6	772·0
1925	10	1829·0	1694·9	5·6	3·2	125·3	108·3	29·1	415·2	327·0	—	204·7	**95·4**	300·6	252·1	811·0
1926	10	1881·7	1744·3	5·8	3·1	128·5	96·9	32·3	417·3	328·7	—	215·9	**109·0**	291·7	243·3	859·9
1927	10	1926·1	1788·1	5·5	2·9	129·6	128·0	33·3	464·1	316·4	—	219·0	**114·0**	273·3	228·5	870·5
1928	10	2014·5	1872·5	5·8	2·2	134·0	220·7	42·6	469·3	336·8	—	243·3	**114·1**	283·8	247·8	924·0
1929	10	1978·1	1836·6	6·6	1·4	133·5	165·9	41·3	457·5	331·3	—	210·7	**103·2**	274·9	228·3	945·0
1930	10	2044·6	1903·4	4·8	1·3	135·1	118·0	44·0	446·8	318·5	—	303·2	**158·2**	316·1	265·1	882·6
1931	10	1893·0	1755·1	12·3	1·2	124·4	97·5	51·6	394·6	271·0	—	224·8	**134**	314·9	262·0	862·9
1932	10	2120·7	1987·8	5·8	1·4	125·7	90·8	44·8	422·2	273·5	—	375·9	**316**	498·5	440·4	714·2
1933	10	2084·0	1950·8	5·6	1·4	126·2	113·4	45·5	424·5	280·6	—	282·8	**228**	587·2	521·7	681·4
1934	10	2122·5	1987·1	5·6	1·3	128·5	112·9	44·5	457·5	292·2	—	244·2	**186**	609·8	548·6	702·2
1935	10	2230·2	2095·5	4·6	1·4	128·7	98·3	45·4	476·6	320·0	—	291·0	**138**	620·3	551·3	723·2
1936[2]	10	2380·7	2245·8	4·3	1·2	129·4	72·7	72·4	541·6	341·7	—	277·2	**215**	663·7	582·9	792·6
1936	11	2465·3	2324·0	4·7	1·2	135·4	80·0	73·9	561·4	356·5	—	283·7	**220**	693·1	609·1	889·8
1937	11	2489·7	2344·3	5·1	1·3	139·0	112·8	44·0	517·7	354·3	—	278·4	**200**	663·9	586·4	985·8
1938	11	2411·4	2265·4	5·6	1·3	139·1	127·9	44·3	497·7	344·2	—	233·1	**158**	650·9	573·4	982·1
1939	11	2581·5	2435·4	7·0	1·4	137·7	115·7	44·2	559·2	384·7	—	333·9	**267**	634·1	551·5	1009·8
1940	11	2941·1	2794·7	4·0	2·2	140·2	108·3	44·6	604·2	445·7	313·5	268·1	**237**	795·2	715·5	919·2
1941	11	3470·3	3324·3	4·3	1·4	140·3	111·1	43·7	657·8	516·5	757·5	171·6	**159**	1022·4	952·4	818·1
1942	11	3771·1	3623·6	5·0	1·6	140·9	93·0	42·9	703·3	561·1	895·0	297·1	**184**	1144·3	1076·6	787·9
1943	11	4175·5	4026·5	4·8	1·5	142·7	100·6	41·8	761·1	610·1	1306·0	131·7	**118**	1178·0	1107·5	755·4
1944	11	4690·4	4539·7	5·5	1·3	143·9	105·1	41·4	878·9	680·3	1665·0	151·5	**132**	1188·7	1117·6	769·5
1945	11	4996·7	4844·6	5·1	1·2	145·8	118·6	41·0	982·9	730·8	1522·0	370·1	**349**	1258·6	1169·3	822·2
1946	11	5833·3	5680·0	4·4	1·1	147·8	195·4	40·7	1181·6	749·7	1558·5	610·5	**582**	1451·4	1359·4	990·8
1947	11	6083·5	5928·2	5·1	1·1	149·1	257·7	107·4	1227·7	754·1	1287·0	793·2	**737**	1509·8	1409·6	1212·0
1948	11	6352·3	6141·0	53·5	0·9	156·9	267·1	44·1	987·5	502·4	1397·0	741·2	**675**	1467·7	1395·7	1356·2
1949	11	6356·4	6145·1	52·6	0·9	157·8	272·5	40·7	1103·2	532·4	793·0	1109·0	**1038**	1501·2	1412·0	1502·7

1950	11	6523·6	6309·8	52·8	0·9	160·1	393·8	44·2	1132·5	540·3	455·5	1408·7	**1318**	1517·0	1426·7	1626·9
1951	11	6509·4	6333·0	15·0	0·9	160·5	474·6	44·0	1129·2	531·5	102·0	971·6	791·0	1965·0	1888·0	1860·0
1952	11	6625·9	6460·0	0·0	0·8	165·1	365·9	45·5	1079·7	550·7	—	1248·5	1182·0	2148·0	2076·0	1665·0
1953	11	6855·9	6694·0	0·4	0·8	160·7	319·2	46·5	1043·0	542·0	—	1417·0	1338·0	2275·0	2194·0	1611·0
1954	11	7110·3	6941·0	1·5	0·6	167·2	232·7	47·6	1069·0	571·0	—	1313·0	1199·0	2353·0	2261·0	1783·0
1955	11	6791·8	6612·0	0·5	0·6	178·7	457·8	49·6	1071·0	565·0	—	1400·0	1271·0	2016·0	1928·0	1747·0
1956	11	6838·6	6656·0	0·6	0·6	181·4	447·8	53·4	1076·0	571·0	—	1416·0	1275·0	1980·0	1893·0	1832·0
1957	11	7115·4	6929·0	2·0	0·6	183·8	498·5	58·1	1126·0	601·0	—	1538·0	1403·0	2049·0	1962·0	1777·0
1958	11	7394·7	7199·0	2·2	0·6	192·9	485·7	63·9	1163·0	586·0	—	1320·0	1185·0	2102·0	1994·0	2126·0
1959	11	8017·4	7767·0	0·5	0·6	249·3	575·3	70·1	1249·0	635·0	—	1380·0	1215·0	1710·0	1584·0	2818·0
1960	11	8110·0	7831·0	0·2	0·6	278·2	691·1	80·3	1369·0	658·0	144·0	1183·0	1017·0	1271·0	1150·0	3323·0
1961	11	8228·4	7928·0	1·9	0·6	297·9	535·3	88·1	1504·0	664·0	221·0	1356·0	1106·0	1120·0	1010·0	3329·0
1962	11	8591·1	8231·0	1·1	0·5	358·5	433·8	102·6	1617·0	700·0	—	1336·0	1067·0	1323·0	1204·0	3609·0
1963	11	9278·5	8851·0	0·5	0·5	426·5	450·7	121·5	1645·0	738·0	—	1307·0	996·0	1286·0	1169·0	4247·0
1964	11	9668·4	9222·0	0·6	0·5	445·3	483·5	145·6	1676·0	771·0	—	1185·0	764·0	1159·0	1038·0	4784·4
1965	11	10390·3	9882·0	0·6	0·4	507·3	546·0	191·2	1940·0	832·0	91·0	1235·0	784·0	1189·0	1048·0	4936·0
1966	11	10463·0	9920·0	3·4	0·3	539·3	561·9	217·2	2227·0	871·0	188·0	1103·0	651·0	1202·0	1061·0	4887·0

Sources

Cols. 3, 4, 6–10, 12, 14–16 (1919–50) extracted from *The Economist*'s 'Banking Supplement' or 'Banking Number' tables on 'English Joint-Stock Banks', and such figures from the same source reported for the National Bank of Ireland. The two series were combined after excluding the assets and liabilities of the non-clearing banks contained in *The Economist* 'Series'. Col. 13 (1919–50) derived from Cmd. 3844 and H. Johnson's *Reprint Series*, No. 54.

Cols. 4, 10–16 (1951–62) extracted from the *Bank of England Quarterly Bulletins*, Dec. 1960 and Sept. 1963.

Col. 5 (1919–50) calculated on a residual basis by subtracting columns 4+6+7 from col. 3.

Col. 5 (1951–62) extracted from the annual issues of the *Bankers' Almanac* by consolidating the clearing banks' 30 June balance sheets given therein and computing the same as for the 1919–50 period.

Col. 3 (1951–66) calculated as being equal to the sum of cols. 4 to 7.

Col. 11 extracted from the *Bankers' Almanac* prior to 1951, and from the *Bank of England Quarterly Bulletin* from there on. It should be noted that the figures reported in col. 12 (Total Discounts) in *The Economist* have been adjusted downwards to allow for this entry.

Cols. 6–9 (1951–62) obtained from the annual issues of the *Bankers' Almanac* by consolidating the relevant items on the 30 June balance sheets of the banks concerned. It should be noted that it is unlikely that cols. 6–9 vary much between 30 June of a year and the following December.

Cols. 4–9 (1963–6) from annual issues of the *Bankers' Almanac and Year Book*.

Cols. 3, 10A–15 (1963–6) kindly provided by the Chief of the Economic Intelligence Department of the Bank of England. (All 31 Dec. figures.)

Notes

[1] London Clearing Banks in 1962: Barclays, Coutts, District, Glyn Mills, Lloyds, Martins, Midland, National Provincial, National, Westminster, Williams Deacon's.

[2] On 1 Jan. 1936 the District Bank became a member of the London Clearing Banks Association.

[3] Except for cols. 6–9, which for the 1951–66 period were extracted from the relevant banks' 30 June balance sheets, all the figures are for 31 Dec. of the relevant year.

[4] Col. 3 (Total Assets/Total Liabilities) does not include either the customers' or the banks' liability for acceptances or endorsements.

[5] Figures in bold type are estimates.

TABLE (A) 1.9 **London Clearing Banks, Annual Average of Monthly Statements 1919–1966 (£ millions)**

Year	Banks	Total Assets or Liabilities[b]	Deposits: Total	Deposits: Current	Paid-up Capital and Reserves	Liability of Customers for Acceptances and Endorsements: Total	Liability of Customers for Acceptances and Endorsements: Acceptances	Cash in Hand and Money at Call and Short Notice: Total	Cash in Hand and Money at Call and Short Notice: Cash on Hand and at B.O.E.	Balance due from Other Banks and Items in Transit: Total	Balance due from Other Banks and Items in Transit: Due from Banks	Treasury Deposit Receipts or Special Deposits	Investments: Total	Investments: British Government and Government-Guaranteed[g]	Bills Discounts: Total	Bills Discounts: Treasury Bills[g]	Loans and Advances and Other Accounts: Total[a]	Loans and Advances and Other Accounts: Loans and Advances
	1	3	4 A	4 B	7	8 A[f]	8 B	A	B	10 C	D[f]	11	12	13	14	15	16 A[a]	16 B
1919	10	—	1510·7	1015·9	—	—	61·5	347·8	216·3	—	—	—	351·4	—	266·0	159·2	—	579·6
1920	10	—	1719·7[e]	1097·6	—	—	75·8	289·6	189·5	—	—	—	367·7[e]	—	259·8	115·6	—	831·6[e]
1921	10	1997	1812	1024·8	—	63	39·4	306·8[e]	206·8[e]	—	—	—	331	—	358·7	224·6	833	790·2
								316	211		48							
1922	10	1953	1774	998·3	—	59	36·5	319	206	—	44	—	391	—	321·3	208·0	750	711·8
1923	10	1874	1674	965·6	119	79	44·7	307	197	—	45	—	356	—	265·9	146·1	761	729·5
1924	10	1887	1671	950·0	122	91	54·5	300	195	—	48	—	341	—	230·3	104·8	808	774·2
1925	10	1888	1662	922·5	123	100	60·5	315	196	—	52	—	286	—	218·6	90·9	856	821·7
1926	10	1888	1665	921·4	127	93	52·1	315	195	—	50	—	265	—	208·7	101·9	892	858·0
1927	10	1942	1713	932·1	129	98	49·5	335	198	—	52	—	254	—	211·0	112·6	928	899·2
1928	10	2069	1766	953·7	133	166	65·3	346	196	—	55	—	254	—	225·9	107·7	948	923·6
1929	10	2139	1800	940·2	134	203	73·6	339	194	—	55	—	257	—	221·2	98·3	991	964·0
1930	10	2073	1801	920·8	134	136	58·0	332	192	—	50	—	258	**235**[c]	255·8	128·6	963	933·4
1931	10	2010	1760	895	135	114	—	303	182	—	46	—	301	**272**	256	156·0	919	
1932	10	2006	1791	867	125	89	—	303	187	—	42	—	348	**320**	308	250·0	844	—
1933	10	2182	1953	978	126	102	—	314	212	—	43	—	537	**500**	354	310·0	758	—
1934	10	2121	1880	953	126	114	—	346	212	—	46	—	560	**520**	230	180·0	753	—
1935	10	2235	1999	1083	128	106	—	357	215	—	48	—	615	**565**	260	**212**[d]	769	—
1936	10	2370	2142	n.a.	129	99	—	379	221	—	54	—	614	**562**	313	**244**	839	—
1936	11	2456	2216	1197	134	105	—	393	228	—	56	—	643	**588**	320	**249**	865	—
1937	11	2542	2287	1233	135	119	—	402	235	—	62	—	652	**597**	281	**196**	954	—
1938	11	2536	2277	1244	139	118	—	392	241	—	60	—	637	**582**	280	**196**	976	—
1939	11	2513	2248	1252	139	125	—	393	244	—	67	—	608	**552**	255	**181**	991	—
1940	11	2765	2506	1522	140	118	—	416	268	—	87	73	666	**612**	370	**315**	955	—
1941	11	3216	2970	1885	140	104	—	445	311	—	107	495	894	**849**	231	**202**	858	—
1942	11	3512	3275	2148	140	95	—	478	345	—	116	642	1069	**1026**	234	**223**	797	—
1943	11	3918	3677	2455	141	98	—	538	386	—	123	1002	1147	**1103**	185	**173**	747	—
1944	11	4396	4153	2740	142	99	—	617	437	—	131	1387	1165	**1118**	171	**154**	750	—
1945	11	4942	4692	3127	144	104	—	698	492	—	141	1811	1156	**1095**	188	**172**	768	—
1946	11	5397	5097	3377	146	153	—	823	523	—	165	1492	1345	**1279**	457	**439**	888	—
1947	11	6032	5650	3690	148	233	—	923	473	—	186	1308	1474	**1398**	723	**685**	1107	—
1948	11	6311	5913	3850	149	248	—	959	486	—	199	1284	1479	**1402**	744	**671**	1319	—
1949	11	6387	5974	3940	153	259	—	1006	496	—	202	983	1505	**1424**	914	**850**	1440	—

1951	11	6787	6162	4095	156	468	—	1080	511	—	232	247	1624	1888	1228	1082	1822	—
1952	11	6667	6083	3907	156	427	—	1034	505	301	226	7	1983	2076	1062	957	1838	1776
1953	11	6754	6256	3938	161	336	—	981	509	310	232	—	2163	2194	1219	1156	1732	1666
1954	11	7014	6495	4078	169	349	—	985	528	343	256	—	2321	2261	1206	1119	1804	1731
1955	11	7095	6454	4054	179	462	—	968	529	361	269	—	2149	1928	1130	1016	2019	1941
1956	11	6902	6288	3932	182	432	—	947	516	367	275	—	1978	1893	1270	1156	1897	1820
1957	11	7122	6433	3905	186	503	—	965	526	394	—	—	2008	1962	1291	1143	—	1868
1958	11	7339	6636	3769	196	506	—	977	543	406	—	—	2149	1994	1277	1167	—	1923
1959	11	7783	6936	4064	246	601	—	1054	565	436	—	—	1836	1718	1223	1089	—	2522
1960	11	8259	7235	4207	278	745	—	1150	588	403	—	74	1407	1277	1149	1007	—	3123
1961	11	8471	7395	4157	308	767	—	1213	607	486	—	174	1122	1009	1225	992	—	3357
1962	11	8443	7611	4186	371	461	—	1341	623	527	—	159	1194	1082	1205	933	—	3408
1963	11	8856	7971	4486	429	455	—	1395	647	563	—	—	1244	1128	1140	842		3880
1964	11	9497	8550	4836	457	490	—	1434	696	658	—	—	1220	1098	1155	790	—	4328
1965	11	10044	8989	4869	513	541	—	1649	739	673	—	56	1087	956	1114	653	—	4653
1966	11	10488	9376	4955	544	567	—	1773	767	704	—	137	1137	997	1135	689	—	4732

Sources

Cols. 4A, 10A, 10B, 12, 14, 16A (1919–21), Cols. 4B, 8B, 15, 16B (1919–30), Committee of Finance and Industry, *Report*, Cmd. 3897 (London: H.M.S.O., 1931), pp. 284–9.

Cols. 3, 4A, 8A, 10A, 10B, 10D, 11, 12, 14, 16A (1921–56), B. R. Mitchell and Phyllis Deane, *Abstract of British Historical Statistics* (Cambridge University Press, 1962), pp. 448–9.

Cols. 4B, 7, 10C, 13, 15, 16B (1951–7), C.S.O., *Annual Abstract of Statistics*, No. 98 (London: H.M.S.O., 1961), p. 279.

Cols. 3, 4A, 4B, 7, 8A, 10A, 10B, 10C, 11, 12, 13, 14, 15, 16B (1957–61), *Annual Abstract of Statistics*, No. 99 (London: H.M.S.O., 1962), p. 276.

Cols. 4B, 7 (1935–9), C.S.O., ibid., 1935–46, No. 84, p. 237.

Cols. 4B, 7 (1940–6), C.S.O., ibid., No. 86, pp. 250–1.

Cols. 4B, 7 (1946–50), C.S.O., ibid., No. 90, pp. 276.

Col. 7 (1923–35), Board of Trade, *Statistical Abstract for the United Kingdom*, No. 82 (London: H.M.S.O., 1937), p. 253.

Col. 15 (1935–50), derived from H. G. Johnson, 'Clearing bank holdings of public debt, 1930–50', *Reprint Series*, No. 54 (University of Cambridge, 1952), pp. 1–8.

Col. 13 (1930–50), ibid.

All columns (1962), C.S.O., *Annual Abstract of Statistics*, No. 101, p. 298.

Col. 15 (1951, 1956), Committee on the working of the monetary system, *Report*, Cmd. 827 (London: H.M.S.O., 1959), p. 356.

Cols. 4B, 15 (1931–4), British banks, *Truptil Appendix*.

All columns 1963–6, C.S.O., *Annual Abstract of Statistics*, No. 105 (1968).

Notes

[a] Prior to 1951 total loans and advances include items in process of collection for eight banks.

[b] Total assets are understated as they exclude value of bank premises and investments in affiliated banks and subsidiary companies. These investments were valued as £43·8 million and £23·9 million respectively in 1937: £67·7 million in total.

[c] The clearing banks' British Government and Government-guaranteed holdings from 1930–50 are averages of the end of June and the end of December figures.

[d] Treasury Bill holdings as estimated by H. Johnson are averages of the end of June and the end of December figures. Johnson suggests that his estimates are too high in the 1930s, and too low in the 1940s.

[e] Slight discontinuity between data given in these columns in 1921 by the two sources.

[f] Balance due from other banks not included in Col. 10A.

[g] Figures in bold type are estimated.

Other Points

(1) All Macmillan figures 1919–30 are year averages of monthly returns.

(2) All other figures 1921–39 are annual averages of weekly returns drawn up on various days within the relevant week by the different banks. The Treasury Bill and British Government Securities figures, however, are averages of 30 June to 31 Dec. estimates over the 1930–50 period.

(3) All other figures 1940–6 are annual averages of monthly returns drawn up in the second half of each year at convenient dates within the relevant month by the different banks. The Treasury Bill and British Government Securities figures, however, are for the 1940–50 period as in note (2). From 1951 they are averages of holdings on varying dates at the end of each quarter.

(4) 1946–62: all figures are annual averages of monthly returns drawn up on the same date of each month by the various banks.

(5) London Clearing Banks, 1919–35: Barclays, Coutts and Company, Glyn Mills, Lloyds, Martins, Midland, National, National Provincial, Westminster, Williams Deacon's.

1936–62, as above, including the District Bank.

TABLE (A) 1.10 **Bank Advances in Great Britain, Annual Averages 1936–8, 1946–66 (£ millions)**

Year	*British Banking Association Total Advances*[1]	*Personal and Professional*	*Food, Drink and Tobacco*	*Retail Trade*	*Agriculture and Fishing*	*Chemical*	*Shipping and Ship-Building*	*Iron and Steel and Allied Trades*	*Engineering, etc.*	*Public Utilities including Transport and Communications*	*Textiles, Cotton, Wool and Others*	*Financial* *Stock Brokers*	*Financial* *Other Financial*	*Financial* *Hire Purchase*	*Building Contracting Building Material*	*Local Authority*
	1	2	3	4	5	6	7	8	9	10	11	A	B 12	C	13	14
1936	869·5	—	29·4	60·1	57·7	—		40·7		—	39·9		109·6		61·5	—
1937	961·0	—	32·5	64·0	60·1	—		49·9		—	43·8		118·2		68·2	—
1938*	954·3	—	36·1	66·4	62·5	—		45·9		—	38·1		109·0		68·1	—
1946	896·2	261·4	59·4	68·4	73·7	8·6	10·5	15·5	62·5	18·3	24·9	4·7	77·1		48·9	71·9
1947	1128·6	321·1	75·1	102·3	89·0	15·0	15·1	14·3	82·3	25·3	30·6	4·8	97·2		65·6	78·8
1948	1354·6	365·9	81·7	138·9	115·4	19·7	16·9	17·1	112·4	38·4	44·0	4·0	103·5		73·0	85·9
1949	1494·6	400·0	101·3	159·2	137·2	18·5	16·2	23·5	109·6	42·0	47·9	4·5	125·9		74·5	88·2
1950	1683·9	419·4	121·0	180·1	163·6	22·0	15·5	21·8	93·1	81·5	65·9	5·1	159·5		78·3	90·9
1951	1920·6	434·3	142·7	207·1	190·4	26·3	15·8	17·3	109·5	81·7	99·4	6·4	200·2		88·6	91·7
1952	1930·6	402·2	158·1	189·4	198·9	35·1	11·7	30·9	150·0	116·4	94·8	5·4	177·6		86·6	78·0
1953	1815·8	366·7	132·5	169·6	200·3	25·9	16·0	55·0	153·6	114·2	81·3	6·4	179·1		78·0	78·3
1954	1907·6	374·3	133·6	176·9	213·7	27·0	16·5	48·8	137·7	138·6	88·6	13·3	178·0†	15·1	79·0	89·0
1955	2120·2	389·1	162·5	192·7	233·6	31·0	22·4	30·2	158·7	184·3	99·9	12·7	177·0	38·6	94·6	90·9
1956	1969·7	331·9	155·9	173·1	225·4	33·2	28·0	39·9	197·4	114·8	90·9	10·7	175·1	28·7	90·1	80·0
1957	2016·0	324·0	150·9	166·2	227·4	31·9	34·5	56·0	233·1	78·1	114·7	14·2	188·1	31·4	85·1	83·0
1958	2071·5	340·7	149·7	182·2	228·6	32·7	51·9	50·3	236·2	86·8	111·0	9·8	178·5	32·0	88·1	79·3
1959	2751·9	512·1	185·4	265·4	292·7	35·5	73·9	66·8	284·2	107·2	116·9	16·9	235·9	89·1	120·7	92·1
1960	3446·5	672·8	189·2	357·1	353·8	40·2	85·6	81·5	360·7	119·6	139·2	18·4	313·5	138·6	169·3	87·9
1961	3802·8	691·3	215·1	369·3	383·2	52·3	106·2	96·2	481·6	118·5	159·4	15·1	335·4	138·6	199·5	91·4
1962	3950·7	707·1	212·1	393·7	393·5	69·7	113·7	107·3	529·0	116·3	168·3	8·7	355·5	104·9	210·9	74·3
1963	4495·3	862·9	227·5	460·5	434·8	81·4	101·9	132·8	535·9	138·6	178·7	8·3	452·3	105·0	248·6	80·2
1964	5024·0	991·0	247·0	510·9	488·3	80·9	98·3	146·6	548·7	139·7	217·3	7·7	539·0	133·3	285·6	92·6
1965	5416·6	972·4	283·0	540·9	517·0	92·7	90·6	163·0	678·5	125·9	226·7	6·8	561·9	150·6	343·6	82·9
1966	5597·0	907·2	295·5	545·4	523·6	131·2	90·3	179·0	796·3	141·7	229·0	6·5	532·7	121·6	367·5	86·8

Sources

1936–8, Cols. 1, 3, 4, 5, 7+8+9, 11, 12A+12B+12C, 13, Bank of England *Statistical Summary*, Nov. 1938, p. 131.

1946–50, cols. 1–11, 12A, 12B+12C, 13, 14, C.S.O., *Annual Abstract of Statistics*, No. 93 (London: H.M.S.O., 1956), p. 274.

1951–61, cols. 1–14, C.S.O., *Annual Abstract of Statistics*, No. 99 (London: H.M.S.O., 1962), p. 280.

1962, cols. 1–14, C.S.O., *Financial Statistics*, No. 30 (October 1964), p. 30.

1963–6, all cols., C.S.O., *Annual Abstract of Statistics*, No. 104 (1967).

Notes

† Includes from 1954 onwards, certain short-term lending not previously recorded – £23·5 million (1954).

* 1936–8, advances of London Clearing Banks only.

[1] Averages of figures Feb., May, August, Nov., of members of British Bankers' Association, through offices in Great Britain – Note London Clearing Banks' share (1959) £2,522 million.

Year	Credit Clearings Total	Debit Clearings Total Cols. 3+4+5	Composition of Debit Clearings: Town (London)	Metropolitan and other (General)	Provincial
	1	2	3	4	5
1880	—	—	5794		—
1881	—	—	6357		—
1882	—	—	6221		—
1883	—	—	5929		—
1884	—	—	5799		—
1885	—	—	5511		—
1886	—	—	5902		—
1887	—	—	6077		—
1888	—	—	6942		—
1889	—	—	7619		—
1890	—	—	7801		—
1891	—	—	6848		—
1892	—	—	6482		—
1893	—	—	6478		—
1894	—	—	6337		—
1895	—	7979	7593		386
1896	—	8039	7575		464
1897	—	7974	7491		483
1898	—	8605	8097		508
1899	—	9721	9150		571
1900	—	9593	8960		633
1901	—	10167	9561		606
1902	—	10644	9158	871[e]	615
1903	—	10745	9235	885[e]	625
1904	—	11219	9678	886[e]	655
1905	—	12953	11355	933[e]	665
1906	—	13390	11719	992[e]	679
1907	—	13453	11657	1073[e]	723
1908	—	12772	10408	1712[e]	652
1909	—	14215[1]	11744	1781[e]	690[1]
1910	—	15402	12697	1962[e]	743
1911	—	15388	12596	2018[e]	774
1912	—	16814[2]	13814	2148[e]	852[2]
1913	—	17336	14191	2245	900
1914	—	15496	12434	2231	831
1915	—	14398	13408		990
1916	—	16487	15275		1212
1917	—	20559	19121		1438
1918	—	22975	21198		1777
1919	—	30699	23214	5201	2284
1920	—	42753	32853	6766	3134
1921	—	36716	30268	4662	1786
1922	—	38958	32780	4381	1797
1923[4]	—	38429	32270	4358	1801
1924	—	41414	35039	4494	1881
1925	—	42303	35801	4636	1866
1926	—	41453	35346	4479	1628
1927	—	43261	36820	4731	1710
1928	—	45877	39311	4893	1673
1929	—	46496	39936	4961	1599
1930	—	44896	38782	4766	1348
1931	—	37436	31816	4420	1200
1932	—	33350	27834	4278	1238
1933	—	33381	27715	4423	1243
1934	—	36779	30740	4744	1295
1935	—	38843	32444	5116	1283
1936	—	42011[3]	35039[3]	5578[3]	1394
1937	—	44158	36719	5967	1472
1938	—	40869	33862	5749	1258
1939	—	33953	27539	5245	1169
1946	—	70269	50060	18951	1258
1947	—	74742	52672	20657	1413
1948	—	81947	57424	22786	1737
1949	—	87946	62604	23456	1886
1950	—	96317	69548	24693	2076
1951	—	111057	80687	28086	2284
1952	—	112637	82438	28146	2053
1953	—	125513	94070	29303	2140
1954	—	146634	112923	31365	2346
1955	—	155083	118597	34017	2470
1956	—	163286	125818	35071	2397
1957	—	175173	135428	37274	2471
1958	—	183363	142319	38596	2448
1959	—	201804	156750	42433	2621
1960	2304	228175	179312	46105	2758
1961	5252	245183	195686	46698	2799
1962	6021	275617	224246	48604	2767
1963	6934	305154	250196	52142	2816
1964	7888	358669	297238	58506	2926
1965	8693	411576	346505	62057	3014
1966	9842	455468	384473	67780	3215

Sources

Cols. 3+4 (1880–1901, 1915–18), col. 2 (1895–1938), col. 5 (1895–1938), B. R. Mitchell and P. Deane, *Abstract of British Historical Statistics* (Cambridge University Press, 1962), p. 449.

Cols. 3 and 4 (1902–10), *The Bankers' Almanac and Year Book*, 1924–5 (London: Waterlow and Son, 1927), pp. cxxiii and cxxiv.

Cols. 3 and 4 (1911, 1913, 1914, 1919–24), B.O.T., *Statistical Abstract for the UK*, 1925, No. 70 (London: H.M.S.O., 1927), pp. 180, 181.

Cols. 3 and 4 (1924–37), ibid., No. 82, p. 254.

All columns (1938–9, 1946–9), C.S.O., *Annual Abstract of Statistics*, No. 90 (1953), p. 275.

All columns (1950–60), C.S.O., *Annual Abstract of Statistics*, No. 98 (1961), p. 278.

Cols. 1–5 (1961–2) C.S.O., *Annual Abstract of Statistics*, No. 101, p. 303.

Cols. 1–5 (1963–6). C.S.O., *Annual Abstract of Statistics*, No. 104, 1967.

Notes

[1] First-year records were kept at Nottingham.

[2] First-year records were kept at Bradford.

[3] 1936 District Bank became a member of the London Clearing House.

[4] Figures here closely correspond to those reported by E. H. Phelps Brown and G. L. S. Shackle, 'Statistics in England and Wales 1919–37', *Memorandum*, No. 74 (London: Royal Economic Society, Sept. 1938), pp. 36–9.

[5] Figures are not strictly comparable owing to a change in composition over the years.

[e] Figures were interpolated from Mitchell and Deane, op. cit.

* Amounts cleared in 12 months ending 31 Dec.

TABLE (A) 1.12 **Bank of England, Annual Average Wednesday Balance Sheet 1880–1966 (£ millions)**

Year	Notes Issued	Total Notes held by Public	Notes held in Banking Dept.	Securities held in Issue Dept. 31 Dec.[a]	Coin and Bullion in Issue Dept.	Special Deposits or Treasury Special Account[f]	Total Deposits and Bank Post Bills	Public Deposits	Private Deposits Bankers, Others		Government Securities in Banking Dept.	Other Securities		Coin in the Banking Dept.	Reserves of Notes and Coin and Bullion	Total Coin and Bullion held by the Bank
												Discounts and Advances	Securities			
	1	2	3	4	5	6	7	8	A 9	B	10	11	12	13	14	15
1880	41·7	26·9	14·7	15·0	26·7	—	33·2	6·9	11·0	16·2	16·1	19·2		1·3	16·0	27·6
1881	38·8	26·3	12·7	15·8	23·5	—	31·9	6·5	10·8	14·4	15·0	21·1		1·1	13·8	24·6
1882	36·8	26·0	10·8	15·8	21·0	—	29·8	5·7	10·7	13·4	12·9	23·0		0·9	11·8	22·0
1883	37·1	25·6	11·5	15·8	21·3	—	30·0	6·6	10·3	12·9	13·4	22·1		0·9	12·4	22·2
1884	37·8	25·4	12·4	15·8	22·0	—	31·5	7·3	10·5	13·5	13·8	22·6		0·9	13·3	22·9
1885	38·7	24·7	14·1	15·8	23·0	—	33·6	6·2	12·8	14·4	14·7	21·2		1·1	15·1	24·2
1886	35·5	24·7	10·9	15·8	19·8	—	29·4	5·2	11·1	12·9	14·4	20·7		1·2	12·1	21·0
1887	36·4	24·4	12·0	16·2	20·5	—	29·6	5·4	11·4	12·6	14·4	19·6		1·4	13·3	21·8
1888	35·6	24·3	11·4	16·2	19·4	—	31·1	6·4	11·1	13·4	16·4	19·9		1·3	12·7	20·8
1889	36·7	24·4	12·3	16·5	20·5	—	32·9	7·2	11·7	13·7	15·8	21·6		1·0	13·2	21·4
1890	37·2	24·6	12·6	16·5	20·8	—	33·6	5·8	12·2	15·3	14·4	23·4		1·0	13·7	21·8
1891	39·8	25·1	14·6	16·5	23·4	—	38·2	6·6	15·3	16·1	10·9	29·7		1·0	15·6	24·4
1892	40·7	25·9	14·9	16·5	24·3	—	36·4	5·9	15·6	14·7	11·9	26·2		1·2	15·7	25·5
1893	41·1	25·9	15·2	16·5	24·6	—	36·2	5·7	15·2	15·1	11·5	25·6		1·8	17·0	26·4
1894	48·7	25·3	23·4	16·8	31·9	—	41·1	7·0	16·9	17·1	11·4	21·3		2·3	25·8	34·3
1895	53·2	25·8	27·3	16·8	36·4	—	48·3	7·6	17·9	22·7	14·1	22·1		2·6	29·9	39·0
1896	58·8	26·5	32·3	16·8	42·0	—	59·9	10·4	17·7	31·7	14·8	29·3		2·4	34·0	44·3
1897	50·0	27·2	22·8	16·8	33·2	—	50·0	10·0	18·1	21·7	13·9	29·4		2·3	25·1	35·6
1898	48·0	27·4	20·6	16·8	31·2	—	49·9	10·5	19·3	20·0	13·0	31·8		2·3	22·9	33·6
1899	47·1	27·9	19·3	16·8	30·3	—	49·7	10·0	21·4	18·1	13·6	32·7		1·9	21·2	32·3
1900	49·2	29·4	19·8	17·8	31·7	—	50·0	9·3	22·7	17·9	17·1	29·5		1·7	21·5	33·3
1901	51·6	29·6	22·0	17·8	33·8	—	50·6	9·7	23·3	17·4	15·7	28·8		2·0	24·0	35·8
1902	51·3	29·4	21·9	18·2	33·4	—	52·1	11·0	23·9	17·1	16·2	29·7		2·3	24·2	35·6
1903	50·6	28·9	21·7	18·5	32·3	—	50·2	8·8	24·4	16·9	16·4	28·0		2·1	23·8	34·4
1904	50·9	28·3	22·6	18·5	32·5	—	49·9	8·5	23·9	17·5	17·0	26·3		2·0	24·6	34·5
1905	52·3	28·8	23·5	18·5	33·9	—	56·1	11·8	23·4	18·9	16·7	30·1		1·8	25·3	35·7
1906	51·0	28·6	22·1	18·5	31·9	—	53·0	10·2	23·7	19·1	15·7	32·1		1·4	23·2	33·4
1907	52·0	28·9	23·1	18·5	33·6	—	53·6	9·2	25·7	18·8	15·2	32·1		1·3	24·4	34·9
1908	54·1	28·9	25·3	18·5	35·7	—	53·4	9·2	26·2	17·9	14·9	29·6		1·5	26·7	37·2
1909	54·4	29·2	25·2	18·5	35·9	—	54·3	10·5	25·7	18·1	15·5	30·1		1·5	26·7	37·4
1910	54·2	28·2	25·9	18·5	35·7	—	54·9	13·1	24·2	17·6	15·5	30·2		1·2	27·1	36·9
1911	55·5	28·6	26·9	18·5	37·1	—	55·5	13·1	24·3	18·1	14·9	30·5		1·1	28·0	38·2
1912	57·8	28·8	27·1	18·5	37·4	—	59·6	17·8	24·2	17·5	14·0	35·1		1·3	28·4	38·8
1913	54·6	29·1	25·9	18·5	35·7	—	54·9	13·3	24·6	16·9	12·7	32·8		1·4	27·3	37·1
1914	64·3	31·6	32·7	18·5	45·9	—	99·3	19·6	47·0	32·7	15·7	67·7		1·1	33·9	47·0
1915	77·7	33·8	43·4	18·5	58·7	—	189·2	85·9	48·0	55·3	36·3	126·6		0·9	44·2	59·6
1916	73·4	35·5	38·0	18·5	55·0	—	153·5	55·3	33·6	64·6	38·8	93·1		1·5	39·4	56·5
1917	71·7	40·2	31·5	18·5	53·2	—	179·5	49·5	39·1	90·8	62·5	100·5		2·1	33·5	55·3
1918	84·0	56·8	29·2	18·5	65·5	—	162·2	35·8	41·4	84·9	58·9	100·1		0·8	30·0	66·3
1919	103·3	79·9	24·5	18·5	84·9	—	144·7	23·9	52·2	68·6	54·7	81·8		1·6	26·1	86·5
1920	134·4	115·3	19·1	18·5	115·9	—	145·1	19·1	83·3[c]	42·7	59·8	83·0		1·2	20·4	117·1
1921	145·0	127·3	17·7	18·5	126·6	—	139·8	16·7	85·9	37·1	53·3	84·8		1·8	19·5	128·4
1922	144·8	122·8	21·9	18·5	126·3	—	134·4	16·7	80·1	37·6	51·9	76·6		1·8	23·7	128·1
1923	145·4	124·2	21·2	19·8	125·8	—	125·0	15·4	70·0	39·5	47·8	72·1		1·8	23·0	127·6
1924	146·2	125·3	20·9	19·8	126·4	—	127·2	14·2	69·9	33·1	45·8	76·1		1·8	22·7	128·3
1925	165·3	138·4	26·9	19·8	145·6	—	126·9	14·1	71·7	41·1	41·1	75·0		1·8	28·7	147·4
1926	168·4	140·7	27·6	19·8	148·6	—	123·7	16·0	68·6	39·1	39·3	73·6		1·4	29·0	150·0
1927	169·9	137·0	32·9	19·8	150·1	—	119·5	16·4	66·4	36·7	43·6	59·5		1·5	34·3	151·6
1928*	183·0[h]	135·1	47·9	19·8	163·3	—	117·5	15·2	65·5	36·9	33·9	52·3		1·8	49·6	165·0
1928†	416·5[d]	377·1	39·4	245·8[b]	156·5	—	116·8	12·4	67·5	37·0	60·0	15·5	19·2	0·5	39·9	157·0
1929	[illegible]	[illegible]	[illegible]	[illegible]	[illegible]	—	[illegible]	[illegible]	[illegible]	[illegible]	[illegible]	[illegible]	[illegible]	[illegible]	[illegible]	[illegible]

1931	406·1	354·8	51·3	262·2	139·7	—	118·3	15·4	64·7	38·3	45·5	10·7	27·8	1·0	52·3	140·8
1932	405·4	359·5	45·9	271·3	130·4	—	131·8	16·3	81·3	34·3	64·0	12·8	26·2	0·8	46·7	131·2
1933	440·4	371·2	69·1	260·1	176·6	—	157·8	17·7	99·9	40·1	79·6	11·8	14·1	1·1	70·2	177·7
1934	451·5	378·7	72·8	256·7	191·5	—	155·6	18·6	100·3	36·7	81·1	7·9	11·1	0·7	73·6	192·2
1935	453·7	394·7	59·0	258·2	193·7	—	150·1 [g]	15·3	96·7	38·1	87·0	9·6	11·8	0·7	59·6	194·3
1936	484·3	431·4	52·9	256·0	227·7	—	151·4 [g]	16·7	96·2	38·5	88·8	9·8	17·1	0·9	53·7	228·6
1937	524·0	479·6	44·5	202·7	321·4	—	153·9	19·5	97·2	37·2	98·4	6·9	21·2	1·1	45·5	322·4
1938	529·5	485·6	43·9	203·0	326·4 [e]	—	160·7	18·2	106·2	36·2	103·2	9·6	21·0	1·0	44·9	327·4
1939	547·9	507·3 [i]	40·6	403·1 [h]	212·3 [i]	—	161·9	21·3	102·5	38·0	107·0	8·5	22·9	0·8	41·5	145·1
1940	608·1	574·7	33·4	607·5	0·2	—	185·0	27·3	110·3	47·4	141·4	4·2	22·9	1·0	34·4	1·2
1941	685·9	652·2	33·7	685·5	0·2	—	192·3	16·7	122·6	52·9	144·4	9·6	21·2	1·3	35·0	1·5
1942	884·7	808·3	36·4	843·8	0·2	—	197·5	10·8	136·9	49·8	150·3	5·4	22·4	0·9	37·3	1·2
1943	1003·1	966·3	36·8	1002·8	0·2	—	223·4	8·7	158·9	55·8	179·8	4·4	19·1	1·2	38·0	1·4
1944	1166·6	1135·7	30·9	1166·3	0·2	—	250·5	9·9	184·4	56·2	214·0	6·0	16·3	1·2	32·1	1·4
1945	1310·8	1284·2	26·6	1310·6	0·2	—	285·7	12·8	217·9	55·1	251·8	9·2	15·0	1·0	27·6	1·2
1946	1403·1	1357·8	45·4	1402·9	0·2	—	322·5	12·6	254·7	55·1	260·2	15·6	18·3	1·1	46·5	1·3
1947	1450·2	1383·8	66·4	1450·0	0·2	—	397·8	12·8	295·9	89·1	313·1	14·8	20·2	1·5	67·9	1·7
1948	1312·7	1253·7	59·0	1312·5	0·2	10·8 [f]	422·1	14·0	304·6	92·7	340·8	15·0	24·2	1·2	60·3	1·5
1949	1314·7	1269·0	45·7	1314·4	0·3	28·6	432·0	12·3	296·4	94·6	354·3	19·7	25·8	4·6	50·3	4·9
1950	1328·7	1287·4	41·3	1327·1	0·4	195·6	596·8	14·7	292·3	94·3	519·8	22·4	26·6	4·8	46·1	5·1
1951	1383·0	1342·4	40·6	1379·4	0·4	4·2	406·2	20·2	297·6	88·5	341·4	14·8	26·8	0·8	41·5	1·2
1952	1475·8	1435·2	40·7	1472·0	0·4	12·5	376·7	25·6	277·2	73·9	314·8	15·5	22·2	1·5	42·2	1·9
1953	1570·6	1531·9	38·7	1566·9	—	29·7	390·4	43·2	277·6	69·6	341·4	8·9	17·4	2·1	40·8	—
1954	1662·4	1630·3	32·1	1658·5	—	5·8	368·8	20·6	281·1	67·2	327·4	9·4	15·7	2·4	34·5	—
1955	1795·1	1760·0	35·1	1791·0	—	3·9	340·6	19·2	254·0	67·5	283·4	22·3	15·6	2·4	37·5	—
1956	1911·5	1875·1	36·4	1907·3	—	1·4 [f]	317·5	16·1	228·0	73·3	257·8	22·7	16·8	2·0	38·4	—
1957	1992·5	1960·3	32·2	1994·3	—	—	303·6	13·3	216·2	74·0	239·4	28·1	19·8	2·3	34·5	—
1958	2068·3	2034·6	33·7	2064·2	—	—	303·0	12·6	217·9	72·6	245·4	19·7	20·4	1·9	35·6	—
1959	2140·7	2104·5	36·2	2137·1	—	—	313·9	13·0	236·0	64·9	258·0	15·5	21·5	0·9	37·1	—
1960	2250·9	2210·7	40·2	2248·0	—	72·1 [b]	403·0	12·0	248·3	65·5	331·9	28·9	19·3	0·8	41·0	—
1961	2341·2	2306·2	35·0	2339·4	—	182·1	516·2	13·0	250·0	71·1	423·8	55·8	18·9	0·8	35·8	—
1962	2374·0	2327·3	46·7	2372·6	—	172·0	502·3	13·1	246·2	71·0	403·7	49·8	19·5	0·8	47·5	—
1963	2440·7	2398·2	42·5	2439·4	—	—	334·3	12·5	249·3	72·5	227·7	60·2	21·1	0·9	43·4	—
1964	2602·2	2561·7	40·6	2600·9	—	—	342·2	12·4	250·6	79·2	251·2	42·9	24·4	0·9	41·5	—
1965	2775·8	2727·4	48·5	2774·5	—	56·4	424·9	12·3	266·6	89·6	311·1	57·1	25·6	0·8	49·3	—
1966	2936·9	2892·5	44·4	2395·5	—	140·7	526·3	13·3	265·4	106·9	410·6	61·9	26·7	0·9	45·3	—

Sources

Cols. 1–5, 7, 8, 10, 11, 12, 13, 14, 15 (1880–1952), 9A, 9B (1929–1952), *Bankers' Almanac and Year Book*, 1954, pp. 1491–2.

Cols. 9A, 9B (1880–1928), interpolated from combined figures in *Bankers' Almanac and Year Book*, 1954, pp. 1491–2, and B. Mitchell and P. Deane, *Abstract of British Historical Statistics* (Cambridge University Press, 1962), pp. 444–6.

Cols. 1–4, 6–14 (1953–61), C.S.O., *Annual Abstract of Statistics*, No. 99 (London: H.M.S.O., 1962), p. 275.

Col. 6 (1962), C.S.O., *Annual Abstract of Statistics*, 101, p. 297.

All columns (1962–6), C.S.O., *Annual Abstract of Statistics*, No. 104 (1967).

Notes

[a] Includes Government debt of £11·0 million.

[b] Deposits called from London Clearing Banks and Scottish banks, not at their free disposal.

[c] Prior to 1920 just covered by deposits of London bankers' head offices. After 1920 it includes branches also.

[d] 1929 includes Treasury currency notes.

[e] Sept. 1939, gold coin and bullion transferred to H.M. Treasury.

[f] These deposits for 1948–56 were designated H.M.T. special account set up under Article IV of the Economic Co-operation Agreement 1948 between the Government of the UK and the USA.

[g] 1936, bank post bills withdrawn.

[h] 22 Nov. 1928, £240,250,000 added to securities in Issue Department on assumption of liability for currency notes and the Fiduciary Issue was raised to £260 million.

[i] 6 Sept. 1939, £280 million transferred to the Exchange Equalization Account, and the Fiduciary Issue raised to £500 million.

* 47 weeks.

† 5 weeks.

TABLE (A) 1.13 **Combined Balance Sheets of Alexanders, National and the Union of London Discount Houses 1890–1966 (£ millions)**

Year-End 31 Dec.	Capital and Reserves	Undivided Profits	Loans and Deposits	Bills Rediscounted	Rebate	Total Liabilities	Cash at Bankers	Bills[b] Discounted: Total	Bills[b] Discounted: Treasury Bills[c]	Investments[b]: Total	Investments[b]: British Government and Government-Guaranteed[c]	Loans and Sundry Accounts
	1	2	3	4	5	6	7	8 A	8 B	9 A	9 B	10
1890	2·8		22·5	13·0	0·3	38·6	0·9	31·2	—	3·8	**2**	2·7
1891	2·8		23·6	8·0	0·3	34·7	0·8	26·1	—	3·5	**2**	4·3
1892	2·8		25·0	9·2	0·3	37·3	0·9	28·5	—	3·7	**2**	4·2
1893	2·8		22·0	9·5	0·3	34·6	0·8	27·7	—	3·5	**2**	2·6
1894	2·8		27·1	8·6	0·3	38·8	0·9	30·4	—	3·9	**2**	3·6
1895	2·8		31·1	8·1	0·3	42·3	1·0	34·0	—	4·2	**2**	3·1
1896	2·8		25·0	9·8	0·3	37·9	0·9	29·1	—	3·8	**1**	4·1
1897	2·8		24·7	8·9	0·3	36·7	0·9	28·0	—	3·7	**1**	4·1
1898	2·8		26·2	9·9	0·3	39·2	0·9	30·2	—	3·9	**1**	4·2
1899	2·8		26·0	7·2	0·3	36·3	0·9	28·4	—	3·6	**1**	3·4
1900	3·0		28·4	9·2	0·3	40·9	0·8	30·7	**4**	5·0	**2**	4·1
1901	3·0		28·4	8·9	0·3	40·6	1·0	30·2	**4**	4·3	**2**	5·1
1902	3·0		27·8	8·3	0·3	39·4	0·9	28·6	**4**	4·6	**2**	5·3
1903	3·0		27·2	7·5	0·3	38·0	0·9	28·4	**4**	4·2	**2**	4·5
1904	3·1		30·5	9·5	0·3	43·4	1·0	31·4	**4**	4·5	**2**	4·5
1905	3·0		32·6	9·7	0·3	46·2	1·0	32·8	**4**	5·9	**2**	6·2
1906	3·1		35·4	10·6	0·3	49·4	1·3	37·2	**4**	6·0	**2**	4·9
1907	3·2		38·8	12·2	0·3	54·5	1·5	45·2	**3**	4·7	**2**	3·1
1908	3·2		36·8	16·3	0·3	56·6	1·5	44·7	**3**	6·4	**2**	4·0
1909	3·2		40·4	14·8	0·3	58·7	1·5	46·6	**3**	6·8	**2**	3·8
1910	3·2		41·6	10·8	0·3	55·9	1·4	42·2	**3**	7·0	**3**	3·6
1911	3·4		41·6	11·9	0·4	57·4	1·5	46·7	**3**	6·2	**2**	2·5
1912	3·4		44·5	14·0	0·5	62·7	1·6	51·9	**2**	5·7	**2**	3·2
1913	3·4		46·6	16·0	0·5	66·8	1·7	58·3	**3**	4·9	**2**	2·0
1914	3·8		38·6	5·6	0·5	48·8	1·3	39·0	**2**	5·9	**3**	1·7
1915	3·8		38·9	8·1	0·6	51·7	1·8	43·9	**20**	4·7	**2**	0·8
1916	3·7		47·2	13·3	0·7	65·0	1·9	55·2	**27**	4·7	**2**	3·0
1917	3·8		57·5	15·4	0·8	77·4	2·0	66·4	**33**	5·7	**3**	3·0
1918	3·8		59·5	15·1	0·6	79·3	2·0	64·0	**32**	8·7	**4**	4·4
1919	4·1		69·6	17·2	0·8	92·2	2·1	79·7	**42**	6·6	**3**	2·9
1920	4·2		75·3	27·2	1·0	108·7	2·2	91·5	**38**	5·5	**2**	3·6
1921	4·5		75·1	29·8	1·2	111·1	2·0	94·0	**52**	8·9	**3**	5·2
1922	4·7		74·0	25·2	1·0	105·6	2·3	88·2	**52**	10·5	**4**	2·1
1923	4·8		78·7	27·7	1·3	112·6	2·5	96·3	**48**	10·3	**3**	3·6
1924	5·1		85·5	39·9	1·4	131·9	2·5	115·0	**50**	10·3	**4**	4·0
1925	5·7		87·8	34·0	1·5	128·9	2·5	110·5	**52**	10·5	**7**	5·5
1926	5·7		88·8	41·9	1·4	137·7	2·4	120·5	**58**	11·8	**8**	2·8
1927	5·9		93·9	40·5	1·6	141·8	2·5	121·3	**54**	13·7	**11**	4·4
1928	6·2		93·2	39·8	1·3	140·6	2·4	118·9	**56**	17·3	**14**	1·9
1929	5·2		92·4	40·3	1·3	140·2	2·5	121·6	**62**	13·6	**12**	2·5

1930	7·0	98·4		40·5	1·3	147·3	2·0	125·0	**89**	17·2	**14**	1·9
1931	7·0	86·2		33·9	1·3	128·4	2·3	111·2	**79**	13·5	**11**	1·1
1932	7·0	105·0		28·9	0·9	142·7	2·7	117·0	**91**	20·2	**17**	2·5
1933	7·0	111·8		24·9	0·8	144·4	2·7	111·5	**87**	28·4	**25**	1·8
1934	7·0	105·9		18·3	0·7	132·0	2·9	90·6	**64**	35·4	**31**	3·1
1935	7·0	114·3		25·5	0·7	147·5	3·0	101·8	**63**	37·7	**33**	5·0
1936	7·8	121·9		27·5	0·7	158·7	3·2	110·5	**73**	40·8	**36**	3·7
1937	7·8	120·2		28·3	0·9	158·1	3·2	115·4	**68**	36·0	**32**	3·0
1938	7·9	124·9		19·4	0·5	152·6	3·3	123·7	**73**	21·3	**18**	4·3
1939	7·9	142·8		18·4	0·7	169·7	3·7	145·4	**104**	18·1	**15**	2·6
1940	8·0	1·0	151·6	10·7	0·7	171·9	3·9	114·8	**78**	51·6	**46**	1·7
1941	8·0	1·1	165·1	13·8	0·7	189·2	4·2	128·2	**84**	55·3	**51**	1·4
1942[a]	8·2	1·2	210·3	11·7	0·7	232·1	4·5	172·2	**153**	53·9	**50**	1·4
1943	9·3	1·0	240·6	5·6	0·7	250·8	5·2	186·8	**159**	63·4	**59**	1·4
1944	9·4	1·1	288·4	7·4	0·3	299·1	5·4	222·0	**189**	70·0	**66**	1·6
1945	9·5	1·2	300·8	8·4	—	311·6	5·1	240·2	**204**	64·0	**60**	2·2
1946	14·5	1·4	423·9	18·6	—	439·8	5·8	336·6	**286**	95·1	**88**	2·3
1947	16·0	1·4	440·5	15·2	—	457·9	6·3	339·1	**295**	109·6	**102**	2·9
1948	16·1	1·6	502·7	38·0	—	520·3	6·4	323·9	**253**	185·9	**175**	4·1
1949	16·3	1·6	563·6	38·9	—	581·6	6·6	399·2	**351**	173·2	**163**	2·4
1950	16·4	1·8	634·8	50·6	—	653·0	6·6	432·9	**394**	211·2	**198**	2·1
1951	16·5	2·0	548·1	65·7	—	566·6	6·3	342·3	**311**	214·3	**203**	3·5
1952	16·8	1·9	576·8	33·9	—	595·5	6·7	393·9	**377**	185·6	**175**	4·0
1953	17·5	1·7	571·8	43·0	—	591·1	7·5	327·7	**303**	244·6	**238**	11·1
1954	23·4	1·9	630·9	59·0	—	656·2	7·8	365·9	**340**	264·2	**254**	13·3
1955	18·4	1·6	571·6	50·0	—	591·6	7·5	355·2	**332**	220·2	**196**	8·6
1956	18·4	1·6	516·6	33·0	—	536·6	7·3	324·8	**279**	189·1	**179**	15·4
1957	18·4	1·6	533·9	55·2	—	553·8	8·4	365·1	**319**	158·4	**148**	22·0
1958	18·4	1·9	596·9	60·9	—	617·2	8·8	388·3	**347**	194·1	**186**	25·9
1959	22·3	1·7	660·5	56·7	—	685·5	9·7	440·7	**372**	220·8	**207**	13·2
1960	22·3	1·7	652·2	52·7	—	676·1	9·2	399·8	**332**	239·1	**236**	28·1
1961	22·3	1·8	652·4	58·3	—	676·5	9·1	409·3	**303**	245·8	**241**	12·0
1962	23·3	1·9	641·3	61·5	—	666·8	9·6	405·3	**294**	236·4	**232**	15·2
1963	24·0	2·1	687·8	69·4	—	713·9	9·1	437·1	**242**	246·5	**239**	20·9
1964	24·4	1·8	631·3	69·6	—	657·5	8·9	387·6	**225**	242·6	**232**	18·1
1965	24·5	2·3	681·4	78·2	—	708·2	9·6	396·1	**244**	276·6	**236**	24·6
1966	24·5	3·1	702·0	67·4	—	729·6	9·6	389·9	**253**	306·3	**198**	21·0

Sources

Cols. 2+3, 4, 8A (1890–9, 1901–4, 1906–9) taken from W. T. C. King, *History of the London Discount Market*, 1936, and *The Economist* 'Banking Supplement' in the relevant years.

Cols. 1, 5, 6, 7, 9A and 10 (1890–9, 1901–4, 1906–9) are estimates based on reported figures in the respective years for the assets and liabilities noted above, and on the actual relevant asset distributions in 1900, 1905 and 1910.

Cols. 8B and 9B (1890–1950) are estimates. Thus:

$$\text{Col. } 8B_t = \text{Col. } 8A_t \left(\frac{\text{T.B. Holdings of Combined UK Banks}}{\text{Total Discounts of Combined UK Banks}} \right)_t$$

where $t = 1900, 01 \ldots 1950$.

$$\text{Col. } 9B_t = \text{Col. } 9A_t \left(\frac{\text{Gov. and Gov.-guaranteed Holdings of Combined UK Banks}}{\text{Total Investments of Combined UK Banks}} \right)_t$$

where $t = 1890, 91 \ldots 1950$.

Cols. 8B and 9B (1951–66) based on Treasury Bill and Government-guaranteed holdings of the members of the London Discount Houses Association, reported yearly in the Bank of England's *Quarterly Bulletin*, 1, No. 1, 1960, and 3, No. 3, 1963.

Cols. 1–8A, 9A, 10 (1900, 1905, 1910–51) extracted from the relevant issues of *The Economist* 'Banking Number' or 'Banking Supplement' (usually in May) up to 1946, and from then on in *Records and Statistics*.

Cols. 1–4, 6, 7, 8A, 9A, 10 (1951–62) extracted from the relevant issues of the *Bankers' Almanac and Year Book*.

Cols. 1–4, 6, 7, 8A, 9A, 10 (1963–6) taken from annual issues of the *Bankers' Almanac and Year Book*.

Throughout the period 1951–62 the recorded total liabilities of the sample of three discount houses accounted for an average of 57 per cent of the total assets of the members of the London Discount Houses Association of which they are members. Over the period their share of the Association's total assets varied between 53 and 61 per cent.

Notes

[a] After 1942 accounting procedures were changed so that bills rediscounted and rebates have been excluded from total liabilities and total discounts from 1943 onwards.

[b] Treasury Bills and Government-guaranteed holdings are estimated throughout and as a consequence are presented as whole numbers.

Cols. 8B and 9B (1963–6) are estimated on the basis:

$$\text{Col. } 8A_t \left(\frac{\text{Treasury Bills}}{\text{Total Bills}} \right)_t^D$$

and

$$9A_t \left(\frac{\text{British Government and Government-Guaranteed}}{\text{Total Investment}} \right)_t^D$$

where $t = 1963, 64, 65$ and 1966.

The ratios

$$\left(\frac{\text{Treasury Bills}}{\text{Total Bills}} \right)_t^D$$

and

$$\left(\frac{\text{British Government and Government-Guaranteed}}{\text{Total Investment}} \right)_t^D$$

were derived from Board of Trade *Quarterly Bulletin*, Vol. 7, 1967, p. 68. They reflect the fraction of the bill and security holdings which all discount companies hold in Treasury Bills and Government stock in each year.

[c] All figures in bold type are estimates.

TABLE (A) 1.14 **Compound Rates of Growth of Commercial Banks' Assets, Advances and Debit Clearings**

Items	*Periods*							
	1891–1966	1891–1914	1914–1918	1920–1939	1939–1946	1946–1966	1920–1966	1955–1966
Total assets all UK commercial banks[a]	3·8[e]	2·6	14·0	1·1	12·0	2·8	3·4	3·8
Total assets – all joint-stock banks of England and Wales[a]	4·2	3·3	14·4	1·1	12·4	2·9	3·5	4·0
Total assets – all joint-stock banks of Ireland[a,d]	n.a.	2·4	15·9	−1·0	10·1	3·7	2·7	5·0
Total assets – all joint-stock banks of Scotland[a]	3·2	1·5	13·7	0·9	10·1	2·2	2·8	2·3
Total assets – private Yorkshire Penny and CWS Banks	2·0	−1·0	9·0	2·8	11·8	0·1	2·8	1·2
Total assets – London Clearing Banks[a]	n.a.	n.a.	n.a.	1·4	12·4	2·9	3·7	4·0
Debit clearings[b]	n.a.	n.a.	10·3	−1·1	11·0	9·8	5·3	11·1
Bank advances[c]	n.a.	n.a.	n.a.	n.a.	n.a.	9·6	n.a.	9·2

Notes

[a] End-of-year, approximately 31 Dec.
[b] Annual amounts.
[c] Averages of figures for Feb., May, Aug. and Nov.
[d] From 1920 onwards, Banks in Eire were excluded.
[e] This figure is not strictly accurate due to discontinuity in the series in 1920.

Section 2 UK Non-Bank Financial Intermediaries 1880–1966

The notes at the end of each of the tables explain their composition, though it should be noted that they contain a considerable number of estimates. As in the previous section, these have been set in bold type. In Tables (A) 2.1 to (A) 2.5, for instance, a number of the recorded assets of the Special Investment Department of the trustee savings banks in the pre-1920 period, all of the Government and Government-guaranteed security holdings of the building societies in the 1880–1957 period, and all of the assets of the insurance companies in the two wars are estimates. In contrast, the data in Tables (A) 2.6, (A) 2.7 and (A) 2.9–(A) 2.12 contain few if any estimates. Nevertheless, for interpretative purposes, it should be noted that the funds of the insurance companies represent the valuation of the assets backing each particular type of contract such companies write as required by the various insurance companies Acts. Similarly, the funds reported by the various societies registered with the Registry of Friendly Societies match the collective valuation of the contributions – deposits, shares, etc. – contributed to such societies by the investing members.

Table (A) 2.8 does seem to require some additional explanation with respect to both its inclusion and its composition. It is included as it appears that all the listed societies provide financial services and therefore should be considered to be financial intermediaries; they insure their members against burial, sickness, industrial accident and unemployment contingencies, or alternatively, they provide assurance in the form of life and pension policies. Except for the fund figures, the majority of the entries on the table are estimates. The reports of the Registered Friendly Societies only list the asset breakdowns of such societies for these years: 1929, 1934, 1936, 1946, 1951, 1953, 1956, 1958, 1961–6. For the trade unions, similar figures are given for 1921, 1926, 1931, 1936, 1953, 1958, 1961–6. The asset distributions of the collecting societies are much more complete and are fully documented for the 1934–9 and 1952–66 periods; those of the superannuation and other trusts, however, are fully specified only for 1935. Finally, it should be observed that the superannuation and other trusts were not registered with the Registry of Friendly Societies until 1927, and that the Registry's first recorded fund figure was given in 1929. As a consequence, the fund figures for these societies before that date are estimates.

It should be recorded as well that, owing to the lack of published data, the coverage of the UK non-banking financial institutions is not comprehensive. In particular, the omission of the investment trusts and the unit trusts is unfortunate. These two intermediaries had assets of £2,339 million and £237 million respectively in 1962. It would also have been useful to include a table showing the balance sheet positions of the pension funds which the *Radcliffe Report* estimates to have a value of some £2,500 million in 1958 and to be increasing by £250 million a year. Our sample of these has been limited to those schemes which registered with the Registry of Friendly Societies under the Superannuation and other Trust Funds (Validation) Act of 1927 – about 15 per cent of all the pension funds in 1958. Optimally, of course, all public and private institutionally managed trusts and pension funds should also have been incorporated since they provide financial services and influence the flow and distribution of financial savings. However, with the exception of those funds administered by the Public Trustees and investment and unit trusts, it is unlikely that such accounts will ever be available for the period before the Second World War. Many of the pertinent records have either been destroyed or are not available for inspection; just as significantly, the time and expense of collecting and organizing the presentation of the residual available data would be quite considerable, and well in excess of the normal grant one may obtain from a University Research Committee.

Finally, it should be noted that much of the omitted material is readily available for the post-1953 period in the various publications of the Central Statistical Office. The protests of the Radcliffe Committee at the aridity of the published financial record has had a marked impact on the responsible officials, in much the same way as the Macmillan Committee inquiry had before the publication of Keynes's *General Theory*. As a consequence, researchers who are engaged in empirically based studies of aspects of the growth and role of the non-bank financial institutions over recent years should consult such publications which contain, for example, the balance sheets of the unit trusts and the investment trusts in considerable detail as well as the balance sheets of the superannuation funds and of all the hire-purchase companies.

TABLE (A) 2.1 **Birmingham Municipal Bank Balance Sheets 1920–1967[b] (Assets and liabilities £ millions)**

Year-End 31 Mar.	*Deposits[a,c]*				*Reserves*	*Total Assets and Liabilities*	*Cash in hand and at Bank*	*Deposits with Birmingham Corporation*		*Depo-sits with National Debt Commis-sioners*	*Investments. All British Government or Government-Guaranteed*	*Treasury Bills*	*Mortgages Advanced[d]*	*Accrued Interest, etc.*	*Interest Rates Paid and Received. Paid on Deposits and Charged on Mortgages*			
	Total	*No. 1 Account*	*No. 2 Account*	*No. 3 Account[e]*				*Total*	*Invested in British Governments*						*No. 1 Account*	*No. 2 Account*	*No. 3 Account*	*Mortgage*
	IA	IB	IC	ID	II	III	IV	V A	V B	VI	VII	VIII	IX	X	XI	XII	XIIA	XIII
1920	0·7	0·7	—	—	0	0·7	0	0·7	**0·4**	0	0	0	0	0	3·5	—	—	n.a.
1921	1·4	1·4	—	—	0	1·4	0	0·3	**0·2**	0	0	0·9	0·2	0	3·5	—	—	n.a.
1922	1·9	1·9	—	—	0	1·9	0	0·5	**0·3**	0	0·8	0·2	0·3	0	3·5	—	—	n.a.
1923	2·9	2·9	—	—	0	2·9	0·3	2·3	**1·3**	0	0	0	0·3	0	3·5	—	—	n.a.
1924	4·2	4.2	—	—	0·1	4·3	0·4	3·4	**1·9**	0	0	0	0·4	0·1	3·5	—	—	n.a.
1925	5·6	5·6	—	—	0·1	5·7	0·5	4·4	**2·5**	0	0	0	0·7	0·1	3·5	—	—	n.a.
1926	6·8	6·8	—	—	0·1	6·9	0·6	5·1	**2·9**	0	0	0	1·1	0·1	3·5	—	—	n.a.
1927	7·8	7·8	—	—	0·1	7·9	0·7	5·5	**3·1**	0	0	0	1·6	0·1	3·5	—	—	n.a.
1928	9·1	9·1	—	—	0·1	9·2	0·9	6·5	**3·6**	0	0	0	1·7	0·1	3·5	—	—	n.a.
1929	10·3	10·3	—	—	0·2	10·4	0·8	7·8	**4·4**	0	0	0	1·7	0·2	3·5	—	—	n.a.
1930	11·5	11·5	—	—	0·2	11·7	0·8	9·0	**5·0**	0	0	0	1·7	0·2	3·5	—	—	5.0
1931	12·9	12·9	—	—	0·2	13·1	0·9	10·2	**5·7**	0	0	0	1·8	0·2	3·5	—	—	5·0
1932	13·7	13·7	—	—	0·3	14·0	0·9	11·0	**6·2**	0	0	0	1·8	0·2	3·5	—	—	5·0
1933	15·3	15·3	—	—	0·3	15·6	0·9	12·7	**7·1**	0	0	0	1·7	0·3	3·0	—	—	5·0
1934	17·1	17·1	—	—	0·3	17·4	1·0	14·6	**8·2**	0	0	0	1·6	0·3	3·0	—	—	5·0
1935	18·9	18·9	—	—	0·3	19·3	1·0	16·4	9·3	0	0	0	1·5	0·3	3·0	—	—	4·5
1936	21·2	21·2	—	—	0·3	21·6	1·1	18·5	10·4	0	0	0	1·7	0·3	3·0	—	—	4·5
1937	23·8	23·8	—	—	0·4	24·2	1·1	20·6	11·2	0	0	0	2·1	0·3	3·0	—	—	4·5
1938	26·7	26·7	—	—	0·4	27·1	1·2	23·3	12·4	0	0	0	2·2	0·3	3·0	—	—	4·5
1939	29·4	29·4	—	—	0·4	29·8	1·2	25·9	15·1	0	0	0	2·4	0·3	3·0	—	—	4·5
1940	31·6	31·6	—	—	0·4	32·0	1·5	27·2	15·3	0	0·3	0	2·7	0·4	3·0	—	—	4·5
1941	35·9	35·9	—	—	0·4	36·4	1·4	28·3	15·7	0	3·5	0	2·6	0·5	3·0	—	—	4·5
1942	42·1	42·1	—	—	0·5	42·5	1·6	29·3	15·8	0	8·5	0	2·4	0·7	3·0	—	—	4·5
1943	50·8	50·8	—	—	0·5	51·3	1·7	30·7	15·8	0	16·0	0	2·2	0·7	3·0	—	—	4·5
1944	59·5	59·5	—	—	0·5	60·0	1·6	31·4	15·1	0	24·1	0	1·9	0·8	3·0	—	—	4·5
1945	67·7	67·7	—	—	0·5	68·3	2·2	32·2	15·8	0	31·6	0	1·8	0·5	3·0	—	—	4·5
1946	74·3	74·3	—	—	0·5	74·8	1·6	33·2	15·8	0	37·8	0	1·7	0·6	2·75	—	—	4·0
1947	78·0	78·0	—	—	0·5	78·6	2·0	34·9	14·6	0	40·0	0	1·3	0·3	2·75	—	—	3·5
1948	80·9	80·9	—	—	0·5	81·5	2·3	36·5	13·0	0	41·0	0	1·4	0·3	2·75	—	—	3·5

1951	85·1	86·1	—	—	0·6	86·7	1·4	38·9	13·0	0	43·1	0	2·2	0·2	2·75	—	—	3·5
1952	84·8	84·8	—	—	0·6	85·5	5·4	35·9	13·0	2·5	38·9	0	2·6	0·2	2·75	—	—	4·0
1953	85·4	85·4	—	—	0·7	86·2	4·6	36·0	13·0	3·4	38·9	0	3·0	0·2	2·75	—	—	4·0
1954	86·3	86·3	—	—	0·7	87·1	5·7	36·0	13·0	3·0	38·9	0	3·4	0·2	2·75	—	—	4·0
1955	88·1	88·1	—	—	0·7	88·9	4·5	36·6	19·1	0	42·8	0·5	4·4	0·2	2·75	—	—	4·0
1956	88·6	88·6	—	—	0·8	89·4	4·6	35·5	19·0	0	44·0	0	5·2	0·2	2·75	—	—	4·5
1957	85·9	85·9	—	—	0·9	86·8	5·4	35·4	18·7	0	40·8	0	5·1	0·2	2·75	—	—	4·5
1958	83·6	77·0	6·6	—	1·0	84·6	4·3	29·2	18·5	6·5	39·2	0	5·2	0·2	2·75	2·5	—	4·5
1959	81·9	72·4	9·5	—	1·1	83·0	4·3	24·4	17·5	9·4	39·2	0	5·4	0·3	2·75	2·5	—	4·5
1960	84·2	72·1	12·1	—	1·1	85·3	4·3	26·0	13·3	12·0	37·1	0	5·6	0·2	2·75	2·5	—	4·5
1961	85·3	71·2	14·0	—	1·2	86·5	4·1	25·3	13·5	13·9	37·1	0	5·9	0·2	2·75	2·5	—	4·5
1962	86·7	70·8	15·9	—	1·3	88·0	5·3	23·5	12·9	15·7	37·1	0	6·1	0·2	2·75	2·5	—	4·5
1963	88·8	71·0	17·8	—	1·6	90·4	4·7	24·5	14·6	17·7	37·1	0	6·2	0·2	2·75	2·5	—	4·5
1964	91·2	71·4	19·8	—	1·6	92·9	4·5	25·0	14·8	19·7	37·1	0	6·3	0·3	2·75	2·5	—	4·5
1965	92·8	71·0	21·8	—	1·8	94·7	4·0	25·2	14·6	21·7	37·1	0	6·3	0·3	3·0	2·5	—	5·0
1966	93·9	71·1	22·8	—	1·9	95·9	4·8	24·6	14·6	22·6	37·0	0	6·4	0·4	3·0	2·5	—	5·0
1967	92·3	66·3	22·2	3·9	2·2	94·7	4·3	22·0	13·1	21·9	37·0	0	6·6	0·3	3·0	2·5	5·5	6·0

Sources

Cols. IA to VA, VI to XIII (1920–63), Col. VB (1935–63), Birmingham Municipal Bank, *Annual Report and Statement of Accounts* for relevant years, with the exception of the portion of deposits with the City of Birmingham which was invested in British Government securities from 1923 to 1934; these were estimated on the basis of the post-1934 figures given in the *Annual Reports*.

e.g. Col. VB (1920–34) estimated: $VB_t = \lambda \times VA_t$, where $\lambda = [VB/VA]_{1935} = 0{\cdot}5616$.

All cols. (1963–7) *Annual Reports* from the Birmingham Municipal Bank.

Notes

[a] Established under Finance Bill, No. 2, 1956. First £15 of interest on these deposits exempt from income tax, all such deposits invested by National Debt Commissioners.

[b] Established by Act of Parliament on 1 Sept. 1919.

[c] Regulations on deposits.

1926 Maximum per annum £500, maximum withdrawn without notice £30.

1937 Maximum per annum £500, maximum withdrawn without notice £30.

1946 Government Statutory Rule and Order, maximum individual deposit £2,000.

1952 Government Statutory Rule and Order, maximum individual deposit £3,000.

1957 No. 1 Account, maximum per annum deposits £500, maximum individual deposit £3,000, maximum withdrawal on demand £30. No. 2 Account, no annual deposit limitation, maximum individual deposit £1,000, maximum withdrawal on demand £30.

1960 No. 2 Account, maximum individual deposits £2,000, No. 1 Account £5,000, annual maximum deposit limit cancelled. Maximum withdrawal on demand £50.

[d] Regulations on advances.

Pre-war houses (1914–18) 80 per cent of appraised value to a maximum of £600.

1921 general: not to exceed one-third of total funds. Post-war houses 50 per cent of building costs up to £800.

1922 for a maximum term of 20 years, 80 per cent advance up to £1,000.

1926 up to 99 per cent advanced on municipal houses.

1930 80–90 per cent on all houses, with no limit to the amount.

1934 for a maximum term of 25 years, 90 per cent on all houses with no limit to the amount.

1940 Mortgages given only on freehold or leasehold property in the Birmingham area. All new and surplus monies invested with the Government.

1945 for a maximum term of 20 years, 80 per cent advance on all houses, with no limit to the amount.

1948 term of 20–25 years, 80 per cent advance on all houses, with no limit.

1956 term of 20 years, 80 per cent advance on all houses, with no limit.

[e] Savings Department No. 3 opened on 1 Jan. 1967 and is known as the Investment Department (range of individual deposit limitations £1–5,000 provided at least £100 held in No. 1 account).

TABLE (A) 2.2 **Post Office Savings Bank Balance Sheets 1862–1967 (£ millions)**

Year-End 31 Dec.	*No. of Branches* 1	*Total Deposits and Interest* 2	*Government Stock held for Owners* (Introduced 22 Nov. 1880)* 3	*Total Assets*[c] 4	*Government and Government-Guaranteed*[b] *Total* 5 A	*Treasury Bills* 5 B	*Cash Total*[c] 6	*Premises*[c] 7	*Other Assets*[a,c] 8
1862	2535	1·7	—	1·7	—	—	—	—	—
1863	2991	3·4	—	3·4	—	—	—	—	—
1864	3081	5·0	—	5·0	—	—	—	—	—
1865	3321	6·5	—	6·6	—	—	—	—	—
1866	3507	8·1	—	8·3	—	—	—	—	—
1867	3629	9·7	—	9·9	—	—	—	—	—
1868	3813	11·7	—	11·9	—	—	—	—	—
1869	4047	13·5	—	13·8	—	—	—	—	—
1870	4082	15·1	—	15·5	—	—	—	—	—
1871	4335	17·0	—	17·5	—	—	—	—	—
1872	4607	19·3	—	19·9	—	—	—	—	—
1873	4853	21·2	—	21·8	—	—	—	—	—
1874	5068	23·2	—	24·0	—	—	—	—	—
1875	5260	25·2	—	26·2	—	—	—	—	—
1876	5448	27·0	—	28·1	—	—	—	—	—
1877	5668	28·7	—	29·8	—	—	—	—	—
1878	5831	30·4	—	31·2	—	—	—	—	—
1879	6016	32·0	—	32·8	—	—	—	—	—
1880	6233	33·7	0·1	34·6	—	—	—	—	—
1881	6513	36·2	0·7	36·7	—	—	—	—	—
1882	6990	39·0	1·1	40·1	—	—	—	—	—
1883	7369	41·8	1·5	43·7	—	—	—	—	—
1884	7756	44·8	1·9	46·4	—	—	—	—	—
1885	8106	47·7	2·5	**49·3**	—	—	—	—	—
1886	8351	50·9	2·9	52·5	—	—	—	—	—
1887	8720	53·9	3·3	56·7	—	—	—	—	—
1888	9022	58·6	3·8	61·3	—	—	—	—	—
1889	9353	63·0	4·2	65·3	—	—	—	—	—
1890	9681	67·6	4·7	69·4	60·0	0·0	**0·2**	0·2	**9·0**
1891	10063	71·6	5·1	72·9	63·5	1·8	0·2	0·2	9·0
1892	10517	75·9	5·6	78·6	69·2	0·0	**0·2**	0·2	**9·0**
1893	11018	80·6	6·3	83·5	73·1	4·9	0·1	0·3	**10·0**
1894	11323	89·3	7·0	95·3	84·9	7·4	0·1	0·3	**10·0**
1895	11518	97·9	6·9	105·8	94·4	0·0	**0·1**	0·3	**11·0**
1896	11867	108·1	6·9	119·6	107·2	3·4	0	0·4	12·0
1897	12212	115·9	7·0	128·7	115·8	1·0	0·1	**0·4**	12·4
1898	12582	123·1	7·5	133·9	120·4	0·3	0·3	**0·4**	12·8
1899	12995	130·1	8·4	129·6	113·1	0·5	0·3	**0·4**	15·8
1900	13341	135·5	10·5	133·5	114·1	0·8	0·3	**0·4**	18·7
1901	13672	140·4	12·8	135·3	115·7	0	**0·2**	**0·4**	**19·0**
1902	14048	144·6	14·3	138·7	118·9	0	0	**0·4**	19·4
1903	14362	146·1	16·2	**146·1**	126·3	0	0	**0·4**	19·0
1904	14614	148·3	17·4	148·5	128·8	0·1	0·3	**0·4**	20·5
1905	14862	152·1	17·9	152·2	131·5	0	0·5	0·4	19·8
1906	15055	156·0	19·0	156·1	135·8	0·4	0·2	0·4	19·7
1907	15166	157·5	20·5	157·7	136·3	0·1	0·4	0·4	20·6
1908	—	160·6	20·6	160·8	139·8	0·3	0·4	0·4	20·2
1909	—	164·6	21·6	164·7	143·2	0·2	0·4	0·4	20·7
1910	—	168·9	23·2	168·9	146·3	0·3	1·2	0·4	21·0
1911	—	176·5	24·8	176·6	155·6	0·4	1·0	**0·4**	19·6
1912	—	182·1	26·1	182·2	160·3	0	0·6	**0·4**	20·9
1913	—	187·2	26·6	187·4	164·3	0	0·7	**0·4**	22·0
1914	—	190·5	26·6	190·7	166·0	0	1·2	**0·4**	23·1
1915	—	186·3	54·7	186·5	158·8	5·3	1·5	**0·4**	25·8
1916	—	196·7	104·2	196·8	169·7	0·2	1·1	0·4	25·6
1917	—	203·3	151·0	**203·7**	176·0	0	**1·6**	**0·4**	**25·7**
1918	—	234·6	185·7	235·0	206·7	2·5	2·0	0·4	25·0

1921	—	264·2	209·7	264·4	233·1	0·1	0·9	0·4	30·0
1922	—	268·1	206·3	268·3	239·1	0	0·7	0·4	28·1
1923	—	273·1	202·5	273·3	243·5	0	1·0	0·4	28·4
1924	—	280·4	197·5	280·6	252·5	1·2	1·0	0·4	26·7
1925	—	285·5	183·7	285·7	257·0	0	1·2	0·4	27·1
1926	—	283·7	184·6	283·8	235·5	0	0·8	0·5	47·0
1927	—	284·6	188·6	284·7	236·1	0	0·5	0·5	47·6
1928	—	288·6	191·5	288·6	256·8	0	0·6	0·5	30·7
1929	—	285·0	190·8	285·0	263·8	0	0·2	0·5	20·5
1930	—	290·2	188·3	290·2	272·9	0	0·6	0·5	16·2
1931	—	289·4	191·6	289·4	281·8	0	0·4	0·5	6·7
1932	—	305·7	194·5	305·7	297·5	0·2	2·0	0·5	5·7
1933	—	326·7	186·8	326·7	312·8	0	2·4	0·5	11·0
1934	—	354·8	176·0	354·8	337·3	0	2·9	0·5	14·1
1935	—	390·3	169·7	390·3	359·1	0·5	1·8	0·5	28·9
1936	—	432·4	165·5	432·4	387·7	0	1·5	0·5	42·7
1937	—	470·5	165·9	470·5	423·0	0	1·2	0·5	45·8
1938	—	509·3	202·6	509·3	455·6	0	1·6	0·5	51·6
1939	—	551·4	205·6	551·4	492·4	0	0·8	0·5	57·7
1940	—	654·4	267·6	654·4	593·3	9·2	2·7	0·5	57·9
1941	—	822·9	440·4	822·9	762·9	0	1·9	0·5	57·9
1942	—	1005·4	625·1	1005·4	943·5	0	3·5	0·5	57·9
1943	—	1240·6	747·1	1240·6	1179·3	0	6·0	0·5	54·8
1944	—	1493·9	867·5	1493·9	1452·3	0	7·3	0·5	33·8
1945	—	1776·6	984·9	1776·6	1762·9	15·0	7·7	0·5	5·5
1946	—	1981·9	1183·6	1981·9	1962·8	0	13·3	0·5	5·3
1947	—	1943·2	1310·0	1943·2	1933·7	0	6·3	0·5	2·7
1948	—	1948·0	1237·0	1948·0	1940·1	0	**4·7**	0·5	2·7
1949	—	1947·6	1166·6	1947·6	1941·1	0	3·2	0·6	2·7
1950	—	1934·3	1143·7	1934·3	1929·5	0	1·6	0·6	2·7
1951	—	1875·9	1120·5	1875·9	1873·3	0	2·0	0·6	0
1952	—	1812·3	1067·8	1812·3	1810·1	0	1·6	0·6	0
1953	—	1746·8	1012·5	1746·8	1743·1	0	3·1	0·6	0
1954	—	1727·4	973·1	1727·4	1725·0	0	1·8	0·6	0
1955	—	1700·0	990·6	1700·0	1696·8	0	2·6	0·6	0
1956	—	1688·0	966·4	1688·0	1683·4	0	4·0	0·6	0
1957	—	1677·0	932·0	1677·0	1673·8	0	2·6	0·6	0
1958	—	1645·6	893·0	1645·6	1645·0	0	0	0·6	0
1959	—	1679·0	995·9	1679·0	1676·8	0	1·5	0·7	0
1960	—	1710·2	1137·0	1710·2	1706·9	0	2·6	0·7	0
1961	—	1736·6	1241·4	1736·6	1728·1	0	7·8	0·7	0
1962	—	1760·1	1260·0	1760·1	1754·9	3·0	4·4	0·8	0
1963	—	1791·6	1303·6	1791·6	1783·0	0	7·8	0·8	0
1964	—	1814·4	1320·4	1814·4	1808·5	0	6·7	0·8	0
1965	—	1822·5	1233·4	1822·5	1816·3	0	5·4	0·8	0
1966	—	1739·8	971·3	1739·8	1734·7	0	4·3	0·8	0
1967	—	1672·7	692·6	1672·7	1667·2	2·5	4·7	0·8	0

Sources

Col. 3 (1921–35), Board of Trade, *Statistical Abstract for the UK*, 1913–35, Nos. 79–80, p. 245.

Col. 3 (1880–1905), *Postmaster General Annual Reports*.

Col. 3 (1906–20), Board of Trade, *Statistical Abstract for the UK*, 1906–22, Nos. 67–88, p. 295.

Col. 3 (1936–62), extracted from the National Savings Table in this Appendix.

Col. 3 (1963–6), C.S.O., *Annual Abstract of Statistics*, 1963–6.

Cols. 1, 2, 4–8 (1860–1962), *Postmaster General Annual Reports*.

Cols. 1, 2, 4–8 (1963–6), *Postmaster General Annual Reports*.

Notes

* Includes stock held for benefit of trustee savings banks' depositors.

[a] Includes bonds of Metropolitan Water Board, local loan stocks and temporary accommodation to local authorities.

[b] Valued as average price on or around 31 Dec.

[c] Figures in bold type are estimates. Method: interpolation between given years.

TABLE (A) 2.3 **Trustee Savings Banks of the United Kingdom 1880–1967 (Assets and liabilities £ millions)**

Year-End 20 Nov,	No. of Offices	No. of Banks	Total Deposits, Both Departments	Ord. Dept. Deposits	Special Investment Dept. Deposits[1]	Stock Dept.	Surplus and Reserves: Total	Surplus and Reserves: Special Investment Dept.	Ordinary Depts.' Assets: Total	Ordinary Depts.' Assets: Held by National Debt Commissioners	Ordinary Depts.' Assets: Cash	Other Assets Including Premises	Special Investment Departments' Assets: Total Assets	Total Investments	British Government and Government-Guaranteed	Mun. and Local Gov. Stock	Mortgage	Cash	Other Assets: Accrued Interest, Tax Rebate
	1	2	3	4	5	6	7 A	7 B	8	9	10	11	12	13 A	13 B	13 C	14	15	16
1880	—	442	46·0	44·0	2·0	0·0	1·1	0·1	45·0	44·2	0·3	0·5	2·1[a]	—	—	—	—	—	—
1881	—	437	46·4	44·1	2·3	0·1	1·1	0·1	45·1	44·3	0·3	0·5	2·4	—	—	—	—	—	—
1882	—	430	47·2	44·6	2·6	0·2	1·2	0·2	45·7	44·9	0·3	0·5	2·8	—	—	—	—	—	—
1883	—	421	47·8	45·0	2·8	0·4	1·2	0·2	46·0	45·2	0·3	0·5	3·0	—	—	—	—	—	—
1884	—	411	48·9	45·8	3·1	0·5	1·3	0·2	46·9	46·1	0·3	0·5	3·3	—	—	—	—	—	—
1885	—	409	49·7	46·4	3·3	0·7	1·2	0·2	47·4	46·6	0·3	0·5	3·5	—	—	—	—	—	—
1886	—	405	50·4	46·8	3·6	0·8	1·3	0·2	47·9	47·1	0·3	0·5	3·8	—	—	—	—	—	—
1887*	—	400	51·1	47·3	3·8	0·9	1·2	0·2	48·3	47·5	0·3	0·5	4·0	—	—	—	—	—	—
1888	—	382	50·4	46·4	4·0	1·0	1·2	0·2	47·4	46·6	0·3	0·5	4·2	—	—	—	—	—	—
1889	—	346	49·1	44·9	4·2	1·2	1·5	0·2	46·2	45·4	0·3	0·5	4·4	—	—	—	—	—	—
1890	—	324	48·0	43·6	4·4	1·3	1·4	0·3	44·7	43·9	0·3	0·5	4·7	1·3[h]	1·3	3·3		0·1[c]	0[d]
1891[2]	—	303	47·0	42·9	4·1	1·3	1·3	0·2	44·0	43·2	0·3	0·5	4·3	0·8	0·8	3·4		0·1	0
1892	—	281	46·7	42·4	4·3	1·3	1·4	0·3	43·5	42·7	0·3	0·5	4·6	1·2	1·2	3·3		0·1	0
1893[3]	—	267	46·7	42·2	4·5	1·3	1·4	0·3	43·2	42·5	0·3	0·5	4·8	4·7	4·7	0[b]		0·1	0
1894	—	257	48·1	43·5	4·6	1·4	1·2	0·2	44·5	43·8	0·3	0·5	4·8	4·7	4·7	0		0·1	0
1895	—	245	50·0	45·3	4·7	1·3	1·3	0·3	46·3	45·6	0·3	0·5	5·0[a]	4·9	4·9	0		0·1	0
1896[4]	—	239	51·4	46·7	4·7	1·1	1·3	0·3	47·7	46·9	0·3	0·5	5·0	4·9	4·9	0		0·1	0
1897	—	232	53·1	48·5	4·6	1·1	1·2	0·3	49·4	48·7	0·3	0·5	4·9	4·8	4·8	0		0·1	0
1898	—	231	54·6	50·0	4·6	1·1	1·3	0·3	51·0	50·2	0·4	0·5	4·9	4·8	4·8	0		0·1	0
1899	—	231	56·0	51·4	4·6	1·1	1·4	0·3	52·5	51·6	0·3	0·5	4·9	4·8	4·8	0		0·1	0
1900	—	230	56·0	51·5	4·5	1·4	1·3	0·2	52·6	51·6	0·4	0·5	4·8	4·7	4·7	0		0·1	0
1901	—	230	56·5	52·0	4·5	1·7	1·5	0·4	53·1	52·1	0·4	0·5	4·9	4·8	4·8	0		0·1	0
1902	—	229	57·1	52·5	4·6	1·9	1·5	0·3	53·7	52·8	0·4	0·5	4·9	4·8	4·8	0		0·1	0
1903	—	228	57·2	52·5	4·7	2·1	1·6	0·3	53·8	52·8	0·3	0·6	5·0	4·9	4·9	0		0·1	0
1904[5]	—	224	57·7	52·8	4·9	2·3	0·8	0·3	53·3	52·6	0·4	0·6	5·2	5·1[h]	5·1	0[b]		0·1	0
1905	—	224	58·3	52·7	5·6	2·3	1·7	0·4	54·0	53·1	0·4	0·6	6·0	1·4[i]	1·2	0·2[g]	4·5[f]	0·1[c]	0[d]
1906	—	224	59·4	53·0	6·4	2·4	1·8	0·5	54·3	53·4	0·4	0·6	6·9	1·4[i]	1·2	0·2[g]	5·2[f]	0·2	0·1
1907	—	222	59·2	52·2	7·0	2·5	1·7	0·4	53·5	52·5	0·4	0·6	7·4	1·6[i]	1·4	0·2[g]	5·6[f]	0·2	0
1908	—	222	59·9	51·7	8·2	2·4	1·8	0·4	53·1	52·0	0·4	0·6	8·6	1·9[i]	1·6	0·3[g]	6·5[f]	0·2	0
1909	—	222	62·0	52·2	9·8	2·5	1·9	0·5	53·6	52·5	0·4	0·6	10·3	2·3	1·9	0·3[g]	7·7[f]	0·3	0
1910	—	219	63·2	52·3	10·9	2·7	2·0	0·6	53·7	52·6	0·4	0·6	11·5	2·7	2·3	0·4[g]	8·6[f]	0·2[e]	0
1911	—	215	65·2	53·0	12·2	2·7	2·0	0·5	54·5	53·3	0·5	0·7	12·7	2·9	2·5	0·4[g]	9·5[f]	0·3	0
1912	392	211	67·2	53·8	13·4	2·8	2·0	0·5	55·3	54·1	0·5	0·7	13·9	3·2	2·8	0·4[g]	10·4[f]	0·3[e]	0[e]
1913	402	202	68·7	54·3	14·4	2·8	2·0	0·5	55·8	54·6	0·5	0·7	14·9	3·4	2·9	0·5[g]	11·2[f]	0·3[e]	0[e]
1914	403	196	69·5	53·9	15·6	2·8	2·2	0·6	55·5	54·2	0·6	0·7	16·2	3·7	3·2	0·5[g]	12·2[f]	0·3[e]	0[e]
1915	410	191	66·8	51·4	15·4	6·4	2·1	0·6	52·9	51·6	0·7	0·7	16·0	3·5	3·0	0·5[g]	12·0[f]	0·4	0·1
1916	413	189	68·4	53·8	14·6	9·0	2·1	0·5	55·4	53·7	0·9	0·7	15·1	3·4	2·9	0·5[g]	11·3[f]	0·4	0
1917	411	179	66·4	52·4	14·0	18·3	2·2	0·6	54·0	52·3	1·0	0·7	14·6	3·3	2·8	0·5[g]	10·9[f]	0·4	0
1918	410	171	75·1	61·0	14·1	22·6	2·2	0·6	62·6	60·9	1·1	0·7	14·7	3·3	2·8	0·5[g]	11·0[f]	0·4	0
1919[6]	413	163	86·8	71·9	14·9	25·4	2·3	0·6	73·6	71·7	1·2	0·7	15·5	3·5	2·9	0·5[g]	11·6[f]	0·4	0

1920	414	163	91·3	75·1	16·2	26·9	2·5	0·7	76·9	74·7	1·5	0·7	16·9	**3·7**[i]	**3·2**	**0·5**[g]	**12·7**[f]	0·4	0·1
1921	420	152	92·3	73·1	19·2	27·6	2·7	0·9	74·9	73·0	1·2	0·7	20·1	**4·3**	**3·7**	**0·6**[g]	**15·1**[f]	0·6	0·1
1922	421	148	98·3	75·8	22·5	27·4	3·0	1·0	77·8	76·0	1·0	0·7	23·5	**5·2**[i]	**4·4**[i]	**0·8**	**17·6**[f]	0·6	0·1
1923	417	147	103·2	79·6	23·6	27·5	3·4	1·3	81·7	79·9	1·0	0·8	24·9	5·5	3·6	0·8	18·7	0·4	0·3
1924	421	146	107·0	82·3	24·7	28·5	3·9	1·7	84·5	82·8	1·0	0·8	26·4	5·5	3·6	0·8	20·6	0·6	0·3
1925	428	140	110·4	83·4	27·0	31·7	4·2	1·9	85·7	83·8	1·0	0·8	28·9	5·1	3·4	0·7	22·9	0·6	0·3
1926	437	131	110·8	82·0	28·8	34·0	4·6	2·1	84·5	82·6	1·0	0·9	30·9	5·1	3·5	0·7	24·8	0·6	0·3
1927	443	123	113·9	81·4	32·5	36·1	4·1	1·5	84·0	81·7	1·3	1·0	34·9	5·5	3·9	0·7	28·2	0·8	0·4
1928	450	119	120·5	81·6	38·9	38·4	5·3	2·6	84·3	82·1	1·3	1·0	41·5	5·9	4·3	0·7	34·2	0·9	0·4
1929	466	113	124·4	79·3	45·1	38·0	5·7	2·9	82·1	79·6	1·5	1·0	48·0	7·2	5·6	0·7	39·6	0·8	0·6
1930	494	107	133·2	79·1	54·1	39·3	6·1	3·3	81·9	79·7	1·1	1·0	57·4	8·4	6·9	0·7	46·9	1·2	0·9
1931	504	106	143·0	77·9	65·1	40·7	6·5	3·6	80·8	78·3	1·4	1·1	68·7	12·0	10·5	0·7	54·3	1·2	1·1
1932	519	102	154·8	80·0	74·8	40·8	7·1	4·0	83·1	80·5	1·4	1·1	78·8	12·7	11·4	0·6	62·4	2·4	1·3
1933	538	100	171·4	88·8	82·6	37·6	7·9	4·7	92·0	89·4	1·5	1·1	87·3	13·7	12·1	0·9	68·3	4·1	1·2
1934[6]	560	102	181·9	94·8	87·1	36·8	8·6	5·3	98·1	95·4	1·5	1·1	92·4	13·0	11·3	1·0	74·6	3·5	1·2
1935	585	104	197·4	107·6	89·8	35·9	9·2	5·7	111·1	108·3	1·6	1·1	95·5	15·4	12·1	2·7	76·6	2·3	1·2
1936	609	105	212·1	120·3	91·8	35·4	9·9	6·2	124·0	121·1	1·7	1·2	98·0	15·5	11·8	3·1	79·3	1·8	1·1
1937	648	102	224·6	131·3	93·3	37·1	10·4	6·5	135·2	132·2	1·8	1·2	99·8	15·1	11·6	2·9	81·6	1·8	1·2
1938	680	101	238·9	142·4	96·5	38·3	10·8	6·8	146·4	143·3	1·9	1·3	103·3	14·9	11·4	2·9	85·1	1·9	1·4
1939	699	99	248·3	150·3	98·0	39·8	11·2	7·0	154·5	151·2	2·0	1·3	105·0	13·6	10·4	2·8	87·0	2·8	1·4
1940[7]	698	99	272·5	171·8	100·7	44·7	11·6	7·2	176·2	172·2	2·7	1·3	107·9	14·9	12·8	2·8	87·8	2·5	1·6
1941	697	93	320·1	212·8	107·3	49·5	12·0	7·4	217·4	213·8	2·4	1·3	114·7	21·7	18·7	2·7	88·3	2·7	1·9
1942	710	91	375·2	262·6	112·6	54·2	12·6	7·7	267·5	263·7	2·6	1·2	120·3	30·1	27·0	2·7	86·0	2·3	1·7
1943	723	89	444·7	330·9	113·8	59·0	13·4	7·9	336·4	332·4	2·9	1·1	121·7	35·5	32·9	2·2	82·2	2·4	1·7
1944	741	88	523·2	408·8	114·4	63·7	15·9	9·6	415·1	410·8	3·1	1·1	124·0	39·1	36·9	2·2	80·2	2·6	1·6
1945	770	87	603·1	488·5	114·6	71·7	15·8	8·4	495·9	490·6	4·2	1·1	123·0	41·4	39·3	1·8	77·6	2·3	1·6
1946	811	87	670·3	557·7	112·6	83·1	17·3	8·8	566·2	560·7	4·4	1·1	121·4	41·6	39·8	1·6	75·4	2·8	1·6
1947	870	87	731·5	621·9	109·6	82·6	19·0	8·7	632·2	625·5	5·4	1·3	118·3	42·5	40·8	1·5	71·7	2·7	1·5
1948	985	86	799·2	688·7	110·5	82·6	20·7	8·7	700·7	693·6	5·4	1·6	119·2	42·4	40·8	1·5	72·3	3·0	1·5
1949	1065	85	856·9	744·4	112·5	85·3	21·9	8·6	757·7	749·9	5·7	2·1	121·1	43·4	41·9	1·5	73·3	2·8	1·6
1950	1151	84	908·9	793·7	115·2	87·8	23·1	8·9	807·9	799·5	5·9	2·5	124·1	45·4	44·3	0·8	74·2	3·0	1·5
1951	1270	85	932·3	816·6	115·7	94·0	23·7	9·0	831·3	821·7	6·6	3·0	124·7	45·4	44·0	1·2	74·4	3·3	1·6
1952	1259	85	953·7	831·3	122·4	103·2	23·8	8·6	846·5	836·8	6·5	3·2	131·0	45·8	43·9	1·8	80·2	3·2	1·8
1953	1283	85	968·6	824·9	143·7	109·6	24·3	8·8	840·4	830·2	6·7	3·4	152·5	46·6	42·1	4·7	98·5	5·1	2·3
1954	1303	84	1019·7	827·1	192·6	114·3	25·2	8·9	843·4	831·9	7·9	3·7	201·5	54·7	45·4	9·3	137·1	6·8	2·9
1955	1321	84	1047·5	821·3	226·2	124·6	32·3	9·2	844·4	833·3	7·1	3·9	235·4	63·2	52·1	11·1	162·6	6·2	3·4
1956	1325	84	1094·4	811·6	282·8	134·6	26·8	9·1	829·3	816·4	7·8	5·2	291·9	72·4	56·8	15·5	209·5	5·6	4·4
1957	1333	84	1140·1	823·3	316·8	138·6	27·8	9·3	841·8	827·2	8·6	5·9	326·1	77·6	57·3	20·3	237·4	5·6	5·5
1958	1335	84	1165·4	822·8	342·6	147·7	29·3	9·5	842·6	827·3	9·0	6·2	352·1	95·2	68·4	24·1	244·8	6·1	6·0
1959	1331	84	1239·1	858·6	380·5	166·2	31·2	10·0	879·8	863·8	9·4	6·6	390·5	115·0	81·8	26·1	262·2	7·1	6·2
1960	1340	83	1314·6	880·6	434·0	182·9	32·8	10·5	902·9	884·9	11·0	6·9	444·5	145·7	103·1	34·4	284·4	7·1	7·2
1961	1340	80	1401·4	902·4	499·0	196·1	35·0	11·1	926·3	908·4	10·3	7·5	510·1	177·1	126·7	41·1	316·7	7·7	8·3
1962	1351	80	1517·1	913·6	603·5	200·3	38·2	12·7	939·1	919·4	11·5	8·1	616·2	218·8	149·4	60·0	367·8	8·6	10·6
1963	1358	80	1685·0	951·6	733·4	201·4	42·0	14·7	978·9	958·5	11·6	8·7	748·1	275·0	173·0	89·1	450·4	11·0	11·6
1964	1362	80	1880·7	995·6	885·0	208·9	45·6	15·9	1025·3	1003·1	12·8	9·5	900·9	351·1	211·1	123·6	523·2	12·3	14·1
1965	1374	79	2021·4	1027·4	994·6	212·9	50·8	17·9	1060·3	1035·3	14·9	10·2	1011·9	400·0	240·5	142·4	582·7	12·0	17·2
1966	1405	78	2145·7	1038·7	1107·0	202·2	58·5	19·8	1077·4	1050·0	15·6	11·0	1126·8	449·4	262·5	167·3	642·5	14·5	20·3
1967	1427	77	2261·0	1045·6	1215·4	196·2	64·8	21·9	1088·5	1057·3	17·9	12·6	1237·3	524·0	296·0	203·0	676·3	14·2	23·7

Notes to Table (A) 2.3. overleaf.

Sources

Col. 3=cols. 4+5, col. 7A=col. 8−4+7B, col. 7B= col. 12−5.

Col. 1 (1912–62), cols. 2, 4, 5, 9, 10 (1890–1962), col. 6 (1919–62), cols. 8, 11 (1880–1962), col. 12 (1896–1962), cols. 13A+14 (1900–15), col. 15 (1906–11), cols. 8 to 16 (1923–62), cols. 13C+14 (1890–3), cols. 15, 16 (1915–22), cols. 13A+13C+14 (1921–22), contained in *Annual Reports of the Inspection Committee of Trustee Savings Banks* (London: H.M.S.O.).

Up to 1921 these reports were published in *Parliamentary Papers*. After 1921 these reports were published separately through the Treasury Department, except for the period 1939–48. For this period, no reports were published, but the secretary of the Inspection Committee kindly submitted unpublished reports for these years for inspection. Also: cols. 2, 4–6 (1880–1944), H. O. Horne, *A History of Savings Banks* (Oxford University Press, 1947), pp. 386–91.

Cols. 2, 4–6 (1944–62), cols. 8–16 (1932–62), *Trustee Savings Bank Year Book*, relevant years. For the period 1920–4, col. 6 differs from the figures found in Horne, as Horne's figures include 'Stock Holdings' of the Special Investment Department for these years which were as follows: 1920 £0·3 million, 1921 £1·8 million, 1922 £3 million, 1923 £2·8 million, 1924 £2·4 million. In addition, the figures for the Ordinary Department differ from Horne's and the *Trustee Savings Bank Year Book* for the years 1939–45 as the Inspection Committee left out the banks in Guernsey and Jersey from its report for this period.

All columns (1963–7) *Annual Report of the Inspection Committee of Trustee Savings Banks* (London: H.M.S.O., 1963–8).

Notes

* Cardiff failure.

[a] Col. 12 (1880–95) = col. $5_t.\hat{\lambda}$ where

$$\lambda = \frac{\text{Special Inv. Dept. Total Assets}}{\text{Special Inv. Dept. Deposit}}$$

and estimate $\lambda = \hat{\lambda}$;

$$\hat{\lambda} = 1{\cdot}06 = \frac{\sum_{i=1896}^{1900} \left(\frac{\text{Special Inv. Dept. Total Assets}}{\text{Special Inv. Dept. Deposits}}\right)_i}{5}$$

[b] Cols. 13C+14 (1894–1904). Under the Act of 1891 and until the Act of 1904, these types of fund placements were prohibited. As a consequence it is assumed the banks eliminated their holdings of the same which were given as noted for the 1890–3 period in the Inspection Committee's *Report* of 1894.

[c] Cols. 15 and 16 (1890–1905) estimated on basis cash/total assets and other assets/total assets for the years 1906–10.

[d] As above.

[e] Cols. 15 and 16 (1912–14) estimated as (*c*) and (*d*) above on basis of the relevant ratios for the years 1915–18.

[f and g] Cols. 13C and 14 (1905–22), cols. 13C and 14 were estimated on the basis of the mortgage–total asset and municipal and local-government stock/total asset ratios of 1923.

[h] Cols. 13A and 13B (1890–1904) estimated on a residual basis on the assumption that there was no other medium in which the Special Investment Department could hold their unaccounted assets.

[i] Cols. 13A and 13B (1905–22) as for the period 1890–1904. It should be noted though, with respect to col. 13B, that the *Reports* did give the combined total holdings of investments and mortgages for the period 1906–22, e.g. col. 13A and col. 14. These, plus the 'Stock Holdings' of the Special Investment Department noted above, formed the basis for the estimates contained in col. 13B.

[1] Special Investment Department established under authority of Section 16 of the *Trustee Savings Bank Act* of 1863.

[2] *Savings Bank Act* 1891 restricted deposits in Special Investment Department and placed a maximum on such deposit accounts of £500. In addition it confined the placement of Special Investment funds to British Government securities and other trustee investments. It excluded land or any interest on the same.

[3] *Industrial and Provident Societies Act* 1893 eased deposit restrictions somewhat, and removed maximum deposit limitation on Industrial and Provident Societies' deposits.

[4] *Savings Bank Act* 1896 removed maximum and annual deposit restrictions on Friendly Societies' holdings of trustee savings bank deposits.

[5] *Trustee Savings Bank Act* 1904, Special Investment Department allowed to invest in any security issued under *Local Government Loans Act* or loans secured on a local rates. In addition, trustee savings banks with ordinary deposits over £200,000 allowed to apply for permission to open new Special Investment Department.

[6] Investment powers of Special Investment Department enlarged in these years.

[7] After 20 Nov. 1940, the five Irish trustee savings banks were no longer included in the *Inspection Committee's Report*. In total, the ordinary deposits and stock holdings of these banks amounted to £2·3 and £0·1 million respectively in 1940. They held no special investment deposits.

TABLE (A) 2.4 **Building Societies in Great Britain 1880–1967 (Assets and liabilities £ millions)**[5]

Year-End[3] Varies, usually 31 Dec.	No. of Societies	Total Assets or Liabilities[8]	Composition of Liabilities						Mortgages		Investments[6]			Other Assets	
			Shares	Deposits	Loans from Banks	H.M. Government Advances	Other Liabilities and Provisions	General and Specific Reserves	Total	Amount Advanced During Year	Total	Government and Government-Guaranteed[1,4]		Total	Cash[2]
	I	II	III	IV	V	VI	VII	VIII	IX	X	XI	XII		XIII	XIV
1880	1853	54·3	27·1			25·7[10]		1·5	—	—	—	—	—	—	—
1881	2157	59·0	31·6			25·7		1·7	—	—	—	—	—	—	—
1882	2518	66·5	36·0			28·4		2·1	—	—	—	—	—	—	—
1883	2789	68·6	38·2			28·2		2·2	—	—	—	—	—	—	—
1884	3014	68·9	39·5			27·2		2·2	—	—	—	—	—	—	—
1885	3202	70·1	41·0			26·7		2·4	—	—	—	—	—	—	—
1886	3261	70·3	41·5			26·4		2·4	53·0	—	—	—	17·3[9]	—	—
1887	3446	71·2	42·7			26·0		2·5	54·3	—	—	—	16·9	—	—
1888	3523	70·3	42·5			25·3		2·5	53·4	—	—	—	16·9	—	—
1889	n.a.	69·9	42·1			25·3		2·5	53·0	—	—	—	16·9	—	—
1890	4472	69·6	41·6			25·3		2·7	52·6	—	—	**0·2**	17·0	—	**0·6**
1891	4320	67·1	40·2			25·2		2·5	51·1	—	—	**0·2**	16·0	—	**0·6**
1892*	n.a.	64·1	39·5			22·1		2·5	47·6	—	—	**0·2**	16·5	—	**0·6**
1893	4485	58·1	36·5			18·9		2·9	43·9	—	—	**0·3**	14·2	—	**0·6**
1894	4320	56·6	35·9			18·0		2·7	41·1	—	—	**0·3**	15·5	—	**0·6**
1895	3642	54·5	34·4			17·5		2·6	43·1	—	—	**0·3**	11·4	—	**0·6**
1896	2983	55·8	34·4			18·9		2·5	42·8	—	—	**0·4**	13·0	—	**0·6**
1897	2616	56·4	34·0			19·9		2·5	42·9	—	—	**0·4**	13·5	—	**0·8**
1898	2494	58·1	34·0			21·3		2·8	43·6	—	—	**0·4**	14·5	—	**0·8**
1899	2378	59·8	34·5			22·3		3·0	47·7	—	—	**0·4**	15·1	—	**0·8**
1900	2286	60·0	35·0			21·6		3·4	45·6	—	—	**0·6**	14·4	—	**0·8**
1901	2208	60·9	35·4			22·1		3·4	46·8	8·9	—	**0·6**	14·1	—	**1·0**
1902	2145	62·7	36·4			22·8		3·5	48·1	8·9	—	**0·6**	14·6	—	**1·0**
1903	2073	65·0	37·5			23·9		3·6	50·3	9·7	—	**0·6**	14·7	—	**0·9**
1904	2018	66·8	38·5			24·5		3·8	52·0	9·4	—	**0·6**	14·8	—	**1·0**
1905	1950	69·1	39·8			25·4		3·9	53·2	9·0	—	**0·6**	15·9	—	**1·1**
1906	1916	71·0	41·2			25·8		4·0	54·5	9·2	—	**0·5**	16·5	—	**1·1**
1907	1863	72·0	42·3			25·6		4·1	56·2	9·6	—	**0·5**	15·8	—	**1·1**
1908	1829	72·8	43·6			25·3		3·9	57·3	8·9	—	**0·4**	15·5	—	**1·2**
1909	1777	75·2	44·6			26·0		4·0	58·3	9·0	—	**0·5**	16·9	—	**1·3**
1910	1723	76·3	45·6			25·9		4·2	59·7	9·3	—	**0·4**	16·6	—	**1·2**
1911[7]	1611	63·5	43·9			16·0		3·7	59·7	8·9	—	**0·1**	3·8	—	**1·1**
1912	1588	64·1	44·5			15·9		3·7	60·0	8·3	—	**0·1**	4·1	—	**1·0**
1913	1550	65·3	45·6			16·0		3·8	60·7	9·1	—	**0·1**	4·6	—	**1·1**
1914	1501	66·1	46·5			15·9		3·8	61·0	8·8	—	**0·1**	5·1	—	**1·5**
1915	1454	65·7	46·4			15·3		4·0	59·9	6·5	—	**0·9**	5·8	—	**1·4**
1916	1408	65·2	46·7			14·4		4·1	57·1	4·9	—	**1·6**	8·1	—	**1·7**
1917	1362	64·4	46·6			13·6		4·2	54·5	4·5	—	**2·8**	9·9	—	**1·6**
1918	1336	68·5	50·1			14·1		4·3	53·2	7·0	—	**5·4**	15·3	—	**1·4**
1919	1308	77·2	56·6			16·2		4·5	57·8	15·8	—	**7·7**	19·5	—	**1·6**

1920	1271	87·0	63·9	16·1		2·2[11]		4·9	68·8	25·1	—	7·6	18·2	—	1·6
1921	1255	95·3	70·9	17·2		1·9		5·3	75·5	19·7	—	8·4	19·8	—	2·0
1922	1180	107·4	80·4	19·3		1·7		6·0	83·7	22·7	—	10·9	23·7	—	2·2
1923	1143	124·7	93·5	21·8		2·6		6·8	98·8	32·0	—	11·3	25·9	—	2·6
1924	1112	144·9	109·0	24·5		3·6		7·8	119·7	40·6	—	10·4	25·1	—	3·0
1925	1092	169·2	127·8	27·3		5·1		9·0	145·9	49·8	18·2	9·1	—	5·1	3·5
1926	1064	193·9	147·7	30·5		5·2		10·4	171·2	52·2	—	8·4	22·6	—	4·0
1927	1054	223·3	172·8	33·4		5·2		12·0	197·7	55·9	—	8·9	25·6	—	5·7
1928[3]	1035	268·5	213·2	36·0		5·4		13·8	227·5	58·7	—	13·0	40·9	—	6·0
1929	1026	312·7	250·2	38·9		7·9		15·7	268·1	74·7	33·9	12·7	—	10·7	7·7
1930	1026	371·2	302·8	44·6		6·1		17·6	316·3	88·8	—	14·9	54·8	—	9·1
1931	1013	419·2	341·8	50·4		6·9		20·1	380·2	90·3	—	14·6	59·0	—	19·1
1932	1014	469·3	380·8	61·5		5·3		21·7	388·4	82·1	59·3	21·0	—	21·3	19·2
1933	1013	501·1	395·5	75·5		6·0		24·1	423·5	103·2	60·8	16·3	—	16·8	12·3
1934	1007	555·6	424·3	97·3		6·8		27·2	476·2	124·6	57·7	13·4	—	21·7	17·3
1935	999	602·0	447·2	114·8		9·4		30·6	529·7	130·9	55·7	13·8	—	16·6	11·8
1936	985	656·2	480·7	128·4		12·9		34·2	586·7	140·3	52·3	12·6	—	17·1	12·3
1937	977	710·4	517·5	143·3		11·5		38·1	636·4	136·9	55·2	11·7	—	18·8	13·9
1938	971	758·9	548·3	155·7		13·4		41·6	686·7	137·0	53·2	11·7	—	18·9	14·3
1939	960	773·7	559·4	152·0		18·4		43·9	706·1	94·3	48·5	10·2	—	19·2	14·6
1940	952	756·2	552·2	142·3		16·2		45·6	677·8	21·2	54·2	19·3	—	24·2	22·7
1941	947	749·1	548·7	138·8		15·6		46·0	643·9	10·0	78·2	29·1	—	27·0	22·6
1942	931	753·0	550·9	140·0		14·8		47·3	608·4	16·3	109·8	44·4	—	34·8	22·7
1943	924	769·5	564·9	143·1		12·6		48·9	576·2	28·1	158·6	62·9	—	34·6	23·1
1944	905	795·4	585·2	148·8		10·8		50·6	561·9	52·9	199·1	80·3	—	34·5	22·5
1945	890	824·0	605·2	155·2		11·0		52·6	573·3	97·6	216·1	93·9	—	34·6	24·0
1946	874	876·9	646·1	163·7		11·2		55·9	640·4	188·2	202·3	84·7	—	34·2	22·2
1947	858	954·5	702·4	179·8		12·9		59·3	733·4	242·5	179·5	71·4	—	41·6	23·3
1948	847	1037·8	768·6	192·0		15·3		62·6	836·9	264·0	162·0	71·9	—	39·0	25·4
1949	835	1142·0	855·6	201·9	5·4	11·8[12]		67·3	953·7	276·0	146·0	53·3	—	42·3	31·4
1950	819	1255·9	962·3	205·9	4·6	12·8		70·8	1059·8	269·7	150·4	56·7	—	45·6	32·6
1951	807	1357·0	1057·0	208·1	4·0	13·8		74·1	1158·2	367·6	145·5	65·3	—	53·4	40·0
1952	796	1478·1	1186·1	197·5	2·6	14·5		77·4	1263·1	266·1	158·4	60·5	—	56·6	44·2
1953	782	1642·6	1338·4	202·7	1·9	16·2		83·3	1396·2	299·5	184·2	68·3	—	62·2	49·9
1954	777	1867·4	1535·1	222·1	1·8	18·6		90·1	1573·5	373·2	221·5	89·1	—	72·3	57·5
1955	783	2065·4	1732·3	216·5	2·1	18·7		95·7	1751·9	394·4	240·2	107·2	—	73·3	57·0
1956	773	2230·1	1969·3	193·5	1·1	24·2		101·4	1878·6	334·9	275·5	145·5	—	76·1	60·1
1957	755	2414·6	2085·0	189·0	1·4	31·3		107·8	2032·4	374·1	304·7	157·7	—	77·6	58·5
1958	744	2621·3	2268·6	198·5	0·9	36·5		116·8	2178·6	374·7	351·0	193·0	—	91·8	69·5
1959	732	2907·1	2523·0	213·8	0·7	6·1	35·9	127·7	2406·1	517·3	398·2	211·8	—	102·8	72·3
1960	726	3166·4	2720·8	222·0	0·8	43·3	39·9	139·3	2647·5	559·8	414·7	231·9	—	104·3	71·4
1961	706	3436·8	2920·9	225·6	0·6	89·6	46·9	153·3	2870·6	545·8	455·5	241·0	—	110·6	74·8
1962	681	3815·3	3264·9	242·2	0·6	83·3	54·3	170·7	3138·6	613·0	556·4	268·0	—	120·9	80·7
1963	662	4331·0	3732·8	271·1	0·3	79·7	57·8	189·9	3556·0	849·4	643·6	291·7	—	131·9	86·2
1964	635	4863·0	4218·6	293·1	0·4	73·9	68·0	209·0	4091·9	1042·5	630·7	299·6	—	140·0	86·6
1965	605	5531·9	4848·6	294·8	0·2	71·3	84·4	232·6	4544·4	955·4	823·0	350·8	—	164·3	103·4
1966	576	6305·8	5595·0	299·2	0·4	68·5	81·1	261·6	5218·8	1244·7	905·5	386·3	—	181·5	112·6

Notes to Table (A) 2.4 overleaf.

Notes to Table (A) 2.4

Sources

Cols. I (1880–9), IX (1886–8), XI+XIII (1886–8), II (1880–8, 1891, 1893–8), III, IV+V+VI+VII, XI+XIII (1880–8, 1890, 1891, 1893–9), VIII (1880–8, 1891, 1893–9), Board of Trade *Statistical Abstract*, 51, pp. 250–2. Figures prior to 1895 in cols. I, X, XI–XII, IV–VII, VIII multiplied by 1·6, 1·1, 2·9, 1·2, 1·7 and 1·4 respectively to adjust for the fact that unincorporated societies were excluded from returns before 1895.

Cols. I–III, IX, X, XI, XIII (1925, 1930–60), *Building Society Yearbook* 1961, (London: Fancey and Co.), pp. 34–5.

All columns (1889 and 1892) estimated, method by arithmetical interpolation between 1888 and 1890 and 1891 and 1893 respectively.

Cols. X, XI+XIII (1901–29) III, IV+V+VI+VII (1901–29), Bank of England, *Statistical Summary*, July 1932, p. 11.

Col. I (1890–1929), col. II (1915–19, 1938–9, 1946–62), col. IX (1890–91, 1893–1920), kindly provided by the Registrar of Friendly Societies.

Cols. II (1910–14), III, IV+V+VI+VII (1918, 1919), cols. II, III, V+VI+VII, VIII (1920–37), Board of Trade, *Statistical Abstract for the UK 1937*, No. 82 (London: H.M.S.O., 1938), p. 188.

Cols. III, XI+XIII (1930–5), ibid., p. 266.

Cols. IV+VI+VII (1920–5), ibid., p. 266. When adjusted for Fund figures: shares+deposits+reserves, this makes it possible to derive deposit and loan figures.

Cols. I, II, VIII, IX (1900–50), *Building Society Yearbook* (London, 1959), pp. 48–9.

Cols. IV, VI+VII (1926–9), Registrar of Friendly Societies, *Building Society Statistical Summary 1929–39* (London: H.M.S.O.).

Cols. III, IV, V+VI+VII, VIII, XI, XIII (1936–45), C.S.O., *Annual Abstract of Statistics 1935–46*, No. 84 (London: H.M.S.O.), p. 243.

Cols. III, IV, XI, XIII (1946–50), V, VI, VII (1946–8), cols. V, VII (1948–50), C.S.O., *Annual Abstract of Statistics*, No. 91 (1956), p. 289.

Cols. V, VI+VII (1949–50), Registrar of Friendly Societies, *Report*, 1951, Part 5.

Cols. III–V, VIII, IX, XI, XIII, XIV (1951–61), VI+VII (1951–8), VI, VII (1959–61), Registrar of Friendly Societies, *Report*, 1961, part 5 (London: H.M.S.O.), p. 30.

Col. XII (1954–9), Registrar of Friendly Societies, *Report*, 1959, part 5.

Col. XII (1960), Registrar of Friendly Societies, *Report*, 1961, part 5, p. 25.

All columns 1961–2 not mentioned above, found in either C.S.O., *Annual Abstract of Statistics*, No. 100, p. 294, or C.S.O., *Financial Statistics*, No. 30, p. 30.

Cols. XI, XII, XIV (1925, 1929, 1932–8) derived from figures reported in the 'Building Society Supplement', *The Economist*, 1 July 1939. The figures contained in *The Economist* represent the balance sheet figures of 108 large societies accounting for 90 per cent of the total assets of all societies in the relevant years.

Cols. I–IV, VI–XI, XIII and XIV (1963–6) from C.S.O., *Annual Abstract of Statistics*, No. 104, 1967.

Cols. V and XII (1963–6), Registrar of Friendly Societies, *Report*, part V (1963–6) and part ii (1967).

Notes

* Liberator failure.

[1] Figures in col. XII (1890–1924, 1926–8, 1930, 1931, 1939–54) are estimates. Method of estimation:

$$(\text{Govt. Gty.})_{Bt} = \lambda.\theta_t.\text{I}_t.\epsilon,$$

where

$$\theta_t = \left(\frac{\text{Govt.-Gty. holdings of Ins. Comps.}}{\text{Ins. Co. Total Assets} - \text{Mortgages} - \text{Personal Loans}}\right)_t$$

where

$$\lambda = \frac{\sum_{t=1954}^{1961}\left(\dfrac{\text{Gov. and Gov.-Gty. Building Soc.}}{\text{Total Assets Building Soc.} - \text{Mortgages}}\right)_t}{\sum_{t=1954}^{1961}\left(\dfrac{\text{Gov. and Gov.-Gty. Ins. Comp.}}{\text{Total Assets} - \text{Mortgages} - \text{Personal Loans Ins. Comp.}}\right)_t} = 1{\cdot}55$$

$$\text{I}_t = (\text{Total Assets Building Soc.} - \text{Mortgages})_t$$

and

$$\epsilon = \text{Adjustment or Splicing Factor,}$$

e.g.

$$\epsilon \text{ in } 1953 = \left(\frac{\text{Actual Gov. and Gov.-Gty. 1954}}{\text{Estimated Gov. and Gov.-Gty. 1954}}\right) = 0{\cdot}54$$

[2] Figures in col. XIV cash (1890–1924, 1926–8, 1930, 1931, 1934–51) are estimates. Method of estimation:

$$C_{Bt} = \phi\left(\frac{\text{Cash Holdings Joint-Stock Banks England and Wales}}{\text{Total Assets Joint-Stock Banks England and Wales}}\right)_t.A_{Bt}.\epsilon$$

where

$$\phi = \frac{\sum_{1951}^{1961}\left(\dfrac{\text{Cash Holdings Building Soc.}}{\text{Total Assets Building Soc.}}\right)_t}{\sum_{1951}^{1961}\left(\dfrac{\text{Cash Holding of Banks}}{\text{Total Assets of Banks}}\right)_t} = 0{\cdot}22$$

A_{Bt}=total assets of building societies in period t, and ϵ is the adjustment or splicing factor, e.g.

$$\epsilon \text{ in } 1951 = \frac{\text{Actual Cash Building Soc. 1951}}{\text{Estimated Cash Building Soc. 1951}} = 0{\cdot}93.$$

[3] Accounting change. Year-end moved from 31 Dec. to 31 Jan. in 1928. As a consequence, the figures reported reflect the consolidation of balance sheets struck from 1 Feb. of that year to 31 Jan. of the succeeding year.

[4] Government and Government-guaranteed holdings include tax reserve certificates and Treasury Bill holdings of societies.

[5] Figures reported below may not add because of rounding. In addition, they are the consolidated totals of several hundred societies, some of which undoubtedly prepare their balance sheets on different dates.

[6] After 1 Jan. 1961, investments of building societies ruled by Authorized Investment Order: I, II, III.

[7] Birbeck failure caused unincorporated societies to lose £10·8 million in deposits.

[8] Societies incorporated in Ireland had assets of £1·3 million in 1906 and £0·8 million in 1920.

[9] Sum of cols. XI+XIII.

[10] Sum of cols. IV to VII=IV+V+VI+VII.

[11] Sum of cols. V to VII=V+VI+VII.

[12] Sum of columns VI and VII=VI+VII.

TABLE (A) 2.5 **Insurance Companies Established in the United Kingdom 1880–1966 (£ millions) All classes of business: Life, Industrial, Accident, Bond, Employer liability, Fire, Motor Vehicle since 1931**

End of Year	*Total Assets* 1	*Mort-gages* 2	*Loans on Public Rates and Local Government Securities* 3	*Loans on Policy and Personal Securities* 4	*British Government and Government-Guaranteed Securities* 5	*Other Commercial and Municipal Securities* 6	*Foreign Government and Municipal Securities* 7	*Deben-tures* 8	*Preference and Guaranteed Stocks* 9	*Ordinary Stocks and Shares* 10	*Land Insurance Property and Ground Rent* 11	*Cash and Stamps* 12	*Other Assets, Residual* 13
1880	155·1	70·9	19·5	9·0	5·0	7·1	4·4	10·6	7·9		8·1	4·5	8·1
1881	159·9	71·3	19·6	8·8	5·3	8·3	4·3	11·4	8·7		9·2	4·6	8·4
1882	165·0	72·7	21·6	8·9	5·1	8·8	4·3	11·6	9·8		9·4	3·9	8·9
1883	169·7	74·4	22·0	9·2	5·0	9·4	4·1	12·3	9·9		10·0	4·3	9·1
1884	174·8	75·0	22·6	9·3	5·3	10·8	3·9	12·6	10·4		10·7	4·7	9·5
1885	179·3	75·6	23·1	9·5	5·6	11·3	4·1	13·2	11·4		11·4	4·6	9·5
1886	184·3	77·3	23·4	9·6	5·8	11·6	4·0	14·2	11·3		12·4	4·9	9·8
1887	189·7	77·8	23·6	9·8	6·0	11·8	3·7	15·8	12·0		13·4	5·6	10·2
1888	196·0	78·2	23·6	10·0	6·2	12·6	3·6	18·1	12·5		14·4	6·6	10·2
1889	203·6	79·1	23·8	10·3	6·4	12·8	3·5	20·3	13·1		14·8	8·4	11·1
1890	211·3	83·1	22·5	10·5	6·4	12·8	3·5	23·3	13·1		15·8	8·7	11·6
1891	217·5	83·9	22·3	11·0	5·8	13·6	3·7	24·6	13·7		16·3	9·6	13·0
1892	223·4	84·8	24·7	11·3	5·5	14·4	3·9	26·5	13·6		17·2	8·9	12·6
1893	231·4	85·1	26·2	11·9	5·5	15·8	4·1	28·8	14·4		18·3	8·0	13·3
1894	240·4	84·8	27·9	12·0	5·7	17·1	4·6	30·8	16·3		19·3	8·0	13·9
1895	251·3	83·4	28·3	12·2	5·7	17·1	5·5	35·3	20·4		20·5	8·4	14·5
1896	263·8	82·0	28·9	12·6	6·2	17·4	7·0	40·9	25·1		22·0	6·9	14·8
1897	277·0	82·2	29·1	12·9	6·4	18·2	7·9	45·3	28·8		23·6	6·9	15·7
1898	288·8	84·1	28·7	13·5	6·7	18·5	9·0	47·8	32·2		25·5	6·3	16·5
1899	300·4	82·7	31·4	13·8	6·7	18·8	10·6	51·2	34·6		27·1	6·0	17·5
1900	311·1	85·2	33·1	14·4	7·7	19·3	10·9	60·0	35·1		30·0	6·1	9·3
1901	321·3	86·6	35·0	15·4	9·1	19·4	10·7	54·1	35·9		30·2	5·7	19·2
1902	336·8	88·8	37·2	16·5	9·8	19·8	10·8	58·1	38·3		31·6	6·3	19·6
1903	352·6	91·8	39·5	17·9	9·7	19·7	10·5	63·1	39·9		33·9	6·0	20·6
1904	366·7	96·1	42·6	19·3	9·4	19·9	10·4	65·3	40·5		35·8	5·9	21·5
1905	384·4	96·9	44·8	20·5	9·2	20·1	11·7	72·3	42·1		37·2	6·7	22·9
1906	395·8	99·2	45·1	21·5	7·9	20·3	12·3	77·8	42·3		39·2	7·0	23·2
1907	413·8	101·9	46·9	23·1	8·2	20·2	13·5	84·9	42·8		40·9	6·4	25·0
1908	429·3	102·3	49·6	24·8	8·0	19·1	15·0	91·8	44·5		42·7	6·9	24·6
1909	447·3	103·3	53·1	25·8	7·3	20·3	17·4	99·5	42·1		44·2	7·2	27·1
1910	467·3	102·4	31·7	27·4	6·9	38·0	29·3	108·5	44·8		44·5	6·9	26·9
1911	491·3	107·3	31·3	28·0	5·0	38·8	33·2	118·3	29·5	18·1	44·9	6·6	30·3
1912	511·0	109·7	31·4	29·3	5·8	40·3	36·6	125·8	30·1	19·2	45·6	7·4	29·8
1913	530·1	113·9	31·3	31·5	5·3	42·0	39·3	131·5	30·5	18·4	46·1	8·3	32·0
1914	551·0	114·1	30·7	32·6	6·1	44·4	44·8	137·0	30·5	19·0	46·8	11·3	33·7
1915	**564·9**	**108·7**	**36·0**	**45·4**	**52·9**	**44·0**	**53·2**	**90·0**	**24·0**	**15·4**	**45·9**	**14·3**	**35·1**
1916	**584·4**	**103·2**	**33·3**	**44·5**	**76·8**	**44·6**	**55·0**	**80·6**	**22·2**	**15·0**	**44·6**	**9·4**	**55·7**
1917	**600·9**	**100·4**	**32·8**	**44·5**	**116·1**	**47·2**	**54·1**	**77·3**	**22·5**	**15·3**	**45·1**	**9·9**	**35·7**
1918	**635·4**	**98·8**	**32·0**	**24·4**	**162·0**	**50·9**	**50·9**	**82·3**	**26·1**	**18·0**	**45·2**	**11·1**	**33·7**
1919	**673·6**	**93·6**	**29·6**	**22·9**	**200·1**	[illegible]	[illegible]	[illegible]	[illegible]	[illegible]	[illegible]	[illegible]	[illegible]

1921	757·4	87·8	35·2	34·0	243·4	51·4	53·8	77·7	22·3	20·8	47·2	16·4	67·4
1922	803·6	91·2	36·1	29·7	281·4	62·4	52·2	79·5	22·6	25·2	49·5	18·2	55·6
1923[1]	850·1	91·3	35·6	30·0	285·8	77·2	60·0	90·6	27·4	29·0	49·9	19·4	53·9
1924	934·7	96·9	37·2	33·1	298·2	83·6	71·8	106·4	32·8	33·7	53·5	20·2	67·3
1925	1005·1	106·3	43·9	40·9	303·1	87·9	73·9	124·4	41·2	44·3	53·3	22·3	63·6
1926	1065·6	116·1	49·6	48·3	299·5	90·1	77·6	143·0	48·4	50·0	54·7	23·4	64·9
1927	1127·0	128·1	57·7	58·5	286·7	91·8	80·6	165·7	56·3	55·5	55·9	26·1	64·1
1928	1187·9	134·3	58·2	71·6	272·6	93·7	89·0	185·8	67·3	66·2	57·6	24·7	66·9
1929	1252·0	151·3	58·4	86·4	252·1	97·4	89·6	201·3	79·4	82·0	59·3	26·4	68·4
1930	1292·7	162·4	60·8	76·1	249·9	97·2	91·7	222·1	87·5	89·9	61·3	26·0	67·8
1931	1340·9	165·7	63·1	73·8	275·6	99·9	87·8	226·6	90·8	92·5	64·3	29·1	71·7
1932	1389·4	179·5	69·1	70·2	302·4	106·8	79·9	225·9	89·7	92·6	67·0	36·8	69·5
1933	1449·6	162·2	85·1	65·7	344·2	115·4	80·9	231·5	94·9	99·0	71·5	31·9	67·3
1934	1516·3	163·8	91·1	60·6	363·4	120·4	82·3	244·8	104·1	108·0	76·0	30·9	70·9
1935	1586·7	167·7	101·2	55·8	364·6	119·4	86·4	257·9	119·9	126·8	83·4	35·0	68·6
1936	1664·7	182·2	112·7	51·8	367·3	116·6	91·9	266·6	132·9	150·5	91·6	33·0	67·6
1937	1744·7	191·3	121·1	51·3	373·6	115·5	92·0	280·1	143·1	172·5	96·6	41·4	66·2
1938	1824	201	124	55	386	117	94	631			103	40	73·0
1939	1883	206	147	56	373	121	90	651			109	82	48·0
1940	1934	191	240		497	114	97	698			106	75	−84
1941	2009	185	239		590	106	98	647			106	54	−16
1942	2101	176	219		695	103	99	640			105	55	9
1943	2204	170	203		780	104	104	641			108	53	41
1944	2316	162	178		896	100	109	642			111	51	67
1945	2374·2	149·6	122·8	27·2	983·5	99·2	109·0	252·4	170·0	205·5	110·9	53·4	90·7
1946	2526·3	149·2	124·1	25·8	1007·4	102·0	112·1	259·6	200·1	241·7	118·3	71·6	114·4
1947	2717·8	163·8	125·3	25·6	976·5	106·9	128·7	283·0	243·3	292·2	135·2	90·7	146·6
1948	2904·0	188·0	104·5	26·6	1131·4	112·9	142·9	249·1	223·5	306·5	151·0	103·5	164·2
1949	3148·2	215·4	101·8	28·8	1166·7	129·5	174·0	268·5	245·0	340·8	174·3	114·1	189·3
1950	3370·3	258·5	96·8	31·4	1116·6	146·1	184·9	329·4	256·7	373·3	196·8	117·4	262·4
1951	3589·7	310·9	99·8	34·8	1139·6	149·8	195·9	372·9	265·9	411·8	229·1	133·2	246·0
1952	3809·2	362·4	98·8	41·6	1145·4	159·6	209·3	410·5	264·4	456·4	256·9	143·5	260·4
1953	4086·8	395·9	98·5	46·3	1212·7	169·1	217·2	463·6	279·1	506·8	285·7	140·7	271·2
1954	4436·5	430·3	101·7	49·0	1247·1	182·7	219·0	543·7	311·8	618·8	311·9	131·3	289·2
1955	4822·9	505·8	109·4	54·6	1232·6	189·0	222·1	603·5	335·1	736·3	376·8	134·5	323·2
1956	5206·6	594·3	131·2	63·5	1215·9	188·5	244·0	669·2	347·6	826·6	409·0	144·2	372·6
1957	5579·9	658·5	139·4	70·8	1195·1	194·4	236·5	762·1	355·1	943·4	450·2	148·9	425·5
1958	5998·7	715·7	162·0	76·7	1232·2	210·0	234·5	821·9	355·7	1082·4	499·3	150·2	458·1
1959	6554·2	773·7	193·4	78·6	1256·0	232·4	243·3	909·9	365·2	1310·8	553·7	154·8	482·4
1960	7156·0	885·8	195·8	84·2	1325·3	239·0	249·4	977·0	367·8	1513·5	611·7	178·5	528·0
1961	7854·4	1019·6	203·8	94·0	1332·3	256·2	280·6	1089·0	372·9	1721·6	714·1	186·5	583·8
1962	8463·5	1130·6	217·3	101·2	1485·8	246·7	304·1	1178·0	372·8	1834·5	779·5	182·0	630·0
1963	9211·0	1129·4	251·2	105·0	1579·4	264·3	324·3	1337·2	393·0	2020·2	847·3	195·4	764·3
1964	10102·0	1393·7	253·3	101·5	1674·5	277·0	332·1	1535·0	408·7	2253·4	910·7	223·3	738·8
1965	10979·0	1575·5	279·5	127·3	1724·3	284·6	335·0	1745·7	434·1	2418·7	1037·7	217·5	799·2
1966	11787·7	1762·7	284·4	152·4	1742·1	293·1	347·0	2012·0	435·6	2534·7	1107·2	232·7	883·8

Notes to Table (A) 2.5 overleaf.

Notes to Table (A) 2.5

Sources

All cols. (1880–1914) British Parliamentary Papers LXV, 1882, p. 388; LXVI, 1883, p. 278; LXXV, 1884, p. 345; LXXII, 1884–5, p. 276; LXI, 1886, p. 309; LXXVI, 1887, p. 377, XCII, 1888, p. 393; LXXI, 1889, p. 393; LXIX, 1890, p. 304; LXXIX, 1890–1, p. 364; LXXIV, 1892, p. 392; LXXXV, 1893–4, p. 266; LXXX 1894, p. 390; XC, 1895, p. 312; LXXVII, 1896, p. 365; LXXI, 1897, p. 422; LXXXVI, 1898, p. 262; XC, 1899, p. 331; LXXX, 1900, p. 354; LXXI, 1901, p. 370; XCV, 1902, p. 369; LXV, 1903, p. 444; LXXXVIII, 1904, p. 402; LXXIV, 1905, p. 360; XCI, 1906, p. 420; LXXVII, 1907, p. 539; LXXVII, 1909, p. 539; LXXXII, 1910, p. 473; LXXIV, 1911, p. 821; LVIII, 1914–16, p. 743.

(1922–37), Board of Trade, *Summary of Statements of Assurance Business* (London: H.M.S.O., 1938).

(1945–9), C.S.O., *Annual Abstract of Statistics*, No. 93, 1956.

(1950–9), ibid., No. 98, p. 293.
(1960), ibid., No. 99, p. 290.
(1961), ibid., No. 100, p. 291.
(1962), ibid., No. 101, p. 313.
(1963–6), ibid., No. 105, 1968.

Col. 1 (1915–21), derived from fund figures of life and industrial insurance companies multiplied by factor K_t, where t=1915, 1916, 1917, 1918, 1919, 1920 and 1921, and our estimates of K_t were, respectively 1·25, 1·27, 1·29, 1·31, 1·33, 1·35, and 1·36. It should be noted:

$$K_t = \frac{\text{Total Assets of all UK Life Insurance Companies}}{\text{Total Life, Annuity and Industrial Insurance Funds all Companies}}.$$

This was equal to 1·21 in 1913, 1·23 in 1914 and 1·36 in 1922.

Cols. 2–13 (1915–17), devised from aggregate balance sheet figures of a sample of five large UK life insurance companies, whose combined total assets = 31 per cent of our estimate of all UK insurance company assets in 1915, e.g. 176·0/574·9 million. The percentage distribution of each particular group of assets for the sample of the combined total assets was found for each year. These percentages were then corrected by a factor $\hat{\theta}_i$; where:

$$\hat{\theta}i = \frac{\dfrac{\%\text{ of }i\text{th Assets all Companies}}{\text{of their Total Assets in 1922}}}{\dfrac{\%\text{ of }i\text{th Assets Sample Cos.}}{\text{of their Total Assets in 1922}}}.$$

These adjusted percentages were then multiplied by the total asset figures found in col. 1 for the respective years. The companies chosen were as follows: North British and Mercantile Insurance Company, Prudential Life Insurance Company, Alliance Insurance Company, Royal Insurance Company.

Cols. 2–13 (1918–21), derived from aggregated balance sheet figures of fifteen large UK insurance companies representing 55·8 per cent of assets of all UK life insurance companies in 1918. The various entries in the respective columns were estimated as for the years 1915–17, the corrective factor, $\hat{\theta}$, however, was recomputed for the fifteen as opposed to the five companies in the earlier years. The additional companies are the Commercial Union, Eagle Star, Liverpool, London and Lancs., Scottish Provident, Scottish Widows, Standard, Sun Life.

Balance sheet data of sample insurance companies drawn from British Parliamentary Papers.

Col. 1 (1938–44), derived from fund figures of Life and Industrial Insurance Companies which were multiplied by factor K_t=1·32 in 1938 and 1939 and 1·33, 1·34, 1·35, 1·36, 1·37 in 1940, 1941, 1942, 1943, 1944 respectively. K_t=1·32 in 1936 and 1937, and 1·38 in 1945 and 1·36 in 1946, where

$$K = \frac{\text{All Insurance Companies Assets}}{\text{All Insurance Companies Funds}}$$

in each year.

Cols. 2–13 (1940–4), derived aggregate balance sheet figures of all insurance companies whose funds exceeded £40 m in 1942. The percentage asset distributions found in the sample were multiplied by a splicing factor $\hat{\theta}_i$,

$$\hat{\theta}_i = \frac{\%\text{ of }i\text{th Asset in 1945 of all Companies total Assets}}{\%\text{ of }i\text{th Assets in 1945 of Sample of 14 Companies total Assets}}$$

The sample for these years was as follows: Alliance Insurance Company, Britannic, Commercial Union, Co-operative Insurance Society Ltd, Legal and General, North British and Mercantile, Norwich Union, Phoenix Assurance Company Ltd, Prudential, Pearl, Refuge, Royal Insurance, Royal London Mutual, Sun Life Assurance. In 1945 these fourteen companies held 49·7 per cent of the assets of all assurance Companies – Bourne's *Insurance Year Book*, 1941, 1946.

Note

The figures prior to 1924 do not include the non-life insurance companies' balance sheet data. The total assets of such companies were £39 million and £64 million in 1922 and 1927 respectively.

TABLE (A) 2.6 Life and Other Type Insurance Funds, Great-Britain-Based Companies and Societies only 1880–1966 (£ millions) excludes Lloyds

Year-End	Totals: Cols. I+III	Totals: Total All Insurance Funds[2]	Life and Annuity Assurance Funds	All Industrial Assurance Funds	Co. Industrial Assurance Funds[1]	Co. Capital and Redemption and Sinking Funds	Co. Accident Insurance Funds	Co. Fire Insurance	Marine Aviation Transport	Motor Vehicles	Miscellaneous Insurance: Total	Miscellaneous Insurance: Employers' liability	Collecting Societies Industrial Assurance Fund
	A	B	I	II	III	IV	V	VI	VII	VIII	IX A	IX B	X
1880	125·2	—	123·7	—	1·5	—	—	7·6		—	—	—	
1881	129·6	—	127·7	—	1·9	—	—	7·7		—	—	—	—
1882	134·1	—	131·9	—	2·2	—	—	7·6		—	—	—	—
1883	138·4	—	135·6	—	2·8	—	—	8·3		—	—	—	—
1884	143·1	—	139·5	—	3·6	—	—	8·4		—	—	—	—
1885	147·2	—	142·8	—	4·4	—	—	9·2		—	—	—	—
1886	151·5	—	146·1	—	5·4	—	—	9·5		—	—	—	—
1887	155·8	—	149·9	—	5·9	—	—	9·9		—	—	—	—
1888	161·8	—	154·9	—	6·9	—	—	10·2		—	—	—	—
1889	168·5	—	160·5	—	8·0	—	—	10·4		—	—	—	—
1890	174·8	—	165·9	—	8·9	—	—	10·4		—	—	—	—
1891	180·1	—	170·5	—	9·6	—	—	11·0		—	—	—	—
1892	186·6	—	176·4	—	10·2	—	—	10·8		—	—	—	—
1893	194·2	—	183·0	—	11·2	—	—	10·3		—	—	—	—
1894	202·7	—	190·2	—	12·5	—	—	10·4		—	—	—	—
1895	212·9	—	199·3	—	13·6	—	—	10·7		—	—	—	—
1896	223·6	—	209·2	—	14·4	—	—	10·6	0·7	—	—	—	—
1897	235·6	—	219·8	—	15·8	—	—	10·8	0·6	—	—	—	—
1898	246·1	—	228·9	—	17·2	—	—	10·9	0·6	—	—		—
1899	257·0	—	238·2	—	18·8	—	—	10·8	0·6	—	—	—	—
1900	266·6	—	246·1	25	20·5	—	—	10·8	0·7	—	—	—	5
1901	277·4	—	255·3	28	22·1	—	—	10·9	0·7	—	—	—	6
1902	289·2	—	265·0	31	24·2	—	—	12·9	0·9	—	—		7
1903	297·5	—	274·2	33	23·3	—	—	13·6	0·9	—	—		7
1904	309·8	—	284·5	37	25·3	—	—	14·4	1·1	—	—	—	8
1905	323·1	—	296·0	39	27·1	—	—	14·9	1·4	—	—	—	8
1906	335·8	—	306·4	42	29·4	—	—	13·6	1·5	—	—	—	8
1907	352·4	—	315·4	47	37	—	—	14·7	1·5	—	—	—	10
1908	365·9	—	325·9	48	40	—	—	16·0	1·5	—	—	0·7	8
1909	379·4	—	336·4	52	43	—	—	17·6	2·5	—	—	0·8	9
1910	394·6	—	348·6	56	46	—	—	19·1	2·6	—	—	1·3	10
1911	408·8	—	359·8	59	49	—	—	*	*	—	—	*	10
1912	422·5	—	370·5	63	52	—	—	*	*	—	—	*	11
1913	437·3	—	381·5	67	55·8	—	—	27·8	*	—	—	3·5	11
1914	448·8	—	390·1	70·8	58·7	—	—	*	*	—	—	*	12
1915	451·9	—	390·5	73·9	61·4	—	—	*	*	—	—	*	13
1916	460·2	—	395·2	78·1	65·0	—	—	*	*	—	—	*	13
1917	465·8	—	396·4	83·4	69·4	—	—	*	*	—	—	*	14
1918	485·0	—	411·0	88·7	74·0	—	—	*	*	—	—	*	15
1919	506·4	—	425·9	96·7	80·5	—	—	*	*	—	—	*	16
1920	527·2	—	437·5	107·6	89·7	—	—	*	*	—	—	*	18
1921	556·9	—	456·6	121·3	100·3	—	—	—	—	—	*	*	20·0
1922	591·0	721	479·5	133·9	111·5	—	—	—	—	—	*	*	22·4
1923	629·5	767	506·3	148·6	123·2	13·6		79·3			*	5·6	25·4
1924	669·1	810	532·7	165·7	136·4	14·3		94·2			*	6·0	29·3
1925	721·9	872	570·1	183·6	151·8	14·8		96·7			*	6·4	31·8
1926	771·4	929	605·6	200·9	165·8	15·6		104·0			*	6·4	34·7
1927	819·5	986	640·4	217·1	179·1	16·7		109·0			*	6·3	37·7
1928	866·3	1040	674·3	223·4	192·0	18·3		115·3			*	6·4	40·9

1931	980·6	1163	754·3	276·7	226·3	20·8		109·6			*	*	50·4
1932	1036	1217	793·0	296·4	243·0	—		*			*	*	53·4
1933	1092	1279	833	316·2	259·3	—	*	*	*	*	*	*	56·9
1934	1136	1342	868	338·1	277·5	—	*	*	*	*	*	*	60·6
1935	1200	1405	903	360·6	296·7	29·6	3·4	47·1	16·2	14·1	*	7·4	63·9
1936	1260	1474	943	385·1	317·1	32·1	3·8	46·1	16·3	14·9	*	7·8	68·0
1937	1321	1545	984	409·7	337·3	33·8	4·1	46·7	17·2	15·8	*	8·5	72·4
1938	1382	1617	1023	435·4	359·2	35·7	4·2	45·4	17·7	16·0	31·4	8·6	76·2
1939	1416	1653	1042	455·1	374·4	37·1	4·2	45·5	20·0	15·5	*	9·0	80·7
1940	1443	1687	1054	473·4	388·6	37·9	4·2	45·3	25·6	14·1	32·4	9·9	84·8
1941	1488	1746	1081	496·8	406·9	34·4	4·4	47·6	32·1	15·1	35·0	11·9	89·9
1942	1545	1815	1115	525·9	430·4	34·8	4·7	47·1	37·1	13·0	36·9	12·5	95·5
1943	1609	1896	1153	558·4	456·0	34·9	4·9	48·5	41·4	11·6	43·2	18·6	102·4
1944	1678	1980	1193	594·3	484·9	34·9	5·2	50·9	43·1	12·4	46·4	20·5	109·4
1945	1771	2086	1244	643·4	526·9	35·0	5·5	53·1	41·0	15·3	48·3	—	116·5
1946	1882	2233	1313	692·5	568·6	39·6	6·2	60·1	48·2	20·6	52·5	—	123·9
1947	1995	2395	1391	736·6	604·1	47·8	7·2	69·4	56·0	26·4	60·3	—	132·5
1948	2118	2552	1478	781·7	640·0	53·9	7·6	78·9	68·4	30·2	53·4	—	141·7
1949	2244	2734	1573	821·5	671·1	58·7	7·7	96·8	82·1	38·2	56·4	—	150·4
1950	2378	2913	1675	862·3	703·0	62·8	9·8	108·7	88·5	43·6	59·6	—	162·6
1951	2511	3079	1786	892·0	724·9	62·7	10·7	118·7	95·4	50·4	63·3	—	167·1
1952	2661	3261	1914	919·0	746·5	69·5	11·9	125·7	101·0	57·7	62·2	—	172·5
1953	2864	3497	2078	969·1	786·5	71·7	13·9	128·9	101·6	65·2	68·3	—	182·6
1954	3113	3772	2273	1034·3	840·1	75·3	14·8	128·8	102·3	69·5	73·6	—	194·2
1955	3374	4063	2484	1093·3	889·9	76·5	15·8	136·1	103·1	75·8	78·5	—	203·4
1956	3617	4369	2681	1150·2	936·5	74·0	17·7	162·6	106·0	87·7	89·7	—	213·7
1957	3880	4668	2907	1197·4	972·7	69·7	19·4	167·6	109·3	100·5	96·4	—	225·3
1958	4238	5052	3211	1262·7	1026·9	65·6	20·9	169·6	110·9	111·6	99·3	—	235·8
1959	4648	5495	3557	1339·6	1090·6	61·0	22·4	175·1	115·4	118·3	106·6	—	249·0
1960	5114	6005	3951	1425·5	1162·5	57·1	24·8	180·5	124·7	127·9	113·5	—	263·0
1961	5512	8454	4384	1602·0	1127·5	54·6	28·1	193·0	133·3	139·3	119·7	—	274·5
1962	6137	7105	4840	1577·1	1296·6	53·1	30·1	196·0	133·7	150·1	125·1	—	280·5
1963	6777	7786	5408	1664·8	1368·7	49·5	33·8	197·8	135·2	164·4	131·6	—	296·1
1964	7504	8572	6046	1770·9	1458·5	48·3	37·3	207·2	136·6	185·7	140·0	—	312·4
1965	8242	9354	6680	1890·9	1561·5	46·4	34·0	218·7	132·9	202·1	148·5	—	329·4
1966	8955	10112	7315	1983·8	1640·0	44·0	36·0	227·5	134·0	211·0	160·2	—	343·8

Sources

Col. II (1924–53), col. I (1881–1953), col. III (1914–53), J. Johnston and G. W. Murphy, 'Growth of life assurance in the UK since 1880', *Transactions Manchester Statistical Society*, Nov. 1956, pp. 285–9.

Cols. IV–VIII (1938–47), C.S.O., *Annual Abstract of Statistics*, No. 86, p. 261.

Cols. IV–VIII (1948–9), IXA, IXB (1938), C.S.O., *Annual Abstract of Statistics*, No. 92, p. 281.

Col. III (1903–6), *Insurance Register* (*Life*), first edition (London: C. and E. Layton, 1912), pp. 59 and 61.

Cols. III, VI, IXB (1913), III (1914–30), IXB (1923–30), *Bank of England Statistical Summary*, 1932.

Cols. I, IV–IXA (1950–60), C.S.O., *Annual Abstract of Statistics*, No. 99, 1962, pp. 285–9.

Col. III (1961–2), *Insurance Directory and Yearbook*, 1963–4 (London: Buckley, 1963), pp. 421–5.

Col. X (1930–4), *Report Industrial Assurance Commission*, 1935, p. 51.

Col. II (1914–23), *Report Industrial Assurance Commission*, 1925, p. 129.

Col. III (1912–13), Board of Trade, *Assurance Companies' Returns*, 1922, p. 482.

Cols. I (1880), III, VI+VII (1880–1912), Board of Trade, *Statistical Abstract*, No. 43, p. 226.

Cols. II, III, (1954–60), X (1935–62), Registrar of Friendly Societies, *Report on Industrial Assurance Companies*, 1963, p. 31.

Cols. IV to IXB (1935–7), C.S.O., *Annual Abstract of Statistics*, Nos. 84–5, pp. 244–7.

Cols. IV, V+VI+VII+VIII (1923–31), Bank of England, *Statistical Summary*, Dec. 1932, p. 12.

Cols. I, II, IV–X (1961–2), C.S.O., *Annual Abstract of Statistics*, No. 101, 1964.

Cols. IXB (1908–10), VI, VII (1896–1910), Board of Trade, *Statistical Abstract*, 1959–60, p. 368.

Cols. B (1922–37, 1939), II (1900–13), X (1900–29), IV (1932–4) kindly provided by J. Revell of the Department of Applied Economics at Cambridge. The figures were originally extracted from the *Annual Abstract of Statistics* and from the *Reports of the Registrar of Friendly Societies*.

Cols. I, III–IX (1963–6), C.S.O., *Annual Abstract of Statistics*, No. 104, 1967.

Cols. II, X (1963–6), *Reports of the Industrial Assurance Commission*, 1963–7.

Col. III (1880–1902) kindly provided by the Registry of friendly Societies.

Col. B (1963–6)=col. A+ $\sum_{i=IV}^{X}$ col. *i*.

Cols. IXB (1939), IXA and IXB (1940–9), C.S.O., *Annual Abstract of Statistics*, No. 87, pp. 275–6.

Notes

* Figures not available.

[1] In the 1887–1911 period, the Prudential Life Insurance Company held 78 per cent of the corporate industrial assurance business.

[2] Col. B (1938–66)=Cols. A+IV to IXA+X.

TABLE (A) 2.7 **Life and Other Types of Insurance Premiums Paid Yearly to UK-based Companies and Societies on Business both Inside and Outside the UK 1880–1966 (premiums in £ millions)**

Year-End	*Totals*[1] *Premiums* *Life, Annuity, Industrial Assurance IB+III*	*Totals*[1] *Premiums* *All Premiums IB+II+IV+V to IXA*	*Life and Annuity Assurance Premiums* *Life Only*	*Life and Annuity Assurance Premiums* *Total Premiums*	*All Industrial Assurance Premiums*	*Company Industrial Assurance Premiums*	*Company Accident Premiums**	*Company Capital and Redemption and Sinking Fund**	*Company Fire Insurance*	*Marine, Aviation, Transport**[2]	*Motor Vehicle*	*Miscellaneous Insurance* *Total*[3]	*Miscellaneous Insurance* *Employers' liability*[3]	*Collecting Societies' Industrial Assurance Premiums*
	A	B	I A	I B	II	III	IV	V	VI	VII	VIII	IX A	IX B	X
1880	—	—	—	—	—	—	—	—	—	—	—	—	—	—
1881	—	—	—	12·5	—	—	—	—	—	—	—	—	—	—
1882	—	—	—	12·8	—	—	—	—	—	—	—	—	—	—
1883	—	—	—	12·9	—	—	—	—	—	—	—	—	—	—
1884	—	—	—	13·2	—	—	—	—	—	—	—	—	—	—
1885	—	—	—	13·4	—	—	—	—	—	—	—	—	—	—
1886	—	—	—	13·7	—	—	—	—	—	—	—	—	—	—
1887	18·0	—	—	14·4	—	3·6	—	—	—	—	—	—	—	—
1888	18·7	—	—	15·0	—	3·7	—	—	—	—	—	—	—	—
1889	19·5	—	—	15·5	—	4·0	—	—	—	—	—	—	—	—
1890	20·4	—	—	16·0	—	4·4	—	—	—	—	—	—	—	—
1891	20·6	—	—	15·7	—	4·9	—	—	—	—	—	—	—	—
1892	22·9	—	—	17·9	—	5·0	—	—	—	—	—	—	—	—
1893	23·8	—	—	18·3	—	5·5	—	—	—	—	—	—	—	—
1894	25·1	—	—	19·4	—	5·7	—	—	—	—	—	—	—	—
1895	26·9	—	—	21·0	—	5·9	—	—	—	—	—	—	—	—
1896	28·3	—	—	21·9	—	6·4	—	—	—	—	—	—	—	—
1897	28·8	—	—	22·2	—	6·6	—	—	—	—	—	—	—	—
1898	30·4	—	—	23·2	—	7·2	—	—	—	—	—	—	—	—
1899	31·0	—	—	23·4	—	7·6	—	—	—	—	—	—	—	—
1900	31·6	—	—	23·5	—	8·1	—	—	—	—	—	—	—	—
1901	32·8	—	—	24·4	—	8·4	—	—	—	—	—	—	—	—
1902	34·3	—	—	25·0	—	9·3	—	—	—	—	—	—	—	—
1903	35·4	—	—	25·8	—	9·6	—	—	—	—	—	—	—	—
1904	37·6	—	—	27·3	—	10·3	—	—	—	—	—	—	—	—
1905	38·1	—	—	27·5	—	10·6	—	—	—	—	—	—	—	—
1906	39·2	—	—	28·1	—	11·1	—	—	—	—	—	—	—	—
1907	40·5	—	—	28·9	—	11·6	—	—	—	—	—	—	—	—
1908	42·4	—	—	30·0	—	12·4	—	—	—	—	—	—	—	—
1909	45·0	—	—	31·9	—	13·1	—	—	—	—	—	—	—	—
1910	44·6	—	—	31·3	—	13·3	—	—	—	—	—	—	—	—
1911	46·0	—	—	31·9	—	14·1	—	—	—	—	—	—	—	—
1912	—	—	—	32·8	—	—	—	—	—	—	—	—	—	—
1913	51·2	—	—	33·9	—	17·3	2·1	—	29·2	—	—	—	—	3·7
1914	52·3	—	—	34·3	—	18·0	2·1	—	28·9	—	—	—	—	3·8
1915	52·4	—	—	33·8	—	18·6	2·0	—	30·0	—	—	—	—	3·7
1916	53·6	—	—	34·0	—	19·6	2·0	—	31·9	—	—	—	—	3·9
1917	55·5	—	—	34·5	—	21·0	2·2	—	36·0	—	—	—	—	4·3
1918	61·0	—	—	38·6	—	22·4	2·2	—	41·7	—	—	—	—	5·2
1919	68·9	—	—	43·5	—	25·4	2·6	—	49·5	—	—	—	—	6·3
1920	76·8	—	—	47·5	—	29·3	2·7	—	58·5	—	—	—	—	8·9
1921	80·1	—	—	49·0	—	31·1	2·9	—	54·2	—	—	—	—	7·5
1922	83·1	—	—	51·5	—	31·6	—	—	—	—	—	—	—	—
1923	87·5	—	—	54·3	—	33·2	3·2	—	57·7	14·5	—	—	5·2	—
1924	92·9	—	—	58·8	42·3	34·1	3·3	—	58·3	14·6	—	—	5·5	4·8
1925	102·4	—	—	65·8	45·2	36·6	3·3	—	60·6	13·3	—	—	5·7	5·0
1926	102·2	—	—	65·4	45·4	36·8	3·4	—	60·9	13·3	—	—	5·7	5·1
1927	110·2	—	—	71·4	48·1	38·8	3·6	—	59·1	13·8	—	—	5·8	5·5
1928	116·9	—	—	76·0	50·5	40·9	3·9	—	59·0	13·7	—	—	5·8	5·7
[illegible]	[illegible]	[illegible]	[illegible]	[illegible]	[illegible]	[illegible]	[illegible]	[illegible]	[illegible]	[illegible]	[illegible]	[illegible]	[illegible]	[illegible]

1930	119·3	—	71·7	75·5	54·2	43·8	4·0	4·6	55·1	12·8	—	—	5·8	6·1
1931	120·8	269·4	70·6	75·4	56·1	45·4	3·7	4·0	51·9	12·0	32·5	28·4	5·4	10·7
1932	132·8	276·2	73·1	86·4	57·3	46·4	3·7	3·0	50·8	11·4	31·8	26·8	5·0	11·0
1933	137·8	277·7	76·8	90·1	58·9	47·7	3·6	3·7	48·4	9·9	31·3	26·9	4·9	11·3
1934	142·0	287·0	77·3	91·9	61·9	50·1	3·8	4·0	48·8	10·2	31·9	29·2	5·3	11·8
1935	147·1	296·4	80·7	95·6	63·7	51·5	4·0	5·1	48·8	10·1	33·3	30·0	5·8	12·2
1936	151·7	310·2	84·2	98·1	66·4	53·6	4·2	3·2	48·9	10·5	35·3	31·4	6·1	12·7
1937	155·5	316·5	87·8	99·7	69·2	55·8	4·5	2·8	49·8	12·6	37·4	33·8	6·7	13·4
1938	160·1	323·2	91·3	102·1	71·8	58·0	4·6	3·3	49·5	12·8	37·9	34·1	7·1	13·8
1939	159·3	—	91·7	99·5	74·2	59·8	4·6	2·4	49·6	14·8	36·6	—	6·9	14·3
1940	158·6	325·3	89·9	96·4	76·8	62·2	4·0	2·0	51·0	22·6	31·9	33·2	7·4	14·6
1941	159·1	339·8	91·2	95·5	78·6	63·6	3·9	1·7	54·5	24·8	34·0	37·2	9·6	15·0
1942	167·8	362·2	94·6	99·8	83·8	68·0	4·1	1·7	56·3	39·2	28·4	39·5	9·4	15·9
1943	175·8	372·2	98·6	103·6	89·2	72·2	4·3	1·7	59·9	30·0	24·6	45·6	13·3	17·0
1944	185·2	389·4	103·3	109·5	93·5	75·7	4·7	1·8	65·1	26·3	26·4	48·2	13·9	17·8
1945	196·9	414·2	109·1	117·5	97·8	79·4	5·1	2·3	71·8	22·6	33·8	49·9	13·4	18·4
1946	218·1	481·7	121·3	134·5	103·2	83·6	6·2	3·2	88·3	27·1	46·9	58·0	14·3	19·6
1947	250·1	566·8	140·9	158·9	112·4	91·2	7·7	3·6	108·6	40·9	61·5	73·2	17·7[3]	21·2
1948	270·1	627·4	156·6	173·0	119·9	97·1	8·6	3·2	127·6	50·5	70·7	73·9	—	22·8
1949	286·1	686·7	171·3	185·8	124·1	100·3	9·6	3·1	148·2	55·6	84·7	75·6	—	23·8
1950	307·4	759·5	188·6	203·9	127·6	103·5	10·5	2·1	168·5	58·4	102·7	85·8	—	24·1
1951	340·6	855·5	212·6	232·4	133·1	108·2	13·0	2·0	190·5	68·0	119·4	97·1	—	24·8
1952	365·6	937·0	234·2	253·6	137·6	112·0	14·5	1·8	202·7	73·0	142·2	111·6	—	25·6
1953	391·3	986·0	253·5	274·7	143·1	116·6	16·6	1·8	205·5	66·5	155·3	122·5	—	26·4
1954	421·7	1038·0	278·6	300·8	148·4	120·9	17·6	2·0	209·7	63·1	165·1	131·3	—	27·5
1955	458·5	1112·8	305·6	331·1	156·0	127·4	19·0	2·1	218·9	65·4	180·5	139·8	—	28·6
1956	490·7	1235·3	328·7	356·2	163·8	134·5	21·6	2·0	249·8	69·5	210·1	162·3	—	29·3
1957	537·0	1348·8	355·4	396·9	170·4	140·1	23·5	2·1	260·5	77·6	240·1	177·7	—	30·3
1958	584·9	1439·5	387·5	438·3	177·9	146·6	26·0	2·1	266·4	78·1	266·7	184·0	—	31·3
1959	632·1	1532·4	422·9	478·6	186·1	153·5	28·6	2·1	277·9	80·4	283·8	194·9	—	32·6
1960	693·3	1649·3	460·5	532·3	195·8	161·0	31·6	2·2	286·7	84·5	307·5	208·7	—	34·5
1961	757·9	1777·6	508·4	589·3	203·6	168·6	35·8	2·6	302·9	91·2	333·8	218·4	—	35·0
1962	832·1	1900·8	549·8	650·9	216·1	181·2	38·6	2·9	314·8	91·9	354·8	230·8	—	34·9
1963	944·2	2076·1	596·7	759·1	221·2	185·1	42·2	2·2	317·2	95·5	390·7	248·0	—	36·1
1964	1030·3	2262·6	663·1	836·1	231·6	194·2	46·3	2·3	338·9	100·2	440·7	266·5	—	37·4
1965	1053·3	2381·3	726·9	849·3	242·8	204·0	48·6	2·3	368·1	104·4	478·2	287·6	—	38·8
1966	1142·1	2559·9	790·7	928·1	254·2	214·0	50·6	2·1	395·3	114·1	501·2	314·3	—	40·2

Sources

Cols. IA, II–IXA (1961), C.S.O., *Annual Abstract of Statistics*, No. 101, pp. 311–12.

Cols. IB (1881–1953), II (1924–53), IV (1913–53), J. Johnston and G. W. Murphy, 'Growth of life assurance in the UK since 1880', *Transactions Manchester Statistical Society*, Nov. 1956, pp. 285–9.

Cols. IA, IV, V, VI, VII, VIII (1938–47), C.S.O., *Annual Abstract of Statistics*, No. 86, p. 261.

Cols. IA, IV–VIII (1948–9), IXA (1938–49), ibid., No. 92, p. 281.

Cols. IA, IV–IXB (1930–6), IA (1930–7), Bank of England, *Statistical Summary*, 1938.

Cols. IV, VI, X (1913), VI–VII (1923–9), IXB (1923–9), Bank of England, op. cit., 1932.

Col. III (1887–1911), *Insurance Register (Life)*, first edition (C. & E. Layton, London, 1912), pp. 59–61.

Cols. IXB (1937–47), IXA (1950), IB, III–VIII (1954–62), *Insurance Directory and Year Book* 1963–4 (London: Buckley, 1963), pp. 421–5.

Cols. IV, VI, X (1914–21), Board of Trade, *Return*, 1922, p. 482.

Cols. IV, V, VI, VII, VIII, IXA (1937), Bank of England, *Statistical Summary*, May 1939, p. 60.

Col. X (1924–66), Extracted from various *Reports* of the Industrial Assurance Commissioner.

Cols. IA, II, III–IXA (1950–61), C.S.O., *Annual Abstract of Statistics*, No. 99, 1962, pp. 285–9.

Cols. IA, IB, II–IXA (1962–6), C.S.O., ibid., No. 105, 1968.

Cols. III (1912, 1913–37, 1944–50) kindly provided by J. Revell of the Department of Applied Economics at Cambridge.

Notes

* Excludes reinsurance.

[1] Excludes one company completely engaged in reinsurance.

[2] Marine Insurance only until 1930.

[3] As from 1947, Employers' liability included in miscellaneous insurance under S.I. 1948, No. 1839.

Column headed 'Total, all Insurance Premiums' – to 1946 inclusive, sum of cols. IB, II, IV–IXB; from 1947–66, sum of cols. IB, II, IV–IXA.

Col. II = col. III + col. X.

TABLE (A) 2.8 **Funds and Assets of the Various Societies Registered with the Registra**

Year-End Approx. 31 Dec.	**PART 1.** *Registered Friendly Societies*							**PART 2.** *Trade Unions*							**PART 3.** *Certified Loan Societies*	
	Funds	*Total Assets*	*Investments*			*Mortgages*	*Cash and Deposit*	*Funds*	*Total Assets*	*Investments*			*Mortgages*	*Cash and Deposit*	*Funds*	*Total Assets*
			Total	*Brit. Govt. Govt.-Gty.*	*Other*					*Total*	*Brit. Govt. Govt.-Gty.*	*Other*				
	A	B	C	D	E	F	G	A	B	C	D	E	F	G	A	B
1920	71·6	67·3	41·5	16·0	25·5	13·8	3·3	16·0	18·6	9·2	2·2	7·0	1·5	5·4	0·2	0·2
1921	74·4	69·9	43·1	16·6	26·5	14·3	3·5	10·9	12·7	6·3	1·5	4·8	1·0	3·7	0·2	0·2
1922	80·0	75·2	46·4	17·8	28·6	15·4	3·8	10·0	11·8	5·0	1·2	3·8	1·0	3·4	0·2	0·2
1923	83·4	78·4	48·4	18·6	29·8	16·1	3·9	10·9	13·0	6·6	1·6	5·0	1·2	3·8	0·2	0·2
1924	87·7	82·4	50·8	19·5	31·3	16·9	4·1	11·6	13·9	7·1	1·7	5·4	1·3	4·0	0·2	0·2
1925	91·1	85·6	52·8	20·3	32·5	17·5	4·3	12·7	15·4	8·0	1·9	6·1	1·5	4·4	0·2	0·2
1926	97·4	91·6	56·5	21·7	34·8	18·7	4·6	8·7	10·7	5·3	1·4	3·9	1·1	2·2	0·2	0·2
1927	100·5	94·5	58·3	22·4	35·9	19·4	4·7	9·9	11·8	6·1	1·5	4·6	1·2	2·6	0·2	0·2
1928	106·2	99·8	61·6	23·7	37·9	20·5	5·0	10·8	12·4	6·2	1·5	4·7	1·2	2·9	0·2	0·2
1929*	109·7	103·1	63·7	24·5	39·2	21·2	5·2	11·6	12·9	6·3	1·5	4·8	1·3	3·1	0·2	0·2
1930	115·3	108·4	69·8	25·5	44·2	21·7	5·4	11·9	12·7	6·0	1·4	4·6	1·3	3·2	0·2	0·2
1931	119·8	115·0	75·9	26·5	49·3	23·0	5·8	11·5	12·0	5·5	1·3	4·2	1·2	3·1	0·2	0·2
1932	126·1	123·6	82·0	27·5	54·3	24·7	6·2	11·5	12·0	5·7	1·3	4·2	1·1	3·3	0·2	0·2
1933	131·4	131·4	88·1	28·6	59·4	26·3	6·6	12·1	12·5	5·8	1·4	4·4	1·1	3·8	0·2	0·2
1934*	136·8	140·2	94·8	29·9	64·9	28·0	7·2	13·2	13·5	6·2	1·5	4·7	1·1	4·4	0·2	0·2
1935	142·1	146·0	99·4	32·5	66·9	28·2	7·2	14·5	14·6	6·7	1·6	5·1	1·2	5·2	0·2	0·2
1936*	148·3	151·3	102·9	33·6	69·3	29·2	7·4	16·4	16·4	7·5	1·8	5·7	1·2	6·0	0·2	0·2
1937	153·6	156·7	106·7	34·8	71·8	30·2	7·7	18·5	18·5	8·4	2·0	6·4	1·4	6·8	0·2	0·2
1938	159·3	162·5	110·5	36·1	74·4	31·3	8·0	20·4	20·4	9·3	2·2	7·1	1·5	7·5	0·2	0·2
1939	163·3	166·6	113·3	37·0	76·3	32·2	8·1	22·6	22·6	10·3	2·5	7·8	1·6	8·4	0·1	0·1
1940	167·5	172·5	134·4	56·9	77·5	30·8	8·1	25·1	25·1	12·0	6·3	5·7	1·6	8·8	0·1	0·1
1941	175·4	180·7	140·8	62·1	78·7	29·4	8·1	28·0	28·3	14·2	8·0	6·2	1·6	9·3	0·1	0·1
1942	182·4	187·9	146·3	66·4	79·9	28·0	8·0	31·8	32·1	17·0	10·2	6·8	1·6	9·7	0·1	0·1
1943	190·6	196·3	152·9	71·8	81·1	26·6	8·0	35·6	36·0	19·6	12·0	7·6	1·6	10·0	0·1	0·1
1944	197·5	203·4	158·4	76·1	82·3	25·2	7·9	39·5	39·9	22·6	14·3	8·3	1·6	10·3	0·1	0·1
1945	203·8	209·9	163·5	80·0	83·5	23·8	7·9	43·1	43·5	25·6	16·5	9·1	3·1	10·4	0·1	0·1
1946*	210·5	217·1	169·2	84·7	84·5	22·3	7·9	46·9	47·8	29·2	17·2	12·0	3·4	10·4	0·1	0·1
1947	217·6	221·9	170·2	86·8	83·5	24·3	7·5	50·8	51·8	32·8	16·6	16·2	3·6	10·2	0·1	0·1
1948	220·5	224·9	171·3	88·8	82·5	26·3	7·1	55·2	56·3	36·9	19·2	17·7	3·9	9·9	0·1	0·1
1949	222·1	226·5	172·4	90·9	81·5	28·3	6·7	58·9	60·1	40·7	19·2	21·5	4·1	9·3	0·1	0·1
1950	224·5	228·9	173·4	93·0	80·5	30·3	6·3	63·0	64·9	45·4	19·1	26·3	4·3	8·6	0·1	0·1
1951*	227·3	231·8	174·5	95·1	79·4	32·4	6·0	65·6	67·6	48·8	21·2	27·6	4·4	7·6	0·1	0·1
1952	231·9	238·9	178·5	93·6	84·9	33·7	5·9	68·4	70·4	52·4	21·8	30·6	4·5	6·4	0·1	0·1
1953*	236·7	243·8	182·5	92·1	90·4	35·0	5·9	71·5	73·3	56·1	22·4	33·7	4·6	5·5	0·1	0·1
1954	240·5	247·7	186·5	90·6	95·9	36·3	5·8	74·8	77·0	59·6	24·0	35·6	4·5	5·6	0·1	0·1
1955	242·5	249·8	190·5	89·1	101·4	37·6	5·7	77·5	79·8	60·7	24·6	36·1	4·2	5·6	0·1	0·1
1956*	249·1	256·9	194·3	87·4	106·9	39·0	5·7	80·4	82·8	65·6	26·8	38·8	4·1	5·7	0·1	0·1
1957	251·1	258·6	188·7	84·9	104·0	39·3	6·1	81·7	84·2	67·5	27·8	39·7	3·9	5·7	0·1	0·1
1958*	256·1	264·7	183·0	81·8	101·2	39·6	6·6	85·2	87·7	71·2	29·6	41·6	3·5	5·9	0·1	0·1
1959	261·8	267·0	198·3	87·8	110·3	40·7	6·7	87·2	88·9	69·7	29·5	40·2	3·3	8·7	0·1	0·1
1960	272·5	275·2	214·2	94·8	119·4	41·9	6·9	91·3	93·1	70·4	30·4	40·0	3·2	11·9	0·1	0·1
1961	279·5	282·3	231·2	102·7	128·5	43·1	7·1	96·2	97·3	70·9	31·1	39·8	3·0	15·4	0	0
1962	287·8	287·4	235·2	101·9	133·3	43·3	7·2	102·0	104·0	77·6	32·2	45·4	2·9	14·8	0	0
1963	296·1	302·0	245·1	100·2	144·9	44·5	7·2	107·3	109·4	82·1	29·0	53·1	2·5	14·3	0	0
1964	304·8	310·9	252·5	96·7	155·8	46·0	7·4	112·5	114·8	87·9	29·6	58·3	2·4	13·5	0	0
1965	326·5	330·0	262·4	94·2	168·2	48·4	8·1	118·8	121·2	94·4	30·4	64·0	2·6	14·4	0	0
1966	341·6	348·4	269·5	91·3	178·2	49·3	8·5	123·2	125·7	100·5	31·2	69·3	2·7	12·5	0	0

of Friendly Societies, which are Financial Institutions in Great Britain 1920–1966 (£ millions)

PART 4. *Collecting Societies*							PART 5. *Superannuation and Other Trusts*							PART 6. *Railway Savings Banks*				PART 7. *All Societies and Companies*		
Funds	*Total Ass.*	*Investments*			*Mort.*	*Cash and Deposits*	*Funds*	*Total Ass.*	*Investments*			*Mort.*	*Cash and Deposit*	*Funds*	*Total Ass.*	*Investments*		*Total Assets*	*Mort.*	*Gross Private Credit*
		Total	*B. Gov. G.-Gty.*	*Other*					*Total*	*B. Gov. G.-Gty.*	*Other*					*Total*	*B. Gov. G.-Gty.*			
A	B	C	D	E	F	G	A	B	C	D	E	F	G	A	B	C	D	A	B	C
17·9	18·6	12·2	2·9	9·3	4·0	0·5	3·1	3·1	*	1·7	*	*	0·3	10·3	10·3	10·3	0	118·1	19·3	85·8
20·1	20·9	13·9	3·3	10·6	4·1	0·6	4·3	4·3	*	2·2	*	*	0·3	11·1	11·1	11·1	0	119·1	19·4	87·4
22·5	23·4	15·8	4·0	11·8	4·5	0·7	5·8	5·9	*	3·2	*	*	0·4	11·8	11·8	11·8	0	128·3	20·9	93·8
25·4	26·4	19·1	4·3	14·8	4·8	0·7	7·8	7·9	*	4·1	*	*	0·5	13·0	13·0	13·0	0	138·9	22·1	101·4
30·9	32·1	23·7	5·0	18·7	5·7	0·9	10·3	10·4	*	5·2	*	*	0·6	14·1	14·1	14·1	0	153·1	23·7	112·1
33·7	35·2	26·4	4·6	21·8	6·1	0·9	13·4	13·5	*	6·3	*	*	0·8	15·0	15·0	15·0	0	164·9	25·1	121·4
36·8	38·6	29·3	4·0	25·3	6·7	0·8	17·1	17·3	*	7·4	*	*	1·0	15·2	15·2	15·2	0	173·6	26·5	130·5
40·0	42·1	31·2	3·5	27·7	8·1	0·8	21·5	21·7	*	8·5	*	*	1·4	15·5	15·5	15·5	0	185·8	28·7	140·4
43·6	45·9	32·6	3·6	29·0	9·4	1·0	26·4	26·6	*	9·6	*	*	1·5	16·0	16·0	16·0	0	200·9	31·1	152·1
46·7	48·2	33·1	3·6	29·5	10·2	1·0	31·9	32·2	*	9·9	*	*	1·9	16·3	16·3	16·3	0	212·9	32·7	162·2
50·2	52·1	35·8	3·8	32·0	10·8	1·2	38·0	38·3	*	11·1	*	*	2·1	16·8	16·8	16·8	0	228·5	33·8	174·8
53·9	56·1	38·4	4·1	34·3	11·9	1·0	42·8	43·1	*	14·2	*	*	2·5	17·2	17·2	17·2	0	243·6	36·1	185·1
57·3	59·8	40·3	4·0	36·3	11·9	2·0	49·9	50·3	*	17·1	*	*	3·7	17·7	17·7	17·7	0	263·6	37·7	198·5
61·5	64·2	43·6	4·4	39·2	11·6	1·7	55·5	55·9	*	20·7	*	*	3·5	18·8	18·8	18·8	0	283·0	39·0	212·3
65·7	68·6	46·7	4·5	42·2	12·2	1·2	60·3	60·8	*	22·4	*	*	3·4	20·5	20·5	20·5	0	303·8	41·3	229·3
69·6	72·8	48·6	4·9	43·7	12·2	1·8	65·0	66·2	50·9	23·7	27·2	1·5	4·2	23·1	23·1	23·1	0	322·9	41·6	241·8
74·5	78·2	51·2	4·9	46·3	13·7	1·6	70·5	71·1	*	24·0	*	*	3·8	25·4	25·4	25·4	0	342·6	44·1	259·5
79·9	84·1	52·5	4·8	47·7	16·0	1·5	75·9	76·6	*	24·7	*	*	4·7	27·4	27·4	27·4	0	363·5	47·6	276·5
84·8	89·3	55·1	5·1	50·0	17·5	1·6	83·1	83·8	*	26·3	*	*	4·6	29·5	29·5	29·5	0	385·7	50·3	294·3
90·5	95·4	58·3	5·5	52·8	18·5	3·1	89·4	91·1	*	26·5	*	*	7·4	30·9	30·9	30·9	0	406·7	52·3	308·2
95·7	100·5	73·6	23·1	50·5	20·3	2·7	97·3	99·2	*	36·9	*	*	8·6	32·0	32·0	32·0	0	429·4	52·7	278·0
101·8	106·9	76·4	28·2	48·2	20·3	1·9	105·0	107·1	*	44·9	*	*	5·9	33·8	33·8	33·8	0	456·9	51·3	288·5
108·9	114·3	79·8	33·9	45·9	19·7	1·7	114·3	117·7	*	55·0	*	*	5·8	33·8	33·8	33·8	0	485·9	49·3	295·2
117·3	123·2	82·8	39·2	43·6	19·6	1·8	123·5	127·3	*	62·6	*	*	5·2	35·8	35·8	35·8	0	518·6	47·8	308·0
125·9	132·2	87·1	45·8	41·3	18·9	1·9	133·9	137·9	*	73·0	*	*	4·6	38·5	38·5	38·5	0	552·0	45·7	318·1
134·7	141·4	91·6	52·6	39·0	18·4	1·8	143·3	150·4	*	84·2	*	*	4·4	44·3	44·3	44·3	0	589·6	45·3	331·8
143·4	150·6	94·1	53·9	40·2	18·1	2·4	154·8	161·0	*	85·2	*	*	5·0	44·7	44·7	44·7	0	621·3	43·8	354·6
154·6	162·3	96·4	52·4	44·0	20·1	2·9	166·6	173·3	*	81·4	*	*	5·1	43·8	43·8	43·8	43·8	653·2	48·0	346·5
165·7	174·0	103·9	60·9	43·0	23·0	3·1	184·0	193·2	*	97·0	*	*	4·8	44·4	44·4	44·4	44·4	692·9	53·2	357·7
176·6	185·4	109·7	61·7	48·0	26·1	3·3	197·7	207·6	*	97·8	*	*	3·7	44·1	44·1	44·1	44·1	723·8	58·5	387·1
187·6	197·0	116·3	61·3	55·0	30·9	3·2	210·6	221·1	*	95·5	*	*	2·2	43·6	43·6	43·6	43·6	755·6	65·5	422·8
197·9	207·8	129·2	69·8	59·4	37·0	3·5	228·9	243·3	237·3	112·1	125·2	0	1·5	41·3	41·3	41·3	41·3	791·9	73·8	433·8
205·2	218·4	136·6	73·0	63·6	42·9	3·4	247·1	260·7	256·8	118·6	138·2	0	1·3	41·5	41·5	41·5	41·5	830·0	81·1	464·5
217·9	231·5	143·7	74·0	69·7	45·5	3·3	269·1	283·9	281·1	127·8	153·3	0	1·1	42·2	42·2	42·2	42·2	874·8	85·1	500·5
232·1	246·0	151·3	73·0	78·3	47·3	3·7	290·6	306·6	305·0	136·4	168·6	0	0·9	42·9	42·9	42·9	42·9	920·3	88·1	537·4
244·0	259·5	159·2	73·8	85·4	49·3	3·0	319·6	335·0	327·6	144·1	183·5	0	0·6	43·4	43·4	43·4	43·4	967·6	91·1	577·7
251·8	273·7	172·2	93·2	79·0	54·2	3·0	341·1	354·7	353·7	157·8	195·9	0	0·9	43·1	43·1	43·1	43·1	1011·3	97·3	587·7
270·9	288·9	182·3	93·3	89·0	54·4	3·6	369·7	384·5	383·5	171·1	212·4	0	1·0	44·2	44·2	44·2	44·2	1060·5	97·6	622·9
284·3	304·7	189·4	93·1	96·3	57·7	3·8	402·5	418·6	417·6	186·3	231·3	0	1·0	44·3	44·3	44·3	44·3	1120·1	100·8	667·7
300·6	322·0	199·0	93·4	105·6	59·9	4·1	436·6	454·1	453·1	202·1	251·0	0	1·1	44·3	44·3	44·3	44·3	1176·8	103·9	699·1
318·1	341·5	207·6	94·0	113·6	66·5	3·8	476·4	493·0	483·0	212·7	270·3	0	1·4	44·6	44·6	44·6	44·6	1247·5	111·6	747·0
332·4	358·6	213·6	94·2	119·4	74·5	4·0	502·7	518·7	507·1	220·0	287·1	0	2·7	44·9	44·9	44·9	44·9	1301·8	120·6	779·7
340·2	367·3	215·6	91·7	123·9	78·2	4·9	525·6	525·6	515·1	212·9	302·2	0	2·0	44·6	44·6	44·6	44·6	1328·9	124·4	816·7
359·0	385·7	223·0	93·0	130·0	79·6	4·5	565·1	565·1	553·8	224·3	329·5	0	2·3	43·7	43·7	43·7	43·7	1405·9	126·6	887·4
378·6	406·7	230·5	93·9	137·1	87·4	4·4	595·1	595·1	583·1	241·0	342·1	0	2·4	43·4	43·4	43·4	43·4	1470·9	135·8	939·1
399·4	428·7	237·5	93·0	144·5	93·6	4·7	652·4	652·4	639·4	264·2	375·2	0	2·6	41·4	41·4	41·4	41·4	1576·7	144·6	1023·6
416·6	447·3	244·1	93·4	150·7	100·3	4·8	688·4	688·4	674·6	278·8	395·8	0	2·8	37·5	37·5	37·5	37·5	1647·3	152·3	1086·5

Notes to Table (A) 2.8 overleaf.

Notes to Table (A) 2.8

Sources

Part 1. *Registered Friendly Societies*

Col. A (1920–62): *Reports of the Registrar of Friendly Societies*, Part I, various years.

Cols. B–G (1929, 1934, 1936, 1946, 1951, 1956, 1958, 1961, 1962): interpolated from sample returns published by the Registrar of Friendly Societies in his *Reports* of 1930, 1934, 1936, 1952, 1957, 1959, 1962, 1963, respectively, multiplied by an expansion factor K_T, where $K_{1929}=1{\cdot}86$, $K_{1934}=1{\cdot}74$, $K_{1935}=1{\cdot}72$, $K_{1946}=1{\cdot}53$, $K_{1951}=1{\cdot}53$, $K_{1956}=1{\cdot}51$, $K_{1959}=1{\cdot}54$, $K_{1961}=1{\cdot}59$, and $K_{1962}=1{\cdot}56$.

$$K_T = \left(\frac{\text{Total Funds of All Societies}}{\text{Total Funds of Sample Societies}}\right)_t$$

Col. B (1920–8, 1930–3, 1935, 1936–45, 1947–50, 1952–5, 1957, 1959–60) is estimated. Method: known fund figures were multiplied by an interpolation of the asset/fund ratio λ_{ft} where this ratio was derived from published statistics for the years 1929, 1934, 1936, 1946, 1951, 1956, 1958, 1961 and 1962. It should be noted that λ_{ft} was quite stable throughout the period being 0·94 in 1929, 1·02 in 1934, 1·02 in 1936, 1·03 in 1946, 1·02 in 1951, 1·03 in 1953, 1956 and 1958 and 1·01 in 1961 and 1962.

Cols. C–G (1920–8): entries estimated on the assumption that the relevant asset ratios in each year were identical to those of 1929.

Cols. C–G (1930–3): entries estimated by interpolation between the relevant column ratios given for 1929 and 1934.

Cols. C–G (1935): entries estimated by interpolation between 1934 and 1936 figures.

Cols. C–G (1937–9): entries estimated on assumption that the relevant asset ratios in each year were identical to the relevant ratios in 1936.

Cols. C–G (1940–5): entries estimated on assumption that the relevant ratios in each year were identical to those in 1946.

Cols. C–G (1947–50): based on an arithmetic interpolation between 1946 and 1951 figures.

Cols. C–G (1952–5): based on arithmetic interpolation between 1951 and 1956 figures.

Cols. C–G (1957): based on interpolation between 1956 and 1958 figures.

Cols. C–G (1959–60): based on interpolation between 1958 and 1961 figures.

Col. A (1963–6): *Report of the Registrar of Friendly Societies*, Part 1, 1966.

Col. B (1963–6): estimated – Col. A multiplied by expansion factor of 1·02.

Cols. C–G (1963–6): based on sample of Friendly Societies' asset distributions reported in Part 2 of the Registrar's *Reports* in each year.

Part 2. *Trade Unions*

Col. A (1920–62): *Reports of the Registrar of Friendly Societies*, Part I, various years.

Cols. B–G (1921, 1926, 1931, 1936), *Report of the Registrar of Friendly Societies*, 1937, Part 4, H.M.S.O., p. 5.

Col. B (1920, 1922–5, 1927–30, 1932–5), estimates:

Method $\quad \text{Col. } B_T = \hat{\lambda}_{TAt}.\text{Col. A}_t$

where $\lambda_{TAt} = \left(\dfrac{\text{Total Assets Trade Unions}}{\text{Total Funds Trade Unions}}\right)_t$

and $\hat{\lambda}_{TAt}$ was interpolated from λ_{TAt} found in base years.

Cols. B–G (1953, 1958, 1961, 1962) given in *Reports of the Registrar of Friendly Societies*, Part 4, in 1954, 1959, 1962 and 1963 respectively.

Col. B (1937–52, 1954–7, 1959–60), estimated:

Method $\quad \text{Col. B}_t = \text{Col. A}_t.\hat{\lambda}_{TAt}$

where $\hat{\lambda}_{TAt}$ interpolated between λ_{TAt} in recorded years, e.g. $\lambda_{TA1936}=1{\cdot}00$, $\lambda_{TA1953}=1{\cdot}03$, $\lambda_{TA1958}=1{\cdot}03$, $\lambda_{TA1961}=1{\cdot}01$, $\lambda_{TA1962}=1{\cdot}02$.

Cols. D–G (1920, 1922–5, 1927–30, 1932–5, 1937–9), estimates: Method as for Col. B using data for base years to determine $\hat{\lambda}_{TGt}$, $\hat{\lambda}_{TOt}$, $\hat{\lambda}_{TMt}$ e.g. $D_t=\hat{\lambda}_{TGt}.B_t$, $E_t=\hat{\lambda}_{TOt}.B_t$, and $F_t=\hat{\lambda}_{TMt}.B_t$, where $\hat{\lambda}_{TGt}$, $\hat{\lambda}_{TOt}$ and $\hat{\lambda}_{TMt}$ are interpolated from the values of the observed ratios of Government securities, of other investments and of mortgages to total trade union assets in certain years.

Col. D (1940–52, 1954–7, 1959–60), estimates:

Method $\quad D_t = B_t.\hat{\lambda}_{SGt}.\hat{\lambda}_{TGt}$

where $\hat{\lambda}_{SGt} = \left(\dfrac{\text{Super Ann. G.G. Gty.}}{\text{Super Ann. Total Assets}}\right)_t$

and $\hat{\lambda}_{TGt} = \left(\dfrac{\text{T.U. Gov./T.U. Total Assets}}{\text{S. Gov./S. Total Assets}}\right)_{1953} = 0{\cdot}68.$

Col. C: total investments (1920–62) = col. D + col. E.

Cols. E–G (1940–52, 1954–7, 1959–60): estimated by interpolation between base years; however, it was assumed that mortgage figures were constant throughout the war.

Col. A (1963–6): *Registrar of Friendly Societies Report*, Part I, 1966.

Col. B (1963–6): Col. A. 1·02 – expansion factor used in 1962.

Cols. C–G (1963–6): *Registrar of Friendly Societies Reports*, Part 4, 1963–6, based on 'Analysis of trade unions with assets exceeding £¼ million'. These trade union assets accounted for over 90 per cent of all trade union assets during these years.

Part 3. *Certified Loan Societies*

Col. A (1920–62): *Annual Report of the Registrar of Friendly Societies*, 1920–63.

Col. B (1936–7, 1952–62): ibid.

Col. B (1920–35, 1938–51):

$$\text{estimated } B_t = A_t.\hat{\lambda}_{clst},$$

where $\lambda_{clst} = \left(\dfrac{\text{Total Assets Cls}}{\text{Total Funds Cls}}\right)_t$

and $\hat{\lambda}_{clst}$ = average of λ_{clst} in all recorded periods = 1·00.

Cols. A and B (1963–6): *Registrar of Friendly Societies Report*, Part I, 1966. The total assets of these societies did not exceed £40,000 in 1966.

Part 4. *Collecting Societies*

Cols. A–F (1924–34, 1935–9, 1952–62), *Reports of the Industrial Assurance Commissioners*.

Col. A (1920–3, 1940–51), *Reports of the Registrar of Friendly Societies*.

Col. B (1920–3, 1940–51), estimates. Method: $B_t=A_t.\hat{\lambda}_{CAt}$, where for 1920–3 $\hat{\lambda}_{CAt}=\lambda_{CA1924}$

and $\lambda_{CA1924}=\left(\dfrac{\text{Assets of Collecting Societies}}{\text{Funds of Collecting Societies}}\right)_{1924}=1{\cdot}04$

For the period 1940–51, λ_{CA1952} was used as an estimate of $\hat{\lambda}_{CAt}$.

Col. G (1924–39, 1952–62), assumed to be equal to 'other assets' in the *Annual Reports of the Assurance Commissioner*.

Col. G (1940–51), estimated. Method: ratio of cash holdings to total assets held by insurance companies in each year multiplied by Col. B and by a splicing factor

$$=\lambda_{CCt}, \text{ where } \lambda_{CC1939}=\left(\frac{\text{Cash/Total Assets of Coll. Soc.}}{\text{Cash/Total Assets of Ins. Cos.}}\right)_{1939}=0{\cdot}74$$

and $\lambda_{CC1952}=0{\cdot}43$, where $\hat{\lambda}_{CCt}$ was interpolated for each year between 1939 and 1952 on the assumption that it fell by equal increments over the period.

Cols. D–F (1920–3, 1940–51) estimated as follows: Col. B multiplied by the relevant asset ratio reported by life insurance companies for the relevant year after it had been multiplied by splicing factors λ_{CGt}, λ_{COt} and λ_{CMt} which were found as follows:

In the 1920–3 interval,

$$\lambda_{CGt} = \left(\frac{\text{Collecting Soc. Gov. Gov. Gty.}}{\text{Est. Coll. Soc. Gov. Gov. Gty.}}\right)_{1924} = 0{\cdot}49$$

$$\lambda_{COt} = \left(\frac{\text{Coll. Soc. Other Investments}}{\text{Est. Coll. Soc. Oth. Invests.}}\right)_{1924} = 2{\cdot}1$$

$$\lambda_{CMt} = \left(\frac{\text{Collect. Soc. Mortgages}}{\text{Est. Collect. Soc. Mortgages}}\right)_{1924} = 1{\cdot}7$$

In the 1940–51 interval, $\lambda_{CG1952}=0{\cdot}90$, $\lambda_{CO1952}=1{\cdot}42$, and $\lambda_{CM1952}=2{\cdot}07$, were used as estimates of λ_{CGt}, λ_{COt} and λ_{CMt} respectively. Note: between 1940 and 1944 life insurance companies' holdings of other investments was not available so Col. E was estimated over these years by interpolating between the 1939 and estimated 1945 figures using equal annual decrements.

Col. C (1920–3, 1940–51) = col. D + col. E.

Col. A (1963–6): *Registrar of Friendly Societies Report*, Part I, 1966.

Cols. B, D, F (1963–6): *Report of the Industrial Assurance Commissioner*, 1966.

Col. E (1963–6): estimated: $E_t = B_t$. (Coll. Soc. Other Invests./Coll. Soc. Total Assets)$_{1962}$.

Col. C = col. D + col. E.

Part 5. *Superannuation and Other Trusts*

Col. A (1929–62): *Annual Reports of the Registrar of Friendly Societies*, 1930–63.

Cols. B–G (1935): ibid., 1936.

Col. A (1920–8) estimated by interpolated growth rate backwards from 1929 to 1922 – 2 per cent p.a.

Col. B (1920–34, 1936–62) estimated $B_t = A_t . \hat{\lambda}_{St}$,

where $$\hat{\lambda}_{St} = \left(\frac{\text{Superann. Soc. Tot. A}}{\text{Superann. Soc. Tot. F}}\right)_{1935} = 1{\cdot}0.$$

Cols. C–G (1951–5, 1961, 1962) are derived from a sample of three societies extracted from the societies' *Reports* deposited with the Registry of Friendly Societies. These reports are not available for public inspection, but the Registry kindly collected a sample from their files which recorded the asset distributions of three societies. The combined funds of the societies in the sample amounted to £54·0 million, £59·9 million, £66·1 million in 1960, 1961 and 1962, and to £23·1 million and £32·7 million in 1951 and 1955. The recorded asset distribution in each of the above years was then multiplied by K_t.

$$K_t = \frac{\text{Total Funds of All Super. Soc. in } t}{\text{Total Funds of three Soc. in } t}.$$

In 1951,

$$K_t = K_{1951} = \frac{228{\cdot}9}{23{\cdot}1} = 9{\cdot}91.$$

Cols. C–G (1952–4, 1956–9) estimated by interpolation between the data found for 1951, 1955, 1961–2.

Cols. D and G (1920–34, 1936–50) estimated. Each column was estimated by taking the total assets in each year, Col. B, and multiplying it by the Government security/total asset ratio and the cash/total asset ratio as reported by insurance companies in each year after adjusting these ratios by two splicing factors λ_{SGt} and λ_{SCt}.

$$\lambda_{SGt} = \frac{\left(\dfrac{\text{Gov. plus Gty. Hldgs. Sup. Soc.}}{\text{Tot. Assets Sup. Soc.}}\right)_t}{\left(\dfrac{\text{Gov. Gov. Gty. Hldgs. Ins. Co.}}{\text{Total Assets Ins. Cos.}}\right)_t}$$

$$\lambda_{SCt} = \frac{\left(\dfrac{\text{Cash Hldgs. Sup. Soc.}}{\text{Tot. Assets Sup. Soc.}}\right)_t}{\left(\dfrac{\text{Cash Holdings Ins. Co.}}{\text{Total Assets Ins. Co.}}\right)_t}.$$

$\lambda_{SG1935} = 1{\cdot}55$ and $\lambda_{SC1935} = 2{\cdot}3$ were used in the 1920–34 period, whereas, in the 1936–50 period, the splicing factors used in each year were adjusted from their 1935 values by equal annual increments to their 1952 values $-\lambda_{SG1952} = 1{\cdot}24$ and $\lambda_{SC1952} = 0{\cdot}2$.

Col. A (1963–6) *Registrar of Friendly Societies Report*, Part I, 1966.

Cols. B–G (1963–6) estimated: Col. A_t.relevant estimated asset distribution in 1962.

Part 6. *Railway Savings Banks*

Col. A (1920–62), *Annual Reports of the Registrar of Friendly Societies.*

Col. D (1954–62), C.S.O., *Annual Abstract*, No. 101 (1964), p. 273.

Col. B (1920–62), Col. C (1920–62), Col. D (1920–53), completed on the basis of information supplied by the British Transport Commission.

(1963–6) *Registrar of Friendly Societies Report*, Part 1, 1966.

Part 7. *All Societies and Companies*

Col. A, Cumulated Sum of Col. B in Parts 1–6.

Col. B, Cumulated Sum of Col. F in Parts 1–6.

Col. C, Cumulated Sum of Col. B – Sum of Col. D + G in Parts 1–6.

TABLE (A) 2.9 **The Funds[4] and the Number of Societies Registered Under the Friendly Societies and Provident and Industrial Assurance Societies Acts (Great Britain only) 1900–66 (Funds in £ millions)**

Year-End Approx. 31 Dec.	Gross Totals All Societies: No. Socs[12] ('000)	Gross Totals All Societies: Funds	All Societies Registered under Friendly Societies Act[1,5,6]: No. Socs. ('000)	All Societies Registered under Friendly Societies Act[1,5,6]: Funds	Industrial and Provident Societies (Co-operatives)[7]: No. Socs.	Industrial and Provident Societies (Co-operatives)[7]: Funds[3]	Building Societies' Funds	Registered Trade Unions: No. Unions[9]	Registered Trade Unions: Funds	Workmens' Compensation Societies' Funds	Certified Loan Society[10] Funds	Railway Savings Banks[2,11]: Banks	Railway Savings Banks[2,11]: Funds	Superannuation and Other Trusts[8]: No.	Superannuation and Other Trusts[8]: Funds	Collecting Societies (Industrial Assurance): Socs.	Collecting Societies (Industrial Assurance): Funds	Industrial Assurance Companies: Cos.	Industrial Assurance Companies: Funds	Net Total all Societies and Companies: No. ('000)	Net Total all Societies and Companies: Total
	I A	I B	II A	II B	III A	III B	IV	V A	V B	VI	VII	VIII A	VIII B	IX A	IX B	X A	X B	XI A	XI B	XII A	XII B
1900	—	—	—	—	—	—	—	—	—	—	—	—	—	—	—	—	—	—	18·4	—	—
1901	—	—	—	—	—	—	—	—	—	—	—	—	—	—	—	—	—	—	20·0	—	—
1902	—	—	—	—	—	—	—	—	—	—	—	—	—	—	—	—	—	—	21·8	—	—
1903	—	—	—	—	—	—	—	—	—	—	—	—	—	—	—	—	—	—	23·3	—	—
1904	—	—	—	—	—	—	—	—	—	—	—	—	—	—	—	—	—	—	25·3	—	—
1905	—	—	—	—	—	—	—	—	—	—	—	—	—	—	—	—	—	—	27·1	—	—
1906	—	—	—	—	1803	30·7	—	—	—	—	—	—	—	—	—	—	—	—	29·4	—	—
1907	—	—	—	—	1821	32·6	—	—	—	—	—	—	—	—	—	—	—	—	31·8	—	—
1908	—	—	—	—	1826	33·7	—	—	—	—	—	—	—	—	—	—	—	—	35·2	—	—
1909	—	—	—	—	1870	34·6	—	—	—	—	—	—	—	—	—	—	—	—	37·8	—	—
1910	—	—	26·9	52·4	1918	35·6	—	548	5·9	—	—	—	—	—	—	—	—	—	40·0	—	—
1911	—	—	**27·2***	**52·9***	1939 / 2858	37·3 / 46·4	47·4	542	6·3	0·1	—	—	6·9	—	—	—	—	—	42·9	—	—
1912	—	—	**27·6***	**53·4***	2987	48·8	48·9	613	5·6	0·1	—	—	7·1	—	—	—	—	—	53·0	—	—
1913	33·6	238·9	**28·0**	**53·9***	3086	53·6	50·1	616	6·5	0·1	0·2	19	7·4	—	—	—	11·2	19	55·8	—	—
1914	33·7	251·0	**28·1***	**56·2***	3151	58·0	51·1	620	7·0	0·1	0·2	19	7·7	—	—	52	12·0	19	58·7	—	—
1915	33·9	266·6	**28·3***	**58·5***	**3243***	**63·5***	**53·8***	**613**	**8·6**	**0·1***	**0·2***	**19***	8·1	—	—	52	12·4	19	61·4	—	—
1916	34·0	283·7	28·4	60·8	3335	69·1	56·5	611	10·6	0·1	0·2	19	8·4	—	—	53	13·0	19	65·0	—	—
1917	33·8	306·3	28·1	63·2	3429	72·3	66·4	609	12·8	0·1	0·2	19	8·0	—	—	54	13·9	19	69·4	—	—
1918	34·2	343·8	28·1	65·2	4066	95·7	70·1	621	15·1	0·1	0·2	19	8·7	—	—	54	14·7	19	74·0	—	—
1919	34·5	361·3	**27·6***	66·7	4661	96·2	75·8	644	16·1	0·1	0·2	19	9·6	—	—	52	16·1	19	80·5	—	—
1920	34·8	400·5	27·1	71·6	5522	109·9	84·9	656	16·0	0·1	0·2	19	10·3	—	—	51	17·9	18	89·7	34·8	400·5
1921	35·3	413·7	27·0	74·4	5717	103·5	93·4	621	10·9	0·1	0·2	19	11·1	—	—	53	20·1	18	100·2	35·3	413·7
1922	34·6	443·0	26·2	80·0	5851	101·2	105·7	607	10·0	0·1	0·2	19	11·8	—	—	53	22·5	18	111·5	34·6	442·4
1923	34·4	484·4	26·1[1]	83·4	5830	106·1	122·1	583	10·9	0·1	0·2	19	13·0	—	—	53	25·4	16	123·2	34·4	483·7
1924	33·4	537·1	25·3	87·7	5980	114·9	141·3	571	11·6	0·1	0·2	12	14·1	—	—	185	30·9	17	136·4	33·4	535·1
1925	33·3	591·1	25·4	91·1	5904	122·5	164·1	579	12·7	0·1	0·2	12	15·0	—	—	182	33·7	18	151·8	33·3	589·7
1926	32·8	640·3	25·0	97·4	5889	127·5	188·6	577	8·7	0·1	0·2	12	15·2	—	—	171	36·8	18	165·8	32·8	637·9
1927	32·8	701·3	24·9	100·5	5891	137·9	218·1	578	9·9	0·1	0·2	12	15·5	—	—	164	40·0	17	179·1	32·8	698·7
1928	32·3	782·0	24·5	106·2	5888	150·1	263·1	567	10·8	0	0·2	12	16·0	—	—	155	43·6	17	192·0	32·3	779·1
1929	32·4	886·6	24·5	109·7	5853	162·2	304·9	557	11·6	0	0·2	12	16·3	149	31·9	151	46·7	17	203·1	32·4	882·2
1930	32·0	987·7	24·1	115·3	5821	172·9	365·1	560	11·9	0	0·2	12	16·8	183	38·0	151	50·2	17	217·3	32·0	982·5
1931	31·6	1064·1	23·7	119·8	5793	180·2	412·0	552	11·5	0	0·2	12	17·2	207	42·8	153	53·9	16	226·3	31·6	1058·2
1932	31·4	1159·6	23·5	126·1	5752	189·8	464·1	549	11·5	0	0·2	12	17·7	219	49·9	155	57·3	15	243·0	31·3	1152·2
1933	31·1	1216·2	23·3	131·4	5728	190·4	495·0	547	12·1	0	0·2	12	18·8	222	55·5	155	61·5	15	251·3	31·1	1221·5
1934	30·8	1329·1	23·0	136·8	5673	206·2	548·7	537	13·2	0	0·2	10	20·5	237	60·3	155	65·7	15	277·5	30·1	1319·3
1935	30·7	1454·4	22·9	142·1	5691	250·0	592·6	537	14·5	0	0·2	10	23·1	254	65·6	151	69·6	15	296·7	30·7	1442·9
1936	30·7	1558·7	22·9	148·3	5699	263·1	643·3	535	16·3	0	0·2	10	25·4	268	70·5	152	74·5	16	317·1	30·5	1549·9
1937	30·3	1672·9	22·6	153·6	5693	281·5	698·8	526	18·4	0	0·2	10	27·4	281	75·8	151	79·9	15	337·3	30·3	1657·9
1938	30·1	1777·4	22·3	159·3	5682	295·3	745·5	521	20·4	0	0·2	10	29·5	292	83·1	149	84·8	15	359·2	30·1	1760·4
1939	29·8	1828·2	22·2	163·3	5599	301·8	755·3	522	22·6	0	0·1	10	30·9	304	89·4	149	90·5	14	374·4	29·8	1809·4

1940	29·3	1846·7	22·0	167·3	5427	300·4	746·0	515	23·1	0	0·1	10	32·0	303	97·3	147	95·7	14	388·6	29·3	1823·4
1941	29·2	1905·6	21·8	175·4	5349	320·9	733·5	516	28·0	0	0·1	10	33·8	306	105·0	147	101·8	14	407·0	29·2	1881·2
1942	29·0	1990·7	21·7	182·4	5307	350·8	738·2	522	31·8	0	0·1	10	33·8	313	114·3	147	108·9	14	430·4	29·0	1963·0
1943	28·9	2108·5	21·6	190·6	5328	392·6	756·9	520	35·6	0	0·1	10	35·8	321	123·5	145	117·3	14	456·0	28·9	2077·1
1944	28·8	2235·4	21·4	197·5	5362	430·4	784·6	520	39·5	0	0·1	9	38·5	342	133·9	140	125·9	14	484·9	28·8	2200·1
1945	28·7	2374·5	21·3	203·8	5445	465·4	812·9	529	43·1	0	0·1	6	44·3	353	143·3	138	134·7	14	526·9	28·7	2334·3
1946	28·7	2533·4	21·1	210·5	5629	498·7	865·7	527	46·9	0	0·1	6	44·7	367	154·8	138	143·4	14	568·6	28·7	2489·7
1947	28·5	2693·1	20·7	217·6	5777	513·9	941·5	512	50·8	0	0·1	6	43·8	383	166·6	136	154·6	14	604·1	28·5	2644·3
1948	27·7	2854·8	19·7	220·5	5981	522·3	1022·6	512	55·2	0	0·1	6	44·4	403	183·9	133	165·7	14	640·0	27·7	2800·7
1949	26·8	3010·1	18·8	222·1	6112	514·6	1124·8	513	58·9	0	0·1	6	44·1	417	197·7	128	176·6	14	671·1	26·8	2952·4
1950	26·2	3192·0	18·0	224·5	6204	521·2	1238·4	512	62·9	0	0·1	6	43·6	426	210·6	123	187·6	14	703·0	26·2	3128·3
1951	25·3	3335·7	17·2	227·3	6246	510·5	1339·2	513[9]	65·6[9]	0	0·1	6	41·3	432	228·9	118	197·9	14	724·9	25·3	3273·2
1952	24·8	3514·9	16·5	231·9	6365	513·3	1460·9	506	68·4	0	0·1	6	41·5	438	247·1	115	205·2	14	746·5	24·8	3457·6
1953	24·3	3782·0	16·0	236·7	6415	533·6	1624·4	512	71·5	0	0·1	6	42·2	436	269·1	111	217·9	14	786·5	24·3	3718·7
1954	23·8	4127·7	15·5	240·5	6438	559·3	1847·3	515	74·8	0	0·1	6	42·9	436	290·6	107	232·1	14	840·1	23·8	4057·1
1955	23·5	4452·0	15·2	242·5	6442	590·4	2044·5	510	77·5	0	0·1	6	43·4	432	319·6	102	244·0	14	890·0	23·5	4372·9
1956	23·1	4730·5	14·8	249·1	6434	619·2	2204·2	506	80·4	0	0·1	6	43·1	426	341·1	100	256·8	14	936·5	23·1	4644·0
1957	22·8	5010·3	14·5	251·1	6409	638·9	2381·9	504	81·7	0	0·1	6	44·2	426	369·7	97	270·9	14	972·1	22·8	4905·5
1958	22·6	5342·9	14·2	256·1	6511	659·6	2583·9	501	85·2	0	0·1	6	44·3	423	402·5	96	284·3	14	1026·9	22·6	5224·1
1959	22·5	5790·3	14·0	261·8	6765	704·1	2863·0	494	87·2	0	0·1	6	44·3	414	438·6	93	300·6	14	1090·6	22·5	5656·1
1960	22·4	6191·5	13·6	272·5	7021	745·6	3080·0	491	91·3	0	0·1	6	44·6	410	476·4	91	318·1	14	1162·5	22·4	6046·6
1961	22·1	6568·1	13·2	279·5	7117	787·5	3297·3	484	96·2	0	0·1	6	44·9	405	502·7	91	332·4	14	1227·5	22·1	6403·6
1962	21·9	7080·7	13·0	287·8	7257	808·9	3675·7	476	102·0	0	0	6	44·0	386	525·6	90	340·2	15	1296·6	21·9	6903·3
1963	21·8	7755·0	12·7	296·1	7418	823·1	4192·1	457	107·3	0	0	6	43·7	378	565·1	86	358·9	15	1368·7	21·8	7561·1
1964	21·6	8475·5	12·4	304·8	7606	863·6	4719·0	452	112·5	0	0	6	43·4	371	595·1	84	378·6	15	1458·5	21·6	8263·6
1965	21·5	9383·2	12·2	326·5	7882	909·0	5374·5	437	118·8	0	0	5	41·4	369	652·4	81	399·4	15	1561·2	21·5	9148·6
1966	21·4	10328·1	11·8	341·6	8145	928·7	6152·0	432	123·2	0	0	5	37·5	361	688·4	80	416·7	15	1640·0	21·4	10069·9

Sources

Cols. IIIA, B (1906–11), Board of Trade, *Statistical Abstract*, No. 67, p. 300. Fund figures are share capital only, and financial, land and building co-operative societies are excluded from the return.

Col. XIB (1900–12), see insurance fund figures. Cols. XIA and B (1913, 1920–32), *Report of Chief Registrar for Friendly Societies*, 1933, pp. 8–9. Col. XIB (1914–36), J. Johnston and G. Murphy, 'Growth of life assurance in UK since 1880', *Transactions Manchester Statistical Society*, Nov. 1956, pp. 285–9.

Cols. XA and B (1913–19), *Report of Registrar of Friendly Societies*, 1923, Part A, p. 39.

Cols. IIA–XIIB (1937–51), Registrar of Friendly Societies, *General Statistical Summary*, 1940–50, 1937–47, 1938–48, 1941–51 (London: H.M.S.O.).

Cols. IIA and B (1910, 1916–18), *Report of Registrar of Friendly Societies*, 1932, Part 2.

Cols. IIIA and B, IV, VA and B, VI, VII to VIIIB (1911–14), *British Parliamentary Papers*, LXXVI, 1914, p. 80.

Cols. IIIA and B, IV–VIIIB (1916–19), *Registrar of Friendly Societies*, 1918–19, Part A, p. 38.

Cols. VIIIA and B (1915), *British Parliamentary Papers*, XXIV, 1916, p. 83.

Cols. VA and B (1910–36), B. Mitchell and P. Deane, *Abstract of British Historical Statistics* (Cambridge University Press, 1962), p. 70. Fund figures adjusted to include funds of employers' unions.

Cols. IIA and B (1920–4), cols. IXA and B (1929–35), *Report of Registrar of Friendly Societies*, 1936, pp. 36, 40 and 41.

Cols. IIIA and B (1924–34), Board of Trade, *Statistical Abstract for the United Kingdom 1937*, No. 82 (London: H.M.S.O., 1938).

Cols. IIA and B (1936), cols. IIIA and B (1935–9), cols. XA and B (1935–9), C.S.O., *Annual Abstract of Statistics*, 1935–46, No. 84, p. 249.

Col. XIA (1933–6), cols. IA and B (1913, 1920, 1925, 1930, 1935, 1938–51), cols. IV, VIIIA and B, IXA to XB (1933–6), kindly provided by the statistician of the Registry of Friendly Societies.

Cols. XIIA and B (1920, 1930, 1935–7), *Report of Registrar of Friendly Societies*, Part 1, 1939.

Col. XII (1921–9, 1931–4), *Report of Registrar of Friendly Societies*, Part 1, 1937.

Col. XII (1938, 1951, 1952), *Report of Registrar of Friendly Societies*, Part 1, 1952.

Cols. IIA–VIIIB, XA and B (1920–35), Registry of Friendly Societies, *General Summary 1936*, Part 1 (London: H.M.S.O., 1937), p. 41.

Cols. IA–XIIB (1952–1966), *Annual Reports of the Registrar of Friendly Societies*, Parts 1–5.

Notes

[1] By the Industrial Assurance Act 1923, 129 Friendly Societies with a total of £0·8 million funds were transferred into Collecting Societies.

[2] Railway Savings Banks funds = deposits of members.

[3] A good 80 per cent of these societies are members of the Co-operative Trading Societies.

[4] Funds: Generally defined as = share capital + deposits + loans from members + net balance of disposable reserves. The fund figures are abstracted so as to represent combined savings of members. They are adjusted to eliminate inter-investment between societies so far as possible; thus, for instance, share capital and deposits of Co-operative Wholesale Societies are omitted as they belong to the Retailing Societies. In the same way the funds of the Co-operative Wholesale Societies' Bank and the Co-operative Insurance Society are omitted.

[5] Includes Branches of Orders.

[6] Some societies registered as Friendly Societies do industrial assurance business.

[7] Industrial and Provident Societies; these figures include funds and number of societies of the Retail Co-operative Societies.

[8] Registered under superannuation and other trust funds (Validation Act) 1927.

[9] Includes both employees and employers up to 1951, after which the employers' associations were excluded.

[10] Loan Societies Act 1840, maximum $i = 12$ per cent maximum loan £15, limit on loan 1 year, exempt from stamp duty and provisions of Money Lenders Act.

[11] Formed under Railway Savings Bank Act.

[12] Cols. IA and B (1914–19, 1921–4, 1926–9, 1931–4, 1936–8),

$$\sum_{i=II}^{XI} (\text{col. } i_A) \quad \text{and} \quad \sum_{i=II}^{XI} (\text{col. } i_B)$$

respectively in each year.

* Estimates interpolated for years contained between reported figures.

TABLE (A) 2.10 **Balance Sheets of Hire-Purchase Finance Houses – Sample of Eight Companies 1920–1966 (Assets, liabilities in £ ,000)**

Year Figs. for End of Period	*Total Liabilities (or Assets)*	*Liabilities*					*Assets*						
		Deposits	*Bankers' Loans and Acceptances*	*Share Capital Issued and Paid up*	*Reserves*	*Other Liabilities*	*Hire-Purchase Credit*	*Cash in Hand and at Banks*	*Investments*		*Fixed Assets*	*Interests in Subsidiaries and Other Assets*	*Number of Finance Houses*
									Total	*Government Securities and Stock*			
	1	2	3	4	5	6	7	8	9 A	9 B	10	11	12
1920	1013	40	11	130	190	642	910	51	—	—	—	52	1
1921	1007	83	—	130	195	599	887	—	—	—	—	120	1
1922	993	28	27	130	195	613	923	—	—	—	—	70	1
1923	1191	727	81	130	195	58	1116	—	—	—	—	75	1
1924	1524	935	150	130	200	109	1438	—	—	—	—	86	1
1925	2204	1093	496	280	224	111	2044	79	—	—	—	81	2
1926	2540	1220	629	280	253	158	2355	112	—	—	—	73	2
1927	3067	1299	954	280	319	215	2821	146	—	—	—	100	2
1928	3536	1435	1147	380	435	139	3058	164	50	50	3	261	2
1929	4274	1596	1599	380	473	226	3696	207	50	50	3	318	3
1930	6454	1628	2507	1383	533	403	5372	226	171	50	14	671	5
1931	6600	1674	2375	1416	577	558	5451	310	123	—	15	701	5
1932	6475	1850	2195	1483	612	335	5424	346	120	—	15	570	5
1933	6626	2334	1786	1483	649	374	5434	398	124	—	14	656	5
1934	8344	2859	2479	1916	713	377	6714	554	126	—	13	937	6
1935	9233	3290	2249	2011	824	849	7343	556	151	—	15	1158	7
1936	10619	4206	1876	2488	1604	445	8688	568	152	—	17	1194	7
1937	16013	4676	5035	3675	1812	815	13089	795	158	—	100	1871	8
1938	18214	5059	6221	3968	2212	754	15000	930	162	—	99	2023	8
1939	18269	4259	7240	3988	2095	687	15007	999	22	—	103	2138	8
1940	11655	3020	2470	4272	1820	73	8857	529	233	227	109	1927	8
1941	8051	1540	376	4272	1541	322	5316	451	400	392	85	1799	8
1942	8044	1424	569	4272	1533	246	4516	538	869	867	103	1978	8
1943	8541	1288	895	4272	1566	520	3626	764	1011	1006	88	3052	8
1944	8693	1246	791	4282	1627	747	3876	707	1054	1051	84	3172	8
1945	9234	1587	1395	4282	1626	344	5133	696	810	805	85	2510	8
1946	14421	3228	4267	4282	1784	860	10339	649	594	591	87	2752	8
1947	23028	4548	9516	4411	2339	2214	16924	741	24	19	88	5251	8
1948	28806	5232	12877	4456	3122	3119	18435	868	421	418	226	8856	8
1949	32383	3258	15501	5089	3291	5244	20261	1060	369	366	374	10319	8

1950	36651	6776	15680	5211	3799	5183	22696	999	366	366	380	12210	8
1951	42144	4728	21703	5299	4215	6199	26201	1331	339	339	386	13887	8
1952	45590	6796	21843	5424	4644	6883	28559	1453	339	339	433	14806	8
1953	52039	7126	26393	5572	5077	7871	32393	1545	338	338	460	17303	8
1954	65126	9589	34955	5635	5714	9233	41555	1808	494	338	560	20709	8
1955	102018	13167	60174	9904	6398	12375	61800	2766	474	328	639	36339	8
1956	102503	45384	28171	9962	7078	11908	56740	3885	474	328	674	40730	8
1957	125540	58656	33736	10501	10661	11986	72202	5671	475	328	731	46461	8
1958	166449	92326	29175	14112	16499	14337	94778	7608	492	328	788	62783	8
1959	243434	116540	63654	25566	15799	21875	121946	9913	349	328	935	110201	8
1960	334367	204400	63696	30554	18825	16892	146177	13821	350	328	1782	172237	8
1961	446042	263246	76820	34555	31401	40020	322572	24205	2583	663	6419	90263	8
1962	436183	284763	59586	33055	32584	26195	332638	26202	4196	817	15781	57636	7
1963	450332	313641	46829	32296	23421	34145	340343	28167	5558	853	18089	60141	6
1964	544743	399954	42936	37346	25083	39424	415010	27944	7147	872	24593	70092	6
1965	721672	514014	69308	42541	27142	68667	555837	33447	9772	1003	29397	90559	6
1966	749122	552879	51404	42783	30260	71796	572313	30741	16316	2034	33996	95841	6

Sources

Bowmaker, United Dominions Trust: *The Bankers' Almanac and Year Book*.

All other companies: company files, reports and balance sheets for the relevant years, held by the Registrar of Companies.

Col. 9B (1963–6), Government securities estimated on the basis of col. $1 \times \lambda_t K$, where:

$$\lambda_t = \left[\frac{\text{Securities other than Trade Investments}}{\text{Total Assets}}\right]$$

ratio of all hire-purchase companies in each year (as derived from C.S.O., *Annual Abstract of Statistics*, No. 105, 1968, p. 320), and K is a splicing factor.

$$K = \left[\frac{\text{Government Securities/Total Assets}}{\lambda_{1962}}\right]$$

$$= \left[\frac{817/436453}{17/725}\right] = \frac{0{\cdot}00187}{0{\cdot}02345} = 0{\cdot}08.$$

All other columns (1963–6), found from annual issues of *Bankers' Almanac and Year Book*.

Col. 1 = cols. 2+3+4+5+6.

Col. 2, Deposits, consists of current and deposit accounts.

Col. 5, Reserves, includes reserves for capital revenue and income tax.

Col. 6, Other liabilities, includes profit balance, accounts with subsidiaries, minority interest, unearned finance charges, etc.

Col. 7, Hire-purchase credit; includes hire-purchase credit, bills and notes receivable, advances, short-term loans, etc.

Col. 10, Fixed assets; includes land, buildings, plant, etc.

Col. 11, Interests in subsidiaries and other assets; investments in and current accounts with subsidiaries; also includes some minor items of sundry debtors, secured advances, repayments and interest accrued, etc.

Discontinuity in 1963 due to reduced sample size of six companies – United Motor Finance deleted; and also a different accounting format.

Notes

Companies	*Year of First Entry in Table*[2]	*Date of Balance Sheet*
Bowmaker Limited	1937	31 Oct.
British Wagon	1920	31 Dec.
Forward Trust	1935	1958 30 Apr. 1959 31 Oct.
Mercantile Credit Co. Ltd.	1934	30 Sept.
Midland Counties Motor Finance	1929[1]	1958 31 Dec.
Mutual Finance	1930	1959 30 Sept.
United Dominions Trust Ltd.	1925	30 June
United Motor Finance	1930	30 June

[1] Midland Counties Motor Finance ceased trading in 1962.

[2] Wagon Finance Corporation Ltd, and North Central Finance (formerly North Central Wagon Ltd) were both operating in 1920, and date well back into the nineteenth century.

— Indicates sum involved is less than £500.

TABLE (A) 2.11A **Government-Sponsored Financial Institutions: The Finance Corporation for Industry Balance Sheet 1946–1966[1] (£ millions)**

Date 31 March	*Capital*	*Reserves*	*Retained Profits*	*Retained Earnings*	*Loans from Banks*	*Special Deposits*	*Total Liabilities, Total Assets*	*Loans*	*Current Assets*	*Other Assets*
	I	II	III	II+III	IV	IVA	V	VI	VII	VIII
1946[2]	0·5	—	—	—	—	—	0·5	0·3	0·1	0·1
1947[2]	0·5	—	—	—	1·5	—	2·0	1·9	0·0	0·1
1948[2]	0·5	—	—	—	4·5	—	5·0	4·7	0·1	0·2
1949	0·5	—	—	—	10·8	—	11·4	11·0	0·3	0·1
1950	0·5	—	0·1	—	32·8	—	33·4	32·7	0·6	0·1
1951	0·5	—	0·1	—	55·3	—	55·9	54·5	1·3	0·1
1952	0·5	—	0·1	—	53·7	—	54·3	52·8	1·3	0·2
1953	0·5	—	0·1	—	62·0	—	62·5	60·9	1·5	0·1
1954	0·5	—	0·1	—	60·1	—	60·7	58·9	1·7	0·1
1955	0·5	0·3	0·2	—	54·2	—	55·2	53·9	1·3	0
1956	0·5	0·8	0·2	—	41·2	—	42·6	41·2	1·4	0
1957	0·5	0·8	0·2	—	42·9	—	44·3	42·4	1·9	0
1958	0·5	0·0	0·1	—	30·5	—	31·1	29·3	1·8	0
1959	5·5	0·0	−2·2	—	35·2	—	38·5	37·0	1·4	0·1
1960	5·5	1·0	0·3	—	39·1	—	45·9	44·5	1·3	0·1
1961	5·5	1·8	0·1	—	54·7	—	62·1	59·8	2·2	0·1
1962	5·5	2·3*	0·1*	2·4*	53·7	—	61·6	60·5	1·1	0
1963	5·5	—	—	2·9	56·2	—	64·6	62·9	1·7	0
1964	5·5	—	—	3·4	60·9	—	69·8	69·0	0·8	0
1965	5·5	—	—	4·0	61·3	25·4	96·2	94·8	1·4	0
1966	5·5	—	—	4·4	61·3	26·1	97·0	95·4	1·6	0

Sources

Annual issues of the *Bankers' Almanac and Year Book.*

Notes

* After 1962 'Reserves' and 'Retained Profits' combined under 'Retained Earnings'.

[1] Authorized to commence operations 19 May 1945.
[2] Balance taken at 30 September.

Date *31 March*	*Capital* I	*Reserves* II	*Loans from Banks* III	*Retained Profits* IV	*Total Liabilities, Total Assets* V	*Loans* VI	*Current Assets* VII	*Other Assets* VIII
1946[2]	1·5	0·2	0·1	—	1·8	1·3	0·5	—
1947[2]	3·0	0·2	3·0	—	6·2	5·7	0·5	—
1948[2]	6·0	0·4	5·0	—	12·4	10·8	1·4	0·2
1949	6·0	0·2	6·7	—	12·9	12·4	0·5	—
1950	7·5	0·1	8·2	0·1	15·9	15·7	0·2	—
1951	7·5	0·5	12·5	0·2	20·7	20·3	0·3	0·1
1952	7·5	0·6	15·5	0·4	24·0	23·7	0·3	0·0
1953	7·5	0·9	17·8	0·6	26·8	26·3	0·4	0·1
1954	7·5	1·1	19·8	0·6	29·0	27·8	1·2	—
1955	7·5	1·8	20·0	0·6	30·1	28·6	1·4	0·1
1956	7·5	2·3	22·0	1·0	32·8	32·2	0·5	0·1
1957	7·5	2·8	22·8	0·9	34·0	33·1	0·9	—
1958	7·5	3·3	25·0	1·0	36·7	34·3	2·4	—
1959	15·0	3·8	19·0	0·9	38·7	35·7	3·0	—
1960	15·0	4·0	25·0	1·2	45·2	38·4	6·8	—
1961	15·0	4·3	25·0	1·4	45·9	42·1	3·8	—
1962	15·0	4·5	32·5	1·7	53·7	46·6	7·0	0·1
1963	16·6	5·8	30·8	1·2	54·5	50·4	4·0	0·1
1964	20·0	8·0	33·3	1·4	62·7	56·9	5·7	0·1
1965	22·5	5·8	39·0	2·3	69·6	63·7	5·8	0·1
1966	30·0	9·5	36·7	4·7	80·9	75·5	4·2	1·2

Sources

Bankers' Almanac and Year Book, annual issues.

Notes

[1] Authorized to commence operations 20 July 1945.

[2] Balance taken at 30 Sept.

TABLE (A) 2.12 **The Compound Rates of Growth of the Total Assets of Various UK Non-Bank Financial Intermediaries**

Item	*1880–1966*	*1880–1914*	*1914–1918*	*1920–1939*	*1939–1946*	*1946–1966*	*1920–1966*	*1955–1966*
Total Assets Birmingham Municipal Bank	n.a.	n.a.	n.a.	21·8	14·1	1·2	11·2	0·7
Total Assets Trustee Savings Banks (a) Ordinary Department	3·8 / 4·3[1]	0·6 / 1·0[1]	3·0	3·7	20·4	3·3	5·9	2·2
(b) Special Investment Department	7·6 / 7·7[1]	6·2 / 5·8[1]	−2·4	10·6	2·1	11·8	9·6	15·8
Total Assets Building Societies	6·2 / 6·3[1]	0·6 / −0·1[1]	0·9	12·2	1·8	10·4	9·7	10·7
Total Assets Insurance Companies	5·2[2] / 5·4[1,2]	3·8 / 4·2[1]	3·6	4·8[3]	4·3	8·0	6·3[3]	8·5
Life and Annuity Funds	4·8 / 5·0[1]	3·4 / 3·7[1]	1·3	4·7	3·6	9·0	6·3	10·3
Life and Annuity Premiums	5·0 / 5·5[1]	3·0 / 3·4[1]	2·9	4·0	4·4	10·1	6·7	9·8
Total Assets of Selected Friendly Societies	n.a.	n.a.	n.a.	6·7	6·2	5·0	5·9	4·7
Funds of all Friendly and Provident Societies	n.a.	n.a.	8·2	8·3	4·9	7·3	7·3	7·9
Total Assets Hire-Purchase Co. Sample	n.a.	n.a.	n.a.	16·5	−3·4	21·9	15·5	19·9
All Insurance Funds	n.a.	n.a.	n.a.	5·0[4]	4·4	8·0	6·2[4]	8·6
Post Office Savings Bank	4·7	5·1	5·4	3·9	20·0	−0·7	4·2	0·2

Notes

[1] These annual rates of growth are computed from 1891 and not from 1880.

[2] Not strictly accurate owing to discontinuity in coverage of series.

[3] These annual rates of growth are computed from 1924, not 1920.

[4] These annual rates of growth are computed from 1922, not 1920.

Section 3 UK Money, Liquid Assets, National Savings and Institutional Private Credit Series 1880–1966

The first table, *United Kingdom National Savings*, and the third and fourth tables, *UK Money Supply and Households' Liquid Assets 1880–1966* and *UK Financial Institutions – Credit Series 1880–1966*, have been derived from the contents of the other two sections of this Appendix. The second table, *Coin and Currency in Circulation in the UK 1880–1966* and the fifth, sixth and seventh tables, *New Capital Issues in the UK 1920–1966*, *Stocks Quoted on the London Stock Exchange 1930–1966*, and *UK Rates of Interest 1860–1966*, are based on other sources. As in the other two sections, however, each table is fully footnoted, so it should be easy to ascertain how the statistics in each column have been derived.

The data contained in the last three tables (A) 3.5, (A) 3.6, (A) 3.7 were extracted from these published sources; the *Midland Bank Review*, the Bank of England *Statistical Summary* and the Bank of England *Quarterly Bulletin*, the *London Stock Exchange Official Year Book*, and the Central Statistical Office *Annual Abstract of Statistics*. They have been included in this section primarily to draw attention to their availability. The data in Tables (A) 3.1–(A) 3.4, however, either have not been published or are difficult to reconcile with statistics which are currently published in the Bank of England *Quarterly Bulletin* or the Central Statistical Office *Financial Statistics* (see for example the latter's 'Money Supply' series which began in 1963). Detailed notes are given below on the composition of the data in each of these four tables.

Table (A) 3.1, *United Kingdom National Savings 1880–1966*, represents the book value of various forms of State-issued or State-regulated issues of negotiable and unnegotiable savings instruments held by the private sector – mainly households – as of a certain date in each year. The statistics in the table reflect quantitatively the extent of the State's efforts to stimulate the growth of 'small savings' by setting up its own savings bank, stimulating the growth of State-regulated savings banks, or by launching direct savings placement schemes to encourage thrift and of course provide finance for the Exchequer. To be sure, the statistics are not completely comprehensive in that they omit various State-sponsored annuity schemes run by the Post Office Savings Bank up to 1928, and, much more importantly, the funds of the State-run national assurance and insurance schemes. Nevertheless, the data in the table do reflect the vast majority of household savings which the State has attracted through voluntary means.

In this table, it should be noted that dates at which the various stocks of 'savings' were measured vary according to the column chosen. The data in column 1, Post Office Savings Bank Deposits, are recorded as of 31 December in each year; the data in columns 2, 3 and 4, the ordinary deposits, the special investment departments' deposits, and the Government stock holdings of the trustee savings banks, are recorded as of 20 November each year. All of the data in the other columns, except the data in columns 9 and 10 which are consolidated totals, reflect the noted forms of 'savings' outstanding as of 31 March in each year. These varying year-end dates prevent this National Savings table from being directly comparable with the table entitled *National Savings* carried in the more recent issues of the Central Statistical Office's *Annual Abstract of Statistics*, in which all of the data are recorded as of 31 March of each year. Naturally too, as column 10 ('Total Savings') is composed of the total of savings banks' deposits as posted on 20 November or 31 December, plus the State's direct savings placements outstanding as of 31 March in each year (columns 6A+7A+7B+8), it provides only an approximate total of these forms of savings outstanding between March and December in any one year up to 1920. From 1920 on, noting that the deposits of the Birmingham Municipal Savings Bank, which are posted as of 31 March, are included in column 9 and therefore in column 10, both the consolidated total of savings bank deposits and of total savings are measured composed of items which were on three different dates during the last nine months of each calendar year. In Table (A) 3.3, *UK Money Supply and Households' Liquid Assets*, the incorporated National Savings instruments which are posted as of 31 March in Table (A) 3.1 have been lagged so as to reflect approximately the totals of such savings outstanding as of the end of the immediately preceding calendar year, before they were inserted along with the other year-end data.

In Table (A) 3.2, *Coin and Currency in Circulation in the UK 1880–1966*, this type of problem recurs inasmuch as some of the data are posted as of the end of the calendar year while the rest are represented as a yearly average. In column 1 (the coin series), for example, the data were recorded as of the end of the calendar year up to 1932; after 1932 annual averages are given. Again, all the note issues recorded in column 10 are annual averages, while the note issues of the Scottish, Irish and other UK banks as posted in columns 11–13 are recorded as of the end of the calendar year. Finally, column 16, 'Notes and Coin held by Banks', are annual averages or estimates of these, and of course columns 15 and 17, 'Total Notes and Coin Outstanding' and 'Currency outside the Banks', which are composed of the totals in the other columns, are of a mixed vintage.

In this table, however, the effect of these varying dates is less serious, as the coin and currency issued was most carefully regulated by the State over the whole period. Moreover, after the First World War, the greater part of the data in the table was measured on an annual basis. As a result, the statistics given in column 17, 'Currency Outside the Banks', are generally almost identical to the same series given in Government publications which are recorded as annual averages. For example, in the June 1941 issue of the Bank of England's *Statistical Summary*, the annual average of such a stock in 1940 is given as £545 million; in Table (A) 3.2, column 17, the figure in 1940 is £546 million. Again, later on in the series, the Central Statistical Office's *Annual Abstract of Statistics* records that the annual average stock of currency outstanding was £1,551 million in 1954 and £2,161 million in 1962. Column 17 gives the currency outstanding as £1,552 million in 1954 and £2,156 million in 1962. To be sure, the discrepancy is somewhat larger in the pre-1940 issues of the *Statistical Summary* – the data given in column 17 are slightly smaller than the corresponding totals given in the *Summaries*. However, this discrepancy is due to the fact that the Bank of England included the note issues of the Southern Irish banks as well as that of the Northern Irish banks in their computations up to 1940. In Table (A) 3.2, such note issues were deleted as of 1920. In all, the data in column 17, 'Currency Outside the Banks', may be regarded as the annual average stock outstanding from 1920 on and as a mixture of such an annual average and a year-end stock in the pre-1914 period, with the bias in favour of the year-end owing to the preponderance of coin as opposed to notes in these earlier years.

In Table (A) 3.3, *UK Money Supply and Households' Liquid Assets 1880–1966*, the accuracy of the data is again somewhat distorted by the necessity for using stock figures which were recorded at different dates during the year or which are annual averages of these stocks on various dates during the year. Where possible, as in column 10, 'Defence Bonds, National Savings Certificates, Accrued Interest on such Savings Certificates, Premium Savings Bonds and all bonds held for savers by the Post Office Registrar', and in column 7, 'Savings Banks' Deposits', the totals were adjusted so they more nearly reflected the balance outstanding as of the end of the calendar year. All savings bank deposits recorded as of 31 March in one year were presumed to be the total outstanding as of 31 December in the previous year, and similarly, all Government savings instruments outstanding as of 31 March in one year were presumed also to be equal to the outstanding stock as of 31 December in the preceding year. Nevertheless, such adjustments could not be made in some cases – columns 2, 3, 5 and 8 ('Inter-Bank Deposits', 'Private Deposits at the Bank of England', 'Currency outside the Banks' and 'Building Societies' Deposits and Shares') – and so the data in these columns are not strictly comparable with the data in columns 1, 7, 10 and 11 which were recorded approximately on an end-calendar-year basis. This variability as to the date or average of dates when the items in the successive columns were recorded does introduce errors in the recorded estimates of net deposits of all banks in the UK (column 4), of the net money supply (column 6), and total quasi-money and total potential encashable assets (columns 9 and 12, respectively), as such columns are composed of the columns which are to the left of them. Nevertheless, as an inspection of the table shows, relatively, the weight of these induced errors decreases with the passage of time as the end-year balance sheet statistics become increasingly dominant.

The variability in the dates to which the statistics in the various columns refer does make it difficult to reconcile, say, the net money supply statistics, in column 6, with the totals published under the same heading by such international institutions as the International Monetary Fund, in its monthly *International Financial Statistics*, or, for that matter, with those of the Central Statistical Office, in its monthly issues of *Financial Statistics* over recent years. It should be noted that no money supply statistics are published for the early years by these official agencies. However, the task of reconciliation is made much more difficult by differences in the definition of the 'money supply'. The Central Statistical Office's estimates, for instance, include only deposits of UK residents in their totals; whereas my estimates include all deposits and other accounts at UK-based banks. Again, the Central Statistical Office's estimates include all such deposits of UK-based banks plus all such deposits of the accepting houses, of the discount houses and of overseas banks operating in the UK; in my series deposits in these other institutions were excluded from the total in column 1. Moreover, from June 1966, the Central Statistical Office's statistics included negotiable dollar certificates of deposits issued by such accepting houses and overseas banks, that is the portion of these issues which were owned by UK residents, whereas again these items were not included in the total in column 1. In effect, the errors introduced in the money supply series in this table through the use of different dates only make the comparison of this series with the official series difficult; whereas the variation in the definitions of what components should form this important financial stock makes the comparison completely impracticable.

These official money stock series, which provide end-year, annual average, and quarterly estimates of the money stock over the past ten years or so, are undoubtedly more accurate than mine. They have been collected on a consistent basis, and, perhaps more importantly, they reflect the actual rougher estimate of the net money stock which was owned by residents and non-residents alike. In this sense, such statistics should be used instead of mine in any analysis of the role money played or how this stock itself was determined in the post-1962 period. Again, it is partly for this reason that the post-1962 data recorded in this Appendix have not been used in the previous chapters.

Nevertheless, as the author of the February 1969 issue of the *Midland Bank Review* asserts, a certain amount of caution should be employed in using any 'money stock' statistics, for the component stocks which compose it are often selected rather arbitrarily.[1] For example, the Central Statistical Office's definition of the money stock includes deposits at the accepting houses, at the discount houses and at overseas banks which are owned by UK residents. These deposits, however, as the author of the article in review points out, are mainly composed of time deposits which have to be withdrawn and re-deposited in the domestic banking system before they may be used as a means of payment – one of the main functions which money is said to perform.[2] As a consequence, the inclusion of such financial claims might be said to stretch somewhat the traditional definition of the money stock, and in any event, whether this stretching is relevant or not, the inclusion of such deposits leads to certain inconsistencies in that the savings deposits at other domestically based institutions, such as the building societies, the trustee savings banks and the Post Office Savings Bank, are excluded. As a result, inasmuch as the deposits at these foreign banks are 'term' deposits which may not be directly used to make payments, it would seem that these deposits which are owned by UK residents should be included under the caption 'quasi-money' (see the International Monetary Fund's *International Financial Statistics* and column 9 of this table) rather than under the category of net money stock. Finally, of course, whatever category these particular financial claims are slotted under, it should be noted that between 1914 and 1958 the growth of UK residents' deposits in such foreign banks and domestic accepting houses was probably minimal if not actually negative – it is only in the post-1958 period that these banking entities have expanded rapidly.[3]

In Table (A) 3.4, *UK Financial Institutions – Credit Series 1880–1966*, the variation in the date during the year when the balance sheets of the constituent institutions were struck is less serious than in Table (A) 3.3; at least to All the data reflect end-year balance sheet positions; though some of the institutions, particularly the smaller building societies, drew up their balance sheets at widely different dates over the year. Again, though, the omissions in the coverage, particularly of the foreign banks operating in the UK in the pre-1914 period and the post-1958 period, undoubtedly reduce the aggregate totals – columns I, II, III, XI, XIII, XIV, XV and XVI. These institutions played an active part in the money market and in the capital market in these periods.

The recorded data in this table are also distorted by other factors. The total assets/liabilities statistics of the banks and discount companies are undoubtedly inflated to some extent by what one might call 'end-year balance sheet window dressing' – the totals undoubtedly include a certain amount of intra-group finance which made the dressing-up somewhat easier. Again, too, the commercial banks' loans and advances (column I), and the total private credit and the net private credit extended by the money market institutions (columns XV and XVI), are probably somewhat upward biased in the pre-1914 period owing to the bank amalgamation movement. Moreover, the recorded total private credit and net private credit statistics, columns XIII–XVI, have not been adjusted to exclude bank advances to the public corporations; though Table (A) 1.10 in the first section of this Appendix suggests that the omission was of no particular significance.[4] Finally, of course, differences in the method of asset evaluation undoubtedly also have an effect on the recorded data. The banks, given their exempt status under the Companies Act, chose a conservative method in appraising the value of their assets; as a consequence these figures probably more nearly reflect their book than market value. In contrast, the assurance companies are required by law to post returns which reflect the market value of their assets as of certain prescribed intervals. Naturally, then, the totals in columns II and VIII are not strictly comparable. These considerations, coupled with the fact that in the earlier years the Government and the Government-guaranteed securities, banks and other financial institutions held were estimates, mean that the derived private credit figures are certainly not exact; at best they may be taken as only a general index of the amount of private credit the UK financial sector extended in each of the years over the 1880–1966 time period.

[1] 'Money supply and the banks', *Midland Bank Review* (February 1969), pp. 3–9.
[2] Ibid., p. 4.
[3] 'The UK banking sector 1952–67', *Bank of England Quarterly Bulletin* (June 1969), p. 176.

[4] Banks' advances to the nationalized sector, 'Public Utilities, including Transportation and Communication', were shown to have just increased from £18·3 million to £116·3 million over the 1946–62 period. In contrast, total bank advances are shown to have increased from £896 million to £3,951 million over that time interval.

TABLE (A) 3.1 **United Kingdom National Savings 1860–1967 (£ millions)**

Year	Irish P.O. Savings Bank, included in Col. 1	Irish Trustee Savings Bank, included in Col. 2	Birmingham Municipal Bank 31 March	P.O. Savings Account 31 Dec.[1,4]	Trustee Savings Banks: Total 20 Nov.[8]	Trustee Savings Banks: Ordinary Department 20 Nov.	Trustee Savings Banks: Special Investment Department 20 Nov.[7]	Stock Department 20 Nov.[3]	National Savings Certificates, Principal and Accrued Interest 31 Mar.: Amount A / Interest B	Defence Bonds and Other Securities on P.O. Register 31 Mar.[2,5]: Defence Bonds A / Other Securities B	Premium Savings Bonds 31 Mar.	Total Savings Banks Deposits[9]	Total Savings[10,11]
	A	B	C	1	2	3	4	5	6	7	8	9	10
1860	—	—	—	—	41·5	41·3	0·2	—	—	—	—	41·5	41·5
1861	—	—	—	—	41·7	41·5	0·2	—	—	—	—	41·7	41·7
1862	—	—	—	1·7	40·8	40·6	0·2	—	—	—	—	42·5	42·5
1863	—	—	—	3·4	41·2	41·0	0·2	—	—	—	—	44·6	44·6
1864	—	—	—	5·0	39·5	39·3	0·2	—	—	—	—	44·5	44·5
1865	—	—	—	6·5	39·0	38·7	0·3	—	—	—	—	45·5	45·5
1866	—	—	—	8·1	36·7	36·4	0·3	—	—	—	—	44·8	44·8
1867	—	—	—	9·7	36·8	36·5	0·3	—	—	—	—	46·5	46·5
1868	—	—	—	11·7	37·2	36·9	0·3	—	—	—	—	48·9	48·9
1869	—	—	—	13·5	37·9	37·6	0·3	—	—	—	—	51·4	51·4
1870	—	—	—	15·1	38·3	38·0	0·3	—	—	—	—	53·4	53·4
1871	—	—	—	17·0	39·2	38·8	0·4	—	—	—	—	56·2	56·2
1872	—	—	—	19·3	40·3	39·7	0·6	—	—	—	—	59·6	59·6
1873	—	—	—	21·2	41·2	40·5	0·7	—	—	—	—	62·4	62·4
1874	—	—	—	23·2	42·3	41·5	0·8	—	—	—	—	65·5	65·5
1875	—	—	—	25·2	43·5	42·4	1·1	—	—	—	—	68·7	68·7
1876	—	—	—	27·0	44·6	43·3	1·3	—	—	—	—	71·6	71·6
1877	—	—	—	28·7	45·6	44·2	1·4	—	—	—	—	74·3	74·3
1878	—	—	—	30·4	45·9	44·3	1·6	—	—	—	—	76·3	76·3
1879	—	—	—	32·0	45·6	43·8	1·8	—	—	—	—	77·6	77·6
1880	—	—	—	33·7	46·0	44·0	2·0	—	—	—	—	79·7	79·7
1881	—	—	—	36·2	46·5	44·1	2·3	0·1	—	0·7	—	82·6	83·3
1882	—	—	—	39·0	47·4	44·6	2·6	0·2	—	1·1	—	86·2	87·3
1883	—	—	—	41·8	48·2	45·0	2·8	0·4	—	1.5	—	89·6	91·1
1884	—	—	—	44·8	49·4	45·8	3·1	0·5	—	1·9	—	93·7	95·6
1885	—	—	—	47·7	50·4	46·4	3·3	0·7	—	2·5	—	97·4	99·9
1886	—	—	—	50·9	51·2	46·8	3·6	0·8	—	2·9	—	101·3	104·2
1887	—	—	—	54·0	52·0	47·3	3·8	0·9	—	3·3	—	105·1	108·4
1888	—	—	—	58·6	51·4	46·4	4·0	1·0	—	3·8	—	109·0	112·8
1889	—	—	—	63·0	50·3	44·9	4·2	1·2	—	4·2	—	112·1	116·3
1890	—	—	—	67·6	49·3	43·6	4·4	1·3	—	4·7	—	115·6	120·3
1891	—	—	—	71·6	48·3	42·9	4·1	1·3	—	5·1	—	118·6	123·7
1892	—	—	—	75·9	48·0	42·4	4·3	1·3	—	5·6	—	122·6	128·2
1893	4·1	1·9	—	80·6	48·0	42·2	4·5	1·3	—	6·3	—	127·3	133·6
1894	4·7	1·9	—	89·3	49·5	43·5	4·6	1·4	—	7·0	—	137·4	144·4
1895	5·3	2·0	—	97·9	51·3	45·3	4·7	1·3	—	6·9	—	147·9	154·8
1896	5·9	2·1	—	108·1	52·5	46·7	4·7	1·1	—	6·9	—	159·5	166·4
1897	6·4	2·2	—	115·9	54·2	48·5	4·6	1·1	—	7·0	—	169·0	176·0
1898	6·9	2·2	—	123·1	55·7	50·0	4·6	1·1	—	7·5	—	177·7	185·2
1899	7·5	2·3	—	130·1	57·1	51·4	4·6	1·1	—	8·4	—	186·1	194·5
1900	7·8	2·3	—	135·5	57·4	51·5	4·5	1·4	—	10·5	—	191·5	202·0
1901	8·3	2·3	—	140·4	58·2	52·0	4·5	1·7	—	12·8	—	196·9	209·7
1902	8·7	2·4	—	144·6	59·0	52·5	4·6	1·9	—	14·3	—	201·7	216·0
1903	9·4	2·5	—	146·1	59·3	52·5	4·7	2·1	—	16·2	—	203·3	219·5
1904	9·6	2·5	—	148·3	59·5	52·3	4·9	2·3	—	17·4	—	205·5	222·9
1905	10·0	2·5	—	152·1	60·6	52·7	5·6	2·3	—	17·9	—	210·4	228·3
1906	10·4	2·5	—	156·0	61·8	53·0	6·4	2·4	—	19·0	—	215·4	234·4
1907	10·6	2·5	—	157·5	61·8	52·2	7·1	2·5	—	20·5	—	216·8	237·3
1908	10·6	2·4	—	160·6	62·3	51·7	8·2	2·4	—	20·6	—	220·5	241·1

1910	11·7	2·5	—	168·9	66·0	52·5	11·0	2·7	—			23·2		—	232·2	255·4
1911	12·2	2·6	—	176·5	67·9	53·0	12·2	2·7	—		24·8		—	241·7	266·5
1912	12·7	2·6	—	182·1	70·0	53·8	13·4	2·8	—		26·1		—	249·3	275·4
1913	13·0	2·6	—	187·2	71·5	54·3	14·4	2·8	—		26·6		—	255·9	282·5
1914	—	—	—	190·5	72·3	53·9	15·6	2·8	—		26·6		—	260·0	286·6
1915	—	—	—	186·3	73·2	51·4	15·4	6·4	—		54·7		—	253·1	307·8
1916	—	—	—	196·7	77·5	53·8	14·7	9·0	1·4	—	104·2		—	265·2	370·8
1917	—	—	—	203·3	84·8	52·4	14·1	18·3	74·5	0·0	151·0		—	269·8	495·3
1918	—	—	—	234·6	97·7	61·0	14·1	22·6	137·7	3·7	185·7		—	309·7	633·1
1919	—	—	—	266·3	112·2	71·9	14·9	25·4	227·0	11·5	215·2		—	353·1	795·3
1920	—	—	0·7	266·5	118·6	75·1	16·2	27·3	273·5	24·0	204·3		—	358·5	836·3
1921	—	—	1·4	264·2	121·8	73·1	19·3	29·4	285·0	35·0	209·7		—	358·0	852·7
1922	—	—	1·9	268·1	128·8	75·8	22·5	30·5	342·0	45·0	206·3		—	368·3	916·6
1923	—	—	2·9	273·1	133·5	79·6	23·6	30·3	353·8	65·0	202·5		—	379·2	935·5
1924	—	—	4·2	280·4[4]	137·9	82·3	24·7	30·9	366·1	80·0	197·5		—	391·6	955·2
1925	—	—	5·6	285·5	142·2	83·4	27·0	31·8	368·8	90·0	183·7		—	401·5	954·0
1926	—	—	6·8	283·7	144·8	82·0	28·8	34·0	375·6	100·0	184·6		—	401·3	961·5
1927	—	—	7·8	284·6	150·0	81·4	32·5	36·1	371·8	121·0	188·6		—	406·3	966·7
1928	—	—	9·1	288·6	159·0	81·7	38·9	38·4	362·4	121·0	191·5		—	418·3	972·2
1929	—	—	10·3	285·0	162·4	79·3	45·1	38·0	361·2	122·0	190·8		—	419·7	971·7
1930	—	—	11·5	290·2	172·5	79·1	54·1	39·3	358·0	121·0	188·5		—	434·9	981·4
1931	—	—	12·9	289·4	183·7	77·9	65·1	40·7	371·6	124·5	191·6		—	445·3	1008·5
1932	—	—	13·7	305·7	195·6	80·0	74·8	40·8	378·9	98·0	194·5		—	474·2	1047·6
1933	—	—	15·3	326·7	209·0	88·8	82·6	37·6	383·7	90·5	186·8		—	513·4	1083·9
1934	—	—	17·1	354·8	218·7	94·8	87·1	36·8	389·3	98·5	176·0		—	553·8	1119·1
1935	—	—	18·9	390·3	233·3	107·6	89·8	35·9	393·0	107·3	169·7		—	606·6	1169·3
1936	—	—	21·2	432·4	247·5	120·3	91·8	35·4	391·4	116·3	165·5		—	665·7	1222·6
1937	—	—	23·8	470·5	261·7	131·3	93·3	37·1	390·1	124·0	165·9		—	718·9	1274·9
1938	—	—	26·7	509·3	277·2	142·4	96·5	38·3	385·9	130·9	202·6		—	774·9	1363·4
1939	—	—	29·4	551·4	292·7	152·4	99·4	40·9	381·5	137·4	205·6		—	832·6	1419·7
1940	—	—	31·6	654·4	321·3	173·6	101·9	45·8	430·5	143·2	60·1	207·5	—	961·5	1659·6
1941	—	—	35·9	822·9	373·9	214·8	108·6	50·5	605·5	154·3	250·5	189·9	—	1182·2	2228·1
1942	—	—	42·1	1005·4	433·8	264·6	113·9	55·3	831·4	171·6	429·0	196·1	—	1426·0	2882·5
1943	—	—	50·8	1240·6	508·3	333·0	115·2	60·1	1033·8	193·5	542·2	204·9	—	1739·6	3520·5
1944	—	—	59·5	1493·9	591·6	411·0	115·8	64·8	1291·8	223·0	651·2	216·3	—	2080·2	4239·5
1945	—	—	67·7	1776·6	674·8	488·5[6]	114·6[6]	71·7[6]	1511·2	259·4	762·1	222·8	—	2447·4	4943·5
1946	—	—	74·3	1981·9	753·4	557·7	112·6	83·1	1603·7	296·4	— 1183·6 —		—	2726·5	5513·8
1947	—	—	78·0	1943·2	814·1	621·9	109·6	82·6	1673·0	327·9	1100·6	209·4	—	2752·7	5735·7
1948	—	—	80·9	1948·0	881·8	688·7	110·5	82·6	1741·5	362·5	1033·4	203·6	—	2828·1	5806·6
1949	—	—	83·4	1947·6	942·3	744·4	112·5	85·3	1737·2	399·0	975·7	190·9	—	2887·9	5791·7
1950	—	—	85·1	1934·3	996·7	793·7	115·2	87·8	1713·4	432·2	955·5	188·2	—	2928·3	5785·4
1951	—	—	85·1	1875·9	1026·3	816·6	115·7	94·0	1709·7	460·6	934·1	186·4	—	2893·3	5723·5
1952	—	—	84·8	1812·3	1056·9	831·3	122·4	103·2	1725·7	487·0	877·2	190·6	—	2850·8	5644·3
1953	—	—	85·4	1746·8	1078·2	824·9	143·7	109·6	1748·6	507·6	821·3	191·2	—	2800·8	5561·9
1954	—	—	86·3	1727·4	1134·0	827·1	192·6	114·3	1767·6	523·0	783·2	189·9	—	2833·4	5574·1
1955	—	—	88·1	1700·0	1178·1	827·3	226·2	124·6	1813·6	544·4	806·2	184·4	—	2841·6	5645·8
1956	—	—	88·6	1688·0	1229·0	811·6	282·8	134·6	1833·3	556·4	776·9	189·5	—	2871·0	5670·7
1957	—	—	85·9	1677·0	1278·7	823·3	316·8	138·6	1907·4	525·9	742·1	189·9	66·4	2903·0	5808·8
1958	—	—	83·6	1645·6	1313·1	822·8	342·6	147·7	1887·3	505·8	702·1	190·9	147·7	2894·6	5822·6
1959	—	—	81·9	1679·0	1405·3	858·6	380·5	166·2	2017·5	484·3	810·0	185·9	215·8	3000·0	6229·2
1960	—	—	84·2	1710·2	1497·5	880·6	434·0	182·9	2084·1	491·6	955·4	181·6	253·3	3109·0	6583·4
1961	—	—	85·3	1736·6	1597·5	902·4	499·0	196·1	2138·7	504·7	1059·4	182·0	309·6	3223·3	6913·0
1962	—	—	86·7	1760·1	1717·4	913·6	603·5	200·3	2122·5	521·8	1075·5	184·5	351·7	3363·9	7098·1
1963	—	—	88·8	1791·6	1886·4	951·6	733·4	201·4	2133·8	551·3	1122·5	181·1	393·6	3565·4	7396·4
1964	—	—	91·2	1814·4	2089·5	995·6	885·0	208·9	2110·2	592·2	1142·1	178·3	437·2	3786·2	7654·0
1965	—	—	92·8	1822·5	2234·3	1027·4	994·0	212·9	2076·4	623·4	1055·3	178·1	491·4	3936·7	7737·9
1966	—	—	93·9	1739·8	2347·9	1038·7	1107·0	202·2	1927·5	673·0	793·7	177·6	546·7	3979·4	7424·9
1967	—	—	92·3	1672·7	2457·2	1045·6	1215·4	196·2	1982·5	581·8	508·6	184·0	585·8	4026·0	7286·9

Notes to Table (A) 3.1 overleaf.

Notes to Table (A) 3.1

Sources

Cols. 1, 3, 4 (1860–1939), Mitchell and Deane, *Abstract of British Historical Statistics*, 1962, pp. 453–4.

Cols. 7A+7B (1910–24), 6A, 6B (1916–23), Board of Trade, *Statistical Abstract for UK 1925*, No. 70 (London: H.M.S.O., 1927), p. 188.

Cols. 7A+7B, 6A, 6B (1924–37), Board of Trade, ibid., 1937, No. 82 (London: H.M.S.O., 1938), p. 265.

Cols. 1, 3, 4 (1940–62), see other tables. Col. 5 (1945–62), see Tables (A) 2.2, (A) 2.3.

Cols. 7A, 7B, 6A, 6B (1938–46), C.S.O., *Annual Abstract of Statistics*, No. 85, p. 257.

Cols. 7A, 7B, 6A, 6B (1947–53), C.S.O., *Annual Abstract of Statistics*, No. 93, 1956, p. 279.

Cols. 7A, 7B, 6A, 6B (1953–62), ibid., No. 101, p. 276.

Col. 8 (1957–62), C.S.O., *Annual Abstract of Statistics*, No. 99, p. 284.

Cols. 7A, 7B (1881, 1885, 1890, 1895, 1900, 1905), P. Woodruff, 'British savings banks', *Bankers' Magazine*, CXXXII, 1931, p. 370.

Cols. 7A+7B (1880–1910), *Annual Reports of Postmaster General.*

Col. 5 (1881–1944), and an alternative source for cols. 3 and 4, H. C. Horne, *A History of Savings Banks* (London: Oxford University Press, 1947), pp. 386–91.

Cols. A and B (1893–1913), Department of Agriculture and Technical Instruction for Ireland, *Banking, Railway and Shipping Statistics*, Ireland, H.M.S.O., pp. 5–21.

Col. C. (1920–62), the deposits of the Birmingham Municipal Bank chartered in 1919 are extracted from the annual reports.

Col. 6B (1917–37), Pember and Boyle, *British Government and Securities in the Twentieth Century*, Second edition, June 1950, p. 317.

Cols. 6A to 8 (1963–7), C.S.O. *Annual Abstract of Statistics*, relevant years.

Cols. 3 to 5 (1963–7), *Trustee Savings Bank Reports*, relevant years.

Col. 1 (1963–7), *Post Office Savings Bank Reports*, relevant years.

Col. C (1963–7), *Birmingham Municipal Savings Bank Reports*, relevant years.

Notes

[1] Post Office Savings include accrued interest.

[2] Defence Bonds are at nominal value.

[3] Figures in col. 5 included in cols. 7A, 7B.

[4] Post Office Savings Bank deposits included accounts opened in Eire before 1923.

[5] Nominal value.

[6] Five savings banks in Eire included to 1945.

[7] Figures before 1891 not complete and slightly understate actual sum on account of air-raid damage to records.

[8] Col. 2=cols. 3, 4 and 5.

[9] Col. 9=1+3+4+C.

[10] Col. 10=cols. 1+3+4+6A+7A+7B+8+C.

[11] Excludes col. 6B – accrued interest on National Savings Certificates.

TABLE (A) 3.2 **Coin and Currency in Circulation in the United Kingdom 1880–1966 (£ millions)**

Year	Coin in Circulation					Coin held by Banks				Bank of England Notes Outstanding[2]	Notes in Circulation				Total Notes and Currency Outstanding	Notes and Coin held by Banks	Currency Outside Banks[1]
	Total	Gold	Silver	Nickel, Brass	Bronze	Total	Gold	Silver	Others		Scot-tish Notes	Irish	Other Banks	Total Notes			
	1	2	3	4	5	6	7	8	9	10	11	12	13	14	15	16	17
1880	121	**103**	16·4	—	1·4	—	—	—	—	26·9	5·6	6·0	3·4	41·9	162·9	**10**	153
1881	124	**106**	16·6	—	1·4	—	—	—	—	26·3	5·6	7·2	3·3	42·4	166·4	**10**	156
1882	127	**109**	16·7	—	1·5	—	—	—	—	26·0	5·8	8·3	3·4	43·5	170·5	**11**	160
1883	129	110	17·3	—	1·5	—	—	—	—	25·6	5·9	6·7	3·3	41·5	170·5	**12**	158
1884	121	**102**	17·6	—	1·6	—	—	—	—	25·4	5·9	6·1	3·2	40·6	161·6	**11**	151
1885	118	**99**	17·6	—	1·6	—	—	—	—	24·7	5·8	5·9	3·0	39·4	157·4	**11**	146
1886	111	**92**	17·7	—	1·7	—	—	—	—	24·7	5·7	5·9	2·7	39·0	150·0	**13**	137
1887	108	**88**	18·0	—	1·7	—	—	—	—	24·4	5·8	5·5	2·5	38·2	146·2	**14**	132
1888	100	80	18·2	—	1·7	—	—	—	—	24·3	5·8	6·3	2·5	38·9	138·9	**16**	123
1889	102	**81**	19·7	—	1·8	—	—	—	—	24·4	6·2	6·7	2·4	39·7	141·7	**18**	124
1890	108	**85**	20·6	—	1·9	—	—	—	—	24·6	6·5	6·6	2·3	40·0	148·0	**18**	130
1891	116	**93**	21·0	—	2·0	—	—	—	—	25·1	6·6	6·2	2·2	40·1	156·1	**18**	138
1892	114	90	21·5	—	2·0	—	—	4·5	—	25·9	6·5	5·9	2·1	40·4	154·4	**20**	134
1893	114	**90**	22·0	—	2·1	—	—	—	—	25·9	6·5	6·1	2·0	40·5	154·5	**18**	136
1894	118	**92**	23·5	—	2·1	—	—	—	—	25·3	6·6	6·2	1·8	39·9	157·9	**22**	136
1895	117	92	22·6	—	2·1	—	—	—	—	25·8	7·0	6·1	1·7	40·6	157·6	**20**	138
1896	118	**93**	23·2	—	2·2	—	—	—	—	26·5	7·3	6·1	1·6	41·5	160·5	**12**	148
1897	121	**95**	23·5	—	2·3	—	—	—	—	27·2	7·5	6·1	1·4	42·2	163·2	**21**	142
1898	124	**98**	23·8	—	2·4	—	—	—	—	27·4	7·8	5·9	1·4	42·5	166·5	**26**	140
1899	122	95	24·1	—	2·5	—	—	—	—	27·9	7·9	6·5	1·3	43·6	165·6	**25**	141
1900	131	**104**	24·6	—	2·7	—	—	—	—	29·4	8·1	6·7	1·2	45·4	176·4	**28**	148
1901	128	**101**	24·7	—	2·8	—	—	—	—	29·6	8·0	6·3	1·1	45·0	173·0	**31**	142
1902	127	**100**	24·5	—	2·9	—	—	—	—	29·4	8·0	6·8	0·9	45·1	172·1	**34**	138
1903	127	100	24·4	—	3·0	—	—	—	—	28·9	7·8	6·8	0·7	44·2	171·2	**28**	143
1904	129	**102**	24·0	—	3·0	—	—	—	—	28·3	7·7	6·3	0·6	42·9	171·9	**33**	139
1905	{124 121	**97**	23·9	—	3·1	—	—	5·3	—	28·8	7·5	6·0	0·6	42·9	{166·9 163·9	**36**	{131 128
1906	122	—	24·2	—	3·3	—	—	4·7	—	28·9	7·6	6·4	0·5	43·4	165·4	**35**	130
1907	124	—	24·4	—	3·5	38·4	33·3	5·1	—	28·9	7·4	6·6	0·5	43·4	167·4	**34**	133
1908	125	—	24·6	—	3·6	57·2	50·4	6·8	—	28·9	7·2	6·4	0·4	42·9	167·9	**39**	129
1909	129	—	24.6	—	3·6	56·3	49·2	7·1	—	29·2	7·2	6·6	0·3	43·3	172·3	**41**	131
1910	133	113	25·2	—	3·7	51·2	44·2	7·0	—	28·3	7·1	7·2	0·3	42·8	175·8	**43**	133
1911	141	—	25·9	—	3·8	60·0	54·0	6·0	—	28·6	7·3	7·1	0·2	43·2	184·2	49	135
1912	147	—	27·2	—	4·0	66·6	60·6	6·0	—	28·8	7·7	7·2	0·2	43·9	190·9	50	141
1913	156	—	28·2	—	4·3	77·4	69·5	7·2	0·7	28·7	7·7	8·1	0·2	44·7	200·7	59	143
1914	165	—	33·9	—	4·6	91·8	82·8	8·2	0·8	60·9	9·5	10·9	0·4	81·7	246·7	**72**	175
1915	146	—	41·0	—	4·7	121·1	110·2	10·0	0·9	89·8	12·6	15·0	0·1	117·5	263·5	**61**	203
1916	149	—	48·4	—	5·1	97·9	87·1	9·8	1·0	155·5	15·5	19·1	0·1	190·2	339·2	**115**	224
1917	135	—	51·2	—	5·5	110·8	98·5	11·3	1·0	206·2	19·0	22·3	0·1	247·6	382·6	**93**	290
1918	141	—	59·1	—	6·0	9·2	—	8·2	1·0	310·8	25·1	30·9	0·2	366·8	507·8	**125**	383
1919	140	—	62·4	—	6·4	16·0	—	15·1	0·9	414·1	28·0	29·1	0·2	471·4	611·4	**170**	441
1920	99	—	63·7	—	7·0	16·0	—	14·9	1·1	449·2	29·4	{24·7 7·7	0·2	{503·5 486·5	{602·5 585·5	{**139** 127	{463 459
1921	94	—	64·1	—	7·5	19·1	—	17·3	1·8	436·7	25·2	5·2	0·2	467·3	561·3	153	408
1922	91	—	60·9	—	7·6	18·3	—	16·2	2·1	400·4	23·3	5·0	0·2	428·9	519·9	144	376
1923	89	—	56·0	—	7·4	16·3	—	14·1	2·2	387·7	22·1	5·0	0·2	415·0	504·0	138	366
1924	89	—	55·9	—	7·4	16·1	—	14·1	2·0	390·8	22·2	4·9	0·1	418·0	507·0	136	371
1925	87	—	56·8	—	7·3	16·6	—	14·7	1·9	383·9	21·7	4·4	0·1	410·1	497·1	135	362
1926	88	—	56·9	—	7·3	17·6	—	15·7	1·9	376·4	20·7	4·1	0·1	401·3	489·3	133	356
1927	86	—	56·8	—	7·5	18·0	—	16·1	1·9	374·6	21·2	4·0	0·1	399·9	485·9	134	352
1928	84	—	58·4	—	7·6	15·6	—	13·7	1·9	371·9	21·1	3·9	0·1	397·0	481·0	134	347
1929	84	—	57·0	—	7·7	14·7	—	12·7	2·0	362·3	21·4	3·7	0·1	387·5	471·5	129	343

Year	1	2	3	4	5	6	7	8	9	10	11	12	13	14	15	16	17
1931	78	—	59·0	—	7·8	18·2	—	15·8	2·4	354·8	21·4	3·2	0·1	379·5	457·5	119	339
1932	69	—	58·7	—	7·8	19·2	—	16·7	2·5	359·8	21·0	3·2	0·1	384·1	453·1	115	338
1933	71	—	58·6	—	7·7	17·4	—	15·1	2·3	371·2	19·2	3·2	0·1	393·7	464·7	121	344
1934	72	—	59·6	—	7·7	16·1	—	14·0	2·1	378·5	21·4	3·4	0·1	403·4	475·4	123	352
1935	69	—	60·4	—	7·8	16·4	—	14·4	2·0	394·7	21·7	3·6	0·1	420·1	489·1	128	361
1936	70	—	62·1	—	8·2	18·0	—	15·9	2·1	431·2	23·1	3·7	0·1	458·1	528·1	135	393
1937	74	—	64·5	0·5	8·6	20·3	—	17·9	2·4	479·6	23·5	3·9	0·1	507·1	581·1	141	440
1938	76	—	66·0	0·7	9·0	21·4	—	18·4	3·0	485·6	23·8	3·9	0·1	513·4	589·4	144	445
1939	79	—	70·7	0·8	9·2	20·3	—	17·3	3·0	507·3	26·2	4·6	0·1	538·2	617·2	155	462
1940	86	—	75·6	1·0	9·2	20·1	—	17·2	2·9	574·7	30·2	6·0	0·2	611·1	697·1	151	546
1941	93	—	80·9	1·7	9·2	22·7	—	20·2	2·5	653·9	38·5	8·6	0·2	701·2	794·2	176	618
1942	101	—	90·8	2·9	9·2	22·6	—	19·9	2·7	808·4	49·3	10·8	0·2	868·7	969·7	193	777
1943	112	—	96·7	4·1	9·2	23·5	—	20·8	2·7	966·1	57·1	11·7	0·2	1035·1	1147·1	210	937
1944	120	—	103·2	5·0	9·4	20·8	—	18·1	2·7	1135·5	63·3	11·5	0·2	1210·5	1330·5	222	1108
1945	128	—	110·3	5·3	9·7	18·7	—	15·9	2·8	1283·2	65·8	10·7	0·2	1359·9	1487·9	236	1252
1946	130	—	118·0	5·3	9·9	21·0	—	17·9	3·1	1357·6	70·4	10·2	0·2	1438·4	1568·4	238	1330
1947	135	—	123·1	5·2	10·0	27·5	—	24·2	3·3	1383·3	69·6	8·9	0·2	1462·0	1597·0	254	1343
1948	148	—	144·5	5·2	10·0	22·4	—	18·4	4·0	1253·5	67·0	7·8	0·1	1328·4	1476·4	250	1226
1949	160	—	144·5	5·1	10·0	38·3	—	34·0	4·3	1270·4	69·0	6·6	0·1	1346·1	1506·1	266	1240
1950	156	—	141·1	5·0	10·0	37·7	—	33·2	4·5	1283·6	71·1	5·8	0·1	1360·6	1516·6	274	1243
1951	151	—	140·1	5·0	9·6	34·2	—	30·1	4·1	1342·4	77·3	5·4	0·1	1425·2	1576·2	284	1292
1952	151	—	139·8	5·0	9·5	35·0	—	31·0	4·0	1435·2	85·6	5·4	0·1	1526·3	1677·3	305	1372
1953	155	—	146·3	5·5	9·3	35·4	—	31·2	4·2	1531·9	92·3	4·2	0·1	1628·5	1783·5	321	1462
1954	159	—	149·6	5·9	9·0	37·5	—	33·2	4·3	1630·3	97·7	4·3	0·1	1732·4	1891·4	339	1552
1955	163	—	154·1	6·4	8·8	37·7	—	33·5	4·2	1760·0	104·8	4·2	0·1	1869·1	2032·1	373	1659
1956	169	—	163·4	6·8	8·7	36·9	—	32·9	4·0	1875·1	112·8	6·0	0·1	1994·0	2163·0	395	1768
1957	176	—	167·7	6·9	8·5	39·9	—	36·0	3·9	1966·3	118·5	5·9	0·1	2090·8	2266·8	425	1842
1958	182	—	169·7	7·1	8·3	45·3	—	41·3	4·0	2034·6	119·7	5·4	0·1	2159·8	2341·8	438	1904
1959	184	—	171·5	7·3	8·3	46·8	—	42·8	4·0	2104·5	122·4	5·2	0·1	2232·2	2416·2	448	1968
1960	187	—	175·9	7·4	8·3	42·6	—	38·9	3·7	2210·7	125·3	4·9	0·1	2341·0	2528·0	467	2061
1961	198	—	187·1	8·5	8·4	43·4	—	39·9	3·5	2306·2	127·8	5·0	0·1	2439·1	2637·1	490	2147
1962	209	—	195·3	9·0	8·8	48·6	—	44·9	3·7	2327·4	123·1	4·7	0	2455·2	2664·2	508	2156
1963	209	—	194·2	9·2	9·1	52·9	—	48·9	4·0	2398·2	125·9	4·7	0	2528·8	2737·8	530	2208
1964	217	—	202·4	9·7	9·7	57·4	—	53·2	4·2	2561·7	129·4	4·6	0	2695·7	2912·7	583	2330
1965	228	—	214·1	9·9	10·4	59·9	—	55·8	4·1	2727·4	132·2	5·0	0	2864·6	3092·6	609	2484
1966	244	—	227·8	10·3	11·0	66·1	—	61·9	4·2	2892·5	130·9	6·1	0	3029·5	3273·5	641	2632

Sources

Col. 1 = sum of cols. 2 to 5 (1880–1905); col. 6 = sum of cols. 7 to 9; col. 14 = sum of cols. 10 to 13; col. 15 = col. 1 + col. 14; and col. 17 = col. 15 − col. 16.

Col. 2 (1883, 1888, 1892, 1895, 1899, 1903, 1910), cols. 3, 4, 5 (1880–1962), col. 7 (1907–17), col. 8 (1892, 1905–62), col. 9 (1913–62), were kindly provided by A. Dowling, Esq., of the Royal Mint. It should be noted that some of these statistics may be found in the annual *Reports* of the Royal Mint, and from the pre-1914 Board of Trade, *Statistical Abstract for the UK*.

Col. 1 (1905–31), Bank of England, *Statistical Summary*, Nov. 1932, p. 12. (1932–53), E. Coppieters, *English Bank Note Circulation 1694–1954*, Louvain: I.E.S.R., 1955, p. 100. (1954–62), C.S.O., *Annual Abstract of Statistics*, relevant issues.

Col. 2 (1880–2, 1884–7, 1889–91, 1893–4, 1896–8, 1900–2, 1904, 1905) are estimates. The net gold coin issued (after withdrawals) was obtained from the Mint and adjusted for the import or export of gold coin for the relevant years; these figures were obtained from the Board of Trade, *Statistical Abstract*. These 'net' stock figures were spliced in with the Mint's estimates noted above.

Col. 10 (1880–1928), *Bankers' Almanac and Year Book*, 1930–1, No. 86, p. 2409. This series is identical to those in Mitchell and Deane's *Abstract of British Historical Statistics*.

Col. 10 (1929–39), col. 13 (1880–1939), Mitchell and Deane, *Abstract of British Historical Statistics* (Cambridge University Press, 1962), pp. 445–6. Col. 10 (1940–62), C.S.O., *Annual Abstract of Statistics*.

Cols. 11, 12, 13 (1880–1962), extracted from *The Economist's* 'Banking Number' and 'Banking Supplement', and after 1950 from the Bank of England *Quarterly Bulletin* and the *Bankers' Almanac*.

Col. 16 (1921–62), Note Holdings of Banks (1921–38), Bank of England *Statistical Summary*, Jan. 1939, p. 4. (1939–62), C.S.O. *Annual Abstract*, No. 84, p. 235; No. 88, p. 283; No. 101, p. 301.

Col. 16 (1880–1920), estimated on the following basis. Banks' cash as recorded in annual balance sheets × $\hat{\lambda}$ Where $\hat{\lambda} = 0{\cdot}562$, and:

$$\hat{\lambda} = \frac{\sum_{1921}^{1925} \text{Actual Bank Currency Holdings}}{\sum_{1921}^{1925} \text{Balance Sheet Bank Cash}} = 0.562.$$

Cols. 1, 10 and 16 (1963–6), C.S.O. *Annual Abstract of Statistics*.

Cols. 3–5, 8 and 9 (1963–6), *Reports of the Royal Mint 1962–1967*.

Cols. 11–13 (1963–6), from *Bankers' Almanac and Yearbook*.

Notes

[1] Currency outside the banks is probably biased upwards as the currency and coin holdings of foreign banks and British banks mainly operating abroad have not been included in col. 16.

[2] Includes Treasury currency notes from their issue in 1914. These notes were not issued after 1928.

TABLE (A) 3.3 **United Kingdom Money Supply and Households' Liquid Assets 1880–1966[2] (£ millions)**

Year	*Gross Deposits All UK Commercial Banks 31 Dec.*	*Annual Average of Inter-Bank Deposits*	*Annual Average of Private Deposits at Bank of England*	*Net Deposits All Banks in UK*	*Annual Average of Net Coin and Currency Outside Banks*	*Net Money Supply UK*	*Savings Banks' Deposits*	*Building Society Shares and Deposits*	*Total Quasi-Money*	*Defence Bonds, National Savings Certificates, Premium Savings Bonds*[1]	*Insurance Company Funds. Life 31 Dec.*	*Total Potential Encashable Assets*	*Cols. 6/12*	*Cols. 9/12*
	1	2	3	4	5	6	7	8	9	10	11	12	13	14
1880	342	**8**	**8**	342	153	495	80	50	625	1	124	750	0·66	0·83
1881	360	**9**	**8**	359	156	515	83	54	652	1	128	781	0·66	0·83
1882	377	**9**	**8**	376	160	536	86	61	683	2	132	817	0·66	0·84
1883	392	**10**	**8**	390	158	548	90	63	701	2	136	839	0·65	0·84
1884	406	**9**	**8**	405	151	556	94	63	713	3	140	856	0·65	0·83
1885	414	**10**	**9**	413	146	559	97	64	720	3	143	866	0·65	0·83
1886	414	**11**	**8**	411	138	549	101	65	715	3	146	864	0·63	0·83
1887	425	**11**	**8**	422	132	554	105	66	725	4	150	879	0·63	0·82
1888	454	**12**	**8**	450	123	573	109	65	747	4	155	906	0·63	0·82
1889	479	**13**	**8**	474	124	598	112	64	774	5	161	940	0·64	0·82
1890	499	**13**	**8**	494	130	624	116	64	804	6	166	976	0·64	0·82
1891	524	**14**	**10**	520	138	658	119	62	839	6	171	1016	0·65	0·83
1891	595	**15**	**10**	590	138	728	119	62	909	6	171	1086	0·67	0·84
1892	608	**16**	**11**	603	134	737	123	59	919	7	176	1102	0·66	0·83
1893	600	**15**	**10**	595	136	731	127	53	911	7	183	1101	0·66	0·83
1894	632	**18**	**11**	625	136	761	137	52	950	7	190	1147	0·66	0·83
1895	677	**18**	**14**	673	138	811	148	50	1009	7	199	1215	0·67	0·83
1896	701	**18**	**17**	700	148	848	160	51	1059	8	209	1276	0·66	0·83
1897	722	**19**	**13**	716	142	858	169	52	1079	8	220	1307	0·66	0·83
1898	749	**20**	**13**	742	140	882	178	53	1113	8	229	1350	0·65	0·82
1899	774	**20**	**13**	767	141	908	186	55	1149	11	238	1398	0·65	0·82
1900	799	**22**	**14**	791	148	939	192	55	1186	13	246	1445	0·63	0·82
1901	797	**23**	**14**	788	142	930	197	56	1183	14	255	1452	0·64	0·81
1902	809	**24**	**14**	799	138	937	202	58	1197	16	265	1478	0·63	0·81
1903	790	**22**	**14**	782	143	925	203	60	1188	17	274	1479	0·63	0·80
1904	802	**23**	**14**	793	139	932	206	61	1199	18	285	1502	0·62	0·80
1905	828	**25**	**14**	817	131 128	948 945	210	64	1222 1219	19	296	1537 1534	0·62 0·62	0·80 0·79
1906	854	**25**	**15**	844	130	974	215	65	1254	21	306	1581	0·62	0·79
1907	862	**25**	**15**	852	133	985	217	66	1268	21	315	1604	0·61	0·79
1908	884	**27**	**14**	871	129	1000	221	67	1288	22	326	1636	0·61	0·79
1909	900	**28**	**14**	886	131	1017	227	69	1313	23	336	1672	0·61	0·79
1910	939	**28**	**14**	925	133	1058	232	70	1360	25	349	1734	0·61	0·79
1911	978	**30**	**14**	962	135	1097	242	58	1397	26	360	1783	0·62	0·78
1912	1012	**31**	**14**	995	141	1136	249	59	1444	27	370	1841	0·62	0·78
1913	1059	**33**	**14**	1040	143	1183	256	60	1499	27	382	1908	0·62	0·79
1914	1163	**49**	**26**	1140	175	1315	260	61	1636	55	390	2081	0·63	0·79
1915	1272	**51**	**34**	1255	203	1458	253	60	1771	106	390	2267	0·64	0·78
1916	1473	**71**	**33**	1435	224	1659	265	60	1984	226	395	2605	0·64	0·76
1917	1737	**71**	**43**	1709	290	1999	270	59	2328	327	396	3051	0·66	0·76
1918	2024	**82**	**41**	1983	383	2366	310	63	2739	454	411	3604	0·66	0·76
1919	2398	**93**	**41**	2346	441	2787	353	71	3211	502	426	4139	0·67	0·78
1920	2538	**88**	43	2493	463	2956	358	80	3394	530	438	4362	0·68	0·78
1920	2398	**83**	43	2358	459	2817	359	80	3256	530	438	4224	0·67	0·77
1921	2420	**86**	37	2371	408	2779	358	88	3225	593	457	4275	0·65	0·75
1922	2261	**78**	38	2221	376	2597	369	100	3066	621	480	4167	0·62	0·74
1923	2210	**80**	40	2170	366	2536	380	115	3031	644	506	4181	0·61	0·72
1924	2194	**86**	33	2141	371	2512	393	134	3039	643	533	4215	0·60	0·72
1925	2184	**92**	41	2133	362	2495	403	155	3053	660	570	4283	0·58	0·71
1926	2223	**90**	39	2172	356	2528	402	178	3108	681	606	4395	0·58	0·71
1927	2275	**92**	37	2220	352	2572	407	206	3185	675	640	4500	0·57	0·71
1928	2352	**97**	37	2292	347	2639	419	249	3307	674	674	4655	0·57	0·71
1929	2315	**97**	37	2255	343	2598	421	289	3308	668	710	4686	0·55	0·71

1931	2226	**82**	38	2182	339	2521	445	392	3358	671	754	4783	0·53	0·70
1932	2510	**74**	34	2470	338	2808	476	442	3726	661	793	5180	0·54	0·72
1933	2485	**77**	40	2448	344	2792	515	471	3778	664	833	5275	0·53	0·72
1934	2526	**82**	37	2481	352	2833	556	522	3911	670	868	5449	0·52	0·72
1935	2673	**86**	38	2625	361	2986	609	562	4157	673	903	5733	0·52	0·73
1936	2856	**96**	39	2799	393	3192	669	609	4470	680	943	6093	0·52	0·73
1937	2888	**105**	37	2820	440	3260	722	661	4643	719	984	6346	0·51	0·73
1938	2810	**102**	36	2744	445	3189	778	704	4671	725	1023	6419	0·50	0·73
1939	2962	**114**	38	2886	462	3348	835	711	4894	841	1042	6777	0·49	0·72
1940	3360	**147**	47	3260	546	3806	963	695	5464	1200	1054	7718	0·49	0·71
1941	3974	**183**	53	3844	618	4462	1188	688	6338	1628	1081	9049	0·49	0·70
1942	4345	**198**	50	4197	777	4974	1433	691	7098	1975	1115	10188	0·49	0·70
1943	4840	**210**	56	4686	937	5623	1747	708	8078	2382	1153	11613	0·48	0·70
1944	5440	**223**	56	5273	1108	6381	2086	734	9201	2756	1193	13151	0·49	0·70
1945	5822	**241**	55	5636	1252	6888	2453	760	10101	3084	1244	14429	0·48	0·70
1946	6764	**282**	55	6537	1330	7867	2749	810	11426	3311	1313	16050	0·48	0·71
1947	7074	**316**	89	6847	1343	8190	2747	882	11819	3341	1391	16551	0·49	0·71
1948	7313	**339**	93	7067	1226	8293	2830	961	12084	3303	1478	16865	0·49	0·72
1949	7306	**344**	95	7057	1240	8297	2891	1058	12246	3289	1573	17108	0·48	0·72
1950	7476	**346**	94	7224	1243	8467	2930	1168	12565	3291	1675	17531	0·48	0·72
1951	7465	**394**	89	7160	1292	8452	2892	1265	12609	3281	1786	17676	0·48	0·71
1952	7590	389	74	7275	1372	8647	2853	1384	12884	3269	1917	18070	0·48	0·71
1953	7848	402	70	7516	1462	8978	2803	1541	13322	3264	2078	18664	0·48	0·71
1954	8175	442	67	7800	1552	9352	2835	1757	13944	3348	2273	19565	0·48	0·71
1955	7783	459	68	7392	1659	9051	2840	1949	13840	3356	2484	19680	0·46	0·70
1956	7806	461	73	7418	1768	9186	2869	2103	14158	3432	2681	20271	0·45	0·70
1957	8102	497	74	7697	1842	9521	2903	2274	14698	3434	2907	21039	0·45	0·70
1958	8367	507	73	7933	1904	9837	2891	2457	15185	3714	3211	22110	0·44	0·69
1959	8888	538	65	8415	1968	10383	3004	2737	16124	3966	3557	23647	0·44	0·68
1960	9043	598	66	8511	2061	10572	3110	2943	16625	4194	3951	24770	0·43	0·67
1961	9172	608	71	8635	2147	10782	3324	3146	17252	4256	4384	25892	0·42	0·67
1962	9507	647	71	8931	2156	11087	3366	3507	17960	4382	4840	27182	0·41	0·66
1963	10189	680	73	9582	2208	11790	3568	4004	19362	4460	5408	29230	0·40	0·66
1964	10608	787	79	9900	2330	12230	3788	4512	20530	4425	6046	31001	0·39	0·66
1965	11325	818	90	10597	2484	13081	3938	5143	22162	4118	6680	32960	0·40	0·67
1966	11402	861	107	10648	2633	13281	3973	5894	23153	3843	7315	34311	0·38	0·68

Sources

Col. 1 (1880–66), derived from end-of-year balance sheet figures of UK banks found in *The Economist*'s 'Banking Number' and 'Banking Supplement' up to 1950, and in the post-1950 period from the Bank of England *Quarterly Bulletin* and the *Bankers' Almanac and Year Book*.

Col. 2 (1952–66), C.S.O., *Annual Abstract of Statistics*, Nos. 99, 101, 105. (1921–51), partial estimates; based on 1936–51, C.S.O., *Annual Abstract of Statistics*, Nos. 37, 39; 1921–35, Board of Trade, *Statistical Abstract for the United Kingdom*, Nos. 72, 81. The recorded data for the 1936–51 period cover only inter-bank deposits of the London Clearing Banks. As a consequence, these were spliced to the post-1951 series by a factor $\lambda = 1{\cdot}70$.

$$\lambda = \frac{\text{Recorded Inter-Bank Deposits and Transit Items in 1952}}{\text{Recorded London Clearing Bank Inter-Bank Deposits in 1952}}.$$

On the same grounds, the 1921–35 data were adjusted by multiplying by a factor $\theta = 1{\cdot}78$, to reflect this and the exclusion of the District Banks in the pre-1936 period. For the 1880–1920 period, the reported 'Bank Cash' figures given in the banks' balance sheets were used as the basis. These were multiplied by a factor $\alpha = 0{\cdot}22$.

$$\alpha \text{ estimated} = \frac{\sum_{1921}^{1926} \text{Inter-Bank Deposits reported by Board of Trade}}{\sum_{1921}^{1926} \text{Bank Cash as recorded on Balance Sheets of London Clearing Banks}}.$$

Col. 3 (1880–1966), see col. 9B, Table (A) 1.12 (Bank of England Annual Balance Sheet). The pre-1920 series was adjusted to exclude certain bankers' deposits.

Col. 4 = col. 1 + col. 3 − col. 2.

Col. 5 (1880–1966), see col. 17, Table (A) 3.2, 'Coin and currency in circulation in the United Kingdom'.

Col. 6 = col. 4 + col. 5.

Col. 7 (1880–1966), deposits of the Post Office Savings Bank, the trustee savings banks and Birmingham Municipal Savings Bank derived from the *Reports of the Postmaster General*, *Reports of the Inspection Committee of Trustee Savings Banks*, and from the *Annual Reports* of the Birmingham Municipal Bank. As the Birmingham Municipal Bank strikes its balance sheet on 31 Mar., its registered deposits in that year were assumed to be the same as those on 31 Dec. in the previous year.

Col. 8 (1880–1966), extracted from the Board of Trade *Statistical Abstract* and the *Building Societies Year Book*.

Col. 9 = col. 6 + col. 7 + col. 8.

Col. 10 (1880–1966), extracted from the Board of Trade *Statistical Abstract* and the C.S.O. *Statistical Abstract*. The amounts of National Savings Bonds and Certificates are also recorded as of 31 Mar. Here too, the 31 Mar. positions were taken to reflect the level outstanding on 31 Dec. in the previous year.

Col. 11 (1880–1966), extracted from the Board of Trade *Insurance Company Returns*.

Col. 12 = col. 9 + col. 10 + col. 11.

Col. 13 = col. 6/col. 12.

Col. 14 = col. 9/col. 12.

Notes

[1] Includes accrued interest earned on National Savings Certificates.

[2] The data in the various columns were generally recorded as of the end of the calendar year, 31 Dec., or as of 31 Mar. in the following year. However, the data in columns 2, 3 and 5 are annual averages of the amounts outstanding on a certain day in each week or each month. As a result, cols. 5, 9 and 11 do not reflect the actual money stock, the stock of quasi-money or the stock of encashable assets as of 31 Dec. in each year.

TABLE (A) 3.4 **UK Financial Institutions – Credit Series 1880–1966[1] (Funds in £ millions)**

Year-End Approx. 31 Dec.	Bank Loans and Advances	Total Assets of Various Institutions									Consolidated Accounts all Financial Institutions				Commercial Banks and Discount Cos.	
		Commercial Banks and Discount Cos.[7]	Non-Bank Financial Institutions	Post Office Savings Bank	Trustee Savings Banks	Birmingham Municipal Bank	Building Societies	Insurance Companies	Various Registered Friendly Societies	Hire-Purchase Cos.[8]	Total Assets	Total Mortgages	Total Gross Private Credit[5]	Total Net Private Credit[6]	Total Gross Private Credit[5]	Total Net Private Credit[6]
	I	II	III	IV	V	VI	VII	VIII	IX	X	XI	XII	XIII	XIV	XV	XVI
1880	219	432	291	35	47	—	54	155	—	—	723	112	—	—	318	308
1881	222	453	304	37	48	—	59	160	—	—	757	116	—	—	330	320
1882	242	475	321	40	49	—	67	165	—	—	796	124	—	—	354	347
1883	239	492	332	44	49	—	69	170	—	—	824	126	—	—	365	352
1884	255	509	339	45	50	—	69	175	—	—	848	127	—	—	380	371
1885	248	517	349	49	51	—	70	179	—	—	866	129	—	—	382	369
1886	252	517	359	53	52	—	70	184	—	—	876	130	—	—	378	366
1887	259	527	370	57	52	—	71	190	—	—	897	132	—	—	387	376
1888	268	559	379	61	52	—	70	196	—	—	938	131	—	—	406	395
1889	282	586	390	65	51	—	70	204	—	—	976	132	—	—	420	411
1890	290	611	399	69	49	—	70	211	—	—	1010	136	690	649	437	424
1891	307	641	406	73	48	—	67	218	—	—	1047	135	711	668	456	443
1891[2]	342	760	406	73	48	—	67	218	—	—	1166	135	798	748	543	523
1892	339	777	414	79	48	—	64	223	—	—	1191	133	808	756	550	529
1893	347	767	421	84	48	—	58	231	—	—	1188	129	800	748	543	525
1894	345	802	441	95	49	—	57	240	—	—	1243	126	822	768	560	540
1895	368	853	463	106	51	—	55	251	—	—	1316	126	874	817	604	583
1896	392	872	493	120	53	—	56	264	—	—	1365	125	912	855	630	610
1897	406	893	516	129	54	—	56	277	—	—	1409	125	940	877	646	624
1898	421	925	537	134	56	—	58	289	—	—	1462	128	971	905	665	642
1899	442	950	547	130	57	—	60	300	—	—	1497	128	1007	938	689	665
1900	456	983	562	134	57	—	60	311	—	—	1545	131	1022	958	695	671
1901	443	980	575	135	58	—	61	321	—	—	1555	134	1016	939	680	653
1902	442	994	598	139	59	—	63	337	—	—	1592	137	1033	952	682	652
1903	455	972	623	146	59	—	65	353	—	—	1595	142	1054	973	682	657
1904	450	985	642	149	59	—	67	367	—	—	1627	148	1057	980	670	651
1905	447	1018	665	152	60	—	69	384	—	—	1683	154	1099	1013	690	664
1906	470	1048	684	156	61	—	71	396	—	—	1732	158	1141	1053	718	693
1907	479	1058	705	158	61	—	72	414	—	—	1763	164	1179	1086	735	710
1908	464	1080	725	161	62	—	73	429	—	—	1805	165	1197	1104	739	713
1909	469	1098	751	165	64	—	75	447	—	—	1849	169	1229	1134	752	729
1910	508	1137	777	169	65	—	76	467	—	—	1914	171	1264	1164	793	765
1911	511	1175	799	177	67	—	64	491	—	—	1974	177	1295	1191	815	787
1912	532	1219	826	182	69	—	64	511	—	—	2045	180	1353	1254	857	834
1913	552	1272	853	187	71	—	65	530	—	—	2125	186	1403	1283	891	850
1914	581	1361	880	191	72	—	66	551	—	—	2241	187	1426	1313	903	871
1915	535	1480	887	187	69	—	66	565	—	—	2367	181	1255	1143	779	747
1916	527	1701	917	197	71	—	65	584	—	—	2618	171	1261	1127	786	754
1917	628	1991	938	204	69	—	64	601	—	—	2929	165	1370	1255	923	890
1918	641	2301	1016	235	77	—	69	635	—	—	3317	163	1455	1337	1020	981
1919	1055	2704	1107	267	89	[illegible]	77	674	—	—	3811	164	1815	1692	1377	1348

1920	1177	2880	1160	267	94	—	87	712	—	—	4040	173	2080	1930	1619	1571
1920[3]	1115	2713	1316	267	94	1	87	748	118	1	4029	192	2092	1927	1542	1496
1921	991	2731	1371	264	95	2	95	795	119	1	4102	202	1989	1815	1385	1348
1922	940	2567	1448	268	101	3	107	840	128	1	4015	219	1881	1710	1260	1224
1923	978	2521	1542	273	107	4	125	893	139	1	4063	236	1977	1815	1311	1275
1924	1039	2530	1633	281	111	6	145	935	153	2	4163	263	2123	1939	1389	1349
1925	1099	2520	1749	286	115	7	169	1005	165	2	4269	301	2257	2073	1430	1386
1926	1146	2571	1844	284	115	8	194	1066	174	3	4415	340	2396	2205	1474	1432
1927	1162	2630	1952	285	119	9	223	1127	186	3	4582	385	2525	2329	1495	1451
1928	1199	2712	2086	289	126	10	269	1188	201	3	4798	429	2702	2487	1545	1494
1929	1223	2676	2209	285	130	12	313	1252	213	4	4885	494	2851	2623	1558	1502
1930	1125	2770	2341	290	139	13	371	1293	229	6	5111	561	2897	2667	1483	1433
1931	1072	2569	2464	289	150	14	419	1341	244	7	5033	618	2830	2588	1338	1278
1932	924	2865	2612	306	162	16	469	1389	264	6	5477	670	2776	2535	1202	1155
1933	881	2842	2764	327	179	17	501	1450	283	7	5606	695	2796	2543	1144	1093
1934	917	2877	2949	355	191	19	556	1516	304	8	5826	758	2968	2696	1196	1135
1935	939	3039	3140	390	207	22	602	1587	323	9	6179	817	3186	2902	1285	1222
1936	1016	3231	3353	432	222	24	656	1665	343	11	6584	894	3396	3101	1341	1284
1937	1124	3271	3568	471	235	27	710	1745	364	16	6839	959	3675	3365	1471	1414
1938	1122	3187	3775	509	250	29	759	1824	386	18	6962	1025	3795	3463	1459	1397
1939	1140	3360	3925	551	260	32	774	1883	407	18	7285	1053	3873	3559	1472	1416
1940	1034	3767	4105	654	284	36	756	1934	429	12	7872	1013	3615	3476	1351	1301
1941	921	4409	4421	823	332	43	749	2009	457	8	8830	971	3466	3232	1200	1139
1942	885	4837	4792	1005	388	51	753	2101	486	8	9629	921	3347	3080	1100	1045
1943	853	5365	5261	1241	458	60	770	2204	519	9	10626	878	3338	3034	1069	1026
1944	870	6033	5773	1494	539	68	795	2316	552	9	11806	852	3384	3033	1101	1050
1945	930	6428	6267	1777	619	74	824	2374	590	9	12695	848	3500	3118	1222	1169
1946	1118	7517	6787	1982	688	79	877	2526	621	14	14304	909	3949	3517	1476	1424
1947	1372	7837	7125	1943	751	82	955	2718	653	23	14962	1018	4505	4014	1760	1689
1948	1542	8222	7516	1948	820	84	1038	2904	693	29	15738	1152	5202	4316	2360	1934
1949	1732	8277	7959	1948	879	86	1142	3148	724	32	16236	1302	5583	4692	2447	2075
1950	1882	8535	8372	1934	932	87	1256	3370	756	37	16907	1460	6158	5112	2619	2214
1951	2161	8415	8699	1876	956	86	1357	3590	792	42	17114	1620	6830	5672	3025	2528
1952	1940	8536	9039	1812	978	86	1478	3809	830	46	17575	1789	6830	5746	2681	2175
1953	1877	8796	9483	1747	993	87	1643	4086	875	52	18279	1989	7233	6071	2672	2134
1954	2080	9218	10149	1727	1045	89	1867	4436	920	65	19367	2233	8186	6881	3030	2401
1955	2034	8772	10827	1700	1080	89	2065	4823	968	102	19599	2517	8799	7408	2970	2379
1956	2139	8738	11447	1688	1121	87	2230	5207	1011	103	20185	2785	9463	8014	3079	2508
1957	2092	9081	12112	1677	1168	85	2415	5580	1061	126	21193	3030	10154	8490	3122	2450
1958	2472	9427	12830	1646	1195	83	2621	5999	1120	166	22257	3246	11225	9390	3570	2844
1959	3254	10075	13915	1679	1270	85	2907	6554	1177	243	23990	3552	13072	11037	4522	3720
1960	3804	10264	15048	1710	1347	87	3166	7156	1248	334	25312	3935	14585	12305	5134	4259
1961	3855	10426	16300	1737	1436	88	3437	7854	1302	446	26726	4335	15674	13452	5153	4418
1962	4198	10812	17449	1760	1555	90	3815	8464	1329	436	28261	4767	16964	14618	5547	4793
1963[9]	4892	11628	19010	1792	1727	93	4331	9211	1406	450	30638	5269	19120	16477	6421	5591
1964	5500	12022	20816	1814	1926	95	4863	10102	1471	545	32838	6151	21477	18672	7246	6323
1965	5667	12081	22801	1823	2072	96	5532	10979	1577	722	34882	6854	23609	20447	7617	6569
1966	5654	12992	24529	1740	2204	95	6306	11788	1647	749	37525	7783	25134	21798	7471	6631

Notes to Table (A) 3.4 overleaf.

Notes to Table (A) 3.4

Sources

Col. I (1880–1966). Table (A) 1.1, col. 16.

Col. II (1880–1942). The sum of col. 3 in Table (A) 1.1 and col. VI in Table (A) 1.13.

Col. II (1943–66). The sum of col. 3 in Table (A) 1.1 and cols. IV+V+VI in Table (A) 1.13.

Col. III (1880–1920). The sum of cols. 4 (Table (A) 2.2), 8+12 (Table (A) 2.3), col. II (Table (A) 2.4), col. 1 (Table (A) 2.5).

Col. III (1920–66). The sum of cols. 4 (Table (A) 2.2), 8+12 (Table (A) 2.3), col. II (Table (A) 2.4), col. 1 (Table (A) 2.5)+col. V (Table (A) 2.1), Part 7, col. A (Table (A) 2.8), and col. 1 (Table (A) 2.10).

Col. IV (1880–1966), Table (A) 2.2, Col. 4.

Col. V (1880–1966), Table (A) 2.3, Cols. 8+12.

Col. VI (1920–1966), Table (A) 2.1, Col. V.

Col. VII (1880–1966), Table (A) 2.4, Col. II.

Col. VIII (1880–1966), Table (A) 2.5, Col. I.

Col. IX (1920–1966), Table (A) 2.8, Part 7, Col. A.

Col. X (1920–1966), Table (A) 2.10, Col. 1.

Col. XI (1880–1966), sum of cols. II+III of this Table.

Col. XII (1880–1966), sum of col. XI (Table (A) 2.1), col. 14 (Table (A) 2.3), col. IX (Table (A) 2.4), col. 2 (Table (A) 2.5), and col. B, Part 7 (Table (A) 2.8).

Col. XIII (1880–1966), the sum of the residuals found as follows: [Table (A) 2.1, cols. V−(VI+VIIB+VIII+IX+X)]+[Table (A) 2.3, cols. 8+12−(9+10+13B+15)]+[Table (A) 3.4, cols. II−(XII+XIV)]+[Table (A) 2.5, cols. 1−(5+6+7+12)]+[Table (A) 2.8, Part 7, col. C]+[Table (A) 2.10, col. 1−(9B+8)]+col. XV of this table.

Col. XIV (1880–1966), col. XVI of this table plus the following amounts: [Table (A) 2.1, cols. VIIA+XI−VIIB]+[Table (A) 2.3, cols. 13C+14+16]+[Table (A) 2.4, cols. (IX+XI−XII)+[Table (A) 2.5, cols. 2+3+4+8+9+10]+[Table (A) 2.8 Parts 1–6, cols. C+F−D]+[Table (A) 2. 10, cols. 9A−9B+7].

Col. XV (1880–1966), Commercial Banks' and Discount Companies' Gross Private Credit, is the residual sum of [Table (A) 1.1, col. 3−(cols. 10B+13+11+15)]+(Table (A) 1.13, cols. VI−(cols. VII+VIIIB+IXB)].

Col. XVI (1880–1966), Commercial Banks' and Discount Companies' Net Private Credit, is the sum of [Table (A) 1.1, cols. 12+14+16−13−15]+[Table (A) 1.13, cols. VIIIA+IXA+X−VIIIB−IXB].

Notes

[1] The series composed as follows: commercial banks and discount houses: *The Economist*'s series, 'Banks of England and Wales', the banks of Ireland and Northern Ireland, the banks of Scotland, the Yorkshire Penny Bank, Co-operative Wholesale Society Bank, and such banks as British Mutual and Erlangers and those banks incorporated in *The Economist*'s Private Bank Series. The discount houses consist of the following sample – Alexanders, National and Union of London, and their joint total assets amounted to 57 per cent of the total assets of the members of the London Discount Houses Association in the 1950s. Other financial institutions: building societies of Great Britain, Post Office Savings Bank, trustee savings banks, insurance companies based in the UK, Birmingham Municipal Bank, and selected Registered Friendly Societies (Registered Trade Unions, Friendly Societies, Collecting Societies, Railway Savings Banks, Superannuation Funds), and a sample of eight hire-purchase companies from 1920.

[2] In 1891 *The Economist* Private Banks, the three discount houses, the Yorkshire Penny and Co-operative Wholesale Society Bank were incorporated in the series.

[3] In 1920 the banking series was adjusted by the exclusion of the Southern Ireland banks. In the same year, both the Registered Friendly Societies and the hire-purchase companies were incorporated in the series, and from the same year the insurance company figures have been adjusted to reflect the non-life UK-based insurance company assets which were previously excluded.

[4] The slight discontinuity in the total net private credit series in 1951 is due to the availability of a greater breakdown of the superannuation funds registered with the Registry of Friendly Societies.

[5] Total Private Credit: this was calculated by subtracting from the consolidated total assets of each set of institutions, the cash, the Treasury Bills, the Government and Government-guaranteed stock and such loans, which as in the case of insurance companies, were clearly made abroad, and summing the residual totals.

[6] Net Private Credit: this was calculated by adding all the clearly identified assets such as mortgages, non-Government investments, loans and advances, commercial paper, debentures and equities of each set of institutions and summing the totals. It specifically excludes such items as other assets, premises, cash, Government and Government-guaranteed investments and Treasury Bills.

[7] The total assets of the banks excludes customers' liabilities for acceptances and endorsements, and the total assets of the discount companies have been adjusted to include 'bills rediscounted' after 1942 in order to maintain the consistency of the series.

[8] Sample of hire-purchase companies.

[9] In 1963 the sample of hire-purchase companies was reduced to six.

TABLE (A) 3.5 **New Capital Issues in the United Kingdom 1920–66 (£ millions)**

Year	*Midland Bank Series*[2]							*Bank of England Series*[1]				
	Total 1	*Home* 2	*Public Authority* 3	*Production* 4	*Trade* 5	*Transport* 6	*Finance* 7	*Total* 8	*Home* 9	*Local Authority* 10	*Industry* 11	*New Issues on London* 12
1920	384	331	—		263		—	—	—	—	—	368
1921	216	100	—		64		—	—	—	—	—	389
1922	236	101	—		75		—	—	—	—	—	574
1923	204	67	—		67		—	—	—	—	—	271
1924	224	89	—		76		—	—	—	—	—	209
1925	220	132	—		109		—	—	—	—	—	232
1926	253	140	—		100		—	—	—	—	—	231
1927	305	176	—	103		43	—	317	166	25	141	355
1928	363	220	—	138		64	—	361	210	17	193	369
1929	254	160	—	111		45	—	268	166	2	164	285
1930	236	127	—	55		10	—	244	131	29	102	268
1931	89	44	—	21		4	—	95	45	7	38	102
1932	113	84	—	36		9	—	118	88	10	78	189
1933	133	95	—	51		4	—	137	96	25	71	245
1934	150	107	—	61		3	—	165	123	28	95	169
1935	183	162	—	88		33	—	199	138	23	115	236
1936	217	191	—	90		33	—	245	212	42	171	256
1937	171	139	—	76		11	—	187	154	33	121	252
1938	118	93	28	48		12	5	132	104	26	78	180
1939	66	43	12	19		11	2	72	51	15		92
1940	4	4					—	3	3	—	3	—
1941	2	2					—	2	2	—	2	—
1942	4	4	4	18		1	—	4	4	—	4	—
1943	9	7					—	8	7	—	7	—
1944	8	6					—	9	7	—	7	—
1945	20	17	—	13		3	1	24	18	—	18	—
1946	131	112	—	74		27	11	154	137	—	137	—
1947	151	118	5	82		26	5	187	155	—	155	—
1948	251	213	100	76		33	5	278	240	—	240	—
1949	138	96	—	80		8	8	157	115	—	115	—
1950	313	262	154	94		9	5	360	308	—	308	—
1951	252	203	76	108		13	7	292	242	—	242	—
1952	370	323	206	94		15	8	387	335	—	335	—
1953	396	337	246	56		27	9	435	378	19	358	—
1954	471	410	225	138		11	37	531	451	18	433	—
1955	567	525	306	166		25	29	635	571	9	562	—
1956	296	265	54	158		18	34	366	313	54	259	—
1957	383	321	27	250		16	28	367	302	26	276	–
1958	316	255	76	143		12	25	360	285	61	224	—
1959	480	435	50	180		68	137	541	493	45	448	—
1960	557	514	57	247		96	115	608	559	53	507	—
1961	609	554	29	295		97	132	666	599	29	570	—
1962	605	565	179	163		102	121	632	568	136	432	—
1963	593	535	103	199		132	100	650	525	92	433	—
1964	508	464	80	224		99	62	743	597	90	507	—
1965	771	764	264	379		81	40	826	752	261	491	—
1966	857	836	205	431		74	127	1080	1038	316	722	—

Sources

Cols. 1–7 (1920–62), *Midland Bank Reviews.*

Cols. 8–11 (1927–39), *Bank of England Statistical Summaries*, various years.

Cols. 8–11 (1946–62), *Bank of England Quarterly Bulletin.*

Col. 12 (1920–39), B. Mitchell and P. Deane, *Abstract of British Historical Statistics* (Cambridge, 1962), p. 762.

Cols. 1–7 (1963–6), *Midland Bank Review* (February, issue).

Cols. 8–11 (1962–6), *Bank of England Quarterly Bulletin.* A new series was begun in 1962 for cols. 8–11.

Notes

[1] Recent series published by the Bank of England are not comparable with earlier series, and are therefore not incorporated.

[2] Pre-1920 new issue figures may be found in *The Economist* to the year 1870. Figures also found in the *Statist* to the year 1907.

TABLE (A) 3.6 **Stocks Quoted on London Stock Exchange 1930–1966[1,2] (Fund figures in £ millions)**

Date		Number of Securities Listed			Value all Securities: Market		Value all Securities: Nominal		Value Listed British Government Funds								New Listing British Funds Guaranteed and National Stocks	
Year	Month/Day	Total 1	Daily List 2	Supplementary List 3	Daily List 4	Total 5	Daily List 6	Total 7	Nominal 8	Market 9	Value British Government and Government-Guaranteed. Nominal 10	UK Corporation Stock, Public Boards. Market Value 11	Dominion and Foreign Government and Corporation Stock. Market Value 12	Total Company Securities. Market Value 13	Total New Listing. Nominal 14	New Money 15	Total 16	New Money 17
1930	—	—	—	—	—	—	—	—	—	—	6053	—	—	—	—	—	—	—
1931	12/31	—	5927	—	—	—	18458	—	6430	—	6018	—	—	—	259	—	—	—
1932	12/31	—	5959	—	—	—	18371	—	6327	—	6036	—	—	—	783	—	—	—
1933	3/24	—	5951	—	—	—	18684	—	6642	—	6203	—	—	—	812	—	—	—
1934	3/24	—	5875	—	—	—	18582	—	6653	—	6220	—	—	—	455	—	—	—
1935	3/24	—	5882	—	—	—	18601	—	6673	—	6471	—	—	—	586	—	152	—
1936	3/24	—	5443	—	—	—	17375	—	6433	—	6362	—	—	—	743	—	312	—
1937	3/24	—	5522	—	19475	—	17698	—	5724	6767	6418	—	—	—	697	—	108	—
1938	3/24	—	5629	—	17347	—	17950	—	6848	6860	6485	—	—	—	570	—	161	—
1939	3/24	10297	5693	4604	16824	18520	17976	19789	6923	6598	6527	901	1427	9593	300	—	81	—
1940	3/24	10014	5681	4333	—	19224	18209	19470	7213	7093	7097	823	949	—	429	366	306	305
1941	4/7	9821	5551	4270	—	16474	16977	18143	7201	7321	8218	818	914	—	559	291	534	288
1942	4/7	9827	5501	4326	—	18694	18421	19577	8951	9185	9533	821	784	—	672	591	589	589
1943	4/5	9885	5465	4420	—	21328	19557	20731	10080	10361	10684	832	770	—	911	837	837	831
1944	4/3	9848	5422	4426	—	22719	20496	21666	11143	11296	11225	830	773	—	381	340	328	328
1945	4/3	9615	5313	4302	—	24370	—	22160	11864	12168	12569	839	765	—	514	396	386	385
1946	4/1	9615	5236	4379	—	26141	—	23021	12888	13301	12455	798	704	—	679	479	490	428
1947	4/8	9941	5184	4757	—	28078	—	23392	13130	13716	12967	791	693	—	1543	1082	1233	893
1948	4/5	9821	—	—	—	26573	—	22973	14248	14167	12640	584	679	—	1410	269	1063	0
1949	4/4	10053	—	—	—	26163	—	22904	14395	14613	12660	594	908	—	811	253	539	100
1950	4/3	9711	—	—	—	25067	—	22949	14589	13683	12982	535	847	—	1322	183	1001	40
1951	4/2	9706	—	—	—	26991	—	23623	15211	14367	13897	520	872	11142	1724	727	1389	507
1952	3/21	9708	—	—	—	25443	—	24894	16349	13882	14131	460	820	10221	1534	1298	1162	1078
1953	3/31	9752	—	—	—	27130	—	25624	16799	14783	14748	575	870	10908	1922	792	1478	619
1954	3/31	9861	—	—	—	30503	—	26653	17402	16019	14791	522	988	12887	2717	1036	2075	729
1955	3/31	9954	—	—	—	33796	—	27749	17582	15533	14852	508	988	16646	2851	766	1798	399
1956	3/29	9988	—	—	—	33634	—	28852	18338	14678	15194	452	938	17497	2088	1257	1337	884
1957	3/29	9979	—	—	—	35795	—	29674	18676	15157	14643	524	943	19102	2054	825	1211	443
1958	3/31	9893	—	—	—	33102	—	30127	18623	14485	15380	520	892	17141	1758	1420	900	892
1959	3/31	9800	—	—	—	39020	—	30503	18203	14778	15043	593	993	22588	2032	390	903	0
1960	3/31	9591	—	—	—	45068	—	31293	18175	14287	15761	620	946	29149	2261	933	969	353
1961	3/31	9355	—	—	—	50951	—	33332	19214	14900	15697	653	887	34450	3209	1708	1584	1070
1962	3/31	9175	—	—	—	50224	—	33621	18588	14251	16690	714	836	34359	2273	712	500	0
1963	3/31	9134	—	—	—	55309	—	35738	19828	16306	—	915	903	37108	3019	1953	1592	1257
1964	3/31	9191	—	—	—	59841	—	37696	20027	16257	—	1033	1006	41469	3523	2092	1300	1260
1965	3/31	9299	—	—	—	75155	—	39168	19648	15202	—	1116	1392	57359	3323	1603	850	822
1966	3/31	9431	—	—	—	78164	—	40214	19771	15220	—	1287	1516	60095	3884	2462	1811	1271

Sources

(1931–62), all columns except col. 9 from annual reports published by the London Stock Exchange, *Statistics Relating to Securities quoted on the London Stock Exchange*, various years.

Col. 10 (1930–62), Pember and Boyle.

Cols. 5, 6 and 11 (1900–1920), kindly provided by A. J. Murray, public relations officer, London Stock Exchange. These figures are extracted from the *Stock Exchange Official Intelligence*, now called the *Stock Exchange Official Year Book*. They are as follows:

	1900	1901	1902	1903	1904	1905	1906	1907	1908	1909
Col. 5	8358	8903	8789	8834	9057	9303	9324	9692	9935	10201
Col. 6	803	878	916	936	964	966	981	987	987	979
Col. 11	261	509	408	455	377	273	282	451	315	459

	1910	1911	1912	1913	1914	1915	1916	1917	1918	1919	1920
Col. 5	10649	10817	10990	11262	11442	11745	12297	13277	13391	15382	16626
Col. 6	1005	1009	1012	1013	1011	1221	1715	2955	2970	4495	5418
Col. 11	n.a.	n.a.	n.a.	n.a.	n.a.	n.a.	n.a.	n.a.	n.a.	n.a.	n.a.

Figures for the years 1921–30 were not published.

Cols. 1–9, 11–17 (1963–6), annual reports of the London Stock Exchange, *Statistics Relating to Securities quoted on the London Stock Exchange*.

Notes

[1] Not all securities are British-owned or -created. Some have par value in foreign currency, some have no par value at all.

[2] Wholly owned subsidiaries companies' listed stock excluded from valuation.

TABLE (A) 3.7 **United Kingdom Rates of Interest 1860–1966**

Year	Bank Rate I	Consols 3% II	Long Dated III	Medium Dated IV	Short Dated[c] V	Treasury Bills[a] VI	Market Rate on High-Class Bills VII	Call Rate[d] VIII
1860	4·18	3·19	—	—	—	—	4·00	—
1861	5·27	3·28	—	—	—	—	5·00	—
1862	2·53	3·23	—	—	—	—	2·25	—
1863	4·41	3·22	—	—	—	—	4·25	—
1864	7·40	3·33	—	—	—	—	7·00	—
1865	4·77	3·35	—	—	—	—	5·33	—
1866	6·99	3·41	—	—	—	—	6·41	—
1867	2·54	3·23	—	—	—	—	2·67	—
1868	2·10	3·20	—	—	—	—	2·29	—
1869	3·21	3·23	—	—	—	—	3·37	—
1870	3·10	3·24	—	—	—	—	3·28	—
1871	2·88	3·23	—	—	—	—	2·89	—
1872	4·10	3·24	—	—	—	—	4·09	—
1873	4·79	3·24	—	—	—	—	4·70	—
1874	3·69	3·24	—	—	—	—	3·55	—
1875	3·23	3·20	—	—	—	—	3·14	—
1876	2·60	3·16	—	—	—	—	2·26	—
1877	2·90	3·15	—	—	—	—	2·62	—
1878	3·78	3·15	—	—	—	—	3·60	—
1879	2·52	3·08	—	—	—	—	2·14	—
1880	2·77	3·05	—	—	—	—	2·53	—
1881	3·50	3·00	—	—	—	—	3·05	—
1882	4·13	2·98	—	—	—	—	3·55	—
1883	3·57	2·97	—	—	—	—	3·22	—
1884	2·95	2·97	—	—	—	—	2·58	—
1885	2·88	3·02	—	—	—	—	2·40	—
1886	3·05	2·98	—	—	—	—	2·33	—
1887	3·35	2·95	—	—	—	—	2·65	—
1888	3·30	3·02	—	—	—	—	2·53	—
1889	3·55	2·88 2¾%	—	—	—	—	2·85	—
1890	4·52	2·85	—	—	—	—	3·88	—
1891	3·26	2·87	—	—	—	—	2·77	1·19[b]
1892	2·53	2·85	—	—	—	—	1·77	1·38
1893	3·05	2·79	—	—	—	—	2·31	2·00
1894	2·11	2·72	—	—	—	—	1·19	1·00
1895	2·00	2·59	—	—	—	—	0·96	1·06
1896	2·48	2·48	—	—	—	—	1·57	2·00
1897	2·63	2·45	—	—	—	—	1·93	1·44
1898	3·24	2·48	—	—	—	—	2·65	1·88
1899	3·75	2·58	—	—	—	—	3·25	2·75
1900	3·96	2·76	—	—	—	4·00	3·71	2·75
1901	3·72	2·93	—	—	—	3·48	3·17	2·69
1902	3·33	2·91	—	—	—	2·96	2·97	2·50
1903	3·75	2·83	—	—	—	3·45	3·38	2·63
1904	3·30	2·83 2½%	—	—	—	2·90	2·68	2·44
1905	3·01	2·78	—	—	—	2·20	2·62	2·13
1906	4·27	2·83	—	—	—	3·00	3·97	3·63
1907	4·93	2·97	—	—	—	3·76	4·49	3·00
1908	3·01	2·91	—	—	—	2·25	2·29	2·75
1909	3·10	2·97	—	—	—	2·14	2·28	—
1910	3·72	3·08	—	—	—	3·06	3·16	—
1911	3·47	3·15	—	—	—	2·83	2·91	—
1912	3·77	3·28	—	—	—	3·04	3·62	—
1913	4·77	3·40	—	—	—	3·48	4·37	—
1914	4·04	3·34	—	—	—	3·01	2·91	—
1915	5·00	3·82	—	—	—	3·82[e]	3·66	—

Year	Bank Rate I	Consols 3% II	Long Dated III	Medium Dated IV	Short Dated[c] V	Treasury Bills[a] VI	Market Rate on High-Class Bills VII	Call Rate[d] VII
1916	5·46	4·31	—	—	—	5·18	5·20	—
1917	5·15	4·57	—	—	—	4·79	4·79	—
1918	5·00	4·40	—	—	—	3·59	3·57	—
1919	5·15	4·63	—	—	5·24	3·48	3·93	3·01
1920	6·72	5·32	—	—	6·23	6·21	6·41	4·47
1921	6·12	5·21	—	—	5·70	4·58	5·17	4·32
1922	3·69	4·43	—	—	4·78	2·57	2·64	1·98
1923	3·49	4·31	—	—	4·39	2·62	2·72	1·96
1924	4·00	4·39	—	—	4·36	3·39	3·46	2·43
1925	4·55	4·43	—	—	4·51	4·09	4·14	3·47
1926	5·00	4·55	—	—	4·35	4·51	4·48	4·01
1927	4·65	4·56	—	—	3·98	4·25	4·26	3·71
1928	4·50	4·48	—	—	4·73	4·15	4·16	3·56
								3·52
1929	5·50	4·60	—	—	5·08	5·26	5·26	4·47
1930	3·42	4·48	—	—	4·31	2·48	2·57	2·27
1931	3·93	4·40	—	—	4·54	3·59	3·61	2·94
1932	3·00	3·75	—	—	3·64	1·49	1·87	1·61
1933	2·00	3·39	—	—	2·09	0·59	0·69	0·69
1934	2·00	3·10	—	—	1·78	0·73	0·82	0·82
1935	2·00	2·89	—	—	2·46	0·55	0·58	0·50
1936	2·00	2·93	—	—	2·45	0·58	0·60	0·50
1937	2·00	3·28	—	—	2·90	0·56	0·58	0·50
1938	2·00	3·38	—	—	2·72	0·61	0·63	0·51
1939	2·26	3·72	—	—	3·30	1·21	1·22	0·96
1940	2·00	3·40	—	—	2·78	1·03	1·04	1·00
1941	2·00	3·13	—	—	2·47	1·01	1·03	1·00
1942	2·00	3·03	2·96	2·89	2·32	1·00	1·03	1·00
1943	2·00	3·10	3·04	3·02	2·45	1·00	1·03	1·00
1944	2·00	3·14	3·05	3·02	2·37	1·00	1·03	1·00
1945	2·00	2·92	2·94	2·99	2·45	0·90	0·95	0·92
1946	2·00	2·60 2½%	2·48	2·55	2·08	0·50	0·53	0·50
1947	2·00	2·76	2·60	2·67	2·18	0·51	0·53	0·50
1948	2·00	3·21	2·81	2·79	2·02	0·51	0·56	0·50
1949	2·00	3·30	3·55	2·83	1·94	0·52	0·63	0·50
1950	2·00	3·54	3·77	2·99	2·03	0·52	0·69	0·50
1951	2·08	3·78	3·98	3·59	1·85	0·56	0·91	0·54
1952	3·71	4·23	4·55	4·25	2·98	2·20	2·71	1·79
1953	3·88	4·08	4·30	3·95	3·03	2·30	2·77	1·94
1954	3·17	3·75	3·99	3·55	2·61	1·79	1·84	1·42
1955	4·29	4·17	4·37	4·24	3·81	3·75	3·75	2·54
			4·24	4·11				
1956	5·33	4·73	5·13	5·14	4·67	4·95	5·05	3·58
1957	5·54	4·98	5·46	5·11	5·15	4·81	4·98	3·79
1958	5·42	4·98	5·54	5·25	4·75	4·56	4·74	3·76
1959	4·00	4·82	5·23	5·09	4·16	3·38	3·49	2·38
1960	5·42	5·42	5·77	5·78	5·44	4·89	5·05	3·71
1961	5·83	6·20	6·27	6·33	5·71	5·14	5·41	4·20
1962	4·90	5·98	5·98	5·79	5·24	4·17	4·40	3·22
1963	4·0[h]	5·58	5·43[g]	5·17[g]	4·83[g]	3·66[f]	3·83[f]	2·38[h]
1964	5·0	6·03	5·98	5·70	5·54	4·61	4·81	3·41
1965	6·4	6·42	6·56	6·55	6·57	5·91	6·29	4·80
1966	6·5	6·80	6·94	6·87	6·77	6·10	6·43	4·84

Sources

Cols. I and VII (1860–1900), R. H. Palgrave, *Bank Rate and the Money Market* (London: J. Murray, 1903), p. 33.

Col. I (1901–52), *The Economist, Records and Statistics*, 1953, p. 438.

Col. I (1953–66), C.S.O., *Annual Abstract of Statistics*, various issues.

Col. II (1860–1966), Board of Trade, *Statistical Abstract of the UK*, and C.S.O., *Annual Abstract of Statistics*, various issues.

Cols. III, IV (1942–66), C.S.O., *Annual Abstract of Statistics*, various issues.

Cols. V, VI (1919–62), London and Cambridge Economic Service, *Key Statistics of the British Economy*, various issues.

Col. VI (1900–1914), Pember and Boyle, *British Government Securities in the Twentieth Century* (supplement).

Col. VI (1915–19), E. V. Morgan, *Studies in British Financial Policy, 1914–25*.

Col. VII (1901–27), Mitchell and Deane, *Abstract of British Historical Statistics* (Cambridge University Press, 1962), p. 460.

Col. VII (1928), Balogh, *Financial Organization*, p. 131.

Col. VII (1929–41), Bank of England, *Statistical Summary*, various years.

Col. VII (1942–66), *Annual Abstract of Statistics.*

Col. VIII (1917–28), London and Cambridge Economic Service, *Monthly Bulletin.*

Col. VIII (1928–41), Bank of England, *Statistical Summary*, various years.

Col. VIII (1942–66), C.S.O., *Annual Abstract of Statistics.*

Col. VIII (1891–1908), C. A. E. Goodhart, unpublished dissertation (Cambridge University, 1963).

Cols. I–VIII (1963–6), C.S.O., *Annual Abstract of Statistics*, No. 104, 1967.

Notes

[a] Treasury Bill rates are averages of weekly allotments between 1900–14 of six-month bills. From 1921–66 they are averages of three-month or 91-day bills. Between these periods the rates were mostly fixed.

[b] Figures from Goodhart's tables are averages of maximum and minimum monthly figures.

[c] Short-dated Government securities have about four years to maturity.

[d] 'Call rate' is also labelled 'call money' and 'day-to-day loans'.

[e] The figures from Morgan are averages of monthly averages, hence partly unweighted.

[f] Averages of monthly averages.

[g] Averages of end-month yields.

[h] Averages, using duration in weeks as weights.

TABLE (A) 3.8 **The Compound Rates of Growth of National Savings, Money and Near-Money Stocks, and the Assets of the Financial Institutions**

Items	*Periods*							
	1880–1966	*1880–1914*	*1914–1918*	*1920–1939*	*1939–1946*	*1946–1966*	*1920–1966*	*1955–1966*
UK National Savings	5·4 5·6[1]	3·8 3·7[1]	21·9	2·8	21·4	1·5	4·8	2·5
Savings Banks' Deposits	4·7 4·8[1]	3·5 3·5[1]	4·4	4·5	18·6	1·9	5·4	3·1
Currency Outstanding	3·4 4·0[1]	0·4 1·0[1]	21·6	0·0	16·3	3·5	3·9	4·2
Net Money[a]	4·0[1]	2·6[1]	15·8	0·91	13·0	2·6	3·4	3·5
Quasi-Money[b]	4·4[1]	2·6[1]	13·8	2·2	12·9	3·6	4·4	4·8
Total Potential Encashable Assets[c]	4·7[1]	2·9[1]	13·9	2·5	13·1	3·9	4·7	5·2
Total Assets of the Financial Institutions	4·7[1,2]	2·9[1]	10·3	3·2	10·1	4·9	5·0	6·1
Total Assets of Banks and Discount Houses	3·9[1]	2·6[1]	14·0	1·2	12·2	2·8	3·5	3·6
Total Assets of the Non-Bank Financial Institutions	5·6[1,2]	3·4[1]	3·7	5·9	8·1	6·6	6·6	7·7
Total Gross Private Credit Total Net Private Credit	4·7[1,2] 4·6[1,2]	2·5[1] 2·5[1]	0·5 0·5	3·3 3·3	0·3 −0·2	9·6 9·5	5·5 5·4	9·9 10·2
Bank Advances and Loans	3·8[1,2]	2·3[1]	2·5	0·2	−0·3	8·4	3·6	9·8
Mortgages	5·5[1,2]	1·4[1]	−3·5	9·4	−2·1	11·4	8·3	10·8

Notes

[1] These annual rates of growth are computed from 1891 and not from 1880.

[2] These figures are not strictly accurate owing to the discontinuity in the series in 1920. At that date, the banks of Southern Ireland are excluded, and the hire-purchase companies and some of the societies registered with the Registrar of the Friendly Societies are included for the first time.

[a] Net money = currency in hands of the public + bank deposits – an estimate of inter-bank deposits.

[b] Quasi-money = net money supply + savings banks' deposits + building societies' shares and deposits.

[c] Total potential encashable assets = net money supply + UK National Savings + building societies' shares and deposits + life insurance co. funds.

Bibliography

AKANTHOS. 'Banks and the Finance of Foreign Trade'. *Bankers' Magazine*, Vol. CLXIX (1950), pp. 349–54.

ALDCROFT, D. 'The Early History and Development of Export Credit Insurance in Great Britain, 1919–39'. *Manchester School* (January 1962), pp. 69–85.

ALHADEFF, D. & C. 'The Struggle for Commercial Bank Savings'. *Quarterly Journal of Economics* (February 1958).

ANDERSON, P. 'Yield Curve Hypotheses and a Note on Inverse Carrying Charges'. Unpublished Paper, Federal Reserve Bank of Boston, 1962.

ANDO, A., BROWN, E., SOLOW, R., & KAREKEN, J. 'Lags in Fiscal and Monetary Policy'. *Stabilization Policies*. Englewood Cliffs, N.J.: Prentice-Hall, 1963, pp. 1–96.

ANDO, A., & MODIGLIANI, F. 'Velocity and the Investment Multiplier'. *American Economic Review* (September 1965), pp. 693–728.

'Are Banks Losing Deposits?' *Bankers' Magazine*, Vol. CXCI (1961), pp. 461–3.

AXILROD, S. H. 'Liquidity Preference and Public Policy'. *Staff Economic Comment*. Washington: Federal Reserve System, June 1961.

BALL, R. J., & DRAKE, P. S. 'Impact of Credit Control on Consumer Durable Goods Spending in the United Kingdom, 1957–61'. *Review of Economic Studies*, Vol. XXX (3), No. 84 (October 1963).

'Bankers' Advances and Deflation'. *Bankers' Magazine*, Vol. CX (1920), pp. 649–57.

Bankers' Almanac and Year Book for 1924–25. London: Thomas Skinner, 1926.

Bankers' Almanac and Year Book for 1930–31. London: Thomas Skinner, 1932.

Bankers' Almanac and Year Book for 1933–34. London: Thomas Skinner, 1935.

Bankers' Almanac and Year Book for 1940–41. London: Thomas Skinner, 1946.

Bankers' Almanac and Year Book for 1951–52. London: Waterlow & Son, 1952.

'Banking and Currency After the War'. *Bankers' Magazine*, Vol. CVII (1919), pp. 259–67.

'Banking Links with H.P. Finance'. *Bankers' Magazine*, Vol. CLXXXVI (1958), pp. 176–7.

'Banking Policy and the Cash Ratio'. *The Economist*, 'Banking Supplement', 16 November 1940, pp. 6–7.

BARBER, A. V. 'Assets Structure of the Joint Stock Banks in Relation to the Trend of Deposits'. *Bankers' Magazine*, Vol. CXLVII (1939), pp. 437–49.

BARBER, C. L. 'The Quantity Theory and the Income Expenditure Theory in an Open Economy, 1926–58: A Comment'. *Canadian Journal of Economics* (August 1966), pp. 375–7.

BARRAND, A. R. 'The Assurance Companies Act 1909'. *Journal of the Institute of Actuaries*, Vol. XLV, pp. 257–319.

BARRETT, C. R., & WALTERS, A. A. 'The Stability of Keynesian and Monetary Multipliers in the United Kingdom'. *Review of Economics and Statistics* (November 1966), pp. 395–405.

BATES, J. A. 'Hire Purchase and the Banks'. *Bankers' Magazine*, Vol. CLXXXVI (1958), pp. 361–7.

'The Bills of Exchange Act 1882'. *Bankers' Magazine*, Vol. CLXXIV (1952).

BOARD OF TRADE. *Statistical Abstract for the United Kingdom 1924*, No. 69. London: H.M.S.O., 1926.

BOARD OF TRADE. *Statistical Abstract for the United Kingdom 1925*, No. 70. London: H.M.S.O., 1927.

BOARD OF TRADE. *Statistical Abstract for the United Kingdom 1937*, No. 82. London: H.M.S.O., 1938.

BOARD OF TRADE. *Statistical Abstract for the United Kingdom 1938*, No. 83. London: H.M.S.O., 1940.

'Board of Trade Committee Report: Fixed or Unit Trusts'. *Bankers' Magazine*, Vol. CXLII (1936), pp. 338–48, 370, 477–80.

BRECHLING, F., & CLAYTON, G. *Commercial Banks' Portfolio Behaviour*. National Economic Development Office: University of Liverpool, 1962.

BRECHLING, F., & CLAYTON, G. *Economic Journal* (June 1965), pp. 290–316.

'British Banking'. *The Economist*, 16 June 1956, pp. 1–20.

'British Banking'. *The Economist*, 15 June 1957, pp. 3–23.

'British Banking'. *The Economist*, 14 June 1958, pp. 1–24.

'British Banking'. *The Economist*, 18 June 1960, pp. 1247–68.

'British Banking'. *The Economist*, 30 June 1962, pp. 1327–51.

BROIDA, A. L. *Liquidity as a Variable in Monetary Analysis.* Preliminary Draft Thesis. Chicago, 1962.

BRUNTON, J. 'Money and Credit'. *Bankers' Magazine*, Vol. CXLIII (1937), pp. 901–6.

'Building Societies'. *The Economist*, 11 April 1936, pp. 3–28.

BUILDING SOCIETIES ASSOCIATION. *Annual Meeting*. 1914.

BUILDING SOCIETIES ASSOCIATION. *Report of Council.* 1942–3.

BUILDING SOCIETIES ASSOCIATION. *Report of Council.* 1946–7.

BUILDING SOCIETIES ASSOCIATION. *Report of Council.* 1948–9.

BUILDING SOCIETIES ASSOCIATION. *Report of Council.* 1949–50.

BUILDING SOCIETIES ASSOCIATION. *Report of Council.* 1953–4.

BUILDING SOCIETIES ASSOCIATION. *Report of Council.* 1954–5.

BUILDING SOCIETIES ASSOCIATION. *Report of Council.* 1955–6.

BUILDING SOCIETIES ASSOCIATION. *Report of Council.* 1956–7.

BUILDING SOCIETIES ASSOCIATION. *Report of Council.* 1959–60.

BUILDING SOCIETIES ASSOCIATION. *Report of Council.* 1960–1.

BUILDING SOCIETIES ASSOCIATION. *Report of Council.* 1961–2.

BUILDING SOCIETIES ASSOCIATION. *Report of Council.* 1962–3.

Building Society Year Book 1959. London: Franey & Co., 1959.

CATT, A. J. L. 'Credit Risk and Credit Rationing: A Comment'. *Quarterly Journal of Economics* (August 1963), pp. 505–10.

CENTRAL STATISTICAL OFFICE. *Annual Abstract of Statistics*, No. 84. London: H.M.S.O., 1947.

CENTRAL STATISTICAL OFFICE. *Annual Abstract of Statistics*, No. 90. London: H.M.S.O., 1953.

CENTRAL STATISTICAL OFFICE. *Annual Abstract of Statistics*, No. 91. London: H.M.S.O., 1954.

CENTRAL STATISTICAL OFFICE. *Annual Abstract of Statistics*, No. 98. London: H.M.S.O., 1961.

CENTRAL STATISTICAL OFFICE. *Annual Abstract of Statistics*, No. 99. London: H.M.S.O., 1962.

CENTRAL STATISTICAL OFFICE. *Financial Statistics*, No. 13. London: H.M.S.O., May 1963.

CLAPHAM, SIR J. *The Bank of England 1797–1914*, Vol. II. Cambridge: Cambridge University Press, 1944.

CLAYTON, G. 'British Financial Intermediaries in Theory and Practice'. *Economic Journal*, Vol. LXXII (December 1962), pp. 869–80.

CLAYTON, G., & OSBORN, W. T. *Insurance Company Investment*. London: Allen & Unwin, 1965.

CLEARY, E. J. *The Building Society Movement*. London: Elek Books, 1965.

COHEN, J. 'Circular Flow Models in the Flow of Funds'. *International Economic Review* (May 1963).

COMMITTEE ON FINANCE AND INDUSTRY. *Minutes of Evidence*, Vols. I and II. London: H.M.S.O., 1931.

COMMITTEE ON FINANCE AND INDUSTRY. *Report*. Cmd. 389. London: H.M.S.O., 1931.

COMMITTEE ON THE WORKINGS OF THE MONETARY SYSTEM. *Principal Memoranda of Evidence*, Vol. I. London: H.M.S.O., 1960.

COMMITTEE ON THE WORKINGS OF THE MONETARY SYSTEM. *Principal Memoranda of Evidence*, Vol. II. London: H.M.S.O., 1960.

COMMITTEE ON THE WORKINGS OF THE MONETARY SYSTEM. *Principal Memoranda of Evidence*, Vol. III. London: H.M.S.O., 1960.

COMMITTEE ON THE WORKINGS OF THE MONETARY SYSTEM. *Report*. London: H.M.S.O., August 1959.

'Comparative Statement of Investments of British Assurance Companies'. *Journal of the Institute of Actuaries*, Vol. LVI (1925), pp. 118–19.

'The Convertibility Fiasco'. *Bankers' Magazine*, Vol. CLXIV (1947), pp. 135–9.

COPELAND, M. A. 'Tracing Money Flows Through the United States Economy'. *American Economic Review* (May 1947), pp. 31–49.

COPPACK, D. J., & GIBSON, N. J. 'The Volume of Deposits and the Cash and Liquid Assets Ratios'. *Manchester School* (September 1963), pp. 203–22.

COPPIETIERS, E. *English Bank Note Circulation 1694–1954*. The Hague: Louvain Institute of Economics and Social Research, 1955.

CRAMP, A. B. 'Banks and Their Competitors'. *The Banker* (February 1963), pp. 89–95.

CRAMP, A. B. 'Financial Intermediaries and Monetary Policy'. *Economica*, Vol. XXIX (May 1962), pp. 143–51.

CRICK, W. F. 'British Monetary Policy, 1931–37'. *Bankers' Magazine*, Vol. CLXV (1938), pp. 221–38.

CRICK, W. F. 'The Genesis of Bank Deposits'. *Readings in Monetary Theory*. London: Allen & Unwin, 1962.

CRICK, W. F. 'Monetary Policy and Banking Practice'. *Bankers' Magazine*, Vol. CXXXV (1933), pp. 907–16.

CROUCH, B. C. 'The Growth of Trustee Departments and their Future Prospects'. *Bankers' Magazine*, Vol. CLXIII (1947), pp. 431–6.

CROUCH, R. L. 'A Re-examination of Open Market Operations'. *Oxford Economic Papers* (July 1963).

CRUMP, N. 'Banking and Monetary Conditions in England and the United States'. *Bankers' Magazine*, Vol. CXXI (1926), pp. 675–85.

CRUMP, P. C. 'Wartime Finance – A Résumé of Financial Conditions During and After the War as They Affected Life Insurance Companies'. *Journal of the Institute of Actuaries*, Vol. LIX (1928), pp. 347–73.

CUTLER, C. G. 'The Requirements of the Building Societies Act'. *Building Societies Association, Report on Proceedings at Annual Meeting* (1910), pp. 71–86.

DACEY, W. M. *Money Under Review*. London: Hutchinson, 1960.

DAY, A. 'Radcliffe Under Scrutiny Now for the Critics'. *The Banker* (June 1960), pp. 404–9.

DEPARTMENT OF AGRICULTURE AND TECHNICAL INSTRUCTION FOR IRELAND. *Banking, Railway and Shipping Statistics, Ireland*. London: H.M.S.O., 1913.

DEPRANO, M., & MAYER, T. 'Tests of Relative Importance of Autonomous Expenditure and Money'. *American Economic Review* (September 1965), pp. 729–44.

DOW, I. 'The Merchant Banks'. *Bankers' Magazine*, Vol. CLXXI (1951), pp. 244–50.

DOW, J. C. R. *The Management of the British Economy*. Cambridge: Cambridge University Press, 1964.

DRAKATOS, C. 'Short-term Fluctuations in the Velocity of Circulation of Money in the United Kingdom, 1954–61'. *The Banker*, Vol. CXCIV (1962), pp. 408–15.

DUESENBERRY, J. *Business Cycles and Economic Growth*. New York, 1958.

The Economist. 'British Banking Survey'. 17 June 1950, pp. 1339–49.

The Economist. 'British Banking Survey'. 7 June 1952, pp. 689–705.

The Economist. 'Banking Number'. 23 May 1914, pp. 1197–1209.

The Economist. 'Banking Supplement'. 12 May 1934, pp. 1–24.

The Economist. 'Banking Supplement'. 16 May 1936, pp. 3–27.

The Economist. 'Banking Supplement'. 20 May 1939, pp. 4–64.

EINZIG, P. 'Dollar Deposits in London'. *The Banker* (January 1960).

ELLERTON, SIR C. 'Relations Between the Bank of England and the Commercial Banks of the United Kingdom'. *Relations Between the Central Banks and the Commercial Banks*. Frankfurt: Fritz Kropp Verlag, 1957.

ELLIS, H. S. 'Some Fundamentals in the Theory of Velocity'. *Readings in Monetary Theory*. London: Allen & Unwin, 1962.

ENGINEERING AND ALLIED EMPLOYERS' NATIONAL FEDERATION. *Memorandum re Burden of Local Taxation* (March 1928).

'Export Finance from the Banks'. *Midland Bank Review* (August 1962), pp. 10–20.

FEDERATION OF BRITISH INDUSTRIES. *Britain's Economic Problems and Policies*. London: The Federation, 1957.

FEDERATION OF BRITISH INDUSTRIES. *The Control of Industry*. London: The Federation, 1919, pp. 1–9.

FEDERATION OF BRITISH INDUSTRIES. *A New British Financial Policy: Industry's Plan*. London: The Federation, April 1932.

FEDERATION OF BRITISH INDUSTRIES AND THE EMPIRE ECONOMIC UNION. *Report on Empire Monetary and Financial Policy*. London: The Federation, 1931.

'The Finance Act, 1956'. *Journal of the Institute of Actuaries*, Vol. LXXXIII (Part 1), pp. 19–33.

'Finance for Industry'. *Bankers' Magazine*, Vol. CLXXIX (1955), pp. 536–8.

'Financial Facilities After the War'. *Bankers' Magazine*, Vol. CVII (1919), pp. 115–22, 198-207.

'First Interim Report of the Committee on Currency and Foreign Exchange After the War'. *Bankers' Magazine*, Vol. CVI (1918), pp. 587–600.

FORD, J. L., & STARK, T. 'Some Statistical Analyses of the Long-term Rate of Interest in the UK, 1948–63'. *Bulletin of Oxford University Institute of Economics and Statistics* (November 1965), pp. 287–98.

FRIEDMAN, M. 'Demand for Money: Some Theoretical and Empirical Results'. *Journal of Political Economy* (August 1959).

FRIEDMAN, M., & MEISELMAN, D. 'The Relative Stability of Monetary Velocity and the Investment Multiplier in the United States 1897–1958'. *Stabilization Policies.* Englewood Cliffs, N.J.: Prentice-Hall, 1963.

FRIEDMAN, M., & SCHWARTZ, A. J. *A Monetary History of the United States 1867–1960.* Princeton, N. J.: Princeton University Press, 1963.

GALPLIN, L. P. 'Movement in the Value of Bank Deposits in Great Britain'. *Bankers' Magazine*, Vol. CXXVII (1929), pp. 563–84.

GAMBINO, A. 'Money Supply and Interest Rate in Recent Macro-Economic Conception'. *Banca Nazionale del Lavoro Quarterly Review* (September 1954).

GIBSON, A. H. 'Government Credit in Relation to Commodity Prices'. *Bankers' Magazine*, Vol. CLXV (1938), pp. 917–38.

GIBSON, A. H. 'War Finance and the Aftermath'. *Bankers' Magazine*, Vol. CXLIX (1940), pp. 337–53, 495–506, 643.

GOLDSMITH, R. W. *Financial Intermediaries in the American Economy Since 1900.* Princeton, N. J.: Princeton University Press, 1958.

GOODHART, C. A. E. 'The Determination of the Volume of Bank Deposits 1891–1914'. Unpublished Dissertation, University of Cambridge, 1963.

GREENGRASS, H. 'The Discount Market'. *Bankers' Magazine*, Vol. CLXX (1950), pp. 101–8.

GURLEY, J. G., & SHAW, S. *Money in a Theory of Finance.* Washington, D. C.: Brookings Institution, 1960.

HALDANE, A. R. B. *One Hundred and Fifty Years of Trustee Savings Banks.* London: Trustee Savings Banks Association, 1960.

HAMBURGER, M. J. 'The Demand for Money by Households, Money Substitutes and Monetary Policy'. *Journal of Political Economy* (December 1966), pp. 600–19.

HAYES, A. 'Interest Rates and Monetary Policy in Perspective'. *Federal Reserve Bank of New York Monthly Review* (February 1966), pp. 22–6.

HENDERSON, R. F. 'The Economic Effects of Hire Purchase'. *Spring Lectures 1956.* London: Institute of Bankers, 1956.

HENDERSON, R. F. *The New Issue Market and the Finance of Industry.* Cambridge: Bowes & Bowes, 1951.

HICKS, J. R. 'Liquidity'. *Economic Journal* (December 1962), pp. 787–802.

HICKS, J. R. 'A Suggestion for Simplifying the Theory of Money'. *Economica* (February 1935), pp. 1–19.

HIGONNET, R. P. 'Bank Deposits in the United Kingdom 1870–1914'. *Quarterly Journal of Economics* (August 1957), pp. 329–67.

'History of Life Assurance'. *Journal of the Institute of Actuaries*, Vol. XXV (1886), pp. 259–71.

HOLMANS, A. E. 'The Quantity of Money, Gross National Product and the Price Level'. *Scottish Journal of Political Economy* (February 1961), pp. 28–44.

HORNE, H. O. *A History of Savings Banks.* London: Oxford University Press, 1947.

'How to Reduce Prices'. *Bankers' Magazine*, Vol. CX (1920), pp. 658–63.

IMLAH, A. H. 'British Balance of Payments and Export of Capital 1816–1913'. *Economic History Review*, Vol. V (1952), pp. 208–39.

'Instalment Buying'. *The Economist*, 23 April 1962, p. 908.

'The Insurance Market'. *Bankers' Magazine*, Vol. CLXXI (1951), p. 22.

Insurance Register (*Life*). London: Clayton, 1912.

JASEY, A. E. 'The Workings of the Radcliffe Monetary System'. *Oxford Economic Papers*, Vol. XII (June 1960), pp. 170–80.

JAY, P. 'The Economic Challenge from St Louis'. *The Times*, 26 February 1970.

JOHNSON, H. G. 'British Monetary Statistics'. *Economica*, Vol. XXVI (February 1959), pp. 1–17.

JOHNSON, H. G. *Clearing Bank Holdings of Public Debt, 1930–50.* Reprint Series No. 54. Cambridge: Cambridge University Press, 1952.

JOHNSON, H. G. 'Monetary Theory and Policy'. *Money, Interest and Welfare.* Vol. 1 of *Surveys of Economic Theory.* 3 vols. London: Macmillan, 1967.

JOHNSON, H. G. 'Some Implications of Secular Changes in Bank Assets and Liabilities in Great Britain'. *Economic Journal*, Vol. LXI (1951), pp. 544–61.

JOHNSTON, J., & MURPHY, G. W. 'The Growth of Life Assurance in the United Kingdom since 1880'. *Transactions of the Manchester Statistical Society* (1956–7), pp. 1–76.

JUCKER-FLEETWOOD, E. E. 'The Key Role of the Velocity of Circulation of Money and Credit'. *Oxford Economic Papers*, Vol. X (October 1958), pp. 290–315.

KAVANAGH, N. J., & WALTERS, A. A. 'Demand for Money in the UK 1877–1961: Some Preliminary Findings'. *Bulletin of Oxford University Institute of Economics and Statistics* (May 1966), pp. 93–116.

KENDALL, M. G. *The Source and Nature of the Statistics*

of the United Kingdom, Vol. II. London: Royal Statistical Society, 1957.

KERAN, M. W. 'Economic Theory and Forecasting'. *Federal Reserve Bank of St Louis Review* (March 1967), pp. 7–16.

KEYNES, J. M. 'The Problem of the Gold Standard'. *Bankers' Magazine*, Vol. CXIX (1925), pp. 540–5.

KIDDY, A. W. 'Britain's Financial and Commercial Position After the War'. *Bankers' Magazine*, Vol. CXIII (1922), pp. 591–619.

KIDDY, A. W. 'The Tendency Towards State Control of Finance and Industry'. *Bankers' Magazine*, Vol. CXLV (1938), pp. 813–26.

KIDDY, A. W. 'The True Significance of External Debt'. *Bankers' Magazine*, Vol. CXL (1921), pp. 70–87.

KING, W. T. C. 'Should the Banks Bid for Deposits?' *The Banker* (December 1962), pp. 761–72.

KHUSHRO, A. M. 'An Investigation of Liquidity Preference'. *Yorkshire Bulletin of Economic and Social Research*, Vol. 1V (1952), pp. 1–20.

LAIDLER, D. 'The Rate of Interest and the Demand for Money: Some Empirical Evidence'. *Journal of Political Economy* (December 1966), pp. 543–55.

LAMFALUSSY, A. 'Money Substitute and Monetary Policy'. *The Banker* (January 1961), pp. 44–50.

LAVINGTON, F. *The English Capital Market*. London: Methuen, 1929.

LAWTON, C. L. 'Trustee Savings Banks'. *Bankers' Magazine*, Vol. CLXX (1950), pp. 369–79.

LEE, T. H. 'Substitutability of Non-Bank Intermediaries Liabilities for Money: The Empirical Evidence'. *Journal of Finance* (September 1966), pp. 444–58.

LEWIS, P. J. 'Indices of House-Building in the Manchester Conurbation, South Wales and Great Britain, 1851–1913'. *Scottish Journal of Political Economy* (February 1961), pp. 148–55.

LIPSEY, R. G., & BRECHLING, F. P. 'Trade Credit and Monetary Policy'. Unpublished Paper, London School of Economics, December 1962.

LOMBARD. 'Crux of the Savings Bank Argument with Lombard Street'. *Financial Times*, 20 February 1946, p. 11.

London and Cambridge Economic Bulletin. New Series, No. 32. December 1959.

London and Cambridge Economic Service Monthly Bulletin. Bulletin 1, Vol. V. 24 January 1927.

London and Cambridge Economic Service Monthly Bulletin. Bulletin 1, Vol. XI. 23 January 1933.

London and Cambridge Economic Service Monthly Bulletin. Bulletin 1. 23 January 1939.

LYDR, M. 'The Laws Relating to Hire Purchase'. *Spring Lectures 1956*. London: Institute of Bankers, 1956.

LYSON, A. 'The Sources of Finance for Industry and Commerce in Great Britain Since the War'. *Bankers' Magazine*, Vol. CLXXVIII (1954), pp. 217–36.

MACESICH, G. 'Empirical Testing and the Income Expenditure Theory'. *Canadian Journal of Political Economy* (August 1966), pp. 377–9.

MAKIN, F. B. 'Treasury Bills'. *Bankers' Magazine*, Vol. CXLVIII (1939), pp. 399–403.

MARSH, D. R. 'Executor and Trustee Service'. *Bankers' Magazine*, Vol. CLXIX (1950), pp. 452–8.

MASON, J. J., & SACHS, D. 'Statistics Bearing on Financial Investment'. *Journal of the Royal Statistical Society*, Vol. CXVIII, Part I (1955), pp. 67–100.

MATHER, L. C. 'Unsecured Advances'. *Gilbert Lectures on Banking 1957*. London: Institute of Bankers, 1957.

MAY, W. T. 'Some Observations on Currency and Credit and Their Influence on Trade and Exchange'. *Journal of the Institute of Actuaries*, Vol. XLVII, pp. 19–52.

MCLEOD, A. N. 'Credit Expansion in an Open Economy'. *Economic Journal* (September 1962), pp. 611–41.

MEADE, J. E. 'The Amount of Money in the Banking System'. *Readings in Monetary Theory*. London: Allen & Unwin, 1962.

MERRIMAN, C. O. *Unit Trusts and How They Work*. 2nd edn. London: Pitman, 1959.

MITCHELL, B. R., & DEANE, P. *Abstract of British Historical Statistics*. Cambridge: Cambridge University Press, 1962.

MITCHELL, G. W. 'Interest Rates versus Interest Ceilings in the Allocation of Credit Flows'. *Annual Meeting of the American Finance Association*, 28 December 1966, pp. 1–18.

'Money and Banking in the Twentieth Century, Post Office Savings Series'. *Bankers' Magazine*, Vol. CLXXII (1951), pp. 283–91.

'Money Supply and the Banks'. *Midland Bank Review* (February 1969), pp. 3–9.

'Monetary Policy, 1844–1939'. *The Economist*. 'Banking Supplement'. 16 April 1935, pp. 4–8.

MORGAN, E. V., & THOMAS, W. A. *The Stock Exchange: Its History and Functions*. London: Elek Books, 1962.

MORRAL, D. *A History of Industrial Life Assurance*. London: Allen & Unwin, 1955.

MORRIS, F. 'Instalment Buying'. *Bankers' Magazine*, Vol. CXXV (1928), pp. 707–14.

NAYLOR, E. 'A History of the Building Societies Association'. *Building Societies Association Annual Meeting* (1915).

'The New Monetary Weapon – Full Description and Appraisal'. *The Banker* (August 1958), pp. 493–506.

'New Scheme for Home Ownership'. *Bankers' Magazine*, Vol. CLXXVI (1958), pp. 461–2.

'Notes on Friendly Societies'. *Journal of the Institute of Actuaries*, Vol. XXV (1882), pp. 24–35.

OKUM, A. M. 'Monetary Policy, Debt Management and Interest Rates: A Quantitative Appraisal'. *Stabilization Policies*. Englewood Cliffs, N.J.: Prentice-Hall, 1963.

OLIVER, F. R. *The Control of Hire Purchase*. London: Allen & Unwin, 1961.

PAISH, F. W. *Studies in an Inflationary Economy*. London: Macmillan, 1962.

PALGREVE, R. H. I. *Bank Rate and the Money Market*. London: Murray, 1903.

PALUSTER, D. 'Bank Deposits as Trustee Funds'. *Bankers' Magazine*, Vol. CLXVII (1949), pp. 296–303.

PATINKIN, D. 'Financial Intermediaries and Monetary Theory'. *American Economic Review* (March 1961), p. 95.

PATINKIN, D. *Money, Interest and Prices*, 2nd edn. New York: Harper & Row, 1965.

PHELPS BROWN, E. H., & SHACKLE, G. L. S. *Statistics on Monetary Circulation in England and Wales, 1919–37*. Memoranda No. 74. London: Royal Economic Society, September 1938.

PHILLIPS, C. A. *Bank Credit*. New York, 1916.

PLEASE, S. 'Investment by the Nationalized Industries'. *Bankers' Magazine*, Vol. CLXXVIII, pp. 408–11.

POLAK, J. J. 'Financial Statistics and Financial Policy'. *International Monetary Fund Staff Papers*, Vol. VII, No. 1 (1959), pp. 1–8.

PRAIS, S. J. 'Company Finances After the Boom'. *The Banker* (August 1958), pp. 519–28.

PREST, A. R. 'National Income of the United Kingdom, 1870–1946'. *Economic Journal*, Vol. LVIII (March 1948), pp. 31–62.

'The Progress of Banking in Great Britain and Ireland During 1920'. *Bankers' Magazine*, Vol. CXI (1921), pp. 741–7.

'The Progress of Banking in Great Britain and Ireland During 1939'. *Bankers' Magazine*, Vol. CL (1940), pp. 1–16.

RADICE, E. A. *Savings in Great Britain 1922–35*. London: Oxford University Press, 1939.

RAYNES, H. E. *A History of British Insurance*. London: Pitman, 1948.

RAYNES, H. E., HICKSON, C. H., & GOLDING, C. E. 'Life, Fire, Accident and Marine Insurance', *Modern Business Texts*, Vol. VIII. London: Modern Business Institute, 1924.

REGISTRY OF FRIENDLY SOCIETIES. *Report of the Chief Registrar of Friendly Societies for the Year 1957*, Parts 1–5. London: H.M.S.O., 1958.

REGISTRY OF FRIENDLY SOCIETIES. *Report of the Chief Registrar of Friendly Societies for the Year 1958*, Parts 1–5. London: H.M.S.O., 1959.

REGISTRY OF FRIENDLY SOCIETIES. *Report of the Chief Registrar of Friendly Societies for the Year 1959*, Parts 1–5. London: H.M.S.O., 1960.

REGISTRY OF FRIENDLY SOCIETIES. *Report of the Chief Registrar of Friendly Societies for the Year 1961*, Parts 1–5. London: H.M.S.O., 1962.

'The Report of the Canadian Royal Commission on Banking and Finance: A Review'. *Federal Reserve Bank of New York Monthly Review* (August 1964), pp. 151–5.

RIX, M. 'Building Societies in 1958'. *Bankers' Magazine*, Vol. CLXXXVII (1959), pp. 289–93.

RIX, M. 'Trustees and their Investment Powers'. *Bankers' Magazine*, Vol. CLXXXIX (1960), pp. 98–101.

ROBERTSON, D. H. 'A Note on the Theory of Money'. *Readings in Monetary Theory*. London: Allen & Unwin, 1962.

ROBINSON, J. 'Radcliffe's General Liquidity'. *The Banker* (December 1960), pp. 790–5.

ROSE, H. B. 'Another Look at Liquidity'. *The Banker* (March 1960), pp. 160–7.

ROUSE, H. L. 'The Benefit of Amalgamations in Banking'. *Bankers' Magazine*, Vol. CXLV (1938), pp. 624–32.

ROWAN, D. C. 'Techniques of Monetary Control: A Review Article'. *Banca Nazionale del Lavoro Quarterly Review* (June 1963).

RUNCIE, N. 'UK Finance Companies: A Study of Projects, 1949–58'. *Bankers' Magazine*, Vol. CLXXXVIII (1959), pp. 189–99.

RUNCIE, N. 'UK Finance Companies: The Uses and Sources of Funds 1949–58'. *Bankers' Magazine*, Vol. CLXXXVII (1959), pp. 455–64.

RYBERYNSKI, T. M. & FROWEN, S. 'Merchant Banks'. *Bankers' Magazine* (July 1961), pp. 1–10.

SALZYN, V. 'The Competition for Personal Savings Deposits in Canada'. *Canadian Journal of Economics* (August 1966) pp. 327-37.

SAYERS, R. S. 'Alternative Views of Central Banking'. *Economica* (May 1961), pp. 305–20.

SAYERS, R. S. *Central Banking After Bagehot*. Oxford: Clarendon Press, 1958.

SAYERS, R. S. 'The Determination of the Volume of Bank Deposits'. *Banca Nazionale del Lavoro Quarterly Review* (December 1955).

SAYERS, R. S. *Modern Banking*. 5th edn. Oxford: Clarendon Press, 1961.

SAYERS, R. S. *Modern Banking*. 6th edn. Oxford: Clarendon Press, 1965.

SAYERS, R. S. 'Monetary Thought and Monetary Policy in England'. *Economic Journal*, Vol. LXX (December 1960), pp. 710–24.

SCANLAN, F. J. 'War Debts and Peace'. *Bankers' Magazine*, Vol. CXLVII (1939), pp. 567–79.

SELDEN, R. T. 'Cost-Push Versus Demand-Pull Inflation'. *Journal of Political Economy*, Vol. LXVII (February 1959), pp. 1–20.

SHACKLE, C. L. S. 'Recent Theories Concerning the Nature and Role of Interest'. *Economic Journal*, Vol, LXXI (June 1961), pp. 209–55.

SHAPIRO, R. 'Financial Intermediaries, Credit Availability and Aggregate Demand'. *Journal of Finance* (September 1966), pp. 459–78.

SHEARER, R. A. 'The Expansion of Bank Credit: An Alternative Approach'. *Quarterly Journal of Economics* (August 1963), pp. 485–502.

SHEPPARD, D. K., & BARRETT, C. R. 'Financial Credit Multipliers and the Availability of Funds'. *Economica* (May 1965), pp. 198–214.

SILBERMAN, L. 'Rationing Credit; Federal Reserve Banks Urge Banks to be More Choosy in Parcelling out Loans'. *Wall Street Journal*, 3 February 1965, p. 1.

SMITH, W. L. 'Financial Intermediaries and Monetary Controls'. *Quarterly Journal of Economics*, Vol. LXXIII (November 1959), pp. 533–53.

SPRING-RICE, D. 'The Money Market Since the War'. *Bankers' Magazine*, Vol. CXV (1923), pp. 417–31.

STEELE, F. E. 'The Working of the London Money Market'. *Bankers' Magazine*, Vol. CXXVII (1929), pp. 162–7.

STEER, E. T. 'The Role of the Stock Exchange in Raising New Capital'. *Bankers' Magazine*, Vol. CLXXXVII (1959), pp. 20–4.

STRAW, K. H. 'Hire Purchase in the Consumer Sector'. *Bankers' Magazine*, Vol. CLXXXIII (1957), pp. 96–104, 214–19.

TAYLOR, F. S. 'The Scottish Banks'. *Bankers' Magazine*, Vol. CLXXII (1951), pp. 19–23.

TEW, B. 'A Case for Financial Controls?' *The Banker* (January 1960).

TEW, B., & HENDERSON, R. F. (ed.). *Studies in Company Finance*. Cambridge: Cambridge University Press, 1959.

THOMAS, S. E. *British Banks and the Finance of Industry*. London: King, 1931.

TOBIN, J. 'Liquidity Preference and Monetary Policy'. *Review of Economic Statistics*, Vol. XXIX (May 1947), pp. 124–31.

'The Treasury Bill, the Story of an Economist's Invention'. *Midland Bank Review* (February 1961), pp. 3–9.

TYLDESLEY, S. 'Working Class Savings'. *Bankers' Magazine*, Vol. CXXIII (1927), pp. 975–8.

'The UK Banking Sector 1952–67'. *Bank of England Quarterly Bulletin*, Vol. IX, No. 2 (June 1969).

VASSAR-SMITH, R. 'Inaugural Address by the President'. *Bankers' Magazine*, Vol. CVI (1918), pp. 558–84.

VAIT, O. 'Changes in Monetary Policy and their Consequences to Banking'. *Relations Between the Central Banks and Commercial Banks*. Frankfurt: Fritz Kropp Verlag, 1957.

VICKERS, D. 'Hire Purchase Finance'. *Bankers' Magazine*, Vol. CLXXVI (1953), pp. 297–304.

WALTERS, A. A. 'Monetary Multipliers in the UK, 1880–1962'. *Oxford Economic Papers*, Vol. XVIII, pp. 270–85.

WALTERS, A. A. 'Money in Boom and Slump'. *Hobart Papers*, No. 44 (January 1969).

WALTERS, A. A. 'The Stability of Keynesian and Monetary Multipliers in the United Kingdom'. *Review of Economics and Statistics* (November 1966), pp. 395–405.

WARBURTON, C. 'Monetary Velocity and Monetary Policy'. *Review of Economics and Statistics*, Vol. XXX (November 1958), pp. 304–13.

WHELDON, G. F. 'The Central Bank'. *Bankers' Magazine*, Vol. CLXX (1950), pp. 273–82.

WHITE, W. H. 'Inventory Investment and the Rate of Interest'. *Banca Nazionale del Lavoro Quarterly Review* (June 1961).

WHYTE, W. H. 'Stock Markets and the War'. *Bankers' Magazine*, Vol. CXXXII (1923), pp. 603–17.

WILLIAMS, D. 'Some Aspects of Monetary Policy in England, 1952–58'. *Yorkshire Bulletin of Economic and Social Research*, Vol. XII (November 1960), pp. 96–108.

WILLMAN, F. A. 'Hire Purchase and the Banker'. *Bankers' Magazine*, Vol. CXLVIII (1959), pp. 67–71.

WILSON, R. A. 'The History of the Cheque'. *Bankers' Magazine*, Vol. CXLVI (1938), pp. 834–51.

WOODRUFF, P. 'British Savings Banks'. *Bankers' Magazine*, Vol. CXXXII (1931), pp. 37–48, 363–75.

YOHE, W. P. 'The Derivation of Certain Financial Multipliers'. *Southern Economic Journal* (July 1962).

YOUNG, R. A. 'Federal Reserve Flow of Funds Accounts – Recent Developments in Monetary Analysis'. *International Monetary Fund Staff Papers* (February 1957), pp. 323–42.

Index

(**Bold** type indicates references to the tables.)

accepting houses, 1
accident insurance, **158–9**, **160–1**
aggregate expenditure and money stock, 68–73, 81
Agricultural Credit Acts, 9
Agricultural Mortgage Corporation, 14
agriculture, bank advances, **134**
Air Finance Company, 14
Alexanders, **138–9**
Amory, Derick Heathcoat, 11
asset distribution
  Government restrictions, 10
  rigidity of, 13
asset preferences
  banks, **35–6**, 37, 60–4, 113
  early stability, 21
  financial institutions, 10, **35–6**, 40, 60–4
  household, 56–60, 103
  and interest rates, 19, 56, 57–9, 62–3, 106–7
  models, 41, 52, 104
  non-bank financial institutions, **35–6**
asset valuation
  banks, 1*n*.
  unit and investment trusts, 1*n*.
assurance companies
  Government security holdings, 30–1
  overseas investment, 95, 97
  see also insurance companies, life assurance companies
Assurance Companies Act, 7
autonomous expenditure, 87, **90**
  and aggregate expenditure, 72
  in constant price regression models, 106
  and consumption, 71, 74–9
  current and constant prices, 100, 101
  definition, 73–4, 84
  determinants, 92
  and money stock, 71, 72
  and private expenditure, **83**, 84, 87, 100
  regressions, 76, 88, **90**, 92

'b', *see* deposit–reserve ratio
balance of payments, Government policy, 8–9
balance sheets, banks', 13, **116–32**
Balfour Committee, 9
Ball, R. J., 72
Bank Acts, 5–6
bank assets, **3**, **30–1**, **116–40**, **184–5**
  growth, 25, **26**, 27, 92, 114, **140**
  institutional, 4
  and interest rate, 59–60, 62–3
  and investments, 39
  movements, 25, 27
  preferences, **35–6**, 37, 60–4
  and tax rate, 62–3
  valuation, 1*n*.
Bank Charter Act (1694), 7
bank credit
  institutional, **96**
  movement of private, 27, 89, 90, 92
  placement, 27, **28**
  restrictions, 9, 11
  see also bank loans and advances, credit, credit availability, loans
bank deposits, **42–3**, 114, **116–17**, **118–19**, **120–1**, **122–3**, **124–5**, **126–7**, **128–9**, **130–3**, **182–3**
  changes in, 21–2
  current, 59
  and encashable assets, **18–19**
  and high-powered money, 44, **45**, 66, 104–5
  models, 66, 104, 105
  and money stock, 69
  multipliers, 38, 40–1
  regressions, 65–6
bank loans and advances, 25, **26**, 32, 38–9, 60–1, 114, **116–33**, 175, **184–5**
  by sectors, **134**
  diminishing share of private market, 93
  growth, **140**, **192**
  and holdings of Government securities, 39
  and long-term interest rate, 63
  as a proxy for money supply, 92–3
  ratio, 39–40
  see also bank credit, credit
Bank of England, 16, 114
  balance sheet, **136–7**
  co-operation with Government, 9
  entry into London Clearing House, 5
  lender of last resort, 5–6
  nationalization, 10
  role in hire-purchase company and unit trust formation, 9, 14
bank rate, **190–1**
  as proxy for bank interest, 60
Bankers' Industrial Development Corporation, 9, 14
banks, 4, 5, 6, 12–13, 108, **113–40**
  accounting practices, 111
  and additions to money stock, 6
  balance sheets criticized, 13
  bills discounted, 12, 38
  and building societies, 14–15
  cash–reserve ratio, 40, 44, **47**
  clearings, **135**
  combined balance sheets, **116–17**
  England and Wales, **118–19**, **126–7**, **140**
  Government security holdings, **30–1**, 32, 33, 38, 39, 40, 41, 60–1, **116–33**, **136–7**
  growth rate of assets, **192**
  hire-purchase interests, 11, 15

banks (*contd.*)
  and inter-war deflation, 12
  Ireland, **120–1**, **126–7**, **140**
  London Clearing, **130–3**, **140**
  monopoly, 13–14, 16
  notes and coin, **180–1**
  overseas, 1, 15
  portfolio behaviour, 12, 38, 39, 60–1, 63
  private, **124–5**
  private credit, **184–5**
  reserve ratio, 41
  reserves, 42–3
  Scotland, **122–3**, **126–7**, **140**
  statutory framework, 5–6
  total-liability ratio, 40
  see also bank assets, bank credit, bank deposits, bank loans and advances
Barrett, C. R., 41, 72, 75, 79, 104, 105
Becker, G., 75
bills discounted, bank holdings, 38, **116–33**
Birmingham Municipal Savings Bank, 22*n.*, 23, 113, **142–3**, **176–8**
  asset growth rate, **172**
  assets, **184–5**
  banks' opposition to, 14
  restrictions on asset placements, 10
Blind Act, 10
Borrowing Act, 10
Brechling, F., 39, 40, 41, 61, 95, 104, 107
British Empire, 4
  and UK savings, 12
British Trade Corporation, 8
building industry
  bank advances, **134**
  Government encouragement, 9, 10, 11, 103
building societies, 11, 13, 21, 22, 103, **150–2**
  accounting practices, 111
  arrangements with banks and insurance companies, 14–15
  asset growth rate, **172**
  assets, **3**, **150–1**, **166–7**, **184–5**
  deposits and interest rates, 56–7
  deposits and shares as quasi-money, 17, **182–3**
  Government security holdings, **30–1**, 32, **150–1**
  interest rate and asset preferences, 57–8
  interest rates and savers' preferences, 59
  investment restrictions, 8
  rising share of institutional assets, 4
  statutory framework, 6–7
  see also financial sector
Building Societies Acts, 6–7, 9–10
Building Societies Association 13, 14

call rate, **190–1**
capital goods, credit availability and demand for, 71
capital issues
  new series, **187**
  relaxation of Government control over, 11
Capital Issues Committee, 10
cartelization, financial institutions, 13
cash–reserve ratio, banks', 40, 44, **47**
certified loan societies, funds and assets, **162**, **166–7**
charitable trusts, State regulation, 7–8
chemical sector, bank advances, **134**
cheques, 5

Chicago school
  reconciliation with Keynesian theory, 75
  see also Friedman, M.
City of London, changes in position of, 11–13
Clayton, G., 39, 40, 41, 57, 61, 95, 104, 107
Cleary, E. J., 56–7
Cmd. 9052 (bank amalgamation), 9
coin and currency in circulation, 173–4, **180–1**, **182–3**
collecting societies, funds and assets, **163**, **166–7**
Collecting Societies Industrial Assurance Fund, **158–9**, **160–1**
Colonial Stock Act (1900), 12
commercial bills, decline in banks' holdings, 12
Committee on Finance and Industry, *see* Macmillan Committee
Committee of the London Clearing Banks, 13
Commonwealth Development Finance Company, 14
companies, restrictions on borrowing, 10
Companies Acts, 5, 6
company securities, **188**
consumer durables, determinants of demand, 72–3
consols rate, **190–1**
consumption
  and autonomous expenditure, 71, 74–9
  determinants of, 100
  and encashable assets, 77, **78**
  and Gross National Product, 80
  and money stock, 72, 74–9, 107–8
  as a proxy for permanent income, 79
  regressions, **76**, 77, **78**
Co-operative Wholesale Society Bank, 113, 114, **124–5**, **128–9**, 140
Coppietiers, E., 7
corporation stock, **188**
Council for the London Stock Exchange, 14
credit
  and balance on foreign account, 41
  and money stock, 69–70
  selected financial institutions, 27, **28**
  see also bank credit, bank loans and advances, loans, private credit
credit availability, **40**
  and income changes, 87
  and inflation, 87
  interest rate, 86
  measurement, 88
  models, **96**
  and private expenditure, 70–1, 72–3, 87–99, 100
  regressions, 65, 67
  restrictions, 9, 86
credit price, *see* interest rate
Cunliffe Committee, 9, 44, 103
currency, 173–4, **180–1**
  changes in stock, 21, 22
  and encashable assets, **18–19**
  growth rate, 17, **192**
  non-bank holdings, 42–3, 174
currency–deposit ratio, 95*n.*
current accounts *versus* deposit accounts, interest rates, 59

Dacey, W. Manning, 39, 40
Defence Bonds, **182–3**
Defence Regulations, 10
deflationary policy, effect on banks, 12
deposit accounts, 19
deposit controls
  Post Office Savings Bank, 6
  trustee savings banks, 6

deposit–currency ratio, **42–3**, 89, 95*n*.
influence on money stock, 44, 47
movements, 44
and private expenditure, **90**, 91, 92
relative importance in UK and USA, 47–8
deposit–reserve ratio, **42–3**
and money stock, 47
movements, 44, 47
in UK and USA, 47–8
Deprano, M., 77
discount companies
assets, **3**, **30–1**, **184–5**
balance sheets, **138–9**
credit movements, 27, **28**
growth rate of assets, **192**
holdings of Government securities, 29, **30–1**, **138–9**
private credit, **184–5**
Drakatos, C., 80
Drake, P. S., 72
Duesenberry, J., 87

Economist, *The*, 44, 112, 114
employers' liability insurance, **158–9**, **160–1**
encashable assets, 79–87
and bank deposits, **18–19**
and consumption expenditure, 77, **78**
and currency, **18–19**
definition, 73
growth rates, 17, 21, **192**
percentage shares of components, **18–19**
and private expenditure, 17, **74**, 81, 84, 85–6
quasi-money, **18–19**
see also household encashable assets
Enfield Committee, 9
engineering sector, bank advances, **134**
Euro-dollar market, 12, 14, 15
exchange equalization account, 9
expenditure
and credit availability, 72–3
as a determinant of real balances, 106
USA money stock and nominal, 71
see also private expenditure
expenditure determination
constant or current prices, 75
quantity theory approach, 49
Export Credit Guarantee Act, 9
Export Credit Guarantee Schemes, 9
banks' opposition to, 14
export finance, need to stimulate, 8–9

Farrington Committee, 8
Federal Reserve Board, 72
finance, capital issues, **187**
Finance Corporation for Industry, 14, **170**
Finance Houses Association, 15
financial institutions
asset growth rate, 1, 25, **26**, **30–1**, **192**
asset preferences, 10, **35–6**, **40**, 60–4
assets, **184–5**
controls, 8, 10, 11, 102–3
coverage, 1
credit series, **184–5**
and environmental changes, 13
holdings of Government securities, 29, **30–1**, 32
and international conditions, 11–13
loan placements, 13, 27, 28
market-sharing, 15
mortgages, **184–5**
portfolio preferences, 103
private credits, 27, 65, 66, 93, **96**
specialization, 5
State sponsorship, 14
and trade associations, 13, 14–15
see also banks, financial intermediaries, non-bank financial institutions
financial intermediaries, **141–72**
asset growth rate, **172**
asset preferences, 37–8
assets, 64–5
liabilities, 66
as component of money stock, 69–70
see also Birmingham Municipal Savings Bank, building societies, Friendly Societies, hire-purchase companies, insurance companies, Post Office Savings Bank
financial sector
bank advances, **134**
evolution, 4
institutional credits, 96
private credit, **90**
private loans and private expenditure, 87–99
savings and investments, 29–33
financial services, legislative framework, 108
fire insurance, **158–9**, **160–1**
First World War, 4, 8
deflationary finance after, 9
determinants of money stock, 47
see also war years
food, drink and tobacco, bank advances, **134**
foreign stocks, **188**
Foreign Transactions Advisory Committee, 12
Friedman, M., 37, 57, 68, 70, 71, 72, 75, 79, 80, 87, 104, 105, 106
Friendly Societies, 141, **162**, **166–7**
asset growth rate, **172**
assets, **3**, **162**, **166–7**, **184–5**
and Provident Societies, growth rate of funds, **172**
statutory framework, 6
Friendly Society Acts, 6

Gambino, A., 38, 41
giro system, 14
Gladstone, W. E., 7
Gold Standard, 9, 12
Goldsmith, R. W., 38
Goodwin, 41
Government
and autonomous expenditure, 84
and bank lending, 39
as decision-maker, 4
direct-savings placements, 29
expansion of National Debt, 7
expenditure regulation, 87
extension of credit-restricting policy, 15
finance-channelling arrangements, 9, 16
and the financial institutions, 9–10, 102–3
financial intervention by, 8–9
fiscal policy, 63
market for own obligations, 7–8, 10
and market segmentation, 14
policy formation, 106

Government (*contd.*)
and Post Office Savings Bank, 6, 8
suggested stabilization of money stock, 72
Government securities, **188–9**
bank holdings, 38, 39, 60–1, 63, 64, **116–17**, **118–19**, **120–1**, **122–3**, **124–5**, **126–7**, **128–9**, **130–3**
building society holdings, **30–1**, 32, **150–1**
discount company holdings, **138–9**
financial institutions' holdings, 29, **30–1**, 32
financial intermediaries' holdings, **142–51**, **154–5**, **162–3**, **168–9**
see also Treasury Bills
Great Depression, 9
gross domestic private expenditure, *see* private expenditure
Gross National Product
and bank holdings of Government securities, 64
and consumption expenditure, 80
and financial institutions' asset growth, 1
and money stock, 87*n*.
in quantity theory formulations, 80
see also income velocity
gross private credit, *see* private credit

Hambros Bank, 113
Hamburger, M. J., 56, 70
Hayes, A., 88
Hicks, J. R., 69
high-powered money, 41, **42–3**
and bank deposits, 44, **45**, 66, 104–5
components, 66
and money stock, 47
and movement of money, 44, **45**
non-financial-sector preference, **37**
and private expenditure, 88–92
Higonnet, R. P., 71, 114
Hire Purchase Act (1954), 11
hire-purchase companies, 103, **168–9**
asset growth rate, **172**
assets, **3**, **168–9**, **184–5**
and Bank of England, 9, 14
credit relaxation, 11
Government securities, **168–9**
rapid growth, 4
hire-purchase finance, 9
Holmans, A. E., 52, 80
House Purchase Scheme (1958), 11
household encashable assets
components, **18–19**
and money supply, 174, **182–3**
private credit as proxy for, 89
return on, 104
see also encashable assets
households
asset preference estimates, 56–60, 103
savings and interest rates, 56–7
housing, 11
State aid, 9, 10, 103
Housing Guarantee Schemes, 11
Housing and Town Planning Act (1919), 9
Hyde, F., 39, 41

income
and credit availability, 87
relation to money stock, 71–2, 105
income expenditure approach, *see* autonomous expenditure
income tax rate, 10
and credit availability, 89
and income velocity, **54**, 55
income velocity
average and coefficient of variation, 49
estimates, 52–6
and income tax rate, **54**, 55
and interest rate, **54**, 55, 57, 81
marginal and average, **80**
possible correlations, 50
and quantity theory, 48–9
in recession, 50
regression analysis, 53–6
and retail price index, 104
industrial assurance, **158–9**, **160–1**, **166–7**
Industrial and Commercial Finance Corporation, 14, **171**
industry, capital issues, **187**
inflation, demand pull, and credit availability, 87
institutional mortgages, growth after 1914, 27, 29
insurance companies, 103, 141, **154–6**, **158–9**, **160–1**
asset growth rate, **172**
assets, **154–5**, **182–3**, **184–5**
building society links, 14–15
growth, 4
holdings of Government securities, 32
and social legislation, 10
statutory framework, 7
see also assurance companies, financial intermediaries, life assurance companies
insurance funds, growth rate, **172**
interest rates, **190–1**
and bank holdings of securities, 61, 63
and bank rate, 60
and banks' asset preferences, 62–3
and building society deposits, 56–7, 57–8
and changes in money stock, 70
and encashable asset preferences, 19
financial intermediaries, **142–3**
and household asset preferences, 56–7
income velocity and, **54**, 55, 57, 81
and National Savings, 25
and portfolio preferences, 106–7
and preferences for bank deposit or current accounts, 59
and private expenditure, 79–99, 100
regression coefficient, 55
international conditions, effect on financial institutions, 11–13
investment
restrictions on overseas, 12
statutory restrictions on, 8
investment trusts, 1, 141
asset valuation, 1*n*.
credit relaxation, 11
Ireland, banks, **120–1**
Irish Republic, effect on statistics, 112
iron and steel industry, bank advances, **134**

Johnson, H. G., 68, 105
joint-stock banks, *see* banks
Jucker-Fleetwood, E. E., 80

Kaldor, N., 70
Kavanagh, N. J., 53, 56, 104
Keran, M., 87*n*.
Keynes, J. M., 69, 75
Keynesian theory of money, 69
see also autonomous expenditure

Lavington, F., 68, 69, 87
Lee, T. H., 53
lending and borrowing, increased segmentation, 5
life and annuity funds, asset growth rate, **172**
Life Assurance Acts, 7
life assurance companies, **158–9**, **160–1**
  funds, **3**, 21, 22, **158–9**
  as percentage of encashable assets, **18–19**
  premiums, **160–1**
  as quasi-money, 17
  see also assurance companies, insurance companies
liquid assets
  as components of money stock, 70
  see also encashable assets
liquidity, banks' emphasis on, 39
liquidity effect, 89
loans
  financial-sector and private-expenditure, 88
  selected financial institutions' placement, 27, **28**
  see also bank credit, bank loans and advances, credit, credit availability
local authorities, 12
  bank authorities, **134**
  capital issues, **187**
  restrictions on borrowing, 10
London Clearing Banks, 113–14, **130–3**
  Committee, 113
London Clearing House, 5
London Stock Exchange, Council, 14

'M', *see* net money
Macmillan Committee, 9, 13, 38, 44
marine, aviation and transport insurance, **158–9**, **160–1**
Mayer, T., 77
Meade, J. E., 41
Meiselman, D., 70, 71, 72, 75, 79, 80, 81, 87, 104, 105, 106
merchant banks, 12
  expansion, 4, 15
Military Savings Bank, 7
Mitchell, G. W., 56
monetary regulation, 107
monetary stringency, banks' reaction to, 63
money
  balances, *see* money stock
  growth rate, 17
  model, 64
  and movement of high-powered money, 44, **45**
  net, 17, **18–19**
  problem of definition, 108
  quasi-, 17, **18–19**, 21, **182–3**, **192**
money stock, 21, 22, 79–87, **90**
  and aggregate expenditure, 68–73
  asset preference constancy assumptions, 52
  and autonomous expenditure, 71, 72
  averages and coefficients of variation of determinants, **40**
  bank deposits as a component of, 69
  bank loans and advances as proxy, 92–3
  banks' near-monopoly over additions to, 6
  case for Government regulation, 72
  components, 69–70
  and consumption, 71, 72, 74–9, 107–8
  credit as a component, 69
  Cunliffe Committee proposals, 9
  definitions, 80, 81
  demand determination, 105
  and deposit–currency ratio, 44, 47
  determinants, **42–3**
  'direct effect' hypothesis, 68
  estimates, 64
  and household liquid assets, 174, **182–3**
  not an independent variable, 105
  influence on future income and prices, 105
  and level of income, 71–2, 105
  models, 41, 48, 64, 104
  and nominal expenditure in the USA, 71
  effect of oscillations in real value of, 72
  and prices, 70, 105
  and private expenditure, 17, **74**, 80, 81, 83–7, 100
  real and nominal, 72
  effects of reducing, 44
  unsatisfactory nature of statistics, 174–5
money supply, *see* money stock
Montague Loan Bill (1692), 7
mortgage credits, **184–5**
  financial intermediaries, **142–3**, **146–7**, **150–1**, **154–5**, **162–3**
  growth, 27, 29, **192**
motor vehicle insurance, **158–9**, **160–1**
Municipal and General Securities, 14
municipal savings banks, restrictions on asset placements, 10

National Debt, legislative authority for expansion, 7
National Debt Commissioners, 6, 7
  deposits of financial intermediaries, **142**
National Discount House, **138–9**
National Health Insurance Act, 10
national income, in quantity theory formulations, 80
National Insurance Act (1946), 10
National Savings, 8, 21, 22–5, 103, 107, 173, **176–8**
  Bank, 7, **176–7**
  Bonds, **3**, **176–7**
  Certificates, 23, 25, **176–7**, **182–3**
  compound rate of growth, **192**
  direct security sales, 29
  as percentage of encashable assets, 18–19
  as quasi-money, 17
nationalization, financial effects, 10–11
net money
  components, 17
  growth rate, **192**
  as percentage of encashable assets, **18–19**
net money supply, *see* money supply
Net National Income, 59
non-bank assets, growth rate, 92
non-bank currency holdings, **42–3**
non-bank financial institutions
  asset growth rate, **172**
  asset preferences, **35–6**
  assets, 25, **26**, **184–5**
  cash holdings, **30–1**
  credit placement, 27, **28**
  Government security holdings, **30–1**, 32
  private credits, 93, **96**
  private loans and private credit, 92
  see also financial intermediaries
non-financial sector, preference for financial intermediaries' liabilities, 37
Norman, Montague, 9
notes
  holdings, **116–27**
  issue, 5, 9, 174

Old Age Pension Acts, 10
Osborn, W. T., 57
overseas banks, 1
  UK deposits, 15
overseas investment, 95, 97
  restrictions, 12
Overseas Trade Act, 9

'p', *see* deposit–currency ratio
Patinkin, D., 72, 79
peacetime decline in Government security holdings of non-bank financial institutions, 32
pension funds, 1*n.*, 141
Porter Commission, 57
Post Office Register, 22, 23
  acquisition of Government stock through, 7, 8
Post Office Savings Bank, 22, 23, 112, **144–5**
  asset growth rate, **172**
  assets, **3**, **144–5**, **184–5**
  deposits, **144–5**
  interest rate and asset preferences, 57–8
  statutory framework, 6, 8
premium savings bonds, 8, **176–7**, **182–3**
price changes and effects of money stock, 86
prices
  and changes in money stock, 70
  constant, in regressions, 105
  constant and current, in expenditure determination, 99
  constant and nominal, in credit availability model, 95
  constant or current, in expenditure determination, 75
  and foreign debt issues, 97
  and income velocity, **54**, 55
  and lagged previous money stock, 105
  and quantity theory of money, 68–9
primary reserve ratio, banks, 39
private banks, **124–5**
private credit
  and financial ease, 95
  financial institutions, 27, 65, 66, 93, **96**, **184–5**
  models, 104
  movement, 27, **28**
  and private expenditure, 17, 74, 93, 96, 98*n.*
  as proxy for household encashable assets, 89
private expenditure, 79–87, **90**
  and autonomous expenditure, **83**, 84, 87, 100
  credit availability, 70–1
  dependence of variables determining, 105
  and deposit–currency ratio, **90**, 91, 92
  determinants of, 98–9, 100
  and encashable assets, 17, **74**, 81, 84, 85–6
  and financial stocks, 17, 73–4
  and high-powered money, 88, 92
  and interest rates, 79–99
  lagged determinants, 84–5
  and market-tightening techniques, 95
  models, **96**
  and money stock, 17, 74, 80, 81, 83–7, 100
  movement in, 25, 26
  and private credits, 17, 74, 93, 96, 98*n.*
  and private loans, 87–99
  quantity theory and credit availability models, 89
  regressions, 81, **82**, 88, **90**, 94, 95, 97
private sector, average asset preferences, **35–6**
private trusts
  funds, 1
  State regulation, 7–8
production, capital issues, **187**
Provident Societies, **166–7**
public authorities, capital issues, **187**
public utilities, bank advances, **134**

quantity theory of money, 48–9, 68–9
  model, 80, 89
quasi-money, **182–3**
  components, 17
  growth, 17, 21, **192**
  as percentage of encashable assets, **18–19**

Radice, E. A., 56
railway savings banks, funds and assets, **163**, **166–7**
real income and income velocity, 53
Registrar of Friendly Societies, 6
regressions
  autonomous expenditure on money stock, 92
  autonomous expenditure on private credit, 88, **90**, 92
  bank deposits, 65–6
  consumption and autonomous expenditure, **76**
  consumption on encashable assets, 77, **78**
  consumption on money stock, **76**, 77, **78**
  credit availability, 65, 67
  financial institutions' asset preferences, 60–4
  financial institutions' private credits, **65**, 66
  household asset preferences, 56–60
  income velocity, 54–6
  money supply, 64–5
  private expenditure
    and bank private loans, 97
    and non-bank institutional loans, 97
    on encashable assets, 81, **82**
    on high-powered money, 88, **90**, 95
    on interest rate, 94
    on lagged private credit, 94
    on money stock, 81, **82**
    on private credit, 88, **90**
    on short-term interest rate, 81, **82**
    on a time-trend term, 81, **82**
    on Treasury Bill rate, 94
retail trade, bank advances, **134**
Robertson, D. H., 69
Roosa, 61

Salyzn, V., 57
savings
  framework for collection and placement, 6–7
  interest rate and household, 56–7
Savings Bank Acts, 7–8
savings banks
  deposits, 21, 22, **182–3**
    growth rate, **192**
    as percentage of encashable assets, **18–19**
  see also Post Office Savings Bank, trustee savings banks
savings bonds, as quasi-money, 17
savings-investment process, financial institutions, 33
Sayers, R. S., 38, 64, 70, 105, 108
Schwartz, A. J., 37, 57, 105
Scotland, joint-stock banks, **122–3**
Scottish Co-operative Wholesale Society Bank, 113
Second World War

effects on financial sector, 21, 22
see also war years
Securities Management Trust, 9, 14
Selective Employment Tax, 106
Shapiro, R., 71
Shearer, R. A., 40, 41, 56, 61, 71, 72, 87, 95, 104, 107
Sheppard, D. K., 41
Ship Mortgage Finance Company, 14
shipping and shipbuilding, bank advances, **134**
short-term funds, change from net supplier to net absorber, 4
short-term interest rate
and income velocity, **54**, 55
regression coefficient, 55
see also interest rate
small savers, 6, 16
see also Post Office Savings Bank, trustee savings banks
special investment departments, 8
special investment deposits, trustee savings banks, 23
stamp duties, 5
sterling, 4
changes in international position of, 11–13
Sterling Area, 9, 12
stocks quoted on London Stock Exchange, **188**
superannuation and other trusts, **163**, **166–7**
superannuation funds, 1, **163**

tax rate
and banks' asset preferences, 62–3
see also income tax rate
textiles, bank advances, **134**
total aggregate expenditure and money stock, 68–73, 81
total-liability ratio, banks, 40
trade, capital issues, **187**
trade associations of financial institutions, 4–5, 13
trade unions, funds and assets, **162**, **166–7**
transaction velocity, 68
transport, capital issues, **187**
Treasury Bills, 111–12
bank holdings, **116–17**, **118–19**, **120–1**, **122–3**, **124–5**, **126–7**, **128–9**, **130–3**
discount company holdings, **138–9**
financial intermediaries' holdings, **142–3**, **144–5**
as high-powered money substitutes, 48
interest rate, **190**
market holdings, 12
rate as proxy for bank interest, 59–60
see also Government securities
Treasury Deposit Receipts, 47, 113, **116–17**, **118–19**, **120–1**, **122–3**, **126–7**, **130–3**
Trustee Savings Bank Acts, 6
Trustee Savings Bank Association, 13, 14
trustee savings banks, 13, 23, **146–8**
asset growth rate, **172**
assets, **3**, **146–7**, **184–5**
banks' opposition to, 14
Government security holdings, 30–1, 32, **146–7**
and interest rate, 56, 59
special investment deposits, 23
statutory framework, 6, 8

Unemployment Income Act, 10
Union of London Discount Houses, **138–9**
unit trusts, 1, 141
asset valuation, 1*n*.
Bank of England support, 14
credit relaxation, 11
and Government borrowing, 10
United Dominion Trust, 9, 14
United States of America
asset preference ratios, 44
autonomous expenditure and consumption, 75–7
bank holdings of Government securities, 38, 41
bank loans and advances and holdings of Government securities, 41
banks' long-term securities, 61
banks' total-liability ratio, 40
deposit–reserve ratio, 48
income velocity, 50, 53
interest rates and household asset preferences, 56
money stock, 71, 72, 75–7
and consumption, 75–7
and nominal expenditure, 71
and private expenditure, 80

Wadsworth, J., 39
Walters, A. A., 53, 56, 72, 75, 79, 80, 87, 104, 105
War Pension Schemes Act, 10
war years
banks' asset growth in, 25, 27
demand and money stock, 105
Government security sales during, 27, 29, 32
impact on financial structure, 4, 103
National Savings in, 23
Warburton, C., 50, 71
Widows, Orphans and Old Age Contributing Pensions Acts, 10
Woodruff, P., 7
Woolwich Equitable Building Society, 14
Workmen's Compensation Acts, 10
workmen's compensation societies funds, **166–7**

Yorkshire Penny Bank, 113, **124**, **140**